AFIELD

Portraits of Wisconsin Naturalists,
Empowering Leopold's Legacy

Volume One

Sumner Matteson

LITTLE CREEK PRESS
AND BOOK DESIGN
Mineral Point, Wisconsin USA

Little Creek Press®
A Division of Kristin Mitchell Design, Inc.
5341 Sunny Ridge Road
Mineral Point, Wisconsin 53565

Book Design and Project Coordination:
Little Creek Press

Book produced by Blackburnian Press, LLC

First Edition
January 2020

Printed in Wisconsin, United States of America

To order books visit www.littlecreekpress.com

Library of Congress Control Number: 2019935004

ISBN-10: 1-942586-59-0
ISBN-13: 978-1-942586-59-3

On the front cover:
Jim Zimmerman in fen, Jefferson County, September 1992.
Photo credit: Elizabeth H. Zimmerman.

On the back cover:
Aldo Leopold with Frederick and Frances Hamerstrom,
ca, 1939, central Wisconsin.
Photo credit: Robert McCabe and the Aldo Leopold Foundation, WI.

MONARCH

Dedicated to and

in memory of James T. Harris

and

John Bielefeldt, Gilbert Boese, Bill Brooks, John Robert Cary,
Noel Cutright, June Dobberpuhl, Donald Gibson, Jim Hale,
Neil Harriman, Walter Kuhlmann, Beth Arthur Lane,
Andy Larsen, Roy Lukes, Jim Meeker, Steve Miller,
Julie Peltier, Eugene Roark, Bob Russell,
and Pam Troxell

and

Sam and Imogene "Gene" Johnson,
and Terry Kohler

and

Larry David Sperling

Praise for AFIELD,

Portraits of Wisconsin Naturalists, Empowering Leopold's Legacy

❝This work will go down as a very important work.”
—David Gjestson, WDNR Wildlife Biologist (ret.)

❝Reading your chapter on George Becker brought tears to my eyes. He not only changed the direction of my life, we went on to be very close friends. How wonderful that you are doing this project.”
—Michael Dombeck, Chief (ret.), U.S. Forest Service

❝The chapter on Bill Volkert does an excellent job of capturing him as naturalist and philosopher. Well-written and entertaining, you will learn how Bill became a self-taught naturalist and ecologist of the first order.”
—George Meyer, Secretary (ret.), WDNR; Executive Director, Wisconsin Wildlife Federation

❝The chapter on George Knudsen is extraordinary.”
—Charles Pils, Director (ret.), Bureau of Endangered Resources (now Bureau of Natural Heritage Conservation), WDNR

❝You have a marvelous accounting of how my parents focused on life, some of their challenges, and their unique character. I can picture them chatting with you, opening up to you. I think you have a gem here.”
—Elva Hamerstrom Paulson (Daughter of Frances and Frederick Hamerstrom)

"It is a privilege beyond words that you have made it possible for me to have a greater understanding and pride in the great man Sam was!"
—Shirley Robbins (Widow of Sam Robbins)

"The chapter on Marion [Moran] really touched me. It was like she was in the room with me talking."
—Mark Peterson, Executive Director (ret.), Sigurd Olson Environmental Institute, Northland College.

"When I should have been doing something useful, I just sat at the computer and read the whole thing [chapter on Lorrie Otto]. I couldn't stop. It is very well done."
—Mary Kohler (Conservationist, Business Woman, Pilot)

"I don't know how to thank you and commend you for the choices you have made from the journals [of LeRoy Lintereur]. I think people will love this; it is fascinating to see and read, brought together in a beautiful format.
—Judith Lintereur Johnson (Daughter of LeRoy Lintereur)

☀

Wonder is the very engine of life.

—Erling Kagge, *Silence: In the Age of Noise*

"

Every realm of nature is marvelous ... so we should venture on the study of every kind of animal without distaste; for each and all will reveal to us something natural and something beautiful.
—Aristotle, *On the Parts of Animals,* Book One, Part 5

If love did not live in matter,
how would any place have
any hold on anyone?
—Rumi, *Birdsong*

Attentiveness alone can rival the most powerful magnifying lens.... Look in a certain way and a whole new world can be revealed.
—Robin Wall Kimmerer, *Gathering Moss:*
A Natural and Cultural History of Mosses

What being a naturalist has come to mean to me ... is this: Pay attention to the mystery.
—Barry Lopez, "The Naturalist" in Orion,
People & Nature, Autumn 2001

"

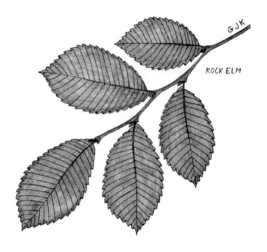

The human eye does more than see;
it stitches the seen and unseen together,
the temporal and the eternal.
It wakes me again and again
to the astonishment of finding
myself in a body moving
through a world of beauty
and dying and mystery.

—Alison Hawthorne Deming,
Writing the Sacred into the Real

Table of Contents

RED OAK ACORN

GJK

Foreword:
Gathering of the Voices

By Curt Meine, PhD, conservation biologist, historian, and writer

Historians and linguists have long debated the meaning of the word *Wisconsin*. The river gave the state its name. Who gave the river its native name? What did it mean to them? We may never know definitely, but the original meaning most in favor lately is among the oldest recorded, and the most poetic: "gathering of the waters."

In this volume, Sumner Matteson provides a gathering of voices of and from Wisconsin. Here we meet the observant students and caretakers of our waters and soils, fish and flowers, trees and birds, critters and crawlers. Like Wisconsin's waters, the voices of these notable naturalists have mingled over time and helped to define the state. Over the generations they helped make Wisconsin synonymous with environmental stewardship. Wisconsin became known far beyond its borders for its conservation tradition and culture of care.

But just as we are prone to take our waters for granted, so can we easily neglect the voices of our elders. Although voices inevitably fade and are forgotten, culture has always worked to counter that loss and to conserve human experience in *story*. Now, however, our collective memory can be overwhelmed by our collective distraction, by our all-absorbing fixation on the newsfeed, the tweetstorm, the livestream.

All the more reason to value this gathering of voices.

For 40 years Sumner has regularly made time to record the stories of Wisconsin field biologists, ecologists, conservation biologists, and land stewards. Among them are the well-known and recognized as well as the more obscure and overlooked. All made vital contributions to natural history and conservation in Wisconsin. Some were scientists and teachers. Others were writers and advocates, public servants and citizens. All, in some way, were wisdom-keepers. Their lives span a century and a half, and many never met. Yet they are connected across their diverse places and times and experiences. They shared a passion for what Aldo Leopold called "things natural, wild, and free." They carried the same conviction that we are bonded to the land and all its inhabitants and to one another upon it.

Sumner's perseverance in gathering their voices has only increased the value of his work. In fact, we need these voices and stories now more than ever.

We need them to remind us that we belong to an ever-evolving community of people who built the fund of knowledge, commitment, and vision that we draw upon daily, if mostly unconsciously.

We need them to serve as antidotes to frustration as our conservation leadership has eroded, our land ethic has been challenged, and our civic life has fragmented.

We need them to ground us as we face a future of rapidly changing social, economic, and environmental realities, most especially the uncertain effects of accelerating climate change.

We need them to encourage us all to assume our responsibilities, defend the public good, and value our shared natural assets for future generations and all our fellow creatures on the land.

We need them, more than anything, to nurture the next generation of citizen-conservationists.

I recently found myself in an end-of-the-workday discussion with a younger colleague about the state of land stewardship in Wisconsin. In response to recent political developments, she was exasperated and bewildered. "When I was in college in the '90s, we looked to the older generation and wondered what there was left for us to do! They'd done clean water and clean air and endangered species and wilderness. It seemed all that was left was for us to fill in the details.... Well, I guess there's more to do."

There is more to do. There is always more to do.

These stories also bear witness to an old truth. Wisconsin's tradition of natural history and conservation commitment has always depended not on a few individuals—even those remembered here. Leadership has always relied on the actions of curious, creative, committed citizens. True conservation leadership has always resided in those who love the land and who work to solve problems, meet needs, and seize opportunities. It expresses itself through all who know that the health of our lands, waters, wildlife, communities, and economies depend on people working together to understand the workings of the land and to make constructive change happen. Every voice in this volume reminds us of this. Listen.

Our elders speak to us in varied tones. They are informed, emotional, experienced, funny, rough, inspiring, bold, quiet, wise, and adventurous. Through their stories, and their many ways of telling them, we can again connect our knowledge and our spirit. We can again demonstrate our respect for one another and our love for the landscape of Wisconsin. ✳

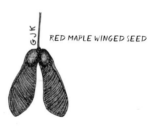

RED MAPLE WINGED SEED

In nature I joyously become a
part of whatever surrounds me.

—Clare Cooley, *Unpublished writings*

Preface:
To Catch a Naturalist

Open to those who are feelingly alive to the majesty of nature.
  —Alexander von Humboldt, 1822

There is a great need to preserve what is left of our
fragile environment before we have passed the point
of no return.
  —Owen Gromme, letter to SM (January 30, 1989)

A landmark UW intergovernmental analysis ... assessed the state of global
biodiversity and finds that devastation is proceeding at a rate that is tens
to hundreds of times faster than during the past ten million years—a rate
never seen before in history.
  —*Forbes*, May 9, 2019

One reason Wisconsin silica sand is so desirable is because it lies very close
to the surface, requiring relatively little digging to get at it.... Once the sand
is all gone, the plan is to restore the hills; they'll just be a third smaller than
before.... From there, it's off to the fracking fields. The sand that used to
make up a Wisconsin hillside will be shot deep into the earth [to free up oil
and gas] hundreds of miles away in Texas or North Dakota.
  —Vince Beiser, *The World In A Grain, The Story of Sand and
  How It Transformed Civilization* (Riverhead Books, 2018).

Recent generations of children have grown up with even fewer meaningful
experiences in the outdoors than those of a century ago, and today's youth
spend far more time indoors or in highly controlled outdoor settings than
ever before.... It's clear that if we are to cultivate knowledge about—and
a sense of responsibility for—nature, we need to begin at a very young

age [with] old-fashioned nature study as one way to offset nature-deficit disorder.

> —Stanley A. Temple, "Rachel Carson and a Childhood Sense of Wonder," *Wisconsin Academy of Sciences, Arts, and Letters* (Fellows Forum, 2015)

A rare wild bison was shot and killed after it wandered into Germany. A local official ordered hunters to kill the animal, which had not been seen there for over 200 years.

> —*The New York Times,* 2017

This book is a beginning—40 years in the making—with no definitive ending to telling the stories of our naturalists. This is, after all, Volume One. I hope these stories inspire you to become more engaged within the natural world, more aware of and sensitive to the wild and untamed and inviolate, as have our Wisconsin naturalists—those men and women who, often alone, study or observe some aspect of nature rigorously or to different degrees—by consistently immersing themselves afield, and then sharing their ardent knowledge and insights through various means, from correspondence, journal entries, and artistic expression, to published papers, books, lectures, and classes, to field trips and family outings.

Whether the focus is on birds, fishes, herptiles, insects, mammals, plants, rocks, soils, or some other area of outdoor interest, this book will attempt to bring to life the journeys and personal challenges of our naturalists.

I will go further. Naturalists are often public interpreters of landscapes, of plant and animal communities, of interrelationships between plants and animals. This is what separates them from other scientific minds—or scientists that may lead a less public life by nature of their chosen area of study. My friend and naturalist Bill Volkert (see Chapter Eleven) put it this way:

> I see my job as an interpretive naturalist as somewhat different; there are many excellent scientists—including field scientists—but they're not all capable of effectively conveying what they know to a broad audience. I'm familiar with a wide range of studies in nature; that's why I take the title of naturalist. I'm not a specialist in one particular field, although I have studied birds more than anything else. But I try to be familiar with a variety of topics. Good communication skills are

essential. It's one thing to know your subject; it's another to get other people to see it and understand it.

𝕫

DURING THE COURSE of a life negotiating peaks and canyons, while stubbornly (some might say blindly) adhering to a vision of what can be accomplished via dogged perseverance and sometimes not-always-quiet tenacity, and not succumbing to the desire to give up, I have had the good fortune to engage and learn from many a fine Wisconsin naturalist. Wide-ranging discussions often occurred, typically at day's end.

For this project, I spoke with more than 40 Wisconsin naturalists, most of whom I interviewed with a portable Marantz tape recorder, starting in 1979 with Sigurd Olson at his cabin on Listening Point near Ely, Minnesota.

For the few naturalists in this book I did not know well or never met, family members and colleagues shared journals or directed me to the Wisconsin State Historical Society to personal correspondence illuminating the breadth of the naturalist's life. But through it all, during the long journey to bring this volume to completion, I have been more intrigued by what the naturalist experienced or felt or believed than what he or she accomplished because in exploring any life a fuller portrait emerges.

As far as how I selected those featured in this first volume, I thought about how different personalities and life stories would fit together under the same literary roof, so to speak. What you have before you is a purposeful selection—elaborated further below—of this first collection of Wisconsin naturalists. Someone else may have selected a different array of personality types. In Volume One, 18 chapters feature 19 naturalists. Nine of these naturalists were inducted into the Wisconsin Conservation Hall of Fame (www.wchf.org). I knew personally eight of the nine and wasn't alive to know the ninth, Increase Lapham.

The Wisconsin naturalists represented here are well known to some, barely known, or not known at all, but, again, I have been more interested in life stories and experiences than in notable accomplishments. How to begin? Who goes first and who last? This volume has to begin with Increase Lapham, the pioneering, self-taught naturalist (and arguably our first well-known ecologist of sorts) who came to Wisconsin before it was a state, and who settled in Milwaukee before it was a city. The near-bookend has to be Eric Epstein, the highly regarded, longtime ecologist for the Wisconsin DNR's Bureau of Endangered Resources—now the Bureau of Natural Heritage Conservation—who retired in 2011 with an understanding of Wisconsin landscapes that few have attained. And in between I will introduce you to extraordinary men and women whose lives are as varied as the subjects that interest them.

Francis Zirrer follows Lapham as the next earliest-appearing naturalist chronologically among those covered in this volume. George Knudsen and Jim Zimmerman follow next, and are paired because they were only two years apart in age (born in the mid-1920s) and often ran into each other early on. Ruth Hine, the Hamerstroms, and Sam Robbins follow because of their friendships and work during the same time period in the middle to later years of the twentieth century. Lorrie Otto follows George Becker because, like Becker (devoted to fishes), she became focused on a singular pursuit: transforming our front lawns into showcases of native plants. Francis Hole is next as the chief spokesperson for our soils. Bill Volkert, LeRoy Lintereur, Lois Nestel, and Marion Moran follow because they are largely self-taught, though each had varying degrees of education, ranging from no college (Nestel), to some college (Volkert and Moran), to a college degree (Lintereur).

Joseph Rose follows Marion Moran because of his indigenous heritage and perspective, a perspective that Marion revered. Michael Van Stappen precedes Eric Epstein because he was at life's end during the time of our interview—a unique circumstance—and because he was a friend of Eric's. The last chapter focuses on Sigurd Olson because of his importance to other naturalists portrayed here, and because his wise outlook and indefatigable spirit provide a fitting anchor to the book.

Most chapters of Volume One begin with a brief biographical sketch followed by the words only of the naturalist I interviewed. I employed this approach to allow the reader to connect immediately with a naturalist. A few chapters contain narratives and selected excerpts from journals or letters. My guiding intention throughout is to honor Leopold's legacy as demonstrated through the journeys and stories of our past and present naturalists, who tirelessly remind us to not lose sight of ecological and human-land relationships.

You will notice men* are featured more than women in this volume. Why? When I began my chosen profession as a conservation biologist with the Wisconsin Department of Natural Resources in the early 1980s, there were far fewer women than men in the wildlife and natural history fields, to say nothing about what wildlife-based professions were like prior to the 1950s (as Fran Hamerstrom could attest). Accordingly, my early field experiences (and later conversations) involved a far greater number of men than women, particularly those individuals older than me. Thankfully, today, the number of women in the wildlife field, and in the sciences in general, has increased dramatically.

*Each a white Caucasian male (except for Joe Rose). We need more people of color in the field to represent the diversity of our culture, and to bring unique perspectives on the natural world.

*

The true value of the Midland lifestyle is that it simultaneously builds and strengthens three levels of existence—individual, community, and Earth. In building character, [founder] Paul Squibb knew it was necessary to avoid the clutter that came as a burden of living in prosperity.... To Squibb, a life of character was an intentional, measured, uncluttered life—a life free from the keeping-up-appearances mentality that burdens us with conspicuous consumption and distracts us towards minutiae.... The means by which Squibb sought to build character in his simple life school almost a century ago are the same ones now advocated by modern-day visionaries for healing our planet from the affliction of "affluenza" and climate collapse.... Uncluttered lives leave smaller ecological footprints.

> —Lise Schickel Goddard. *MIDLAND ~ From Strong Roots Grows a Mighty Oak: The Enduring Educational Model of Midland School, 2016.*

ALTHOUGH I HAVE LIVED in Wisconsin all of my adult life (since 1972), the idea for something akin to this book originated when I was a high school student at Midland School near Los Olivos, California. Before arriving at Midland, I had lost interest in school in Washington D.C., where my father worked for the State Department. I remember only being happy when alone by a stream or pool looking for frogs and turtles or exploring fields looking for bugs and butterflies or walking in a woods listening to birds—wherever I could find a piece of the natural world in a very urban setting. My parents were worried.

Born and raised in St. Paul, Minnesota, they both had a love for remote places and had a primitive cabin on Lake Namakagon in northern Wisconsin. It was here where we were the last to go electric on the lake—preferring to use kerosene lamps—that I grew up during the summers and where I first acquired a passion for birding, awaking during early morns on a screened porch to the calls of an eastern wood-pewee or red-eyed vireo, or listening at night to a distant common loon as a stormfront approached.

My older sister, Adelaide Donnelley, who lives in California, suggested to my parents that Midland School was just the place where I could regain my footing. Midland lay at the knee of the foothills right next to the Los Padres National Forest. The founder of Midland—Paul Squibb—leased land beginning in 1932 during the Great Depression and eventually purchased what amounted to 2,860 acres for the school, which emphasized Spartan values to develop a student's character. We lived in small wooden cabins heated by tiny wood stoves that we collected firewood for during school outings in the surrounding foothills. At Midland, traditional academics were combined with hard physical work and afforded endless opportunities to explore the natural world.

At night, occasionally, I remember sneaking away with a few upperclassmen to the distant reservoir where we would sit on a hillside—a long grass stem in my mouth—listening to a western screech owl or common poorwill.

What I liked best about Midland (a special school, still about 80 in size, and today coeducational), in addition to its unique teachers and students, was the freedom to wander alone in the nearby hills and mountain range on Tuesday, Friday, and Sunday afternoons, when students were free to do whatever they chose. Grass Mountain showed its face every day as an alluring and prominent destination.

On those blessed afternoons off, I often hiked alone as far away as I could, into the chaparral, through sagebrush and oaks, and higher into manzanita, up into cougar and condor range, knowing I needed to be back at school in time for a shower and the school dinner. Oh, and there was the nightly required gathering at the school chapel just before dinner, but I tried to avoid that ritual whenever possible.

During one of these forays, near the summit of Grass Mountain, I remember thinking about naturalist, writer, and explorer John Muir, and what it would have been like to sit with him around a campfire chewing the cud. Here was a man, originally from Scotland, who had spent his boyhood living at a small lake in central Wisconsin, and attending the University of Wisconsin-Madison before leaving for the California wilderness. He famously wrote: "I was only leaving one university for another, the Wisconsin University for the university of the Wilderness."[1] I identified with his fierce independence and need to explore the wilderness, and it got me thinking about the different ways early outdoor experiences, or a paucity of them, have influenced our life's direction. I felt that if I knew more about the inner life of a naturalist such as Muir—what he thought, imagined, suffered through, found joy in—I would understand myself better and find a commonality and purpose in carving a life's direction.

Fast forward to today. What a great pleasure and high reward it has been to have walked—literally and metaphorically—with the naturalists in the pages before you, or to have gleaned insights from their letters and personal journals. I discovered I shared many of the same general attributes that define this set of naturalists: perseverance, need for solitude, love of wild and remote places, need to master one or more natural history subjects (for me, birds), a sometimes quirky but essential sense of humor to survive failures and disappointments, and a desire to share what has been learned through nature study and outdoor experiences.

So, I've been asked many a time, why did I write this book? Other than my intent to introduce to the public the stories and lives of Wisconsin naturalists past and present, what is the greater motivation? The answer is simple and basic: I want others to meet—and learn from—those committed to awakening the wonder, awe, joy, and insight that nature offers through observation, contemplation, and study.

If there are three takeaway themes from the book (and really from the years conversing with all naturalists involved in the **Wisconsin Naturalists Project**), I would venture to say 1) early exposure/interactions with the outdoors were pivotal to influencing a *naturalist's path*; 2) a guiding influence or mentor, and/or literature read early on, were important to encouraging or fostering a career (or an avocation) as a naturalist; and 3) each possessed an unquenchable curiosity for, and a desire to know more about, Wisconsin's natural history.

🍃

There is a danger of becoming too mechanistic, too technological, in our approach to human-land relations. That is why the role of the naturalist is so important: because he or she is in the unique position of not only providing knowledge but guidance in the continuing effort to broaden our creative relations with the land, thereby elevating the importance of conservation in our lives.

A quarter century before Leopold wrote "The Land Ethic" in *A Sand County Almanac*, he wrote what historian Susan L. Flader called his "most significant ... of his unpublished manuscripts"[2] on conservation ethics: "Some Fundamentals of Conservation in the Southwest," published 30 years posthumously.[3] Toward the end of the article Leopold departs from a discussion of erosion and focuses on "conservation as a moral issue."

Paraphrasing the Russian philosopher P.D. Ouspensky, Leopold writes that we try to "regard the earth's parts—soil, mountains, rivers, atmosphere, etc.—as organs, as parts of organs, or a coordinated whole, each part with a definite function.... In such a case we would have all the visible attributes of a living thing, which we do not now realize to be such because it is too big, and its life processes too slow. And there would also follow that invisible attribute—a soul or consciousness—which not only Ouspensky, but many philosophers of all ages, ascribe to all living things and aggregations thereof, including the 'dead' earth."

Here, in these early words, you have a hint of the philosophical underpinnings that shaped Leopold's *Land Ethic*: "A thing is right when it tends to preserve the integrity, stability, and beauty of the biotic community."[4] This ethic was an outgrowth of his love for people and the land, and a desire, I believe, to see a new, broader envisioning for how we regard natural resources and the outdoors, which is a central thesis in *AFIELD*.

Beyond reading this book, I want you to deepen your own special relationship to and with the outdoors. "You don't have to be in a wilderness setting," says Sigurd Olson in the book's last chapter. You can begin anywhere—in a city park or in any landscape free of pavement. Here's an example of note:

On August 7, 2018, I visited wolf biologist Adrian Wydeven and wife Sarah Boles, a professional landscaper, who was working late that day. In a forest opening, Sarah had created a remarkable meadow garden of native plants at their home in rural northwestern Wisconsin.

I arrived about 6 p.m., and as I turned up a road close to their home, I observed a merlin (*Falco columbarius*) darting across the road nearly at eye level. Adrian and I soon sat on a bench and chair at the garden's edge along

SUMNER MATTESON

the upper part of the meadow community next to a small runoff pond. The pond basin had recently filled with water from rains that had fallen a few days earlier.

Quickly we took note of a large number of dragonflies zipping around us. There were hundreds! These were concentrated at three different locations in the garden. The dragonflies were flying so fast we couldn't identify them. What were they attracted to? Answer: concentrations of "hilltopping" black garden ants (*Lasius niger*) emerging from a grassy mound at each location. Adrian commented that he didn't see a single flying ant, except one that had landed on my right shoulder but soon disappeared.

We decided to catch one of these dragonflies, but had no net, so Adrian went inside their home and returned with one of Sarah's shawls—bright orange in color. We stretched it out above the mound, and Adrian flipped it over and caught a dragonfly on our first try. Looking at Karl and Dorothy Legler's *Dragonflies of Wisconsin*, we first guessed variable darner (*Aeshna interrupta*)—a beautiful specimen with turquoise, gem-like markings along its abdomen. The key to darner identification, we later learned, is the shape of the first side-stripe on the thorax because the markings on the abdomen can be similar or appear identical for different darner species. Consulting with naturalist and odonate specialist Bill Smith, we learned its true identity: the Canada darner (*Aeshna canadensis*), which exhibits a deep cut-out on the thorax's first side-stripe.

The merlin I had first seen when arriving, I surmised, might have been attracted to the dragonfly concentrations in the garden area, which likely contained more than one species. We walked around Adrian and Sarah's home in a half-mile radius and found just one other similar gathering of dragonflies and ants but nothing near the numbers observed at the native meadow garden. So, none of this would have happened if we hadn't been in the right place at the right time, but more importantly, none of what we observed would have taken place if Sarah—over several years—had not diligently created the meadow community of native plants outside their home.

Here was a neat, little ecological demonstration playing out before two enraptured adults (one that specialized in mammals and one in birds) awed like kids in a candy store: the merlin (possibly) attracted to the dragonflies; the dragonflies attracted to and feasting on the ants; and the ants emerging from dry grassy mounds of a small native meadow created by a caring native plant enthusiast. (Parenthetically, the same phenomenon—with merlin nearby—occurred here in 2019 just thirteen days later than the 2018 date—on 20 August, about the same time of day, and only on that day, Adrian told me.) Therefore, dear reader, never underestimate the learning opportunities before you when you allow yourself to be open to the creations and teachings of the natural world.

And further with the aid of a local naturalist, or through one of the hundreds of field trips offered by the Natural Resources Foundation of Wisconsin (www.wisconservation.org), and/or by exploring our State Natural Areas (search keywords "wisconsin state natural areas" on internet), discover that you can do or see more than what you thought, maybe more than you ever imagined.

I also hope this book will motivate younger generations to place a greater value in knowing and safeguarding our natural resources when they read the stories and come to know the experiences of our naturalists. By having a glimpse into their private worlds and what obstacles stood in their way, I am certain their life stories will become illuminating and instructive.

This book will proudly proclaim that our stories do not end, even when we are no longer around to share them.

Now, I only ask that you take this book with you to a favorite quiet place, where you can read and re-read the words of these remarkable individuals who, in my mind, are the unsung conservation heroes of our time, of generations past, present, and future. Then, hook up with a like-minded soul, and go explore the natural world! ☀

Sumner Matteson

Van Vliet Hemlocks State Natural Area, Vilas County, Wisconsin. Old-growth northern mesic forest with small bog lakes, kettle depressions, and black ash swamps.
Photo by Thomas A. Meyer, courtesy of Wisconsin DNR.

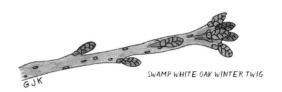

SWAMP WHITE OAK WINTER TWIG

Prologue:
Revelations

Oh that glorious Wisconsin wilderness! Everything new and pure in the very prime of the spring ... young leaves, flowers, animals, the winds and the streams and the sparkling lake, all wildly, gladly rejoicing together!

—John Muir, *The Story of My Boyhood and Youth*

What [Alexander von] Humboldt sees from the mountaintop is more than just a view. Every view reveals a history, from the deep time of geology to the shifting migrations of nations to the personality of the viewer, primed by his time to see beauty, meaning, and hope in the landscape, to read beyond the surface to the dynamic play of crosscurrents surging in the depths.

—Laura Dassow Walls, *The Passage to Cosmos*

This book largely reflects the Western scientific natural history tradition as represented by the naturalists I interviewed during 1979–2017. The one exception is Ojibwe elder Joseph Rose. There is today a growing appreciation of indigenous ecological knowledge, and writers are beginning to take note.[5]

Aristotle (384–322 BC) was among the first curious Europeans to study nature systematically and earnestly discuss his findings. For nearly 2,000 years his observations of the natural world, particularly his observations of animal behavior, dominated scientific understanding. Especially notable was his knowledge of fish (ichthyology), documented copiously in his *Historia Animalium*.[6]

A turning point in the understanding of natural history occurred in the seventeenth century when former British clergyman and college teacher John Ray (1627–1705) became the first to classify plants into species and passionately convey his knowledge of natural history to his students.[7] Following fairly close behind Ray was the unheralded German-born naturalist Maria Sibylla Merian (1647–1717), who made a unique and major contribution to entomology and botanical art through her detailed notes and illustrations of the metamorphosis of butterflies, showing the close relationship between plants and butterfly developmental stages, leading some in recent times to call her the world's first ecologist.[8] (The word *ecology* actually did not begin to crop up until 1873; it was first spelled *oecology*, which came from the Greek word for household, *oikos*.) She also closely observed the behavior, habitats, and uses of insects in Surinam, and her scientific drawings and sketches of tropical insects and animal life are prized possessions today.

Swedish taxonomist Carolus Linnaeus (1707–1778) greatly refined John Ray's work when he published in 1758 the tenth and definitive edition of *Systema Naturae*[9] (the system of nature), which provided the scientific foundation (binomial nomenclature) for the classification of plants and animals. But in the public eye, the individual who first aroused widespread sentiment about natural history study was a contemporary of Linnaeus—the popular Reverend Gilbert White (1720–1793), who spent countless hours in the field and delighted in sharing what he observed with anyone who would listen.

White's *Natural History and Antiquities of Selborne*, published in 1788, consisted largely of letters describing the natural history around his Selborne vicarage in England's southern coastal county of Hampshire. Though he lacked formal scientific training, White impressed scientific minds with his fine eye for detail and a superb capability to capture on paper what he observed in the natural world. So keen were White's observations, and so confident was he, that on at least one occasion he corrected the great Linnaeus who believed a cuckoo to be a bird of prey. White did not personally inform Linnaeus because of modesty, rather White's brother, John, took it upon himself to write to Linnaeus to advise him of the error.[10]

Gilbert White's love for nature study always gave way, however, to his responsibilities as a clergyman. The lure of the church life almost altered the course of another Englishman—Charles Darwin (1809–1892). Having shown little interest in being a physician, as his father desired, Charles, again at his father's behest, chose the next best life—that of a priest. He went to Cambridge University for three years, became somewhat disenchanted, but attained a bachelor of arts degree. While there, however, he came under the influence of a geology teacher, Adam Sedgwick, and a professor of botany, the Reverend John Stevens Henslow. It was Henslow who, recognizing Darwin's greater aptitude for geology and botany and the study of natural history than for ecclesiastical matters, arranged for Darwin's five-year journey on the *HMS Beagle* in 1831 to South America and the Canary and Galapagos islands.[11]

When Darwin returned to England, he detailed his experiences (using Gilbert White as a model) in a book titled *Journal of Researches*, published in 1839.[12] During his southern voyage, Darwin became quite enamored with the animals he observed, especially when visiting the Galapagos Islands. Information on animal ethology and ecology contributed significantly to his theory of natural selection in *On the Origin of Species*, published in 1859.[13]

Another very important and highly regarded (but hardly recognized today) naturalist was a friend of Darwin's, the Prussian explorer and exemplary geographer Alexander von Humboldt (1769–1859), whose popular writings describing his travels and scientific observations in Latin America between 1799 and 1804 influenced not only Darwin, but in the U.S., zoologist and geologist Louis Agassiz, naturalist John Muir, and writer Henry David Thoreau, among several others. Humboldt's detailed work on the relationship between geography and plant occurrences set the stage for the development of biogeography, and he was the first to articulate the concept of climate change based on his observations.[14] His groundbreaking, multi-volume tome, *Kosmos*, which portrayed a unified, ecological, interacting universe, anticipated later work by Aldo Leopold, who viewed the earth as a "coordinated whole."[15]

Still another largely forgotten but highly regarded naturalist of the times was Mary Anning (1799–1847) of southern England. Her love of fossils she discovered initially along England's southern coast when she was only eleven eventually garnered her much attention in academic circles. A notable find was the discovery of the first *Ichthyosaurus*, a dolphin-like reptile. Other "firsts" included the long-necked reptile, *Plesiosaurus*, and a *pterosaur* or "flying dragon," in the late 1820s. Mary tragically died of breast cancer in her late 40s, but her contributions to our understanding of fossils continue to draw praise.

THE STUDY OF AMERICAN NATURAL HISTORY began ambitiously in the late seventeenth century when Jesuit missionary Louis Nicolas (who earlier had joined Father Claude Allouez at Wisconsin's Chequamegon Bay mission on Lake Superior in 1667) wrote "the first comprehensive work on North American birds... [and became] the first writer to attempt to describe all the wildlife of North America."[16] His unpublished work—two manuscripts—vanished for a while after his death, and were not published until the twentieth century.[17]

In the early decades of the eighteenth century, Englishman Mark Catesby (1682–1749) published *The Natural History of Carolina, Florida and the Bahama Islands*—in parts beginning in 1730 and ending in 1748. This exhaustive work contained 220 colored plates, hand-drawn, of everything from mammals to insects to plants—a comprehensive depiction, including descriptions and observations, of the natural history of Britain's southeastern colonies.[18]

After Catesby came John Bartram (1699–1777), the first American-born and largely self-taught naturalist to achieve international recognition. Bartram (as did Catesby) obtained funds from wealthy gentlemen eager to obtain plants for their gardens, and plants from the British colonies were highly prized. But the long voyages between North America and Britain, combined with rats eating seeds of different varieties, spelled disaster. Bartram changed all of that through ingenious packaging methods (he coated seeds to protect them) involving gourds, bottles, and other containers that effectively protected plants from the stressors of long voyages. Owing to this success and his ability as a botanist in discovering rare species, Bartram became King George III's botanist in North America in 1765.[19]

Had the Brits won the Revolutionary War eleven years later, who knows, Aldo Leopold might have been King George VI's ecologist in North America. But more on Aldo later. Preceding him in Wisconsin (which achieved statehood in 1848) were a handful of outstanding nineteenth century naturalists; among these was self-taught naturalist Increase Lapham (1811–1875), whose chapter starts off this book and whose dominant interests were archeology, botany, meteorology, and geology.[20] New York-born Henry Rowe Schoolcraft (1793–1864), self-taught as a geologist, mineralogist, zoologist, and botanist, was another.

In 1820, Schoolcraft accompanied an official U.S. expedition searching for the source of the Mississippi. Traveling from Detroit via St. Mary's River into Lake Superior and along Superior's southern shore, he served as the expedition's official geologist and mineralogist, and he also collected many botanical and zoological specimens.[21] To him we owe the first copious notes on Wisconsin's avifauna—notes taken during trips down the Namekagon, Flambeau, Mississippi, and Wisconsin rivers, up the Bad and White rivers, across the prairies between Galena and Portage, and along Lake Superior. Two of the more notable species he documented: the Arctic three-toed woodpecker (today known as the black-backed woodpecker *Picoides arcticus*), a species unknown to renowned ornithologist Alexander Wilson in New York; and the evening grosbeak (*Coccothraustes vespertinus*), a species unknown to science at the time.[22]

Then there was Ohio-born Dr. Philo Romayne Hoy (1816–1892). He came to Racine in 1846 to open a medical practice and began to collect animal specimens extensively. By 1876, this good friend of Increase Lapham had obtained 318 bird species, eggs of 150 bird species, scores of mammals and reptiles, 1,300 beetles, and 2,000 moths. The Smithsonian Institution's Spencer Fullerton Baird described Hoy's collection of local birds as the largest of its kind. Hoy published extensively on several taxa, was the first to investigate the deep-water fauna of Lake Michigan, and documented changes since settlement in the abundance and occurrence of birds around Racine.[23]

Wisconsin's finest oologist was Captain Benjamin Franklin Goss (1823–1893), who first arrived in Milwaukee from New Hampshire in 1841 to pursue a career as a printer. A jack-of-all-trades, Goss farmed near Pewaukee until 1855, served briefly in the Wisconsin Assembly, became a grocer, turned to real estate, enlisted in the army for three years, started a general store, and worked as a postmaster. His serious collecting began in the late 1860s. By the time of his death in 1893 he had collected over 3,000 eggs representing 720 bird species, and he had traveled throughout North America to obtain them. Eggs were not all that he collected. He donated nearly 2,400 butterflies and beetles caught in the U.S. to the Milwaukee Public Museum, along with his enormous egg collection.[24]

After Increase Lapham, perhaps Wisconsin's most gifted early-day naturalist was Swedish-born Thure Kumlien (1819–1888). Kumlien attended Upsala Academy where, at age 19, he made a series of watercolors of Swedish birds and mammals. At Upsala University, he studied and became steeped in theology, history, geography, philosophy, mathematics, Latin, Greek, Hebrew, and natural history. He soon fled to Wisconsin to escape oppressive parents, who disapproved of his marriage to Christine Wallberg, daughter of a Swedish army officer.[25]

When he arrived in Milwaukee on August 28, 1843—seven years after Increase Lapham arrived in Milwaukee from Ohio (there is no evidence of any correspondence or interaction between the two naturalists)— the Kumliens, along with a small Swedish party, set off on foot for Lake Koshkonong. This amounted to a 60-mile walk to find land where they could settle. They eventually settled on the northern side of the lake amid open fields and an oak forest, about a quarter-mile from the present-day Dane County line.[26]

The notion of making a living through farming held little appeal to Thure, and upon his arrival at the lake he began to collect animal specimens with the idea of eventually supporting his family through the sale of various natural history items. (Collecting and cataloging specimens was the norm of the day for an aspiring naturalist.) Thure eventually built a fine collection of bird skins and eggs that gained wide attention. He was also an avid plant collector. Near his home he collected at least 102 plant species that he later donated to the Milwaukee Public Museum.[27]

Despite lacking authoritative texts on American natural history, Kumlien employed his knowledge of Swedish natural history and eventually developed a comprehensive understanding of southern Wisconsin's flora and fauna, including a thorough comprehension of phanerogams (spermatophytes), ferns and their allies, mosses, lichens, and fungi. The American botanist Edward Lee Greene, who learned a considerable amount of botany from Kumlien, dedicated a new genus—*Kumlienia*—in his honor.[28]

As settlement occurred around him, Kumlien witnessed the destruction of local flora and fauna, something he lamented in a letter to Greene. He noted that a plant-rich tamarack swamp two miles from his home had been drained and converted to a strip featuring "market-garden vegetables."[29]

Kumlien collected in most branches of natural history, including mammals, birds, fishes, reptiles, amphibians, insects, and shells, but there was hardly enough business to sustain him, so he taught at the Albion Academy in Albion (eastern Dane County) between 1867 and 1870. Here, he introduced his students to the science of ornithology.[30]

Hired by the University of Wisconsin and the State Normal Schools to make collections of birds, Thure became in 1881 a taxidermist and conservator for the Wisconsin Natural History Society. In 1883 the Milwaukee Public Museum bought the Society's collections, and he held the same position with the museum until his death in 1888.[31]

SUMNER MATTESON

Overseas, Kumlien gained a reputation as the state's finest collector at a time when one's skill as a collector was equated with one's capability as a naturalist. He was not as revered at home. Local residents thought he was a little odd for venturing out at night with a lantern to capture and collect invertebrates in the fields around his home. But his collections were substantial. He once made a trip to the Milwaukee Public Museum carrying 600 specimens of plants and invertebrates, as well as many birds.[32]

More than any other pioneer naturalist, Kumlien increased our knowledge of Wisconsin's avifauna. Although he did not obtain his first book on American ornithology until 1848, by 1850 he had documented the occurrence of at least 115 bird species in the southern part of the state. More interested in sharing his observations than in publishing papers on his findings, Thure had, in the words of ornithologist A.W. Schorger "an intense and childlike love of natural objects" that contributed to his ability as "a singularly accurate observer."[33]

One of Thure's five sons, Aaron Ludwig Kumlien (1853–1902), was a fine naturalist in his own right, capable of producing beautiful drawings and watercolors of birds, butterflies, fish, and mammals. He taught at Milton College in the 1890s and gained a reputation as an excellent field naturalist who directed and guided his students in the study of nature. Ludwig is perhaps best remembered for his collaboration with naturalist Ned Hollister on the seminal book *Birds of Wisconsin*, published in 1903. It's a work that summarized nearly 60 years of ornithological records collected largely by the Kumlien family. The authors described over 357 bird species and subspecies.[34]

ALDO LEOPOLD,[35] born January 11, 1887, grew up along the banks of the Mississippi in Burlington, Iowa, the son of a furniture manufacturer of German descent. After graduating from the Yale School of Forestry in 1909 and working for the United States Forest Service in Arizona, he accepted a position in 1924 in Madison, Wisconsin, as associate director of the U.S. Forest Products Laboratory. He came to Madison with the understanding that he would soon become director, but it was not to be, and for the next four years he became mired in administration and paperwork. He quit in 1928 and went into private practice as a consulting forester. He also performed game surveys and assisted universities in developing wildlife management programs.

Aldo used his time away from government bureaucracy to write the classic *Game Management*, based on lessons learned over 15 years in the Southwest and Midwest. The same year it was published, 1933, he joined the University of Wisconsin-Madison to fill the chair of game management, created especially for him. Two years later, he bought an abandoned farm on 80 acres of overworked land adjacent to the Wisconsin River. Here with his family he fixed up an abandoned chicken coop—the "shack"—and conducted ecological experiments to restore native vegetation and wildlife.

The refinement of years of natural history observation and interpretation, together with personal reflections, led to the writing of the renowned *A Sand County Almanac*,[36] which was repeatedly rejected by publishers over a period of seven years before the Oxford University Press called on April 14, 1948, to notify him of its acceptance. A week later, Aldo died fighting a neighbor's brush fire. As he realized his heart was failing and death was near, he lay down in a grassy area, folded his hands together across his chest, and passed away, with the fire, which had become light, quickly brushing over his body.[37]

Today, there is no question that Leopold is the most well-known and revered Wisconsin naturalist among the pantheon of American naturalists. More importantly, his work very much represents the broad community of Wisconsin conservation and natural history figures, including those represented in this volume. It is his legacy of keen natural history study combined with a focus on ecological restoration and a consummate ability to communicate widely what he learned and interpreted that is honored through the stories and lives of the 19 naturalists presented in this book. Collectively, their stories serve to empower the Leopold legacy and present a cogent argument for working together to make sure that the conservation of biodiversity* is not imperiled but preserved for posterity. ☀

*A final note: scientific names of plants and animals in this volume are used sparingly, with some exceptions, to make the book more accessible (readable) to the general reader. And since scientific nomenclature is likely to change regularly, instead of an appendix listing the common and scientific names of every plant and animal discussed, I instead have listed in the book's only Appendix, the on-line taxonomic sources for the organisms mentioned. The reader is referred to this Appendix to check an on-line source for the most current common and scientific names of species.

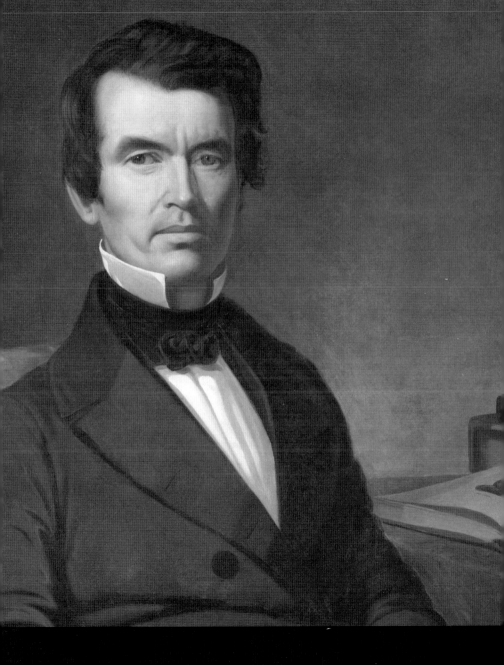

Increase Lapham

PAPER BIRCH

GJK

Chapter One~
Increase Lapham

It is with a great deal of regret that I inform you that I cannot spend this day of rest with you at home, in peace and quiet, instead of in the woods ten miles from any place.

—Letter to wife, Ann Marie Lapham, Sunday, 21 April 1839

Apart from Native Americans, who were the first to know Wisconsin's natural history, there was one who many argue was Wisconsin's premier naturalist—Increase Allen Lapham—the first to promote the state's natural history well beyond the state's borders. Wiry, quiet and unassuming, this self-trained scholar possessed an inexhaustible passion to understand and catalog the natural world.

Today, Increase Lapham is widely recognized as Wisconsin's most accomplished pioneering naturalist, working at a time preceding and following statehood, and initiating investigations into the state's botany, geology, topography, geography, ichthyology, meteorology, history, forestry, and archeology. The Smithsonian Institution published his work on effigy mounds in 1855—the highly acclaimed *The Antiquities of Wisconsin*.[38]

One day, while travelling in an open wagon with a group of reporters to inspect the planned route of a southeastern Wisconsin railway line, he asked the driver to stop and stop again so that he could walk into a field to pick a flower or another plant, or collect a stone. One reporter described Lapham's effect this way: "No sooner had we fairly started, than little was his mind occupied with the question of the railway.... If he secured something rare and new, his face and manner seemed to express the joy of a child in chasing a butterfly. And so we traveled for 30 or 40 miles. The journey was slow, but interesting, and the more we saw of his guileless and child-like life, the more profound was our admiration for the character of the man who seemed to rise above the dross of this world, and soar constantly in the realms of Science."[39]

His seminal work on Wisconsin's forests—*Report of the disastrous effects of the destruction of forest trees, now going on so rapidly in the State of Wisconsin*[40]— warned of the dangers of resource over-exploitation, and he became known as a father of forest conservation for his advocacy of scientific management. Of equal importance was his concern for the effects of weather on farmers and the Great Lakes shipping trade. He became immersed in the study of weather, and in 1870 helped establish a national storm warning system, which was to evolve into the National Weather Service.

Born March 7, 1811, in Palmyra, New York, to Quaker parents and the fifth of 13 children, Increase (named after Increase Allen, his grandfather on his mother's side) originally came to Wisconsin at age 25 as a self-trained Ohio canal engineer. He was invited by a fellow Ohio canal worker, Byron Kilbourn, to join an engineering crew to help build a canal from Milwaukee west into Wisconsin's lead region. Increase learned canal work under his father, Seneca, a contractor on the Erie Canal, and from his brother Darius, an assistant engineer. The Milwaukee-Rock River canal never materialized when railroad transportation took root, but Lapham chose to remain in Milwaukee with his new bride, Ann Marie Alcott.

For the next nearly 40 years, as Milwaukee grew from a frontier village to a prosperous city, Increase went to great lengths to explore the countryside and document the area's natural history, publishing as early as 1836 the Wisconsin Territory's first scientific treatise, *A Catalogue of Plants and Shells Found in the Vicinity of Milwaukee*.[41] Eight years later, he finished Milwaukee's first commercially published book, *A Geographical and Topographical Description of Wisconsin*, which informed new immigrants eager to learn more about their chosen area of settlement. A second edition[42] in 1846 included his first published detailed map of the Wisconsin Territory.

In an unpublished autobiography,[43] Increase told how he first became intrigued by the natural world in Lockport, New York, where his father was working on the locks for the Erie Canal. "I earned some money by cutting stone to be used in the locks. Soon after this, I was employed in the engineer service … in the capacity of rodman for my brother Darius Lapham who had already [achieved] the position of assistant engineer. The beautiful mineral specimens I found in the deep cut rock at Lockport gave me my first ideas of mineralogy and initiated a habit of observation that has continued through all my life. I found amusement and pastime in the study of nature, leading to long walks in the country, and as I found no others of similar tastes, these rambles were usually without companions."

Learning through his "habit of observation" proved rewarding: "The satisfaction of being able to learn some new thing is a sufficient return for the extra effort. Knowledge is power, says the proverb. It is at any rate a pleasure."

Though self-deprecating to a fault, Increase's observation acumen led to his becoming an accomplished botanist. He estimated his botanical collection

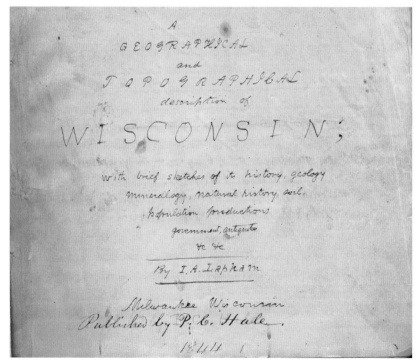

Increase Lapham's handwritten title page for *A Geographical and Topographical Description of Wisconsin*. Wisconsin Historical Society, WHS-101706.

CHAPTER ONE

of specimens to be about 8,000 species at its peak, and he donated more than 1,000 plant specimens to the newly established University of Wisconsin Botany Department. He also filled requests for specimens from botanists overseas and from nationally known scientists, such as Harvard University botanist Asa Gray and naturalist Louis Agassiz.

Increase was also very involved with community and regional affairs, lecturing about science to high school students meeting at the Unitarian Church and to fellow members of the Milwaukee Lyceum, of which he was a founder. He served as the first secretary of the Wisconsin Academy of Sciences, Arts, and Letters and helped found the groundbreaking Milwaukee Female College and what is today the Wisconsin Historical Society, where he served as president for 10 years.

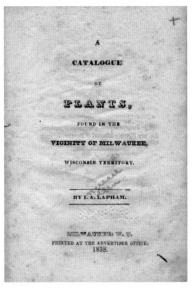

Title page of Increase Lapham's *A Catalogue of Plants Found in the Vicinity of Milwaukee, Wisconsin Territory.* Wisconsin Historical Society WHS-102043.

Lapham's noteworthy contributions are presented in elegant detail in the Lapham biography *Studying Wisconsin* by Martha Bergland and Paul G. Hayes (Wisconsin Historical Society Press, 2014), but it is his impressions of Wisconsin's landscapes, as well as his thoughts and feelings on early Wisconsin life that intrigue me most. These are typically conveyed through family letters, personal journals, and public writings—all wonderfully accessible through the Wisconsin Historical Society.

In the pages that follow, I attempt to shed light on these subjects, largely through correspondence Increase had with his older brother Darius with whom Increase held a special bond and exhibited a sharp but playful sense of humor, and with wife Ann Marie, to whom he turned more and more after Darius' death by cholera in 1850 at age 42; he was only three years older than Increase. It should be noted here that Increase's daughter, Julia, painstakingly edited and typed hundreds of pages of his correspondence, again, all housed at the Wisconsin Historical Society. These are the source for much of the material that follows.

I start, however, with the reflections of naturalist and friend Philo R. Hoy, who knew him for nearly 30 years, and who paid tribute to him in the *Transactions of the Wisconsin Academy of Sciences, Arts, and Letters,* after Lapham's death on September 14, 1875. His piece was titled, "Increase A. Lapham, LLD."[44]

"My first acquaintance with Dr. Lapham was in 1846, when one morning there landed from the steamer *Sultana* a small man with a huge collecting box hanging at his side.

"He came from Milwaukee and intended returning on foot along the lakeshore in order to collect plants and shells, no easy journey, encumbered, as he soon would be, with a well filled specimen box. He spoke lightly of the undertaking, saying he had performed similar feats before.... In after years we were often together, studying the mounds, quarries, forest trees, etc., near Racine, and my first impressions of his energy, perseverance, enthusiasm, accuracy, and extent of information were all deepened by our subsequent meetings.

"He was a quiet, unassuming gentleman, benevolent, and most hospitable, as both strangers and friends can abundantly testify. He had not the advantages of commanding presence, and was not gifted in public speaking, and being modest to a fault, always inclined to underrate his own abilities and labors. He often did not receive that recognition which his knowledge demanded ... [but] he soon became the authority on all scientific subjects and was often appealed to from city, state, and country for information which he alone could furnish....

"No one could doubt his industry who saw his large, valuable, and well used library, and his extensive and systematically arranged collection of minerals, fossils, shells and antiquities; or who examined his Herbarium of three thousand specimens—the finest in the Northwest—and then remembered in connection with all that his work in other directions. His idea of rest was characteristically shown by his once cataloguing my hundreds of insects for future use in some publication, at a time when he visited me under his physicians' orders to take a needed rest and abstain from business.

"Lapham never had the advantages of a college education. But was not the book of nature ever open to impart instruction to this student who knew how to read its pages with delight and profit?...

"To know Dr. Lapham, we must go with him to his workshop—the great out-doors. We stroll out on the prairies. He pulls up the grass and discourses

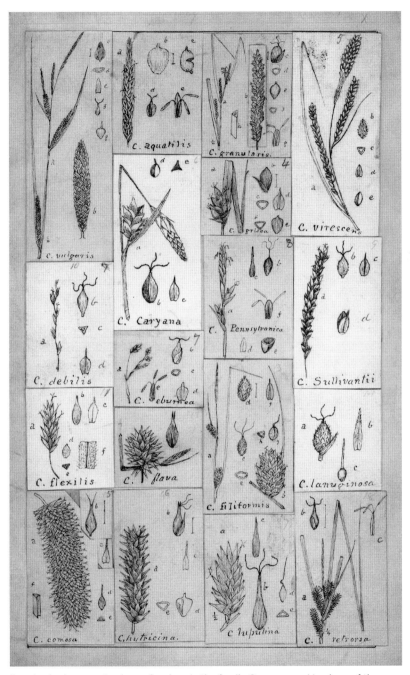

Drawing by Increase Lapham of sedges in the family Cyperaceae. Members of the genus *Carex* may be called "true" sedges, the species-rich genus in the family. Wisconsin Historical Society, WHS-83780.

familiarly of the spikes and spikelets, the rachis and glume, inspects the roots, digs down and examines the soil from which they spring. His tongue is unloosed, and he becomes eloquent in spite of himself. We go into the forest. He talks of the various species of trees, the vines that clamber up their trunks and nestle in their branches. He inspects the lichens that grow on the rough bark, examines the moss that adheres to the roots, and unearths a tiny helix that has found a home there. We go to the rapids, and he immediately interests himself in the rare ferns that festoon the rocks with their graceful fronds or clambers among the quarries, marks the stratification of the Silurian rocks, and chips out rare forms of Crinoids and Trilobites—those wonderful representations of the ocean fauna of the dim past.... He talks of the force of the winds and their velocity and direction and then looks up [at] the clouds and tells their indication, and speaks of the annual rainfall and of the average temperature of the seasons for the last thirty years, during which time he had kept a faithful record of these phenomena...."

In the following correspondence between Increase and his family, "Dear Brother" or "My dear brother" refers to older brother Darius, unless otherwise noted.

Milwaukee, July 7th, 1836

Dear Brother:

Since I left you at Reading [Ohio] I have passed over 1,200 miles! Milwaukee contains about fifty houses, mostly on the east side of the river; it is supposed to contain (with the suburbs) about 1,000 inhabitants! Town lots are worth $500 to $5,500. Lumber is from $30 to $50 per thousand feet. Flour $8.25 per barrel and everything else about the same proportion. Labor is $1.25 per day and boarding, which equals $2.00 per day. The mail arrives and departs once a week and has just brought papers that I saw at Detroit.... I find Milwaukee just about what I expected and have therefore no cause of disappointment or complaint. I suppose I can enjoy myself as well here as among the musketos [sic] on the extension of the Miami canal.

Your affectionate brother,

I.A. Lapham

CHAPTER ONE

Dear Father:

Milwaukee is the site of an Indian town and the remains of their wigwams are still to be seen. The ground is covered with small mounds, resembling large potato hills, on top of which they have planted from year to year their scanty crop of corn. The Indians found about here belong principally to the tribe called Menominee (in English "wild rice eaters").

I shall start in a few days on a geological excursion with Mr. Kilbourn [in whose house Lapham was boarding]. If we do not find gold mines we may find something else equally valuable.

Your dutiful son,

Increase

Milwaukee, Oct. 1st, 1836

Dear Father:

Your letter of July 4th came to hand towards the last of the month and on the very day that I mailed for you my first from this place....

I have already made several jaunts through the country. 1st, to Root river, 25 miles on foot and alone through the woods, 17 miles of it without any house! Saw no Indians but if I had, I should have felt much more safe than if I had met a gang of white men! They are decidedly the most to be dreaded! 2nd, to the Menononee [sic] Falls on horseback with an experienced backwoodsman. Encamped at night on the bank of the river at the falls. This was my first essay in camp duty. Cooked my dinner by hanging a piece of meat on a sharp stick and fastening the end of the stick in the ground before the fire. Slept on the ground under a small cloth tent which we brought on one of our horses. 3rd, went to Chicago; travelled along the Des Plaines river where I saw some of the finest lands that I ever did see.

The river runs through heavily timbered land bordered on both sides by broad, rolling prairies. Chicago is a low, level muddy place.

I have not heard from Darius since I left his house in June, is he still alive? Pazzi [another Lapham brother] says that Darius has a Rachel in his family now, is this his mother?

Don't forget to write me every month.

I remain your dutiful son,

Increase

Reading, Hamilton Co., Ohio
Oct. 30th, 1836

Dear Brother Increase:

You have gone so far to the 'far west' and joined yourself to that outlandish conglomeration of folks called "land speculators" of whom the president has as poor an opinion as I have, that I have been at a loss how to concoct a letter to suit you under the circumstances. By [Ohio businessman] Micajah [T. Williams] I sent you word that we were alive and kicking and by him I received the same important intelligence from you.

Micajah says that you must let "yarbs [herbs] and Mussells" alone and go to making yourself rich. Sam'l Forrer says he is afraid you will forget to get rich in your zeal for shellology. Micajah says he introduced you to Gov. Dodge and told him that his government was commenced under most favorable circumstances for internal improvements having two first rate civil engineers in the territory and that you were one of them!...

I remain yours forever,

Darius

Darius and Phebe (daughter) Lapham.
Ohio History Connection.

Milwaukee, W[isconsin] T[erritory]
Dec. 3rd, 1836

Dear Brother:

After waiting until I had lost all patience and had fairly come to the conclusion that you had determined not to write me again, I received your letter of Oct. 30th. Have you received six letters that I have sent you since I left home?

I regret very much that you do not answer my letters, for I want to give you an account of my numerous jaunts into the country in this vicinity; the woodlands, the prairies, the beautiful lakes surrounded by regular hills and filled with beautiful islands; our rivers and cascades, the rocks, stones and "yarbs;" the ancient mounds made to represent turtles, lions (?), bears and other animals, our native copper, our lead ore and our tremendous agricultural productions. I want you to know how I spend my time, what I am doing, how many canals, railroads and turnpikes I have located and a long list of other things which you formerly (or at least I supposed so) took some interest in knowing....

Your affectionate brother,

Increase

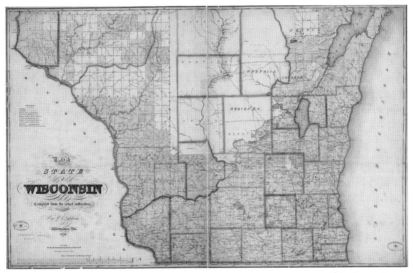

This detailed map outlines mid and southern WI county boundaries, and city/town lines are provided. Other marks include lead mines, copper mines, streams, plank roads, Lake Michigan elevation, Green Bay water depth, and the Milwaukee and Mississippi railroads. Wisconsin Historical Society, WHS-92362.

Milwaukee, W.T., Feb. 25, 1837

Dear Brother:

I have received your letter in which you say that you would read with interest an account of matters and things in general relation to this country. Our town has grown more rapidly than any other town in the United States, and would have grown much faster if we could have procured building material.

In October, 1835, the first lots were sold. There were then only three cabins in town, and not more than half a dozen persons. In one year from that time two hundred buildings were erected, and we have a population of twelve hundred souls. About $30,000 have been expended in grading streets and making other public improvements.

The society here is good, the people are principally from New York and the states east of it; many are from the Canadas. They all possess the enterprising go-a-head spirit of the New Englanders.

The country has not kept pace with the town in its onward march, for the land belongs to the government and cannot be purchased until the president of the U.S. sees fit to bring it into market. However, many people have taken possession of these lands with the intention of purchasing whenever they are brought into market, and in this way we have many fine farms. Merchandise of all kinds is sold here as cheap as at Columbus, O., and you will readily see why this is so when you remember that from Buffalo they are shipped directly to Milwaukee. There is no transfer from schooners to canal boats and no canal tolls to pay. Provisions, on the other hand, are about one hundred percent higher here than in Ohio on account of having to be transported from a distance. This, of course, makes farming a very profitable business.

Our town is very beautifully situated on a plain elevated from five to thirty feet above the lake and enclosed by hills about one hundred feet high. On the slope and projecting swells of these hills are some grand sites for residences commanding a view of the lake and the town. One of the best and most picturesque of these I have selected for myself. This plain is divided into several parts by the Milwaukee and Menomonee [sic] rivers and the Kinnikinnick Creek. The Milwaukee is navigable for the largest vessels on the lakes for two and a half miles above the mouth, but a sand bar thrown up by the lake prevents all vessels drawing more than six feet of water from entering the river. It is expected that the present Congress will appropriate $25,000 for constructing piers at this place.

In our immediate vicinity the land is covered with a dense forest, the timber of which is said by our ship-carpenters ... to be much more solid and firm in its texture than the timber of the Eastern states.

As we travel into the interior we find first the "Openings" and finally the "Prairies" at a distance varying (according to direction) from ten to twenty miles.

It is believed that a canal forty miles long will connect us with Rock River and thence with the lead and copper mines district between this river and the Mississippi, as well as with the whole immense valley of the "Father of Rivers" [Mississippi River Valley]. I shall start out as soon our snow is gone and the weather permits to make an exploration of the route of this canal.

I hope you will write me a history of the journey you propose to take to Columbus and home, and especially in regard to matters and things in general at home.

Your affectionate brother,

Increase

✦

Milwaukee, W.T., March 19, 1837

Dear Father,

I went out with a party a few days since to explore the summit of a canal from Milwaukee to Rock River, about 25 miles from here. When we started the weather was fine and the sleighing in some places rather bad. The next day it rained or snowed nearly all the day, but this did not prevent us from running the necessary levels. At night we encamped wet as we could well be, got our fire started and ourselves warmed and our supper over, and then came on a tremendous gale of wind from the northwest, which blew all the heat from our fire, blew our tent over and sunk the thermometer to ten degrees below zero. You can easily imagine we spent the night rather uncomfortably. The gale continued until noon the next day; and as we could do no more work nor find any more comfort, we came home....

I have enjoyed good health during the winter and my sleeping in the woods when the thermometer is below zero, does me more good than hurt.

Your dutiful son,

Increase

✦

Milwaukee, May 12, 1837

My dear brother:

Your letters of the 15th of March and the 6th of April were duly received.... Are you still in the service of the state? Or are you about to emigrate to the Hoosier state?

I spend two hours every morning (weather permitting) in making a garden for Pazzi, who is to be here within a few weeks with his wife and baby. It is surrounded by a fence made of cedar posts and tamarack poles, and I have planted many of the useful and ornamental plants and shall tomorrow morning put in some of the famous premium potatoes, which you may have seen puffed in the newspapers.... I send you a newspaper by which you will see that I have received the very profitable office of "Register of Claims"; it furnishes plenty of business but no pay.

Did I tell you of my exploration of the route between Pishtaka [today's lower Fox] and Bark rivers when the thermometer was 20 degrees below zero? The length of the winter is one of the principal objections to this country; they are pleasant but too long; they are fine sleighing but we soon become tired of that. We have had very little warm weather yet, vegetation is very much retarded. The summer is too short to suit a botanist.

Your truly affectionate brother,

Increase Allen Lapham

Milwaukee Nov. 27th, 1837

My dear brother,

A few days since on my return from the "Mineral Region" lying on the great Mississippi river, about a hundred and fifty miles west from here, I found your letter of the 24th and have derived more pleasure from reading it (and Hannah's, which accompanies it) than from any thing else which I have seen lately.

I am very glad to learn that there is one who thinks of me "when hands are on the plough" and who sits down to write me a letter "when his summer's work is over." I began to think that I had got so far away from home that I would be forgotten, but am happy to learn that it is not so.

I have been traveling about two weeks through our new country, have visited the famous city of Aztalan, and the new capital [Madison] of Wisconsin on the "Four Lakes." I have been on the ground which was the theater of the Indian War of 1830 [Blackhawk War of 1832], have seen and conversed with persons who were engaged in that war, have been down into the lead mines 90 feet below the surface and followed the drifts for many rods in various directions. All these were new and novel things to me, and I should have liked very much to have had you enjoy with me the pleasure of the trip.

Our cold weather set in about a week ago, and one of our long winters has commenced.

Remember me to all the folks and be assured that I shall always remain,

Your affectionate brother,

I. A. Lapham

✿

Dear Hannah,

You want to know how I get along at Milwaukee. I get along here very well. I sleep on my little mattrass [sic] which you saw at Columbus. I board with a fine family, Mr. Blanchard's, who live in the same house where I sleep and do my office work. Mr. B has one daughter grown and two little children, girls, about as old as Lorana and Amelia. We have plenty to eat and that which is "first rate and good." You have eaten white fish after they have been salted and put in barrels for some time, I have eaten them fresh from the lake. They are much better when fresh. I have [a] neat room to sleep in, well carpeted, a bureau and book case, plenty of books on law, Natural History and miscellany. I do not have to work very hard, my income is about $1,500 or $1,600 a year, maybe more.

When I shall come home is now very uncertain, perhaps in a year or so. But whether you will have a chance to look at my wife when I come is very doubtful. I can't get money enough to pay wedding expenses these hard times.

So good bye. Be a good girl. Your affectionate brother,

Increase

Dear Brother,

I received a few days since on my return from the "Mineral Country" your long epistle on the subject of shooting stars, Pazzi's journey, how to get along in the world, how you are drawing a salary of $3,000, how much you are ahead of the other engineers in Ohio and c&c. and so on, all of which is very interesting to me, and now it becomes my duty to sit down and write as long a letter in reply. But how shall I do it? What subject shall I select which shall be interesting to you? There's the rub! What do you care about our flourishing town, its all a "Humbug!" so I will say nothing about that.

Shall I tell you about the country between here and the Mississippi which I have just visited for the purpose of studying its features, its productiveness, its mines, its water communications, etc.? What are all those to you?

I suppose that an account of my descent into a mine 90 feet deep and extending many hundred feet in various directions, at that depth below the surface, or if I tell you how much I was surprised to find ore lying in horizontal beds instead of veins as had been represented, or if I should tell you of our sleeping in the woods and being awakened by the hooting of an owl instead of the crowing of a cock in the morning, these things I suppose you care nothing about. What then shall be the subject?

If you care nothing about the country I am in, perhaps you will care something about me. Shall I tell you, then, what I am doing and how I do it, how I spend my time, how I amuse myself during my few leisure hours. These you can easily imagine, for I spend my time about the same as all other old bachelors!

Would you like to hear about my private concerns, how I get along in the world? ... If I should tell you how often I go "a courtin," how many pretty lasses we have here and all about our parties and sleigh rides, you would probably think that I was consuming time, pen, ink and paper foolishly, and you would think right enough too!...

Studio portrait of Increase A. Lapham in suit and tie. Wisconsin Historical Society, WHS-43831.

If I should detail the plan proposed to procure the immediate construction of a canal from Milwaukee into the "Mineral Point Region," should tell you what steps have been already taken to bring about that object, or should tell all that has been done in the way of exploring the route, you would perhaps think it was only a visionary speculating project which would never be carried into effect.

In view of all these difficulties I can only conclude by asking, what shall I write about?

Yours affectionately,

Increase

Milwaukee, March 1st, 1838

Dear Father and Mother and Brother and Sisters,

It is now just two months since I wrote you last and I suppose you will begin to expect to hear from me before you get this. You are about the only persons in the world that care enough about me to take any interest in my welfare and so I like to write you letters, but I like a great deal better to receive letters from you.

The short letters from Wm [William] and Hannah giving me an account of their New Years Quilting and Chopping Bee came duly to hand.

It would do my own eyes good to look upon mother "face to face" as well as hers, but I cannot conveniently make arrangements to visit you before next winter. I promise myself then a journey to Ohio and perhaps to the Eastern states which I have long wished to see for myself.

I am not exactly well now and for these reasons, a few days since, after having been for some time engaged in the office I set out on foot and walked 25 miles without stopping and about five of it was through the snow 8 or 10 inches in depth without a path and across marshes, hills and lakes. I was so much fatigued that I have not yet entirely recovered. I also slightly scratched my hand and made it sore, and as I have caught cold in it, or something else, the sore is not very small nor very free from pain. I have strong hopes of regaining my health and soundness without the aid of either calomel [mercurous chloride-used as a laxative]or lobelia!

Since my last I have been appointed by Governor Dodge "by and with the advice and consent of the council" a Notary Publick [sic] for this county and also Engineer to the Milwaukee and Rock River Canal Co., pay $5.00 per day (or $1,825 per annum) when engaged in actual service. So I am now Principal Engineer!

It is probable, though yet uncertain, that the work will be commenced this next season, it will at any rate be surveyed and perhaps located. Whether the work will be commenced depends on whether Mr. Kilbourn obtains a grant of land from Congress. He is now in Washington for that purpose.

I see a new stage line advertised to run from Columbus by Dublin to Bellefontaine. Does this go by way of Mt. Tabor? So that I can come all the way home in the stage?

I shall look for Hannah's letter soon which she promises shall be better written than the last. She might sit down when she has leisure and write me a good long letter and have it all finished before William thinks of starting for West Liberty.

I want you all to remember not to forget me because I am so far off.

Yours very affectionately,

I. A. Lapham

April 18, 1838

Dear Brother Increase,

What would you say to a proposition to return to Ohio? Mr. Forrer is very anxious that you should return, he says you shall have a place in the corps of engineers any time you choose to return....

I remain your affectionate Brother Darius

Milwaukee May 18th, 1838

Dear Brother,

Your letter dated just one month ago is received....

You ask what I would say to a proposition to return to Ohio? A question which I think I answered in my last. The principal objection is a desire to establish myself permanently at some particular place, but I had rather be a principal engineer in Wisconsin than an assistant in Ohio. I believe I told you that I had received the appointment as Engineer of the Milwaukee and Rock River Canal Company. Should anything turn up however, which would make my situation here less agreeable and profitable I shall most certainly return to Ohio, although with the exception of its being the residence of my parents and brothers and sisters I believe Ohio has no higher claim on my affections than several states. I am convinced that a residence in New York or some of the New England states would suit me very well. If I leave Milwaukee I shall probably have to lead a wandering life, a year or so here and a year or so there.

Perhaps I should have a wife and family and build a neat little cottage on a hill, set out trees and shrubs and expend much time and labor in rendering it a pleasant place and then a new appointment will render it necessary for me to leave it for the "smoke and dust" of some crowded city.

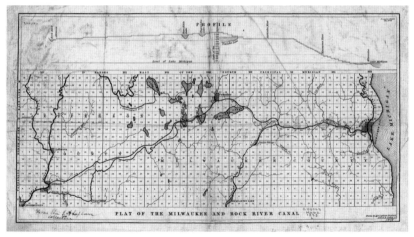

A map of the proposed route of the Milwaukee and Rock River Canal from Fort Atkinson on the Rock River in the west to the city of Milwaukee and Lake Michigan in the east. It shows townships and ranges, sections for portions of Jefferson and Milwaukee counties, as well as identifying a number of rivers, lakes, and streams, some of which include Branch, Fox/Pishtaka rivers, and Johnson's, Oak, and Kinnickinnic creeks. In addition, the map provides a profile of the map showing the elevation of the route above the level of Lake Michigan. Wisconsin Historical Society, WHS-96462.

I was very much surprised a few days ago to find one of my former letters to you printed in one of the publick [sic] newspapers! If that is the disposition you make of my letters I must be more careful in future as to what I write and how I write it, for in the published letter I observe a very awkward experience.

All's well with Increase

*

Milwaukee Oct. 11, 1838

Dear Mother,

Thy letter of the 13th of Sept. came to hand a few days since, and the same mail brought a letter from Ann Marie. We are not married yet but I am now waiting the arrival of a steamboat to take me to Marshall from whence I shall return in about two weeks with a wife!

The times continue to be hard although it does not cost us quite so much to live here now. We are supplied with many necessaries of life from our own soil, so that we do not have to send off all our money to Ohio to buy provisions.

I cannot say when I can make you another visit. I did intend to go on from Marshall but cannot, owing to the pressure of business occasioned by the land sale here.

The next letter I write will probably be accompanied by one from a new daughter of yours.

My love and best wishes to all.

Your dutiful son,

Increase

*

Milwaukee, Nov. 11, 1838

Dear Brother,

I hope you will pardon me for not writing you a letter on the day before I was married! Who ever heard of such a thing!...

We spent a week in traveling from Marshall to Milwaukee having been detained a few days on the road. We are now boarding at a tavern where we are very pleasantly situated, not so pleasantly situated however but that we intend to commence housekeeping in a few weeks, as soon as our house can be prepared for

Drawn portrait of Ann Lapham, wife of Increase A. Lapham. Wisconsin Historical Society, WHS-43832.

us. Then we expect to be perfectly happy. You will not be much engaged during the coming winter and I wish you would find it convenient to take Nancy and Phebe and Harriet in a sleigh and make us a visit! How glad I should be to see you at my house and to introduce you to my wife.

Ann Marie joins me in wishing you to make such a visit.

Dec. 9th at 11 o'clock a.m.

You will see by my date that nearly a month has passed over since I commenced this letter and during that month we have moved into our own house, and I am writing now in my own little family room, and my wife who has just finished dusting and sweeping and otherwise cleaning it has gone into the other room to allow me to write without interruption!...

We have a quarter of an acre of ground for a garden in which I intend to spend the morning hours next summer.

Excuse me for writing so much about myself, I think getting married has had the effect you supposed it would, of making me feel that I was of more consequence in the world than before, for I cannot even write about anything but self.

So good bye,

Increase

Milwaukee, December 18th, 1838

Dear Mother,

Having now settled myself in life I have seated myself at the table for the purpose of writing you a letter.... In October I went to Marshall Mich. and on the 24th of that month was united for life to one of the best "Wild Cat" girls that can be found. We left there on the same day for Milwaukee accompanied by Elizabeth and Caroline Stone, who are to form part of my family, they are nieces....

We have everything we need and plenty of it. It is not a "region of frost, privation and barbarism affording scarcely the necessaries of life" as Dr. J says is supposed at home, for our winters are not longer or more severe than those of New York, we have many of the comforts and elegancies of life, and a peep into our cellar would show that we are not destitute of the "necessaries of life."

I have come pretty much to the conclusion never to move. I have seen so many evils resulting from it, that I am heartily glad to hear that you are finally getting settled in your own house. I leave room for a few lines from Ann.

Your dutiful son,

Increase

My Dear Mother,

Although an entire stranger to you, I feel that I have a right to address you by the above endearing title, and it is with much pleasure I seat myself to improve the opportunity Increase has given me of paying my respects to you.... We are now domesticated in our own house which to me is the pleasantest in Milwaukee.... I have with me the two daughters of a beloved sister, who have for some time been in my mother's family and as she determined upon my marriage to give up the cares of housekeeping she consigned these children among other things to our hands, Increase having kindly consented to my continuing the care I had hitherto exercised over them....

It would add much to our happiness could we see you and father in our home. Please give my respects to father. I was very young when my father died, but old enough to realize what a loss it was....

To all members of your family remember me with much affection.

Your affectionate daughter,

Ann

King's Creek, 1st month, 25th, 1839

Dear Son,

I received thy letter and it was very pleasant to hear of thy happiness and all the good things the Lord has blessed thee with; for every good and perfect gift cometh from His all-bountiful hand, and may thee ever bless Him and let thy first thoughts be offered up to Him in humble gratitude. It is a great while since I had the pleasure of seeing thee, it may be that we never shall meet in this life, but we may so live that we meet in the mansions of peace and rest, where all sorrow shall be done away and we be found worthy to inherit the crown of everlasting life which the Lord the righteous judge shall give to all that love Him and keep his commandments.

Thy affectionate mother,

Rachel Lapham

Dear Daughter,

In looking over the few precious lines from thy pen my heart was filled with love and gratitude and I said in my heart the Lord has not left me comfortless but has given me another daughter in the place of the one taken away by death.

Thy affectionate mother,

Rachel Lapham

Milwaukee, Wis. T., March 17, 1839

To all the folks at home,

I have now received three letters from you since I have written one to you.... Mother and Lorana express some anxiety to know when I shall make you a visit, and Lorana thinks I had better find some business in Ohio and come back there. Now I think differently. It is true that I should prefer being among my own friends and relations, but if I were in Ohio I should have to be always moving about from place to place and not have any particular home. Here it is different. I have a very good little house and should very much dislike to break up and move off to any other place....

I should have written you before, but I have been so busy for the last month or so, that I have scarcely had time to eat or sleep. The great "Land Sale" has just closed. Nearly all the land in the country has been bought from the government within the last four weeks; I have had to go to Chicago twice, riding night and day. On one occasion in a stormy night the driver lost his way on the prairie and we had to remain on the coach till morning. It froze so hard that in the morning the coach could not be moved till we got an axe and chopped away the ice! The poor driver froze his feet, fingers and ears! But I got home alive!

In a day or two I am to start out to survey the Rock River canal, that will take about six weeks. I must "live in tents" and sleep on the ground! What fine times I shall have! I received a few days since the appointment of Engineer and Secretary with a salary of $2,000....

Yours affectionately,

    I. A. Lapham

Encampment near Rock River,
April 5, 1839, Saturday morning.

My Dear wife,

My time has been so completely occupied since I wrote you last that I have really not had time to answer your very interesting letter received by Mr. Hustis.

The news that you write was truly welcome. I hope Mother Alcott will remain with you till I return and a great while afterward!...

Very soon after I closed my last letter to you Mr. Kilbourn came around the hill riding his favorite Katey; he was soon followed by a troop of others carrying long poles. They really looked quite unique as they came riding along the road.

We soon commenced work; it was my duty to do the leveling. I have to talk at the top of my voice, such as this, "Up, up—halt—very light up—halt—fast—right." We ran across Nemahbin lake on the ice, then coasting along Twin and Oconomowoc Lakes also on the ice, and along the creek to Hatch's Mills, thence across to Big Marsh, which extends to the Rock River. We have been more than a week on this endless morass. Its northern shore consists of bays and points of high land running into it which form the first real difficulty in locating a canal. These difficulties are easily overcome however.

Our course led through some immense Tamarac swamps near the south bend of Johnson's Creek and Wingfield's Run. It would have done you good to see us winding about among the Tamaracs, where we occasionally, by making a mis-step, would sink into the mud and water three feet deep.

We shall finish this end of the lane in a day or two and then return to the summit. There is a great deal of interest felt here in the question where the canal shall terminate on Rock River, every house is crowded with visitors all more or less interested in the question and all advocating their claims as the most suitable point. The great question will soon be decided.

We ran a Random level down to the river on Wednesday and gave three hearty cheers on reaching the waters of this beautiful river.

We staid [sic] at Jefferson, a town containing one house (Mr. Darling's)! It is the county seat for Jefferson county.

Yours affectionately,

Increase

❧

Friday evening April 19th, 1839

My dear wife,

I have now seated myself on a bundle of bed clothes and have a small portable desk before me resting on the tongue of our baggage wagon. I have just finished a hard days work in endeavoring to bring our work to the Menominee River.... Although we ran four miles the first day and got to Redfield the next, we had to remain there three days in our endeavors to find the best route for the canal. On Wednesday we crossed at the Fox river and up to last night we were tracing along the margin of an immensely large swamp. Some of the branches or spurs we had to cross and can testify as to the their depth which is not very small. Mrs. Kilbourn of course went around them.

We have now arrived at the Menominee River at a point eleven miles from Milwaukee and shall follow it down tomorrow and next day to Hiram Burdick's....

Sunday morning.

The above was written with the intention of sending it by Mrs. Kilbourn yesterday, but when these few lines were completed it began to grow dark and our "Kitchen girl" gave notice that supper was ready. So I laid by your letter and went to our dining room and supped with Mr. and Mrs. Kilbourn and Dr. Barber, an invited guest.

Yesterday we crossed the Menominee and we are now in the "Forks." Another day's work will bring us within a mile or two of Burdick's so that Tuesday or Wednesday you can ride out and make me a visit if you are so disposed. But I am forgetting your letter of yesterday, a thousand thanks for that. It was handed to me on the field and our whole camp had to stop until I had devoured its contents.

It is with a great deal of regret that I inform you that I can not spend this day of rest with you at home, in peace and quiet, in stead of in the woods "ten miles from any place."

I would like very much to spend another Sabbath in the good old fashioned way.

With all love and regard,

Your affectionate husband,

Increase A. Lapham

Milwaukee, April 10th, 1841

Dear Brother,

Yours of the 25th was received last night and read by my "better half" to me with pleasure to both of us. The duty of reading it fell upon her on account of a sad accident which has just happened to me in the shape of hot maple sugar in a semi-fluid state which was spilt upon my hand so as to actually raise a blister! I have however strong hopes of recovering soon from this dreadful affair!

Our canal affairs are now, agreeably to your last, nearly in the same condition, both waiting for some aristocratic capitalist to take up the bonds which are ready for their acceptance....

As soon as the bonds were printed I mounted [horse] "Adelaide" and in three days was in Mineral Point (the headquarters of Gov. Dodge) 130 miles from here, rather a hard drive considering the newness of the roads. A snow storm prevented me from making the necessary "Geological Survey" to enable me to give you a very satisfactory report in relation to the Mineral Point region, but Mr. S. Taylor supplied me from his beautiful cabinet with as many specimens as I could conveniently carry in my saddle bags. The governor and other officers of state treated me very politely and used every exertion to hasten the business of signing bonds, letters of instruction &c. The governor appointed me "special agent" with pleasure. Had intended to address me on the subject "was very glad I had come."

I got home safely notwithstanding the weight of my saddle bags, which laid me liable to suspicion of having specie aboard, which is rather a dangerous traveling companion!

Now I hope you will make an attempt to visit me! I have tried to visit you several times without success. Your greater energy of character will undoubtedly enable you to succeed. Come by way of home, so as to bring father and mother with you! Should be happy to see you all here! Now don't think I am joking! Do come and see.

Increase

🍂

Milwaukee, April 13th, 1841

Dear Father,

I have not heard from you for some time except through Darius from whom I received a letter a day or two since....

Our spring here is very backward, weather cold and wet, it has been so for some time, keeping everything like vegetation down. This is very disappointing to a botanist who is always anxious to observe the first opening of the spring flowers and who in general prefers to have spring and summer last all the year. I spend much of my leisure time yet in botanical pursuits and now have a very handsome collection of dried plants,

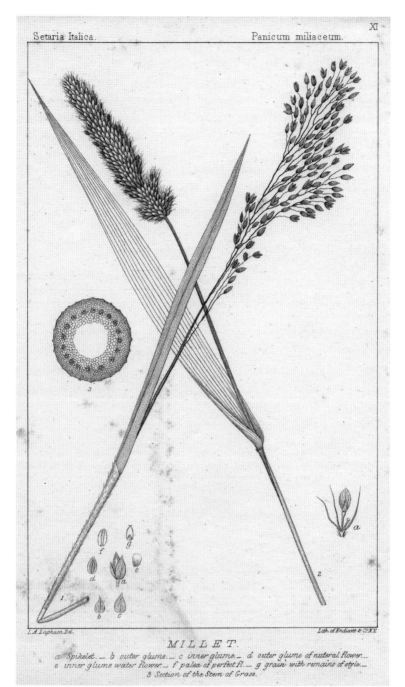

Setaria Italica.   Panicum miliaceum.

I.A.Lapham Del.   Lith. of Endicott & Co.N.Y.

MILLET.

a Spikelet.— b outer glume.— c inner glume.— d outer glume of nuteral flower.—
e inner glume water flower.— f palea of perfect fl.— g grain with remains of style.—
3 Section of the Stem of Grass.

Millet. Increase Lapham's drawing of *Setaris italica* (foxtail millet) and
Panicum miliaceum (proso millet). Wisconsin Historical Society, WHS-4100491.

numbering something over 2,000 species. To this I am adding every now and then by exchanging with botanists throughout the country. We have a great many interesting plants here.

Your affectionate son,

Increase

Milwaukee, May 6th, 1841

Dear Brother,

We are all well....

Spring is still very backward here, took my vasculum along to gather new flowers, of which I found but few. The side saddle flower [northern pitcher plant, purple pitcher-plant], of which I found the leaves, is very interesting. The leaves are tubular and standing erect hold water with which they are generally filled, it is the *Sarracenia purpurea* of botanists.

Found some very beautiful and perfect shells in Rock River but nothing new.

A steamboat is being built at Aztalan to run on Rock River from that place to St. Louis, will start Monday next.

Gov. Dodge, a faithful, honest, capable public officer has been removed. Gen'l Harrison refused to do this deed, but Tyler did it! So we go.

All's well, your brother,

Ink

Milwaukee, Jan'y 30th, 1842

Dear Brother William,

Your letter of the 6th inst. received the very day I mailed to one of the girls. We now have weather warm enough for April (during the day) our snow which a few days ago was two foot deep is now very much reduced and has entirely disappeared from exposed situations.

Our canal is about to be changed into a railroad, a change that can very easily be made before the canal is constructed. I think the change will be rather beneficial to the country than otherwise.

Truly your brother,

Increase

One of the frightful facts of nineteenth century life was the omnipresent threat of death from infectious and parasitic diseases, particularly during winter—"the sickly season" as Lapham called it. The larger cities were especially vulnerable, and that didn't change until the 1890s, when large public sanitation works projects took hold in the form of large-scale sewage disposal and water chlorination systems. Infant mortality was high during this period, and an expected and feared occurrence, and the average lifespan in the nineteenth century was only between 39 and 49 years of age.[45]

The Lapham family was not immune.

Milwaukee, Feb'y 18th, 1842

Dear Parents, Brothers and Sisters,

It is with profound sorrow that I read the melancholy news, in William's last letter, of the death of my dear brother Pazzi. We can now only console ourselves with the hope that we may not only meet him but all other departed friends and relatives in that land where we shall not again be called upon to separate. That such may be the sense is the hope and belief and the object of all our prayers. May the Almighty Ruler of all things grant that it may be so.

Death appears this year to be striking with unusual or rather more than usual severity upon the poor human family. From the president of the United States down to the humblest citizen, he has been doing his work of destruction, without respect of persons. Hence the fact that "we all must die" has been strongly impressed upon our minds of late, and with it the absolute necessity of being prepared for the great change that is then to take place in our circumstances and condition. That the tendency of this feeling will result in our good, in a determination to become better and more useful citizens of this world, we earnestly hope and believe.

We are well here and are very thankful for this evidence of the kindness of Providence. While so many are called upon to give up some member of their families, we have been exempted from this sorrow.

Your dutiful son and brother,

Increase

⌁

Milwaukee, May 23, 1842

Dear Parents,

Lorana's letter containing the painful intelligence of our loss arrived last evening. Although we were in part prepared by William's letter, yet the faint hopes you then had deceived us. We could not realize that Sister Hannah was so low, and trusted the next letter would bring us news of her continued improvement. I will not attempt any words of consolation for I know that from the only true source you have already sought and found that comfort which our Heavenly Father has promised. I can not think of you without seeing Pazzi and Hannah, it seems impossible that a few short months could make such a difference in the little circle that met so happily last summer, how little we realized the possibility of this affliction. Can you not write us oftener? I enjoy your letters much and they do Increase a great deal of good. Believe me as ever.

Your affectionate daughter,

Ann Marie

Dear Father and Mother,

I hardly know what to say by way of consolation or otherwise, in reference to our late accumulated bereavement; the loss of a brother one would suppose was a great loss but add within months, a sister too, is indeed an affliction, and one which should set us all to thinking of the vanity of all our worldly hopes and anticipations; of the uncertainty of human life; and of the great fact that we, too, will soon be called upon to follow in the train.... I hope to hear of the good health of what remains of the family, and regret that my distance from you prevents my visiting you in your troubles.

Your affectionate son,

Increase

❦

Milwaukee, Sept. 15th, 1845

Dear Brother,

We have your letter of the 2nd inst. We are making so many sidewalks and street gravelings that much of my time is occupied in the engineering line, this with selling town lots, collecting rents, &c.... I must make some change in my affairs so as to make my income in some degree proportionate to the labor devoted to business....

By our sun risings and moon risings are beautiful beyond description, rendered so in a great degree by the broad smooth surface of the Milwaukee River lying just before our door towards the east. They set behind some magnificent hills a hundred feet in height adorned by forest trees.

We have hardly been able to speak with composure of the death of our only son Allen [William Allen Lapham passed away July 31, 1845, at age 1 year, 7 months, 12 days], and consequently have not written to our friends relating to him. [Nine years later, his fourth son Samuel Stone Lapham also passed away at a similarly young age, 1 year, 3 months, 23 days.]

Your affectionate brother,

Increase

❦

Always, Lapham returned to public discourse and natural history study to lessen his grief over a family loss. He was in high demand as a public speaker. On February 4, 1848, Increase appeared at the Unitarian Church in Milwaukee to give a lecture to the Milwaukee High School on Wisconsin's diverse landscapes and natural beauty. Here are some excerpts from that lecture, with particular attention to the traveling hardships posed by the extensive prairies of the time:

> Our "Oak Openings" as they are called, afford much scenery of extreme beauty. Thousands of dollars have been expended in European countries to adorn and beautify the estates of the noble and wealthy classes, without producing anything more than a slight approximation towards the beauty and loveliness of our oak openings....

I have spoken of the beauty of the prairies, but it must not be forgotten that although they are beautiful and highly attractive at first sight, they are not, after all, exactly the places for the new settler to fix upon for his future home, unless he can find, what is rarely to be found, a tract of land half covered with timber and half prairie. Upon the first settlement of the country, much search was made for such farms and a few were so fortunate as to find them. But in general it was ascertained that the line

Plants in Flower

March 29th
  Acer rubrum
April 4 · Trillium nivale
    Hepatica triloba

" 18 – Snow 1 inch deep
  25 Arabis rhomboidea
" 26 – 1st Steamboat from Below
  29 – Caltha palustris
    Sanguinaria canadensis
    Claytonia Virginica
    Isopyrum thalyctroides
    Eugenia bulbosa
  + Alnus serulata
    Salix conoides?
    Ranunculus hirsutus?

May 7 Snow —
    Anemone nemorosa
    Ictodes foetida
  + 12 Erythronium Americanum
            album
    Fragaria Virginica
    Viola cucullata
    Phlox divaricata
    Gnaphalium Americanum
    Ranunculus abortivus
    Trillium erectum
    Euchroma coccinnea
  14 Dentaria laciniata
    Mitella diphylla
    Hippophae Canadensis
    Iris cristata?
  18 Xylosteum ciliatum
    Prunus Virginiana
    Panax trifoliata
    Dirca palustris

May 18th Thalyctrum dioicum
    Pedicularis canadensis
    Ribes lacustris
    Viola pubescens
    Acer sacharium
    Uvularia grandiflora
    Caulophyllum thalyctroides
19 Thlaspi Bursa pastoris
    Plantago cordata
    Arum tryphyllum
    Prunus americana
    Crataegus sp. ?
20 Actea alba
    Coptis trifolia
    Aronia botrys pirum
    Corydalis canadensis
23 Leontodon taraxicum
    Populus tremuloides
    Floerkia uliginosa
29 Hard frost
    Veronica peregrina
30 Dodecatheon integrifolium
    Geranium maculatum
    Juncus polycephalum?
    Orchys spectabilis
    Vicea craca
    Zizia aurea
    Carices integerrima
    Aquilegia Canadensis
    Convallaria stellata
    Polygala senega
    Arabis laevigata
    Lathyrus albidus
    Menyanthus trifoliata
    Vaccinium Pennsylvanicum

Page from Increase Lapham's 1838 botanical diary in which he listed plants he observed in flower stage. Wisconsin Historical Society, WHS-100342.

of separation between the prairies and the timber was rather an infinite one. Nature here, as in most other cases, has so graduated one kind into the other, that it is difficult to say precisely where one begins and the other ends; the prairie being usually surrounded by scattered trees and shrubs. Hence a farm to be in the prairie, must be a very extensive one, if it also embraces much woodland.

The bleak winds of winter roam over these proud prairies with as much freedom as upon "Old Ocean" itself, and they are here without the modifying influence of water. They are therefore much dreaded by the luckless persons who are compelled to encounter them. Even in summer, the constant stream of air coming in the same direction unchecked by a single tree, is very inconvenient to persons passing over the prairies. I have known persons to have their cheeks chafed and become sore by the fluttering of their shirt collars while traveling on the prairies! This was, of course, in the prosperous days of shirt collars and before they assumed their present downward tendency.

In winters when there is much snow, the prairies present many inconveniences. The free scope allowed for the wind is extended also to the snow, which never lies still where it falls but is constantly drifted about from place to place. The slopes and summits of the knolls and ridges will be bare of snow while the hollows and low places will be covered to great depths. Grains therefore sown upon prairie land are either not protected by snow from the effects of the severe frosts or they are covered with too much snow. From this cause also, the prairie roads, so fine in summer, are an abomination in winter. A strong wind blowing constantly in one's face when the thermometer is anywhere in the neighborhood of zero is not to be supported by many people but must often be encountered on the prairies. Many persons have lost their lives in this encounter, and it is found to be especially dangerous on those roads which most abound in licensed taverns!

The track of the road in winter can never be smooth and well beaten as in timbered land. The track made by your sleigh is soon filled with drifted snow; other sleighs following in the same track beat down this additional snow and make other tracks to be again filled and again beaten down. Hence every sleigh has to break for itself a new track which is a very real inconvenience, as all know who have attempted it. The result of this process is, that in a short time, if there is much travel along the road it becomes a high ridge of hard beaten snow, just wide enough for your team with soft snow banks on each side. A team with much of a load is constantly liable to be thrown off on either side and tumble over into a soft snow bank some four or six feet deep. These inconveniences with the want of timber, the liability of fires, &c. make the prairies less desirable than they are usually supposed to be....

Increase's occasional poking, but always informative, letters to brother Darius continued.

Milwaukee Feb. 20th, 1848

Dear Brother,

It is now a long time since we have heard from you directly, and when we did hear, your communication being an effort at poetry was not as full and comprehensive as we could wish.

We have had a remarkably mild winter here. No sleighing, the north winds, even, are not very cold, the ice has left our river being a month earlier than usual....

I have a prospect of being employed by the Legislature to draw some large maps of the new state of Wisconsin. If so I shall probably visit all the county seats for the purpose of collecting data. I don't know of any other honors to be conferred on me about which to write, so I must stop here.

Plank roads are "all the go" here now. We shall probably have some before one year goes by. Railroads are lost sight of at present.

Love to all from your affectionate brother and sister,

I. A. Lapham and Ann

Milwaukee March 29th, 1848

Dear Brother,

This year is to be one of great events in Wisconsin. We have just adopted a State Constitution and the whole system of political machinery is about to

This map from 1863 shows the population density per square mile in the entire state; southeastern and southern Wisconsin had the greatest population density. Wisconsin Historical Society, WHS-91008.

be put in motion here. Caucusses and conventions are the order of the day. Next week we shall elect town and city officers throughout the state. In May we elect governor, members of the first state legislature &c....

In about three weeks we will be connected by the telegraph wires by way of Cleveland with your city, when, in cases of enough importance, we can communicate without loss of time. The gap between Michigan City and Kalamazoo is all that remains and this is nearly closed up....

We all send our love and regards for you and yours.

Your brother,

I. A. Lapham

CHAPTER ONE

Milwaukee Aug. 3rd, 1848

Dear Brother,

I own that I have been remiss in my duty in regards to writing letters this summer.... A few days ago I went with Col. Stone, my brother-in-law, by way of East Troy, Janesville and Madison to the Blue Mounds, which we ascended and enjoyed a view of some fifty miles radius in every direction. The mound is a little mountain, being 1,000 feet above the Wisconsin river, a few miles to the north of it. It appears to be composed of a hard flinty rock, which has remained while all the soft limestone around it has been carried away in the course of numerous geological ages. I found several new plants there/the trees look stunted and have quite an Alpine appearance.

Coming home I got some stalactites from the newly discovered cave ... but I did not go into the cave. It has been explored about 1,000 feet and extends further. It is evidently the bed of a subterranean river of muddy water, the stalactites being black and muddy throughout....

My best regards to all,

Your brother,

I. A. Lapham

*

The year 1850 was an eventful but sad one for Increase. It started well enough, with several sojourns, including one noted in his journal.

May 30. Traced the ancient lake beach south from Kenosha to the state line and four miles south; at that point a series of ancient mounds are built upon it.... The prairies west of Kenosha (on which we drove in the afternoon) are diluvial; no rock is found. Near the middle of Sec. 5 in Salem (T. 1, R. 20) we came upon some abrupt gravel knolls, similar to those found about Delafield and elsewhere. On one of those were some ancient works commanding a view of Silver Lake in the town of Salem, Kenosha County, and the fine valley in which it rests....

We were told this evening of an Indian practice to secure "horse blocks" or a step by which women and children can conveniently mount their horses. A small tree is selected by the side of the trail which is cut and bent in two places. The cut is about two feet above the ground. This is done without destroying the life of the tree so that in a few years the "sapling" becomes a tree large enough to use for the purpose indicated. Such trees I have often observed without knowing their origin, but supposed them accidental freaks of nature. They are said to be very common along the trail.

A later trip to the Upper Mississippi elicited a rhapsodic description in a paper he wrote for a publication titled the *N.W. Journal Science and Education.*

"No part of the United States, not even the world renowned Hudson, exceeds the valley of the Upper Mississippi in the beauty of its scenery. From the south line of the state to the [Minnesota] Falls of St. Anthony there is one continued series of fine picturesque bluffs and hills of continually varied form and feature.... Here are prominent cliffs surmounting gentle grassy slopes, the calm and placid waters of the Mississippi (here of crystal purity) winding its way among the hills, a charming admixture of prairie, with here and there groups of trees of native growth, sturdy oak intermixed with spire topped evergreens all well calculated to excite the most agreeable emotions in the mind of the beholder."

Around this time, however, Increase received very sad news. Darius had fallen ill and passed away in late July—a death that left Increase no doubt bereft and inconsolable. Darius shared a similar deft sense of humor and appreciation for all things wild. Increase looked forward to sharing his explorations with him like no other. The only reference to his passing came from a short journal entry: "My brother Darius died of Cholera at Cincinnati, 20th of July, 1850, and was buried at the Home Farm, Mt. Tabor, in Champaign County, Ohio."

Increase's primary family focus in letters then became wife Ann Marie, to whom he wrote whenever away from home for more than a few days. The following letter to Ann, penned one week before Darius's death, displayed his self-deprecating sense of humor and boundless love for adventure as he descended into a lead mine.

Mineral Point, July 13, 1850

My dear wife,

   We have been separated so much at late that I begin to feel that we are quite strangers, I want to renew the acquaintance; writing letters is a poor substitute for personal acquaintance....

   You certainly would not have owned me as a husband if you could have seen me last evening in a miner's trousers, frocked cap; the cap just fitted to cover the hair, made of deerskin. I put one foot in a loop at the end of a strong rope and was lowered fifty-six feet into the earth by a windlass! John could not be persuaded to go down, his courage failed him! I wish you had been there to go down to! I know you would have enjoyed it; it was so romantic!

I went down to a drift or horizontal opening, about 200 feet long that I went through on all fours; it was only 3 feet high; hit my back against the sharp points of the roof.

It was dark as midnight, had a candle set in the soft clay for a candle stick, so that I could stick it down when and where I pleased. Came out covered with mud and dirt and loaded with specimens, all the more valuable for having mined them myself. [In a small sketch] See that man tugging away at the windlass! My life, the happiness of my whole family hangs upon his nerve! Never fear, he is used to it. I stop at every change of rock to study the geology of the mine, no thought of danger, am now safe again!

Your loving husband,

Increase A. Lapham

❦

Natural history observations were important to Increase, whether it was geology, botany, or animal life, and phenological events were something he wanted his children to note, as indicated in the following letter to Ann Marie Lapham excerpted here:

Detroit, Friday afternoon
April 29, 1851

My dear wife,

No remarkable incidents, no hair breadth escapes to relate.

I have thought of the observations every time since I left.... Tell Mary and Julia to keep a sharp lookout for the [purple] martins, so as to note their first appearance. I would like to have them find out when the plum, peach, apple and pear first open their petals....

Yours affectionately,

Increase

Horicon, Oct. 12, 1851

My dear wife,

I am going to spend a few moments in communicating with my dearly beloved wife and family. Whatever comfort it may be to you and to them to hear from me it cannot exceed the satisfaction which I enjoy in writing to you. Next to seeing and being with you, it is my greatest source of happiness....

I send you a sketch of "Lapham's Peak" (as the neighbors around have decided to call it) as it appeared when it first burst upon our "astonished sight." It is about 400 feet above the country around and about 824 feet above Lake Michigan and 1402 feet above the ocean....

The weather is bad, barometer going down so that I fear some time will be lost, for I can not survey in the bushes while it is raining. I have found no acquaintance here yet and do not wish to until tomorrow. My appearance here with compass and other curious apparatus has excited some curiosity among the bar-room loafers; and my negative answers to the questions whether I was on the railroad survey? some plank road? or some village plat? have only tended to heighten the mystery! We have a poor house, poorly kept, with occupants as usual, besides those of the human species! But these things are small matters compared with the delights of "a life in the woods."

Yours affectionately,

Increase

❧

In correspondence with the editors of the Milwaukee Sentinel, Increase presented an informative travelogue of the landscapes he encountered and people observed when away from Milwaukee searching out effigy mounds. Here are brief excerpts about two events:

Kingston, May 29, 1852

Messrs. Editors,

It is a charming ride on a pleasant summer day to leave Waushara and drive around the three beautiful lakes lying northwest of that place, as we did yesterday. They are Fox Lake, Lake Emily and Lake Maria.

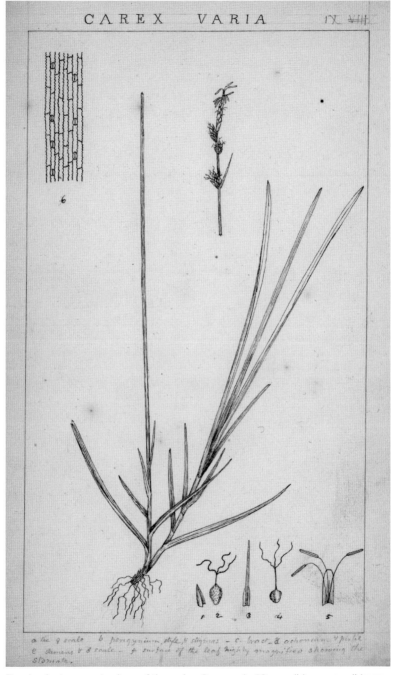

Drawing by Increase Lapham of the sedge *Carex varia*. (*Carex albicans var. albicans*, blunt-scaled oak sedge). Wisconsin Historical Society, WHS-83776.

The bushes are generally high, presenting as we ride along, many beautiful views, worthy of the pencil of the landscape painter. Broad, undulating prairies may be seen in one direction stretching off, far as the eye can reach. The oak openings and the patches of more dense forest, the rocky cliffs, the wooded Islands, all tend to give an agreeable variety. These lakes lie in the dividing ridge between the waters of the Mississippi and those of the Great Lakes....

The favorite evening amusement now about country taverns appears to be playing, jumping and other manly exercises interspersed with rational conversation, by listening to which one may always gain some new ideas, and perhaps useful information....

I. A. L.

Increase Lapham in foreground observing rock formations at Taylor's Glen on an 1869 trip to the Wisconsin Dells. A. Holly seated in background. Photo by H. H. Bennett. Wisconsin Historical Society, WHS-44911.

CHAPTER ONE

A ride of about twenty miles through the woods much of the way with scarcely a track to mark the course brought us to this place, which is one of the most interesting and remarkable localities in Wisconsin.

The Wisconsin River is contracted by steep rocks to a very narrow channel for a distance of about two miles, the water rushing through, especially when high with great violence, dashing against the rocks here and whirling with frightful rapidity there, boiling and foaming at a great rate....

Mr. Parker takes much pains in showing off the many wonders of the place and takes the lead in showing the way along the narrow shelved rocks with the boiling cauldron at a fearful depth directly under your feet, and through the caverns, where it is necessary to use "all fours" and no great man can pass through—we had no difficulty!

This spot is just the place to suit a naturalist. Agassiz would be in ecstasies all the time.

Among the many other new and interesting plants I found the northern scrub pine [*Pinus banksiana*] the Labrador Tea [*Ledum latifolium*] and the wooly *Hudsonia* [*H. tormentosa*] all sub artic [*sic*] plants and seldom or never found south of the Dells of the Wisconsin.

At six last evening we had a storm of wind and rain and hail such as I never before witnesse[d], one hailstone was 1 1/6 inches its longest diameter. The windows on the west side of the Dell House were completely riddled and cattle ran in every direction as if mad. One of the most curious effects was the effect of the hailstones falling in the water of the river, the whole surface being covered with "jets d'eau" a foot high constantly playing—presenting a rare phenomenon which can be compared to nothing else in nature.

Just as the storm broke away a raft made its appearance having encountered the dreadful storm while passing through the Dells! When the water is high the "passage of the Dells" becomes quite a nice job requiring an experienced pilot to prevent everything from being dashed in pieces against the rocks....

I. L.

Not quite two and a half years after beloved Darius passed away, Increase decided to go home to Ohio—alone. It had been years; over 20 since he had spent any part of winter with his mother and father. He delighted in describing the journey and family reunion to Ann and their children.

MT. Tabor, Ohio

Jan. 23rd, 1853

My dear wife and children,

I suppose you will expect to hear from me occasionally while on my present tour, to gratify you I propose to write an occasional letter. After leaving you I had no ill luck until the next morning, when I forgot my black walking stick, which has so often sustained me in times of weakness and which I fondly hoped might sustain my tottering footsteps when old age creeps upon me. I wrote back to Mr. Edgerton requesting him to send it to Milwaukee and to drop you a line so that you would know where to get it.

Had a pleasant stage ride across the prairies from Janesville to Rockford and by railroad to Chicago.

On Thursday I was whirled rapidly over the Southern Michigan and Northern Indiana railroad to Toledo on the Maumee river in Ohio where we had oyster soup for supper.

The next day, was hurried up early, crossed the Maumee on a steam ferry and went forty-six miles by railroad to Belleview on the Sandusky road, where we arrived just one hour after the train had passed, so I was compelled to lay here twenty-three hours, waiting for the next Cincinnati train! But to make the best of a bad matter I had a fire made in a little private bedroom and went to work on the American Paleontology just as naturally as if I had been at home and the hours slipped by.

It was not until Saturday at 2 p.m. that I was set down at West Liberty and looked eagerly about among the crowd thinking it possible that some of "our folks" might be there. "Here I am" said a voice, which proved to be my father's, he having seen me thus employed. After dining at Mr. Runkle's we rode out home in a snow storm, the first they have had here. Mother made so much ado about my coming home that the girls were alarmed and ran to see who was killed, thinking that certainly something dreadful had happened....

CHAPTER ONE

It is now just 22 years since I was at home in the winter and then we had just about as much snow as we have today, and my horse had the same trouble with snow balls collecting under his feet, the snow laying upon mud.

Last evening the first number of the "Oakley Herald" a family newspaper devoted to Literature, Science and the Fine Arts, edited by Wm Lapham Esq., was brought in and read to the family circle. It had some good pieces, good hits and some very queer poetry that made all of us laugh. This paper is in manuscript and to be published or issued weekly. Among the items was mentioned the "carpenter who made use of moonbeams in the erection of houses" and "the mason who tried to find a hen that could lay a brick!"

Your affectionate husband and father,

I. A. Lapham

❧

Among Lapham's travels, one of the most notable trips was to Lake Superior in 1858, which was reached via train, and then steamboat through the Straits of Mackinac. The stated purpose of this trip was to explore on foot the Penokee Iron Range east of Ashland and assess the extent of the iron ore resource. Here are extended excerpts from his personal notes, handwritten in ink on blue-lined notebook paper.

August 31st, 1858

The bay or harbor into which we entered between Madeline Island and the main shore is a magnificent one—perfectly safe for boats to lie in during the most severe storms, land locked on every side. The old buildings at La Pointe, and at the place of the "Old Fort," and of the Middle Fort present a striking and rather picturesque appearance. The old fort is now abandoned, and the middle fort nearly so. The principal part of the present inhabitants being at the most westerly place known as La Pointe....

These "forts" as they are called are the remains of the establishments of the American Fur Company consisting of strongly built stores, surrounded with a fence of high pickets set into the ground. The pickets are mostly of the white cedar [*Thuja occidentalis*] and though they have been in the ground twenty years or more yet retain a considerable degree of soundness and strength.

Sept. 1st, 1858

At La Pointe, Lake Superior. Remained at La Pointe waiting for a steam boat on which to go to Superior which is the name of the embryo city at the head of the lake....

Much of the time was spent in botanizing and checking on a copy of Gray's Manual the plants growing naturally on the island [Madeline Island] thus showing the flora of this northern part of Wisconsin and how it compares with the south part of the same state. There are many remarkable differences in the vegetation of the two localities.

Found two or three small mollusks under the old logs and pond lily leaves in a lagoon near the "Middle Fort."

Sept. 2 and 3

Remained at La Pointe still waiting for a boat. Continued observations on the island. A heavy blow from the South east continued throughout all the time since my arrival here. This has caused the delay in the arrival of the boat, which has been lying by at Copper Harbor waiting for it to pass over.

At length the North Star arrived and we attempted to go to Superior, but in the night the wind increased to such a gale that the boat was put about and run into Bayfield where she remained until the morning of.

Sept. 4th

By half past 12 we were in Superior. On the way we passed among the Apostle Islands and could see the high lands of the "north shore." The steam boat channel is so near the middle of the lake that we could not well make out the character of the shores. From the boat we could see the "Mineral Range" that skirts the south shore at only a short distance from the coast. On the return we saw fishermen here drawing their "gill nets" near the middle of the lake—a dangerous employment, I should think, in these times of stormy weather....

The sandstone brought here from the St. Louis river is of the same character as that examined at La Pointe....

Sept. 5th, 1858

Returned this forenoon in the same boat to La Pointe where we arrived at 1-1/2 p.m., and set off immediately in a small sail boat for a voyage across Cheqwaumegon [sic] Bay to Ashland.

The sail across from La Pointe to the head of this bay was a very pleasant one—the wind being favorable.... The long sandy point [Long Island] that separates this bay from the waters of the lake is a very remarkable one, partly covered with trees. It has a counterpoint on a smaller scale extending from Madeline Island.

Sept. 6th, 1858

At Ashland, at the southern extremity of Chequamegon Bay this morning we doffed our coats, put on red flannel shirts, overhauls, boots &c. to prepare for a tramp of ten days in the woods. Four men were engaged as "packers" whose duty it was to carry large packs on their backs, much in the same manner as an Indian woman carries her child. These packs were to contain our beds (blankets), cooking utensils, and provisions. I carried a tin botanizing box and a mineral hammer and chisel. Col [Cutter] had command. Mr. L.F. Leopold of Cleveland Ohio was one of the party and we were fortunately joined this morning by Prof. E. Daniels, one of three state geologists of Wisconsin. With him I am to explore the Penokee Iron Range lying south and south east from this place—the same that was discovered and described by Col. Whittlesey in Owens Geological Report. The journey was to be made on foot as there are yet no roads made through these dense forests. A very good trail however has been opened so that the walking was easy.

At 10 a.m. got started and walked over a gradually ascending plain, underlain mostly by the red marl. At intervals a short distance is sand—probably an ancient Lake Beach. At Ashland noticed the marl lying in ridges, as if thrown up by the same cause—though this is not probably, their origin. The trail leads directly south from Ashland, on or near a section line, one mile east of the range line between ranges 4 and 5 west of the 4th Principal and in township 47 north.

Six miles brought us to Welton's on [a] branch of the Bad River (here called White River) which runs in a valley perhaps one hundred feet deep, cut mostly in the red marl. The trees on this flat were conifers, poplar, thick almost exclusively. The bark of the white cedar is used to cover houses; also to form an outside lining or additional protection of log houses: surveyors together use it to make a temporary camp under which to spend a night. It is also used in various other ways. Saw much balsam [*Abies balsamea*] with the little warts on the bark under which was to be found the aromatic gum which gave name to this tree. At Weltons first saw [American] elm trees [*Ulmus americana*].

We learned of an adventure of Mrs. Welton with a large black bear which was very much disposed to make himself at home about the house picking up such food as happened to be left within his reach. Not liking his companionship she boldly shot him through the window of the house; though not until she had firmly fastened the door to prevent an attack in case of failure to kill—and as soon as the gun was discharged she ran for the upper story of the house ... hastily pulling up the ladder as a further security against pursuit. Poor bear however was too far gone to think of revenge—he was soon dead.

We passed a large beaver dam and were reminded of the fact that these strange animals are still found in this vicinity....

Sept. 7th, 1858

Started early, for a tramp of 18 miles—six more than we walked yesterday....

At 5 miles south eastwardly from Libbies (where we started this morning) we found the first trap rock in place in the bed of a stream (branch of Bad River) associated with what appeared to be altered sandstone. This last named rock contains much epidote—may be an epidote trap. Probably this epidote the only indication here found of copper. This is called the "Copper range." We saw no copper but these rocks are doubtless the prolongation of the copper bearing trap and conglomerates found on the Montreal river a few miles above the mouth. The same range is said to continue on towards the west and to rise into considerable hills....

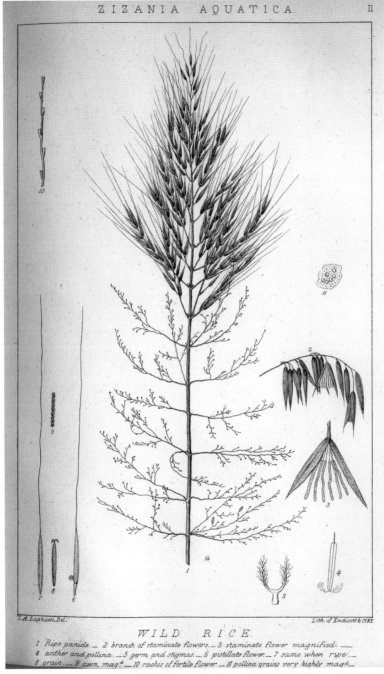

WILD RICE.

1 Ripe panicle.— 2 branch of staminate flowers.— 3 staminate flower magnified.—
4 anther and pollina.—5 germ and stigmas.— 6 pistillate flower.— 7 same when ripe.—
8 grain.— 9 awn, mag.ᵈ— 10 rachis of fertile flower.— 11 pollina grains very highly mag.ᵈ—

Increase Lapham's drawing of *Zizania aquatica* (annual wild rice). Wisconsin Historical
Society, WHS-102200.

The timber is mostly hardwood but some pine, hemlock, basswood &c. As we ascend the ridges we encounter the Ground Hemlock completely covering the ground with their prostrate stems and evergreen foliage, and rendering the walking difficult. The botanist said the name of this troublesome shrub was *Taxus canadensis* [Canada yew]. *Tripus prostratus* would have been a better name said the geologist as his foot became entangled and he was triped [sic] so as to fall prostrate upon the ground...!

Sept. 8th, 1858

Started with 6 men (3 packers) to explore the iron range eastward from Penokee, (Bad River) which is said to extend eleven miles, and perhaps more.

On NE 1/4 of 13-44-3—climbed to the top of a log house to get a view of the country, which cannot be had from the trail even on the top of the Range because of the dense growth of mostly maple trees. A small clearing, and an old "wind fall" here enabled us to see off but only for a short distance. We got no distant view of Lake Superior as I had hoped to do. This could only be done by climbing one of the highest trees, or by clearing away a large opening in the dense forest....

Sept. 10th, 1858

Commenced our return journey over the eleven miles of the iron range this morning by the examination of the outbreak on the S.E. 1/4 of Sec. 32 T45 R1W. The main ridge seems to terminate here....

The ... rock ... proved to be a very pure slaty iron ore, measuring at right angles to the strata sixty feet in thickness. This ore is nearly all suitable for working into iron. Its slaty structure and brittleness will render it easily worked and broken into suitable size for something.

Sept. 11th, 1858

Examined this morning the rapids half a mile below the House (Penokee).... We crossed a short distance below on a tree which we cut for the purpose, to the East or right bank, and on returning saw a number of trees that had been felled by the beaver. There is no trace of a dam here—the stream being too large for this purpose. These beaver that build no dams are called "bank beaver" and are supposed to be of a different kind from the dam builders, but this is probably not the case. The difference is only in habit, owing to different circumstances in which they are placed. Col Cutter informed me that he measured a birch tree that had been cut by these singular animals, and found it 19-3/4 inches in diameter. The trees I saw were 2 to 5 inches in diameter—maple and birch. Quite a number of these animals are still annually caught in this part of the country.

Sept. 12th, 1858

Today we examined the range west of Penokee as far as the west line of Range 3.... From the top of this bluff (about 300 feet high) we had another fine view of the country south, extending to the high lands.... The whole is covered with trees, and we could only see their tops. Or we may say this was an extended view of "tree-tops."

I have now traced this "Iron Range" from near the east line of range one west of the fourth principal meridian to the west line of range three; being therefore across three ranges of six miles each....

We may safely say that here is an Iron Mountain Range twenty miles in length. Judging from the uniformity of the geological formations throughout this whole extent, we may safely infer that the Iron Ore is also continuous though often concealed beneath the surface. We had not the time nor means to make extensive excavation in search of the ores where not visible upon the surface, but wherever a section could be obtained, iron was found in greater or less quantity thus confirming the opinion that the iron is co-extensive with the range....

A pine tree cut in the gap at Penokee was about 160 feet in height.

We saw several temporary tents that had been formed by surveyors and others under which to spend a night. These were made of the bark of the white cedar or hemlock [*Abies canadensis*] supported by small trees bent over and twisted together like so many arches, or by poles raised on an incline plain, like one side of the roof of a house. These temporary encampments are very quickly and easily made, and add much to the comfort of a night in the woods.

We noticed some of the log house at La Pointe where there was an outer protection of bark to form an additional protection against the intense cold of the long winters of this climate and latitude....

The northern part of the State of Wisconsin extending from the central regions usually known as "the pineries" to the shore of Lake Superior is but little known and its importance but little appreciated by the man of the population residing in the southern part of the state.... The small number of inhabitants gives them but little political importance, but yet their rights and the duties of the government towards them are the same as if they had votes enough to attract the attention of political aspirants to office and distinction....

Sept. 13th, 1858

Having completed our examinations of the Penokee Iron Range, we commenced our return journey this morning. Went over the same ground as our way out, as far as Sibley's, 18 miles. Obtained specimens of rocks and minerals on "the copper range," but no copper.

We got back to Ashland at noon, and had a pull over the bay so as to get to La Pointe at 7 p.m. just in time to avoid one of those sudden gales that sprung up half an hour afterwards.

La Pointe, Mad. Isl. Wis. Sept. 15th, 1858

Remained here all day, waiting for a steamboat. Just at night got under way on board the *North Star*, intending to go to Ontonagon— went only a few miles when the captain decided the lake was too rough for him to proceed, and especially too boisterous to enable him to land at Ontonagon where there is as yet no government harbor. Accordingly the boat was run back to La Pointe and lay there all night.

The best general view about La Pointe is from the high ridge east of the "Middle Fort," forming the southern extremity of the island. From here looking towards the west, we see the three places; the old, or middle fort; La Pointe village proper; and Bayfield, all nearly in a straight line; with the bay for a foreground, and the distant forest clad hills for a background.

Increase ends this particular observation with one that calls to mind—if one stands in a similar Madeline Island location—a modern-day scene of piers, sailboats, and perhaps sea kayaks:

CHAPTER ONE

This little bay with its piers, its sailboats, and bark canoes, the old Catholic Church, the white buildings, [and] the remnant of the old stockade of pickets, all unite to make a very fine and unique scene.

Lapham's Wisconsin between 1832 and 1866. Map provided by Dr. David Mladenoff and Monika Shea, courtesy of Forest Ecosystem and Landscape Ecology Lab, Department of Forest and Wildlife Ecology, University of Wisconsin-Madison.

Less than five years after his Lake Superior sojourn, on February 25, 1863, Increase Lapham lost his beloved wife, Ann Marie, unexpectedly at age 46 to unknown causes. He never wrote about this great loss, and likely dealt with her death by working harder on his various projects, watched over carefully by his two daughters, Mary, 24 and Julia, 21. He also had three surviving sons, teenagers Henry and Seneca and six-year-old Charles.

About twelve-plus years later, on a warm day in mid-September 1875, Increase celebrated the completion of a draft paper on Oconomowoc Lake. Here, at the lake, at a farmstead estate ("Minnewoc")[46] he purchased for his children, he decided to end his day by fishing. Taking out a rowboat and fishing pole, he rowed out beyond the lake's marshy edges, not wanting to come in until "he succeeded in getting a good string" of panfish.[47]

He was successful. Around 6 p.m., he rowed back with a large string of fish, but nearing shore he had to deal with dense emergent vegetation, which required his pushing the boat strenuously with an oar. The exertion proved too much. He collapsed face first into the bottom of the boat, still clutching the oar. His youngest son, Charles, found him.

The outpouring of grief was immediate, and newspapers across the state paid tribute. Gone was the state's preeminent naturalist of the times and a man whose unmatched passion for studying Wisconsin's natural history was saluted across the country. ☀

Francis Zirrer
(1885-1968)

Zirrer in cap—the only known photo of him. Photo taken at the 1964 Wisconsin Society for Ornithology Convention, Madison, Wisconsin. Photo provided by Nancy Nabak, courtesy of Wisconsin Society for Ornithology.

YELLOW BIRCH

G J K

Chapter Two~
Francis Zirrer

I am living so far from my rural mailbox that it requires five hours of strenuous walking through a wilderness to go there and back; therefore I do not go often. An enormously interesting country, full of wildlife, but too far from everything.

—FZ

Reclusive, but unabashedly inquisitive, Francis Zirrer[48] spent thousands of hours alone observing the natural world in northwestern Wisconsin. Most of his work, documented in 40 years of field notes, was unfortunately discarded after his death. Nevertheless, there is still an abundance of valuable information on bird and natural history observations in his correspondence with distinguished Madison chemist and ornithologist A.W. Schorger during the 1930s and '40s, and in eight articles written for *The Passenger Pigeon*. He also wrote three natural history articles for the *Milwaukee Journal* in the late 1950s.

His striking natural history observations stirred other naturalists who knew him, though since he was hermetic, he was not an easy man to know. Zirrer's admirers included Smithsonian Institution Secretary Alexander Wetmore, acclaimed ornithologist A.C. Bent, mammalogists H.H.T. Jackson and Paul

Errington, conservationist and historian Walter Scott, and Milwaukee Public Museum ornithologist and wildlife artist Owen Gromme. The distinguished authority on Wisconsin birds, Reverend Samuel D. Robbins, Jr., referred to Zirrer's records in several species accounts in *Wisconsin Birdlife: Population and Distribution Past and Present,* published in 1991.

Born in Austria on December 21, 1885, Zirrer moved to Yugoslavia and became a citizen of that country before emigrating to the United States. It is not known when he arrived in the U.S. The earliest reference is a trip to Glacier National Park in 1915 at the age of 29. In a March 12, 1942, letter to Schorger, he wrote:

"I visited the park in the summer of 1915. Not as a tourist. I was too poor for that, but being young it did not make much difference. I stayed over 6 weeks, camped in the open, and live[ed] from a bag of supplies supplemented by fish and an occasional rabbit. With the mountains (and the water ouzel) I [felt I was back at] my alpine home. So many other things, esp. plants, were alike or very similar. The same *Dryas octopetala* [mountain avens or eightpetal mountain avens] decorated the rockslides; a pretty blue gentian, very much like the alpine *Gentiana acaulis* [stemless gentian or trumpet gentian], colored the meadows above the timber line, and there were others."

Zirrer lived in Milwaukee with his wife Clara Kullmann during the early to mid-1920s. In 1928, they moved to northwestern Wisconsin. For 16 consecutive years, the Zirrers lived in remote parts of northwestern counties, settling in three different locations, each more secluded than the previous one.

From 1928 to 1932, they lived on a "timbered farm" north of Hayward in Sawyer County. From late September 1932 until the summer of 1940, they lived in a one-room cabin in the mixed hardwood-conifer forest of northwestern Rusk County, southeast of Birchwood and "miles from the nearest human habitation."[49] In 1940, the Zirrers moved to the edge of a conifer bog that today is known as the Kissick Alkaline Bog Lake State Natural Area, west of Hayward in northwestern Sawyer County.

Had it not been for Schorger's constant encouragement and support, Zirrer's observations of the natural world may never have come to light. It was Schorger's constant prodding to publish that probably persuaded Zirrer to submit feature articles to *The Passenger Pigeon* beginning in 1944. And he might have published earlier had he not thought himself inarticulate, a person with poor writing skills.

Zirrer's correspondence with Schorger ran intermittently from 1934 through 1949. Owen Gromme stated that it was through him that both men "became acquainted."[50] Thanks to Schorger's foresight, most of Zirrer's letters to him are available for study at the Wisconsin State Historical Society archives in Madison.

ZIRRER WAS OUT AT ALL TIMES OF THE DAY AND NIGHT and in all types of weather. Although anthropomorphic at times in his descriptions of birds, there is no doubt that he possessed a probing scientific mind and was a reliable and accurate observer, as Schorger affirmed in a July 11, 1968, letter to Ruth Works, Zirrer's good friend: "During a [long] correspondence ... I acquired a profound respect for his ability as a naturalist. He was a very careful observer and, if any uncertainty arose in his mind, he sought further information before reaching a conclusion."

Zirrer's earliest known Wisconsin observations occurred on forays to the Namekagon River in northwestern Sawyer County in the late 1920s and early 1930s. In late September 1932 at their secluded woodland home in Rusk County, he described a particularly memorable experience.

"The first night we were disturbed not only inside by many woodland mice but also outside by something continually dropping on and running over the roof. When I went out to see what was causing all that noise, I frightened what it was, and for a while everything remained quiet. The night was almost as bright as the day. The full moon hung like a detached yellow disk in the intensely clear, crisp night sky, making every object, every twig and leaf clearly visible. Rigid, resembling a jagged wall, stood the great trees, hemming in the little dwelling from all sides. Stepping under a big maple, a few yards from the cabin, I waited. Before long, I heard a slight rustle among the trees in the rear. Following the sound with my eyes, I saw something stirring near the top of a tall balsam fir. A dark something leaped into space and floated lightly upon the roof. It was a northern flying squirrel. Then I saw others, from other trees, all around the tiny clearing, following the first one onto the roof or sailing across the clearing from one tree to another. The whole space above the cabin and the clearing had become alive with animated animal forms.

"It was a pleasant, moonlit night, and the pretty woodland creatures were frolicking. But it was also the harvest time. The summer of 1932 had been unusually favorable and bountiful. The trees and the shrubbery were loaded with fruit, seeds, acorns, [and] nuts...."[51]

Another creature that fascinated Zirrer in Rusk County was the northern saw-whet owl. "These little owls visited us upon several occasions, mostly from the latter part of September until the first permanent snowfall, which usually takes place before the first half of November. On warm, autumn nights when windows were left open, we heard them calling, at times from several directions at once, indicating that several of them were around. With a light inside and window shades up, one of them would sit on a branch or a woodpile a few feet away, stare into the lighted window, and call softly. Although they are usually quite tame and often permit a very close approach, they are alert and of very keen hearing.

Northern saw-whet owl (*Aegolius acadicus*) nestling at nest cavity, west of Ashland in Bayfield County. Photo by Ryan S. Brady, May 21, 2016. Photo courtesy of Wisconsin DNR.

"Sneaking through the rear door as noiselessly as possible, I occasionally tried to approach them from the side or from the rear but found this impossible. The owl would let me come to a distance of three to four feet without showing alarm, but when I stretched my hand to get hold of it, it would glide away and disappear into the darkness."[52]

The woods Zirrer inhabited and explored in northwestern Rusk County, beginning in 1932, probably contained patches of old-growth hardwoods. According to Zirrer, some of the yellow birch in his neighborhood had a diameter of two feet, and at least one he mentioned, about a mile and a half from his cabin, was recorded with a diameter of 3 feet, 9 inches. In such areas white pine and hemlock had been selectively harvested prior to hardwood clear-cuts. This was common practice during the lumbering years of the late nineteenth and early twentieth centuries. By 1910, 65 percent of the total land area of 10 northern Wisconsin counties, including Sawyer County, was reported cut-over, with most remaining areas culled for white pine.[53]

IN 1933, ZIRRER MADE AN IMPORTANT DISCOVERY. "While on a field trip through the extensive, heavy hardwood and mixed timber surrounding our log cabin, and stretching for miles in every direction, I heard suddenly a loud, angry *keek, keek, keek, keek, keek*. At the same time, something struck me on the head from behind, knocking my cap off. In the semidarkness, caused by the dense foliage, I saw a dark, shadowy form pass with lightning speed above my head and disappear among the leaves. It was a northern goshawk [*Accipter gentilis*].

"The bird passed above my head and alighted on the lower limb of a big sugar maple about 200 feet away. Getting myself a stick for protection, I scrutinized the neighboring trees for the nest. Of course I had no intention of striking the bird, but when the hawk, screaming at the top of its voice, its eyes ablaze with fury, flew at me again, I raised the stick, which the bird dodged.

"Though knowing that the nest could not be far away, it took awhile before I located it in a crotch of a giant yellow birch, next to the tree trunk about 35 feet above the ground. I saw one nearly fully grown young at the rim of the nest, and, after some search, three others among the foliage of this and a neighboring tree. While thus engaged, I was attacked again and again by the old bird, which, after a few minutes was joined by another, probably the male. Swinging the stick above my head, I was able to keep the attacking birds at a respectful distance. Not wanting to frighten the birds unduly, I went home, while the hawk followed me to the road, screaming. Next day, visiting the nest again, I was attacked so unexpectedly by the angry bird that it not only knocked my cap off, but hit me so severely on the head that it drew blood, and I felt the swelling fully two weeks after."[54]

Until Zirrer's 1933 record, only A.J. Schoenebeck had claimed to have found goshawks nesting in the state (four nests in 1891), but he provided no data beyond the number of nests.[55]

When Zirrer saw the birds returning to the same nest tree in 1934, he knew that the rarity of his find would interest Owen Gromme, widely recognized at the time as one of the leading authorities on birds in the state. He informed Gromme and soon after sent a special delivery letter to him with instructions to contact a Reverend Senger of Rice Lake. Senger, Zirrer's cousin, would direct Gromme to Zirrer's cabin.

In his personal field notes (housed at the Milwaukee Public Museum), Gromme made this entry about Zirrer's correspondence on May 15, 1934:

> "The other day I received his first letter stating that he had under observation last spring and this the nest of a goshawk. He wrote us as a matter of record and invited us to verify his find if we wished. He wrote in the style of a man of some scientific knowledge, and is evidently a confirmed conservationist. He gave me to understand that if we come up there it must be with the understanding that we would not molest the birds unduly, and under no circumstances kill the birds or take the nest."[56]

Zirrer later wrote Schorger (June 10, 1935): "I am not a scientist and not very anxious for a new record, so I hardly ever use the gun. In this I am in accord with the late Hermann Laus:

> 'Lieber eine Lucke in der Wissenschaft, als eine in der Natur.'"

Translation: Rather a hole (or gap) in science than one in nature.

Zirrer was also very sensitive to the plight of raptors. He railed against the predominant negative view of these birds and vented some of his anger towards the Wisconsin Conservation Commission (now Wisconsin Natural Resources Board). In a November 6, 1934, letter to Schorger he wrote:

"This splendid hawk [northern goshawk] as well as his smaller relatives *velox* [now *Accipiter striatus*, the sharp-shinned hawk] and *cooperii* [Cooper's hawk] are condemned to death by the Wisconsin Conservation Commission. That means that every bloodthirsty idiot can empty his gun at everything that looks like a hawk with the excuse that it was a 'bad hawk.' It is tragic that men of that body do not view the natural necessity with a little more understanding and liberality. I do not deny that our fierce bird is at times very destructive, but what is the difference if a few of the grouse or rabbits are destroyed and eaten by it or die through disease as this is the case right now, when there are practically no grouse or rabbits left."

In the latter part of this letter Zirrer was referring to a crash in the snowshoe hare population. Between 1934 and 1949 he never again saw the number of snowshoe hares that were present from 1932 through the summer of 1933 in northwestern Wisconsin. Commenting on the abundance of hares and eastern cottontail rabbits during the early 1930s, Zirrer wrote in *The Passenger Pigeon*:

"It was nothing unusual to see fifty to sixty of them in less than a mile walk.... They also furnished an abundance of food to our goshawks. The thirty to forty acres surrounding the nest tree were at times actually littered with the skeletons and partly devoured cadavers of these hares. Usually they could be found stretched across fallen trees or on the tops of old stumps...

"The end of summer 1933 saw the end of the varying hares and the cottontail rabbits. Suddenly, almost at once, they had disappeared, swept away as by an epidemic. Their smelly cadavers, lying everywhere and persisting a while longer, told of their extraordinary numbers before. The comparatively few that were spared retired then to their original habitat, the sphagnum bogs, swamps, and marshes, especially those with an abundance of willows, where they recuperate, and from whence they populate the upland woods after their renewed increase."[57]

Back to the goshawk story. On May 15, 1934, Gromme traveled north with an assistant, Walter Pelzer. In the late afternoon of 16 May, they arrived at Zirrer's cabin. After meeting him, Gromme made this journal entry:

"Mr. Zirrer is a very quiet man, and after becoming acquainted with him one can understand his reason for seclusion from prying eyes and wagging tongues. He has a peculiar but probably reasonable philosophy regarding human contacts. He is caring for an invalid wife who requires most of his time. During what spare time he has he studies birds, insects and plants, and has an exceptionally keen and scientific mind. He does remarkably well with what few books he has.

"He is a very short but very active man; has keen blue eyes and rugged physique. His little feeding shelter is a source of joy to both he and his unfortunate wife. He never kills anything, not even a rabbit for food. He ... speaks English poorly, but strange enough one does not seem to be aware of this after knowing him."[58]

On May 17, Pelzer and Gromme selected a large yellow birch about 25 feet from the nest tree as a site to erect a photographic blind. Gromme, however, did not like the view from the blind because the nest was partly obstructed by some branches. The following day he asked Pelzer to remove several small branches from the nest tree. Zirrer recalled what happened next:

"Pelzer, armed with a small saw and a hatchet, was sent up. But ... as he began to approach the nest from below, the fierce female struck ... screaming at the top of her shrill, angry and savage voice.... Encumbered with tools, he could not use his hands to ward off the attacking bird. Pounded with hard, powerful wings and slashed with long, razor sharp talons, he bent his head to protect his eyes and face.... Had he not been held to the tree by the strong leather belt, he most certainly would have been knocked from it.... Pelzer reached the nest ... obstructing branches were cut and Pelzer could descend before the bird was ready for another attack. On the ground he looked with a mixture of sadness and amusement at his shirt, which was hanging in tatters."[59]

From the blind, Gromme had caught much of the action on film, including shots of the female at the nest (see photo), but later that day, Pelzer received word that his grandmother had died. He and Gromme quickly departed, their photography unfinished.

On the afternoon of May 26, more than a week later, Gromme, Pelzer, and Warren Dettman of the MPM staff returned to Zirrer's cabin and proceeded to the blind to resume photography. Zirrer described what ensued:

"Although it was late when they arrived, they decided to get some pictures. Somehow the old birds remained quiet and did not fly at us when we approached the nest tree. In fact, the birds were not even seen. So all precautions were foolishly cast aside, and Gromme started up the tree to the blind. He was only halfway up the big trunk when, with a fierce, savage scream, and coming like a bolt of lightning, the female struck. The excited calls of warning from the ground came too late. Gromme, holding to the heavy spike, reeled for a moment as if he had lost his balance and would tumble down, but fortunately, he held and in a few seconds recovered sufficiently to descend. Fortunately for him the female did not strike again. I fear to think what could or would have happened had she kept at it. Our hawk-investigating affair would probably have had a tragic ending. An examination revealed eight deep gashes across his head, one of them across his right temple and dangerously near his eye."[60]

Gromme recalled the incident this way: "I had climbed about halfway up to the platform tree when the boys shouted warning to me just in time for me to see the female bird coming straight at me. I drove my left fist at her, but she deftly 'shot' in between my fist and bare head and struck me a terrific and painful [blow]...."[61] He added: "... by a mere flip of a wing ... she struck a blow that made my senses reel. It felt like a crack across the head with a heavy whip.... She had evidently taken hold with both feet as she struck and dragged her hind claws about four inches. From that time on, all ascents to either tree were made with the head well protected by heavy burlap or a sheepskin-lined leather helmet."[62]

Photo by Owen Gromme of adult female northern goshawk and young at yellow birch (*Betula lutea*) nest site near Birchwood, Rusk County, Wisconsin, May 18, 1934. Photo provided by Milwaukee Public Museum.

CHAPTER TWO

Before Gromme departed for Milwaukee, he had apparently managed to convince Zirrer of the importance of collecting one of the goshawk young for the museum. Pelzer, wearing a sheep wool-lined helmet provided by Zirrer, climbed the nest tree once more, withstood repeated blows to the head by the female, and retrieved one of the young.[63]

It was not long before it became known in the area that a rare bird was nesting nearby and, according to Zirrer, there was "speculation as to the monetary gain that might be made from the hawks." Apparently fearing the worst, Zirrer took it upon himself to prevent the birds from returning to the nest tree. The following spring, in 1935, he knocked part of the nest down with a long pole.

"After this I did not visit the old tree for about a week, but I cannot describe my consternation when I did get to the old nesting site again. Although it was the first week of April, a blizzard was raging and the thermometer stood at zero.... A dark object loosened itself from the top of a yellow birch in front and above me, and before I had a chance to duck, struck me on the head. Then I saw that the hawks had begun to build another nest, not more than 60 to 80 yards from the old one."[64]

He returned the following day and recorded some of the first observations ever published in North America on nest-building by the goshawk:

"Unseen by the birds, I hid behind some storm broken treetops and a group of balsam firs. According to my notes, gathered then and upon many another occasion, the female builds alone. The material for it, for the most part the thin, and when older, easily breakable twigs of the white birch, she finds on the ground or breaks them from the prostrate young trees whose straight white boles, a few inches in diameter, often crisscross the forest floor. After a stick is placed, which usually takes a considerable amount of time ... she flies again downward to find another. The selection of a suitable stick takes at times wholly five minutes and even longer.... All sticks are carried in the beak.... According to my notes she builds only in the forenoon for about an hour."[65]

Zirrer's observations on nest-building and other aspects of the bird's breeding biology are still cited in life histories of the northern goshawk.

OTHER NOTABLE OBSERVATIONS by Zirrer involved the "natural" nesting of chimney swifts and purple martins. On June 10, 1935, he wrote to Schorger:

"It might interest you that [purple martins] occasionally still nest in hollow trees, away from the haunts of man; at least this was or still is the case a few miles from here [in northwestern Rusk County]. This, only on a much larger scale, holds good for [chimney swifts]. These birds sometimes meet death by coming down the stovepipes and burn[ing]. I saved them on several occasions and pulled once one's charred body from our stove. This lasted until I capped the entrance with wire."

Then, apparently in response to Schorger's inquiry about the nesting swifts, Zirrer commented on a particularly unusual swift nesting occurrence (and more) in a July 29, 1935, letter to him:

"The nest in question is built and occupied for a number of years already, in a most ridiculous place. The building is a country style toilet, used probably twice or thrice daily. Under the roof, which is only about 6 feet above the ground, are cut 2 small holes for ventilation. The door is always closed, so the birds enter through those holes.

"Instead of building the nest right under the roof as a person would expect, they insist to build the nest only about a foot above the board and within six inches of the party who happens to use the toilet. Sometimes they use the same nest; sometimes they build a new one a few inches higher or lower. Before the nesting commences, the old birds roost, hanging on the wall above the nest every night. Later the young ones do the same. Mr. Gromme, when here, saw the nest and tried to photograph the old birds at night with the help of the flashlight and long exposure, but apparently without a good result.

"It might interest you that the swift often [builds a nest] inside … a barn or hayloft … but are generally not observed. I have seen a number of nests built this way, since I [have been] living in [northwestern Wisconsin). It might also interest you that the bird builds a nest about the size of a teaspoon, deposits an egg, enlarges the nest a little next day, and deposits another egg and so on until the nest and set is completed. I have seen this on several occasions."

Here was information on the process of nest-building by chimney swifts not previously recorded in Wisconsin. It shows once again Zirrer's special attention to detail.

It is not clear whether Schorger ever visited Zirrer to stay overnight at his Rusk County home. Zirrer repeatedly invited him, and Schorger occasionally expressed an interest in coming. At the end of Zirrer's July 1, 1939, letter, he wrote:

"In your letter of Sept. 16, 1938, you spoke of coming up here this year, if time permits. If you do and care to rough it a little, there is a nice, level spot right here for camping, and the rest can be arranged easily. We are somewhat crowded and live in very primitive fashion, but the woods are almost within arms reach. You can hear the birds singing you to sleep, owls [in] concert at night, and plenty of music at dawn. I shall do my best to make you comfortable, provided you are satisfied with what we have to offer."

Over two years elapsed before Zirrer's next known letter to Schorger. The Zirrers had moved in 1940 to a cabin in northwestern Sawyer County. This was unknown to Schorger, who had sent Zirrer a copy of his latest publication. Zirrer responded on August 24, 1941, with an eight-page letter that provided a window into the bird life at his new home within today's 160-acre Kissick Alkaline Bog Lake State Natural Area.

"If everything is real quiet, and one is patient and lucky, a glimpse of [a] sora [*Porzana carolina*] or Virginia rail [*Rallus limicola*] can be had. (Walking on the shore through the narrow belt of sedges and other weeds, one can raise one or the other of the two rails.) ... During the breeding season red-winged

Kissick Alkaline Bog Lake State Natural Area near Hayward, Sawyer County, Wisconsin. Photo by Thomas A. Meyer. Photo courtesy of Wisconsin DNR.

blackbirds were extremely abundant.... Different species of swallows, swifts, cedar waxwings, and common nighthawks were abundant and some still are. They dart, especially toward the evening, over the placid, sunlit waters. Even the black tern, with its stream-lined body and long, narrow wings visited us daily for several weeks. Needless to say that practically every land bird that I know from N. Wisconsin, and a number of water birds, is often or occasionally seen in, or in the vicinity of, our bog or pond; at times their abundance is astounding.

"In the afternoon of June 19, after a week of almost continuous rain, a male Connecticut warbler was observed in a small oak tree a few feet from one of our windows. The bird was busy picking and carrying away small green caterpillars. It even sang a little! June 28 another was seen in the tamarack bog about half of a mile from here.... I mentioned it to Gromme in a letter, and he informed me that it is perfectly well possible [that it is] breeding here because they had found it breeding at about the same time in the Burnett County.

"In the same letter [to Gromme] I mentioned among other birds the palm warbler as breeding here, and he thinks that it might be another new record. I had not paid much attention to it thinking that it is one of the regular breeders in N. Wisc. I am sorry now because a pair nested here, barely 50–60 yards from the dwelling although I did not see the nest. Watching wild ducks on the pond, I saw and disturbed the bird daily for quite a while, but thinking it [was] nothing unusual, I failed to investigate.... In the evening [of] July 5, I noticed the whole family feeding in small tamaracks a few yards from the house, calling incessantly *zit, zit, zit*.... If it had not been for the parent birds I would have been unable to identify them, for the young birds look very much like some sort of sparrow, excepting for the longer and thinner bills...."

In his August 24, 1941, letter to Schorger, he also made mention of another discovery:

"Last spring I heard another call that puzzled me for a number of weeks. Snow was still plentiful and bogs were flooded. For a number of evenings I stood at the edge of the bog and listened to a call resembling a distant, subdued barking of a heavy dog. One evening, in order to bring the mysterious caller closer if possible, I started to imitate it. Doing this for a while the calling ceased, but I kept on calling. Everything remained quiet, however, and I was just about ready to quit and go home, when all of a sudden something—not over 30 feet away—burst into a weird, maniacal

CHAPTER TWO

laugh, *heh, heh, heh.* This was followed by a sound very much like teeth chattering, and finally like a violent shaking of a heavy, wet garment. The whole performance was repeated several times in succession, and then everything remained quiet. It was pitch dark among the conifers, and I could not see a thing. Several weeks later, however, I learned to know the actor—the long-eared owl [*Asio otus*]...."

It wasn't just the animal world that intrigued him, Zirrer took great delight in investigating the flora of the conifer bog adjacent to his cabin. Orchids were exquisite finds for him, and he became immersed in identifying each species as if each was a new personal discovery:

"Our neighborhood is also very interesting botanically. Orchids are extremely plentiful, and so far I have observed several species, among them such choice beauties as three species of *Cypripedium* [lady's-slippers], *Arethusa* [*bulbosa*, dragon's mouth], *Calopogon* [*pulchellus*, grass pink], and *Pogonia* [*ophioglossoides*, rose pogonia]. [On] June 12 I was lucky enough to find the *Orchis rotundifolia* [*Amerorchis rotundifolia*, round-leaved orchid], so far known only from the Ozaukee, Sheboygan and Door counties. When orchids bloom the whole bog is transformed into a most wonderful wild garden, and these choice varieties bloom literally by the thousands."[66]

Forty summers later, botanist Stephen Solheim visited the Kissick Alkaline Bog Lake. He compiled an impressive list of plant species, including 16 orchids. About *Orchis rotundifolia*, although he was unaware of Zirrer's report, he said, "This bog may well be the historical site for the threatened *Orchis rotundifolia* collected in a bog near Hayward in 1941. This appears to be the only suitable site in the area, but the plant has not been observed, and is thus extirpated if this was the collection site."[67]

Zirrer made no mention of actually collecting this rare orchid in his letters to Schorger. But files in the WDNR's Bureau of Endangered Resources (now Bureau of Natural Heritage Conservation) showed that Zirrer collected the plant on June 10, 1941, and sent it to the Milwaukee Public Museum. It is difficult to speculate whether Zirrer's collection activities or a specific environmental condition or event imperiled this particular species in the 40 years between Zirrer's observation and Solheim's visit. A clue may be found in Zirrer's August 5, 1945, correspondence to Schorger in which he writes:

"The bog, not being protected with snow as usual, froze to a depth of many inches. This in turn had had a bad effect on the orchids: those with shallow root horizon froze out, and some species though plentiful before, were quite rare last spring. Much of the other vegetation was also affected, some of it very badly."

The bog and surrounding land do not appear to have changed significantly since Zirrer's time, mainly because the state acquired 941 acres (today known as the Kissick Swamp Wildlife Area), including the bog, during 1946–1951.[68] Earlier, in the 1920s, mature stands of white cedar, white and black spruce, and balsam fir had been logged uniformly. Zirrer observed in 1944 that the bog was "mostly overgrown with small conifers up to about six inches [in] diameter, [with] some larger trees, esp. cedars and enough firewood to last forever."[69] Today, there is an even-aged monotypic stand of dense conifers over much of the wildlife area. But has the bog lake itself changed? Zirrer[70] put the size of the bog lake (he actually referred to it as a pond) at 30 acres, and yet in 1983 the WDNR described it as only 10 acres in size. Zirrer may have included the adjoining sedge mat in his estimate because it is not likely that the size of the lake has changed significantly since the 1940s.[71]

Bogs were not exactly the favorite haunts of local townspeople in Zirrer's day. And the "pond" itself had quite a reputation. Zirrer commented: "To the casual observer the pond appears very shallow, but underneath there is an enormous layer of soft, black mud, which also reaches for a considerable distance under the adjoining bog. A 16-foot pole forced through the top layer of matted vegetation or pushed into the water next to the shore does not reach the bottom. In the opinion of the neighbors, the pond is bottomless; which belief was strengthened a few years previously by the fact that a cow, venturing too far, broke through the floating *Sphagnum* and disappeared into the mud beneath."[72]

WHILE AT THE BOG SITE, Zirrer also took a considerable interest in mammals. On March 12, 1942, he wrote Schorger: "I find mammals, especially small mammals, just as interesting, and sometimes more so than birds. One can hardly go along with just one branch of nature study; it is advisable, almost essential, to be posted as much as possible on everything else." Zirrer observed the behavior of (common) porcupines, mink, (American) red and (Eastern) gray squirrels, muskrats, and young deer mice. His observations of the muskrat resulted in a four-page, single-spaced, typewritten paper that is now among mammalogist H.H.T. Jackson's papers at the State Historical Society. This paper describes the winter behavior of a muskrat at an ice hole on the bog lake. In the late fall of 1943, Zirrer observed that a muskrat had gnawed a hole through the ice on his pond—something that had never been observed (or known) by H.H.T. Jackson—and was practically unheard of anywhere at the time. Schorger was excited about it. He conducted a literature search and found a 1920 reference to similar behavior.

On July 12, 1944, Zirrer elaborated: "December 5 at 6 a.m., temp. was 8 above, but it rose at noon to 40.... Shortly after 3 p.m, I ... began to carry ... wood to the shore to be hauled across the pond later. Glancing over the icy surface of the pond which, at that particular place is about 320 feet wide, I noticed in the middle of it a small, dark object which was not there before. Going closer I saw that it was a small muskrat, sitting on its haunches and eating something.... [My] first thought, however, was not the rat or where it came from but the condition of the ice....

"Cautiously I approached the animal which, seeing me coming, vanished from sight. Gingerly, afraid to break through, I stepped nearer. In the ice there was an oval hole measuring, when I returned later with a ruler, 4-1/2 inches in length and 3-1/2 in width.... The hole was situated exactly over a large bed of [large-leaved pondweed or broad-leaved pondweed, *Potamogeton amplifolius*] from which the rat lived all winter. It is somewhat peculiar, but the fact is that this plant does not grow anywhere near the shores of the pond; the existence of it in the pond was unknown to me until then."[73]

Schorger passed on Zirrer's observations of muskrats, mink, and other mammals to H.H.T. Jackson, who corresponded with Zirrer to seek additional information. Jackson summarized Zirrer's muskrat observations in his book, *Mammals of Wisconsin*.[74]

IN THE EARLY 1940s, Zirrer was honing his skills as a naturalist. While his knowledge of the natural world increased, so too did his desire to learn more about what he was seeing. Although his personal book collection contained many European and regional (U.S.) publications, as well as several on Wisconsin's flora and fauna, Zirrer's appetite for natural history works had grown insatiable. How could he obtain more books, he asked Schorger. He had exhausted the local library as a source. Besides, he didn't want to borrow books. He wanted to buy them and mark them up with notes as he saw fit.

By 1943, Zirrer had begun to build an impressive library, including many publications in English (though he was still not satisfied), and he had developed a knack for picking up books here and there:

"Since you browse considerably in bookstores it might be of some interest to you to hear that I have exchanged by the way of barter my volume of the *Birds of America*, price $4.00, for six volumes of Bent's *Life Histories [of North American Birds]*, bulletins 121, 126, 130, 135, 142, and 146. That was a 'Lucky Strike!'"[75]

Schorger, besides providing him copies of articles, encouraged Zirrer to contact the Smithsonian Institution. He did so and included "a few of my observations" he thought might interest Secretary Alexander Wetmore. Secretary Wetmore forwarded two of the publications Francis wanted and, to Zirrer's delight, "confirmed some of my observations."[76]

Keenly aware of Zirrer's promise as a naturalist, Schorger took steps to bring him in closer contact with the scientific community. He submitted Zirrer's name for membership to the Wisconsin Society for Ornithology in 1942 and recommended that he become a member of the Wisconsin Academy of Science, Arts, and Letters. It was with great delight that Zirrer later learned of his acceptance by the Wisconsin Academy. He felt indebted to Schorger and profusely thanked him for this and more in a June 10, 1943, letter:

"I have received recently the certificate of membership in the Academy ... which I certainly appreciate and treasure ... greatly. Through your friendly interest and kind recommendation I was introduced to the Wise. Soc. [for] Ornithology, have become a member of the Academy, the supreme court of Wisconsin science and other intellectual activity, and now have joined the Wilson Ornithological Club [later renamed Wilson Ornithological Society].

"Through your friendly advice ... to apply for the technical bulletins on food and food habits of ducks and Bent's *Life Histories* I have not only acquired several valuable, extremely interesting and readable books, but also learned of a source of fine scientific literature largely unknown to me before.... In fact I am taking the monthly catalog of the government publications so as not to miss anything of interest. Not that I have any superfluous money but I would rather skimp on eats than miss a good book if it is within my means.

"I cannot emphasize sufficiently how sincerely I appreciate all this, and wish to thank you. You are not only a scientist and as an ornithologist the best in Wisconsin but also a fine fellow in every other way. How could have you otherwise bothered with such a poor shanty dweller who is really nothing to you."

As Zirrer's mentor, Schorger urged him to publish his observations. But Zirrer was reluctant to do so. In a August 5, 1942, letter to Schorger he wrote: "Although not just so very dumb, and somewhat of a linguist, I am still at war with the English language. I wish sincerely to be able to master English as perfectly as you do. Then perhaps I should not fear to write something for publication, although even then my knowledge of various scientific disciplines could not compare with yours." Schorger later noted ironically: "His command of the English language would put many of our college graduates to shame. Yet, he was very reluctant to prepare his observations for publication."[77]

In 1944, at the age of 58, Zirrer took the plunge and published his first feature article, titled "Bittern," in *The Passenger Pigeon*. A relatively short piece, he reminds us of what bird migration must have been like in its heyday before noticeable declines occurred in the later decades of the twentieth century, but he had fun recalling one incident:

"Our dwelling is situated at an extensive tamarack-cedar-black spruce bog, so close that the branches of tamaracks reach almost to our windows and only a few feet above the high water mark. [American] bitterns are very common with us, so common that occasionally one is seen sitting on one or another of our woodpiles, often not more than a few feet from the house....

"On my trips into the bog evenings and nights, I have, upon several occasions, heard a croaking sound, moving back and forth, coming sometimes from a considerable height, then again low over the bog, but always moving. At times dark, ghostly forms passed with great speed within 10 to 20 feet of me.... May 18 last year I was in the bog just a little before dark. Migration of warblers was at its height, and the birds were actually swarming everywhere. While standing thus on a slightly drier spot and partly concealed by the dense growth of evergreens, I heard that familiar croaking sound again. Two large birds appeared in the distance, chasing one another with unbelievable speed just above and between the treetops, which at that particular place are about 8 to 12 feet high, both birds croaking angrily, excitedly. It was already too dark to place them. Aside from that, the birds flew with such speed above and among the trees that I could only now and then catch a glimpse of them. This went on for a number of seconds. Suddenly, the birds started straight toward me and coming to the small opening, on the edge of which I was standing, dropped right in and started to fight jumping at one another like two roosters, using beaks, wings and feet at the same time. Then I saw that the birds were bitterns and very probably two males.

"I stood like a statue, and at first the birds did not pay the slightest attention to me, if they saw me at all. Before long, however, the larger bird cornered the smaller one, which began to back toward me. In this manner, the smaller bird, with its back turned, came so close that I could have touched it. Now the larger bird became suspicious. Facing me only a few feet away, it apparently began to realize that the dark form standing in front of it was not just a tree stump. The bird froze in its track assuming the well-known pose, and the other bird, without turning, followed suit. For quite some time not one of us moved. Before long, however, the weight of my body began to tell. I was sinking deeper and deeper. Water started to gurgle under my feet, and I was forced to move. This of course put life into the birds; with much flapping of the wings, but without a croak, they rose and disappeared in the distance."[78]

A man of diverse interests, Zirrer also worked hard at cultivating a large garden—something he occasionally mentioned in his letters to Schorger during the 1940s. On November 6, 1943, he wrote:

"[This past summer I] produced 50 of each: cauliflower, broccoli, white and curly cabbage. Many of my cauliflowers weighed 4 and 5 lbs. but some were even a good deal larger, and the rest, broccoli etc., were in proportion. Further, I have produced several bushels of peppers, none smaller than a large lemon, but many were nearly double. I have had potatoes, tomatoes, corn, peas, edible soybeans, lima beans, onions, radishes, parsnips, carrots, beets, turnips, Chinese cabbage, cantaloupes, cucumbers, squashes, and even okra. Does your mouth water? For a while I thought of sending you a box of the fanciest, and I would have, but finally I was afraid that you might say: 'What the!' It goes to show, however, what this soil is capable of producing.... Once the weeds [are] under control, which I have done very effectively, very little time and labor is required to keep the garden going."

From his writings, Zirrer's life in the deep woods of northwestern Wisconsin sometimes sounds bucolic if not idyllic, but it was, in fact, quite difficult. Much of his time was spent caring for Clara, whom he described in a December 24, 1937, letter to Schorger as "helpless ... unable even to get herself a drink of water." The Zirrers were married in 1917. He blamed her condition on a botched medical operation in 1920, and apparently wrote an unpublished (and lost) 510-page novel about the incident.

A SEPTEMBER 26, 1943, letter to Schorger paints a broad picture of Zirrer's bog world near Hayward. The reference to a rubber shortage in the following excerpt quickly reminds us of the war in progress:

"Although I do not own a car [the] rubber shortage affects me too. Since most of our fuel is in the bog (I find that a good sized bog is botanically and zoologically the most interesting formation in Wisconsin—a regular treasure chest. Practically every mammal and bird is found ... and botanically such numbers of rare, beautiful and interesting plants grow there that the flora of the adjoining formations appears drab and trivial in comparison.) and practically all of my tramping is done in there, I need a pair of reasonably high rubber boots. With some reluctance, the rationing board allowed me a pair of boots last year and did so this year again, but they do not last long, and during the summer I was largely without them. Still I have made a considerable number of very interesting observations, some of them I think new or at least not in any book I have or have read.

"From now on my work in the bog consist[s] of cutting or gathering dead or dying tree[s]. Since I cannot stay away from home more than a few hours daily, the work lasts well until the end of December. The trees, mostly cedar, black spruce, and some tamarack, must be carried about 1/4 to 1/2 of a mile to dry land where they are still [far] from the dwelling—very hard and slow work. Even if horses were obtainable, no team can enter the bog until it is thoroughly frozen, which it is not before the end of December.

"In places I tramp through about one foot of mud and water, over various debris, through the dense bog shrubbery and trees, over deep elastic sphagnum and through the matted vegetation of different grasses, rushes and sedges, some of them as sharp as a knife and tough as a wire. Some parts of my path tremble under every step; under and between the grass, shrubs, moss and roots lurk deep hidden holes full of mud and water. Suddenly one or both of my feet break through; I sink into my knees, even up to my belt sometimes. I feel icy cold water running in on the top of my boots. I try to get out as fast as possible, but the tough black mud or the roots hold my feet like in a vise—or perhaps it is the bog witch or the will o' the wisp. I am lucky if by sinking in I am able to keep the balance because otherwise I take a bath and am wet all over. If this happens when my work for the day is nearly done I go home to change and get dry, but if it is at the beginning of it I do not bother. To the merry tune of sloshing water in the boots I only work harder to keep from freezing. Even when once at home I cannot change immediately, my wife and her needs come before my comfort. But I am a reasonably tough guy and used to hardships.

"On my way in and out of the bog and during my work there I see and come across much that is interesting.... Lifting a hollow log a number of *Peromyscus* [deer mice] scamper in all directions—some of them up the nearest tree.... Last winter I have also learned that the muskrats travel extensively under the snow, apparently in search of food. Coming from the direction of the pond they occasionally appear on the surface of the snow there where various channels and deepened deer trails intersect the bog.... With a pole I have followed their trails. Earlier in the fall I see [eastern] chipmunks gather the seed of *Thuja occidentalis* [northern white cedar]. To do this they go to the end of the smallest twigs, often 20 to 30 feet above the ground. Seeing the twigs bending under some weight one expects to see a bird, but getting closer one is surprised to see chipmunks way up in the branches. And yet the seed is so small, hardly worthy of the effort.

"In Nov. 1941, I frightened a family of *Peromyscus* from their snug winter quarters in the hollow roots of a large cedar stump. Among the different seeds and nutlets stored there, there was also a quantity of cedar seeds and about a pint of achenes. I took a few of the latter with me, but for a long time I was not able to place them. During the periods of full moon I sit, if the sky is clear, somewhere in the bog or near the pond to watch various night creatures and listen to their calls. While sitting so about two weeks ago at [the] edge of the bog, I noticed that the fruiting heads of the *Helianthus giganteus* [tall sunflower] moved and bent down. Wondering about the cause of the movement I watched. With the help of my glass, and going a little closer, I saw two of these mice climbing over the tops, very probably gathering the seed. Taking some seed with me home, I compared it with the other of nearly two years ago: it was the same. The same seed ... as long as it is soft and milky, that is from the later part of August until about the 20 of September, the favored, in fact almost the only food of [American] goldfinches, for which they go day after day until it is too ripe. After they cease to come, [black-capped] chickadees take the rest...."

Zirrer concludes his long September letter by sharing in Schorger's grief regarding Schorger's son, apparently killed in the World War, and mentions his own personal sorrow:

"I hope this senseless slaughter would end soon. I can understand, even if you do not say so, how you feel about your son. I have had and have so many sorrows myself that I sincerely feel your anxiety, and hope with you for the best. I ... am not given to hate, but there were times that I could not even look at my German books. However, I realize now that it was not right; one must not condemn everything and everybody, although I have enough cause to do so.

"This letter would have been written sooner, but since the 28 of August we struggle with death. My wife is very seriously ill. It is just this week that there is a slight improvement noticeable. Personally I have not had much sleep since."

Sadly, Zirrer's wife passed away on his 59th birthday (December 3, 1944). He wrote to Schorger of his grief on December 20, 1944:

"I am somewhat late in answering your letter of Dec. 3, but it was not neglect. I have just passed through the most crucial period of my life: my dear wife, my most treasured friend, my faithful companion for over 27 years ... passed away Dec. 3 and was buried in Milwaukee 6 December. Though physically almost entirely helpless, her mind was keen, quick grasping and clear to the very end, which, as a result of slight cold, came so really unexpectedly. No one, not even her doctor, suspected that the end was so near. Although I have gone through an unusual amount of sorrows and tribulations in my life, her death was the hardest blow, and today I doubt that I will ever recover from it; for the time being I am completely lost, have no interest in living and only wish to follow her.

"If I can stand it I shall stay here until May or June—until the rusty blackbirds return and nest, if they do.... How we had both planned for your reception to make your stay here pleasant and interesting, and now she has gone."

Beginning in 1945, Zirrer wrote to Schorger less often. In a May 5, 1945, letter to Schorger he said, "Since the death of my wife ... I have done very little field work; there is not the interest the way it used to be." This would explain the lack of correspondence. Perhaps Zirrer had served as his wife's eyes and ears, describing his observations to her in detail before committing them to letters. Without her presence and companionship, his interest faded.

Zirrer did not correspond with Schorger again until the fall of 1946. He offered this account of the intervening period in a September 25, 1946, letter:

"It is more than a year since I have ... written to you. From the beginning of July 1945, after moving away from Hayward, I have spent nearly eight months in Milwaukee. In the beginning of March 1946 I ... returned to Hayward where I spent 3 month[s]. From there I went to Birchwood and now, since the last week of August, I am in Chicago.

"The purpose of this travelling back and forth was to finish and prepare—for a possible publication—a manuscript (I call it a novel), which I [had] written before moving to Milwaukee.... The manuscript contains about 510 pages with about 260 words to a page."

Zirrer asked Schorger to edit the manuscript and offered to pay him for his services. Schorger replied in late September:

"I have just received your letter of the 25th and its contents were surprising. You are very versatile. I have wondered frequently during recent months what you were doing since I had not heard from you.

"Regarding the manuscript, I suggest that you send it on so that we can form some opinion as to what can be done with it. Mrs. Schorger has had considerable experience with manuscripts, and she will be glad to read it also.

"From your letter I am sure that you realize that you have entered a very competitive field."

On October 10, 1946, Zirrer sent his manuscript to the Schorgers and apologized for the rough draft. By October 27, he had received the first four chapters back and Zirrer sent Schorger $20 "for the postage ... and as part compensation for Mrs. Schorger's work and time ... editing it." Schorger had apparently asked Zirrer's permission to share the chapters on the [northern] goshawk with the Kumlien Club. Zirrer, in his October 27 letter, gives Schorger permission to read it but not to "reveal its source or my name.... I have much more material than this on the goshawks, gathered during eight years of my thorough acquaintance with the same pair, or rather the same female.... If I find time I may perhaps prepare a paper on northern goshawks in the near future for *The Passenger Pigeon*." He did indeed publish an article on goshawks in the July 1947 issue of *The Passenger Pigeon*.

Why would Zirrer choose to live in Chicago, a place so seemingly foreign to him? It could have been that he desired an environment radically different from anything that reminded him of his wife. Although living in the city, Zirrer still caught sight of fall migrants that passed through—or died trying—something that he voiced concern over, decades ahead of his time:

"Four weeks ago I found an ovenbird, warm still, on the pavement at the corner of Lawndale and 26th. I sent it to the Chicago Academy of Science. Not as anything of value, but I thought that it may throw a little light on the migration and the dangers to migrating birds, lost among the maze of buildings."[79]

Schorger returned the $20 Zirrer had sent Mrs. Schorger. Regarding the manuscript, he wrote:

"You have not included too much of your observations on natural history. Both of us feel that they are the best part of the MS. This is your forte, and I hope that you will do much more along this line. It is my advice that you work on popular articles on natural history using the careful observations in your notebooks.... P.S., I do hope that you will eventually donate your notebooks to the Wisconsin Historical Society, Madison. It would be most unfortunate if they should be lost or destroyed."[80]

Zirrer replied on November 4, 1946:

"I [do] not think that my notebooks could be of any value to [the] Wisconsin Historical Society. At any rate, they would have to be rewritten. As they are now, part of my notes would often [not be] understandable to anyone else."

Zirrer, at almost 61 years of age, was hardly living an easy life in Chicago. His job at a large department store apparently involved electrician duties, one of which proved quite hazardous as described in a November 24, 1946, letter to Schorger:

"Two weeks ago I ... contracted a bad cold.... About a week ago we were installing the necessary wiring for television on the roof of a big department store building, where I am employed, and the antenna had to be carried to the top of a water tank, more than two hundred feet above the street. After several employees, ex-service men, refused to climb it, the foreman of the television company asked me to do it, which I did. Climbing itself was an easy affair, but pulling up and fastening the antenna without much support or something to hang on, and [having] both hands occupied, was an entirely different proposition. To make it worse, a strong, cold wind, accompanied by heavy misting, blew. Before long my hands were numb and my clothes wet. I was freezing and shivering. Somehow I managed to fasten the antenna and tightened the wire.... Once inside I actually fainted from my sick condition and exhaustion."

Of course, while dangling 200 feet above the pavement, Zirrer somehow made note of whatever birds were present: "During the work on the top of the tank a large flock of gulls circled above my head. Feeling quite uneasy, I was wondering if the birds were expecting, perhaps hoping for, a meal...."

⁊

AFTER TWO YEARS IN CHICAGO, Zirrer had had enough of city life. In the fall of 1948 he moved back to the Hayward area "to revise, finish, and re-type my manuscript, a task which I could not do in Chicago." He found a remote location near the Totagatic River in northwestern Wisconsin. On May 15, 1949, he wrote Schorger:

"I am living so far from my rural mailbox that it requires five hours of strenuous walking through a wilderness to go there and back; therefore I do not go often. An enormously interesting country, full of wildlife, but too far from everything. I have made many new and interesting observations: Gray squirrels chasing the red ones; red squirrels chasing the weasels; bald-headed [bald] eagles attacking ducks at the river; wood ducks and hooded mergansers swimming within four feet of the [North American river] otters, etc."

Zirrer, ever wary of the approach of the forester's axe, was quick to notice changes in the north due to forestry practices. In a June 2, 1949, letter to Schorger he also wrote:

"This locality used to be a very good, more or less primitive area of fine second and even some old growth timber, but during the last few years most of the saleable trees [have] been cut down, leaving only the young, the useless, the dead and the dying ones.

"Many of these privately owned forties appear as if they had been stricken by a cyclone—the most reckless forest destruction imaginable. If this keeps on a few years longer, not one good tree of more than eight inch diameter will remain. This of course [has] affected the plant and animal life also. Over wide areas the flora [has] greatly changed and many of the choicest plants completely gone. Of mammals as large or larger than a red squirrel, the most common is [white-tailed] deer and porcupine. It is much easier to see five or ten deer than one red or gray squirrel.

"Since I [have come] here (the beginning of October 1948) I [have seen) hundreds of deer and dozens of porcupines but only one snowshoe hare, seven red and two gray squirrels. Of course where would they get the necessary food when all the mature fruit or seed bearing trees [have] been cut away. In their stead I see cottontail rabbits and striped gophers [thirteen-lined ground squirrels, *Ictidomys tridecemlineatus*] invading the woods."

Despite his retreat from society, Zirrer continued his writings for *The Passenger Pigeon*. "The Great Blue Heron," published in July 1951, pulls the reader in like the beginning of a novel:

"In the beginning of April, when northern Wisconsin woods and bogs are yet buried under great masses of powdery, hard packed, discolored snow; when atmosphere drips with misty wetness; when hardly a living creature is seen or heard, and nature itself seems to breathe hopelessness and despair; there perhaps will emerge, from the thick, grayish haze, a pair of big, dark, bluish colored birds, like an apparition from another world. The great blue heron is here again! Bridging the dreary, depressing emptiness of endless woods on great, broad wings, the birds vanish as suddenly as they have emerged, as if they have been swallowed up by the creeping fog."[81]

Zirrer's next piece for *The Passenger Pigeon*, titled "The 'Great' Pileated Woodpecker," appeared in the spring 1952 issue.[82] His last submission to *The Passenger Pigeon* titled "The Great Horned Owl," appeared in 1956.[83] At that time, he was apparently still living in the Hayward area. Some time afterwards, he moved back to Milwaukee, where he worked at the Krueger Lithographing Company until the summer of 1958. Then he moved back once again to the Hayward area. From here, he wrote at least three articles for the *Milwaukee Journal* that appeared in winter and spring, 1958–1959.[84] The last of these was titled "Nature Lover's North Woods Diary" and was subtitled "Isolated Cabin Dweller Tells How He and His Bird, Animal Friends Survived Bitter Winter in Forest Near Hayward, Wis.; Spring Came Late This Year." Zirrer was 73. The article began as follows:

"This was an unusually hard winter. My poorly built cabin is getting poorer every year. With a steady fire, it is warm enough, even in the coldest weather, but at night, when the fire is low, the temperature drops quickly.

"To top it all, I ran out of wood about six weeks ago. I thought last fall that the wood I cut would last all winter. Wood is plentiful around here, but to get it when deep snow covers the ground is a problem.

"Because of the frigid temperature and heavy snows farther south, the birds were slow in returning—even the [American] crows, which usually come before the end of February. This year the first ones—three of them showed up Mar. 15; the main body came back on April 3. About 100 crows appeared at my 'knacker's yard' where I, during the winter, dumped several hundred pounds of meat scraps. These included bear and deer skulls; fox, skunk, raccoon and various other cadavers; deer feet, bear fat and so on—even a two-headed calf that a farmer brought to my neighbor, a taxidermist, for mounting, but later decided to abandon. The cawing crows descended on the dump and fed as if they had eaten nothing for days. Part of a bear carcass, weighing about 50 pounds, was stripped of flesh and fat in less than two days."

Most people wouldn't tolerate mice in their living room, but not Zirrer:

"The cabin ... was the home of several deer mice—cute little beasties, glossy tawny brown above and snowy white under. They ran up and down the walls and beams better than a squirrel. Last fall, after noticing these squatters, I bought a few traps but decided not to use them. Instead, I started to place a bit of food on the floor every night. It did not take them long to discover the new bounty. They approached the food furtively at first—advanced, retreated, advanced again, hesitated, but finally grabbed a piece and ran. Before long, they became accustomed to my presence and the light burning and did not run away if I moved. Now they come, one after another, pick a piece of food, sit on their haunches like diminutive squirrels and, transferring the food from their mouths to their tiny, handlike paws, start to eat daintily. If there is more than they can eat at one sitting, they carry it away and hide it, sometimes in my boots."

Zirrer ended on a mournful note, lamenting the ongoing destruction of the forest he had come to know so well:

"Outside my cabin the forest looks empty and desolate. Before long, however, the chainsaws will be back here. In spite of conservation talk, the woods are still exploited to the limit. Every tree that is not too small must go. There is hardly a day that I don't hear the distant buzzing of the chainsaw. One or two logs are secured; the rest—one-half to two-thirds of the tree—is left to decay."

IT IS NOT CLEAR HOW LONG Zirrer lived in the Hayward area or elsewhere in the Northwoods. At some point, perhaps in the mid-1960s, Zirrer decided to move back to Milwaukee to live out his remaining years. He died on May 30, 1968, at Columbia Hospital in Milwaukee. He had asked long-time friend Ruth Works to handle his affairs after his death. Historian

CHAPTER TWO

and conservationist Walter Scott passed on a request to Schorger for information that could be included in an obituary. Scott noted that Zirrer was "an unusual man and a fine naturalist deserving of recognition."[85] *The Passenger Pigeon* editor Charles Kemper added: "No finer nature writer, in this editor's opinion, has ever appeared in any publication than the contributions of this humble man."[86]

Schorger had a request for Ruth Works that he made in a July 11, 1968, letter:

"I asked Mr. Zirrer to leave his notebooks to the Wisconsin Historical Society. He replied that they were kept in such a manner that he doubted that anyone except himself could get much benefit from them. If you find that these notebooks are still among his papers, it would be a fine thing to send them to the Society as they would be of no value to any heir. Now that Mr. Zirrer is deceased, I intend to donate his important letters to the Society."

Ruth Works responded to Schorger on July 27, 1968.

"I was glad to have your letter of July 11.... He came to Milwaukee, when he was so sick, because he was so fond of a doctor he had seen here a number of times....

"I've almost completed reading his 'novel,' two big typed volumes, and have found only slight reference to the medical malpractice he felt his wife suffered from.... I think it should go to the Historical Society. It gives so many facts on life in northern Wis. during the Great Depression. Not only is the wealth of wildlife in the woods described, but prices of potatoes are given, nationality groups mentioned, etc. Would you please ask the Historical Society if they would like to have it? It is beautifully typed...."

A thorough check of files at the Wisconsin State Historical Society has failed to produce Zirrer's "novel." As to the notebooks that so interested Schorger, they experienced a sad but perhaps predictable fate. Ruth Works explained:

"Mr. Zirrer's things were stored in a warehouse and, having no car, I had to look through the small boxes right there, using vacation time from my job to do so. I did find some notes ... in extremely small handwriting. My impulse was to keep them, but then I thought, "Who is ever going to try to read this?" So I threw them out. On getting home, with the things I did save, I found your letter ... suggesting his notes be given to Hist. Soc. I felt bad!"[87]

Imagine these field notes—perhaps decades of painstaking observations—lost forever. It is fortunate that Schorger saved and donated his Zirrer papers to the Wisconsin Historical Society in Madison. These, Zirrer's few published articles, and miscellaneous references, are the only records we have from one of the most diligent yet unheralded naturalists in Wisconsin's history. ☀

George Knudsen
(1922-2004)

George Knudsen showing a dogbane beetle (*Chrysochus auratus*) to visitors
at his White Pines Nature Center, Hayward, Wisconsin, July 12, 1983.

GREEN ASH

Chapter Three~
George Knudsen

So I'm walking along real quietly. The rain starts to come down. I remember thinking to myself, "This is the day I'm going to get it. I'm going to get killed for sure on a spooky morning like this." My heart starts to beat a little faster. I walk up on a little hill because he is down around the edge of this bog that is curving off to the northwest. I look down and see big bracken ferns. So I yell, "Hey bear!" Oh geez, his head comes up out of the tall bracken ferns and I think, "Hippopotamus? Is *that* a monster! What in hell am I going to do?!"

—GK

George John Knudsen, born May 19, 1922, grew up on a sandy farm near Easton, Wisconsin, just north of Wisconsin Dells. Back then, commercial interests were few in the Dells, and the area's meandering, lazy river and sandstone cliffs provided a unique setting for exploring the natural world. Turtles, snakes, and birds first grabbed young George's attention, and his turtle collection, in particular, gained him considerable local notoriety. Insects, too, fascinated him, and the large collection he established during his high school years became so well known that it came to the attention of Aldo Leopold.

Knudsen graduated from Black River Falls High School in Black River Falls in June 1940. Less than two years later, he joined the Army Air Corps to fight in World War II. He attained the rank of sergeant during his service from December 1942 to October 1945. Then, he returned home to Wisconsin and obtained a bachelor's degree in zoology and botany from the University of Wisconsin-Madison.

In June 1949, George began a 34-year career with the Wisconsin Department of Natural Resources. He started as a wildlife biologist working on pheasant and quail research and management, then turned his attention as a furbearer research scientist to ecological studies of beaver, bear, and otter. In the early 1960s, George secured a naturalist position, and eventually became the department's Chief Naturalist until his retirement on May 20, 1983. He was a strong advocate of converting abandoned railroad beds into state trails.

The author of numerous scientific and popular articles and the recipient of several awards, George served as an advisor to the Scientific Area Preservation Council, the state's endangered species program, and the Ice Age National Scientific Reserve.

After retirement, he threw his considerable energy into establishing the White Pines Nature Center near Hayward, Wisconsin. Here, for over a decade, he led several field trips and lectured on Wisconsin's natural history. At 6 feet, 3 inches and weighing about 230 pounds, this barrel-chested Norwegian commanded everyone's attention when he spoke in a strong and measured voice. Additionally, he conveyed an indefatigable childlike enthusiasm for all creatures great and small and possessed a thorough knowledge of the state's native flora.

George's skills ranged widely from creating scores of fine pen-and-ink drawings of native plants (that publisher, Kristin Mitchell, has skillfully employed at the start of *Afield* chapter headings) to trapping and capturing black bears.

Our interview occurred in January 1984 at his west Madison home, where he lived with his wife, Arlene. George and Arlene, who raised three sons—Jeff, Kirk, and Brad—later moved to Verona.

MY FATHER, SILAS J. KNUDSEN, came from Chicago and started farming alone. One day he met a girl from Chicago named Caroline Graef, and they got pretty thick, so he finally married her.

I was born about 25 miles northwest of the home farm where John Muir had spent his boyhood beginning in 1849. I always like to think that our farm was so doggone near John Muir's home that maybe his spirit jumped into me when I jumped out, you know. I like to think that his spirit remained in those sandy lands and in some way helped influence my love for nature. My dad's parents, in fact, everyone on dad's side, were 100 percent Norwegian, coming from Stavanger; Kristiansund; and Bergen, Norway. They came over here because the moneymaking opportunities were better. All of my mother's kin were German, from the Frankfurt area.

Soon after I was born, my parents moved to Wisconsin Dells and purchased a large rooming house and cottage annex called Oak Villa. This was about 1925. The Dells at that time was a great place for a youngster to study nature. I started a turtle collection when I was just a little bit of a guy, and I kept a large number of them at Oak Villa, where our tourist clientele enjoyed looking at them. People always wanted to see my turtles, so I started talking about nature at an early age.

I began observing birds, too, and had a number of pet crows, English sparrows, and even a little screech owl for a while. When I was about nine, I started collecting snakes and showing them to our "roomers." The Dells had a good population of fox snakes, garter snakes, and milk snakes. I didn't know much about them so I'd go to the public library and read. I had no books then since this was during the Great Depression, and we couldn't afford them. So I used the library to learn more about my pets and used that information when talking to people about them. I suppose you could say that's when I started my career as an interpretive naturalist.

The Dells was a very nice place in those days, with a more rustic, easygoing appeal. People would come to our rooming house, for example, and would stay for many days or even a week. They spent a lot of time just loafing on our huge lawn, taking boat trips, petting my pet crows, and handling my snakes. Many asked me to take them on hikes along the cliff tops to High Rock just upriver from the Dells.

Now the Dells is like Coney Island or Las Vegas. Then, it was basically Native American ceremonials, some souvenir shops, and river trips. My dad purchased six launches and started a boat business. My dad didn't stay in the boat business a long time. See, those were the Depression days.

All through the Depression he was trying to hang on to it. As the Depression was cracking, he sold his part of the business. Had he hung on to it, I might have stayed in the Dells in the boat business!

My father was not an outdoorsman at all. He liked to fish a little, but that was it. He didn't hunt; I don't think he ever hunted. He was just so damn busy making a living. My parents never encouraged me to get outside. I didn't need to be encouraged. For one thing, our rooming house was right on the edge of a ravine that went right down to the Wisconsin River. I could go from the back porch, across our lawn, through a little edge of woods at the top of the ravine, down the slope, and walk about a block to the river. That's where I caught my crayfish, water beetles, water snakes, and turtles on occasion. My mother always used to tell me, "Georgie, don't go in the ravine. There are snakes down there!"

I spent a lot of time in that ravine.

I became interested in insects way back then, too. I can remember one outbreak—I didn't know what the heck an outbreak or a fluctuating insect population was—one day walking down by the river in this old dry gulch. I never saw so many big green beetles. I didn't know what the heck they were. And I thought, "Gee, they're all over the place." I've never seen a concentration like that again. Later, I identified them as *Calosoma scrutator*—a ground beetle, the big green caterpillar hunter. They only build up in concentrations like that when there is an outbreak of larvae to feed on. They seem to come from all over. Lord knows how they detect this; it must be through smell because you'll never see a *Calosoma* unless you're really collecting thoroughly. But here was a concentration of them. The only other time I heard of a concentration like that was on Rock Island in Door County when we had a big outbreak of caterpillars up there.

RARELY COULD I GET MY WHITE FRIENDS to hike with me. They wanted to go down to Stokey's Drugstore and have a Coke. Instead, my pals for outdoor adventures were Chadwick and Miles Yellowthunder, sons of Albert Yellowthunder, Sr., chief of the Winnebago Indians at that time. The Yellowthunder clan was the big clan for centuries in the Winnebago Tribe. And Albert Sr. was the last real chief that knew anything about the Winnebagos.

My pals and I swam, canoed in a couple of old beat-up canoes, and hiked; we just romped around in the woods. I spent a lot of time on Blackhawk Island, now a State Natural Area. That's my island. They don't know that, but that's my island. I claimed it way back in 1932! At least that's the way I look at it. I don't think there was a hemlock in there I didn't see.

I was in the Dells year-round until 1931, when my mother died, except for two winters in Arizona. That's why we went to Arizona. Had we stayed there, she'd have made it. But she had to get back and run that rooming house. She died of tuberculosis. After she passed away, and until 1937, I was in the Dells each summer helping run Oak Villa and in Madison living with relatives and going to school from fall through spring.

Here's an interesting sidelight. When I went to school in Madison from grades five through eight I met Jimmy Zimmerman. He was that little guy who was always collecting something around where Edgewood College now sits. And I was a little guy always looking for snakes and bugs down there. We were always running into one another, so we got to be kind of friendly. He was basically plants and I was basically animals. I couldn't figure out why that little guy was looking at silly plants when there were all kinds of nice creepy crawlers around!

BY THE MID-1930s, Father had sold most of his businesses in the Dells. From about 1935 to 1940, he was the project manager for the Resettlement Administration, a federal program headquartered in Black River Falls. He was the chief honcho. The program goal was to buy farms on the sterile sands of Jackson, Juneau, and Monroe counties, put the farmers on better farms, and convert the sandy lands to forest and wildlife production. He and the feds were responsible for buying up all that land that is now the Black River State Forest, the Central Wisconsin Conservation Area, and the Necedah National Wildlife Refuge. He did a lot of work to get the whole area set up, but he never got any credit for it.

My father remarried in 1937, and they settled into a home in Black River Falls. That was a great place for a budding naturalist. I started my own little library, which included Lutz's *Field Book of Insects*, Holland's *The Butterfly Book* and *The Moth Book*, Pearson's *Birds of America*, and a few others on reptiles, amphibians, and mammals. The most important thing in my life was to identify the different critters I collected. Once, I caught a baby

Cooper's hawk. I was about 10 or 11. I usually walked right along the river, but on this particular day, I cut back into the woods. I can still remember this *kek-kek-kek-kek* call. I looked up and saw old ma Cooper's hawk. Well, I'd read a lot by then, and I realized that I was near a nest. So I looked, and sure enough, there was a nest up there.

She came down and almost knocked me in the bean, and I thought, "There's something crazy here." So I kept looking around and sure enough, over there in some hazel brush, a little Cooper's hawk was sitting. I got close to him, caught him, and took him home. I had a Benjamin air rifle so I popped some mice in our woodshed. I kept him well fed with mice and frogs and finally took him out and flew him. One day he might as well have said, "Ny-ahh, ny-ahh, nuts to you, George," and he took off. That was my first contact with a hawk.

My earliest interests were really reptiles, amphibians, and always insects. But I didn't know one from another. At Black River Falls, that's when I really hit it. Just like that, I turned much more scientific. I was absolutely wild about insects. By the time I was a senior in high school, I had over 7,200 insects in my collection. I had cigar boxes full of insects. I always wanted to learn as much as I could. To this day I'm still puzzled in the field by the small insects I encounter because I never had a really good microscope. Most of the insects I collected were the medium to large ones. And it wasn't 7,200 species; it was 7,200 insects. All total I may have had 1,500 species. And many of those were not classified. The ones I could classify I did with Lutz's *Field Book of Insects*. That was my first technical book. I learned how to use the keys in that book. But oh, how I longed for a microscope and good insect books!

Unfortunately, after I went into the army and returned home, all I had left was powder at the end of needles. Through neglect and poor storage, most of my insects were destroyed by museum beetles and mold. In addition, my field notes on many specimens were lost. I salvaged very few insects.

❦

I SPENT A LOT OF TIME ALONE. I guess you could think of me as kind of a loner. Not anti-social. I like people, but it was difficult to find friends who really wanted to talk about animals or plants for any length of time. When people have no interest in what I have to say, I turn and walk, and I think I recognized this when I was a little kid. I think that maybe because I was that way I became interested in taking these little hikes down by Shaddock's Slough and other places. I was like that in Arizona. We lived right on the edge of Phoenix in a little cabin. I was in the desert every day I was not in school. I collected scorpions and centipedes very carefully. And I can remember finding horned toads.

There isn't a little boy or girl that doesn't like animals when they're young. They're going to be a naturalist or some kind of scientist when they grow up, but then it just fades away, and they get into other fields. It just stuck with me because I had so many learning opportunities in the Dells, where I was right next to the wilderness; in Arizona, where I could see the wonder of the desert; and in Black River Falls, where I had nothing but flat, sandy lands on the east side and driftless area hills to fool around in on the west side. I became completely engrossed in nature study. My drug was nature. The more I learned, the more I wanted to learn. I still feel this way.

My father was very supportive. He always bragged to people: "You know George can walk from Black River Falls to Necedah and back and tell you everything between here and there." It was really embarrassing, but kind of fun at that! Dad was wrong, of course.

One of my dad's first biologists was Fred Hamerstrom. He and his wife, Fran, worked mostly in the Necedah area, conducting surveys on otters, beavers, and game birds. I didn't get to know them very well at that time. I do, however, remember Dad being very much impressed by that young couple.

Bill Schunke, one of Dad's game men who came from Germany, encouraged me to study nature. He loaned me his good Zeiss binoculars a few times. I couldn't believe how I could see birds then! Accompanying my father and some of his men on fieldwork, I also began to get interested in wildlife management. I didn't know you could improve habitat.

Since Dad was trying to convert land to game land and had game men working for him, one of his counsels was none other than Aldo Leopold. I met Aldo a number of times in the office; he'd come up on occasion. I don't know how many times he came up, but Dad and the game men would confer with him. I got to know Aldo then. I can remember when we had him out for dinner and one time, in particular, when I showed him my insect collection. He was flabbergasted. Young kid like this with an insect collection, and they were mounted perfectly! I was always very meticulous about things, and he couldn't get over that. The next time he came up he said, "George, get out the insects." We sat down on the davenport, and the next thing you know we're on the floor with boxes all around and he was pointing asking, "What's this? What's that?" One thing about Aldo, if he didn't know, he would never say, "Oh yes. Marvelous collection, I see." He'd always ask you if he didn't know the name of the critter. He never acted as if he were the know-it-all professor. He was just a great, great man.

Once he told me, "George, you should go into economic entomology."

"What the heck is economic entomology?" He told me about Professor Charles Fluke, who was the chief entomologist at the UW-Madison at that time.

He said, "I'm going to tell Charles Fluke about this collection." We had a turkey farm at the time, in the summer of 1940.

One day a car drives up and if it ain't old Professor Fluke. He said, "Well, I just happened to be up in this country, and Aldo Leopold told me about your insect collection and that you'd be a good candidate for economic entomologist." That's what I had in mind when I started at the university in 1941.

I went for a year and took the fundamental courses for an agriculture major. Then I went into the army for three years. One night while on guard duty in England, where I had become interested in birds and English natural history, I remember thinking, "Well, economic entomology is great, but I love insects, reptiles, birds, mammals, and geology." I wondered about wildlife management. So I wrote a letter to Aldo Leopold. I told him I had more of a naturalist's bent and asked him if I could get into wildlife management when I returned.

He wrote back. "Sure," he said. So I swung into that. I had to major in zoology first. But I took several undergraduate courses in wildlife including Leopold's courses.

I remember once that he argued with me on a gray catbird record I had. "It's a little early, George."

I said, "I know it is, but I saw it."

"Are you sure that was a catbird?"

"Yes!" It was just an early catbird. So anyhow, taking all the courses under him worked out real fine. When we went into the field, I was always his bug man.

If he saw a bug out there, he'd say, "Hey George, what's this bug?" Aldo was a good field person, but he admitted he wasn't able to identify everything. Game management and forestry were his fortes.

Leopold was not forceful in his teachings. He was so sincere and interested that one couldn't help but learn from him. On class field trips we'd sometimes sit down, and he would encourage dialogue, not monopolize the conversation or upstage anyone. I remember going up to the Shack. We'd walk and talk, and we'd go into the pine plantation. We helped him plant pines there one weekend. I remember there was a red-shouldered hawk's nest in one of those pine trees. I climbed up and found three hawks. Leopold thought that was pretty nice to have old George climb up a tree. It was kind of a free-for-all type walk, and we'd talk and look. He didn't do a lot of lecturing. It was just a casual hike. Years later I came up and found a ribbon snake near the river. This is one of Wisconsin's rarest snakes. It was one of the only places I recorded them. I don't know if the population is still there or not.

Professor Fluke was much like Leopold in his sincerity and teaching methods. When I came down in 1941 to study under him, he said, "George, this lab is open anytime to you. The insect collection is open to you. If you want to compare specimens, it's there. By the way, under this shelf over here, you see that little key. That's the key to my microscope. You use mine."

I also studied under Norman Fassett, John Curtis, and Lowell Noland. Fassett was a little live wire. I'm not sure if he hated zoology majors, but he loved his plants, naturally, and every time he talked to us zoology majors he'd have something choice to say about us and our "wigglewerps." He always called animals wigglewerps. In the field he was all business, and he didn't engage in conversation much. Curtis was the hardest to get to know. I got along pretty good with him because he knew I had quite a broad background, but I didn't have anywhere near the feeling for him that I had for Fluke and Leopold. I loved Noland. He was another professor that was really soft-spoken and easygoing. His lectures would just flow from one to another.

I had another professor, Art Hassler. Super egotist. First day in class, "Anybody here read German?" There was one or two who raised their hands. "That's good. You'll never be a scholar until you can read German papers." That kind of stuff. That turned us all off because I think we could have taken him out into the field and showed him a few things.

I'VE NEVER BEEN a note keeper to the extent that many naturalists are. I've seen so many species so many times and have observed them so intensively that I have committed them to my mind. Distribution, habitat types, behavior, etc. are fairly well etched into my mind. I've developed a pretty good mental calendar of events. If I were to sit down and write an exact date, I could give you hundreds and hundreds of species and tell you just about when and where you're going to find them. I have committed species to memory through constant visits and observations. If I'd had to take notes on everything I was interested in, I'd never have gotten far into the woods.

You see, I'm an interpreter. I can write scientifically. I can write a good scientific paper, but I can't write this Aldo Leopold type of philosophical narrative. My scientific writing is thorough and accurate, and my popular writing is thorough and accurate but simple. I write exactly as I talk. And I don't try to make 700-word sentences, so by the time you get to the end you're not wondering what it is I'm trying to say. I'm an interpreter and that's my forte. I think that's why I get things across in the field so well. I can explain it so that the layman can understand it. I use a lot of enunciation, and I have my little idiosyncrasies. I "underline" many of my words when I'm talking. I think that's a good way to interpret.

I've always been more field oriented than book oriented. Many naturalists develop their first interests in nature study by reading, then by observing and studying in the field. I started in exactly the opposite way, which in my opinion is more rewarding and stimulating. I can recall a number of times coming up with things that I later learned were wildlife principles. For example, on our turkey farm we had kestrels on telephone wires. I remember those kestrels diving down to get nice big grasshoppers. And I'm thinking, "It's a lucky thing there are a lot of grasshoppers around because those little rascals may otherwise take birds." I later learned that the grasshopper, an abundant species, is what's called a "buffer species." It protects the birds by serving as a ready and available prey source. And I later learned about carrying capacity, reproductive potential, symbiosis, and endangered species.

On our Jackson County farm, about three miles south of Black River Falls, we always had loggerhead shrikes, which are almost a thing of the past now in many areas. I wish I knew why they declined. Some of it may have been the change to clean farming. There aren't those nice dense hedgerows that there used to be. They were nesting up there in a hazel and *Crataegus* [hawthorn] hedge that I remember, very near County Highway 27. Then I saw them west of there in Spalding Hills country on the way up to Northfield. Never in big numbers. I can remember seeing loggerheads enough to say subjectively that I didn't see anything wrong with the population. That was in 1940–1941. There were a number of loggerheads in the area that I traversed from Black River to Hixton, up toward Bruce Mound, Saddle Mound, Castle Mound, Pray, City Point and from Black River Falls to La Crosse, amounting to eight or ten pairs.

Within the last 20 years, I do not recall having seen one loggerhead, and I'm kestrel-watching all the time, and kestrels and loggerheads practically sit side by side. I observed loggerheads in mostly open farm field edge, but near the forest or where the hedgerow went into the forest. I saw the vast majority, however, on barbed wire fences down at the brush level and often on telephone wires. There are plenty of telephone wires around, and there are plenty of barbed wire fences, but the brush is not there. When the loggerhead shrike was listed as an endangered species in 1979, it corroborated my findings.

ONE OF THE BIG CHANGES along the Wisconsin River I've noticed is in the number of lark sparrows. For some reason, I don't see them as I used to down there in the sands. They used to be fairly common. I don't see them at all now. Of course, the ornate box turtle has declined. Long before I worked for the department, I collected and studied insects near Spring Green. Even back in 1941, I used to go there just to collect insects, and I've seen a host of changes there. The *Megacephala* beetles aren't there anymore and are very rare. Six-lined racerunners are nowhere like they were. Box turtle habitat is really reduced.

When I was a little boy in the Dells, almost any flagstone below the dam could be turned over and there'd be crayfish. Then when there were sulfates dumped into the river, I went down below the Superior Street bridge and turned over a lot of rocks and only saw an occasional crayfish. There was no question that polluters were scumming up the river bottom and fouling the waters.

I don't think I've seen much of a change in bird life overall on the Wisconsin River, except for fewer red-shouldered hawks. I really don't know why that is because the river bottom from Sauk City down to Prairie du Chien has never been heavily logged. One bird that has definitely increased down there is the tufted titmouse. I can remember in the Dells when I was a youngster, I didn't see one tufted titmouse. Then, later in my beaver days, I started seeing "tufties" way up in Adams County. I also saw northern cardinals move into Eau Claire and Chippewa counties. I never saw them there in the early 1950s.

AS I MENTIONED earlier, my fascination with wildlife and wildlife principles swung me into wildlife management, not as an undergrad—I received my BS in zoology—but as a graduate student. I took a number of good courses with Joe Hickey and Bob McCabe. Then the opportunity to work on beaver came along, and I thought I would develop a master's thesis. The Conservation Department hired me to do a little beaver study. Well, it got to the point where it turned into quite a project because of beaver-trout, beaver-forestry, and beaver-wildlife controversies. It developed into a steady job. I worked on beaver intensively for eight years. I wasn't about to quit and go back to writing a master's thesis. All the final reports I did were scientifically written and would have satisfied the requirements for a number of master's degrees.

I studied every phase of the beaver's life history, conducted habitat surveys, determined food preferences, and documented the size of beaver ponds. To determine reproductive potential, I gathered carcasses from the trappers. I dissected over 1,600 beaver carcasses to learn the number of pregnant females in the population, the average size of the litter, age structure, and when they started breeding. I looked at beaver damage, beaver trapping pressure, beaver harvests, and beaver movement rates. It was a complete study of the whole beaver situation from the standpoint of life history, ecology, and distribution. And from that data I fought like hell for a very long season because I knew their tremendous reproductive capacity would keep them going as long as we didn't overtrap them. So I fought for lenient seasons. To make a long story short, we needn't worry about the beaver being wiped out by trappers. We now have a tremendous number of beaver in Wisconsin.

One of my longest and most intensive studies entailed observation of 353 beaver ponds to ascertain their effects on other wildlife, trout, forests, and agriculture. This study led me to the conclusion that the beaver is actually a wildlife manager whose changing of the habitat in and around the beaver pond is unmatched by any other species of animal. They are true ecologists!

One beaver pond I saw led to a brief encounter with Frank Lloyd Wright way back in 1953 or 1954. A little creek came out of his pond, went across Highway C, and under the Wisconsin River by the bridge. I wanted to walk down to that pond and see what the beaver was feeding on, so I went up to Frank Lloyd's house and knocked on the door. A servant came to the door, and I told him I was with the Conservation Department and wanted to see the beaver pond. He said he had to see the master. So he saw the master and lo and behold here he comes, Frank Lloyd Wright!

"Oh, so you're with the WCD," he said. "Let's go up on the veranda." So we went up there and had a two-and-a-half-hour talk. He loved nature. I told him many things about natural history that he didn't know. I told him about the big outbreak of cicadas that was due in a couple of years—the 17-year cicada cycle. He said, "Yes, I remember them from the last time. That was a long time ago. I remember the noise they made." We kicked around a lot of words that afternoon, had some lemonade, talked about beaver, talked about my interests. He definitely incorporated his interest in nature into his work; he was a real organic architect!

I CONDUCTED RESEARCH on beaver, bear, and otter during the years 1950–1962. I studied the three species in all parts of their range because the DNR wanted to obtain as much information as possible for future management purposes. I put in very long hours, often starting at five or six in the morning and finishing at dusk.

The work on black bear occurred from 1958 to 1962. At that time we didn't know much about our black bear population. I was asked if I wanted to switch over to studies on them for a year or two. I said, "Yes!" As with all research projects, when you don't know that much about a species, you study every aspect you can. So I plunged ahead with a status survey, a range survey, and a study on food habits.

Series of black bear photos from northern Wisconsin, July 1958—October 1962, depicting use of a "three-foot-long stick" with hypodermic needle by Knudsen (top), assistant Alvin "Dewey" Jaeger (center left), bear in leg-hold trap (bottom left), and processing (bottom right and center right). Photos courtesy of the Knudsen family.

The bear study was basically in the northern two tiers of counties, all the way across the north. But we concentrated our trapping efforts in Bayfield, Douglas, and Washburn counties in the northwest and in Forest, Vilas, and Oneida counties in the northeast. We ran 35 traps a day; it would take three to four days to set them out. Lots of careful work. We'd set them and tend them daily for two to three weeks. We'd have to move them on occasion. We were stuck more than we were moving half the time because of the muddy roads from the constant rain on all these back trails. You'd like to get a hold of those guys that built those roads in the first place. They were pretty awful. We'd get up early and sometimes wouldn't get in until 10 or 11 at night.

We wanted to study movements because in those days there were people worried about shooting all the bears. I wanted to find out as much as I could about bear movements for the simple reason that we trapped—and the DNR still does—"complaint bear." I wanted to know how far we had to haul a bear and release it so it wouldn't raise another complaint. I didn't want to trap a bear and shoot it. That had been happening a lot. I couldn't see wasting bears like that when we could determine how far we had to go to release them. I wanted to find out how far they moved in a certain period of time.

We found out that there was a tremendous amount of movement, especially among the males. With males, we got an average yearly move of 18 miles. That's half a county. They'd go across that county, find a few female residents, and have cubs to bolster the bear population. When you have a good viable population, that's the time to study them, not when they're going downhill. I trapped in many different areas and amassed my data to obtain averages on a county-by-county basis. Bruce Kohn, about 20 years later, wanted to take a very small area in Iron County and see how many bears he could trap out of that area, which he did for three years. He had all kinds of repeat trapping. The interesting thing is the movements were about the same as mine 20 years after my study. In the best bear habitat I had one bear for every one to two square miles. His saturation study came out with 1.6 bear per square mile. That's when research really means something—when it's corroborated somewhere down the line by somebody else.

What were the techniques we used? Just run into the woods, grab a bear, throw him on his back, lift him up—"Ah, weighs about 370 pounds." No. We ear-tagged them, live-trapped them with steel traps, and I designed the traps so they would only catch the foot and not break any bones. They broke a few bones fighting the traps, but out of 181 bears we only had 7–8 percent that showed broken bones at all. They're so tough.

We only had one bear lose his foot. Right up in Drummond (Bayfield County) country. He was up a tree and he hung himself, and his foot was up in the air. When I got him out of that tree, which was quite a job at 250 pounds, I saw that his paw was all pink. I said to my helper Alvin Yeager, nickname Dewey, "God, he's going to lose that foot!" I was ready to kill him. But I thought, "No, let's just see how tough this old boy is." So I ear-tagged him and let him go. Two and a half months later people in Drummond were concerned that there was a bear at the dump coming into town to tear into people's garbage cans. So George Phillips, the warden up there, shot it and saw the ear tag and the bear's missing right front foot. He called Yeager, and he went over and got the carcass. To make a long story short: that bear moved about 14 miles in a two-and-a-half-month period, lost its right foot, and gained 65 pounds. They're tough old boys, I tell you.

A word or two about Yeager. He lived in northwestern Wisconsin at the time. He was a fantastic live-trapper of beaver, coyote, and bear. He handled all the bear complaints and did that for years. He was really ingenious; he could think up things so fast to help you out of a situation. He always carried his share of the workload and often much more. Great guy!

One of my favorite stories involves a bear at the Dairy Farm Resort up by Boulder Junction. There was a dump right behind the resort that bears used. So we thought we'd come up and try to livetrap around the dump. They were open dumps in those days. We really had a bonanza with bears. So we drove to this dump. The tourists staying at the resort knew we were coming somehow. We drove into the dump and looked over the bear sign. People came up to us telling about the big tracks, the little tracks, about the weight of this one and that one. We told them that maybe we would come back in a few days and set one of our big culvert traps. So we did. We came back a few days later, and, of course, we drove in, the tourists saw us coming, and the whole dang bunch got in their cars. Some walked from the resort down to the dump.

We must have had 15–20 people down there. When we approached the dump, there was a bear there that was a pretty tame old gal. I turned to Dewey and said, "Gosh, there's only that one tree. Maybe if I chase her, she'd go up that tree, and we can get her without even trapping her." So I took off out of the truck. People started yelling and clapping. Me after the bear. The bear scooted out and up the dang tree just as nice as could be. So here's the bear sitting up in the tree with no trap, nothing to keep the bear from coming down. But when there's a crowd like that, you know, and you've got a chance to get a bear for free, I thought, "Hell, it's worth the chance." So I climbed up under this bear with my needle and got right up under her fanny and gave her a little shot. She blew at me and I thought, "Boy, if she starts climbing down she's going to use me as part of the tree." But she just stayed up there and pretty soon she started quivering. Well, then she started slipping and down she came right beside me. She was a big one, probably about 180 pounds. I put my arm around her, and both the bear and I skidded down that tree.

Those people watching had eyeballs *that big* watching me, a big Norwegian, coming down the tree with that bear! Of course I couldn't hold 180 pounds; it was mostly a scrambling fall for about 15 feet. The bear was out when we got down there.

I was a big hero that day. So from that time on, every time I was up in that country club area, people would say, "There's the guy that climbed the tree and got that live bear!"

WE WERE ALWAYS very careful. We always figured out exactly how far a bear could reach beyond the trap. When they're in a trap, they'll tramp down all the vegetation just to see how far they can go. So we'd stay outside what we called the "zone of influence." We had a real simple approach. No guns. Yeager would usually talk to the bear and try to get the thing to look at him, and I would sneak around and stab it in the fanny with my three-foot-long stick with a needle on the end. Very simple.

When you're camping in bear country, you shouldn't have food in your tent. You put it outside. Hang it up on a line so they can't get to it. There's quite a structural difference between grizzly bears and black bears, and there is probably quite a psychological difference because black bears are the most timid things in the woods. We trapped 181 of them, and very few of them were very aggressive. Females are more aggressive than males. Unless you come between a mom and her cubs, that bear is going to leave every time. Rarely is anybody attacked in the wilderness by a black bear. They'll bluff you sometimes.

The biggest bear we ever trapped was something else. It was up at the Lake Nebagamon dump in Douglas County. We walked into the dump and here's this giant bear standing there. He was BIG! He took off. I walked up to

CHAPTER THREE

where he had been and said to Dewey, "Look at that track! Are we going to get him in that damn little trap?"

"Oh, I don't know, George!"

Well, we set the trap. It was a 150 double-spring trap. We always set our traps way back so people wouldn't step in them. We always put wires and signs around the traps. I stepped into them to see how they'd hurt. They gave you a good whack, but they didn't have teeth in them. I designed them so that they'd just hold, not dig in nor tear hide and flesh. Of course, we lost bears that way too; they'd just pull out.

About a week later, I walked into the same dump. It was a rainy, drizzly, foggy, miserable morning in August—muggy and absolutely dead calm. I walked up to the cubby where we had this trap set and the trap was gone! Instead, there was a great big skid mark where he had stepped in with his left foot, pulled the foot out, skidded out, and taken off on the run. He left a big track there. I'm telling you, it was really something! It had been raining so the leaves stirred up by his dragging the trap chain made it difficult to figure out where he'd gone. So I went back to the truck and said to Yeager, "You might as well sit tight because I'm going in there to see if I can figure out where that fool bear went."

Once in the woods, I finally found enough sign to lead me down to a trail going around a bog. On the trail there was enough scuff marks from the hooks and chains that hadn't been settled by the rain, so I figured out where he went. And once they're on a trail, they usually use it.

So I'm walking along real quietly. The rain starts to come down. I remember thinking to myself, "This is the day I'm going to get it. I'm going to get killed for sure on a spooky morning like this." I was real edgy. So I walked in about a quarter of a mile on an old deer trail. Then I hear *clink-clank* up ahead. Uh-oh, he's hooked up. My heart starts to beat a little faster. I walk up on a little hill because he is down around the edge of this bog that is curving off to the northwest. I look down and see big bracken ferns. So I yell, "Hey, bear!" Oh geez, his head comes up out of the tall bracken ferns, and I think, "Hippopotamus? Is *that* a monster! What in hell am I going to do?"

I walk down there and look. He's hooked on a tree root from a red pine. It isn't a very big root, but it had stopped him momentarily. He could have tore that thing right out. But he had such a big paw that the trap jaw was right across the pad instead of behind the pad because his foot just wouldn't fit in far enough. So I thought, "Well, that's nice! Root won't hold, and if the root holds, the damn trap won't! When I stick him with the needle, I'm going to get eaten up right there." So I went back to the truck and said, "Yeager, we got our work cut out for us."

"Did we get the big one?"

"We got him!"

We carried our equipment in. We had a .35 Remington semi-automatic that we carried only when we thought we would have trouble. I said, "When I stick him, he's going to be raising hell as big as he is. I don't know about this. If he grabs me, be sure to shoot me! I don't want to suffer!"

When we found him, I estimated his weight at about 475 pounds. Then I gave him a jolt, and I figured all hell was going to break loose. But the funny part is he wouldn't face me. He kept looking out into the bog. I walked around to face him and he looked over here. And Yeager walked around and the bear looked back out into the bog. He would not face us, and I thought, "Well, he's just saving up all his energy. So, well, I guess I better stick him." I gave him a stab in the upper part of his ham. I was ready for him to explode, but he didn't even move. He turned around and backed out into the bog. I said, "Ho boy!" He should have gone down within two and a half minutes, but he didn't. He wasn't even quivering. So I thought I had underdosed him or something. Well, I looked at the syringe, which had a #14 needle. It was somewhat plugged by fat. Then we had to wait an hour because if you give him another shot too soon you can overdose and kill him.

So there we stood out in the rain, waiting for an hour. I said to Yeager, "Well, this has got to be it. He's really going to be mad the second time I stick him." After an hour, I loaded up the gun again and tried to get him up by the hip where there wasn't quite as much fat. I let him drive this time. He was still looking out into the swamp. He turned around once, then looked back out into the bog again, and I thought, "What's the matter with this big old fool?" Then all of a sudden, down he fell. When he was down, I gave him a big syringe full of Nembutal, which is the sleeper drug that keeps them out quite a while. But then to move him, that was something else. They don't have any handles, you know!

I finally moved him to this big red pine up the hill, just by sheer muscle. He weighed 525-plus pounds. That was minimum because the scale only went to 500 pounds. It got stuck at 500, so I lifted up the bear a little. I figured I was lifting a good 25, maybe 40 pounds, to get the thing back up. The state record in the fall after they put on all their fat is about 735 pounds. And this guy would have gone beyond that because this was early August. When a man shot him that fall, about eight miles south of there, he hog-dressed him, took the head off, the hide off, cut off all the fat, all the entrails and paws, and the carcass still weighed 390 pounds. So putting all that back and all the fat, he probably would have gone 675 pounds, which is near the record size. If he had lived a couple of more years—he was in good shape—he could have reached 750 pounds. I felt so bad after he was shot because he was such a nice, docile old bear!

✿

I GOTTA TELL YOU one more. We were called by the warden at Mercer one day. He asked if we'd come up and trap a few bears out of the dump because they were getting too thick in there. They were coming into town at night and disturbing and scaring people. We trapped three or four of them and took them varying distances and released them. The last one we caught was a big male. He weighed maybe 375 pounds. As we became more experienced, we only gave them enough of the drug to take them where we wanted to release them and let them go.

So we drugged this 375-pounder relatively lightly and headed toward Bass Lake, about a half-hour away. We struggled to lift him into the back of the pickup, closed the tailgate, and left the dump. We hit a bunch of bumpy roads. All of a sudden the truck lurched, and I looked through the back window just over the stock rack. That big fool was trying to climb out of the back of the truck—right on the highway! So I yelled, "Yeager, stop this damn truck!" He stopped and I jumped back there. I knew I could do this because a drugged bear is just like a drunken man for at least 45 minutes and won't try to bite. He struggled to climb out, however, and I tried to pull him back in. What a struggle!

I wrestled with the bear. The bear broke one of the boards on the stock rack. I yelled to Yeager to get going. I continued to fight, when all of a sudden, I was aware of a car right behind the truck! I looked up and there were two elderly people, a man and a woman in a big Chrysler. I swear I saw four saucer-sized eyeballs. They couldn't believe that there's a man in the back of a moving pickup wrestling a bear! Shortly after that, we turned off toward Bass Lake and headed into the woods. "He's getting too smart," I yelled out. "Stop!" We came to a halt, and I kicked him in the rear. He wandered off, stumbling through the brush.

I often wonder what those two people had to say about this incident. They didn't follow us, but I bet to their dying day they told that story many times. Silly fool in the back of a pickup wrestling a big bear!

I'VE OFTEN SAID that I wouldn't trade my life for any other person I know. And now I'm more convinced of it than ever. Thing is, I'm the luckiest guy in the world to have a wife that is 100 percent supportive. I asked her once about all those times when I got back from snowshoeing way up north. "Sometimes I was gone a week and didn't call or write you. Were you ever worried?"

She said, "I learned a long time ago not to worry. If it's going to happen, it's going to happen. I have confidence in you as an outdoorsman and figure you won't take chances."

I didn't take chances after I was married. Before that I couldn't have cared less! I'd take off into the forest, carefree, and forget my compass. I'd have a heck of a time figuring out where I was and how to get out. But when I had a family, my attitude changed. She's always been 100 percent supportive to the point where in order to photograph a frog or a snake, I had to put them in the refrigerator to cool them down. What other wife would allow that?

I HAD SOME CLOSE CALLS with snakes. I picked up a fox snake one day right outside of a den. My foot was about 18 inches from where I picked him up. He was sunning himself. What a beauty! I started stuffing him in my bag, and then I saw a rattler right where I had picked up the fox snake. The fox snake had crawled on top of the rattlesnake to sun.

I've seen three rattlesnakes on top of one another sunning themselves. Rattlers want to be near the den so they can zip right in there in case of danger. Other snakes don't bother them either. The ground is warm by the time they come out, so that feels warm. They're getting warmth from below, warmth from above. The sun is shining on their sides; they're as cozy as hell!

I caught a big timber rattler, probably close to 50 inches, on one of the bluffs near Millville, Wisconsin. I didn't have my snake-pack basket with me. I just took a regular muslin sack. I caught the snake, put it in the sack, and then I came down the hill to the car—a station wagon. I opened the tailgate and threw the sack in there. I usually put it in my snake proof carrying case. I took off my Red Wing boots and put on my tennis shoes. By this time it was late afternoon, so I stopped and ate. It was dark when I started heading back to Madison on County Highway C. Driving along I felt something crawl across my right foot, and at the same time I felt it going across my left foot. What the heck? It was the rattler! So what do I do now? I guess I move real slow. So I gradually moved and waited until the thing was off my left foot. I moved my left foot slowly to the clutch and moved my right foot slowly to the brake, not knowing where the snake was. Chances are it might be under the seat. So I moved slowly to the right and opened the door. When I opened the door the dome light went on, and he was coiled right where my left foot had been! I had moved slowly enough so he wasn't disturbed.

I think that one of the things that may have saved me is that Highway C was kind of a bumpy old blacktop road. I think that the snake had become used to all of the motion in the car. Also, the heat from the motor was coming through the firewall there, and the snake did not detect my leg as being warmer than anything else. Had it been a cool evening and the snake escaped from the sack, it might have been an entirely different situation. He'd have nailed me right there!

🍂

AFTER I FINISHED WITH THE BEAR STUDIES, I went on to the Bureau of Parks and Recreation as Chief Naturalist. When I developed the DNR's interpretive program in 1962, I created four sections. The most important one of all was the guided hike. That's where you see nature firsthand. You can smell it, touch it, watch it wave in the breeze, see its beauty, its grace, its color, and its adaptations. Every time I talked about a species, I tried to put a value on it; for instance, its value as wood, fruit, seeds, or as a useful chemical. I emphasized the aesthetic value, too. Take a mushroom like the *Amanita*, which so many people like to destroy. I'd say, "Look at it! Isn't it beautiful! Wouldn't it make a beautiful photograph with the sun shining on it through the maple leaves." I did a lot of that.

Next in importance in my interpretive program was the labeled nature trail. In the beginning, I was trying to figure out the best way to lay out a nature trail for the guided hikes. What was the best way to lay out a nature trail to hold labels? What are the best labels? I spent one whole winter with plastics and laminates trying to come up with durable labels. The one I finally came up with is weatherproof and vandal-resistant. There's nothing that's really vandal-proof. Then I studied audio-visual techniques—how to make displays and exhibits. After I studied these things, I began to put them into our first small nature centers. It was just a matter of developing all the methods and techniques for self-guided hikes, writing my nature hike theme booklet, and writing instructions for each naturalist. I trained the season naturalists that come in June and go through Labor Day. And I trained the permanent naturalists as we hired them.

The very first trail I put in was located right behind the nature center in the pine stand at Devil's Lake State Park. That didn't last very long. It was vandalized. That's when I realized that I had better get some better labels than what I had. I had used plywood with a label varnish overcoat. The vandals peeled this off in nothing flat.

The next trail was in Governor Dodge State Park, then Wyalusing and Peninsula. I hit the big properties first. They had priority. I designed the entire trail at Governor Dodge and put up the labels. Initially, I had designed them as a post with a cross-arm, screw eyes, and a nice 9 x 11 hanging panel of ponderosa pine with a tan enamel. I buffed the surface with jewel's rouge and used India ink for lettering. I personalized those things. I printed every word by hand and did all the drawings. That was a mistake because the vandals would get the label, bend it right over the cross-arm, and break it right off; they just smashed it up. After reading about vandalism problems in the national parks, I thought, "Well, we can't go to photo-aluminized labels because that's awfully expensive. Plus, it's easily scratched because it's aluminum. I'm just going to experiment."

I came up with a label that was a photograph rather than a print because printed lettering overcoated with varnish just dissolves. With a negative, I had instant replay. So then we put the photographs on plywood, but the waterproof plywood still allowed water to get into and under the lamination.

Then I experimented with other things such as putting vinyl over them, urethane, varathane, and every kind of plastic. I made several labels and threw them out on the ground in winter. I let them get rained on, snowed on, frosted on, and even put them under the birdfeeder so the birds would crap on them. In the spring I looked them over, and I had to throw most of them out. I placed the few that remained facing the sun all summer long.

Only one label, with polygloss and fiberglass, came through. Polygloss is one of the most outstanding weatherproof and vandal-resistant plastics there are. Then I bolted each one on 4 x 4's and put a steel frame around them, making them almost indestructible.

When I went to the parks, I'd often get up at the crack of dawn and wouldn't leave until after dark sometimes. I studied the layout of the parks to figure out where to design a nature trail, where to build a nature center, what was unique about that park. Never did anyone ask me how many hours I was spending doing all of this work, including all of the nature trail drawings I did at home during nights, often until midnight!

Giant Swallowtail Butterfly

I've always been artistically inclined. I like to draw. When I was a youngster, I'd lie on the living room floor on cold winter days and draw things. And then in entomology, I did several detailed drawings. The more I drew an insect, the more I knew it.

For the self-guided trails I used black ink in quill pens or various tube-tip pens even though I had trouble at times. I would do the minimum of line work with them, and I would use a pencil to shade. All of my nature trail drawings are ink with pencil shading. In photographing the drawing you get your shading in your negative. So I used pencil as my shading and I used ink for my outline. Then when I had my negative made, I could use it over and over for photo prints. But my narratives were always different. I always changed my narratives.

When we finally hired LTEs (limited term employees), I knew what to tell them. Many didn't know much about interpretation, but they had a lot of coursework. They were tremendously interested in the outdoors. Often on the trail I told them I was going to quiz them: "I'm going to tell you what this is, its value, how it fits in, what its phenology is, whatever. Down the line I'm going to point it out again, and you better remember!" I always had them carry a Sears Catalog with them. That way when they found a plant they didn't know, they could pick a leaf or whatever was characteristic, place it in there, and write a name on that page. Then they'd go home and on occasion flip through the pages. They would not look at the name first but look at the plant and remember. This was a good way to teach them quickly.

I feel good about all those people I hired and trained. And I feel good about having helped develop 60 self-guided nature trails by the time I retired. I personally developed about 48 of them. I gave it my best shot. That's about all you can do.

🌿

ONE OF THE MOST IMPORTANT THINGS I've learned from all of the years in the field is that nature is involved in a great big struggle. It's a struggle of life against death, and every insect, every whale, every seal, every tern, is on a razor's edge right now. We never know when we will fall off and die. In a 24-hour period, there are millions of deaths because it's been shown by an English study that in a diversified acre of open field with some shrubbery there are 100 to 400 thousand spiders and spiderlings, and each of them is feeding on something each day. Plus you have the dragonflies, the ambush bugs, the swallow, the bat. The diversity of nature is a miraculous thing.

George Knudsen teaching about "insects, spiders, and relatives, and their habitats" at his White Pines Nature Center, Hayward, July 12, 1983. Photos by Sumner Matteson.

But the natural fact of mortality in the natural world is not an excuse for permitting habitat destruction. I'll put money toward environmentally sound programs to buy that marsh or buy that forest edge or buy that bog, whatever it might be, especially to protect endangered species. If we don't have a diversity of species so that they're buffering one another, we're going to end up with a monotype of corn, wheat, robins, red-tailed hawks, black bears, and deer. What happens when an epizootic comes along? When you've got monotypes like this, you can always expect your big epidemics to hit because there's a kindling point reached that can spread through the whole forest so to speak. But if you've got isolated populations and great diversity, there are always buffers between them. The point is there's always been a diverse ecosystem, and we can't afford to lose all kinds of species.

🍃

UP UNTIL RECENTLY the earth has been big enough to prevent gigantic scars on our ecosystems. But from here on, we're going to create big scars, and there's the possibility that pollution will kill off major portions of oceans. We are definitely not going to live in harmony with the land if we continue that way. Now, the alternative is to get back to more natural living. Well, how do you do that? I suppose by taking every family and giving them five acres, a sack of seeds, a hoe, and say, "Now get out there and make a living!" If they're so busy planting seeds and harvesting crops, they won't have time to fight with one another. Ha!

The best-case scenario for all the countries on this great planet is for them not to argue about their religions and other ideologies and form a federation of world countries with a super governing Congress. Through computer networks we could hopefully figure out who is short of what, who has a surplus of what, and how we can help countries that have very little. Everybody make up their minds to cooperate! We could make a utopia out of this present mess.

The worst-case scenario is a worsening of the greenhouse effect and the loss of our natural resources. We're in it right now. We're losing our wetlands, forests are being destroyed, and species never classified are going or are gone. We're going to have tens of thousands of extinct species within 20–30 years if nothing changes in tropical countries to alter destruction of the forests.

The total ecosystem is not as healthy as it was 2,000 years ago. There are compounds, organic and inorganic, that are in the system now that nature never intended. And we keep pouring these things in, so the total system is in trouble. If this greenhouse effect takes hold, it can bring about tremendous climatic changes. That might be something we can survive in the short term, but in the long pull we're weakening the ecosystem. There's going to come a time when it's just going to give its last gasp, and life will start all over again.

Urban sprawl is a problem, especially in view of the fact that it sprawls on to land that is most acceptable to homes—level land! The level land is very often outwash or inwash or other glacial alluvium in Wisconsin, which means that you've got layered alluvium and you've got pebbles and gravel and aquifers. The more toxic wastes you get in aquifers, including salt and oils from the bottom of the car, pesticides from lawns and gardens, the more these wastes get into the water table.

The more you sprawl, the more land you take out of cultivation. So it's knocking out the farmland we need. Not that we couldn't restore some lands. For example, I've recommended to the department to buy Duscheck's Marsh[88] out here by Sun Prairie. That used to be a beautiful place. Least bitterns and yellow-headed blackbirds and Virginia rails. They drained it and they got a great big cornfield. I'd like to buy that land, plug those tiles, let the water table build up again, and watch what would come back. It wouldn't be the same as it was before, but it never was the same from one day to the next anyway. You'd be surprised at what that reclaimed wetland would do. Even the old landfill sites, the old dumps that were put into a swamp; if someday we had the energy sources so we could bulldoze the old rusted tin cans and broken glass, we'd get back down to the original topography. We might be surprised once that water sat there 10 years and purified. We'd get cattails back and all kinds of plants and animals.

Wasteful use of resources is one of our biggest problems. Look at the plastic packaging we have. You buy a screw and it's enclosed in plastic. Plastic is from petrochemicals. Petrochemicals are finite resources. Why can't we go in and pick out a couple of screws and throw them in a paper sack? We've got forests to give us the paper. See, those are the things that if I was dictator I'd straighten out. Don't you agree? Paper sacks, you beggar!

IF GOOD NATURALISTS and good interpreters could get a hold of every person on this earth and spend a week with them, we would have a much better chance of saving species and saving communities. I sincerely feel that if people desire to save themselves and our ecosystems they must learn more about them. With study comes understanding, with understanding comes appreciation, and with appreciation comes reverence for and the desire to protect.

I WAS AN ATHEIST for a while, but after putting everything together and seeing just how wonderful everything is, I can't help but feel that there is a preconceived plan for everything. Who knows? The way I'm looking at it now is that God created the physical laws that manifest themselves in the universe. He gave us this earth, the physical laws that go with it, and the medicine to cure ourselves. Putting everything together, I just figured that everything is just *too* orderly and *too* much to our advantage to be chance alone.

I'll tell you about one coincidence that still makes me wonder about what the heck is going on. One fall in New Glarus, my wife, Arlene, entered the New Glarus arts and crafts show. I helped her set up and was there all day. As is usually the case, I'll take a walk and look at all the other crafts, then she'll do the same. We take turns stretching our legs. That fall the woman right next to us was a calligrapher and an artist. So I'm sitting there and finally felt compelled to go over and read what she had on this one painting. The painting was a beach scene with trees; it broke into a strand and then into a scene where there were unicorns—a stylized, mythological rendition. That caught my eye. I went to the calligrapher and said, "You do nice work." Then I read the poem she had calligraphed onto the painting. I got a lump in my throat. It spoke to what I've always felt about where I'm going after I leave this earth.

Here's the poem. It's called "Part of the Sky":

This body I live in is not really mine
Just a home that I've borrowed
I'll return it some time
Death does not haunt me
I will never die

Because I'm part of the earth
And I'm part of the sky

When my body lies empty
I'll find a new home
Give back to the earth
My flesh and my bones
Return what was borrowed
But don't stop to cry
Because I'm part of the earth
And part of the sky
And on some dark night
When you start wondering why
Look at the stars in the clear midnight sky
We all move in circles
It's just something you learn
Death is not dying
It's just my time to return

And if you start wondering
Just where I might be
Look at the showers and leaves on the tree
Look at the rivers and mountains and seas
That's where I am and that's where I'll be
I'll be in the thunder and the rain and the night
I'll be in the sunrise and the first song of light
I'll be in the forest and the birds as they fly
'Cause I'm part of the earth and part of the sky.

I read that and nearly bawled right there because it so perfectly mirrored what I have thought and communicated to people. I told her it was the most beautiful thing I ever read. I asked her who wrote it. She said it was written by a 25-year-old man named Sydney Makepeace Wood III just before he died in 1975.

Then, last fall, Arlene and I took an old army buddy and his wife to where we thought we could find Frank Lloyd Wright's grave. We found it. There were nice big bricks around it. Many of his relatives and non-relatives were buried in the same cemetery. We spent about a half an hour there, and then we started heading back to the car. Off to the right, out in the grass, there was a lone gravestone. I felt a compulsion to go over and see who was buried there. I walked over and yelled for Arlene to come over. On the gravestone's heading was "Sydney Makepeace Wood III, part of the sky." Out of all the places in the U.S. where he could have been buried, and after that poem, here I had been drawn right over to that grave! Incredible.

I keep thinking that maybe someday he'll materialize and I'll get a chance to talk with him. To write that poem he had to have a feeling at his young age for something that I have developed all through these years. The thing is he's buried on the same property with Frank Lloyd Wright; maybe he was family.

I've always felt that I don't want to be buried. I want to be cremated and want to get back into the earth's system. I feel I am from everywhere on this earth. I've thought this many times. There are molecules of me from Australia. There are molecules I sweated out two years ago that are probably passing by a gray whale right now. We all come from somewhere; this has been a part of my philosophy of life. My wife's of the old school. She wants us to be buried side by side.

I'd like to go by wandering off into some bog, and have moss grow over me so I could never be found. But they'd say, "We don't want you Norwegians polluting the Northwoods!" No, the only way I really want to go is down here on a sandbar. Line my canoe with some nice, big, creosoted railroad ties, lay me on it, light that baby afire, and shove it out into the river. That's the way the Norwegians went to Valhalla! ✳

Surrounded by his family, George passed away in Verona, Wisconsin, on October 24, 2004, at age 82. Can there be any doubt he was warmly received in Valhalla?

CHINQUAPIN OAK

GJK

146

Jim Zimmerman
(1924-1992)

SILVER MAPLE

Chapter Four~
Jim Zimmerman

When I went to Madison to go to school from grades five through eight, I met Jimmy Zimmerman. He was that little guy that was always collecting something down there around where Edgewood College now sits. I couldn't figure out why that little guy was looking at silly plants when there were all kinds of nice creepy crawlers around!

—George Knudsen

James Hall Zimmerman was an unusual and brilliant naturalist who influenced several of the naturalists featured in this book. Though born in a Chicago hospital on October 11, 1924, to Katharine Hall Zimmerman and James Garfield Zimmerman, because they wanted to ensure a successful birth,[89] Jim grew up and resided all of his life in an ivy-covered, gray hollow-tile house on the near west side of Madison, Wisconsin. Jim graduated from Wisconsin High School in 1943 and the University of Wisconsin-Madison with degrees in botany—a BA in 1947, an MA in 1952, and a PhD in 1958. He specialized in plant taxonomy.

From 1959 to 1961, Jim wrote college biology study guides for the United States Armed Forces Institute in Madison. Also in 1959, Jim began a six-year association with the Madison Public Schools as naturalist at the Madison

School Forest. He taught ecology and prepared and evaluated outdoor education materials. Beginning in 1961, he developed a popular vocational course called *Reading the Landscape,* which he taught winter evenings at Madison Area Technical College until 1971.

From 1965 to 1976, Jim worked as a naturalist and consultant for the University of Wisconsin-Madison Arboretum. During this time, he helped develop a master plan for restoring the arboretum's 30 biotic communities. Working with his wife, Elizabeth (Libby), a wildlife artist and naturalist, and with graduate student Barbara Bedford, he directed a comprehensive survey of Dane County wetlands, which resulted in the 1974 publication of *The Wetlands of Dane County, Wisconsin.*

In 1977, he became a lecturer in the Department of Landscape Architecture with the University of Wisconsin-Madison. Here, he taught about the natural history, ecology, and management of Wisconsin's grasslands, forests, and wetlands. His course *Understanding Wetlands* earned consistent praise from undergraduate and graduate students.

Jim co-authored (with botanist Booth Courtenay) one book, *Wildflowers and Weeds* (1972), which was re-published as *Wildflowers and Weeds: A Guide in Full Color* (1990), and he began writing two others—one on the natural history of the Midwest and the other on the taxonomy and ecology of Wisconsin sedges.[90] He also authored numerous popular articles on natural history subjects ranging from prairies to the vegetation of the Baraboo Hills. With Libby, he penned a weekly column for the *Wisconsin State Journal.* Finally, Jim was asked by the Reverend Samuel Robbins (Chapter Seven) to contribute to Sam's 1991 landmark book *Wisconsin Birdlife: Population and Distribution Past and Present.* Jim came through splendidly with an ecological chapter titled "The Landscape and the Birds."

An active environmentalist, Jim co-founded the Wisconsin Phenological Society (1959), the still very active Wisconsin Wetlands Association (1969),[91] and the Wisconsin Inland Waterways Association (1975). And he served as an environmental consultant to government, university, and private organizations. An inveterate outdoor enthusiast, Jim canoed, hiked, and camped with Libby throughout much of the country into Ontario, Canada.

A studio in the countryside of Jefferson County allowed the Zimmermans to continue their work away from the distractions of a hectic urban life. An avid gardener for over 50 years, Jim also enjoyed growing a variety of native plants.

Friends and colleagues knew Jim as a complex and highly talented individual who, if he had a particular fault, often stretched himself thin over too many subject areas: botany, ecology, ornithology, entomology, phenology, wetland dynamics, environmental problem-solving, and the restoration and management of woodlands, grasslands, and wetlands. Oh, and according to the late naturalist Harold Kruse, Jim sometimes could be a tad tardy to his own presentations—when he traveled to them by bicycle. So who should Harold, late for Jim's UW-Madison Arboretum presentation, pass on the road? Jim pedaling furiously on his bike.

The principal interview with Jim occurred at his home on a relatively mild night in late January 1981, and a second of sorts—more as observer—as a class guest during a field trip in late March 1982 along the northeastern wooded edge of Lower Mud Lake, southeast of Lake Waubesa in southern Dane County, and to Goose Pond and Mud Lake in Columbia County. A small man with dark hair, a prominent forehead, and thick glasses, he proved loquacious, at times animated, and began in January by focusing on a difficult childhood and the formative influence of his mother.

❦

WHEN I WAS AN INFANT, Mother placed me outside in a baby carriage for hours each day. So I grew accustomed to fresh air and solitude. Later, she saw that I had an interest in nature and especially in plants. I had a garden[92] when I was eight.

All through my youth, I biked everywhere. I stopped and looked at plants or listened to birds. I had a natural environment at hand all the time. Until World War II changed Madison radically, the city was quiet, and many places were a nature paradise. There was an area four blocks west of home that was later developed; it had all the prairies and woodlands that you could imagine. The neighborhoods were unusual around here. We had all the forest birds, and until the 1940s there was almost never the sound of a motorcar.

Something unusual happened when I was in sixth grade. A combination of difficulties came to a head; I think my parents weren't getting along too well at the time. Had my father not died shortly after, I probably would have witnessed a divorce. There was a strain because my father wasn't bringing in any money, and he wasn't too well either—all kinds of problems. On top of that, I wasn't doing too well in school because I was like my father and, in a sense, like my mother. I listened to a different drummer.

I didn't do well in school because they made you do things—physical education, math tests, and so on. If I did things differently, I wasn't understood. I was penalized, received bad marks, or sent home. To top it off, my sixth grade teacher at Randall School was a librarian who substituted for a biology teacher that the school lost, so she had to teach biology. The only thing she knew how to do was to have you read books, so we didn't look at a single plant or animal in that class. We did book reviews and book reports! And because I was a slow reader anyway, this was the last straw. I'd come home in tears, not being able to finish any assignments. I was also suffering from hypoglycemia, which never was fully diagnosed until about five years ago. It made me tire too easily because I went too long without food. I would suffer many difficulties, including anxieties, headaches, and confusion.

Mother sensed something was wrong so I took along some supplementary food, but I was still emotionally upset for all these different reasons. She finally decided to take me out of school over my father's objections. She was the kind of person who did things her own way. She said, "Let's let Jim have his gardening for a year or two and let him straighten out his problems." Well, gardening and fresh air were my salvation. As long as I was outside, I was healthy and happy. I just took off and had the greatest time. I was actually out of school for three years: sixth, seventh, and eighth grades. The truant officer kept coming around, and mother had to convince him that I was making progress. The school tolerated this breach of the system, but, of course, any person who succeeds while operating outside society's institutions is a threat to all institutions! The other kids in the neighborhood wondered why I could be out of school and they couldn't. I had even fewer friends after that; it was a bad situation. I'd get taunted, and there were all kinds of grumblings going on.

Then I went back after a summer of tutoring, and in one summer I caught up to the rest of the kids my age.

Fortunately, instead of sending me to West High next door, which was a big school, my parents sent me to Wisconsin High School, a small university experimental school. I entered as a freshman, did fine, and had a great time.

I want to say something else related to my mother's influence. She did very good things for me, but I think she had some psychological problems of her own, which I acquired and had to overcome. I've gradually had to learn from people that you have to be very sympathetic to their feelings. Not that mother wasn't sympathetic to other people's feelings, but I think she just didn't know how to react.

IT TOOK ME A LONG TIME to do well in front of an audience. I was shy and frightened. It took many years to develop my own system, my own synthesis. I think whatever success I've had in reaching audiences is due to an extreme sensitivity to how other people feel. What I do is prepare in advance, but not until a few hours before a talk, then I can remember it for a few hours without referring to notes, and it comes out fresh and natural. If I prepare too far ahead, I forget it. If I try to look at notes, it's cold and doesn't make any sense to me anymore. I'm one of those people—like my father— who does things differently each time and doesn't stick with a thing very long. This makes it difficult to teach the second section of a college class the same way as I did the first. I'll rework the material in a new way.

Probably the most important thing a teacher has is personality. You've also got to be committed, well-informed, authoritative, and correct most of the time. If you're not, kids—particularly high-schoolers—pick up on this fast. One strategy for reaching them is to show them you're relaxed and to let them discover nature for themselves. Kids are interested in everything, especially little things that they see on the ground. You don't work with birds very much because the amateur or novice has to be trained to see birds. I had to train myself to see birds. You start with something they all can see, show them some plants, tell stories about them, and soon they say, "Oh, gee, I thought those were just weeds out there!" I discovered that a weed in most people's vocabulary was a plant that was unfamiliar. So I pick a few plants, tell about them, and people get all excited about them.

Many people in my field classes remember that while they were studying botany in the arboretum, I would stop and point out an indigo bunting or some such bird singing overhead. Very often students were unaware of this bird singing right over us, and they had to shift gears from plants to birds; that's not easy for most people.

When we took kids out to the School Forest in buses, it was very important to go on the buses with them, whether high school or grade school, it didn't matter. They became a screaming mob if left by themselves. The minute you departed the schoolyard, you began priming them for what they were going to see. You had them look out the window and see some things on the way, and you murdered them if they made any noise. After you got them out there, you turned the motor off and said, "All right, nobody's going to say anything, not even move a foot for five minutes." And having primed them beforehand, you only had to stop for one minute. The birds were all singing, right in view.

Another important thing was to talk at different levels. Even with a class of sixth graders, there was everyone from the mentally challenged to the bright lights in the class, who were mostly troublemakers because they were bored. You had to find something for each of these people. What I did was to start with everyone looking at an insect or spider. I had it crawl around on me. Some people were shocked that I would let an insect do this, but they began not only to see what I was trying to tell them, but also to learn to be respectful toward all life. Ethics were taught by inference.

I've also incorporated a little P.T. Barnum in doing things. I was at Corkscrew Swamp in southern Florida once, and it was time for closing. Here came a couple of college kids who didn't know what to do with themselves. They found a mother alligator and her young, and they started badgering her and making her hiss at them. At the same time, a stork was performing his fantastic feeding dance. He dabbled a pink foot under a lily pad to attract fish, and then he'd put his beak in the water, snap them into his pouch, and try again. To get the kids' attention, I yelled, "Look at this fantastic thing going on over here!" I was all alone and felt a little foolish yelling in the middle of this silence, but I had to entice them. I had enough experience in the School Forest to know that teenagers sometimes will respond to somebody who is showing some authority yet acting a bit. So I went into a spiel about how what this bird was doing was wonderful, but they didn't listen. So I repeated it a second time. Finally, one of them looked over, and I said, "If you'll be quiet, you'll see the greatest show on earth."

I told them this was something that they would never see again in their lives—a bit exaggerated—but finally, they saw him perform the feeding ritual, and I said, "Now here's what he's going to do," and he did, and that finally got them. They would never have seen it otherwise. They then sat transfixed for about half an hour watching this bird. They couldn't stop watching. I was lucky enough to do the right thing at the right time. I've had a lot of failures. Once in a while, you hit the right things to do and it works.

IN HIGH SCHOOL I had a physics professor, Ira Davis, who put on a terrifically terrorizing front—you had to produce or get out—but I was ready for him. He did a lot for me because he taught me self-discipline and how to think.

Probably the most important influence on me, however, was UW-Madison botany professor Norman Fassett. He was an extremely fine teacher as well as a dedicated conservationist. It has been said, although it's only rumor, that he influenced Leopold more than anyone else. Since Fassett was a botanist, I ate up everything he taught. He taught in a remarkable way. He had a sense of the dramatic, and every lecture he pounded home a single point. He threw his whole self into a lecture. There were deep ideas, not shallow ones, and often it took a long time for the students to understand what he was trying to say. But he would get across his feelings about these things as well as good scientific information.

I remember my first field trip with him; he invited me to accompany some of his graduate students. I must have been about 14 at the time. We went in May to Apple River Canyon State Park in Illinois, which was a beautiful place full of wildflowers. At the time, I had only recently become interested in native plants. Fassett was in his element as an actor. There were some young women in the group, and exhibiting chivalry, he carried them across a stream—not all at once!—to this cliff where some rare primroses were growing on an overhanging cliff above about a foot of water. He had a great time performing in the outdoors.

I was with Fassett for 10 years—five years as an undergraduate and five years as a graduate student. My master's was titled "A Key to Sedges." The herbarium was in such disarray at that time that I didn't know which species were correctly identified, so I wasted a couple of years until I got that in order. People began to grumble, saying, "When is Jim Zimmerman ever going to leave college?" A perennial student, but I was just having a ball!

Fassett and Leopold were role models for me. I think about two-thirds of teaching is being a role model for people. The other third is enthusiasm for your subject. Leopold, a very charming but earnest person, was the third major influence. He lived only two blocks away. His daughter, Nina, knew of me, but I didn't remember her. I wasn't really aware of the Leopold family until I took his course. He taught in some ways like Fassett because he made you think creatively. His first exercise threw me for a loop. He had a bunch of pictures of trees that had lost their lower branches over a pond. How? To deer. Why? Well, you were supposed to figure out how the deer got out there. The answer, quite naturally, was that they walked out there and browsed off the branches, which told you that the pond had frozen over.

Leopold's teachings sparked my interest in phenology. I have maintained a daily record of natural events continuously from 1943 to the present. They're records from a variety of different places in and around Madison. At the arboretum, for example, I kept records for eight years from the late '40s through the '50s, after taking Leopold's course. I biked to the arboretum twice a week and tried to cover every part and then started over again. I watched over 800 species of plants. I kept records of their unfolding, blooming, seeding, and fall color. I kept records of the arrival, nesting, hatching, fledging, and song dates of over 75 species of birds. I also observed turtles, frogs, snakes, and insects. Leopold knew this was good training, and I have my students do it now. They have to take an area and tell me what's happening each week.

It took me two years of keeping phenological records before I realized that I was changing my way of life. I studied upstairs with the window open and stopped if I heard a bird outside. I'd spend the whole morning chasing the darn bird down if I couldn't identify it!

Jim with a handful of asters at the Zimmermans' prairie. Photo by, and courtesy of, Elizabeth H. Zimmerman, mid-1980s.

Plants and animals have to tolerate an incredible amount of variation in weather. The problem with any interior continental climate is its instability; it's extremely capricious. Nevertheless, plants form their reproductive parts and their foliage buds according to a solar clock just as punctual as the bird migration schedule. Any summer blooming plant that blooms in June and July is usually a plant that has formed its buds only a couple of weeks previous to bloom. All the spring blooming plants form their flowers the year before. Spring flowers, formed during the shorter days of the year, have to go through a dormancy-breaking period where the temperature is first very cold, then warm, before they can bud out and flower. That's why winter is so important to our plants and trees here in Wisconsin. You can't grow, for instance, apple trees and tulips south of the Mason-Dixon line because there isn't enough cold to break the dormancy of the buds that were pre-formed the previous summer.

Insects follow the schedule of flowering plants closely because they depend on them for food, and in those years where the birds are on schedule, but the plants bloom late, the birds have a hard time finding food. In a year like this one [1982] where the spring is early, the plants bloom early, and the insects soon will bust out. When the birds come, more or less on schedule, they will have more than enough to eat.

I THINK I'VE LEARNED more by teaching than I did as a student. The learning has come from trying to explain things in a way that will reach others. I've found that one of the most difficult tasks has been to communicate my understanding of ecology to students. Values are just as important as facts, but when I launch into developing philosophical ideas about nature, I've lost a good many people because they aren't trained to listen for more than five minutes. So the way I maneuver around that is to get people involved; get people out looking at a field and see how many kinds of grasses they can find. Then they come back with unanswered questions and an appetite for another lecture from me! In this way, they develop their own powers of concentration and observation. It's ironic, but when I was in grade school having all those troubles, the biggest criticism I received was that I didn't concentrate on anything! But that was because I was so nervous and upset. Once I could do my own thing, I spent hours doing one thing and didn't get tired.

I've noticed that as I train students to become more perceptive, I've become sharper myself. And every time you do something with somebody else, you have to know more than they do! When you're out in the field, you have to be one step ahead, so you keep working hard to understand and interpret more. Becoming a naturalist means establishing a 50/50 interplay between receiving information through reading, listening, studying, and receiving information by learning directly from nature through personal observation. I tell my students to go out on the weekend, look at a marsh, and then tell me what they saw, and when we talk about things in class, they learn more, but even better—get students to teach each other!

Jim in fen near Cambridge, Jefferson County, Wisconsin. September 1992.
Photo by, and courtesy of, Elizabeth H. Zimmerman.

You know, Leopold asked me in his first oral quiz how I recognized a field sparrow without hearing it first. I didn't remember the pink bill! I'll always remember that! He conducted these personal oral quizzes so that he could get to know you. As an example of his charm, instead of sitting there like he was going to grill you, he'd come in and first ask you for your advice on something. Once, when I came in, the first thing he said was, "You're working with Fassett over in botany, and I've got a problem with my research on plants near the Shack. Can you tell me what this plant is?" Knowing the student's background, he would ask a particular question of each student. He was extremely clever in putting you at ease, and he was sincere, too; it wasn't just a put-on for show. He did want to know, but he wouldn't ask the student who knew the most about the question, but the student who would grow the most in answering that question. In other words, he tailored every single question to a particular personality. That takes talent!

At six weeks, Leopold insisted on having a personal interview with everybody in his class; he had 40 people. It must have taken him all week. Instead of having a particular week when my students see me, they just come in when they're ready, and so I get to see them all. This is extremely important to me.

A fourth major influence was Paul Olson, a conservationist, former high school teacher, and principal. My first job as a naturalist in the Madison School Forest was under his supervision. Paul understood people. He always made you feel as if you were the greatest person in the world, and without you his program couldn't fly. He taught me perhaps as much about human psychology as any one person. He didn't have a strong education, yet he picked up the ethics of Leopold and the philosophy of conservation. In a sense, he outdid Leopold. He'd get out in the woods with high school kids and inspire them with a little lecture of his own, and he had a vision. He's the one who, with the Hamerstroms, saved the prairie-chicken in Wisconsin through superb salesmanship.

A fifth person who influenced me was Lowell Noland. I first met him through his son Wayland, a chemistry professor in the Twin Cities. Wayland was a loner, and he and I hit it off in high school. He was one of the maybe five friends I had in high school and college. At the university, I took freshman zoology in 1943, and Lowell taught that course. He was probably the finest teacher I ever had in that he was a stickler for good work, but at the same time he had the milk of human kindness, more than anyone I ever met. He was gentle. The students loved him. The best thing about his teaching was that he always respected your ideas. If he didn't like an idea, he'd turn it around and come up with a better one.

One of the things that Noland would do to prepare for lectures was manicure his yard. He'd weed his yard by hand; get out there on all fours and dig into his dandelions while thinking about his lecture. Almost every lecture was related to some personal story, which, of course, is a very good technique. On top of that, it was always fresh. It was always something that he had thought about only a few hours earlier. Leopold did this, too. Both of these men were excited about new ideas, and they were always eager to share them with us. This, of course, kept everyone on the edge of their chairs. Students wouldn't miss their lectures; attendance wasn't a problem.

Noland was so understanding. If there were students having trouble, he'd have them in and talk to them personally. Leopold and Fassett did this, too. I saw a lot in common among the three. Everything was fresh and new and creative all the time, and it was important for my own development to be with people who were so creative. Also, there was almost a religious feeling about nature and natural resources. They all had very strong convictions, and they knew how to communicate and to think! Leopold liked to smoke his pipe while pondering matters and then come up with an idea. He would do this at his seminars. He'd puff awhile as a student was presenting his report, and then he'd jump up and say, "Is this what you mean?" He'd write it on the board and get all excited about it. Something had clicked, and he had to share his discovery with other people.

In 1956, Noland asked me to teach in his integrated liberal studies program in biology. Since I really didn't want to stay narrowly in botany anyway, I jumped at the chance. That was a real eye-opener because now I could teach under a good teacher, which was even better than having been a student under him. We'd have our weekly conferences on how the course was going and what we should do next week. There were several other good TAs [teaching assistants] working for him, so I interacted with some very fine people. We'd all have suggestions to make things better. He was very funny because he'd say, "Well, I'll think about it." He wouldn't agree, but he'd come back the next day, and we'd find that he had incorporated all of our suggestions to problems. He not only made us happy but inspired us to work with him because he was so considerate.

Noland hardly got any sleep. He was up half the night thinking about different problems and approaches to problems, and he'd get up early in the morning just to keep up each day. When I got my PhD, he paid me the ultimate compliment by asking me to take his place and run that course because he was retiring. I had to make an agonizing decision. I declined because I wanted to work outdoors. Although this was a fine biology course—the nicest course I'd ever taught in—it didn't leave much time for the outdoor work I wanted. Many people didn't understand why I instead took the job as naturalist in the Madison School Forest and at the University of Wisconsin-Madison Arboretum. There was less prestige attached to that position in the eyes of certain people on campus

You see, what I value most about my work as a naturalist is reaching other people, turning them on, getting them interested in nature. If I can get people involved, I feel satisfied because I feel I'm helping people enjoy a

Jim with sedges south of Red Cedar Lake, Jefferson County, Wisconsin.
Photo by, and courtesy of, Elizabeth H. Zimmerman, mid-1980s.

more enriched life. The hope is that they would then become more involved and more responsible inhabitants of the planet. It's a matter of getting one naturalist per so many 100 people everywhere, and you'd have most of our environmental problems solved; this was Paul Olson's idea. He had me teach May Theilgaard Watts' *Reading the Landscape* [*of America*] for 10 years as part of the Madison School Forest program, and it became extremely popular. We figured we reached 2,000 people in 10 years, many of whom are now business people and doctors on city councils and county boards.

I've concluded that people's interests are more emotional than rational, and if you give people an emotional experience, they will carry away more and have more interest and involvement than if you give them some kind of intellectual experience. I've had so many good experiences outdoors that I want other people to have these same experiences, but I want them to develop their own philosophy, not because I think they should, but because they can't fail to develop an ecological attitude toward the land if they have contact hours in the field. I've directed my efforts to help people acquire those contact hours one way or another.

I believe I have to be half scientist and half artist. Science and art are very close. The artist is generally perceived to be more spontaneous and the scientist more methodical—everything planned for the next 20 years. Well, scientists aren't like that, and artists aren't so flighty either. A good artist

CHAPTER FOUR

does a lot of planning, and a good scientist does a lot of creative thinking. So there really is no significant difference between science and art; they're both trying to get at the truth, but institutionalized science is anathema to most art-oriented people, and vice versa. It's one of those typical splits of human nature, like between the managers and the ivory tower researchers; neither one understands the other, and they think the other is no darn good.

If you can't be a good communicator, you're only a narrow specialist. It's better to be a jack-of-all-trades so you can put into perspective what the specialists say, and I know which specialist to go to if I need more knowledge and how to adapt what they advise. And to be an effective naturalist, you have to have a grasp of the physical and biological sciences, as well as be an adept communicator. Supposedly being a good communicator ought to happen if you're a good observer, a good synthesizer, because I regard human nature as part of nature. If you're sensitive to one part, you ought to be sensitive to all of nature. Sensitivity, however, requires two steps: perceiving with your senses—good ears, eyes, nose, and so on—and perceiving with your heart. If you're receptive to what's going on around you, then you should be as receptive to people and their feelings as you are to a bird, a plant, the wind, the clouds, or whatever. But that takes some training, and you have to get into the right mental position. You have to bore a hole from inside out until it reaches the holes on the outside coming in so that you make connections.

One of the interesting things Leopold tried to do in his seminars was to have state land managers attend along with his students. He had to work hard to keep them working together, but it made a nice cross-fertilization of different points of view.

🖋

I DON'T KNOW ENOUGH to know whether there is a God or not. I never had a strong religious training or environment. My parents were free-thinking Unitarians. They never took religion too seriously because they felt there was so much hypocrisy in religion. I'm trying to learn what other people, like Native Americans, believe. I've read more about their approaches. They're so different from our European culture that I don't feel I understand them at all, and yet there's something there that appeals to me greatly—a feeling of oneness with nature and birds and plants, which might open a lot of hearts.

I'VE LEARNED that the pace of nature is more restful and more conducive to creative work than the pace of economic society. In nature there are laws, inexorable laws, but somehow the pace is gradual enough. The only time I fully experienced that kind of pace was when Libby and I spent two weeks in the Quetico Superior wilderness. It took an entire week for us to shed the usual white man's schedule, and then I began to look at living in a whole different way. I didn't worry about what time it was; I knew well enough from the sun. If things took a little longer to complete, it didn't matter.

I like Peter Matthiessen's approach in *The Snow Leopard*. I believe his experience in the mountains must have given him a higher state of consciousness—higher than he had known before his trip to the Himalayas to forget his wife's death and to search for the snow leopard, as well as himself.

Nature enters my dreams, enters my thoughts, a lot of the time. I can't get enough of it. It gives me an inner calm and a feeling of fulfillment. I like René Dubos's idea that man and land create a marriage, which is different with each piece of land and with each individual. But there is an inherent problem. When taken at face value, it means chaos because each person is doing his own thing with his own piece of land, with no regard for the overall picture. That's happening right now. Furthermore, right now it's man against nature instead of man with nature; that is not an ethical relationship or a synthesis. I don't think we can force everybody into a mold though and say there is only one way to have a relationship with the land. I think everyone has to figure it out for themselves. As a criterion, you need to say that the land should remain productive for those special things the land can produce best indefinitely without depleting the resource base. The fact that the land can be treated like a used car—get all you can out of it, beat it up, and junk it when you're through with it—this is the opposite of a land ethic.

Regarding a land ethic, there's one fight to preserve land I'd like to mention. In the early 1970s, there was a proposed dam impoundment in the Kickapoo River canyon of west-central Wisconsin's Driftless Area. There was a proposal by the United States Army Corps of Engineers to control flooding and create a lake for recreation in the Kickapoo Valley, but a University of Wisconsin study clearly showed that the project had a low benefit-cost ratio. There were many flaws in the estimated benefits, and the area contained outstanding geologic and botanical features that could be destroyed by such a project. When I first learned of it and talked to people who were trying to prevent the dam, it seemed pretty hopeless. But after canoeing the river, I realized that there was much more at stake; this was a real jewel. I began to get angry. I organized a small group to contact senators and get other people involved. Finally, through the help of Senator Gaylord Nelson's assistant in Washington, we got Nelson out here and then commanded more attention from Washington.

I took an ecology class to the Kickapoo three years in a row, and in each of those years we canoed, camped overnight in Wildcat Mountain State Park, and invited the Army Corps of Engineers to present their side of the story. They always sent two people—like nuns when they are allowed to go out in the world so if one wants to stray from the fold the other can watch over her. The Corps always sent two people so we wouldn't convert one of them to our cause.

One of the people they sent was a biologist. It was always a different person each year because the biologists were driven crazy by the Corps of Engineers' approach to things. The third year, things were getting pretty close to the wire, and the third biologist they sent us was clever. He took me aside and told me, "You know, if you really want to fight this thing, the new endangered species law has just been enacted. If you think there are any endangered plants down there, you ought to work up that angle, because as owner of much of the land, the Corps is responsible for the welfare of any endangered species." So I thanked him, made a list, and got six professors to sign a legal affidavit. We sent it to Washington saying that certain plants should be considered for protection under the Endangered Species Act, and if they were so designated, the Corps had to include them in an environmental impact statement.

The Endangered Species Act was particularly restrictive for public agencies, and so this was important to our efforts, although it probably constituted only 10 percent of the effective opposition to the dam. But the dam was halted. Discussion of a dry dam followed, but without a lake for recreation, the cost-benefit ratio was even lower than that from the original plan, and we succeeded in preserving this marvelous area.

🌿

March 28, 1982, Lower Mud Lake, Dane County

Alone with his thoughts in the chilly early morning, Jim Zimmerman stands along a wooded edge, one hand in his pants pocket, the other resting lightly on a spotting scope. He bends forward to observe a group of ducks drifting about a hundred yards offshore. Dressed in gray khakis, a dark wool sweater, and faded brown jacket, he notes each duck species bobbing about in the blue-black water. About 8:00 a.m., 15 students arrive from Madison. Jim greets each warmly, sets up a second scope, then points to some high branches overhead. There, a golden-crowned kinglet—a tiny, nondescript bird—calls in a thin voice as it wisps from one branch to another searching for grubs and insect larvae. "The kinglets are among the first of the spring migrants," he says. "They'll be nesting in the spruce and fir forests of the far north."

Jim turns around to adjust the scope overlooking the lake. "Oh! The redheads have their heads way up! Take a look." Some students have binoculars and try to pick out the redheads—ducks with rufous-colored heads, grayish bodies, and black breasts—among the huddle of ducks offshore. "Unfortunately, because of our presence the ducks are beginning to move further out, so you'll get a better look with the scopes." After a few more minutes, Jim steps back, both hands in his pockets, and begins to discuss the layout of the land surrounding the lake.

"Lower Mud Lake, largely surrounded by wetlands, is actually a natural widening of the Yahara River. The east side is primarily sedge meadow over peat. The west side, which is wetter, has dominant stands of cattail, bur-reed, bluejoint grass, red-osier dogwood, willow, and various wetland forbs and shrubs. Narrow-leaved cattail borders the lake edge in many places. Because the lake is open in spring before any other in Dane County, migrating waterfowl come here to feed. You might get over 2,000 ducks out here in March and April." Just then, a bugling cacophony comes forth from the lightening western skies.

"Listen!" he calls out. "The sandhill cranes are calling over to the west!" There is a murmur from the group as they study the western horizon for a chance to see these elegant long-necked birds. "Each year, the annual census of sandhill cranes is conducted on an early spring morning. At dawn they do a lot of territorial calling."

Jim turns the scope slowly and identifies American coots, ring-necked ducks, scaup, American wigeon, northern pintail, and a small brownish duck with white cheeks (male) and a stiff, vertically-facing tail—the ruddy duck.

"This isn't just a duck breeding area for a few pairs in the summer," he notes. "This is an area on the Yahara River that acts as a vital resting and feeding location for thousands of migrant birds in the spring and fall. Some of these ducks will be going to shallower marshes when they feed. One reason that they may be hanging in here is that it's too early in the year for them to be moving out, so they're probably just marking time. But also, many of the shallow marshes are dry this year, so they don't have too many places to feed."

Jim and Libby (standing) observing waterfowl at Goose Pond, Columbia County, Wisconsin. March 28, 1982. Photo by Sumner Matteson.

"How is the lake's water quality," one woman asks, "and how has that affected use by waterfowl?"

"Actually, it's in pretty decent shape," says Jim, rubbing his nose. "Let me give you the bigger picture. There are three reasons why this area offers refuge from disturbance and provides some food for waterfowl. First, one of the four big wetlands left on the Yahara River exists across the water here to the west—Lower Mud Lake Marsh. It's nearly a square mile in size. The other three wetlands are Cherokee Marsh, South Waubesa Marsh, and Pheasant Branch Creek. Because of the proximity of these marshes to each other, there is a large natural area that offers safe harbor to migratory birds.

"Second, the water from most of the Yahara River watershed—something like 250 square miles of farmland and urban areas—gets filtered out by three basins: Lake Waubesa, Lake Monona, and Lake Mendota. Therefore, the water has a chance to get cleaned up, and nutrients and pollutants get filtered out or absorbed by these basins. There isn't much of an upland watershed at this point, so the water quality of Lower Mud Lake is pretty good. Also, since the 1950s, Madison sewage has been diverted around all of the lakes. Even though the lake isn't shallow enough to attract many of the shallow-water birds, such as the northern pintail and the blue-winged teal, we always get a few in here along with the diving ducks.

"There are two major kinds of ducks: the marsh ducks or dabblers and the diving or bay ducks. Marsh ducks feed on aquatic plants and invertebrates by upending their bodies as they submerge their heads to search for food. These ducks include the black duck, mallard, pintail, wigeon, wood duck, gadwall, northern shoveler, blue-winged teal, and green-winged teal. There are a few other marsh ducks, but you're not likely to see them around here during migration. Diving ducks dive below the water to search for similar types of food or fish. The ducks seen around here commonly during migration include canvasback, redhead, ring-necked duck, lesser scaup, common goldeneye, and bufflehead.

"The third reason the lake is in decent shape is that there's a good buffer of grasses, tussock meadows, cattail marshes, and this place here where we stand—what was once originally a prairie oak opening, now pastured but showing signs of invasion by oak and aspen.

"In the tall cattail marsh on the northwestern side of the lake, you'll find yellow-headed blackbirds, rails, gallinules, and coots nesting during summer. Rails, gallinules, and coots belong to the *Rallidae* family. Rails are secretive marsh waders, while gallinules and coots feed along the shore or in the open water.

"Duck diversity will be declining on the lake as the breeding season approaches, but there will be some additional species coming in, such as both teal species. And the coots have not yet reached the peak of their migration. There will be a solid mass of coots in here through April. There might be a few loons, too, during April. Then most ducks will pull out, and you'll have teal, mallards, shovelers, and maybe wood ducks hanging around the area during the summer."

As mid-morning approaches, Jim suggests that everyone move on to Goose Pond in southern Columbia County, but not before Libby, who has recently arrived, offers Girl Scout cookies and cider. At Goose Pond—owned and managed by the Madison Audubon Society—the group takes in a variety of waterfowl, including scores of tundra swans foraging in the shallows. After a lunch break at Goose Pond headquarters, Jim gently suggests they head north to Mud Lake, approximately seven miles distant. But something has caught his eye; a platoon of leopard frogs—as many as 50—are hopping west across the warm asphalt. "There are bunches of them!" shouts one woman. Most humans stand—transfixed. Soon, however, feelings of curiosity and amazement turn to alarm. Everyone kneels, crouches, claps, and waves the frogs along.

Libby with her painting of Black Terns at Red Cedar Lake, Jefferson County, Wisconsin. Photo by Jim Zimmerman, mid-1980s. Photo courtesy of Elizabeth H. Zimmerman.

Just when many of the frogs approach the center of the road, a pickup truck appears noisily from the north. It must have struck the driver as rather odd to see people bent over, some on hands and knees, in the middle of the road. He slows to a halt about 15 meters from the group, and one student, wearing sunglasses, his hair blowing wildly across his face, tells the driver the group is engaged in an exercise program. The mustachioed driver, wearing sunglasses and looking stone-faced, does not smile. Once the road is clear of people, he roars on, his wheels flattening three frogs.

"You know," remarks Jim, "when there weren't any roads here, the frogs could move around at will. Roads were built on section lines, and the section line happens to go across this body of water. Libby brought up an interesting point one day. If we had gone metric when North America was settled, we would have had roads every kilometer, instead of every mile; that's two-thirds as far and would have meant half again as many roads."

Jim follows a final contingent of frogs as they cross the road. "As far as I know, no one knows for sure why they come out all at once like this. The same phenomenon has been observed between Cedar Lake and Lake Ripley over in Jefferson County. In the fall and spring, there have been large migrations of leopard frogs. Here, it may be that they breed on one side and winter on the other. It may be that the release of hormones is all synchronized so that they breed together. Because of this synchronization, perhaps due to day length or water temperature, they are all set to go on the same day. Usually, frogs move only on wet nights, but for some reason they've decided to move today."

THE CARAVAN OF VEHICLES leaves the Goose Pond area and passes by flooded fields and marshes, then slows to a crawl to allow for scrutiny of wet fields and ephemeral ponds. "Are these temporary bodies of water of any importance to migratory waterfowl?" I ask.

"Yes," Jim says. "They need fast-food joints along the way for refueling as they head north, and these will do just fine for that purpose. Small, temporary bodies of water lack fish. The food chain, therefore, abounds in snails and crustaceans that the dabblers and even divers can consume."

One flooded marshy spot attracts Libby's eye, and she asks Jim to pull over. Under a bright sun, Libby, donning hip boots, angles slowly along the shallows of the marsh edge. She crouches low, remains still for a moment, then scoops up a coffee cup full of tiny organisms. Excited, she brings back her catch and shows it to the class. A small contingent immediately surrounds her. "What is it?" asks one crew cut, bespectacled fellow.

"*Daphnia!*" replies Libby. "*Daphnia*, a water flea, is the best known of a group of freshwater arthropods. Look at the way they move; it's kind of a jerking motion. They use their antennae to maneuver about and their legs to filter out the bacteria, protozoa, algae, and organic detritus on which they feed from a water current drawn through the shell."

"They're transparent and kind of oval-shaped, aren't they?" asks one smiling woman wearing a red bandana around her brown hair. "Yeah.... Wait a minute! What do we have here? It's a copepod!" exclaims Libby. "See the two tails, the two egg sacs, the two long antennules?"

"Okay, what am I looking at now?" interjects another fellow who has just joined the group.

"Copepods and *Daphnia*," Libby says, and she proceeds to point out and distinguish between the two kinds of organisms. "The copepods are very active feeders, sometimes preying on the bodies of dead animals."

Jim, smiling, indicates that it's time to move on, and the caravan gets ready once more to proceed. Libby remains for a short while longer by the marsh edge. "Libby is in her element," he says to me, proudly.

Reaching Mud Lake in Columbia County (not to be confused with Lower Mud Lake in Dane County) that contains about a mile of open water, the class seems happy, talkative. For an hour they observe different sandpiper species including a Wilson's snipe (formerly common snipe) at the east end, where mud flats border a sedge meadow. In the lake, there are coots and several of the same waterfowl species observed earlier in the day.

About 4:30 p.m. the class disperses, thanking the Zimmermans for the fine day. With everyone gone, Jim sits down on a hill overlooking the east end of the lake, his elbows resting on his knees. He doesn't speak or move. Libby stands beside him and silently watches through a scope the drift of ducks fading west, dark silhouettes against the early evening light. ✳

On September 28, 1992, while working alone on prairie restoration at their Red Cedar Lake country home near Cambridge, Wisconsin, Jim Zim (as his students affectionately called him) suffered a massive heart attack, dropped to the earth face down, and quickly passed away. He was 67. Of the moment, Libby wrote: "A small man lay on the ground, but a giant has fallen." [93]

In 2003, James Hall Zimmerman was inducted into the Wisconsin Conservation Hall of Fame.

Ruth Hine
(1923-2010)

Ruth Hine showing a common garter snake (*Thamnophis sirtalis*) to
a natural history class at Bethel Horizons Camp and Retreat Center near
Dodgeville, Wisconsin, May 1984. Photo by Sumner Matteson.

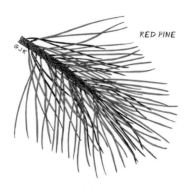

RED PINE

Chapter Five~
Ruth Hine

It wasn't until I went into my doctoral program that I was able to link up with wildlife as a minor. I still couldn't major in it. Why? Remember this was the 1940s. I barely got a job, much less did what I wanted to do. To be perfectly fair, they said at the time that there were no PhD majors in wildlife. I'm not sure if that meant for women only or all majors. I don't dwell on this. People like Fran Hamerstrom and I lived with this so much that we just took the situation for granted at the time.

—RH

Ruth Louise Hine preferred to refer to her ancestry as a "four-part lineage: English, German, Scot, and Irish," with her mother's side contributing all but the English. Born in Columbus, Ohio, on August 19, 1923, Ruth attended high school in Springfield, Massachusetts, graduating in 1940. She went on to Connecticut College, graduating with a bachelor of arts in zoology in 1944, then achieved a master of arts in zoology from the University of Wisconsin-Madison (UW-Madison) in 1947, before earning a doctorate from UW-Madison in zoology in 1952—one of the few women at the time to do so, and the first woman to earn a PhD in zoology at the University of Wisconsin.

From 1949 to early January 1986 (when she retired), Dr. Hine worked for the Wisconsin Department of Natural Resources (WDNR)—formerly the Wisconsin Conservation Department. She began as a conservation biologist, spent many years as a research publications editor, and ended her career as a natural resources specialist.

Ruth edited innumerable WDNR publications, but she also co-authored four WDNR technical bulletins: "Food Habit Studies of Ruffed Grouse, Pheasant, Quail, and Mink in Wisconsin" (1952, with B.P. Stollberg); "Wisconsin Fox Populations" (1953, with S.H. Richards); "Seasonal Variation in Stress Resistance and Survival in the Hen Pheasant" (1956, with C. Kabat, R.K. Meyer, and K.G. Flakas); and "Leopard Frog Populations and Mortality in Wisconsin, 1974–76" (1981, with B.L. Les and B.F. Hellmich). Under her leadership, the WDNR initiated a statewide frog and toad survey in 1981 to monitor populations of the state's 12 frog and toad species.

Ruth in March 1959 at her Wisconsin Conservation Department office, where she served as editor of research publications and was responsible for putting out "The Conservationist," a monthly newspaper for the department's staff. Photo courtesy of Lisa Gaumnitz, WDNR.

Not well known, except among her peers, is the fact that Dr. Hine was instrumental in initiating Wisconsin's Endangered Species Program in the early 1970s as chair of the WDNR's Endangered Species Committee. And except for a late, lateral transfer by another colleague, she most likely would have become Wisconsin's first director in 1978 of the DNR's Office of Endangered and Nongame Species, which became the Bureau of Endangered Resources in 1981, then the Bureau of Natural Heritage Conservation in 2013.

Dr. Hine was universally admired within the WDNR for her skills as a research biologist and editor, and for her kindness and grace as a person. In 1984, she received the second annual Virginia Hart Special Recognition Award, the highest award given to a state female employee for outstanding public service. The award was presented by Wisconsin Governor Anthony Earl. That year she also began to work part-time for Lutheran Outdoor Ministries of Wisconsin and Upper Michigan, developing natural history programs for Lutheran church camps.

Top left: Wisconsin Governor Tony Earl presents Ruth with the second annual Virginia Hart Award on October 1, 1984, to honor Ruth's leadership, community service, pioneering spirit and technical expertise. **Top right:** Virginia Hart, here greeting Ruth, later wrote to her: "I am truly honored to have this great association with you." **Middle:** October 1, 1984. Susie Nehls (assisted Ruth for 16 years as Research Publications Specialist), Ruth, and then-Director of WDNR's Bureau of Research, Kent Klepinger. Photos courtesy of Lisa Gaumnitz, Wisconsin DNR. **Bottom left:** Governor Earl proclaimed October 12, 1985, as "Ruth Hine Day." **Bottom right:** C.D. Besadny letter congratulating Ruth on receiving the Virginia Hart Award.

Commenting on her Lutheran camp work to a reporter ("Know your Madisonian," *Wisconsin State Journal*, Sunday, March 10, 1985), Ruth said: "I think religious stewardship is a process you build step by step. As you become aware of the outdoors, as you begin to experience God's creation, then taking care of it follows. By helping the camps develop first-step programs for campers, you start a process that leads, eventually, you hope, to a greater sense of reverence for all of God's creation."

I first became acquainted with Dr. Hine early in 1974 (the year she won the Citizens Natural Resources Association of Wisconsin Silver Acorn Award for outstanding effort and achievement in Wisconsin conservation), when she offered strong encouragement to myself and James T. Harris for a proposed pioneering study of nesting gulls and terns along the Wisconsin shore of Lake Superior (funded that spring/summer by the University of Wisconsin Sea Grant College Program, today the Wisconsin Sea Grant Institute). When I began work at the WDNR in 1981, I thoroughly enjoyed our interactions and discussions and was sad when she retired on January 3, 1986.

For years after she retired, Dr. Hine worked as a naturalist at the Bethel Horizons Camp and Retreat Center near Dodgeville, Wisconsin. Her field outings were always full and much appreciated by participants.

One quiet wintry evening, in January 1981, we sat down to talk in the living room of her then near westside Madison home that she shared with her dearest friend and companion, Hazel Hiemstra. The following account comes from that interview.

Ruth and long-time companion, Hazel Hiemstra. Photo courtesy of Hazel Hiemstra.

✿

MY PARENTS WERE TWO EXTREMELY DEVOTED PEOPLE who met as kids when they were eleven years old at a summer religious happening in New York State. That was it from then on; they got married and had three of us.

My dad had a lot of tough breaks. He was working at Wesleyan University in Ohio when I was born, and then because of my brother's poor health, headed south to Florida. After six years they decided that the best thing to do was to come back up north; that was in 1929. He was in business as a property manager and had to start all over again. His influence on me is growing stronger and stronger. He never made a great deal of money, never achieved great goals, but he was a neat person, as was my mother. They were very family oriented, deeply religious Methodist people, and they enjoyed their life together very much. We didn't read the Bible much, but we all went to church together. I took it as a matter of course then; it was a part of my life, but they never imposed their beliefs on me. They let me go my own way.

Years separated the ages of the kids. I am the youngest, and there's seven years between me and my brother and four years between my brother and sister. This was probably because of my mother's health. I had an older brother who died at birth, and so it may have been my mother's health that accounted for why the children were spaced so far apart. It's entirely possible that I was an afterthought.

Two years after I was born, we went to Orlando, Florida. One incident stands out. Orlando has many lakes, and Mother and I would take walks around a lake. There were many big black swans [*Cygnus atratus*] there, and they would get very aggressive. I remember once that one of the swans came after me, so Mother swooped me up to get us out of there.

We were in Orlando for about six years, then we moved back up to Ohio for five years. Our Florida home was on the edge of town. There was a field of scrubby pine and grapefruit trees on either side of the house. Now it's just

Ruth's interests in nature started early. Orlando, Florida, ca. 1927.
Photo courtesy of Hazel Hiemstra.

CHAPTER FIVE

a city street. I loved being out there with my brother and his friends as they dug tunnels. They had pulleys and little baskets, and I tagged along and did the same things. When we moved to Cleveland, Ohio, I was at an age when I might have paid more attention to what was around me, but I lived surrounded by a big city, and I simply didn't get out. I explored back streets on my bike, but that was the extent of my roaming.

So I wasn't a kid that started off collecting things in the natural world. I was simply interested in going to school, playing, and doing the usual things kids do. Other than a general liking to be outdoors because my parents liked to be outdoors, it wasn't until I got to high school in Springfield, Massachusetts, that my interest in natural history began.

In Springfield, I recall coming back from school after having faced my first opportunity to choose an elective. The electives were history or biology. I decided to choose biology. I think that decision was based on an inherent liking for biological life. That course really started me going. I don't remember much about it, but I remember my teacher Ellen Fitzgerald. She was quite an influence because I think she recognized that I had a keen interest, and she worked with me after school. At a natural history museum in Springfield, a woman named Mrs. Grimheisen, under whose wing I crept, had a great influence. I was 13 or 14 at the time. She allowed me to study mounts and take home some of the carcasses. I realize now how important a museum experience is in sparking a child's interest in nature. It certainly was in my case.

It was in Springfield that I really began to read books. I remember Jack London's work and Richard Halliburton's travel books. And I was very captivated by Martin and Osa Johnson's safaris. They were Springfield people who wrote about their adventures. I also remember reading books on Africa by Carl Akeley and Ivan Sanderson. They were the early naturalist types. I never really got into Thoreau. I don't know why, because some of his ideas sounded great, but he never really appealed to me. I visited Walden not too long ago and was really sorry I did. It's just a little pond lying in stone. There's no wilderness aspect to it at all. Too bad.

In my senior year in high school, I had two considerations to mull over in determining where I was to attend college. One was that we were financially limited, and that limited the selection process. The other was that I couldn't hack math. So I had to find a college that wasn't going to require three years of math. I narrowed it down to two that I was interested in: Radcliffe or Connecticut College.

The next factor I considered was a strong biology program. Connecticut College had a field biology course, and there was almost nothing on the horizon for that; and they only required one year of math. In 1940, the year I went there, they unfortunately dispensed with the field biology course, but those college years deeply influenced me. They gave me a marvelous biology background—all lab courses, however. But I did have a course in ornithology through which I had several field experiences, and also there was an arboretum.

I spent a summer up at Maine taking invertebrate zoology at the University of Maine right on the Maine coast. I worked as a waitress and went to

summer school. There, I had access to unlimited animals. I can still remember a Solasteridae starfish, a ten-rayed bright red thing, rich and abundant in clear, cold gorgeous water. I don't know if there's the same abundance now that you had then.

Some time later, I worked for a professor at Wesleyan University after I graduated from Connecticut. He went to Bermuda one summer and asked me to go along as his assistant. So I got the chance to study an entirely different ecology. We worked on tropical fish, and I went out and helped catch them.

Connecticut College student majoring in zoology (B.A., 1944). Photo courtesy of Lisa Gaumnitz, Wisconsin DNR.

Once, when out there, the collector allowed us to explore a coral reef. It was a brilliant mass of color and animal life. Unbelievable. I almost went into marine biology because I loved the sea so much.

Then the war came along. There was a strong feeling that everyone wanted to be involved in this effort because it was so global in nature. It happened my sophomore year, and I was swept right toward medicine. I sent in applications for medical school when I graduated because I had the hope of becoming a doctor, but then something inside me told me to slow down, to not go so fast with this. So I got a job for two years as a laboratory assistant. It only took me a few months before I realized that medical school wasn't what I really wanted.

CHAPTER FIVE

I decided to go back to school. I applied to the University of Wisconsin-Madison and the University of California. I really wanted to go to the University of California because I had never been that far before, but then I got offered an assistantship at the UW. I had written Lowell Noland, chairman of the zoology department, about the possibility of an assistantship, and I had written Aldo Leopold about the same thing. Leopold wrote back and pointed out that they didn't take women as graduate students in wildlife, but he put it in a way that didn't really bother me. He mentioned that the zoology department had brought in a new professor to handle mammalogy, zoology, and ornithology and that zoology was probably the best place for me. I didn't know much about Leopold at the time, and I really didn't know much about ecology, and even less about wildlife. They weren't taking women in wildlife ecology.

Well, it was good advice. Noland wrote me the same thing, and the new professor turned out to be John Emlen, Jr. He became my major professor. That was a bright light because birds have always been my deep love. It wasn't, however, until I went into my doctoral program that I was able to link up with wildlife as a minor. I still couldn't major in it. Why? Remember this was the 1940s. I barely got a job, much less did what I wanted to do. To be perfectly fair, they said at the time that there were no PhD majors in wildlife. I'm not sure if that meant for women only or all majors. I don't dwell on this. It's been hammered back into me because of the women's lib movement, but people like Fran Hamerstrom and I lived with this so much that we just took the situation for granted at the time.

I arrived at the UW in 1946, and Leopold taught his famous *Wildlife Ecology 118* in the spring of 1947. I had the blessed good sense to take it right off the bat. He died in 1948.

Leopold was just tremendous. His course opened up concepts all over the place, the most exciting of which was plant succession. It was exciting in the first place just to know that there were plant communities. I was used to seeing trees, plants, and shrubs. I never "saw" a community. Then there was the concept that these communities change, that a grassland becomes a woods and goes through different stages along the way to a climax forest.

Leopold was an excellent lecturer. He often used the blackboard and had many handouts. He had a marvelous way of explaining things. He was interested in us as a class and as people. Aligned with that, I was in the right place at the right time and so doggone lucky that my path crossed with Estella Leopold, who was an undergraduate in botany at the time. We

Ruth and Frederick ("Hammy") Hamerstrom at the Hamerstrom home near Plainfield, Wisconsin, ca. 1950. The Hamerstroms were close friends. Fran Hamerstrom on Ruth: "She combines the qualities of Saint Francis, *Girl Friday*, and a leader of men and women [but] she is so modest that most people don't realize they are being led." (*WDNR magazine*, November/December 1985, Volume 9(6):5). Photo courtesy of Elva Hamerstrom Paulson.

took Fassett's "Spring Flora of Wisconsin" class together, and she invited me to the [famous Leopold] Shack. Several times I would go up with her and Mr. Leopold, and the three of us would go off for a walk. Mr. Leopold was a completely different person. He was quiet within himself. That's what he needed up there. Before Estella and I would take off for the woods he might say, "Don't go into the woods now Estella, it's deer season." Just a quiet comment, and we wouldn't go into the woods.

Estella and I had good times together up at the Shack. We also went up north together a few times, camping and trapping mice. She's a fine botanist who went into paleobotany. I remember a good heart-to-heart talk we had one night that wasn't about plants but which, if I had to label it, was about religion. We talked all night. We had driven down from a camping trip one afternoon and went to the Shack. I can remember that we made supper and a fire outside the Shack. We had a long discussion about morals, behavior, right and wrong. We were at it all night; we never went to bed. Finally, we made breakfast and drove home.

Aldo Leopold's field trips, generally, were excursions to the Shack. My first example of what plant succession was came in the form of his description of a sandbar—how [quaking] aspen and [eastern] cottonwood seedlings got

Ruth kneeling beside Mrs. Leopold near the Leopold Shack, and getting ready to plant a pine, 1947. Photo courtesy of Hazel Hiemstra.

started in the sand, then water levels rose and set the whole process back again. We went right down to the Wisconsin River edge, right up by the Shack, and saw it.

Aldo was a superb, patient, and kind teacher with a dedication and belief in what he said. The poetic side that you see in his book must have been there all the time. I knew him as very factually oriented, but when he would talk about the life and habits of [northern bobwhite] quail [*Colinus virginianus*], he would present information on habitat and food cover of the covey in semi-prose rather than through straight facts. He had us read *The Canvasback on a Prairie Marsh* by H. Albert Hochbaum, Frank Fraser Darling's *A Herd of Red Deer: A Study in Animal Behaviour*, about deer in Scotland, and David Lack's *The Life of the Robin* on the territory of the robin, albeit the British bird, but my first introduction to the notion of territory. I think these were unusual books, and he was employing unusual teaching techniques back then, getting us to think broadly about ecology and conservation.

I had three of the finest profs I've ever had in those first couple of years at the UW: Leopold, Norman Fassett, and John Curtis.

Fassett was a character. He was fun-loving and a real good botanist. He really knew his stuff. What a sense of humor he had. When we were on one of his field trips, of which there were many, he would build a campfire, cook the meal, and then go from there. I remember that he cooked a pork chop once, and somewhere in my early photo collection, I have a black and white photo of him standing with a pork chop on the end of his stick while he recited an ode to a pork chop. What a crazy character. He was so much fun. You know, I can't remember his lectures as well as I remember his field trips.

On his field trips, he would talk all about a plant, where it lived, and fun things about the plant. He was kind of a poetic botanist. "Spring Flora," his famous spring course, which was very popular, focused on plants of the area. He was very interested in ecology, in ecological relationships, but not the kind of ecology I got from the third major influence on my academic life, John Curtis.

Curtis was the complete opposite of the other two in temperament. He was stern, taciturn, somewhat sarcastic, but absolutely marvelous as a teacher. He really knew his stuff. He taught the concept of the community. I got down on my hands and knees and learned what oak and maple forests were through quadrats and study. After the excitement of finding out what it was all about in Leopold's course, I was able to translate it all into scientific facts, ecological facts, through Curtis.

There's something important here. I think back to what my interests were and how they have pointed me toward what I'm doing now. Quite a logical thought at this point is why didn't I go into natural history study instead of ending up as an editor. But as far as I can think back, to 1949, there wasn't anything for women. I don't know whether I had a strong enough feeling that I could fend for myself in some way, but when you're down to rock bottom, what do you do? I had used up my assistantship.

Cy Kabat of the old Wisconsin Conservation Department hired me as a conservation aide, but it was at least two years before I could get a biologist rating. All of the fellows I knew were all placed. Cy kept trying to get something for me. Finally, I was classified as a biologist and became a permanent full-time employee. But there's no doubt that there was a blatant

Ruth atop vehicle examining the back teeth of a white-tailed deer for wear to estimate its age. Buzz Besadny, future DNR Secretary, to her right, takes notes. Fall 1951. Photo courtesy of Lisa Gaumnitz, Wisconsin DNR.

CHAPTER FIVE

kind of sexism that existed at the time. That's just the way it was. It was the old fashioned notion that women couldn't hack it in the field.

As far as the position of director of the Office of Endangered Species [now Bureau of Natural Heritage Conservation], which I had applied for, it was a case where I was simply a victim of the system even though that sounds melodramatic. But it was simply that; the only way I could have been hired was if the head of the Division of Resource Management had decided that the person who had transferred laterally wasn't capable of doing the job, and that just wasn't the case. Jim Hale came in at the last minute as a lateral. I was in the same classification as Jim, so I put in for a lateral transfer. But then I heard that I couldn't lateral transfer because the NRS-7 position as director of the Office of Endangered Species was in management, and my NRS-7 was in research. The starting salary was the same, but the maximum salary was $50 higher and that made it a promotion for me. I had to start with everybody else and apply for the job.

So after working 30 years for the department, I filled out an application for employment. But that's the system, and not too many people would get caught in that rather ridiculous situation. But I really didn't think too much about it and went ahead and filled out the application.

I knew some really good people would be applying, but I thought that since I had quite a bit of experience in that field, and probably more than others, that I would probably have a pretty good chance of getting it. Then at the last minute somebody else lateraled over into the position and was accepted. I don't hold it against Jim because it probably was a big career move for him, but it was kind of a shocker. The bottom kind of fell out after that. I was really disappointed because I had put a lot of thought into what I was going to do and had pages of ideas. I thought ahead a little too fast.

The reason why the endangered species and nongame programs appealed to me so much is that you are dealing with the whole breadth of programs, not just huntable and sports fishing species that most DNR research people must focus on because of federally supported projects. Now, I'm not saying I'm against hunting and fishing, but it's only a piece of the action. I'm more interested in the forest than in the ruffed grouse's place in the forest, and I'm more interested in how you can maintain a forest community than in how you can best harvest that population of ruffed grouse.

Despite it all, I am a firm believer that if a door is closed, a window is open somewhere else. I've been primarily a technical editor, editing reports by researchers. I took some journalism in graduate school. It gave me the foot in the door toward writing and editing rather than going into the field and becoming a field biologist. But it has been a happy combination of editing and biology because I'm often in the field.

I've worked with a wide variety of stuff from plants to clams, to trout, to reptiles and amphibians. I've done a considerable amount of work with the University of Wisconsin over the years. So it's been extremely varied and interesting. I'm a little restless now because I feel the job is a little too

Ruth in 1949 conducts necropsies of mice, shrews, and voles as part of her pioneering PhD study on the ecology of small mammals in the Madison area. Photo courtesy of Lisa Gaumnitz, Wisconsin DNR.

CHAPTER FIVE

restrictive relative to what I consider as extremely important in the world today, that is, the conservation of the community of organisms as a whole.

What I would really like to do is get more into the educational end of things and tell people how terrific it is out there, how they are a part of it, and how they've got to understand it.

In the early years I had no particular philosophy about the land—just a love for the outdoors. So for years I just went along happily studying and having field trips. Yes I had my faith, but it was just some sort of oblong blur out along the edge. As early as 1959, however, I became involved with the Bethel Series—a teaching program for Bible study that did many things to me as it does to many of us who seriously study the Bible for the first time.

For the first time, I began to understand what the Bible was all about, and more importantly, by understanding the concept of the land ethic, I understood what Genesis was about. So for the first time I brought together what was compartmentalized in my mind—the Genesis story of creation and my knowledge and love for the theory of evolution. These used to be in two sides of my head, and they just didn't come together. This is something I would like to help people with who have conflicts reconciling the two sides. My whole approach to the land and the development of a land ethic is firmly rooted in what the Bible tells me to do if I take the first step in believing the Bible in the first place. That first step tells me that I must be a responsible steward with no ifs, ands, or buts. So it all fits together beautifully.

AS I LOOK BACK, I can't text-proof my life, but I can see all the steps developing, and I can see at the least a little bit of a pattern. I'm not saying somebody up there is pulling the strings and leading me on, but as I look back and begin to see how I've grown and developed, I see my life pointing toward something, and I seem to think that I know where I'm pointing. I believe that the Lord is guiding my life, and I try to the best of my ability to keep open and be guided as to what it is that He wants me to do. How it will work out, I'm not sure. But little things are happening.

There are two major outlets that I have. One is Bethel Horizons, which is the camping and retreat center affiliated with Bethel Lutheran Church. I've been named its naturalist. I've finally been named a naturalist after some 30 years!

Ruth talks about prairie restoration with a natural history class at the Bethel Horizons Camp and Retreat Center near Dodgeville. May 1984. Photo by Sumner Matteson.

The other outlet is the Adult Christian Education Foundation, which has its headquarters at the Yahara Center. The foundation formed to promote the Bethel Series Bible study. I'm on their board of directors and am quite involved with that. My dream is to develop an outdoor education awareness program that would be an outgrowth of the Bethel Series and would deal with religion and environment-type issues. It has to start somewhere, and it starts very simply by taking the teachers and pastors and getting them outdoors, getting them aware of their environment, and getting them to build on the creation relationships. By creation relationships I mean the dominion concept where we are given dominion over all. This means stewardship so that each of us is given a responsibility to take care of the earth—a God-given responsibility. I feel you go from awareness to understanding, and from understanding to love. Leopold talked about love—love for the land. And you go from love to personal responsibility to action.

More recently, Leopold's writings have had more of an effect on me than anything in developing my thinking. As I look back, it's been a very slow growth toward where I think I'm going now. As a Christian, I see an audience that can be reached, and based on that, I see the idea of stewardship as something that must be taken or developed in a much broader way than it is now. I think there's a tremendous biblical base for that, and I would like to spend all my time working out ways of helping people understand that responsibility, helping them to understand the proper Judeo-Christian philosophy that is so often misinterpreted. It's not exploitation but

CHAPTER FIVE

management of resources that the Bible addresses. Now we have to develop the proper tools to get people to become good stewards.

What I "preach" is creation ecology. I list simple but major ecological concepts and then parallel those with concepts from the creation story. For example, if you start from the creation story, the world was created in an orderly fashion. That's the basis for why the world was created in seven days—to manifest orderly creation in an orderly way. If you look at ecological relationships, there are several things—succession, community, relationships—all orderly in the environment where humans have not interfered. So the parallel is logical.

☙

AS A NATURALIST, I *love* teaching, and having the opportunity to work with a group and explain to them what I see and what it means is probably the part I like the best. But I'm an eclectic ... I take up other people's ideas. I never figured myself as being necessarily a very good self-starter, but I guess I am if I get really excited about something. And boy, am I learning! For a long time I've been strictly the lecturer type. I take somebody out on a nature hike and they'll ask questions—fine. But usually I tell them this and a little bit of that, and in class, I lecture. But am I ever learning how to teach!

My Bible study class on awareness has kids crawling on their hands and knees to pick up things, put them in little envelopes, and listen and smell and taste!

Learning is a dynamic, unfinished process. So is teaching, and all of it is rooted in love. There's a statement by Leopold, something to the effect that there's no great social movement or movement of any kind that's not rooted in love. You want to advocate that you've got to love it enough to push it. You've got to love the land if you're going to do anything for the land. Leopold said, too, that it's taken us 2,000 years to just attempt to get at the human-to-human relationship. It's about time we turn to the human-to-land relationship!

☙

IT'S NOT HARD to get people excited about nature. I lead nature walks out at Bethel Horizons whenever I can. People are fascinated with what they see around them. You just have to show them a flower or have them take a hand lens and look at it, and they just love it. Sometimes I give a slide show at church. People say, "Oh I love to see the trilliums in the woods! It reminds me when I was a child back on the farm." But many don't go any further than that. So my big question is: What are the tools for leading a person from awareness to understanding? A child does not love intrinsically.

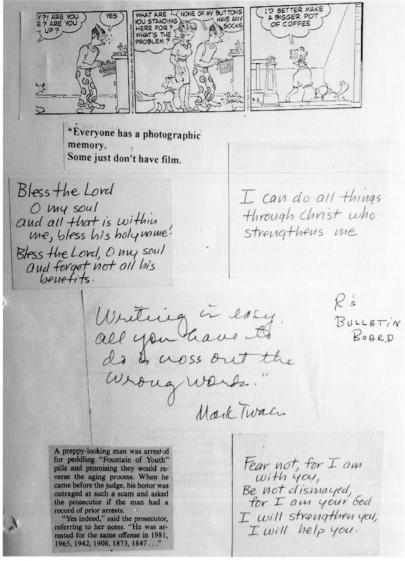

"Ruth loved puns and had a keen sense of humor," notes Hazel Hiemstra about *R's Bulletin Board*, provided courtesy of Hazel.

CHAPTER FIVE

A child is very selfish, has to be taught love, has to be taught sharing, and I think the same thing applies in our attitude toward the land. You have to learn it, learn it from other people. That's why each one of us is very important.

I have to feed people knowledge. I know that, and they learn. In my view, as you get more knowledge you begin to have love aborning. When I learned about a woodland in Curtis's plant ecology class and then went out and walked through a maple-basswood forest, I never would have had the same deep appreciation if he hadn't drilled the principles into me first. I really think you have to study and then experience nature to get that appreciation.

🍃

I'M REALLY IN THE MIDST of a learning and discovery process now, with a different attitude toward why I want to learn something, mostly because I want to transmit what I learn so badly. So it's a whole new relationship. Everything I experience outdoors now is just brighter than it has ever been.

When it comes down to specifics, what I want to do is become more involved in the molding of attitudes toward the building of an ecological conscience. I think I'm much more aware of what has been given to me, and I'm much more aware of a desire to have others understand and grow through a thorough and proper understanding of human-land relationships.

I guess you would say that ultimately my approach is grounded in a strong belief in God, with a focus on fostering a love of the land through education and hands-on experiences. If I can help others open the door to a new relationship with the land, then in some small way I feel rewarded. It is a kind of blessing! ✳

Dr. Hine passed away in Madison on February 23, 2010, and was inducted in April that year into The Wisconsin Conservation Hall of Fame to honor her nearly four decades of conservation work for the WDNR's Bureau of Research and her visionary campaign as a champion of programs to benefit the state's endangered species.[94]

AMERICAN ELM

GJK

Frances and Frederick Hamerstrom
(1907-1998) (1909-1990)

At home near Plainfield, Wisconsin, November 1980. Photo by Sumner Matteson.

BALSAM FIR

GJK

Chapter Six~
Frances and Frederick Hamerstrom

The Norse God Thor took himself a hammer and struck a stone, which produced a stream "strom." This, according to family legend, is how the Hamerstroms got their name.

—Elva Hamerstrom Paulson, *Hamerstrom Stories*

The interaction of these two personalities in long years of collaboration in a loving partnership was key, for each of them accomplished much more than either one of them could have alone.

—Helen McGavran Corneli, *Mice in the Freezer, Owls on the Porch: The Lives of Naturalists Frederick and Frances Hamerstrom*

F rances Carnes Flint Hamerstrom, born in Needham, Massachusetts, on December 17, 1907, to Laurence Bertram Flint and heiress Helen Chase Flint, didn't fit into the mold of a socialite. She failed to complete high school (Milton Academy) and college (Smith College) and was a highly paid fashion model with a passion for collecting insects when she met Frederick Nathan Hamerstrom, Jr., at a Dartmouth College house party one cool autumn evening in 1928.

Frederick, born in Trenton, New Jersey, on July 8, 1909, to Frederick Nathan Hamerstrom, Sr. and Helen Harper Davis Hamerstrom, attended Winchester High School, Dartmouth College for two years, and then graduated from Harvard College in 1931 with a bachelor's degree in English. However, he didn't fit the mold of the typical Ivy Leaguer of the times. He wanted a career in the outdoors.

Engaged on the third date, they married in secret less than three years later on February 18, 1931, then publicly on a rainy June 10, 1931.[95]

In the fall of 1931, the Hamerstroms enrolled at the Game Conservation Institute in Clinton, New Jersey, to study the artificial propagation of game birds, particularly pheasants. While there, they met, and were inspired by, Professor Aldo Leopold from the University of Wisconsin-Madison[96] and learned of fieldwork on game birds and raptors conducted by Dr. Paul Errington, director of the Cooperative Wildlife Research Unit at Iowa State College (renamed Iowa State University in 1959). A year later, in late fall, Frederick received a research fellowship from Iowa State.

For three years the Hamerstroms worked under Errington, studying the nesting of the ring-necked pheasant *(Phasianus colchicus)*, ecology of the northern bobwhite *(Colinus virginianus)*, and food habits of the great horned owl *(Bubo virginianus)* and northern harrier *(Circus hudsonius)*. Their paper (Fran's first scientific publication), co-authored with Errington, on great horned owl food habits won them the Wildlife Society's Terrestrial Publication Award in 1940.[97]

In 1935, Frederick received his master's degree and Fran her bachelor's, both in zoology, from Iowa State College. Then they headed north. From 1935 to 1937, Frederick served as project game manager of the United States Resettlement Administration in Necedah, Wisconsin. Fran, though not officially recognized as a member of the staff, supervised field technicians while performing wildlife research with her

Frederick Hamerstrom, winter of 1934-35, near Ames, Iowa. Photo courtesy of Elva Hamerstrom Paulson.

husband on the greater prairie-chicken *(Tympanuchus cupido pinnatus)*, sharp-tailed grouse *(Tympanuchus phasianellus)*, ruffed grouse *(Bonasa umbellus)*, and sandhill crane *(Antigone canadensis)*, as well as white-tailed deer, river otter, beaver, red fox, muskrat, mink, and other furbearers. They also continued their food habits study of the great horned owl.

During the fall of 1937, they began a research fellowship under Leopold and studied the ecology of prairie-chickens and sharp-tailed grouse. In 1941, Frederick received his PhD in zoology and game management. A year earlier, Fran had received her master's in game management, the only woman to receive a graduate degree under Leopold.

For the next nine years, except for a nearly three-year stint as aviation physiologist with the United States Air Corps during World War II, Frederick was the curator of the Edwin S. George Reserve at the University of Michigan's Museum of Zoology. While Frederick served during the war, Fran did her darndest to stay close to him, becoming at one point a medical technician at the U.S. Army Beaumont General Hospital in El Paso, Texas.

. Let me pause here for a moment. Little known, though mentioned in Elva Hamerstrom Paulson's *Hamerstrom Stories* (2013 Second Edition), but portrayed by writer and illustrator Lita Judge in an international award-winning picture book titled *One Thousand Tracings* (2007) was Fran's heroic role in organizing American ornitholgists to aid the families of European ornithologists and zoologists with shoes, clothing, and food—post-WWII. Lita is Elva Hamerstrom Paulson's talented daughter—the Hamerstroms' granddaughter. The book's title is taken from the tracings of feet for shoes—Fran had suggested in a January 1947 letter to German biologist Gustav Kramer that people who needed shoes send tracings of their feet. A *Committee for the Relief of European Ornitholgists* was formed, with the Hamerstroms in charge of CARE clothing/shoe packages and Dr. and Mrs. John T. Emlen in charge of food packages. By the late 1940s, over 2,300 packages had been sent to Germany, Austria, Hungary, Poland, Finland, England, France, Greece, Czechoslovakia, Italy, Yugoslavia, Rumania, and Holland.

From 1949 to 1972, the husband-wife Hamerstrom team worked as project leader and assistant leader, respectively, of the Prairie Grouse Management Research Unit for the Wisconsin Conservation Department (later Wisconsin Department of Natural Resources—DNR). Their joint field research on prairie-chickens led to a management plan for the preservation of the greater prairie-chicken in central Wisconsin through an innovative

UW grad students and friends at the Hamerstrom field headquarters in "the Pines." George Becker, Bruce Stollberg, Fran Hamerstrom, Frederick Hamerstrom, and Bob McCabe; Hancock, Wisconsin, spring 1940. Photo courtesy of Elva Hamerstrom Paulson.

emphasis on establishing a "scatter pattern" of breeding habitat in central Wisconsin. In their classic treatise, *A Guide to Prairie-chicken Management*,[98] they put it this way: "Ethologically speaking, most species will be most benefited by a scatter pattern of relatively small land parcels, rather than by an equal acreage in one solid block.... Birds distributed throughout the area in a scatter pattern are always in a position and ready to take advantage of favorable developments in neighboring habitats, such as lessened grazing pressure in the next pasture, a hay meadow left idle, etc. In the aggregate, this could be very important. Birds in one large block would have many fewer chances of finding such new habitats."

Their management guide earned them the Wildlife Society's Terrestrial Publication Award, again, in 1957 for the most original and distinguished contribution to the preservation of wildlife.

Among their several wildlife and conservation awards, they also received the Wildlife Conservation Award of the National Wildlife Federation in 1970 for distinguished service to conservation. In 1973, they earned the WDNR's Bureau of Research Award for their decades of prairie grouse studies.

After leaving the DNR in 1972, instead of abandoning their field research, the Hamerstroms expanded it. Fran continued a study of breeding northern harriers, mainly in Portage County, Wisconsin, and she and Frederick (called "Hammy" by friends and close associates) banded over 1,200 Harris's hawks *(Parabuteo unicinctus)* in south Texas and counted osprey *(Pandion haliaetus)* nests in Sonora, Mexico, during 17 winters. Regarding her harrier work, Fran and her assistants banded almost 300 adults and 650 nestlings. She discovered that food abundance influenced harrier mating systems and affected population density. Fran also initiated a long-term breeding study of American kestrels *(Falco sparverius)* using nest boxes.

Both she and Hammy lectured and wrote over 150 technical and popular articles, as well as about 140 ornithological reviews. Frederick also edited technical papers for several ornithological journals and was principal referee for *Raptor Research*, a journal on the biology and ecology of birds of prey.

Fran went on to write 12 books,[99] including three for children. *Walk When the Moon is Full* is a widely acclaimed national and international children's book. Her fourth book, *Strictly for the Chickens*, won the 1980 August Derleth Award of the Council of Wisconsin Writers.

During the course of their illustrious careers, the Hamerstroms examined almost all of the main range of the greater prairie-chicken, as well as parts of the range of the lesser and Attwater's prairie-chickens *(Tympanuchus pallidicinctus* and *Tympanuchus cupido attwateri)* in the United States, and most of the range of sharp-tailed grouse races *campestris* and *jamesi* in the United States and Canada. The range of their wildlife and ecological interests, however, was not restricted to North America. They spent summer months in Germany, Austria, Finland, Lappland, Norway, Sweden, Denmark, and Scotland, studying European grouse, continental hunting traditions and ethics, and general conservation practices. They lectured at universities and meetings of ornithological societies and were invited speakers to six International Ornithological Congresses.

Due to her flamboyant style and the popularity of her natural history books, one might overlook Fran's scientific work. She, in her own right, received notable scientific awards: the Josselyn Van Tyne Award from the American Ornithologists' Union (AOU), the Chapman Award from the American Museum of Natural History, the United Peregrine Society Conservation Award, and the Edwards Prize from the Wilson Ornithological Society. For her extensive bird research, she also received an honorary doctor of science degree (in 1961) from Carroll College in Waukesha, Wisconsin. Beginning in 1972, both Hamerstroms were adjunct professors in the College of Natural Resources at the University of Wisconsin-Stevens Point.

Fran's work with raptors reflected more than a scientific curiosity, for she held a lifelong interest in the sport of falconry, and she and Hammy

Fran playfully posing with an eastern foxsnake *(Pantherophis vulpinus)* along the banks of the Wisconsin River, 1958. Photo courtesy of Elva Hamerstrom Paulson.

helped to legalize falconry in the United States and Wisconsin.[100] Fran was only 12 when she successfully flew a kestrel in falconry. Many years later she helped pioneer the artificial insemination of golden eagles *(Aquila chrysaetos)*. Close to several falconers throughout her life, she maintained memberships in the Wisconsin Falconers Association, North American Falconers Association, Great Lakes Falconers Association, and the British Falconers Association.

An early supporter of the Raptor Research Foundation (RRF), she served as its central director during 1975–'76, and she received the Foundation's President's Award in 1980 for "exceptional service" to RRF. In 1990, the RRF established an award in the Hamerstrom name to recognize outstanding contributions to raptor ecology and natural history.

Among the many positions held, both Hamerstroms served as presidents of the Wisconsin Society for Ornithology, co-vice presidents for science with the Wisconsin Academy of Science, Arts, and Letters, and directors of the Citizens Natural Resources Association.

In 1996, they were inducted into the Wisconsin Conservation Hall of Fame.[101]

In addition to their myriad of duties as wildlife biologists, the Hamerstroms raised two children, son Alan, born in 1940, and daughter Elva, born in

1943. Alan became a successful yacht salesman in Maryland and Elva a distinguished Oregon wildlife artist, who illustrated several of Fran's books.

Finally, the Hamerstroms took into their Plainfield homes over 100 students in a time-honored European tradition of teaching aspiring apprentices, in this case field biologists, not only about rigorous scientific field techniques but about the finer aspects of social etiquette and appreciation for the arts. These apprentices were known affectionately as "gabboons," meaning those who performed the lowest menial form of labor. Fran or Hammy performed the role of disciplinarian and did not hesitate to correct, sometimes abrasively, any misdeed, the memory of which for the offender might later be tempered by one of Fran's wild game (or roadkill) dinners, topped off by one of her treasured homemade pies.

"It's rather like the old apprentice system," Fran told me. "People come and work for little or nothing. Some people pay to work for us, and they get magnificent training, but we're very hard on them. It's a rough go. They're up sooner than 4:00 a.m. Of course, 4:00 is late compared to when we were getting up during 'booming season.' We were often up at 2:30.

"We usually have two gabboons with us during the summer and have had as many as four. Then there are the weekend warriors—people that come in and help us for a short time. It gives us the chance to see whether these people are good gabboon material. It's said that the word gabboon came from an under privileged African tribe enslaved by a more powerful tribe

Fran briefing "boomers," ca. 1954. Photo by Robert T. "Buz" Holland.
Photo courtesy of Elva Hamerstrom Paulson.

CHAPTER SIX

"Boomers Plus"—**Back row:** Frederick Hamerstrom Jr., Os Mattson, Fred Greeley, Dan Thompson. **Middle row:** Gustav Kramer, Frances Hamerstrom, unknown, John Emlen, Ruth Hine, Cy Kabat, Joe Hickey. **Front row:** May Bea Jorgensen in front of Elva Hamerstrom, Alan Hamerstrom, and Bob McCabe (squatting), who added cutout of himself to the photo. Photo by Robert McCabe, ca. 1950. Photo courtesy of Elva Hamerstrom Paulson.

and forced to do all the dirty work while receiving almost no food. Actually, we feed our gabboons very well and try to give them training in whatever they most need. So we're probably not being totally true to tradition. On the East Coast, they're called 'boobies.'"

I interviewed the Hamerstroms at their two-story farmhouse on November 15, 1980, and again on August 3 and 4, 1981. At that time, they had lived in their Waushara County home for over 30 years, and during those years, over 7,000 people (nicknamed "boomers" after the booming sounds the male prairie-chicken makes during courtship in early spring) had stayed with them at one time or another to assist with prairie-chicken observations.

The account and interview below are written in the present tense in an attempt to capture a feel of the times, as well as something of the marvelously infectious Hamerstrom spirit.

The Hamerstroms live simply. Their water is hand pumped from a well, and they heat their 120-year-old home with four cast-iron stoves. On the day of my November visit, a huge conical pile of oak lies split and aging in the bright sun. Adjacent to the farmhouse entrance, a three-seat privy sits about 30 yards west of the house, and an old red barn, a temporary home for injured raptors, stands about 75 yards further south. To its west is a long rectangular machine shed that has one end partitioned off with wire screening. Here, Ricardo, a mentally impaired great horned owl, lives quietly. The faint staccato of typing and the acrid smell of burnt oak greet me.

Fran, medium height with reddish shoulder-length hair, dressed in red-wine colored slacks and a red plaid cotton shirt, welcomes her guest in an assertive Bostonian voice and says that she is working on a paper with University of Wisconsin graduate student Charlie Burke, who continues to type in an adjoining room.

Soon, Frederick emerges from the dining room and greets me courteously in a soft baritone. He has a full shock of wavy snow-white hair and a thick mustache and beard to match. His large face, broad shoulders, and stocky build momentarily bring to mind the countenance of a Confederate Civil War general, but chestnut-brown corduroy trousers, blue denim shirt with red hand-embroidered loops on the shoulders, and especially a prominent turquoise necklace dispel the thought. Both Hamerstroms exhibit a fondness for turquoise. They both wear turquoise rings; one that Fran has is a present from Aldo Leopold. Fran also wears a turquoise bracelet given to her by Frederick to replace a wedding ring worn out after years of manual labor.

Paintings, almost all done by friends or relatives in pen and ink, watercolors, oil, and acrylics, each with a memorable story behind it, many of birds of prey, hang on the walls of almost every room in the house. In the "train room" upstairs, an entire painted wall depicts a pastoral scene of bluffs, sky, river, and lake. The scene was a backdrop for a toy train town complete with hills made of paper mâché and rock that Alan, the Hamerstrom's son, built using the entire expanse of the 10 x 15-foot room for his setting.

And there are watercolors by Fran, mostly on the stairway between the first and second floors. Three watercolors are particularly striking: a dungeon at Flint (Fran's family name) Castle in northern Wales, a spectacular prairie fire in central Wisconsin, and a prairie scene (painted in acrylic with wall paint used for the sky) of a peregrine falcon stooping a prairie-chicken.

Another of her watercolors of a Finnish landscape brings forth an amicable story from Fran. "In 1958 we attended the International Ornithological Congress in Helsinki and afterward went across northern Lappland with a Finnish guide, a German, and a Swiss. We followed a route taken by scores of Lapps and thousands of reindeer. We traveled in the most improbable manner; we took a taxi. It was the cheapest way to travel. Hammy and I had wanted to get acquainted with the Lapps, but the guide said, 'These are very shy people. You can't get anywhere near them; it's hopeless so just forget it.'

I said, 'All right. Just leave us here and come back in a few hours.'

"So the guide dumped us, and I sat on a rock with my back to the Lapp encampment and started painting mountains. Well, first the children came out of the tents. Next came the women. The men stayed in the longest. Such a shy, wild people. Finally, the children came up to see what I was doing, and one of them wanted me to paint his mother. He communicated this to me in sign language. So I painted her. Gradually, the women came up, the men came out, and I went down into the encampment. Soon everyone started doing their own thing. The women were scraping hides, so Hammy decided that he would help them. Well, everyone thought that this was the funniest thing they'd ever seen because that was women's work! They just shrieked with laughter anytime he did anything. When our guide came back, the Lapps were all in a huddle, and in the middle were the two Hamerstroms!"

There seems to be a story behind everything the Hamerstroms own. Their standing floor lamps throughout the house are no exception. When they decided to put in electricity in 1949, Fran went to a second-hand store and "took each floor lamp and rocked it back and forth to see which ones were steady enough so if an owl sat on the lampshade, it wouldn't tip over. Well, the clerk didn't ask me any questions. He had never seen anyone examine lamps in this strange way before. But then when Hammy walked in and started to do the same, he didn't know what to do! All of the Hamerstroms' lamps have solid bases; they seldom tip over!"

FRAN AND FREDERICK lead me into the dining room where Hammy stokes a wood stove before sitting down at an oval-shaped walnut table. To my surprise, a great horned owl peers in through a glass window above a door to a screened-in porch on the east side of the house. This is my first view of Porfirio, the Hamerstroms' highly respected trapping owl used by

Hammy holding Porfirio behind Plainfield home, ca. 1985. Photo by Ilse Dietsche.
Photo courtesy of Elva Hamerstrom Paulson.

Fran to provoke an attack by a territorial harrier (on her northern harrier study area), which flies into a net suspended between two poles over Porfirio's head.

The Hamerstroms had made no mention of the owl before, as if it is as familiar as a house cat.

Throughout our discussion, Porfirio either flies back and forth between perches or peers through the window to follow human movements.

From time to time, Hammy rises to throw another log onto the fire, and he or Fran occasionally leave for a short while to go over something with Charlie Burke.

Throughout our interview, both Hamerstroms take special care to acknowledge the accomplishments of the other, demonstrating a respect that has solidified their marriage and careers. Fran begins.

FRAN: My father was an international criminologist, so I lived in seven countries before I was seven years old. I spoke three languages and two dialects and was expected to speak them all correctly. I had gone to Europe at the age of three and came back to the United States at age seven expecting all children to be learning the same things that I had been learning. They had other skills, like chewing gum!

One of my earliest natural history experiences involved a dead blue jay. I was seven at the time. We lived in Brookline, a suburb of Boston, and the boy next door decided to give the blue jay a funeral. So we brought out a little express wagon, and he had my brother Bertram and me heap flowers on the express wagon. Then we went up the hill on my grandmother's property and buried the blue jay, sang hymns like "Eternal Father, Strong to Save," put a cross up, and went away.

Even though I was just a little thing, I wanted to see the insides of that blue jay. So after this was all over and the boy next door had gone home, I kept wondering, "Does a blue jay have a heart, have a liver, have lungs?"

So I dug up the blue jay. I think I've been like that all of my life as far as having to find out certain things. Once in Dresden, Germany, when I was five, there was a hare in a fenced-in garden that I wanted to have as a pet. So I got my nurse and brother to scare the hare. I hand-grabbed it as it came out through the gate, took it upstairs, then went down to the kitchen and got the cook to give me some spinach leaves. But the hare jumped out the window, and I never saw it again.

I've always wanted to live with living animals; that's why I have an ethological bent.

FREDERICK: My earliest outdoors memory, which probably had more of an influence than I realized at the time, was walking with my grandfather along Darby Creek near Philadelphia. It was a place he was very fond of that had a wooded creek bottom. He enjoyed the birds there. I knew nothing about birds at the time, but because he had a special feeling for the woods, he gave it to me. These walks occurred over a period of a few years when I was younger than 10. At age 10, we moved to New England from New Jersey, so such walks were no longer possible. I did not become a bird-watcher, however, and never have. I became involved with birds through hunting and fishing.

In New England, I placed quite a bit of importance on exploring nature, and my parents were very much in favor of the idea. We were living in Winchester, Massachusetts, outside of Boston, for a number of years, and there is a very fine parkway system there called the Middlesex Fells. It had a number of roads that were used by people, mainly for Sunday driving. But it also had a fairly large chunk of wild land. In winter I would go off all day and knock around on snowshoes. My parents thought this was great because I was getting outdoors and staying out of mischief.

FRAN: My parents were very much against the idea of me getting out. They didn't want me to have anything to do with creepy crawly animals. When I was 11 years old, however, I had bird and mammal specimens in the National Museum. Those people didn't know that it was just a little girl sending in specimens. I hid some guns secretly so that I could continue to collect specimens. I had a BB gun, then a .22, and then a 20-gauge shotgun.

You see, I was raised very strictly. I had a governess and tutors and rather powerful parents, aunts, and grandmothers. They all tried to force this little girl to have the proper skills of a real lady so that she could become an international hostess and play the piano. I had lessons in almost everything: walking, talking, dancing, tennis, horseback riding, skiing, lace making, knitting. You name it—there were lessons. I couldn't go out and do just anything; there always had to be a lesson. And so I pursued my real interests in secret. I climbed out of my window and slept in the woods at night and got back with my specimens in time to be awakened in the morning.

At what age did I start doing this? Eight. I continued it all of the time while living under my parents' roof. I kept the guns underneath the stables. I remember that my governess was much upset one day. She went to my father, and she said, "Mr. Flint, I feel that I should tell you something. Frances appears to be eating cold cream!" And so I was called onto the carpet.

What I was doing was taking the cold cream to grease my guns so that they wouldn't rust. I knew that they needed some kind of oil. And they thought that I was eating it! So I kept taking my punishment for eating cold cream. I didn't mind as long as they didn't find out I had a gun!

FREDERICK (smiling): You'll find her the much more interesting storyteller.

FRAN: Why did I have such a keen interest in the natural world? I can't say. I just know that I seized every opportunity to do anything with animals.

FREDERICK: Leopold was interested in that question. He would ask, "How did your interest start? Why are you here?"

FRAN: Roger Tory Peterson once asked me, "Why is it that you, Fran Hamerstrom, an attractive girl, are so passionately interested in the outdoors and animals?" I couldn't answer, but I didn't mind having him point out that I was attractive!

I came from an unhappy household. I didn't feel close to either of my parents. My three brothers were younger. I felt very alone as a child and didn't trust anybody. I didn't expect to trust anybody; then I met him. I didn't have many friends. I had a fair number among the boys. I played football, climbed trees. I did all of the tomboy things. Those were the kinds of relationships I had. But as for intimate friends or confidants—none.

I didn't respect my father because he had tantrums, and he wasn't fair. I thought that my mother was weak because once I was accused of telling a lie and she knew that I hadn't; she didn't stand up for me. So with that absolute judgment that a child makes, I said I couldn't trust either of them.

I think that it was very good that I lived a double life. I think that I would have had a nervous breakdown and been a cowed little creature otherwise. I had to swing one way or the other with that type of pressure. It was a beastly childhood. I wouldn't be a child again for anything under the sun. But I had a wonderful governess. She didn't have a deep interest in natural history, but she was a tolerant person, and she taught me good work habits.

And I have been lucky. There were some important influences in my life. Charles Johnson of the Boston Museum of Natural History had a profound influence on me. I had a very good insect collection, especially one of parasitic wasps. Johnson had a perfect understanding of me. He knew that this little girl knew how to handle specimens and could key a lot out. I had two long braids, and I'd go into his office, and he'd tie my braids so that they wouldn't fall into the insect trays, and then I could go anywhere and look at any specimen. He trusted me. I used to think how could I honorably get a toothache so that I could get brought to the dentist because the dentist's office was near the museum.

So I took a pencil and twisted it around in my gums and tried to get my gums all swollen so I could go to the museum by way of the dentist's office. This occurred between the ages of 8 and 12.

🍃

FRAN: MY FATHER WOULDN'T LET ME go to Cornell, which was strong in my field. He thought that I was boy-crazy and that I shouldn't go to a school where there were men. He insisted that I go to Smith College.

But Smith wasn't the place for me. Charles Johnson came out when he was an old man and argued with my father, which takes a great deal of courage; my father was known as the "fire-eater." He begged my father to let me go to Cornell, where I would develop and get the great teachers, but my father wouldn't let me go. He wanted me to marry an ambassador or something like that and be an international hostess. This had been the family tradition. We were a very cosmopolitan family and widely traveled. They didn't want me to go off into the country and do all these bizarre things.

So I spent two years at Smith taking the courses that I wanted to take, going to most of the proms up and down the East Coast, and I was doing a little hunting, keeping up my collections. I continued to collect insects and birds for a museum. No specimens went to Smith; I had other contacts.

FREDERICK: My father was a businessman. He never understood how we chose this sort of life, but he was an unusual sort of businessman. He would take on an ailing company, become a member of the board, get the company back on its feet again, and when that was done, he'd find another one. He was a hardworking Norwegian.

My mother's people were British. My paternal grandmother and grandfather also were Norwegian.

I don't know the family history very far back because my grandfather came over as a young man dissatisfied with the Old World. According to the rules of primogeniture, which still apply in some places, only the eldest son could take the family name. All the rest are "son." As a younger son, his inheritance was one gold watch—no family name, none of the land—and so he said, "To hell with this business." My grandfather took the watch, nailed it to the wall and said, "I'm going to the New World with a new name." So he took the family name Hammerstrom and chopped out one of the middle m's.

When my father came along and became curious about things, he asked my grandfather where we came from, and my grandfather simply told my father, "I have cut all ties!" So when I was born and later asked the same question, my father said, "My father told me nothing. That's good enough for me, and if that's good enough for me, it's good enough for you!" Fran's people have been in this country for 300 years.

FRAN: Yes. All my blood is from the British Isles. I am happy to say my children have more mixed blood!

FREDERICK: Our parents were difficult at times. They weren't pleased with our decision to get married. We had no idea that either one of us was interested in anything to do with the outdoors.

FRAN: It was priceless! We both knew the first time we met that this was it. It was like an irreversible chemical reaction, but we didn't know what the other one thought. I finally confessed to him that I had an insect collection. I thought that he might not like that, and he said, "Lay off that insect stuff! We're going to work on game animals!"

FREDERICK: When we decided to get married after the third date, and both sets of parents and both sets of friends knew, everybody said, "This can't be! Don't do it!"

FRAN: He had no future, you see. My father called him "that whippersnapper" or "that nincompoop," and his side said I was a butterfly, a useless doll, and would never do anything.

FREDERICK: Well, I didn't become aware that the scientific life was what I wanted to pursue until quite far along. It came to a showdown when I was a senior in college. We were married commencement week so that as graduation approached, I had to figure out what to do next. We both realized that we didn't want the standard "go into the city and work in the bank" type of job. We wanted something to do with the outdoors but didn't know exactly what it was. So we decided to go to the Game Conservation Institute to learn how to raise game. It was run by More Game Birds, the forerunner to Ducks Unlimited.

In those days, the idea was that you raised upland game on game farms and turned them loose. The fish and game movement started out with the idea of restocking game farm birds, so we went to learn how to do that. While there, we learned of a job as graduate students with Professor Paul Errington at Iowa State College.

We had never known that there was such a thing as a graduate fellowship. The only graduate students we'd ever known were fellows at Harvard and Princeton whose fathers were presidents of big companies. The scenario was something like this: Junior was coming along, and father realizes that Junior is still pretty green, and he doesn't want to bring him right into the company into a big position that he's going to inherit. Father doesn't know what the devil to do with this character, so he sends him back to school for a few more years. Those were the only kind of graduate students we knew.

The idea that there was such a thing as a graduate assistantship that actually paid money so you could stay alive and study was a brand new idea. It was the most wonderful thing that we had ever heard of, so we jumped at it.

Iowa State College was the first institution with a Cooperative Wildlife Research Unit, and I was the second graduate student in the program. Logan J. Bennett, who studied blue-winged teal, was the first. That's where we really began our formal entry into the wildlife field.

My first assignment was to find out where and how many pheasants were nesting. But they had a regulation: no nepotism. Only one member of the family may be on the payroll, so they would not pay Fran. This was in 1932. They would not put Fran on as an official, formal employee, but they paid me an extra $15 a month expecting—clearly understood but not in writing—that she was to work full-time, too. So we had the princely sum of $90 a month to live on. It wasn't so bad. When we got to Wisconsin, we got $50 a month!

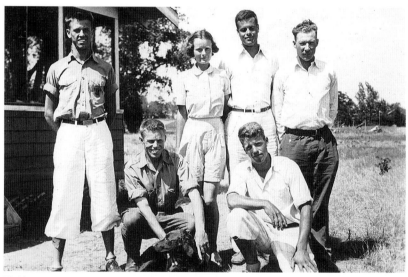

Field crew at the Ruthven Summer Station, Iowa; July 4, 1933. Fran and Hammy stand next to Prof. Paul Errington. Photo courtesy of Elva Hamerstrom Paulson.

In Iowa, we worked primarily on pheasant nesting. Errington, seeing that we were eager and interested, also had us studying the food habits of raptors, great horned owls and harriers, and in winter he put us on his quail census. So we had a good deal to do in addition to the pheasant assignment, which, of course, meant much broader training. We were happy to have this because the pheasant training was the least interesting of all.

CHAPTER SIX

FRAN (turning to Frederick): Would you care to tell the story of when you were caught reading the *Saturday Evening Post*?

FREDERICK: Ah, yes. Iowa in summer is pretty damn hot, and looking for pheasant nests in the middle of the day with that Iowa sun pounding down got to be pretty grim. So we had the brilliant thought: Let's get up early and do most of the fieldwork while it's still cool and then do as the Mexicans and the people of South America do in the heat of the day, knock off, and then go out again in the evening. As far as hours were concerned, we were working considerably more than the standard eight-hour day, but it started a lot earlier than was required of us.

One day during this siesta time, I was reading the *Saturday Evening Post*. Paul had been away on assignment. But he came back, found me reading the *Saturday Evening Post* at twelve o'clock in the middle of the day, and blew a gasket!

FRAN: He wasn't working! Errington, wonderful man that he was, was an absolute slave driver; there's always work to be done! It wasn't a matter of hours.

FREDERICK: He made it very clear that this was not proper procedure. We explained what we were up to, and one of the fascinating things about Paul was that he was always looking, always listening, always thinking. We explained the situation and "that it was too damn hot out there, Paul, at twelve o'clock, and it was a lot cooler at five o'clock in the morning, and we started at five o'clock and not at eight o'clock."

He said, "Well, I guess that's not such a bad idea." So he came around when presented with the evidence.

From the start, the Iowa program was shakily established. Jay N. "Ding" Darling had put his money into it to start the thing off, but the original three-year program was coming to an end, and we weren't sure that arrangements were going to be made to continue it. This was an experiment, the first of its kind. So, at the end of our three years, we didn't know what was going to happen, and I took a job as project game manager with the Resettlement Administration, which brought us to Necedah, Wisconsin.

The Resettlement Administration was one of the New Deal fiascos. The idea was: Here are all of these poor people in rural slums—slums aren't limited to the city—and so good old Uncle Sam was going to find them, buy up their farms, give them a little money, and move them to a place where they would have a much better shake. As a sociological dream, it was lovely.

But, hell and damnation, part of that Necedah country had been selected earlier as a place to move people into! And when they started drawing boundaries around the rest of it that was poor, they figured that they'd draw the boundary around everything.

So the place where people were supposed to go became the place they had to vacate, and they moved them out. Well, we know that in some cases families went back. One fellow, in particular, someone that I got to know better than the rest, was on the boundary and was not essential to the project. Well, Resettlement put the squeeze on him, as they did the others, and told him that he didn't have to sell, but if he didn't, the roads were going to be closed, everyone was going to be moved out, and the schools would be closed. That got to most of them. But this fellow, because he was on the edge, said, "I don't give a damn what you do."

But his wife became ill with cancer, so he came to me one day and said, "I am ready to sell, but on one condition: I will sell only to you. I will give you first chance because I know you want this farm, but I must get the money within 30 days because I've got to get my wife to the Mayo Clinic. If you can't pay me within 30 days, I will take it to somebody else who will."

I sent the request along to the land buyers with the whole story that the man must have the money within 30 days. I said, "If you can't give it to him, tell him." Well, the Resettlement folks were all so keen to straighten the boundary edge that they promised him the money in 30 days. But they knew damn well they couldn't get it to him for a year. And he didn't get it for a year. That's the sort of thing that makes us bitter about Resettlement.

We stayed in Necedah for a short period of time, until we had enough money to go down to Madison to become Aldo Leopold's students.

FRAN: Another thing about that Necedah experience. We learned that a farming community could well be interspersed among wild lands. We realized that a very nice balance had been worked out. For sure, a great many of the families were poor, but so had the city folk been poor. But there had been a relationship between those farms and the countryside; this was being destroyed. It had taken years to build. People had found their niche, and the government was destroying the whole thing. We realized that there was something very wrong there, so we almost wrote a hard article for the *Saturday Evening Post*. But Aldo Leopold said, "Don't get involved in politics. Stick to your wildlife at this stage in your lives." I think he was probably wise. We might have become activists too soon as so many people are these days. They don't have the background and the wisdom to know which bandwagon to choose. I think he did well to hold us back.

FREDERICK: Then there was the practical question in his mind that we didn't know enough about, and that was if you attacked the federal government and the state wildlife people, you've cut off all the jobs there are. So he advised us that this sort of criticism comes later, not now. The best use of the land that was to be vacated was for wildlife; wildlife always gets the second shot. So I served as the game manager at Necedah. Remember, there wasn't any women's lib back in those days. The Resettlement Administration wouldn't allow Fran on the payroll.

Ordinarily, in the federal service a woman couldn't even ride in a government car. That's just the way things were. You'd get into pretty serious trouble if you had an unauthorized female in a government car, and the chance of getting one authorized was just about zero.

FRAN: I described this to a young woman biologist who was working here, and I told her how Hammy had made arrangements so that I could work on that federal project for two years full-time without salary and how lucky I felt just to work with him. She replied, "Well, I guess you didn't know any better." But there was no alternative! I did it, felt lucky, and eventually became a professional. I worked a good many years without a salary to get there. I realized that I had to go to school and get the labels or else I just would have become a tag-along wife. That was hard because I had flunked out of Smith. When we got to Iowa, I was so afraid that he wouldn't love me if I flunked out of Iowa, too. I was very unsure of my ability to put up with the school discipline and study things I hated including all of the prerequisites that one had to take. But I straightened out and got good grades.

FREDERICK: At Necedah, despite the fact that there could be no official recognition, Fran was given permission not only to ride in the car but actually to direct some men. None of this appeared in writing anywhere. So at any moment it could be denied. If somebody higher up in the echelon got the word, he would simply say, "Well, I know nothing about this. I know that it's improper, and of course, I'll put a stop to it at once." They wouldn't even allow us to publish together. I could acknowledge her help, but I couldn't put her name on the paper. We got her name on one paper on great horned owl food habits because she had directed two boys named Os Mattson and Bud Truax. Mattson and Fran published the paper, and that was considered all right, but she could not appear as a co-author with me.

This is the original photo of Aldo Leopold with Hammy and Fran. (The cropped photo is on the back cover of AFIELD.) The original photo, taken by Robert McCabe in central Wisconsin around 1939, includes an unidentified woman (Ruth Durgin?). Photo courtesy of Elva Hamerstrom Paulson and the Aldo Leopold Foundation.

FRAN: He has never gotten over this injustice!

FREDERICK: I was mad as hell.

FRAN: You should be here when a paper is about to be co-authored by the Hamerstroms! Our house guests sit and tremble. There is a fight going for days about senior authorship, and people sit in shocked amazement. Then they listen to the words: "Darling, you should be a senior author! You did most of the work!"

"No, you be senior author; you had the idea." We've just finished one of those fights. We'd fight and fight. We're co-authoring a paper with Charlie Burke who's in the other room typing.

FREDERICK: I'm a third author. I wouldn't know how to do this any other way now. I just write the paper, send it off, and say, "To hell with you buster."

FRAN: Before I forget to mention him, one person that influenced me profoundly in Necedah was Jimmie Blake, a half-breed Indian. He knew the outdoors in a way that I never had the opportunity to know it. Working in the field with him I learned an enormous amount. We went hunting

CHAPTER SIX

together, we did fieldwork together, and he could see much more than I could. In addition to seeing muskrat tracks, he knew what the muskrat was doing. I had never been exposed to anyone like him before, with that degree of sophistication. He was so utterly tuned in, and working with him I realized I was getting a whole new set of skills and appreciation.

FREDERICK: We were very close to Leopold, too. He had an arrangement whereby if you wished to become one of his students, you had to get his approval. Nobody had any scholarship the first year; you came strictly on your own. If he figured you could hack it, he would try to scrounge up some money from somewhere, but there was never any guarantee of success. There was no nicely funded system in operation. His department was brand new. The money that came to his students came from the Wisconsin Alumni Research Foundation or some private source.

When Leopold accepted us, our research headquarters was up here about eight miles from this Plainfield house. We used our car because prairie-chicken research required a lot of automobile travel. For instance, we had to check a 30-mile trap line twice a day. We only went down to Madison for seminars and periodic consultations with Leopold. We had $50 a month for our food, shelter, mileage, and everything else we wanted to splurge on.

Leopold had a wonderful relationship with his students. He'd come up and stay in these abandoned farmhouses, and we'd sit outside if it was warm enough, otherwise around the stove. We'd develop ideas. Leopold

The Hamerstrom Wisconsin home, originally known as "The Walker Place," built by the first judge of Waushara County and shown here in 1960 before Dutch elm disease wiped out the elms planted by Judge Walker. Photo courtesy of Elva Hamerstrom Paulson.

formulated his "land ethic" and was writing *A Sand County Almanac* while we were his students. He gave us a lot of his time. He'd come up every autumn and go hunting with us.

FRAN: Leopold was superb. He knew how to reduce concepts to simple principles, and he knew how to communicate. All of his students had to write, give public talks, and give radio talks; we couldn't get by only doing good biological work. I got my master's under Leopold. I was the only woman who ever got a degree under him. He never held my sex against me. Errington never did either, but the majority did in those days.

Leopold was the one who could pull everything together and see it as if from the top of a mountain. He could learn from anybody. That's one of the things that I learned from him: you can learn from anybody and any animal.

FREDERICK: We were Leopold's students until February 1941. We were on campus one year and were up here working on the Leola Marsh, rather than on the Buena Vista Marsh, for two years. By this time [1941], we had been married for 10 years and decided that if we were going to have children, now was the time or we'd write it off.

When our son Alan was born, $50 a month began to get a little skimpy. The prairie-chicken thesis work was done, and we decided that we'd have to get a job. So we went off to Michigan, to the University of Michigan, where I was curator of the Edwin S. George Reserve. The George Reserve was set up and advertised as an undisturbed natural area where it would be possible for people to study short-term and long-term, but most particularly where you could start a long-term study with the assurance that there would be no disturbance to the land. Natural succession proceeded undisturbed. That was great. Only, the University of Michigan treasured a benefactor, Colonel George, who had given the land in the first place. He had retained 40 acres of land in the center, and this was his land where he had his country house. All the rest belonged to the university.

Colonel George had the right in the deed of grant to enjoy the rest of the land. This meant that he could ride horseback over it, which he was very fond of doing. This horseback riding involved a little bit of trail cutting that wasn't particularly serious. But he had some pretty grand ideas about how and in what shape he wanted to leave the property when he finally kicked off. The fact that it wasn't his anymore and was supposed to be a natural area—well, he knew better. He brought in a dragline and dredged a ditch all the way around the edge of a hardwood swamp because he thought that open water would be nice. Of course, it bollixed up the swamp on which George Sutton had a 20-year study.

Then, the colonel thought it would be nice if visiting scientists could simply fly into the reserve and land there. So he built a small-plane airstrip on the central plateau and around the edge of it a trotting track for racehorses. The racetrack and airstrip were on Walter Howard's small mammal census plot! Then the old boy thought that the tamarack swamp down in the southeast corner could be improved by throwing up a dike and digging in another pond. Most of this had been going while I was away in the Air Corps [during World War II].

When we got back and found out how things were going, I went to one of the regents that I knew and said, "Look, this can't continue. You know what the reserve is supposed to be; what's happening here is wrong."

He said, "I'll see what I can do."

Finally, the word came back, "Hands off!"

I bitterly regret that a university as fine as the University of Michigan allowed these things to go on. Nobody ever denied what was happening. They simply said, "Just think of what we can do with all that money." It was a disgraceful situation, and I resigned.

At the time I resigned, I didn't know where the next job was going to come from. We were hoping to go back to Wisconsin to work on prairie-chickens for the Conservation Department, but nothing came through, and there were obstacles to our returning. So we went to Europe. It was right after the war, and we were among the first to go to Germany without military government auspices, which meant we were not allowed to go to the PX or ride the government-sponsored trains. We traveled third class with its broken windows.

When we were hungry, we went down to the store without any ration stamps and bought food, but doing all of this had its advantages. We didn't have to be, nor did we want to be, tied into the military government lecture circuit. Those poor devils; every minute was programmed. They were handed their tickets and told to be at the station at such and such an hour, that they would be met and have dinner with so and so, and that their lectures would be at so and so.

People were very much astonished. They called us the "free Americans."

That trip lasted about a month, and when we came back, we made a tour of potential jobs. We were very much interested in going to either North Dakota to work on prairie-chickens under Roy Bach, an able fellow, or to Montana to work on sharp-tailed grouse. Montana told us that they would be glad to hire us both, but there was a catch: "Fran could work in the field, only there would be a little problem," they said. "Officially (indignation in his voice), we'll have to take her on as a secretary and not as a field biologist, since she's a female."

It was a rather amusing potential scenario: the secretary caught out in the field with her husband, and some legislator saying, "What is some secretary doing out here?"

So we said, "To hell with this business."

In 1949, we went to Manitoba where I was practically offered the job of Chief Naturalist, but things were still a little sticky for females. She would not have been permitted to come with me into places like the far north. Well, that just wouldn't do. Then we heard that the Wisconsin program had shaped up, and since this was the one we wanted, we were most happy to come back here and pick up the prairie-chicken and sharp-tailed grouse work we had left some years before.

As biologists for the DNR, we worked on the breeding biology of the prairie-chicken and sharp-tailed grouse, trying to identify and protect their habitat. But we quit after the work was done; we didn't retire. We quit rather than retire because of union foolishness. We were told that we would be subject to disciplinary action if we worked more than five days a week, eight hours a day. Try to tell that to prairie-chickens, who are on display seven days a week for eight to ten weeks. So when the department said, "Now that the prairie-chicken work is finished, we're going to transfer you to some other operation," we quit. We hoped by quitting they'd say, "Well, maybe this isn't such a good system after all." It was wasted because now the [work] requirement is essentially overlooked.

We've been freelancing since we quit the department, but we've continued with wildlife research on our own including Fran's breeding study of the harrier here, and Fran has her writing. We're publishing technical papers, Fran is writing popular books, we're doing field research, and I'm editing other people's manuscripts. We're just as involved as we ever were.

FRAN: I married my editor! He does marvelous popular writing and conservation writing, but he doesn't do it often. He'd rather help other people. I can't do a thing with him!

FREDERICK: There's no point in being here just for a free ride. There's no point—and this may be an unkind thing to say—in being an ice cream salesman just living to make money, watch TV, play golf, and go to the movies. You might as well not be here if that's all there is. Research is adventure; you're moving into something unknown, and that's a good bit of the fascination of it after all. You're not following steps that have already been laid out. You find out what the steps are.

FRAN: I think we both have the same attitude. It's a combination of adventure and public service. It's a hard-to-beat combination. Paul Errington set a tremendous example. He was such a dedicated person, and he never told us what to think. During that period, we both caught the spirit of public service, and once having caught that spirit, it has never left us.

Some people tell us: "You're the most deeply religious people we've ever met!" Well, we want to leave the world a better place than we found it.

I think that the real land ethic that we need to consider is: What are we leaving to our children? People must learn to look farther ahead. I try to look 300 years ahead in my thinking. I think that a long-time viewpoint is essential. But this isn't taught anywhere. It's not taught in the schools and in the churches.

I'm a natural optimist. Furthermore, it's part of my moral code that you don't get defeated.

🖋

I am a baby boomer, born in 1953, and that makes me part of a very unusual cohort. Not since Adam met Eve and gave birth to Cain and Abel has any generation been able to say what I and my fellow baby boomers can say: the population of the world doubled in our lifetimes.

—Thomas Friedman, *Thank You for Being Late*.[102]

FRAN: I THINK THE GREATEST HAZARD we face is overpopulation. I feel very deeply about this. I think that we have got to learn not to overpopulate the world. We decided that in 1935 the world was overcrowded and to have only two children. I keep trying to get in my two-bits worth on such matters. I'll walk right up to a pregnant woman with two babies in the laundromat and ask her if she knows about birth control. I do everything I can. I try to get in the overpopulation message in everything I write. I slide in the needle. I think that we should say, "You want food? Okay, get sterilized. Your whole family gets sterilized, and we will feed you for a given length of time." I think that we have got to be hard right now because it's kind in the long run both to our earth and to people.

To put it simply, I may be driving through a marsh with a duck hunter, and I'll say: "See that marsh? If the Hamerstroms had one more child, it might have been drained." That simplifies it so he can understand.

Furthermore, we must have smaller land units, then people get more intimately involved with them. Smaller land units would be much healthier. You wouldn't have the pest problems that you encounter with stands or rows of monotypic crops, and you wouldn't have an increasing reliance on herbicides and pesticides to prevent disease and losses. The government is subsidizing big agribusiness instead of encouraging small family units of farmland. And if a crop fails, the government bails them out.

FREDERICK: The proportion of people living on the land to people living in the city has so drastically changed now. Such a whacking big chunk of our total population is now city, and these city people have theoretical knowledge, but they don't have practical knowledge. Even if they have first-rate practical knowledge, the balance of power is wrong. They're not on the land. They're not directly concerned with it. They help get laws written and that sort of thing, but people are as far removed from the land as they are from each other and other parts of nature in our modern civilization. Unfortunately, there isn't a strong likelihood of any big change in a hurry. It all adds up to deep trouble.

If nothing else, apart from any mystique, we ought to have brains enough to realize that land is the basic resource. It's what keeps us going and makes us happy or unhappy depending on how we use it. We ought to get away from the feeling that good things come from the store. What's the store? It's a middleman, and so many of our city people don't have the foggiest notion where food comes from. As long as it's there on the shelf, that's all that matters. And how many acres have been washed down the Mississippi to get it there they'll never know.

We mustn't look at our species as being apart from the rest of nature, and most particularly, we must rid ourselves of the notion that we are not subject to its rules. We damn well are. We should know that and live by it. If we continue to exploit our natural resources so we can have more ice cream cones, more TV, more radios, with little regard for the consequences, it certainly doesn't look very good for tomorrow, and tomorrow is there.

Within limits, one lives in a practical world. You can't always have what you want because someone else wants things differently, and so you come to an agreement. But if the agreement proposed is such that it compromises principles, then you say no. There is no exception.

FRAN: It's one of the reasons that I admire him so. At the Edwin S. George Reserve that Frederick mentioned earlier, we had security, tenure, and we had two children. Frederick felt that what was going on was wrong, and he left that job with no place to go; he wouldn't compromise. He wrote a marvelous letter of resignation, and we pulled out. He knew what was going on was wrong. It took a lot of courage.

We pick our fights carefully. It depends on what we think we can get away with, how hard we want to fight, and if we're willing to fight on until the last ditch. On the battle to save the sharp-tailed grouse range in Wisconsin, we spent years gathering information through research. Ernest Swift, director of the Wisconsin Conservation Department, said, "Well, you've done your research; now you've got to sell it to the public." And we learned that a research biologist couldn't just do research and find things out. There's got to be that extra step or what he does may never bear any fruit. But in that particular battle, the department's administration just gave us crumbs.

FREDERICK: We got licked.

FRAN: We got licked. They threw us some pacifiers, but we learned a great deal. Any time we lose a fight, we learn. We're more skilled fighters afterward.

FREDERICK: It came down to a conflict between forestry interests and wildlife interests.

FRAN: The conflict between trees that are planted as commercial crops and wildlife. People seem to think that planting trees is always noble. It isn't.

FREDERICK: Sharp-tailed grouse, a pioneer bird, needs the open sun, but not to the degree that open grassland birds do. Sharptails are more the savannah type where you have plenty of open grassy areas. On the other hand, you also have some thickets and scattered trees. As the forest becomes older, taller, denser, more mature, you move into ruffed grouse range. But ruffed grouse are not deep-forest birds as spruce grouse are. At the turn of the century, when Wisconsin was primarily forest in the north and oak openings and prairies in the south, there were some sharptails, but there weren't many. But then with farming, lumbering, and civilization moving into the north, more open country was created, rather abruptly too. Sharptails began to increase in numbers. But as pioneer farming became more advanced, everything settled down into a pattern.

People farmed certain parcels of land, and the edge between farmland and the woods was no longer a rough, gradual edge; it was a sharp edge that went right straight up. Here are the woods, here's the opening, with no rough, brushy edge between. This resulted in no sharptails. Fires and the old burns, as well as some of the old sodded-over clearings that were slow to come back to timber, were keeping the sharptails going.

As it happened, such areas were duck soup for the foresters. Here were nice open pieces of land, sometimes flat, and their planting machines could just go *zip-zip-zip*. So they wiped out what the sharptails needed, and the foresters were the boys who had the clout.

Well, we made a plan and named specific areas that would have to be protected to save the bird, and we said that it was an absolute rock-bottom proposal: "You cut this below what we have given you, and you'll knock out the sharptails."

The forest people and the game people were far apart despite all the sweet talk about working together for the same outfit. Each outfit was fighting for its own empire. And game was weakest in the '50s. Because the department

Elva Hamerstom Paulson's stunning "Painting of a booming ground."
Photo courtesy of Elva Hamerstrom Paulson.

Hammy providing counsel to UW-Stevens Point Master's student Robert Rosenfield in 1982. Both Hammy and Fran served on Bob's graduate committee. Bob would later earn a PhD in zoology and become professor of biology at Point. Photo courtesy of Elva Hamerstrom Paulson (made from a slide provided by Rosenfield).

chose to subsidize tree planting, sharptail habitat disappeared, and as a result, the sharptails are disappearing. It's as simple as that. It didn't have to be that way—simply because the department chose to subsidize tree planting.

With Os Mattson, we once wrote[103] that a rich and varied landscape is the healthiest landscape for all forms of wildlife, and for people as well. We also noted that Wisconsin has a forest crop law designed to provide incentives for the production of timber. Well, why not a wildlife crop law to encourage the production of game and other forms of wildlife?

FRAN: Then we had the battle to save the prairie-chicken. Through the 1950s, the bluegrass seed industry had harvested seed annually in the drained Buena Vista and Leola marshes. This had allowed the prairie-chicken to survive both intensive agriculture, forest, and brush regrowth dominating the landscape elsewhere. Hammy and I encouraged competing foundations to purchase scattered parcels of grassland to save the bird. This wasn't such an easy sell because it was commonly thought that vast contiguous areas of nest habitat were needed to save the bird. But the idea caught fire. I think that there will always be prairie-chickens in Wisconsin, and we played an important part in determining the outcome.

FREDERICK: Our children call this place Grand Central West.

FRAN: We both stimulate a great deal of other research. This place almost always has one or more young people who are learning and participating. In the early years, it was only biologists that came here. Now it's artists, actors, actresses, as well as biologists. We take in more of the world now. But sometimes I feel as though we are just animals on display. We had a whole Greyhound bus full of people come in to look at us not long ago. On a nice Sunday afternoon, people keep coming. One day last summer Hammy said, "I had 20 minutes free today to read!"

FREDERICK: I get a good deal of satisfaction in working with manuscripts. I get some that plainly have potential but are so badly written that they're not going anywhere. I take something like that and make something out of it. That's an accomplishment. When a piece of research comes to fruition and you begin to see where it's leading, what it means, that's certainly rewarding.

FRAN: Our research is rewarding, but it is highly demanding. About three or four years ago, we were in a rainforest near San Andrés Tuxtla, Mexico. We had never done fieldwork in the tropics before. There was such heat that we had trouble seeing because perspiration poured into our eyes. In addition, there were poisonous plants, poisonous snakes, the steep hills, and we had to carry equipment up steep terrain. We were taken to the limit of our strength and came close to dying a number of times. Experiences like that have been unique. It gives one an appreciation. It's something we've tried to tell the starry-eyed young people who want to come into this. It isn't all fun and games out there.

FREDERICK: And the people who read Thoreau and the other "nice" writers are never going to get it that way. You can see something different, and you can get a mystical feeling, but if you want the real thing, you've got to go for the real thing. You don't get it through books and lectures.

FRAN: Thoreau never had much of an impact on me. Why?

FREDERICK: Dreamy.

FRAN: Good Lord, he never really looked at things! He couldn't identify things. A little bird comes and sits on a bush, and you don't know the bird's name, and you don't know the bush's name. And he's considered this great naturalist and is put on a stamp? He goes and lives way off. It sounds so wonderful, but he's within a half-mile of a farmhouse where he goes and mooches meals and pencils! Thoreau just makes me want to spit! Now, in *Civil Disobedience* I think he did some good thinking, and he impresses me, but as a naturalist ... ugh!

John Burroughs was a good naturalist. He performed some fine research; things ring right. Ernest Thompson Seton is one of the great ones that influenced me.

FREDERICK: Yes, one of the strongest ones. Those that influenced me the most were Fraser Darling, Leopold, Niko Tinbergen, and Konrad Lorenz. They comprised the cornerstone.

FRAN: Darwin had a pronounced influence on me. By the time I was 11, I had read all of Darwin in the public library. Here was somebody writing firsthand about the things that had aroused my curiosity. I used to run away from home, get on my bicycle, and go down to the public library. I read books on falconry and all sorts of things. Then I'd go home and take my punishment for having run away to the library. [She walks to a bookshelf.] This is the very book that started me off: *The Insect* by Jules Michelet, published in 1875. I used to look at that book before I could read properly. [It contains exquisite engravings.] It's always been one of my treasured possessions. I think it influenced my taste.

People like Edwin Way Teale and Joseph Wood Krutch are good writers, but they don't go into things in depth.

FREDERICK: And neither of them are telling us things we need to know. We have so much that we need to read that we have very little time to read for fun except when we're on camping trips. In camp we're more apt to read something that doesn't strain the machinery, something like a "whodunnit." Krutch has some beautiful prose expressing some very nice ideas. But the scientific journals are of more immediate concern and deal with problems at hand. Even with the tools of our trade—there are so many—we have to skim and move fast and pick what seems to be most important.

FRAN: We never go for a walk. We hate going for a walk. We always have a purpose. And reading Teale is like going for a walk. We don't have time for that sort of thing. We always have a purpose when we go out, such as to see how the drought is affecting the woods.

FREDERICK: Or to collect plants.

FRAN: If we should start out exploring, well, the first thing, you know, we're working. Sometimes if work gets a bit thick, I go and lie down in the woods and think it through. It puts my troubles in perspective. This evening we're going dancing! That's what we do for fun. In my early twenties, I got a seldom-described disease then known as dendritic keratitis, a herpes virus. And it's flared up off and on throughout my life. Sometimes it's affected both eyes—a sympathetic reaction. I then went from that to glaucoma. Then I had the damn eye taken out. Now I have two fake eyes—one for evening and TV and one for everyday use. So whenever Frederick wants to take me dancing, I ask, "Which eye would you like me to wear?"

FREDERICK: Ballroom dancing is something we're extremely fond of and have very few chances to do. When we first started in this field, we realized that you couldn't be a field biologist back in the boondocks and go to the Copley Plaza for tea dancing. They don't quite fit, and there aren't many chances to go dancing. So when the chance comes, we do. When we travel south in the winter, and when we travel back from Texas and Mexico in the spring, we arrange our travels so that we can dance at night. That's the greatest amount of dancing we do the whole year. There aren't many plays, but when a play comes along we have season tickets at Stevens Point, and we go. Other than those sort of things, we hunt or celebrate anniversaries.

FRAN: He's joking, of course. We don't usually pay much attention to any of our anniversaries. I'll give you a beautiful example. We were driving along a country road one day. My birthday is on December 17, and on November 18, Frederick stopped the car, put his arm around me, and kissed me. I said, "What's this all about?"

He said, "I'm sorry, I forgot your birthday!" My birthday was still a month away! So we've given up on that sort of business!

🖋

Plainfield, Wisconsin, August 3, 1981

THE HAMERSTROM HOME appears burnt-gray in fading twilight, and everywhere in deep grasses, a drone of crickets and katydids punctuate the humid evening air. Hammy, dressed in a faded denim shirt, khaki shorts, and soft leather Haband shoes, and Fran, wearing a paisley shirt with sleeves rolled up, dark blue shorts, and walking barefoot, usher me into their sparse dining room lit only by a standing floor lamp. Fran laughingly

CHAPTER SIX 🦅

says that someone had just tried to sell her a rug shampoo. (There are no carpeted floors in the Hamerstrom home.)

Frederick sits down at an oval walnut table, leans back in a wooden chair, and ponders what's ahead.

The winter of 1981–1982 will be his and Fran's tenth year of study in Sonora, Mexico, he says. When they return the following spring, they will have to sit down and analyze 10 years of data. Their study area, near the village of El Desemboque along the Gulf of California (Sea of Cortez), is approximately 23 miles long. When they first started to count osprey nests here in 1971, they found 30 nests. Since then, they have documented close to 80 nests.

"But," says Hammy emphatically, "one of the things we're going to have to do this coming winter is to go back to the original 30 nests and see exactly what shape they're in and how many are still standing. They nest in columnar cacti that have a way of busting down from time to time. Either the arm that holds the nest, and the nests are enormous, or the whole cactus itself may come down."

"We do quite a lot of walking," remarks Fran dryly, still standing, "because the roads are miserable."

"I've been working on a map for the last several years," adds Frederick. "There is no decent map of the area." He explains that the roads are simply two rough tracks that wind around in a convoluted manner, and they are the only landmarks he can use in making the maps. Recently, he obtained three or four Mexican government geological maps he had requested, and though these didn't show the trails, they at least identified peaks and shorelines, making his job somewhat easier.

Change is slowly creeping into the Mexican study area, perhaps the wildest area they'd ever seen. "It has some of the most beautiful sand beaches that one can imagine," he continues, "and it has not been turned into a tourist resort yet because water is not available for consumption on a large scale." But about

Cardón sahueso *(Pachycereus pringlei)* with osprey nest. Photo courtesy of Elva Hamerstrom Paulson.

30 miles to the north, a gigantic electric generating plant and a deep-water port were under construction. Along with these, the government was slowly building a new highway that could eventually stretch hundreds of miles down the Gulf of California coast.

The Hamerstroms discovered their study area and nesting ospreys by chance. They had been going to fishing villages in the area for a few years when one day they discovered tire tracks in the desert heading north up the coast and decided to follow them. From a map, Frederick saw that the river in San Ignacio came out of the desert and figured that where a river met the sea there had to be one interesting place. But no one could tell him how to get there. He and Fran ended up taking one back road after another, going as far as a tank of gas would take them before returning to refill their tank. Finally, they found a way in and discovered that the river estuary was practically non-existent. So seldom had the riverbed contained water that no riparian fringe existed at all, and a sandbar lay across the river mouth. In the process of discovering the river mouth, they found the ospreys.

"An osprey nesting in the desert seemed like a pretty weird deal," he notes, "but they're so close to water that they hunt in the sea." They found the ospreys nesting in two types of cacti: saguaro and sahueso. The sahuesos occur at a lower elevation than the saguaros, and in mountainous Mexico, there are many more saguaros than sahuesos, says Hammy.

When Fran and Frederick traveled back roads down into Sonora during the winter of 1980, they crossed the beginning of the new highway and were appalled at what they saw.

"Here you are about 100 miles back in the desert," he recalls, "with a little village of 40 or 50 people every 50 or 60 miles. We saw two cars in that 100-mile stretch, and it took us two days to travel the distance on those roads. All of a sudden we came through a little pass and heard this hellacious racket up ahead. It was the LeTourneau earthmovers, the big scrapers, the bulldozers, the tractors, and the sheepsfoot compactors blazing their way across country.

"So, in a very short time, our lovely study area is simply going to be wiped out."

Hammy steps into his study and retrieves a batch of black and white photos, each with a number on the back identifying the nest site of an osprey pair. The ospreys in Sonora are non-migratory, unlike those breeding in Wisconsin that he believes to be a different subspecies.

CHAPTER SIX

After nine years of study, he thinks that the northwest coastal osprey population in Sonora is relatively stable. As for protecting the area from development, the chances are slim. "The Mexican government is too gung-ho for development," he says. "There are very few national parks, and the country to the south and east has increasingly intensive agriculture.

"Of the major rivers flowing into the Gulf of California, none or possibly one reaches the sea. These are big rivers that have been dammed so thoroughly, there is no river water left. And there are new government-sponsored agricultural developments called *ejidos*. We run into them when we come from the north to El Desemboque. The people that farm, however, don't own the land and are allowed to stay as long as they produce, but what's going to happen to them when the water supply for irrigation is depleted? So far the highway is far enough back that it's not going through the osprey country, but who knows where it will go.

"I sometimes get the impression that the engineers just take a site somewhere and say, 'Okay boys, let's go in this direction.' Then when they get down the road a ways, they stop and say, 'Well, let's go off this way.' The highway will go close enough to El Desemboque to mean better access for tourists. Sooner or later condominiums will crop up in the area."

When the Hamerstroms first entered El Desemboque, they discovered hunting and gathering Indian people known as the Seri that had been present perhaps for centuries as an enclave along the northern seacoast. The Seri, numbering between 400 and 500 at the time, had experienced very little contact with the Mexican government until the early 1970s. Since then, the government had built houses, put in streetlights, and dug a well, so the life of the people had begun to change.

"This is an extremely interesting group of people. They've gone straight from the Stone Age to the Nuclear Age in one generation. They have no agriculture and never have. They say that no one could ever starve in the desert, and there's an ethnobotanist there now who showed us what they eat. Sure enough, there are all kinds of things around if you know how and what to look for and know how to prepare them."

He pulls out the original worn-out map of the area he had drafted and points out old trails, the valley of the San Ignacio, the Gulf Coast, Cape Tepoca formed by a mountain coming out into the sea, a long rocky point called Sarjento, an estuary with no river near, and a sand pit with a miniature mountain at its end. Scattered along the coast and inland were osprey nests.

Next year they will have to walk tracts that formerly were drivable to check some of the original 30 nests.

🖋

PORFIRIO. How did he get his name? "He was named after Porfirio Carlos Estrada Arras, the Mexican doctor who saved Hammy's life in 1971," says Fran. "Hammy developed a kidney infection, pneumonia, and a whole slew of things all at once. I rushed him out of camp and went to Hermosillo, the capital of Sonora, and fortunately found this brilliant doctor. We named the owl after him and then discovered that it was about as tactless a thing as one could do because in Mexico owls are bad luck. They're considered witches, and if people find a dead owl, they'll stick pins in it and cut off its wings and legs. They hate owls! Fortunately, he realized that we meant well."

🖋

August 3, 1981. 4:30 a.m.

AT A GRASSLAND AND MARSH study site not too far from their home, Fran and gabboon Dan Groebner, a University of Wisconsin student, discuss trapping a harrier using Porfirio, the great horned owl, as the lure.

"When you've got harrier trapping to do, you have to get out early and set up your net [called a *dho-gaza*, pronounced doe-gaza] before the sun rises so that the harrier can't see you putting up the net," says Fran. "Beneath the net stretched between two aluminum poles, you place either a stuffed owl or a live owl on a perch. Harriers do not like having an owl in their territory, so they dive-bomb it. If all goes well, they whiz into the net, the net collapses, and we rush out and catch the harrier, band it with a U.S. Fish and Wildlife Service band, weigh and measure it, mark it with colored feathers and anklets, and release it.

"When we mark the bird, we cut off the primary wing feather most recently grown, close to the skin. That leaves the hollow butt of the shaft, We then test to see if we have a good fit of a colored feather. If we've got a good fit, we plunge it into Duco household cement and then put it in, where it will be held until the next molt. That means that next spring when the harriers come back, we'll be able to spot our 'imped' [from the Latin *imponere*, to place within] birds even though the color may be somewhat faded. I usually can do all of this business, plus perform a biopsy to determine pesticide levels in the bird's tissues, in about 24 minutes."

If Fran's harriers had not been color-marked and banded in previous years, it would make it difficult to determine whether she was following the same birds year after year. Parts of the approximately 49,000 acres of marsh, meadow, and forest that comprise her Wisconsin study area requires a good deal of patience and effort to locate nests, especially new nests.

"How many adult harriers is it possible to trap in a day? If you get two in one day then there's a celebration. But trapping is not a day-long affair," explains Fran, "because one can't keep a live owl out in the heat for too long without harming it. If you keep the adult harriers away from the nest when the young are small, there's a chance the young will die from lack of food or overexposure to heat or cold.

"You're always thinking about the harrier young and your owl. If you're not successful after 40 minutes, you give up and try again another day. The best weather is an overcast day with a wind of about five to ten miles an hour. The harriers are much more apt to feel like flying and attacking an owl if there's a wind, and if there's an overcast day, they can't see the net so well."

Fran waits by parked vehicles to mount a spotting scope on a tripod while Dan, with Porfirio on his gloved right hand, sets out into the marsh, Sumner following behind. Soon, they become submerged in the grasses that rise cold and wet shoulder-high.

Fran, wearing a winter parka and shorts, prefers to walk barefoot because it's easier to move through the morning dew. Porfirio utters a chittering call. "What we usually do in spring," said Dan, "is look for birds carrying nest material, or we watch a male and see him bring in food to the female during the incubation or rearing period. When the male brings in a mouse or other prey, he circles over the nesting female. She gets up off the eggs and rises into the air to meet him. Sometimes they'll be pretty high up in the air, and sometimes not. The male then drops the mouse in mid-air, and the female grabs it and takes it down to the nest. That tells us where the nest is."

The mosquitoes are voracious. The beasts rise from the grasses in swarms, and at the spot where Dan erects the net, they are especially bothersome. Slapping his neck, he explains that Porfirio has enough leash (fastened to jesses on his legs) to get down into the grasses if the temperature becomes too warm. He raises the net perpendicular to the wind direction because it's easier to catch an attacking bird.

"So long, kid," says Dan to a perched and chittering Porfirio as we depart for the cars where the watch begins.

Back at the car, Fran is alert to the first sight or sound of a harrier. "Sometimes," she says, "when a net is strung up as far away as Dan's, two people work in tandem. A gabboon might hide in the grasses, sometimes within six feet of the net, and listen for the car horn—the signal that the other person, who has been watching through a spotting scope, has seen the net fall. This either means the harrier is caught or has knocked the net down. When the net has dropped, you have to work fast. You quickly put the bird and the net into one end of a metal tube punctured with holes, and then you reach into your pocket, pull out another net, and put that up. While you're weighing and processing the first bird, you may catch the other adult. It takes split-second timing to be a good trapper.

"We've been in a beautiful position to see how little our processing bothers the birds because they go right back to feeding their young or to whatever their business is."

Dan interrupts to say he hears the female. "There she is!" cries out Fran as a chestnut-colored hawk with long pointed wings, long tail, and a white rump lazily approaches Porfirio.

What is the danger to Porfirio? "Very slight," remarks Fran. "We've caught hundreds of raptors by this method, and we've never had an owl hurt, though we have had an owl dusted, just barely touched."

Through the spotting scope, Dan notices that the hawk, now starting to stoop at Porfirio, is still quite far from the net. "This is a pretty smart bird," he winces. "We couldn't ask for better conditions than I had two days ago when it was cloudy and colder. She was stooping then, but not intently."

Fran (ca. 1959) atop her VW van, searching for a harrier. Photo courtesy of Elva Hamerstrom Paulson.

CHAPTER SIX

Altocumulus clouds began to drift in from the north, and a slight northerly wind kicks up a coolness from the grasses. "The weather can be frustrating," ponders Fran while scanning the skies. "Looks as though it's getting better for us. You can be in a thick fog until nine o'clock in the morning, and at nine thirty the fog lifts completely, but at ten, a heat wave puts you out of business—too hot for the owl. As far as I know, no other raptor study in the world has gone on as long as this using marked breeding adults on a study area of substantial size.

"We've found out all sorts of things. For one, the population of harriers is highly influenced by the fluctuations in numbers of voles. When there are lots of voles, the old male harriers become polygamous and may take up to four mates, while the young males breed during their first year. It seems that the voles are an extremely powerful aphrodisiac. When there aren't voles, there is still plenty of food. They switch to birds, amphibians, and small mammals like young rabbits or ground squirrels. But it isn't the abundance of food that causes the male harriers to be polygamous. Rather, it may be something in the intestinal flora of the vole that produces a physiological effect. Or it may be that when there are lots of voles, the male presents the female with food far more often than normal, and this may stimulate her gonads, because he keeps bringing her all these little presents during courtship. I sometimes compare this to someone who is dating a girl. If he gives her a rose a day for 12 days, it's apt to be more effective than if he gives her a dozen roses in one bunch."

Do harriers, as a rule, usually breed during the first year? "The females are quite apt to, but the males do only during a vole high. Otherwise, the male breeds during the second or third year. Also, if the adults raise young successfully, they tend to come back to the study area but not to the same nest. If they are unsuccessful in producing young, we may never see them again in the study area. It's as if successful breeding was almost a form of imprinting in getting them to come back here. They have a very long breeding season. Our earliest eggs hatch in late May, and our latest hatch in late July or early August. The birds tend to nest near willow, and this year, aster. They are important components of nest cover."

Harriers usually lay four or five eggs, sometimes three. The incubation period usually lasts about 31 days, and no trapping occurs until the young have hatched. Because the bird nests on the ground, mothballs are dropped along the path near the nest and when researchers leave, so mammalian predators don't follow a scent trail to the eggs. "We've had very good luck for the most part in not losing any nests," she says. "But we have a new and different problem this year. We found two dead young with mites and then worked quickly and discovered what looked like mites in the nest litter. Apparently, mites have been responsible for two nest failures. We're hoping to collect more nests to see how widespread the problem is.

"Lots of people think that these birds mate for life. That's how this study got started. We had a harrier nest in front of our house, and I wondered about this business of mating for life. So in 1957, I spent a good part of the summer catching one adult, and the next summer I caught another. We hadn't developed any good trapping techniques then; it was exhausting. And then I was reading Christian Brehm's *Compendium of Trapping*—an old German book published in 1885. He mentioned that the French used owls. They put four nets around the owls, but he poo-pooed the technique. But I knew that the French and Germans weren't getting along in those days, so I thought it was worth a try. The gabboon on the project that summer went out with me, and on the first morning we caught two pairs—a feat that has never been duplicated.

"Two pairs by ten o'clock, and we came home singing," she laughs. Dan asks who baked the pies because if a gabboon traps a harrier or finds a nest, he/she gets an apple, cherry, lemon meringue, or blueberry pie from Fran as a reward.

"My pies are worth $55 each," she asserts. "I know an eccentric bachelor in Berkeley who runs a chemical laboratory, and it costs $55 to get a chemical analysis of pesticide residues. Well, he's absolutely gone on my pies. So I ship them to him airmail, and even-steven he'll run an analysis of pesticide residues in exchange for a pie.

"The way I ship them is rather interesting: I bake the pie in the cheapest pie plate that I can buy, then wrap it in foil, put it in a nylon stocking, take the toe of the stocking and put it on one side of a big box and the top of the stocking on the other side so that the pie is hanging in a hammock. You can send a delicate crust all the way to California that way. We send injured raptors to a major rehabilitation center in much the same way. It's absolutely safe!"

THE CAGEY FEMALE harrier half-heartedly stoops several times at Porfirio but pulls up each time before striking the net. Soon she loses interest in Porfirio and disappears to the west. "Probably hunting," says Dan. While waiting for her to return, Fran discusses the loss of harrier habitat to large commercial farms. "If it weren't for the lands managed for prairie-chickens, the harriers would essentially be gone. Two foundations worked to save the greater prairie-chicken from extirpation in the state: the Prairie-chicken Foundation and the Society of Tympanuchus Cupido Pinnatus, the latter borrowing the species' scientific name for its title. Together they bought about 11,400 acres—managed by the state of Wisconsin under a 99-year lease.

"Most of the land that the two foundations purchased were parcels that occurred not as a block but which were scattered throughout the Buena Vista Marsh. By having a scattered pattern through the marsh, it has helped create conditions where harriers can hunt over prairie-chicken habitat. We can do a lot more for the harriers by simply having purchases scattered through the area. Hammy devised the *Hamerstrom Scatter-Pattern Plan*. It's being used for a number of species elsewhere in the country."

Suddenly, two other harriers appear, flying in the direction of the female. "It's the kids!" exclaims Dan.

"Good, they may stimulate her to greater efforts," Fran suggests. "And we may also catch one of them." But the two young drift to the west and disappear behind a hummock without showing any interest in Porfirio.

As the birds meander out of sight, Fran says she hopes that the federal government will eventually take over the project and standardize her procedures. "This project is a tremendous investment, and I don't know of a more sensitive way of measuring the environment than what we've got on hand here. Birds of prey are very sensitive indicators of human impacts on the environment. There's a phenomenal correlation between vole population dynamics, particularly their four-year cycle, and harrier breeding success. No one knows why voles have such a cycle, and it isn't a precise cycle. But harriers have many nests in the area when voles are plentiful, otherwise not. We trap voles to monitor their population levels in different places where harriers are likely to be hunting, using 120 traps at each place. The traps are baited with peanut butter and stretch in a straight line. This gives us 1,200 trap nights for a breeding season. The traps are set out late in the afternoon, and we pick them up fairly early in the morning.

"Back in the late 1960s and early 1970s, when DDT was posing such a horrendous problem for raptors, it was the peregrine's thin eggshells that received most publicity, but the harriers were suffering too. They simply failed to hatch eggs.

"Everybody was saying, 'Fran, why don't you collect some eggs?' And I was saying, 'Listen, I'm trying to tell you something: they aren't laying any eggs!' Not only that, but their behavior was abnormal. They failed to sky-dance during courtship, and there were frantic talon-to-talon food transfers instead of lovely aerial transfers where the male brings food to the female. They set up weak territories. They simply appeared listless, and the number of nests in the study area dwindled to two. I thought that the species might be doomed.

"Everybody was talking about the peregrines, and I was writing about the harriers. Well, the harriers started to recover about a year before the ban on DDT because the use of DDT had been reduced by about 90 percent in the year before the ban."

The female adult harrier does not return. Fran instructs Dan to take down the net and continue his search for new, late-season nests.

After returning home, Fran places a pot of coffee on the stove, removes her sandals, and sets up her typewriter so that she can finish a cover letter that will accompany the sample of mites obtained from harrier nest litter. It is not yet eight o'clock.

"I really want to do more writing," she muses. "Not just scientific papers, but writing more children's books and books for adults. I've got one in mind. I think I'll call it *Birding with a Purpose*. I'm rather against all of these people who go helling all over the place running up bird lists. And because they've seen a lot of birds, they think that they're authorities. But they never watch birds. They're not bird watchers; they're listers. I think that I'll write it rather like *Strictly for the Chickens* with a whole bunch of entertaining episodes. And by the time you are through, you will have learned something!"

DO THE HAMERSTROMS ever think about retiring? Later, over a lunch of curry, brown rice, and Fran's special homemade chocolate pie, Hammy bristles at the suggestion. "Retiring? I can't imagine such a thing.

"The notion that so many people in our society have bought about putting in so many years making money and then retiring, retirement being somewhere off in the distance like a carrot at the end of a stick, is ridiculous. Now that the chore is finished, the thinking goes, people will have the rest of their life to do whatever they please. But so many of them haven't the foggiest notion of what they want to do, and a good many of them drop off rather quickly.

"We've gone at it from another approach right from the start. There are some things that we want to do, and we will put up with a great deal to make it possible to do them. But there is no time at which we will have finished this and then can stop and play bridge or play golf. What a thought!"

🍃

THERE HASN'T BEEN ANYONE quite like the Hamerstroms among our naturalists in the history of Wisconsin conservation.

I never gave any thought to the day when they would no longer be with us.

On March 28, 1990, Hammy, suffering from pancreatic cancer, passed away in a secluded cabin along Oregon's North Umpqua River—a site mutually agreed on with Fran when his death was near. She then turned to a new area of research and spent the next six winters studying the hunting techniques of Zaire pygmies and Peruvian Indians. She also canoed the Amazon River. ✳

Fran continued to live in their old, pre-Civil War farmhouse until a few days before her death. A bout with lung cancer had weakened her to the point where she was unable to care for herself, and she passed away in Port Edwards, Wisconsin, on August 29, 1998. She was 90.

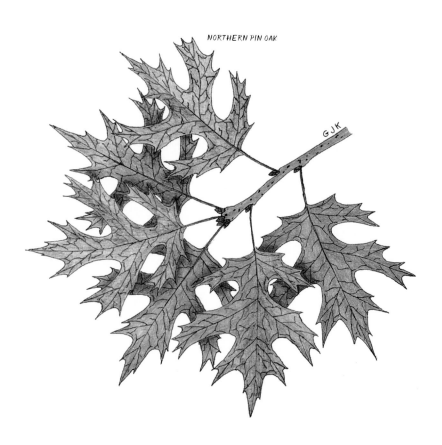

NORTHERN PIN OAK

GJK

Sam Robbins
(1921-2000)

BLACK OAK

GJK

Chapter Seven~
Sam Robbins

While admitting to the full extent the agency of the same great laws of organic development in the origin of the human race as in the origin of all organized beings, there yet seems to be evidence of a Power which has guided the actions of those laws in definite directions and for special ends.

> —Alfred Russel Wallace (Co-discoverer with Charles Darwin of the *Theory of Natural Selection*)

The more I have come to know birds and their habits and migration patterns, the more convinced I am that all of life is a part of the whole creative process I associate with God.

> —Reverend Samuel D. Robbins, Jr.

I will never forget the first time I met Sam Robbins. It was during the 1984 WSO convention in Fond du Lac. The group I was with was taking a field trip to Horicon Marsh. The trip was an early morning affair. We arrived at the marsh in the pre-dawn hours. As we walked along listening to the pre-dawn marsh chorus, a couple of odd flight calls seemed to rise above the other revelers. Immediately in his calm, confident voice Sam said, "short-billed dowitchers." I never said a word. I just walked along silently thinking to myself, "Short-billed dowitchers? You've got to be kidding me." Well, as we headed back to our vehicles at the end of our trip I introduced myself to Sam and asked him how confident he was that the flight calls we heard four hours earlier were indeed short-billed dowitchers. Sam's reply was simply, "very confident." And, as if Sam had a direct line to the Almighty himself, three short-billed dowitchers rose above the marsh grass from some hidden mudflat and immediately revealed their secret with the same flight calls we heard four hours earlier. I looked at Sam and he had that twinkle in his eye and an ever-so-slight "I told you so" smile.

—Scott Baughman (Birder Extraordinaire)

In December 1996, at the time of his 75th birthday and the 50th anniversary of his ordination as a minister, I sat down with the Reverend Samuel D. Robbins, Jr. at his west Madison home to discuss his lifelong passion for bird observation and study, his prodigious book *Wisconsin Birdlife*, as well as his views and beliefs shaped by decades as a small-town minister in Wisconsin.[104]

Born December 16, 1921, to Rosa Margaret Seymour Robbins and Samuel Dowse Robbins in Belmont, Massachusetts, Sam came to Madison, Wisconsin, in 1939, soon after the formation of the Wisconsin Society for Ornithology (WSO). He graduated from the University of Wisconsin-Madison in 1943 with a bachelor of science degree in natural sciences from the School of Education, and then promptly entered the Chicago Theological Seminary. Three years later he began his ministry in Neillsville, Wisconsin, and resumed his involvement with WSO.

Little known about Sam's academic achievements was a master's degree in counseling that he received in 1968 from UW-Stout. From 1968 through 1977, he served as a high school counselor at the Cadott High School in Cadott, Wisconsin. His involvement with WSO, however, remained constant. He served as associate editor of WSO's *The Passenger Pigeon* from 1946 to 1951, and again from 1960 to 1969. He also served as editor from 1953 to 1959.

In addition to writing *Wisconsin Birdlife*, in 1997 Sam updated Owen Gromme's *Birds of Wisconsin* for the University of Wisconsin Press, making all necessary changes to bird nomenclature, range maps, phenology, and descriptions of status, as well as writing a new introduction. During this later period, he also served as a regional coordinator for Wisconsin's first *Breeding Bird Atlas*, which began in 1995 and ended in 2000.

Those who knew the Reverend Robbins knew well there were three loves in his life: his family (wife Shirley and their four children Betsy, Dan, Rick, and David), his ministry, and WSO—a perfect trinity, some birders might say.

During my youthful and later years in Wisconsin, Sam Robbins was the preeminent authority on Wisconsin's birds and possessed the best ears for hearing birds of anyone I've ever known. Once, at Wyalusing State Park in Grant County, I remember him picking

Sam showing Rick and Betsy Ann Robbins, and Carol Scholl, a yellow-bellied sapsucker *(Sphyrapicus varius)* in the kitchen of the parsonage at Roberts, Wisconsin. April, 1963. Photo courtesy of Rick Robbins and Robbins family.

out amid a cacophony of migrating birdsongs a very distant sound—seemingly beyond the hearing ability of our group—the partial song of a rare worm-eating warbler *(Helmitheros vermivorum)*.

A reserved and quiet fellow, you sometimes wondered how he became a minister with the voice needed to command an audience *until* he made his presence known at the annual evening gathering of ragged and tired Madison Audubon Society Christmas Bird Count volunteers assembled at the UW-Madison Arboretum's McKay Center. While everyone waited to begin with their count reports and welcome late arrivals, suddenly out of nowhere came the booming voice of the Reverend Samuel D. Robbins calling the meeting to order.

Here, now, are reflections on the birding and ministerial life from one of Wisconsin's most distinguished and beloved ornithologists—perhaps WSO's greatest champion.

Sam, late 1930s, relaxing after field trip to Cape Ann, Massachusetts. Photo courtesy of Robbins family.

I started to make my first daily bird lists in Belmont, Massachusetts, back in 1932. I was 10 years old, and I did this because I wanted to keep up a bit with my older brother, Chandler, who was doing a little of the same thing. I received lots of encouragement from my parents. Mother and Dad were naturalists, and they took us out for hikes in the neighborhood. Mother's father, Arthur Bliss Seymour, was a world-famous botanist, and although my dad was in an entirely different field—speech pathology—he liked his nature hikes, and he took us kids along. I marveled at what he knew and learned a great deal from him. They had no car, so whatever we did was done on foot or by public transportation. Mainly, we hiked around the woodlands and some of the open fields within a mile of our home.

Dad was a very good teacher. He had exceptional ears and a good memory for bird sounds. One little incident I remember occurred on one of our hikes when we came across a bird that sang *bee-bz-bz-bz*. Dad said, "Sam, remember that. That's a golden-winged warbler." From that moment on, I have recognized that song instantly whenever I've heard it. Both Chan and I were blessed with unusually good ears. I have had mine tested several times, and people doing the testing say they have rarely seen ears that are as sensitive to high pitches as mine. I feel that this was a great gift. Along with a better than average memory, my hearing ability has given me a great deal of enjoyment and resulted in an eagerness to learn more and more.

Sam and Chandler Robbins birding along the Maine coast at Biddeford Pool during summer, 1998. Photo by Jane Robbins, courtesy of Robbins family.

What we had back then was Ralph Hoffman's *A Guide to the Birds of New England and Eastern New York* and Frank Chapman's *Handbook of Birds of Eastern North America*. Now those were field guides that predated Peterson's by a long time. They would describe museum specimens, you might say, more than live birds, but they were the only field guides we had, and we used them a great deal. No such books were available for my dad whose interest in birds was going strong as a teenager. I never knew this until I was working on my own book and Walter Scott came across an old manuscript in *The Oologist*. Walter found that around 1905, Dad wrote an article about an osprey nest in Maine. He was then a 17-year-old kid. How he learned his birds, I don't know. I do know that he did have a couple of birding companions in those days; whether one taught the other or whether they were just fellow learners, I don't know. I think in retrospect that Dad had the ears and the memory that it took to learn the sounds. He passed on to us this importance of listening for these sounds.

Many things I learned from my dad, not only about the identification of birds but also about their behavior. In the spring of 1932, which was the first year that I was really seriously keeping bird lists, Dad took my brothers and me up to what we called "Rock Meadow" to listen for woodcocks. It was late enough in March. We figured there should be woodcocks there. Dad knew exactly where to go to find them, and when we got near the area—before we heard any woodcocks—we met up with a fellow who was also out birding. While we were conversing, a woodcock sounded up, and this other birder called out, "That's a nighthawk!"

Dad corrected him and said, "No, that's a woodcock." And then he went on to explain that the woodcock arrives in late March, while a nighthawk couldn't be expected until May. He said if we listened, we would hear it follow up with its flight song, and that's exactly what happened. This fellow became thoroughly convinced that Dad was right and he was wrong, and here we kids were learning some things about both woodcocks and nighthawks from that experience.

Dad had pet names for certain birds. A white-breasted nuthatch was "John the Clown Bird" because it would go down the tree trunk headfirst. A pileated woodpecker was "His Royal Highness." He helped us set up a small birdfeeder right outside our bedroom window and taught us how to hold seeds in our hands and have the birds feed from them. I think that Dad's expertise was pretty much with local birds because I don't think he went on many extended field trips to other places.

In those early days, the Massachusetts Audubon Society invited people to send in annual lists at the end of the year, and Chan and I very faithfully did this. Interestingly, the society's checklist had a column for "seen" and a column for "heard." I don't think I ever saw that distinction made in any other checklist, but the implication was that a bird that was only heard was kind of a second-rate citizen. People had accepted the idea that you could identify birds by sight, but there was not nearly the acceptance that birds could be identified by ear.

Ludlow Griscom, the accomplished ornithologist from Harvard's Museum of Comparative Zoology, was the one who proved to collectors that you could identify by sight and sound. He did plenty of collecting himself, and I suspect that what he did was to identify birds by sight and sound and then collect the specimens to prove the point. Most of the scientific work in those days was done under the assumption that if you had the collected specimens, you had proof of its occurrence; sight identifications were not trusted. I think Peterson built very much upon what Griscom did and then developed his field guide on that basis.

There's a little story about Griscom collecting a bird in my hometown of Belmont, Massachusetts. One time, on a Sunday morning, when the discharge of firearms was strictly forbidden, Griscom came across a rarity. I think it was a blue-winged warbler. He collected the bird, and he hadn't any more than got the specimen and his gun back in the trunk of his car when a police car drove up. The policeman asked him, "Hey, did you hear a shot around here someplace?"

Griscom's replied, "I certainly did, officer! It was off in that direction!"

MY INTEREST IN NATURE was pretty much restricted. I learned plant life to some extent, and I think I probably learned that from my mother as much as from my father, but I didn't pay near the attention to plant life that I did to bird life.

One time, before I was a teenager, the author Thornton Burgess once had a radio program for a few weeks in which he featured birdsongs. He ended the series of programs with a contest. He invited his listeners to send him on a postcard the names of 25 birds whose songs he was going to imitate. So he whistled each of these birds, and my mother, my brothers Chan, Roger and I, all put down our answers on postcards. When we sent our cards in, we assured Burgess that we had all worked independently, that we were not in cahoots. Burgess was going to award a prize—his own leather-bound *Birds You Should Know*—to the 25 highest scorers. Well, our family won four copies. I think Chan had every answer right, and the rest of us each missed one. The prize was a nice little book to have.

⟡

I REMEMBER my first bird glasses. I still have them here: little four-power opera glasses. There were two pairs, and they were for the entire family. Both of them had the same magnification, but one had a nice, wide eyepiece, and the other one didn't, so we always wanted the one with the eyepiece. I don't think we ever fought over these glasses, but we waited impatiently for our chance to use them if we were on a hike and one of us had it and one didn't. Prism binoculars were available in those days, but they were too expensive for our family, and so we got along as best we could.

Birding was very much a side hobby for my father; he was a hiker. Mother and Dad were very faithful, regular church members, so what hiking we did was mainly on Sunday afternoons. We had no car in our family. My parents weren't wealthy by any stretch of the imagination, and Dad's work did not require him to have a car. Public transportation served for going back and forth to his job every day. He had his own private school for stammerers called the Boston Stammerers' Institute. Dad was a real pioneer in the field of speech correction, and he saw that field develop a great deal during his lifetime. There's a clinic at Boston's Emerson College named in his honor.

⟡

I WAS THE YOUNGEST of the three boys. Chan is three and a half years older than I, and so we often went out together. I'd say he was a mentor; we got along very well. Roger (two years older) was interested in birds but not to the extent that Chan and I were. It was partly because Roger was into athletics in school and neither Chan nor I had the athletic gifts, so we spent more time out on bird hikes and began keeping our lists.

Cemeteries were our favorite places to see birds. The bigger the cemetery and the bigger the city, the more important a cemetery is because it's an island of greenery in the midst of a concrete jungle. I grew up a couple of miles from the famous Mount Auburn Cemetery that attracted birds the way Central Park in New York has done. This cemetery was one of the most favorite places to go to see warblers in spring. There were also a couple of ponds nearby that we would visit that were good for waterfowl. We didn't have very much in the way of open fields; it was pretty much woodland birding that we did. Chan was still living at home most of the time when I was still in high school. He went to Harvard, and we lived only four miles from the Harvard campus. Chan and I used to hike around and listen for any bird sound or watch for any movement. He was the one who taught me the value of "pishing." If we felt there were some birds nearby in some shrubbery, he would get on one side and I'd get on the other, and we'd do some pishing, and then we'd call out to each other what we were seeing.

🍂

WANDERLUST—the desire to be out on my own—is the reason I left Belmont for Madison. During my first two years of college in Madison, I stayed with my mother's sister and her family. I arrived in 1939, just about the time *The Passenger Pigeon* and WSO got going. I missed by just a few months being a charter member.

Local bird clubs had only recently started in Milwaukee, Green Bay, Madison, Racine, and Waukesha. In Madison, we had basically two clubs: The Madison Bird Club—a forerunner of an Audubon chapter—and the Kumlien Bird Club. The more professional scientists all gravitated to the Kumlien Bird Club, which was connected to the university. This had people like Leopold, [A.W.] Schorger, Leon Cole, and a good many other people who were involved in ornithology on a professional level. These were almost entirely university people. But the Kumlien Bird Club members didn't get out in the field very much; they were doing more in the way of research. In terms of just getting out and observing birds and keeping records of when they arrived and departed, very few people were doing this. When I came on the scene, I got the feeling right away that I was more experienced in bird identification.

🍂

AS A YOUNG BIRDER, I was not yet involved in the ministry, but the history of ornithology is full of examples of ministers and other religious people who excelled in the study of birds. Gilbert White, for example, is renowned for his *The Natural History and Antiquities of Selborne*. What was it about the ministry that attracted me? Here's a round-about answer. My parents were faithful church-goers, and so we kids went to church and Sunday school regularly. I can't say that I had any inkling or desire to enter the ministry during those years. As a matter of fact, I kind of chafed at it.

While I had no desire to be a minister, I think my parents had instilled in me a desire to use my life in some kind of an occupation where I could be of service to people. I really thank my parents for that great emphasis. A person who chooses to be a minister needs to feel at some point that God calls that person to enter the profession. I felt all along a sense of a real relationship to God. My parents had helped me feel that God was calling me to a life of service. The question was, what kind of service, how to channel that sense of calling. The channeling didn't come until I was between my junior and senior year in college, but before that I had a period of wandering in "no man's land." I had started college with the idea that I wanted to be a math teacher, but I struggled with calculus to the point that I decided that math was not for me. This would have been 1939–1940. Having that idea knocked out of me, there was nothing to take its place.

🖋

ONE SUNDAY, I sat in church, and Alfred Swan preached a sermon that dealt with the duel between Alexander Hamilton and Aaron Burr, and how the minister at that time in the funeral oration had spoken so powerfully against dueling that dueling practically disappeared in the country after that time. I thought to myself, "By golly, if a minister can really make that kind of a difference, then maybe that's what I really should do." Alfred Swan, incidentally, presided over Joe and Lola Hickey's marriage, and on his 25th wedding anniversary he did the same for Shirley and me!

I eventually went to A.H. Edgerton, who was a counselor to students, and he gave me a whole battery of tests during my sophomore year. In one of these tests, he scored my aptitude or interest. After one test and another, he finally said, "Let me score you for a minister. Oh, this scores very high!" And I said, "Well, that's interesting, but I'm really not interested there." As a result of all of this, I decided to change my major to the natural sciences; I would study to teach science in high school. But a few months after that and after contact with Alfred Swan, I began to think seriously about possibly training to be a minister. What had shown up on Professor Edgerton's tests came back to me, and it gave me great encouragement. And, Sumner, I needed that encouragement because as soon as I breathed to my friends that I was considering this, the universal reaction was: "No, don't do it! Not you!"

I asked why, and they said that a minister had to be able to communicate and talk effectively. He needs to be an orator. I said, "I agree that I am no orator, but I just wonder whether with the right kind of training, I could learn some better speech habits." The chorus of discouragement that I got at that point was loud and clear.

You see, I mumbled. I didn't articulate my words well at all. I didn't project my voice. I had taken a speech course in college, but it hadn't really done that much good. Next chance back home, I talked this over seriously with my dad because of his interest in speech. He referred me to a friend on the Emerson College faculty who could help evaluate my chances of developing acceptable speech habits. So I spent an hour with him, and at the end of the time, he asked me point blank: "How badly do you want to be a minister?" I was able to say, "I want it more than anything else in the world."

Then he said, "Then, you can do it, but it's going to take a lot of hard work."

Another thing. When I was ready to start my senior year in college, World War II was going, and I was getting pretty close to being drafted. I had already received a notice from the Belmont draft board for a physical exam, so my dad questioned whether I should even try to start my senior year in college, but start I did. Soon after I began, however, the draft board sounded like it was ready to draft me. Well, my parent's minister heard about this, and he stormed the draft board and said, "You've got no business drafting that guy! He's been accepted in Seminary. Seminary students receive deferments!" He convinced the draft board to leave me alone. I had registered as a conscientious objector, however, and so I would not have been active; I would have participated in some kind of alternative service. I simply felt that God had intended that this be a world of peace based upon love. While I could understand that there were forces of evil that threatened our world, and that some pretty strong measures had to be taken to restrain such evil, I also felt that nobody wins a war. We've got to learn to find different solutions.

I finished college with a bachelor of science degree in the School of Education. Then I started seminary; indeed, my mind was made up.

Fortunately, I got a first class speech teacher in Seminary who did much to help me undo some bad habits and replace them with good ones. I still slip into some of my old habits in conversation and let my voice drop to a level that somebody can hardly hear, but when it comes to conducting a church service, my voice really booms out. I think I made the grade in that department.

I have always tried to put the church career first. To do this through the years when we had WSO conventions that would last a whole weekend, I would stay through a Saturday night banquet and leave for home about 10:00 or 10:30. I might not get home until 3:00 or so the next morning and then catch a few winks, but I would always be in my place in the pulpit on Sunday morning. I did not miss what I would call my primary responsibility to enjoy some bird occasions, and if I had to choose between something that I was expected to do with the church and going to chase a rare bird that had just been spotted, I would put the church first. I think I've been consistent in that all through my ministry.

Sam on college graduation day in Madison, Wisconsin. Photo courtesy of Robbins family.

* * *

ONE OF THE FIRST THINGS that WSO did in *The Passenger Pigeon* was to publish field notes. WSO received field notes from only a few people, and when I started putting my field notes into the hopper, my name appeared in some of these field notes reports more than anybody else's, which simply meant that I was a more active field observer than most. This eventually changed. The bird clubs became stronger, and eventually we got more local clubs started in different cities, and the interest gradually broadened.

CHAPTER SEVEN

In those early years of WSO, the ornithological interest was pretty much centered in southeastern Wisconsin. We used to speak about the Racine-Madison-Green Bay triangle; all the bird clubs were in that area. The Racine club was called the Hoy Nature Club. I believe the Green Bay Bird Club was started by Earl Wright at the museum at Green Bay. Members helped to organize WSO, and they hosted one of the first WSO conventions.

Even as late as 1960, relatively little birding was being done in northern and western Wisconsin, except by conservation wardens and some research individuals. Another thing that illustrates how narrow the interest was can be traced back to the late 1950s, when I was asked to be editor of *The Passenger Pigeon*. I was associate editor from about 1946 or so until the late 1950s, when I was asked to serve as editor. I can well remember that when I took over as editor, the barrel was empty. There wasn't a manuscript of any kind for me to use in the first issues. This meant thinking up new ideas and convincing people to do some writing. One of these ideas was to have a series of articles devoted to birding hot spots—some of the prime places to go in Wisconsin to look for birds. So I wrote up the Mazomanie area and a couple of others, and other people did the same. We planned to save these pieces and eventually put them out in book form. In a few years, we had 25 or 30 collected, but most of them were within the southeast triangle; we had very few spots in the northern half of the state. This was because birders hadn't been there; they didn't know where the hot spots were.

So we put out the first edition of *Wisconsin's Favorite Bird Haunts*. I think we covered about 30 areas. Thankfully, Daryl Tessen took this project over 15 years later and made a much more complete volume out of it, but that's the difference between 1960 and 1976—we just didn't know much about what was happening in northern Wisconsin. There were people out in other areas doing some very good work. Wallace Grange was a real fine researcher; he investigated the status of woodland birds in Wood County. There was a fellow up in Sawyer County, near Hayward, named Karl Kahmann, who was quite active in the early years of WSO, but again I don't think he had a bird club there. He was just someone who had an interest in birds, and he managed to keep in touch with people from the triangle. There were scattered individuals like that, but no other clubs that I knew of in those early years.

NOW, let me say something about some of the interesting individuals I have known. Let me start with Aldo Leopold. I first met him at Kumlien Club meetings, and we got to know each other reasonably well. It was my regret, in retrospect, that I never took a course under him. I thought the world of Leopold. I was a youngster compared with everybody else he was involved with, but he never treated me as just a little kid; he treated me like an adult before I really was one. I have really warm feelings toward him and much respect. I don't remember that we did any fieldwork together other than we paid attention to the birds near the Leopold Shack.

At Kumlien Bird Club meetings, members always asked for a recent bird observation by anybody. I don't think Leopold hardly ever contributed to this, and I just assumed this was because of his work. He just didn't have time for birding trips, hikes, just for the sake of seeing birds. He was too busy with more important things. I was the guy out in the field a lot. I think, at first, when I reported a few rarities, they were met with a certain amount of questioning. If somebody said that they thought my report was of a very unusual bird and asked how I identified it, I would describe what I had used for identification field marks. People like Walter Scott of the Wisconsin Conservation Department, and ornithologist Norv Barger, came to my aid and helped people accept what I said at face value.

Walter Scott was a remarkable bundle of enthusiasm; he seemed to have boundless energy to put into many different causes. He really did have some wide interests, but I remember him also as a very sincere and friendly person. To illustrate the kind of thing that Walter did that isn't done by many people, if some newspaper pointed out something good that somebody had done, Walter would sit down and write a little note to that person and congratulate them. Now how many people do that? He was just an appreciative and outgoing person. He was also instrumental in organizing WSO; he was anxious not only that this organization get started, but also that we'd get started doing a bunch of worthwhile things.

It was when I was a sophomore at the university that Walter assembled a team to prepare a preliminary bird checklist with migration graphs. He included Earl Loyster from the Conservation Department, Norv Barger, who had just joined the department, me, and Elton Bussewitz—a grad student from Watertown. I thought, "What am I doing on this committee supposedly talking about Wisconsin birds when I'm only in my second year here?" But I think Walter appointed me because he felt that I was such an active birder and had so much experience with birds in Massachusetts that

I probably had a better grasp of Wisconsin birds than many of the people here. We published the checklist booklet, and now it's been through four more revisions.

Walter also envisioned *The Passenger Pigeon* becoming a fine magazine. It had to start out as a mimeographed newsletter, but you start small; he was its first editor. Then he went into the service. He served in the Pacific during WWII, and Norv Barger became the editor at that time.

Walter was a very competent birder in the field, but he didn't get out very much because of the pressure of so many other things that occupied his time. His responsibilities with the Conservation Department increased through the years. When the time came for his retirement, one of the people who spoke at his retirement party referred to him as the "conscience of the Conservation Department"—an interesting term to use, but a very apt one in his case. I was never privy to some of the meetings where decisions were made, but people who felt that Walter was the person who, more than any other, kept them on track as to what their fundamental purpose was as custodians of the land and all its creatures. He was such a sincere person, and his interest in history was well known. He wrote one hundred-year summaries of conservation activities.

When I started work on *Wisconsin Birdlife*, I knew right away whom I wanted to do the bibliography, and he did an outstanding job. This became quite difficult in his last years because he lost his hearing, and in some of the last conversations I had with him, I had to write down what I wanted to say. He'd read it and then orally respond to what I was writing, but he couldn't understand a word I said unless I wrote it down.

To illustrate how he and I shared similar beliefs, in my first parish in Neillsville, I was planning what we called, "Layman Sunday." This was a Sunday, when a service would be conducted and a sermon preached by a layman. I asked Walter to preach. He drove from Madison to Neillsville and delivered an

Sam wrote of this photo: "Working on a weekly column, or on next Sunday's sermon?" 1940s, Cadott, Wisconsin. Photo courtesy of Robbins family.

outstanding sermon. I think he was addressing the stewardship theme that we on the earth are not owners of it; we are custodians of it. God didn't intend it for just one generation but for all generations. This was around 1947 or 1948, long before the idea was popular.

A.W. Schorger was another remarkable individual. I didn't know him nearly as well, but again I had great respect for him. He was the dean of the field birders during the time I was here in college [at UW-Madison]. Everybody looked up to him and knew that he had the last word. Anything that Schorger said he saw, you believed right then and there. He was a collector. He would usually identify his birds without collecting them, but when he came across something rare, he wanted to collect the specimen. This didn't go over all that well with some of the other field birders during those days, but you might say that Schorger belonged in the transition age between the collector and the field observer.

⟡

NORV BARGER was the person more than any other who took me under his wing when I came here [UW-Madison] as a college freshman. It was shortly afterwards that he joined the staff of the Wisconsin Conservation Department. He was a real field birder. I think I got acquainted with him because he knew my aunt and uncle with whom I was staying. Norv showed me some of the nice places to see birds; we enjoyed fieldwork together. He encouraged me and helped me get to know other birders here. There were times that he would take me to WSO conventions when I probably wouldn't have gone otherwise.

Norv was much more of a field man than Walter had been. Again, maybe because of various time commitments, but Norv just loved to get out in the field. He was instrumental in collecting and publishing seasonal field notes in *The Passenger Pigeon* and was the one who held that these field notes ought to be preserved. So, soon after I settled in Wisconsin, he asked me to be the field notes editor of *The Passenger Pigeon*. He wanted to encourage individual research projects, but he was dealing much more with the amateur rather than with the professional on college campuses.

One of the funniest experiences occurred during a late afternoon in May when I was going out to Hoyt Park. My college friends and I used to call it Sunset Point and go there for supper picnics. I had left a little early because

I wanted to stop at the nearby cemetery to look and listen, but I didn't have my binoculars. I'd do what I could with my ears.

When I got to the cemetery, I detected a strange song I didn't know. So I listened and thought, "How do I get a look at this bird?" The only way to do it was to crawl under the wrought iron cemetery fence. I crawled under the fence and walked to the trees where the bird was singing. The bird was up so high in the tree that I still couldn't tell what it was, but the bird kept singing repeatedly. It was driving me nuts because I thought, "This is a rare bird, and I can't identify it!" The best thing I could do was to write down how the song sounded to me. I almost always carried paper and pencil with me but had none that day. I crawled under the fence again, and just as I did, a bus stopped and a bunch of the kids heading to the same picnic were getting off. What in the world was I doing crawling under a fence? I told them I had heard a rare bird, and I begged from them pencil and paper. So they went on to the picnic, and I sat there at the side of the road writing down a description of the birdsong.

Then I heard a car pull up. I fully expected the driver to be a policeman; it was Norv Barger. I told him what I was doing. He listened to the bird. We both crawled under the fence to try and get a look at it, but we couldn't see it any better, so Norv said, "You stay here, and I'll go back." Pretty soon, he came back with his wife and two pairs of binoculars. The singer turned out to be a yellow-throated warbler. Norv was from North Carolina originally, and I think he probably recognized the song, but he wanted to be sure. With the binocs, we finally confirmed the identification, and in short order, half of Madison's ornithologists were out at the cemetery looking at that bird!

❧

ON SEVERAL OCCASIONS, I've heard a bird that I hadn't heard for eight or ten years and recognized it just like that. I'm lucky that way; it's just a gift. When I first met up with yellow-headed blackbirds, however, which I hadn't come across out in New England, I had to learn a new song that I hadn't experienced previously. But in terms of birds that I had once learned, forgotten about, and then run across, it would be hard to remember a time that that has happened—relearning a song.

Right now, with some hearing loss, I can hear a song that does not register with me as a song that I learned before, but it is the same song. There are certain overtones that I'm not picking up, so what I'm hearing is different than what I learned. In a sense, I have to relearn a few songs of birds that I once knew perfectly well, but now I can't catch the full song that I once could hear. For example, I can't hear the high-pitched sounds of cedar waxwings, brown creepers, and golden-crowned kinglets, and for some reason I also can't hear the low-pitched *peent* call of the American woodcock, nor distant calls of black-capped chickadees. But all in all, I have been blessed with a combination of unusual hearing and an unusual memory. This memory generally extends to call notes. I think this is one of the things that has been a source of amazement to a lot of other people when I've been out on field trips. If I can hear a call note and can identify the bird right away, for example as a red crossbill, some people are amazed, but it comes with experience. I don't know how you can teach call notes to other people very well.

LOCALLY, I like to bird the U.W. Arboretum, the Middleton ponds, and various places around the Madison lakes. Also, Mazomanie, the Pine Bluff area, Lodi Marsh, and Fish and Crystal lakes, the Norway Grove area, Goose Pond, and more distant spots like Horicon, Milwaukee, and Two Rivers.

Particularly memorable, however, are the times I have gone to Plainfield and experienced the booming of the greater prairie-chicken. You would show up at the Hamerstroms' house about two in the morning, if you didn't happen to be staying overnight. Here was a place that looked as if it hadn't had a coat of paint for a good many years, but here lived a lovely couple of scientists. They fed us a little bit of breakfast and sent us out in the dark. I didn't know where in the world I was. They'd direct us to follow such and such a line to get to a blind. You'd get in the blind and you'd think that you couldn't possibly sit in such cramped conditions for a couple of hours straight. But once the excitement developed out on the dancing ground before your eyes, you would forget about how cramped you were and just sit amazed to see those birds dancing, courting, confronting, and booming. To me, that was a memorable thing the first time I did it, and I think the wonder was only slightly less with each repetition.

There is another experience that I recall very fondly. When we lived in Adams County, we became acquainted with the birds on the Leola Marsh. We knew what it would be like to be out there on an early spring morning just as it was getting light. I had with me for an overnight guest, S. Paul Jones from Waukesha. I took him out on the marsh the following morning, and the ruffed grouse were drumming, the prairie-chickens were booming, the sandhill cranes were trumpeting. Over Paul's face came the most wonderful look of recollection. I wish I had a photograph of his face as he listened to that marsh music. He said, "We used to hear things like this in Waukesha County years ago!" He was reliving something that had been very precious to him in those early days. I have never forgotten that experience; how privileged I was to help open up this book of memories for Paul.

In connection with my book, I went to the Historical Society library and dug out many of his old field records. They helped me improve my understanding of what bird life was like back in his heyday. There is a club named after him in Oconomowoc. Paul was a very likeable fellow. I never knew that much about what research he did, but he would submit his field notes quite regularly to *The Passenger Pigeon*, and I had an occasion to look over those notes when they came in. I felt that he was a very active and accurate field observer, and he was one who pretty much limited his fieldwork to his own local area.

🌿

I CAN STILL REMEMBER quite vividly the day we discovered Wisconsin's first ruff [*Calidris pugnax*]. I was with a carload of people from Madison. Norv Barger was driving, and his wife, Clara, was along. I think Mary Walker may have been with us. We stopped at the Norway Grove pond in the middle of May, and right away we were aware of a lot of shorebirds. One of the first sounds I heard came from a dowitcher, so I looked for it. In so doing, I passed over a bird that seemed like a pigeon in the water, but I had to check out that dowitcher first to satisfy my ears. Then, I went back to look at the pigeon. Well, it wasn't a pigeon. It was a shorebird that had a pretty inflated area around its neck and throat. We didn't know what in the world that bird was at first. We didn't know for sure until we got back home and borrowed a couple of European field guides from Bill Foster. Then we confirmed that this bird was a ruff. So discovering the first ruff in Wisconsin was a moment that will linger in my memory. Many people eventually saw that bird, but I'll think twice before I ever give up on a pigeon wading in water.

Good friend Bill Foster and Sam birding on the east side of the UW-Madison Arboretum, May 1991. Photo by Sumner Matteson.

I FOUND OWEN GROMME to be a very interesting person to talk with, and I wish to high heaven that I would have had many more conversations with him than I did. Once I got started on *Wisconsin Birdlife*, I traveled to the Milwaukee Public Museum and read his notebooks. We had known each other for a long time. Gromme was enthusiastic, very dedicated to his work, and a very talented person. He was a real conservationist at heart, and I felt we had a lot in common. I don't think I shared his appreciation of hunting, but that didn't make any difference.

The time came when Gromme decided that he didn't want to write the narrative parts of his book on Wisconsin birds, which became a book of his paintings; he wanted to devote his years to painting. He must have thought highly enough of me to ask me if I would takeover the writing project. At the time he asked me, I was so engrossed in preparing a master's thesis that I couldn't take on another project, but I said that if he would still be interested at the time I finished that, I would consider it. So the very day I sent my thesis off to my faculty advisor at UW-Stout, I sent a note to Gromme and told him that I finished the thesis. "Do you still want me to take over the writing of the book?" I asked.

"Yes, we do," he replied.

CHAPTER SEVEN

[THE LATE UW-MADISON PROFESSOR OF WILDLIFE ECOLOGY]
Joe Hickey was another fine individual, and Joe had a sense of humor. Joe had a New York accent, and he used it to play games with me. Whenever we saw a marsh hawk [northern harrier], he referred to it as a "mash" hawk. I think this was his way of pointing out that he could detect in my speech the New England tendency to mispronounce an *r*. Joe was a lot of fun. He was a very good field observer. He loved to be out in the field watching birds, much more so than other university professors.

I can remember one time when he and somebody else and I were going to do a big May Day count, and I was living down on North Murray Street [in Madison] on the third floor of a house. I had set my alarm clock to go off so I would be ready when they picked me up, but the alarm clock did not awaken me. I don't know if this was the clock's fault, or if I slept right through it, but I became aware of a flashing light. I wasn't wide enough awake to fully grasp the situation, but I was aware that they were there to pick me up. They were flashing a spotlight from their car through my bedroom window; the light reflecting off the ceiling awakened me, but I was not wide awake enough to let these people know that I was now awake. So I went over to the window and started waving my hands up and down, and only then did it dawn on me to turn on a light in the room. So I turned the light on and quickly dressed. I don't recall what birds we found, but I remember the stupid way in which the day began. I'm sure he rubbed that one in. Joe had trained early as a field ornithologist. He was part of the Bronx County gang of young birdwatchers that eventually also included Roger Tory Peterson in their membership.

Joe grew up with a lot of confidence in bird identification both by sight and sound, much more so than many native Wisconsinites. I really didn't see very much of Joe, but he was very supportive and interested when I began *Wisconsin Birdlife*, and he was very encouraging to the point of asking whether I could take a sabbatical from my minister's job for a year to work on the book. I had to write him and say that the question of a sabbatical was not possible. I just had to plug away on it in my spare time. Nowadays, ministers are given sabbaticals, but I never had one.

Carl Richter was another unique individual. He never came to WSO meetings. He was not exactly a recluse, but he acted a little bit that way. I think he felt that he didn't have very much in common with the other birders in the Green Bay area because he felt that they didn't appreciate oologists. He was an oologist and a very competent one. One of the first things I did when I undertook *Wisconsin Birdlife* was to contact Carl. I knew that he had kept extensive field records, and I knew he was getting along in years. I wanted to get his data as best I could. So I designed a special kind of report form just for him to report his egg work. He was very accommodating. I went up to see him, and we went out in the field one morning. He and I enjoyed this because we were both quick to pick up things with our ears. We had a glorious morning together, and he showed me different areas where he used to do his egg collecting. These were Oconto Marsh and Peshtigo Marsh. Many of the egg records he shared hadn't been reported, so this turned out to be a fortuitous move that really paid off and made the book a better one, and we did it just in time because he died before I finished the book.

LET ME SAY a few words about Roger Tory Peterson; he was a very likeable man, soft spoken, very sincere, very creative. At the time that I knew him, his fame was already established. I did not feel that he was a person who would not associate with beginner-type people simply because he had reached the prominence he had. I can recall in the early 1980s when Chan came out with his revision of his field guide just as Peterson did—I think they were just two or three years apart. Some of the reviewers made the point that these two fellows were competing against each other, and that they were potential rivals. My impression was just the opposite—that they were friends much more than rivals.

One issue I brought up with Roger, and I was surprised by his opinion, was cowbird control—the issue about whether we needed to take measures to control cowbirds was being batted around quite a bit in 1993. I wondered what Roger's point of view on this was. He felt that we should do little or nothing in the way of cowbird control; he felt that it wasn't as big an issue as some people were making it out to be. I didn't agree with him on that. I think the situation with Kirtland's warblers and golden-cheeked warblers [in the west] is pretty well documented, at least when you're dealing with some endangered species and very limited habitat. We almost have to choose between cowbirds and those warblers. I'm afraid it's reached a point where we need to be making those choices.

I also have spoken out on the wise use of pesticides for a long time. I did it when I was editor of *The Passenger Pigeon*. This was primarily during the DDT era when we lost elm trees and robins. We devoted an entire issue of *The Passenger Pigeon* to this subject. We had articles written by four different people, and we had reprints of these sent to all of the chemical companies in Wisconsin. We didn't realistically expect we would change any minds and practices, but we felt that we wanted our voices to be heard, and we wanted people in these chemical companies to know that they were dealing with something that was a lot bigger than what they were recognizing at the time.

There were communities that had special town meetings on whether or not to use DDT. There was an option at that time to use methoxychlor instead of DDT; it had much less effect on other creatures, but it was more expensive. Some communities did decide to go to the more expensive stuff to try to control Dutch elm disease. I think I became interested in this issue partly through Chan because he was part of a team that was studying some of the effects of DDT on wildlife shortly after World War II when the use of DDT was in its infancy. He knew more about it, and I think he was raising some issues on this, but being a government employee, I don't know whether some of the reports that he made got shoved under the table for political reasons.

I first took note of DDT when the robin situation first came to light. The widespread use of DDT coincided with the spread of Dutch elm disease, and when Dutch elm disease reached southeastern Wisconsin, communities were gung ho on trying to do something to save their elm trees. I would say that this probably centered around Milwaukee and its suburbs and Madison and its suburbs, as much as any other place. The people who were trying to stop Dutch elm disease were using DDT like crazy. It was only as this was going on and people began seeing dead robins all over their lawns that the picture began to emerge that DDT was, first of all, not stopping the spread of Dutch elm disease, and secondly, it was having a serious effect on some of our songbirds.

It was most noticeable with the robins because the elm trees that people were trying to save were in suburban areas where robins were particularly conspicuous. When people began finding dead robins all over their lawns, they began to be much more concerned.

I remember attending a hearing one time when I thought it was very obvious that there was a link between DDT use and songbird loss. One fellow from the university here, I forget his name, was traveling around the state to all of these different hearings and promoting the idea that these chemicals should be used. He was denying that there was any evidence this was the cause of the decline of some songbirds. I just felt like throwing mud in his eye; how could he stand up there and say something that was blatantly wrong?

BEFORE MY BROTHER CHAN conceived the idea of the federal Breeding Bird Survey and began to organize it, we talked with the WSO board of directors about trying to organize some kind of a summer count for Wisconsin. At the time, we were envisioning getting these going in a linear way so that you could compare figures from 1960 with 1961, '61 with '62, and so on for the same given areas. When I presented this to the board of directors, they said it would be a very desirable thing but asked if I really thought that I would get many people involved. This would have been in 1960. I realized that most people put their binoculars away at the end of the spring migration and didn't take them out again for a few months, but I felt they were missing a great bet because of the summer birds that we have, particularly during the month of June before the song period ceases. We could get some significant information.

So the WSO directors finally said, "Go ahead and do one count, and we'll find some others." So we began this project in 1961 and ran it for five years. By the fifth year, we had 75 different areas covered. I summarized the counts in The Passenger Pigeon each year. I learned by 1965 that Chan was developing the federal Breeding Bird Survey project. I recognized right away that his methods were far superior to the ones we were following because they would give comparisons between different areas. I encouraged Chan to do this, but he, too, had been fearful that he couldn't get people to go out birding in June. When he saw what success we were having in Wisconsin, he decided that it was worth a try. So in a way I think we gave him a boost in organizing that project, which has proved to be successful. We gave up on our first project as soon as Chan's got started, so by 1966 we switched from our "summer bird survey" to the North American BBS. The summary we finished is a 26-year summary, 1966–1991.

I HAVE WRITTEN a column every week for backyard bird lovers through *The Country Today*. I began writing that in January 1977. Rarely a week goes by that I haven't received a letter. These letters are so appreciative that if there was such a thing as an apostle to the backyard bird watcher, I probably fulfill that role to some extent. My editor thinks the best one I ever wrote was "Still Singing," about the hermit thrush, as well as about the young girl who lost her life. I had been involved in this girl's life. She was a parishioner of mine. I discovered the bird near the time that this girl died, and I just naturally put two and two together. I wrote a poem at the end. I agree that it

Sam working on an article for *The Country Today*. Medford, Wisconsin, 1980. Photo courtesy of the Robbins family.

was one of my best. My editor was very much touched by it, and several people wrote very appreciatively about that piece.

I don't get into poetry very much, but it does happen on occasion. I wrote a poem once after I saw a tree cut down. In that case, I was just struck by how in just a few minutes time you could take down a tree that probably had been growing for 100 years or more. The stark contrast between the slowness of the growth and the quickness of the fall really got to me. I think that most anyone who reads my *Country Today* articles would recognize that there are religious overtones to what I write. The word stewardship covers a lot of my feelings—we here on earth don't really own anything; all of creation essentially is God's and is intended for all God's creatures and all generations. I feel that I am very much a part of God's creation and that God intended that we have a harmonious relationship with all of nature. I accept the idea that I

Sam showing daughter Betsy Ann a yellow-rumped warbler *(Setophaga coronata)* (formerly myrtle warbler), which "got in on back porch." Photo courtesy of Robbins family.

am responsible to try and keep the natural world in as good condition as possible, so I have taken a deep interest in conservation matters. I feel that the coming generations have just as much right to enjoy the things that I enjoy, so I want to be sure that I do my part to keep things in good shape. For one particular moment in time, I may be responsible for a particular plot of ground that I own, but I don't really own it. I have the responsibility for it because some previous owner passed it on to me, and I want to pass it on to people who come after me.

THE MORE I HAVE COME TO KNOW birds and their habits and migration patterns, the more convinced I am that all of life is a part of the whole creative process I associate with God. I remember once coming across a kid who was trying to shoot a snowy owl. We got to talking, and he said, "I know that owl's around, and I am looking for it." I asked him if he would actually shoot that owl if he found it, and he began to feel a little sheepish about it. I told him a few things about snowy owls, about how they migrate from Canada, how they feed on other creatures and so on, and told him about the feathering that an owl has. To make a long story short, he decided that killing a snowy owl was a very bad idea.

AS MUCH AS I LIKE BEING WITH PEOPLE, I also like equally well the times when I can be alone, and the times when I'm alone, I think I've become more observant. I wish to high heaven that I knew more about what I am looking at. I see plant life, but I don't know much about botany. I think about my uncle, Frank Seymour, who combined a career as a minister with that of a botanist. Most of his life was spent in Massachusetts, but he did come out here for pastorates at Appleton and Tomahawk for a few years. He wrote a book on the flora of Lincoln County while he was here. He wrote books on the flora of New England. He really was an outstanding botanist. How I wish I had his knowledge and understanding of plant and animal life! I feel as if I know only a tiny fraction of the natural world. If I knew more, I would appreciate more of it, but every new level of appreciation I have makes me think more reverently of a divine Creator.

I HAVE QUITE a few places that I would love to travel to, but I realize that when it comes to trying to go to new places and see new birds, my energy limitations are going to restrict me to what I call roadside birding. I couldn't begin to do the things that you do when you go out and collect trumpeter swan eggs; that sounds to me like something for athletic gymnasts and that kind of thing. I have more and more become a roadside birder simply because of my limited strength. I could explain this very nicely and say that I am just plain too big around; it has made a lot of fieldwork difficult. Even when I was younger and healthier, I did not particularly enjoy some of the more difficult hiking. This business of climbing hills and really getting back into the brush where you have to go to see some birds is simply beyond me now health-wise, so I have got to live with certain limitations. I realize that something can happen any moment that may make a major change in my health condition, but if I continue to have sufficient strength, health, and energy, I am anxious to visit new places and try to see birds that I am less familiar with.

I made it a point during my first two or three years of work on *Wisconsin Birdlife* to get out into some of the areas. I think I filled in the worst of the blanks in terms of statewide coverage. I had an advantage that lots of other people didn't have: I moved about every 10 years from one location to another. This gave me a good chance to sample bird life in quite a variety of locations. I am sure that there are still places in the state that I don't know nearly as well as I might, such as the national forests up north where I have never really spent much time. But, overall, I am probably more familiar with most areas of the state than most people.

One hankering that I've had that I've never fully satisfied is to be up on Wisconsin Point in Superior at a time when there's a "fallout"—a large number of visiting migrants exhausted after a long travel. I have been there and camped overnight when I thought the migration would be good, but I have never seen a real fallout there. There are hawk observation points I would like to spend more time at, and I would like to spend some time at night in areas where they trap owls. I haven't done much of any of that. Another place that I have visited only rarely that intrigues me is Seagull Bar up in Marinette, but there again the trouble is it's a long hike over soft sand, and I don't think my energy level would permit this now the way it used to.

ONE OF MY FAVORITE AREAS that I did visit often was the area around Roberts and Hudson in St. Croix County. I did a lot of birding there in the 1960s and have returned a few times since then. That is an area I never tire of because of the nice variety of birds, especially during migration and the summer season. Another thing that I remember enjoying so very much and that I never get enough of is canoeing on the Bois Brule River. John Degerman used to take me down the river once every year, just out of the goodness of his heart. He wanted to learn the birds, and he knew I could teach him the birdsongs, so we would canoe the river. The chorus of birds you get, with the winter wrens and the parula warblers, is just heavenly. So that became really an all-time favorite trip of mine.

There is another area that intrigues me from a mysterious point of view, but I would want to go with somebody who knows the area very well; that area is the Wolf River Bottoms between New London and Hortonville. My interest in that area comes from reading the reports of prothonotary warblers that Father Dayton used to write. These were reports that he used to send in to Owen Gromme. He did his observations in the early years of the twentieth century, but he described year after year prothonotary warblers in those river bottoms. In the early 1970s, I had no idea whether the habitat was still adequate; nobody had been reporting from there for years. I stopped there one July day on my way to Green Bay and found that not only was the habitat still acceptable, but I heard a prothonotary warbler singing, and this was past the song period, about the 20th of July! I made it a point a couple of years after that to get over there in June. There were prothonotary warblers there every time, so I am presuming that these birds were probably present as breeding birds, and they were also present during those early years. To really get a handle on this, a person needs to go in a canoe. There are so many backwaters out there that I would get lost if I tried it myself. I talked with Daryl Tessen about this, and he had the same feeling. He doesn't know that area well enough to pilot a canoe through there, but with someone who is familiar with the area, we might discover more prothonotary warblers and other southern river bottom birds, such as yellow-billed cuckoos and cerulean warblers, too.

I keep going afield. I'm not an avid bird lister. I keep lists, and if you give me time, I will count up a list and tell you how many I've got on my life list, but right now I don't know what I've got. I enjoy seeing a lifer almost as much as the next fellow, but I enjoy just as much seeing a rare bird I have seen before, so I keep going afield often.

Speaking of rare birds, when I think of species that have declined, one of the prime cases that comes to mind is the Bewick's wren. I rarely encountered Bewick's wrens before I moved to Adams County in 1951. I was very pleasantly surprised when I moved to Adams to find that I could hear Bewick's wrens from my backyard every year. There were four or five singing males scattered around the city. Here was this bird that seemed to be so rare other places; it seemed to be present in some numbers, however, up our way. This continued for much of the time that we lived there. I noticed that by about 1958 or so, I wasn't hearing these birds as much as I used to. When I made trips back there after moving away in 1960, I couldn't find one anymore. It took a while for it to sink in that this bird had just plain disappeared. I think it's disappeared from Wisconsin. I don't think we have had a state record for years now, and when the DNR was asking for recommendations for what birds to consider as endangered, I pointed this out to them. Bewick's wren wasn't on their list at first. It has disappeared over this whole part of the country, and I really have no explanation for it.

The pronounced decline in grassland species has been staring us all in the face. I think what made me aware of that was not so much my field observations as my analysis of the Breeding Bird Survey data. I can recall when I first noticed that these species were declining. I called DNR's attention to it, and they followed through and saw that the western meadowlark particularly had declined seriously. I have looked back at my records from when we lived in Mazomanie from 1948 to 1951; on almost every May/June field trip, I heard six or eight or more Henslow's sparrows in that area. I haven't heard a Henslow's sparrow out in the Mazomanie area for years and years. Again, this is evidence of a decline; we might attribute some of that to changes in land use, but I suspect it's more than that.

I also suspect that we are getting declines in whip-poor-wills, and I'm suspicious that there are declines in eastern screech owls, which are numerous in the southern part of the state, but I rarely find screech owls farther north. Regarding waterfowl, I find [northern] pintails are awfully hard to find nowadays. Loggerhead shrikes? The decline was quite pronounced. I didn't see many loggerhead shrikes until we got to St. Croix County in 1960, but then for three to four years, I found loggerhead shrikes on almost every summer field trip I took. I don't know if it was 1964 or 1965, but I was noticing that the places that had them in previous years no longer had them. When I moved away from there in 1968, I think I had probably been through a couple of years without seeing one; so, definitely, that picture has changed since the 1940s–1950s.

When I came to Wisconsin in 1939, I heard people talk about prairie-chickens and about how they used to be everywhere, but by the late 1930s they had just about disappeared from the southern counties. There was some indication out in the Mazomanie grasslands that you might still hear one. I made a point of going out there a couple of times with friends, and we heard prairie-chickens just a few times, probably around 1940 or so and that was the last. So I got in on just the tail end of the stand of the prairie-chicken in southern Wisconsin.

Let me say a few words about the peregrine falcon. One vivid experience I remember occurred in the summer of 1937. I came out from Massachusetts and spent a few weeks with relatives here. I camped out on a sandbar in the Wisconsin River one night, right below Ferry Bluff. All night long the screaming of the peregrine was going on. I don't know if we got any sleep that night or not. I presume that the parents were feeding young all that time, and it just seemed as if they were doing it around the clock; they put on a great show. I'd have to check my records as to how many times I saw peregrines out there after that time, but they soon disappeared.

🍃

WHEN I LIVED in St. Croix County in the early 1960s, I would make two or three trips up to the northwestern part of the state every year. One particular June morning, I was driving along a stretch of road east of Solon Springs with the window down when I heard a Connecticut warbler. I recognized that song instantly. At that time, the Connecticut warbler was thought to be a very rare summer resident. Owen Gromme had a nesting record of it on one of his museum expeditions, but the bird community thought of the Connecticut warbler as being a bird of the swamps. Here I was in dry jack pine area when I heard a song that surprised me. I drove a little bit further. By golly, I heard another one, and I got the idea to make the trip a Connecticut warbler expedition. To make a long story short, in two hours driving—maybe 12 miles in that jack pine area—I found 41 singing Connecticut warblers. I just drove back and forth on some of the side roads. Then I wrote this up and took a few other occasions to go to some other jack pine areas. I found Connecticut warblers there, too. I read the literature to see if other people had been finding this bird in jack pines, and I couldn't find any references. So I wrote an article in *The Passenger Pigeon* called "New Light on the Connecticut Warbler." I began getting feedback from people in Minnesota and received a letter from Earl Godfrey in Canada. Earl said that he had started finding Connecticut warblers in jack pine, and when other people read this article, they started checking jack pine areas, and they began finding Connecticut warblers, too. Now we've got quite a different idea as to its habitat preferences. In certain jack pine barrens in northern Wisconsin, this is a fairly numerous bird.

Related to my scholarly efforts, I feel that my role in research has been more the collecting and compiling of data that we get from other people, such as with the Breeding Bird Survey, than individual research studies of my own. I think, however, I have made some discoveries about Connecticut warblers that were new to the ornithological community. I did the same thing with LeConte's sparrows some years back, but those instances are few and far between. I accomplish more by collecting data from many people, putting these together, and then analyzing them in a way that makes sense. In the case of the LeConte's sparrow, I had mistaken its song. I had heard it several times over a period of years and assumed that it was an abbreviated savannah sparrow song, but one morning while I was in St. Croix County, I heard the song real well and recognized it was not that of a savannah sparrow. I finally hunted the singer down, and I got a look at it. For the first time in my life I felt that I knew the song of the LeConte's sparrow. Having learned that song, I found that if I was out real early in the morning, I could hear that song in quite a few places. So I deliberately explored extensive grass meadows in a few places in the northern counties, and I found LeConte's sparrows all over the place. Again, this was a habitat that people had not associated with this bird; they thought of it as a marsh bird, and here I was in dry upland grass meadows. I corresponded with Carl Richter about this, and he mentioned that most of his observations were in swampy areas, but that he had sometimes found them in dry grass areas, too. So eventually I began examining all of my records obtained by hearing this bird. I noticed that most of the records that I had were real early, before it got light, and that anytime after about six in the morning, I stopped hearing this bird. That was another reason why other people hadn't been hearing this bird.

On some WSO convention trips up north, I began to point out the song to other observers. Once other people learned the song, they found it in more places. So I wrote an article called "New Light on the LeConte's Sparrow."

FINALLY, in 1973, the American Ornithologists' Union decided to split the alder and willow flycatchers. Once this was done, the question became: Which of these do we have in Wisconsin? I had some information in my field notes that I could draw upon to help answer this question because the identification is mostly by sound. You can hardly tell these birds apart by looking at them. But the songs were different enough that I could recall my first experience with what we now call the willow flycatcher. That was out here near Black Earth in the summer of 1937. I met up with this bird, and for the life of me I didn't know what it was. It looked like an alder flycatcher, but it did not sound like the alder flycatchers I had grown up with in New England. What finally tipped me off was a statement in Peterson's first field guide that said that birds west of Ohio sing a different song. He verbalized *Wee-bee-o* for the alder and *Fitz-bew* for the willow. He didn't call them alder and willow; he simply called them different songs of the alder flycatcher. So from that time on, I put down in my notes any time I heard an alder flycatcher an "E" for east or "W" for west.

I had a lot of data at the time the split was made, so I went back over my records. It seemed to me as if the east-west designation was wrong, that it was more of a north-south designation, so I put all of this together for an article in *The Passenger Pigeon*. I wrote that article primarily upon my own observations, and I concluded that northern Wisconsin had alders, southern Wisconsin had willows, and that there was quite a band of overlap, rather narrow in the western part of the state, but becoming broader as you moved east in the state. I think that time has proved this a fairly accurate assessment. There are a few more areas of overlap than what I anticipated at that time, but the general picture has held true. We were ahead of just about all of the other states in determining which flycatchers were present, simply because I had these data going back several years.

SHIRLEY has been a great partner throughout all these years. She has her interests, and these are somewhat different from mine. We've learned how to encourage each other in exploring our own interests.

The fact that we've been in love with each other is a very natural answer to our long marriage, but I would point out as I have pointed out to a great many couples, it's one thing to love each other, but it's much more important to develop a feeling that you love each other because you share the same objectives in life, the same hopes and dreams.

I think Shirley and I have done that right from the word go. We're going to walk together hand-in-hand, arm-in-arm, and heart-in-heart toward these goals. Inevitably, the time is going to come when one of us is gone, but if you have that sense of direction in life, life doesn't stop when you lose your partner. You continue on toward

Sam with beloved wife, Shirley.
Photo courtesy of Robbins family.

your life goal. So we discuss this often with couples that I have married, and Shirley and I started out that way and we're still doing it—serving God is our same life goal—trying to practice in this world the principles of love that we think ought to be universal. I think the thing that probably affects me most deeply is something that's very hard to put into words, Sumner, but I'd like to think and hope that when the final curtain comes down for me, I will hear some divine voice say, "Well done, good and faithful servant." ✳

Sam passed away peacefully at his Madison home in the early morning hours of February 19, 2000, with Shirley, his wife of 53 years, nearby.

SLIPPERY ELM

GJK

George Becker
(1917-2002)

WHITE OAK

Chapter Eight~
George Becker

I was so deep into German ... that I continued a year longer, and that got me the master's in Germanic philology. Toward the end of that year, 1939, somebody mentioned a guy over in the Game Management Department by the name of Aldo Leopold. Well! That was the beginning of my death right there! ... Aldo Leopold not only changed my knowledge, but he changed my direction.

—GB

George Charles Becker, a Renaissance guy with boundless energy and ability to match, was born in Milwaukee, Wisconsin, on February 26, 1917, to Peter and Theresa Becker, of Austrian and Romanian lineage, respectively. He had one sibling, Arthur ("Artie"), born a year later.

Becker graduated from Washington High School in Milwaukee in 1935 and began an impressive and diverse academic career that eventually culminated in the seminal 1983 publication, *Fishes of Wisconsin*.[105] His study of Wisconsin fishes, however, came well after he finished college—the Milwaukee State Teachers College (today the University of Wisconsin-Milwaukee), where he majored in music (playing violin) and minored in German (1935–1937). He went to graduate school at the University of Wisconsin-Madison, but not in ichthyology. He studied Germanic philology. In his last graduate school year, he audited Aldo Leopold's class "Game Management" and was captivated. "The year 1939 was my turn-around from languages to biology and related topics." He earned a master's degree in Germanic philology in 1939, then taught high school languages in Port Edwards, Wisconsin, in 1940 and 1941. But the influence of Leopold remained with him.

On June 21, 1941, George married Cedarburg native and children's literature teacher, Sylvia Klenk. (They had fallen in love while reading works by Schiller in a college German class.) Service in the U.S. Army followed in July 1942. He was sent to the United

Theresa and Peter Becker with sons Arthur and George, 1923. Photo courtesy of Becker family.

States Army Signal Corps radio operator school in Kansas City, Missouri, where he mastered Morse code. He later attained the rank of master sergeant and commanded the first Radio Station Section in Australia, New Guinea,

"It's called 'crackin' a smile." Circa 1970. Photo courtesy of Becker family.

and the Philippines (Island of Leyte) for General MacArthur's forces.

In November 1945, Becker was honorably discharged from duty, and he returned to Port Edwards to rejoin Sylvia. He taught high school there through the 1946–1947 school year and from the fall of 1947 through the 1948–1949 school year. Becker served as principal of Clintonville High School ("not my cup of tea") before becoming a full-fledged student at UW-Madison in pursuit of a master's degree in botany and zoology. He and Sylvia lived south of Baraboo in Badger Village—university housing for married veterans—from the summer of 1949 through the summer 1951, with sons Kenneth, born 1946, and Dale, born 1948. Their third son, David, was born in 1952.

By summer's end in 1951, not only had Becker met the requirements for an MS degree in zoology and botany, but by attending summer sessions over three years he had also earned all of the credits necessary for a PhD, except he had no thesis. The fall of 1951 found the Beckers relocated to a 78-acre country retreat they called Windy Knoll, which included portions of Rocky Run Creek. Comments Sylvia in her 1951 Christmas card (begun in 1948, the annual Christmas card or letter serves as the source of information for most of this biographical sketch): "We Beckers have bedded down in a home of our own once again. Badger Village with its mumps and measles and leaky water pipes is just a vague memory."

For the next five years, Becker taught foreign languages at Madison West High School (including Greek on his own during the noon hour) and studied the trout of Rocky Run Creek, processing thousands of fish. That wasn't all, according to Sylvia, who notes in 1952 that "gardening and chickens are George's current passions. What melons and potatoes! He's found time to teach Sunday school, sing in the choir, and help finish the new church too...." Windy Knoll served as an inviting refuge for the Beckers' friends during a tranquil if not bucolic period. Notes Sylvia in her 1953 Christmas card: "We thrill to the warbles and trills of countless songbirds in the surrounding marshes and meadows and stand arm in arm in the soft moonlight enjoying the bubbling of our stream. We've achieved a leakless roof, windproof siding, indoor plumbing, furnace heat, kitchen cabinets, and a knotty pine study with our many books at our fingertips. Windy Knoll Manor thrives on visitors and can sleep 13 with nary a toe stretched on the floor."

In 1957, George switched his career focus to science and began his long association with the University of Wisconsin at Stevens Point, teaching biology and comparative anatomy, with ichthyology becoming his specialty. The Beckers moved to a farm along the banks of the Tomorrow River, 14 miles from Stevens Point. Around this time, George built his first fish shocking boat and equipment (motor and electrodes) for sampling "all streams and waters of the state."

1954 Christmas card portrait of George, Dale, Kenneth, Sylvia, and David, Portage, Wisconsin. Photo courtesy of Becker family.

CHAPTER EIGHT

"The Becker basement was transformed into a "scientific whirlpool," says Sylvia in her 1958 Christmas letter. "Hundreds of minnows, captured with shocking equipment, swim aimlessly about in aerated aquariums and more hundreds stare glossy-eyed from jars of preservative. He aims to explore the life cycle of a species called the long-nosed dace, and at times we wonder if he is not simultaneously trying to prove that man can live without sleep."

In 1959, she observes that "months ago his research data spilled over from his den to the adjoining room. There in his free moments [he] sits ... pondering the analysis of variance. Calculations spew steadily from the electric computer, are transposed into graph and chart form, and added to the reams of earlier deductions. Intermittently, little wedges of time are snatched for family fun or a stint on the violin. As a very special treat, he allowed himself the pleasure of playing with the Stevens Point Symphony orchestra for one month...."

In 1960, the Beckers moved into town "after nine years in idyllic pastoral settings," residing at 413 Prais Street—"a domain measured in feet instead of acres," says Sylvia in her annual Christmas letter. Here, the family adjusted to urban living relatively smoothly, immersing themselves in a variety of activities, including the "Pro Familie" Quartet, with Ken and Dale on the violin, Sylvia on viola, and George on the cello.

Family string quartet. George (cello), Sylvia (viola), Kenneth (violin), Dale (violin), with David (soon-to-be viola player). Photo by George for the 1960 Christmas card. Photo courtesy of Becker family.

The Beckers performed at several small gatherings. "We are still puzzling over the dubious compliment proffered by one sweet coed," notes Sylvia. "Said she, 'I certainly enjoyed your quartet. I've been laughing ever since.'" Throughout this period, Becker continues his fish studies assiduously, but he realized he needed help if he was to complete his mission.

On June 21, 1961, George and Sylvia celebrate their twentieth wedding anniversary, and Sylvia somewhat prophetically comments in her annual Christmas letter: "God willing, we'll spend the next 40 years holding hands together." In January 1962, George received his PhD in ichthyology from

UW-Madison. That same year he was named the outstanding teacher on campus at UW-Stevens Point.

By the end of 1962, his fish research, as Sylvia drolly observes in the annual Christmas letter, was going full bore: "George's research took our caravan to southern Wisconsin where for two months Father and his willing slaves explored the mighty Wisconsin and sundry smaller streams, collecting thousands of minnows for future study." By 1963, the thought that he could complete a book on Wisconsin fishes had clearly taken hold in George's mind. Says Sylvia: "He has bypassed several opportunities for administrative positions because he truly prefers to teach and desperately hopes for a bit of spare time in which to compile his fish research into book form."

The year 1965 found Becker highly engaged in teaching and very much appreciated for it. Point's student newspaper (May 1965) lauds "his dynamic personality, fairness, knowledge of subject matter, and real concern for the individual student." (One student that fell under Becker's considerable influence and enduring friendship was Stevens Point native and former chief of the U.S. Forest Service, Michael P. Dombeck.)

A 1965 summer vacation included fishing trips to Isle Royale and Glacier National Park. Among other extracurricular duties, he began his second of three years as Conservation Committee chair for the Wisconsin Society for Ornithology (WSO). In 1966, he served as vice president of the WSO. In 1967, he was awarded the university's Johnson Award for Excellence in Teaching, and he began a two-year stint as president of the WSO. Then, in 1968, the university named him curator of fishes for the new Museum of Natural History.

"His newest hobby," notes Sylvia in the 1967 Christmas letter, is "snake catching, and the four prairie rattlers that he and the boys bagged in Montana this summer are proudly displayed in the school museum." Trips out West have become regular occasions. From Sylvia's 1968 Christmas letter: "Anyone familiar with the migratory habits of the Beckers knows that each summer there is that irresistible pull to the rich trout streams of Wyoming and Montana." Self-taught in the art of fly tying, George passes on his knowledge to his three sons, and they spend several summers together fly fishing in remote western streams and at sites in Wisconsin.

In 1969, both George and Sylvia become swept up in the tide of the Vietnam anti-war movement. George publicly decried the "chemical attacks on the cropland and forests of Vietnam." In 1970, Sylvia observes that "George's excess energy has been directed toward one major goal: eliminating all water pollution in the Wisconsin River basin." In 1971, we first learned of Becker's longstanding argument with the Wisconsin DNR over the use of piscicides to control carp. He filed two court suits, including one before the State Supreme Court, both eventually unsuccessful. His main beef was with the department's use of carp poisons, rotenone, and also antimycin, which is no longer used today.

In 1972, George was elected president of the Citizens Natural Resources Association (CNRA), which at that time was arguably the state's leading and most prominent environmental advocacy group. The CNRA led the charge to ban DDT from Wisconsin in 1970, the first state to do so, with the federal government following suit in 1972. In 1973, George received the CNRA's Silver Acorn Award for "outstanding effort and achievement in conservation." George continued his fish research, and by 1974 he had completed a 500-page manuscript titled *The Suckers of Wisconsin*.

Sylvia in white hat explains solar heating panels to a school group, 1975. Photo courtesy of Becker family.

During the summer of 1975, the Beckers successfully converted their oil-heated home to solar heating. According to retired UW-Stevens Point Professor Charles Long, Becker's solar heater was the "first in central Wisconsin."[106] In 1976, Becker completed his first book, published by the Argonne National Laboratory and the U.S. Energy Research and Development Administration, titled *Inland Fishes of the Lake Michigan Drainage Basin*. He also had made significant progress with his *Fishes of Wisconsin* manuscript, aiming to publish it by 1979.

In 1977, Becker took a yearlong sabbatical to work on the *Fishes* manuscript, often spending 14 hours a day on it. Sylvia begins her 1978 Christmas letter: "GREETINGS! If you see a finny vamp spouting greetings you are not hallucinating. I've spent such endless hours typing the final draft of *Fishes of Wisconsin* that I fully expect to metamorphose into a fish myself." Becker's

George in his beloved "basement museum," wearing his homemade corduroy shirt and showing off fish specimens, ca. 1960. Photo courtesy of Becker family.

goal was to get the manuscript to the University of Wisconsin Press by February 1979.

ON DECEMBER 20, 1979, George Becker officially retired from UW-Stevens Point after 22 years of service. The university's four-page press release announcing the occasion stated: "As a curator of fishes for the museum, he gathered more than 250,000 fish representing about 700 species including about 75,000 specimens of Wisconsin fishes which is the most complete collection in existence." This collection is appropriately titled the George C. Becker Ichthyology Collection. And, very satisfying indeed, Becker met his goal of delivering the final pages of his *Fishes of Wisconsin* manuscript to the UW Press.

The year 1979, however, was a bittersweet one for the Becker family. "Inevitably a bit of bad luck overtakes the good," writes Sylvia in her 1979–1980 Christmas letter. "Ken took the first punch with the diagnosis that his delusions and depression were really chronic schizophrenia. Finally, after years of misery the illness had a name and could be treated with medication ... Graciously Dale and [wife] Sharron built him a little cabin of his own (La Casa Pequena) in their Ozark 'Garden of Eden.' For variety and urban experiences he spends several months of the year with us. My own bout with misery began several years ago, but I grimly denied having problems and finished out the final semester with forced enthusiasm.

Once I reached [our winter home in Rockport] Texas the game was over. The tremors and muscle tension which made sleep impossible were in fact Parkinson's disease.... After much trial and error and an extended stay at the Corpus Christi Hospital the magic combination of drugs that I could tolerate evolved."

Sylvia's condition did not slow her enthusiasm for traveling, and she and George spent the next few years visiting refuges and remote sites in Texas, the Ozarks, New Mexico, Arizona, and California, and they even took in the sights and sounds of New York City. George's 1982 summer, notes Sylvia in the 1982 Christmas letter, is "one endless proofreading chore made doubly strenuous by the total loss of reading vision in one eye. The malady bears the lofty name ischemic optic neuropathy. Bluntly stated, that means the optic nerve is dead and there is no cure."

Christmas 1983 brought welcome news from Sylvia's annual letter: "Rejoice, rejoice, the book *Fishes Of Wisconsin* is born! ... After a gestation period of some 25 years a beautiful 'baby' emerged, weighing 7 pounds and covering 1,050 pages.... It is dedicated to 'four wonderful, long-suffering people ... Sylvia ... and sons Kenneth, Dale, and David.' The author modestly omits the fact that most of those 157 life histories and countless maps, charts, and drawings were executed by him while the four of us were nestled in our beds. The biggest strain in family relations came just before publication. I, Sylvia, can soberly testify that any partnership which survives indexing a book of such magnitude in three days and nights is welded in concrete and need not fear dissolution."

Christmas 1984 found the Beckers in Jamaica. Sylvia writes: "We find the Jamaican way of life refreshingly unsophisticated. 'Soon come' may mean anything from five minutes to five hours. Even a seemingly hopeless situation evokes a cheerful 'No problem.' The slow pace is ideally suited to someone with Parkinson's disease who can't hurry under any circumstances. However, their unhurried pace applies only until they get behind the wheel of a car. Then, grab the nearest support and pray!" In 1985, the Beckers sold their Wisconsin summer home and their Texas winter mobile home. They instead bought mobile homes in Florida and Arkansas, the latter to be near sons Ken and Dale. By Christmas 1986, Sylvia seems pleased that their respective "physical ailments are fairly well under control," but she notes that "instant recall now eludes us and names in particular require teamwork." In the end, "laughter is the best medicine, and [we] make the most of every opportunity to laugh, mostly at ourselves."

In 1989, back in Wisconsin, George's work on fishes was honored. He received the first award presented by the University of Wisconsin-Stevens Point's Society of the Sigma Xi for outstanding research. A strong sense of loss and limited time, however, are the focus of Sylvia's 1989 Christmas letter: "Elderly friends and family members are quietly slipping away into the next world, and we miss them terribly.... It also reminds us that our own days are numbered. There are so many things we haven't yet seen or done. A tiny voice inside counsels, 'Do it NOW!' We've begun to heed that advice.... This fall we chose to leisurely revisit Gulfport, Miss. We walked barefoot on the white sand beach and watched seagulls by the hundreds spiraling above our heads."

In 1990, Becker revived "what was once a passionate interest in ornithology. We both joined the local [Kissimmee, Florida] Audubon Society, and he participated in the annual bird count.... We enjoy sporadic visits to local parks and pastures where we've been lucky enough to see such rare birds as the snail kite and the wood stork and our favorites, the resident sandhill cranes who nest in the swamp across the road and krill loudly as they fly directly over our heads to feed in surrounding pastures."

The Beckers celebrated 50 years of marriage on June 21, 1991. Observes Sylvia in the Christmas letter: "Like a pair of snow geese, we mated for life, and birds have always been a part of that union. Even during our five years of courtship, I seldom saw George without a pair of binoculars dangling from his neck. For a while I thought he was born that way. Then, for some 30 years fish fever supplanted bird mania as he struggled to get his knowledge of fishes between the pages of a book. With retirement came stays in Texas, Florida and Arkansas, all rich in birdlife, and a mania was reborn."

Sylvia's 1992 Christmas letter reveals that George's life had changed markedly: "George suffered a cruel blow to his love of life in April when a mysterious optic nerve affliction severely impaired his sight despite delicate state-of-the-art surgery. Gone is his chief enjoyment in retirement, daily bird hikes in the fields and along the shores of nearby lakes and streams.... Gone, too, is the facility to read the dozens of books and magazines that surround us. But here I come to the rescue. I've read entire books aloud.... We've also discovered the magic of the *Talking Books* program, making hundreds of titles available on tapes and discs free for the asking, a truly magnanimous government service."

Son Ken assumed much of the reading role in later years, arriving each afternoon for daily readings to his parents.

CHAPTER EIGHT

Sylvia's 2000 Christmas letter brings "the astonishing realization that George and I have lived side by side for over a half a century. Our sedentary life has replaced the hurly burly of yesteryear. Ever mindful of our OLD age, doctors send us home with a stern warning: 'Do not fall!' But every square inch of floor and furniture seems poised to whack us. George survived the most spectacular plunge of all ... twelve steps to the concrete basement floor. It almost proved fatal.... Dealing with Parkinson's for 21 years, I am accustomed to frequent falls and am perpetually covered with colorful bruises, but I seem to have unbreakable bones! Our three sons are putting up a noble struggle to prolong our presence by fortifying us with good cooking, therapeutic massages, clean clothes, good music, and challenging thoughts and ideas. We wonder sometimes about the merits of longevity but are still able to enjoy the good things that life provides."

One of the good things that the Beckers loved to do was sing as a family. "When our son David is here," Becker told me, "he's at what he calls a keyboard—portable, brought in the back end of his station wagon. We have singing fests. Dale's got a beautiful voice. We're all singing the good old chestnuts, the old standards and folk songs. 'Way Down Upon the Swanee River' is one small illustration. What happens is that Davie will start on the piano. He plays entirely by ear, as well as by note, but he plays entirely by ear when he's doing this with us. And I'm seated in my chair, Sylvia's over there in the other chair, and then it doesn't matter where the people are in the room, they join in. You should hear the music that we made a couple of weeks ago when they were here. It's a very wonderful thing. It's a carryover from our early violin and piano—Artie and I—he on the piano and I on the violin. We've always had music as an avocational activity although I no longer play an instrument."

On January 22 and 23, 2001, I interviewed George at his Eureka Springs, Arkansas, home, with Sylvia in a wheelchair nearby. He greeted me with a wide smile and a firm handshake as he ushered me into their living room. I soon learned that George was able to read and write slowly with the aid of special magnifying optics. His enthusiasm and energy level remained surprisingly high as he talked effortlessly for hours about the past and present. Son Dale dutifully arrived at noon each day to take his mom and dad to a nearby restaurant for lunch.

I'm going to be 84 next month, and the last year has been a real problem for me. I'm just dragging along sometimes. I guess people at my age can expect to slow down. You caught me before I died anyway! (Laughs)

Let's go to the beginning. My first language was German. I was born in Milwaukee, of course. Mother and Dad had been only a few years in this country, and both of them had come from Europe. Dad came from Detta, Austria, and Mother from Buziaş, Romania. These communities that they came from were German-speaking communities, but they did not meet in Europe. They met in Chicago. Dad was an excellent tailor. He could make a suit from top to bottom. He had studied it, you know; that was one of the trainings available in Europe at the time, and he learned his trade in Europe. As he moved through Europe, he stopped at Berlin and worked in a tailor shop there; you could get work anywhere. He was a master tailor, and he went to Chicago to visit people who had migrated earlier, but I don't know what brought him to Milwaukee.

Dad was very successful. He was making coats, and the coat is the most difficult part of a suit to make. He was making coats out of wool for custom tailors all over the city of Milwaukee. The customer could pick out what he wanted from a big box of samples with a swatch of whatever it was they wanted to sell you.

After my parents got married, they had me. My mother was a homemaker, and she didn't have any attraction to the outdoors. But my brother and I liked to be outdoors, and we spent a lot of time in Washington Park. We walked everywhere. I was active in the Boy Scouts in Milwaukee, and my brother, Artie, and I listened to music, particularly the Saturday operas that were broadcast on radio. We enjoyed that tremendously. We'd go down to the library and pick up the score of the opera that was to be sung. Artie was a very accomplished piano player. I, on the other hand, struggled with the violin. I managed to get into the local symphony and played first chair in a number of instances. But I was not an accomplished player.

I SPENT a lot of time at the Milwaukee Public Museum. What the zoo didn't have, the museum had. I walked probably three-quarters of an hour to reach it. I became very much interested in the natural history element of the museum, in mammals, and this is the reason why I got interested in birds, too, and stuck with birds. I came to know [curator] Merl Duesing. I came to know him because for one thing I wanted to get the [Boy Scouts] bird study merit badge. I presented to him the list of birds that I was familiar with, and one of the birds was a European bird. He says, "What's this doing here?" And I said, "Well, in 1925, Mom, Dad, and I went to Europe to visit the old country and the parents, and we saw the European stork there, up on the rooftops." I don't believe he had a stork to show me, but he accepted it anyway. He was a great guy.

George at UW-Madison, ca. 1938. Photo courtesy of Becker family.

I stayed in the scouts for a number of years. I was just shy the cooking and camping merit badges; it's hard to get those in Milwaukee. It's a big city, but we don't cook and camp there. I must have had close to 30 merit badges. One of the enjoyable things that I did was go into Washington Park to see the birds. I was about 10, 11, 12, something like that. I had binoculars. And, of course, I started collecting bird books almost immediately—early Peterson—but that didn't suffice. I always picked up a few more. My parents were not ones to encourage this because I don't think Dad knew a robin from Tweety Bird. What he liked was squabs [pigeons]. He was raising squabs in his last few years of life and enjoying it.

My parents were pretty proud of us. We were good in school; we got good grades, and we never got into trouble. These were forward-looking people from the old country. I think they were trying to emphasize the best that was available, and I appreciated my parents. They were very good people. They weren't strict because we behaved. I don't know why it is that we didn't screw up somewhere along the line!

I was also interested in languages. This came about in my high school work. I started taking Latin, Greek, and Spanish, all at Washington High School. I had Greek, by the way, during a noon hour with Professor Gainsley who was teaching the Latin, but he taught Greek on his own, at noon. Eventually, he got a class together at the beginning of the year of people who were interested in Greek, but as time went on I was the last one left, and then I could see that it didn't pay him to spend any more time with me. But he was a very kind, old fellow who knew his languages very well, especially the classical languages.

When I started out at the university, I started out in music for two years down there at Milwaukee State Teachers College, but I found out very quickly that this was not my ball of wax. I transferred, then, to Madison and finished my undergraduate work in Madison, all in languages, all of those three years.

I was so deep into German at the University of Wisconsin when I transferred that I continued a year longer, and that got me the master's in Germanic philology. Toward the end of that year, 1939, somebody mentioned

George in job application photo, 1939/40. Photo courtesy of Becker family.

a guy over in the Game Management Department by the name of Aldo Leopold. Well! That was the beginning of my death right there!

Oh, I've got tears in my eyes now because I went to that first lecture in Game Management, and he made such an impression on me. I could never lose it. And this man, he just gripped me. I don't know why it would be that way, but it was so sincere, and he was teaching these people the whisper songs of birds and testing them in class. You could tell by what he was doing that it was special. No place else would you get the same kind of treatment, would you get the same kind of education. It changed me completely. I suddenly realized that I was in the wrong area. Not that I didn't enjoy the languages; they were fun, and I did real well in them. I got a master's degree. But, that guy was something special. He said, "Come on into the library, and if you have a chance, take a look at my books. If you want to use them for something, for writing up a paper or whatever." He was a very generous man. So I really took advantage of him. Sometimes I was the only one in that library with him!

All of his books had been re-bound. He must have had a real quirk about that, you know. He'd get a book, a brand new book, and take it over to the bookbinders and get it re-bound in buckram [stiff, hard-wearing cotton or linen cloth]. I guess it was green buckram all the way through.

He was so keenly interested in the individual student. He always called me "Becker." I don't think he knew my first name. "How are you, Becker?"

CHAPTER EIGHT

Oh, boy. He was always telling us what to look for, and how to look for it. And he was really a stickler when it came to writing up a paper, report, or thesis or whatever. Oh, it had to be just so. He would almost invariably return a writing to a student, his student, and say, "Work it over, work it over again." Well, it got to the point where he almost had a mutiny from his students who found it illogical that he was so strict in writing. "Now, listen," he said, "I will never submit a paper after I have first written it." He said, "I will never submit it after I have written it a second time, nor a third time, nor a fourth time, nor a fifth time, nor a sixth time." They got the message: This guy wanted results, perfect results, something really good. And this is the reason why his *Sand County Almanac* has endured. It's writing that's inconceivably good, all the way through.

Leopold was so serious. And the guy had a tremendous gift of language. Of course, he never did get to see his *Sand County Almanac* because he died while fighting that fire, the year before. His graduate students, Bob McCabe, the Hamerstroms, and a few others got together, and they worked up how they were going to handle this. They each read the entire manuscript, made recommendations as to what changes should be made, and finally, I think it was Fran Hamerstrom who said, "Hey, let's not make any changes. It's pretty good the way it is." And indeed it was; it was super.

At the end of December 1939, a census of the pheasant occurred in University Bay. Aldo invited the entire class to come along and watch this census, how it was being taken, and so on. Well, on the morning of the census, Becker was the only one who showed up. The reason why is that nobody knew my telephone number, and they couldn't tell me that this had been called off. Well, Aldo Leopold took real pity on me. He reached into his book cabinet, and there he had about 12 new copies of *Game Management*. He reached down for a copy, and then in his inimitable way, opened it up and inscribed, "From Aldo Leopold to George Becker."

❧

HERE'S A FRAN HAMERSTROM STORY. Once, I had called [Wisconsin Conservation Department Game Manager] Wallace Grange and told him that I was watching a sharp-tailed grouse, which was only three miles outside of Port Edwards where I was teaching at the time. I had set a blind up there to watch them because I had learned this from the Hamerstroms. You make a blind first, and then you watch the beast.

Field trip to assist Hamerstroms with prairie-chicken research in central Wisconsin, ca. 1939. George Becker stands in foreground in black jacket, leaning against vehicle. George Knudsen with upturned cap, stands smiling in back. To George K's immediate right in front of him is John Emlen. Photo courtesy of Elva Hamerstrom Paulson.

We then got a phone call from Fran Hamerstrom. "George? [ornithologist, author, and pioneer recorder of bird songs] Arthur Allen is going to be here tonight for a meal with us. Would you like to join us?" So this is where we met Arthur Allen. He was very nice. We had a hunk of steak that was virtually raw and then a sweet roll. That was the meal. Can you imagine that? And we sat on orange crates. It was memorable because of the man who was there, you know.

SYLVIA: She finished her meal first, and she couldn't bear to do nothing, so she went out to the mailbox and picked up a roadkill of some kind. What was it, George, a rat? Anyway, she brought it in, and she proceeded to take it apart.

GEORGE: Skin it out, right there after we'd eaten. But I tell you, there wasn't enough food in my stomach to cause any reaction. The Hamerstroms seemed to eat so meagerly unless they ate out at somebody else's place. They came to see us in Rockport, Texas. I had just brought in a whole bag of oysters. Well, you know what? They just kept eating more. "Oh," they said, "this is very good, very good, delicious." And before you knew it, the whole bag was gone! They had what I would call a bountiful appetite. It just seemed to reach no end.

CHAPTER EIGHT

THE REASON WHY I spent so much time in Leopold's office was that I was very much interested in the black bear in Wisconsin and wondering what its status was. I think I was interested in bear mostly because I'd never seen any in the wild. I told Aldo about my interest. I don't know if we ever really sat down and talked about what could be done, but I think it came from me that what I would do was get a list of all of the Conservation Department wardens in the northern part of the state where the bear occurred, send a letter to them, and ask them about the status of the bear in their county. This was 1940.

So I got from the department a list of all of the wardens, and then I sent a letter to them and told them what my objective was. Then they proceeded to send back these county maps that I sent them, too, with their markings on them. I was interested in range, and I got a pretty good reading on that. Then in 1946, Walter Scott of the Wisconsin Conservation Department duplicated what I had done and published it in his *Wisconsin Conservation Bulletin* side by side, my map and his map, and they pretty much coincided. You know, that was something really special about Walter. He liked to see young people get ahead. This was something that came out of the clear blue. He saw what I had done, and he thought, "Hey, let me try it too, and let's see how good Becker is, baby." Anyway, of course, there were slight changes, but nothing spectacular.

WALLACE GRANGE was always a very busy man; it was one thing or another. He, too, always called me Becker. He was kind of a brusque man but friendly in a rough sort of way. "How're ya doin', Becker?" But I have great respect for what he did because of his work on game management. [Biologist and mussel ecologist] Harold Mathiak used to work for Wallace Grange at the Poynette Game Farm. He had been in a shooting accident; he blew off his arm. He was in a blind and he was pulling the shotgun toward himself. He must have grasped with the right arm and blew off the left arm. This was before we ever got to know him, but he did not let it handicap him at all. As a matter of fact, Wallace Grange said that Harold was stronger and able to do more than any two men. Wallace said he was the best man that he had for putting up those deer-proof fences at the Sandhill Wildlife Area near Babcock. He was doing the work of a man with two arms. I could never figure that out either, but Wallace Grange said he was just phenomenal. Also, can you imagine a person with a mesh on the end of a long pole getting these mollusk specimens in big streams? And he had only one arm to work with! He had to have scooped down into the substrate to get these things, you know. The force of the water alone; nobody could understand how he managed. He picked out one of the toughest of projects to do, and I guess he just wanted to show the world that it could be done.

Harold had a marvelous garden every year, and he was also the only one in Horicon who built a bomb shelter, single-handed. He was no larger than I am, about my size, and he didn't look any more robust that I am. He was simply very strong—an amazing man.

We had a real good relationship with him, and as a matter of fact, I was responsible for getting him his second wife, Julie. When Harold's first wife, Lola, died, he was very despondent and didn't know what to do. He called me up and says, "George, I just can't exist anymore." He was really down in the dumps.

"Well, Harold, hang in there, man," I said. "I'm going to see what I can do up here at Stevens Point." Our youngest son, David, had a teacher, Julie Kasten, that he adored. She was a fine teacher who came from the Cedarburg area, the same area that Sylvia came from. Anyway, I went to see Julie Kasten one day and I said, "Julie, can I come over and talk to you?" I described to her this very good friend; he had handicaps but he was monetarily secure, and he could work.

Then I talked to Harold, and I gave him her phone number. Julie said, "Yes, I would be willing to...." He was a good friend, and we picked out the best one we could find. It was a good match, and they were married within three months. And, of course, he was gainfully employed with the DNR and had been for years. You know what he did? He was working with explosives with the DNR, too. Did you know this? Darned if I know what he did, but all I can say is that it was dangerous work. I think they were blowing out new holes for making potholes, something like that if I'm not mistaken. There was nothing that stopped that guy. He could cook and do, well, everything—all with the right arm.

When Harold published his book on freshwater mussels, he gave us a copy, and we exchanged when I did my work, too. His was the first work in years on mollusks in the state of Wisconsin. He gave our university at Stevens Point a complete set of all the mollusks that he was finding.

WHEN I WENT into the war, I was a radio operator. We were the first Radio Station Section in the U.S. Army. We were MacArthur's ears and nose. He got the messages that we were picking up. We were stationed first in Australia, outside of Townsville, and from there we went to New Guinea. As the Japanese were pushed away, further and further away from these population areas, we were pushed up to get better reception as we got closer to our objective. I was in charge—the master sergeant. We had an outfit of 19 people, including radio operators, boat people, a mechanic—somebody to keep the equipment going.

After I came back from the Service in '45—I was in the Service for three and a half years, '42 through '45—I wrote a note to Aldo Leopold saying that I was very much interested in going ahead with him [as a graduate student]. Apparently he was not there because his assistant wrote a note to me. He had looked over my record and didn't think I was qualified to do this work. I wrote back to Aldo a little later and mentioned I had been turned down

George in uniform in Kansas City, MO, 1942, while training for the Army Signal Corps. Photo courtesy of Becker family.

George in the South Pacific during WWII, serving until November 1945. Photo courtesy of Becker family.

because I was not qualified, and he wrote a nice note to me and wanted me to contact another assistant, or maybe the same guy, and reapply. Well, I didn't. I didn't because I needed to make up my deficiencies in coursework before working with someone as high-powered as Aldo. He was just tops; he was number one. Aldo Leopold not only changed my knowledge, but he changed my direction.

Finally, after teaching at Port Edwards for a couple of years, and then serving a couple of years as a high school principal at Clintonville, I said, "Sylvia, what am I doing here? I don't want to do this stuff anymore. Look. The Service, they will give me money to go to school again," and I went right back to the University of Wisconsin for the next two years and got all of these very interesting biological courses out of the way. That, I think, was one of the smartest things I ever did. Our accommodations at Badger Village, however, were somewhat spartan, but we managed.

While we were living at Badger, I was in graduate school with [future Wisconsin DNR wildlife manager and naturalist] LeRoy Lintereur at the University of Wisconsin-Madison. LeRoy was a very interesting man, and I loved him dearly. As a student he had some problems, academic problems, but I always had great respect for LeRoy and what he learned on his own. When I called a big meeting up on Lake Superior once, he was up there and was a good contributor to our discussions. He didn't confine himself to any specific thing. He was an outdoorsman. Somebody threw a picture on a wall and was calling attention to something that was happening to the vegetation there, and LeRoy popped up and says, "Well, that's windthrow." It was quite evident that it was windthrow, and everybody agreed; there was no contradiction. He was that kind of a naturalist. He was a natural outdoorsman.

Another person I got to know was Harold Kruse. Harold Kruse was instrumental in saving the Baraboo Hills. We really got to know him through the Citizens Natural Resources Association. I don't know how anybody could have done what he did. One thing to his advantage was that he was a farmer in the area, and he was dealing with farmers in the area. He was trying to talk them out of selling a piece of land or into preserving a piece of land here or there. I don't know how many thousands of acres he set aside. I don't think anybody's ever figured that out, but it's just unbelievable. I had tremendous respect for that man. He seemed to have had a severe case of arthritis because when he walked it was just an ordeal to watch him. And we'd hike miles. We'd go into the field on birding trips, and he was always with us; he never got behind.

CHAPTER EIGHT

At UW-Madison I was fortunate to have [Norman] Fassett as a teacher. He was marvelous! The man was a brilliant botanist. I've never seen anything like him. I think LeRoy had a course with Fassett, too, and he swore by Fassett because LeRoy was a flower man, a plant man. He could identify a heck of a lot of things out in the woods.

Every year, Fassett would publish a new plant group. The guy was a prolific and wonderful man. We'd run into him occasionally at the university concerts; he was quite interested in music. I don't recall lecturing as his strong suit. His forte was the laboratory, and he was just tops! Tops! Fassett got me so interested in plants that I did collections of not only plants but mosses. I collected mosses up in Baxter's Hollow, out of that wonderful little trout stream there. I had some marvelous catches of brook trout out of that stream. It was a crime when he died. He died prematurely.

[Botanist John] Curtis was another good one. The best damn organized teacher I had at the university. University teachers generally are not what I call the best teachers in the world, you know. But he was just tops. And clear. Every lecture was very carefully prepared. I don't think he used notes a great deal. He had it up here [points to head].

So, I got a master's degree at the end of that two-year period. I was studying with Professor Art Hassler at the time. He's an ichthyologist. And that is the reason why I got into the fisheries business. One day Hassler called me into the office and says, "George, how would you like to write a couple chapters for my fish book for the State of Wisconsin. We'll consider that as your work for the master's. A couple of chapters." Which I did. This was way back when I was still in school. Then, I really didn't see that he was putting out anything. And I wanted to get my PhD. I got top grades in everything except organic chemistry. It was the nemesis of most of the PhD candidates in biology, and it was the only course in that whole string of courses that I took that I got a B in, and I was thankful for it.

Now, when did Hassler stop thinking about writing a book on the fishes of Wisconsin, and when did George Becker start pushing it? I don't know really when this all happened, except that the notion must have come very early. There was no book on fishes in Wisconsin outside of a 1935 issue by Willard Green, and it did not include a number of specimens that were in the state. So this is where the root of my book began. In my mind, Wisconsin had to have a fish book. I felt embarrassed because Minnesota had several fish books already. And Michigan had Lagler; that was a good book. Iowa and Illinois had a fish book, but not Wisconsin. So I thought this was made to order, and that was my goal. Come 1957, we moved up to the Point area to a farm by the Tomorrow River, and I built myself a shocking boat. I had no plans, but I'd seen shocking boats before, so it was a Becker-style boat. I started building the electro-fishing equipment entirely. I bought the motor separately, and I had the electrodes fashioned in an electric shop. It was homemade. I used this homemade thing all through the years that we collected fishes, and that was a lot of them.

I could not cover the state all by myself. What I did with my students in the fisheries was I would assign two students to a stream on which they were to sample three locales. I supplied them with a map and the three locales and the equipment that they were to use. They did this with seines, you know. They didn't have the electro-fishing equipment; I didn't set that out. But they came back with some wonderful specimens. Now, when each team of two brought those specimens back into the lab, they would get their fish out into a pan of water, and I would go around and tell them what they had. In some cases they knew what they had, or quite a few things, and every now and then Becker let out a whoop, saying, "Holy man, here we got a good one!" And we'd all gather around and take a look at a rare fish.

I don't think that all of the stations the students did were done with the same amount of thoroughness and alacrity. Some of the students were very conscientious. They came back with some really big collections and a lot of variation in fish species. On the other hand, we had a collection with maybe only ten, 15 fish in the bottom of a bottle, which tells me that these students probably were boozing it up somewhere or not really paying attention

UW-Stevens Point student fish sampling crew, 1960s. Photo courtesy of Becker family.

CHAPTER EIGHT

George with son Kenneth seining in a northern Wisconsin lake in the 1960s.
Photo courtesy of Becker family.

because I knew enough about collecting fish to know when the job was haphazardly done. So those sites had to be re-done.

❧

I STARTED my book in 1958 and finished it 25 years later. At the end, it actually took three years of straight writing, getting up early in the morning and working until late at night. Over those 25 years, the family was together a lot, and they were helping out. Up until 1967, my sons, Kenneth, Dale, and David assisted me in collecting thousands of specimens. This was long before the book was anything of shape or substance. I remember the first collecting period. I had built this equipment, and then we would tackle some of the streams in the immediate vicinity of Stevens Point. We began to learn what was in the stream and how to use that electro-fishing equipment properly. Sometimes the seining nets had to be repaired. We weren't really doing a 100 percent job in getting some of the fish that we were interested in getting. I knew before we started at a particular site what I could expect or what I thought would be there.

I had to learn a lot to begin with, but then very soon I had a publication on the fishes of the county that we were in. We traveled around in a camper during the summers. The camper had bunkbeds in it; it was a real tight fit. The kids were on top; that's the way we had to arrange it. It was a very short

George, Kenneth, and Dale seining in the Florida Keys, 1960s.
Photo courtesy of Becker family.

camper and not big at all—no more than 15 feet. We got up around six, seven o'clock right at the site where we were going to do the sampling. So we didn't have to do any traveling. We did a good portion of our sampling in the morning and in the early afternoon, and then we went on to the next site where we were going to do the work the following day.

One of the things that I did with the boys and Sylvia, and later with my students, was to prepare a little "try me" lunch. This was with a paste that we made, with crackers, and we used as the tasting thing, carp. You'd be surprised how many came back for seconds. Every now and then there'd be one who'd sneak away without ever trying it. But this carp, if made properly, was first class.

I got the biggest kick out of teaching kids. I had an open office. Now this is one thing that Hassler did not do. He was kind of a patrician. His door was always locked, and you felt as if you were encroaching on him. I didn't like that about him. I was taking graduate courses under him, and I had to see him for something. I hated like heck to rap on the door and disturb him. Who knows what he's doing back there, you know. I always had an open door policy.

Eventually, the idea for the book on Wisconsin fishes got to the UW Press. I went to the press and told them what my intentions were, and the gal at the press, Elizabeth Steinberg, had somebody look at what I was doing. Who do you think she selected? Hassler! And he okayed it! Oh, I was grateful for that, you know.

CHAPTER EIGHT

George, Kenneth, David, and Dale after sampling local streams and rivers near Boscobel, Wisconsin. July 1962. Photo by Sylvia Becker. Photo courtesy of Becker family.

I can tell you what my regimen was at the time I was writing. For each species account, I would spend three to five days just getting material. I would go through the entire material, wherever this thing was found written up in a fish book. I would look for it and pick out not only the breeding material, which is very important, but also anecdotal material; I was fascinated by anecdotal material. And my book is full of anecdotal material, by the way. I was criticized by a team of Canadian fisheries people for the anecdotal material. I suppose this was something that they were trained not to include in a sincere and honest fish account. Well, I think it's man's experience, and it makes for interesting reading.

It was 25 years of my life. I don't think I've put any more dedication to any specific thing more than I did to that. I enjoyed doing it, and it seemed like the farther I came along with it, the easier it got for me. Now during vacations I'd be over at the school, eight o'clock in the morning. During vacations I was the only person in the building. I would start as soon as I got there, and I would manage to get home for a couple of meals, an hour at each. We were only three blocks away from school, so there was no problem for me to get over there. Sylvia always had a hot meal for me at noon—always—and at night we always had a good meal. I'd get back to the school as soon as I finished my supper. I would work until sometimes eight, nine, or ten o'clock at night.

I had to begin making slides from the specimens I had to determine age and growth information. I had to cut open specimens to look at the spawning ability at particular times and so on. It was a dragged out process. For some species it was very easy because there were only a few specimens that I was able to garner over the years. So it was three days a week of slugging it out with going into the literature and another three days in writing it up. I spent six days on just one species. Well, when you multiply that by 157 species, you've got a lot of time that was spent in writing that book.

For writing an account, I had a whole stack of books or journals that I had to consider. We had a gal over there at Stevens Point who got all of the books that we did not have in the library. She would get these books and articles in various journals that I did not have. I would spend maybe three days going through just those journals, getting the background material and the specific applications to Wisconsin fish. It became more enjoyable as it went along because you begin to develop ideas and concepts, and you suddenly have a better picture than you did initially.

I was reading practically every book that was put out on fisheries in the United States. As a matter of fact, I have every state book available at that time, and there were a number of them. I would spend at least three days a week gathering material from the various books and pamphlets being published all over the country. Then it would take another three days for me to get this in written form. I had a big stack of books, materials, and papers that went to the UW Press, which they had to sort out. So this gal was extremely helpful. We had a fellow by the name of Art Fish who was in the library, and he was up there in the library stacks. He brought along older fish books that I'd never seen, and would never have seen on my own, and let me look at them. So I had several people that assisted me. I was very grateful and acknowledged them in my speeches after the book was published.

I look at that book and I think, "Maybe this is too big. Maybe this is overwhelming. Maybe people don't read it because it's too large, and they're not coming to grips with the key things that may be of value to improving this whole problem in the future." I think I did not know when to quit; that was the problem I had. I could have made it shorter in many ways, but I felt that all of a sudden it just began to write itself. I got into my study and began typing and this just came out.

The most tedious part of the book was compiling the index, page by page. I had these cards packed tight in two shoeboxes, well over 1,000 cards, probably closer to 2,000 that had to be alphabetized initially and then brought into the proper order; that was very difficult to do. When Sylvia and I got down to the last 60 cards, I was blue in the face. I just couldn't go any further. I shipped those cards along with our list to the [UW] Press, and they took care of it from there. But other than that, Sylvia and I did the whole index, which was something I could have not done alone.

As I was writing the book, I sent out several appeals to the Wisconsin Department of Natural Resources. I said, "Would you please tell your biologists, fish biologists who are doing research, to send me copies of their papers, which I'd like to use in connection with my book?" Zero.

Now, the book came out and I made a visit to the department, and all of a sudden a biologist came to me with a stack of his reprints. He said, "Here. I would like to give these to you." I could have used some of that stuff, or they could have made some comment in connection with what they had done. They are doing some good work. But I was an outsider. I was giving them a hard time. I was taking them to court over their use of piscicides in Wisconsin waters to control carp.

Let me say that the finished product has probably been criticized to a degree by many of the reviewers for the pictures. They're not very satisfied with the colored fish pictures that were taken because sometimes they were made from specimens that were taken out of a jar, and they had lost a lot of their color. I tried my darndest to get colored plates, colored pictures of these fish after they were caught, but it's a tough job. And then I resorted to calling upon my friends in Illinois and elsewhere who had fish pictures that were colored, and they contributed some.

I was amazed that it only took a couple of months to get the thing printed. The original printing was about 3,050 copies. Now, I had many letters after the book was published, and most of them were extremely favorable and grateful for the fact that it was published. I had only two bad opinions. I'm grateful that a number of people found my book very important and a bit useful.

When I finally finished the book, Owen Gromme just shook his head. He said, "George, how did you ever get that book out?" He had just seen my book, and he was overcome by it, amazed, you know. He appreciated good things and I appreciated his comments.

There are at least five new species that have come into the state since my book was written. And then I made a couple of mistakes, and those mistakes were corrected in the 2000 update by Lyons, Cochran, and Fago. I misnamed the lamprey. I thought that we were getting all northern brook lamprey. And instead, they were all the southern. Now, I should tell you why this happened, and it's my fault.

As I was writing this book, I would get these lampreys—it's a smaller lamprey, the northern brook lamprey—and it looked fishy to me because it didn't exactly follow the keys that were available. I didn't have enough sense, let's put it that way, to go into the literature. The literature was in my hand, in my possession, and I didn't bother to go and look into this area in the mid-United States. Well, there it was, southern brook lamprey. Phil Cochran, one

George signs his book *Fishes of Wisconsin* in the governor's office with Wisconsin Governor Tony Earl, who received the first copy. October 4, 1983. Photo by Office of Information Services, Bascom Hall, UW-Madison. Photo courtesy of Becker family.

of the fellows involved in the update, was doing a lamprey study and he says, "This is a southern brook lamprey I'm getting up here in northwestern Wisconsin." He says, "And Becker says there is no southern brook lamprey." It was a terrible error that I made because I did not really check carefully. And as I said, I was a little uneasy about it, but I did not check; that was the most serious error that I made. As far as I know, that's the only species error I made, which is enough. It should not have happened, should not have been there. That is not the way I operate. Despite its shortcomings, I'm very proud of it. I don't think there's a book written that doesn't have some mistakes along these lines. But they were not errors that I engaged in purposely. They're honest errors, let's put it that way.

But here, let me quote from the abstract of the 2000 update: "Since the original publication of George C. Becker's landmark *Fishes of Wisconsin* in 1983, many changes have occurred in the Wisconsin fish fauna. Currently 147 native species are recognized, one more than in [Becker's book *Fishes of Wisconsin*]. Two additional native species, southern brook lamprey and channel shiner, have been found in the state, and one former species, longjaw cisco (*Coregonus alpenae*) is now considered merely a distinctive form of shortjaw cisco (*Coregonus zenithicus*).... Six native species, ghost

CHAPTER EIGHT

shiner, ironcolor shiner, creek chubsucker, deepwater cisco, blackfin cisco, and shortnose cisco are extirpated from the state. Two species thought by Becker to be extirpated, skipjack herring and black redhorse have been rediscovered but are rare. Three endangered species, striped shiner, pallid shiner, and slender madtom, have declined greatly in distribution and abundance and are now nearly extirpated. Fourteen non-native species are currently established in the state, with kokanee salmon, threespine stickleback, ruffe, and round goby, newly reported since Becker's book. At least 19 additional non-native species have been reported from state waters but are not currently established. Two of these, red shiner and pink salmon had been tentatively considered by Becker to be established. The scientific names of 16 native and two non-native Wisconsin fishes have been changed, and several others may be changed in the future."

Then there is mention in the update's Introduction that even as my book was being published, new information was being gathered, which was based on surveys under DNR fish researcher Don Fago during 1975 to 1980 from about 5,000 sites on over 1,700 lakes. Dale contributed significantly to this project, but unfortunately, he wasn't mentioned. Well, this is nothing new with the DNR; they will sometimes overlook their best workers.

❧

FISH MANAGERS think that as long as they are hired to handle fish problems that they've got to do something about them, and sometimes the best thing you can do is let the resource alone. Don't bother it at all; just let it alone. Now you may not have the number of fish there that you would like to have, but you know you are not overusing the waters. Let it come back to its own state. But, of course, we never leave anything alone because we fish. It is very seldom, however, that you fish it out completely in wild waters. In a natural scene, you very seldom come to extirpation, but when man interferes, you may.

In my day, I took a strong stand against the use of pesticides and fish poisons, particularly piscicides such as rotenone and antimycin, in the waters of Wisconsin. Now Horicon is virtually a desert, but back in my day, in the '40s and '50s, the Rock River and Horicon area were much richer biologically. There were a number of large fishes that were edible: pike, walleye, perch, bass. You name the fish, and it was there in the Horicon system. And now, of course, they go through the system and try to list what's left. It's practically a desert.

Piscicide antimycin is discharged into the Tomorrow River at Loberg Road in 1971, while UW-Stevens Point students protest on the bridge. Photo courtesy of Becker family.

On the Rock River, after they did that big fish kill [with toxicant Antimycin A in 1970 and 1973], they had the audacity to get a group of us together to show that they had not removed everything. And you know what they did? They took us to a little stream that was a tributary to the Rock River that they had not treated. So there were fish there, you know. And this was the proof that there were plenty of fish there, and the fish species were not obliterated. Well, that stream of course was not touched. The Rock River itself was, however, really socked, but good.

What have you got left after one of those big treatments? The biggest fish are the ones that are gone first, and the tiny fishes—the food source— somehow manage to persist [at a lower number]. The very first time they ran this [chemical] treatment on the river, they reached well up into the river, and they took in a lake that was above Horicon in the federal part. This had a very special minnow in it that is quite rare in the state of Wisconsin. I pleaded with them. I said, "Look, don't," I could tell they were going to run the treatment all the way up the river, embracing this lake. Well, this minnow species was eliminated from the lake, and now it's an endangered species.

So, the fishery manager, who happened to be a former student of mine, sent a couple of his workers up to Stevens Point and said, "We would like to get a hold of some of these fish that were eliminated in this treatment program.

CHAPTER EIGHT

Could you tell us where to find it?"

I said, "No, I can't. I can't tell you where to find them." I had warned them that there was an endangered species up there in that little lake. And sure enough, they went ahead and treated that lake and there was nothing else in it but these little fish. They made it a total loss.

I never got to see that fish manager, nor did he appear at any of the contests I had with the state in front of the judge. He never appeared. As a matter of fact, I took them to court twice. I was appalled. I was appalled especially in the good waters they were using it in, you know. When I took the DNR to court, Sylvia called up Walter Scott and pleaded with him. Well, what could he do? But he was the only ear in the entire department that we ever felt safe with. Of course, a lot has transpired since, and, of course, the carp have just gone out of sight in numbers! Carp are in the system, and they can't get rid of them. And they won't use my method. Get those big carp out that are roiling up the water and creating a problem. Get in there with seines and really bug those things out, but they didn't do that. DNR fish managers avoided me. I was a plague.

For years, commercial fishermen wanted to get into Horicon and seine out the carp. I'm not sure they want to do it any longer. I think that the water is too contaminated. But the commercial fishermen were always ready to come in there with a seine, and boy, they really can haul those things out and get them. They can catch them alive and send them off in big tank trucks. Live carp was a delicacy. But somehow or other the DNR could not countenance bringing in commercial fishermen. It wouldn't have cost them a cent. The commercial fishermen would have done the trick and utilized the product and sent it off and made a little profit.

Rotenone cleans out a system pretty darn well. I think what it probably does is reduce the oxygen content in the water. If you put enough of that stuff in there, there's no way that anything can persist. Rotenone kills for a short period of time. Now, a lot of different things have been used in addition to that, but fish managers always keep coming back to the rotenone. I think it's probably cheaper, and it's just as effective; it kills everything. And I wouldn't be surprised if it kills a little of the plankton down below in a month. Well, now along with the carp, of course, went all the species.

In my book I wrote the following on page 30: "Chemical treatment to control nongame fish in our streams is a management concept which must be evaluated. Initial data in one study show that clams are particularly sensitive to fish toxicants, and that some species may have been eradicated in treated waters. The mass poisoning of waters appears to work contrary to those biological and ecological principles which support the concept that great species diversity leads to the stability of the environment."

In 1972, I was a member of a governor's task force or committee that looked at the uses and impacts of toxicants on fish management. I quoted from the committee's report in my book [page 28 of *Fishes*]: "The primary goal in the management of all our living resources must be to protect and enhance the integrity of ecosystems. A diversity of aquatic habitats and natural communities must be preserved to provide for education, research and esthetic enjoyment. It should be recognized that other generations will follow ours, and that we have the responsibility to maintain a suitable number of untampered ecosystems in representative habitats throughout the state and to place them 'in trust' for the future." That captures my conservation philosophy.

FISHING OFFERS A BRAND OF SOLITUDE that you don't find elsewhere, especially up north. When I got my teaching job up at Stevens Point, I ran into a fellow there who periodically went up to Lake Nipigon in Canada fishing for the speckled trout—the brook trout. When I bought myself a boat and a trailer for the boat, my family went up there, and we fished for a week or two for the speckled trout. Then in later years we took the family and lived on an island until it was time to leave. There was a lake on that island that had a river in it with the most beautiful northern pike. That is the most delicious meal when it is fried in deep fat. The boys just raved about it. I was a hero when we went for a series of years up to Lake Nipigon.

When we lived along the Tomorrow River early in my career at Stevens Point, we had 60 acres of land there. We also had a creek that nobody knew about, or very few people did. I could go out there and catch a dozen brook trout, or whatever the limit was, you know, in a matter of 20 or 30 minutes. Beautiful trout, maybe not as big as from Nipigon, but beautiful and fresh nevertheless. There was a little stream that was controlled in a sense by a farmer about a quarter mile up the stream. It came out of a big spring there. The kids literally grew up on the Tomorrow River—a wonderful trout stream—and they were out on it day and night. "Oh, Dad, look at this big brown trout I got!" We were so glad that they got to take advantage of it.

🍃

THE KIDS were brought up in the Lutheran faith, but we didn't rag on it. I still have my problems with the reality of God, and so I'm not attracted to the church in any way. Experiences with nature are godly. I've read the Bible, but I still think I find more of this godliness in *A Sand County Almanac*. That is the essence of godliness in my book, and still, there is hardly any mention of a deity.

George out West with a rainbow trout *(Oncorhynchus mykiss)* on the left and mountain whitefish *(Prosopium williamsoni)* on the right. 1960s. Photo courtesy of Becker family.

Nature itself is a tremendous attraction. Can you improve on it? It's the best thing we have! Our real feelings are in nature itself, in the trout stream, in the land surrounding the trout stream. This is heaven. Wherever we had a farm, we had to have a trout stream. And, of course, that's what I was interested in—fish and fishing. I didn't care if I caught something, but it was a nice bonus when you did!

George Becker—afflicted by cancer—passed away on November 4, 2002, about seven months after his beloved Sylvia died.

🍃

BUT I CANNOT END HERE. For a final tribute, please read the following eulogy given by former student and lifelong friend Michael Dombeck, who has graciously and kindly granted permission to use it here.

Some Remembrances of
Dr. George C. Becker
by Mike Dombeck

November 9, 2002, Wisconsin Rivers Alliance
Stevens Point, Wisconsin

Standing in the long slow registration line at college, I was a young student fresh out of Hayward High School in 1966. A robust, barrel-chested middle-aged man with a full head of dark hair and neatly dressed in a white shirt and tie said, "Can I help you?" I handed over my registration slip. He glanced at it, and in an energetic voice he said, "Yes, we still have seats left in general zoology." As he handed me a perforated oblong computer punch card, he asked, "By the way, Dombeck, where are you from?"

George in 2001 at Eureka Springs, Arkansas, where George and Sylvia lived during their final years. Photo by Sumner Matteson.

Classes started nearly a month later. As I walked into my first general zoology lecture, a friendly booming voice yelled, "Hello Mike Dombeck, how are things in Hayward?" I looked up surprised, wondering how he knew who I was. That was my second encounter with George Becker, who would later become my teacher, advisor, mentor, fishing partner, and life-long friend. There were about 60 students in the zoology class. He knew every student's name and had the incredible capacity to remember the names of several thousand students his entire life.

George Becker approached all endeavors with boundless energy and tremendous enthusiasm. He possessed a rare intellect and during his life mastered the arts, letters, and sciences. He mastered the violin as a child and played in the Stevens Point Symphony Orchestra as an adult. He taught English, German, Latin and Greek. And his scientific works were far too many to list here. His seminal work was the monumental 1,052 page *Fishes of Wisconsin*. It remains the definitive work of its kind, the ultimate source of information in the state, written for both the scientist and the angler.

George Becker's skill as a teacher was incredible. His enthusiasm was infectious. After a few weeks in Dr. Becker's class, there was no doubt in my mind what I would study. He had an uncanny ability to motivate students to put forth 100 percent and love it. He had a flawless command of his subject and expected the same of his students. There were no easy A's in his classes. I took general zoology, embryology, marine fishes, and ichthyology and got a master's degree under his instruction. He said teaching embryology was his favorite, even though his most highly refined expertise was the study of fishes.

He loved fishing, whether seining fishes for study or fishing with a fly rod on a small brushy mosquito-infested Wisconsin trout stream or going after brookies, walleyes or muskies on a Canadian lake with loons providing the background music. We were on Eagle Lake in Canada and caught a 26-pound musky the day Richard Nixon resigned the presidency and caught a 40-pounder the next day. George gobbled down the walleye fillets cooked on a wood fire and beamed with delight as we discussed the week's events.

He was not a Nixon fan and publicly protested the terrible waste of the Vietnam War. He did not shy away from controversy, was a champion for social and environmental issues and worried about human population growth. He was a critic of fish poisoning programs and was concerned about biodiversity before our nation knew how rapidly species were disappearing. We would stop along the roadside and he would rattle off the scientific names of the plants in the ditch and name birds by their calls. He had the Leopoldian habit of keen observation.

In the 1970s, the Beckers bought 40 acres across the road from my parents. Our families became friends. Sylvia and George gardened organically and worked toward an ecologically sustainable lifestyle. George loved visiting, had a great sense of humor and would erupt in uncontrollable laughter at a funny story.

A champion of clean air, water, and rivers, George loved rivers and revered the Wisconsin River and condemned its pollution. He was a dreamer of the way things should be, not accepting of the way things are. The press dubbed one of his proposals "Becker's Pipe Dream." Or in his own words, "From Lac Vieux Desert to Prairie du Chien, this great Wisconsin River must become a model of cleanliness."

As the years ticked by, I had the great honor of serving as head of this country's two largest public land management agencies, the Bureau of Land Management and the U.S. Forest Service. My mantra became the "health of the land." Immersed in Washington, D.C.'s political landscape, I often quietly wondered what George would do. Even in his later years, he kept in touch, cheering me on during conservation wins as did the entire Becker family, and encouraging me when I was down. I was honored to be treated like one of the family.

He was a dedicated husband, father, teacher and friend. The world is a better place because of him.

George, thank you. ✳

Lorrie Otto
(1919-2010)

Lorrie in her prairie garden, Village of Bayside, Milwaukee, Wisconsin.
July 28, 2001. Photo courtesy of Dorothy Boyer.

RED MAPLE

GJK

Chapter Nine~ Lorrie Otto

One of the experiences I'll never forget occurred in first grade during winter. I came down with the measles, then encephalitis. I lost consciousness. When I awoke, I was lying on my side in a crib, with railings, and I was downstairs in this big kitchen. As I opened my eyes I could see that the rhubarb and asparagus were up. I let out this scream. I said, "It's spring! The rhubarb is up!" My parents were overjoyed!

—LO

Born in Madison, Wisconsin, on September 9, 1919, Lorrie Otto grew up on a dairy farm on Old Middleton Road in what was then undeveloped countryside outside the city of Madison. Her love for wildflowers and native plants took seed during those early years as she worked alongside her father.

Lorrie graduated from Wisconsin High School in 1938 with honors and from the University of Wisconsin-Madison in 1942 with a bachelor of arts in related arts. That summer, she worked briefly as a model in New York, and in the fall she received training as a pilot in the Women Airforce Service Pilots (WASP)—a former branch of the U.S. Air Force during World War II—before quitting due to sexual harassment.

Married in July 1942 to Owen Otto, son of UW-Madison professor Max Otto, she lived in Madison, then Portland, Oregon, for a year while Owen finished a medical internship in psychiatry. After his internship, they lived in Madison for three years. In 1946, she gave birth to a daughter, Patricia, and three years later in Milwaukee to son, George.

During the 1950s, Lorrie's life of relative tranquility as a psychiatrist's wife changed forever when she successfully spearheaded an effort to protect a ravine and woods in her neighborhood known locally as Fairy Chasm. After that successful initiative, she became a major player in the campaign to ban DDT in Wisconsin. This battle, she said "stole ten years" from her life as she worked tirelessly and successfully with a dedicated cadre of scientists and citizens to convince the state of Wisconsin to ban DDT in 1970. The federal government followed suit two years later and banned DDT nationwide.

After the 1970s, Lorrie turned her attention to The Wild Ones, an organization she helped form to reject the use of lawn care chemicals in favor of planting yards with a variety of native plants. For decades, she led Audubon bus tours in Milwaukee to different front yards—formerly lawns.

Lorrie chronicled her battles with the city of Milwaukee to assist others in rejecting traditional lawn care methods during our interview on April 7, 1999, at her rustic home in Milwaukee, part of a private Village of Bayside community bordering Lake Michigan. We met again at her home on May 5, 1999, following her induction into the Wisconsin Conservation Hall of Fame on April 12, 1999.

You've arrived at Lorrie Otto's residence. Photo by Sumner Matteson.

When I first entered the Bayside community to interview Lorrie, I had to remind myself I was still in Milwaukee. Front lawns gradually grew more wild and diverse as I approached Lorrie's home, which was not readily apparent to a weary traveler except for a wooden sign at the corner of her driveway. Lorrie's home itself seemed like something from a more rural scene, with over 30 species of wildflowers and shrubs in her yard, and a "brick" driveway (of perforated pavers that allow water to percolate through) leading to a dark, wooden house set back against a ravine of deciduous trees and conifers. When she and Owen first acquired their home, 64 Norway and Colorado spruce mostly comprised the front yard. It was hard to imagine at the time of my visit.

Lorrie, tall (nearly six feet) and big-boned, with longish, white hair and an infectious laugh, greeted me warmly and seated me by a picture window looking out into the wooded ravine. Several white-throated sparrows, a white-breasted nuthatch, and an eastern towhee caught my attention near birdfeeders a few feet from the window.

◆

I entered the world as Mary Lorraine Stoeber in 1919, and I held that name for 23 years. My father, Ernest Stoeber, had a big dairy farm, owned about 68 acres, and rented another 40 across the railroad tracks in Middleton. Nearby, my uncle maintained a big apple orchard. The farm landscape rolled with beauty and diversity everywhere. Everywhere! Now, you have to look across the rural scene to find interesting places. We had bobwhite quail, western and eastern meadowlarks, red-headed woodpeckers, and eastern bluebirds. At that time, meadowlarks were common. We had barbed wire fences, old fence posts, and the fence posts had either bluebirds or red-headed woodpeckers working them. Hickory nut trees occurred on the farm border, wonderful oak trees grew around our house, and prairie plants hugged the railroad tracks.

We burned areas by the railroad tracks and the roadsides every year. I can remember the old wooden fenceposts catching on fire because grass had grown and matted around them. In the middle of the night, I remember Father saying he saw a glowing fencepost. He tried to put the fire out to save the fencepost.

I loved every minute that I was on the farm. Every day was different, whether we were planting potatoes—my father put a spade in the ground, opening it a little as I dropped the potato roots in; then he stepped gently on the soil, putting in the plant—or picking rhubarb or asparagus to sell to stores in town, working the hay loader, or taking strawberries out of a can of water.

I can remember sitting on a load of hay and driving a team of horses down the row while wearing a big straw hat with daddy long legs crawling around the hat's edge. I reached the end of the row, and I didn't know how to turn! So my father yelled out, "It's just like your kiddy cart!" But I couldn't transfer it in my mind, and he had to jump on at the last moment to prevent calamity.

Father was wonderful. He hand-terraced three hills. In the wintertime, as part of the WPA [Works Progress Administration—renamed Work Projects Administration in 1939—part of FDR's New Deal] program, he would go to other farmers in Dane County to persuade them to rotate their crops. I remember he had a great big wheel with tape around it, so he must have measured something for the farmers. I followed him everywhere on the farm as his shadow. They had no son and I was the oldest girl.

He began life as a skinny little kid without his father, who died before he was born. The last of eight children, my father worked in a candy factory as a thin, little Madison kid. He probably only had an eighth-grade education, but somehow he enrolled in an agricultural short course, and he just loved it and all of his professors. Then he worked as a hired man, and later on, through a land contract, he bought the land from his boss. We had 28 cows—a motley crew—and then in the final stages of the farm, we had all Golden Guernseys. This occurred in an era before people started worrying about the cholesterol content of cream. In our time, the bigger the cream line on a quart of milk, the more wonderful it tasted.

My grandmother lived in our house, and my mother, Bessie, had no influence on me because she worked all the time and couldn't talk about anything seriously at all, not even sex. But my grandmother was a big gardener. She organized and maintained the vegetable gardens and various kinds of flower gardens. I can still see my little fingers at age four. She would make a little ditch with the side of a hoe, a little trench, and then I would plant the peas about two inches apart all the way down that row. She would tamp it in with the rake, and in another place she'd have another very shallow row where she'd sprinkle lettuce down that little trench. I would come along and push a radish seed in about every four inches or so. Then she'd put up a tight, white string.

I remember when haying, we had an old, black workhorse called Roy. I would lead him as the fork would pull up the hay and dump it into milk crates that hung on the horse's sides by way of a pole. I had to be very careful that he didn't step on my feet. Later, we would take these workhorses for bareback rides. My sister and I and my two cousins had a wonderful time racing through the pastures. I lived an ideal life as a child.

Each of those cousins had a cottage on Lake Mendota. On weekends we would fish and swim off their piers.

ONE OF THE EXPERIENCES I'll never forget occurred in first grade during winter. I came down with the measles, then encephalitis. I lost consciousness. When I awoke, I was lying on my side in a crib, with railings, and I was downstairs in this big kitchen. As I opened my eyes, I could see that the rhubarb and asparagus were up. I let out this scream. I said, "It's spring! The rhubarb is up!" My parents were overjoyed. I just kept looking and staring. So, I was a year older than my classmates after all that. I had to redo first grade.

I HAD AN ATTRACTION toward everything in nature, so I couldn't get enough of the outdoor life. My curiosity, too, proved interminable. I wanted to know, for instance, what kind of nests all the meadowlarks had. I'd go to bed at night and could hardly wait to get up in the morning; every day was different. I loved putting in prairie plants while my father spaded the ground. And then during the war, all of the healthy men had to go fight.

My father had this International milk truck, so my sister and I delivered the milk in these glass bottles on the west side of Madison, all over Shorewood Hills. I learned to drive a tractor, an old Dodge truck, and that milk truck before I learned to drive a car!

We never stopped to have midmorning coffee. I couldn't believe that people did that! We got up at six in the morning. We had two hired men, and they got up at four. We had such gorgeous strawberries that we'd take some around to our favorite milk customers—ones that really washed their milk bottles and always paid their bills. During the Depression, many people didn't pay their bills. Dentists who couldn't pay their bills performed all the dentistry in my mouth.

During the Depression, we always ate. But I remember a horrible time when the farmers went on strike, and they would interfere with farmers bringing their milk to market. They would stop the trucks and dump the cans of milk in ditches! That didn't happen to us, and I'm not quite sure why it didn't. Our farm lay on three different hills, with the house on the highest hill. We could look out the window and watch our milk truck go down the hill. All these guys stood there ready with their baseball bats.

Dad wanted to get through to deliver his milk. I don't know what he did, but they let him through, and then men appeared at the door. Mother sliced bread, spread gobs of butter on them with wonderful strawberry jam, and fed these guys. So Dad must have bribed them with Mother's homemade bread and jam!

I remember Mother being terribly sick of cooking the same thing day after day during the Depression. The basement floor consisted of dirt, and then my dad brought in sand because we had a gravel pit on the farm. So we put carrots in the sand and had big barrels of sawdust there. We put the russet apples in the barrels. Mother canned everything. The drought years were awful, just awful. The pastures turned brown, and my sister and I herded the cattle up and down Old Middleton Road. They must have eaten poisonous weeds. What's green in a drought? Nothing grew in the pastures.

WHEN MY MOTHER was growing up, her father never stayed in one place for very long, so she went from school to school. She never developed any friendships, and school must have been awful for her. She might have made it past grade two; I don't know. So she wanted to make sure that her children didn't bounce from school to school. For six years I walked to Mendota Beach, a little country schoolhouse. Then Mother had some idea that she wanted me at Wisconsin High School in Middleton, but the tuition was $18.00, which was a horrendous fee at the time. My father said no way, but Mother took me in to meet the principal to see if there could be some way to get around it. He said, "Yes, by scholarship." And so every year I had to compete. I had my choice of three subjects, and if I got the top grade, I could come to school for nothing. I chose physical education. Easy. I could outrun, out jump, all those city girls. So I earned my scholarship.

We lived five and a half miles from the school, so I rode my bicycle all through high school and college. Eleven miles a day.

When I was in seventh and eighth grades at Wisconsin High School, Wayne Claxton was my art teacher. He would give us assignments to draw at home. I would sit in the manger, right beside a cow, and draw the cow's head with its eyelashes and its nostrils all flared. Wayne Claxton loved those cow head drawings. But I loved the whole scene—the smell of them chewing their cuds, the smell of their breath, the smell of the hay, and the smell of the silage.

I had a wonderful childhood, so unlike Fran Hamerstrom; it was just the opposite.

I had a marvelous high school education, too. We had small classes. I had a wonderful biology teacher named Miss Weber and a great English teacher named Miss Springhorn, who made us read a book a week, write a report on it, and read it aloud. Plus, every week we had to write an essay on what we did over the weekend. I went through everything that Zane Grey wrote. Colette's *Earthly Paradise* had an impact because of its earthy spirituality. I still recommend that book. So I read a book a week through high school, and then, when I got married, I had a mother-in-law who read a book a week. She had walls made of bookcases, and she subscribed to *The New York Times*. So whatever *The New York Times* reviewed was the best, she'd get the book, and we'd all read it.

I couldn't pick out the best book I've read. I love Leopold and John Muir, but I can't pick out a favorite. It's like saying what's your favorite flower or your favorite plant. Each affects you differently, at a different time.

IN COLLEGE, I was such a good girl—so pure. My freshman year, during my second semester, I got a note from the dean's office. I couldn't imagine why. I didn't smoke. I didn't drink. I was still a virgin. I walked into her office, and she said. "What do you think you're doing? Is that all you want to be? Just a biology high school teacher?"

"God," I thought that was a pretty nice thing to be, you know, I really did.

And so she said, "Your sophomore year, take subjects that you know nothing about; don't declare a major for yourself." That's what I did. I took Greek archeology, physiology, psychology, poetry, economics, and art history, which I took every semester. I had an incredible knack for analyzing paintings, so I always received an A.

In those days, women did not have many options. I could become a major in the arts, go into the home economics department as an art major, or go into art education. I learned that one of the things I could take was advanced botany as a related arts major, which became my choice.

I graduated in 1942, and that summer during the war I didn't have any money. I knew in the fall I was coming back to start my master's program in architecture, but I wanted to see the architecture on the East Coast. I answered an ad in the paper to be the second maid at Kittery Point, Maine, for W.D. Howells, an anthropologist who lectured at UW-Madison and later became a professor of anthropology at Harvard. So I interviewed for the job, but Mrs. Howells wouldn't give it to me because she said I was overqualified. So I came home, but then she called me in a week because no one else came to answer that ad. At that time, I was going to drive her children in her station wagon east from Madison to Maine, but then something happened. They couldn't get the number of gas rationing stamps needed for gas, so I went by Greyhound bus to Kittery Point, a submarine harbor.

At night, everything had to be covered or turned off. They didn't want any lights on in that town so that they couldn't be bombed by the Germans or Japanese. At about seven o'clock at night, we pulled the window shades and the flaps on the edge for the little cracks around the side; we really closed down so no lights appeared anywhere. Then I had to turn down their beds and lay out the man's robe and her nighty and their slippers for him or her. When I first arrived, I had to iron 36 formal gowns; they dressed formally for dinner every night, although they ate by themselves.

Mrs. Howells started asking me to do more and more things, so I had absolutely no free time. And I wanted to read at night. Finally, I said, "I can't do this. I have to read. I have to have time to be by myself. If I can't have evenings, then I don't want to do this." So I gave her two weeks notice. She paid me, and I went to New York.

I never ever dreamed I'd be in New York! I can remember walking down the streets and staring at these tall buildings. I got a room at the YWCA for a minimal amount of money. The first day there, I walked down the sidewalk and a man came up beside me. His name was Ben Brooklyn, a short, middle-aged guy who started walking beside me. He asked, "Would you like to have breakfast with me?"

Well, I needed to save money, so I said, "Sure."

We had breakfast, and he said, "Would you like to be a model?"

"Well," I replied, "I've done some modeling in Madison for Manchester's, a women's store. What do you mean by modeling?"

"Well, I'm a buyer, wholesale buyer, and we're short of tall women to model evening gowns."

I said, "Fine, I'll do that." And so he introduced me to his boss, and I was perfect for it. When growing up, I was the tallest girl in high school; in high-heeled shoes I stood six feet tall. I've always worn high-heeled shoes. I loved being tall! So, I was perfect for this job. They taught me how to walk. The walk is different for wholesalers, much snappier. So I began modeling "MacArthur Red." At that time, MacArthur was the big war hero, but MacArthur Red? Don't you think of blood when you put together MacArthur with red?

One day shortly after I began working, I had on this red crepe dress with my hair up. I walked up the stage, and Ben Brooklyn says, "You're hair is coming loose in back. Do you want to step into my room and redo it?"

And I thought, "Oh, gosh, I'll have to do that."

So I walked into his room. You had to go around the corner to get into this teeny little bathroom that had a mirror in it. So I put my arms up to take my hair down, and by God, he grabbed me! He trapped me with my arms up, and I couldn't get them down. But he was a short guy. He put his mouth right over my nipples, over my red dress. He had me squashed in the doorway. I couldn't go backwards, but I finally got myself loose, and I was ready to kill him. I really was. I felt so strong. After all, I'd pitched hay all those years. So we grappled with each other, and I was going to take that guy and throw him through the window! I could picture his body hurtling down to the sidewalk far below, and I could see the headlines in the *Wisconsin State Journal* saying "Ernie Stoeber's Daughter Murders Man in New York!"

I remember standing there, furious and yelling, "What do you think we are? Barnyard chickens?!" I was so angry and upset. Well, I ran outside, left the few clothes that I had in the Y, and they never heard from me again. I had in my purse my return ticket, and I took the Greyhound bus home.

So that happened the summer after I graduated. Meanwhile, I had become hooked on modern architecture, and I thought about graduate school at UW-Madison, but when you went into graduate school back then, they wanted you to also teach college students in the education department. If I was to teach, then I'd need something more than the saddle shoes, skirts, and wool sweaters I'd made. That comprised my wardrobe. At that time, no store fabrics fit; they were all too short, so I went to a dressmaker. I had to have one nice dress I could use when teaching.

While waiting for the dressmaker, a *Vogue* magazine issue caught my eye on the coffee table. I picked it up. Aviator Jacqueline Cochran was looking for what she called "The Cream of the Crop" of women in the United States to fly airplanes from the factory that produced them to where the boys would take them and then fly off to Europe for the war. Somehow, Jacqueline Cochran convinced Congress to establish the Women Airforce Service Pilots (WASP). Earlier, after I had graduated from college, a great plea came over the radio for nurses. Nurses had become scarce for the war effort. I didn't feel like being a nurse, but I was patriotic, and so I thought I would go to nurse's training. By this time I was about to marry Owen Otto, son of Max Otto—Wisconsin Governor LaFollette's speechwriter. And he said, "Oh, no. If you do that, you're through with me. I'm not going to come home and talk shop!"

So I said, "Well, if they ever train women to fly, I'm going!" I never dreamed, of course, this would happen. Lo and behold, I picked up this magazine, and I thought, "I wonder if I'm the cream of American womanhood." But I also thought, "Why not?" She wanted commercial pilots, and I thought to myself, "There can't be very many women in the United States that are commercial pilots. Come on!" So, I thought, "She's going to have to lower her standards." And so I went down to the airport and said, "I want to learn to fly."

I took a night job at Forest Products Laboratory in Madison to pay for the lessons, which were eight dollars an hour. I learned how to fly little Taylorcrafts and Super Cubs. The first time I flew occurred after a rainstorm. Later, you weren't allowed to fly through clouds, and all the time you had to be thinking if something happened to that engine you had to know from what direction the wind blew from so you could make a forced landing if necessary. So, anyway, here was this wonderful day with cumulus clouds in the sky and my instructor down on the ground. I flew up, and I climbed these canyons of white fluffy clouds. I couldn't see the ground anywhere, and I flew around these enormous cloud canyons. Well, it was heaven, just heaven!

As the months drifted by, Jacqueline's requirements lowered until we met on the same level. I squeezed into the last class and took the train down to Sweetwater, Texas. The planes that I flew were the ones that you see being used for crop dusters today, with the two wings and the two open cockpits, no shield. I wore the fancy helmet and the goggles. But it was too loud up there, like driving 10 tractors in the air. I regret that I didn't just go into glider mode where you can be part of the whole thing.

Flight school at Sweetwater, however, turned out to be a nightmare, a disaster. This was the air force, and the men down there in Texas hated us. The colonels didn't want women flying. They wanted their men to have that extra flying time. I never graduated because Congress cut the program, killed it, and that put an end to it. Actually, if truth be told, it didn't matter what Congress did because I quit the day before they acted.

Did you listen to the Anita Hill and Clarence Thomas Supreme Court hearings? That was my instructor. He was worse than how Hill described Thomas. I tell you I sat here and listened to those hearings and thought, "Anita Hill, everything you say is true."

In my case, the flight instructor was white. He was so terrible. Before I'd practice my loops and barrel rolls and whatnot, I had to climb up quite a ways to reach that altitude. So before I could concentrate on what he was asking me to do, there was a little free time. He sat in the cockpit in front of me with a big mirror so he could see my face. At that time I didn't even know what the word *fuck* meant, so when I got home I had to ask Owen what it meant. This instructor said such terrible things to rattle me. He was so awful that I didn't know what to do with what he said, so I laughed. This is the way I've gotten out of a couple of other things in my life. But he became furious because I laughed. I couldn't talk to him up there. I couldn't say anything. He could talk to me, but I couldn't talk back to him.

We were receiving reports from girls who would come back to cry because they couldn't keep up their instrument time because the colonels wouldn't let them fly. That day, when my instructor acted terribly, I landed the plane, and he said, "You're the best goddamn flier on this field!" So I got out, tied my plane down, and just stood there and watched that bastard go in and file his report on me.

When he walked out, I walked in and said, "I'm quitting!" Oh, the uproar in the place. I never told them why—you did not tattle on men! So I didn't tell anybody about his abuse. He was so terrible that I thought the only way I could kick him in the teeth was to have his best student quit right after he gave the report on what a great flier I was.

I don't know how long it took me to get home from Sweetwater, Texas, back to Madison, but I arrived late in the evening. When I rose the next morning, my father was mortified. He couldn't believe I'd walked away. But we turned on the radio, and the very first thing on the news report was that the WASP program had been discontinued. Some of the women did fly. There was a group of women who were way ahead of me and did graduate. There were women also that weren't allowed to fly, and they were the ones that would come back and tell us these terrible stories and cry. No one had any power to do anything about the abuse. And then, six months later, the government really pulled the strings on the women that did get to fly; they didn't even fly them back to their hometowns. They had to find their way back home. It was pretty damn wicked.

🖋

WHEN I CAME BACK, I married Owen, and the dream of graduate school vanished. He was a fourth-year medical student just going into his final exams, and he'd been pleading with me for a couple of years to marry him. When I married him, I had to move into the Otto household because there was no other place to live in Madison. I'm so glad that I didn't meet my mother-in-law until after I married him because I would have fallen in love with his mother instead of Owen. His mother, Rhoda Otto, was the first really interesting woman I had the opportunity to know in my life, and she swept me off my feet.

I don't think women should marry men who hate their mothers, but my husband hated his mother, and he had told me so many terrible stories about her that I was terrified of her. For seven years we went steady before we got married. So I didn't meet her until about a week before the wedding, and I was scared stiff. She was president of the League of Women Voters.

For the social and intellectual and musical leaders of Madison, Rhoda was the glowing light. Every time a visiting dignitary would come to Governor LaFollette's mansion, LaFollette's wife would call up Rhoda and say, "You've got to come to make the party go!" Rhoda had been a history teacher at Wisconsin High School, so she was great for an evening with foreign people. She could talk about anything. She loved music all of her life, and she sang duets with her mother at the governor's mansion any time some big dignitary came to Madison.

🖋

IN THOSE DAYS, you took your husband's name; I was Mary Otto. I moved into the house where his sister Mary Otto also lived. After a week of confusing mail and telephone calls, I said, "Look, this isn't going to do." She lived there first, so I was the one who had to do something with my name. My middle name was Lorraine. I never liked it because there was a girl at Sunday school whose name was Lorraine. I couldn't stand her, which was rare for me, so I took Lorraine and tried to keep as much of it as I could. I dropped off the *n* and the *a*, and that left me with L-o-r-r-i-e.

Eventually, in 1943, we moved out to Portland, Oregon, for his internship. In Portland, Owen only received $50 a month, so I had to go to work to support us. I went down to the employment station, but I wasn't qualified to do anything. "Do you type?" No, didn't type.

Every single thing she asked me, I kept saying, "No." But then I said, "Now wait a minute. I went to college and I know I can learn. Certainly, there must be some job in the shipyards that I can do?"

And she said, "Well, what would you like to do?"

"Well, what's the highest paying job?"

"Welder."

"Okay, I'll learn to be a welder."

You're not born knowing how to weld. So I entered welder's school, and as it turned out, I was very good because the control I had came from all the fine little muscles in my hand. When you're welding, you not only have to move your hand as the lead is melting, you have to move your hand in a straight line. There were special things on these Victory ships that needed to have perfect welds, and I could do it. So I became the chief welder on these Victory ships.

The arrangement during World War II was that the army would pay for your medical education, but Owen finished medical school in three years instead of four, so no break occurred during summer. Then at the end of that, he had to do an internship. He could choose and do an army internship, or he could be a civilian for a year, and then he had to come back and pay back the army. So Owen chose a civilian internship. We came back to Madison, with orders to go to Mendota Hospital, which was just across the lake. That suited me just fine because I was pregnant and all set to have the baby all by myself while my husband was overseas. As it turned out, the army desperately needed psychiatrists, and to make everybody as happy as possible, they stationed them at their home base. So we stayed right there in Madison for three years. We went back to the Otto home on Lake Wingra at Edgewood Avenue. In 1946, I gave birth to my daughter, Patricia, who is now a great gynecologist and avid birdwatcher.

At first, Owen decided he wanted to go into internal medicine, but after about the first month at Mendota Hospital he wanted to practice psychiatry. We hardly ever talked shop, but he came home one night, and said, "The clods don't break down. It's the really sensitive men. And they say such wonderful things, about the colors of stone, and running water." He worked with men really busted up by the war. Well, then, where to do a residency as a psychiatrist? We ended up in Rochester, New York, for two years and lived two years in faculty housing, where I taught other faculty members how to have victory gardens and how and what to plant.

We then came back to Madison for a year and lived in Eagle Heights, where Owen headed up the student health clinic. One night, at a cocktail party with a bunch of other psychiatrists, this older psychiatrist came up to him and said, "You coward. What the hell are you doing working in your father's shadow up here? Why don't you come down to Milwaukee, find out what the real world is like, and go into private practice?"

It was kind of true. People always referred to Owen as "Max Otto's son." Max, quite famous in his own right, gave John Dewey's funeral sermon and sat with Clarence Darrow when Clarence Darrow was dying in Illinois. When Max sat down beside him, Clarence once said, "I want you to know that I think you're the bravest man."

And Papa said, "Oh, nothing compared to you. How can you say that?"

Clarence whispered, "You married a woman taller than you are!" Max was short, and he never let you forget it.

Anyway, this older psychiatrist said, "I'll take care of you until you get established." So late in 1948, he took Owen into his office here in Milwaukee and introduced him to Milwaukee's wealthiest people. First, we lived in an old mansion with seven bathrooms on Lake Michigan, but I'll take an outhouse if it's on a lake. I only needed one bathroom, so I just closed off the other ones. Then my cousin Doris, very well off financially, said, "You go out and find yourself a house. I'll lend you the money at one percent interest."

So, I picked up a paper, and an ad said: "Do you like seclusion?" It was an ad in the paper put in by the woman next door. We only had one car, so I had to wait until Owen came home from the office. Then we drove out and saw the house, with an acre of lawn and a bunch of little evergreen trees on it that were about as tall as we were. Christian Scientists had owned it, and the man came down with pneumonia and died. No one wanted to buy a house where someone had died. He had died unnecessarily because penicillin was already on the market, but he didn't go for medical help. So we—a doctor and a doctor's wife—came along and bought his house for $38,000 in 1951.

For the first three years, I braided rugs and wove drapes. When we bought the house, no one had told us that we were part of an organization called the Fish Creek Park Company, formed in 1892, that you owned stock in, with one vote. We and about 99 other stockholders comprised the voting membership. We knew we had private roads and a private walk to the beach, down an 80-foot bank, and that we jointly owned about 20 acres of land. But I discovered that we owned twice as much land as what we had thought. A stake behind a white pine tree out there beyond the house was where a woman had led me to believe the land ended. Well, it didn't. It went all the way down the bank into that ravine and halfway across the little stream that's down there. That was a gorgeous surprise!

In 1955, I received a notice to go to an annual Fish Creek Park Company meeting to vote on converting 20 acres of land adjacent to ours into a subdivision development—cluster housing. Yaegers and Usingers, all the wealthy big meat and bread people, lived far away, but they wanted to sell the 20 acres, invest the money, and use it to maintain our roads, which had disintegrated into potholes. "Oh," I thought, "20 acres of land? What is this?" And so they voted to do percolation tests, and we'd meet again in a year to decide if and how we should develop it.

The day after the vote, Owen went off to work, and I went over to see this land, and I got lost! I just followed the stream for a couple of blocks, went up a steep bank, and there on the flat land stood a nice big woods. Well, I'd had enough botany to know that this was really something. There were plants there that I couldn't identify, and wherever we'd lived, whenever I asked someone in Portland or Rochester the name of something, no one ever knew. And I thought, "By God, when I settle down someplace, I'm going to know the name of every tree, every shrub, every plant, and every bird that flies through, and every butterfly that goes by."

Here, wonderful, different kinds of plants grew, even though it was early in spring. I thought, "This is just wrong!" I didn't know why it was wrong to

CHAPTER NINE

allow development, but by God, it felt wrong. I picked up an owl pellet, one little pink *Hepatica* bloomed, and I found a British soldiers lichen.

I collected five things, and I put them in my little woolen jacket, came home, and drove down to the university botany department. I asked to see their oldest botanist; it was Alvin L. Throne. So I came in and said, "Do you know anything about this land?" His face turned very red, and the veins in his nose kind of popped. Oh! He was furious.

He stormed out of the room saying, "Come here!" He threw open tin doors where he had specimens, and he pulled out these sheets with *Pterospora* [woodland pinedrops] glued onto them. This is the only place in Wisconsin where this plant had ever occurred. He found it in 1922. He couldn't believe it; he thought it a fluke.

So for five years he took his students and found them easily. He wrote a report, which he gave me. And I thought, "Gosh. This has got to be special!"

So then I went to the *Milwaukee Journal* to see if something could be done, but I was terribly shy. You wouldn't believe it today. But I was so upset because it was such beautiful land. So I asked to see their suburban reporter, but he seemed disinterested. Then he said, "Well, who is it that owns this land?" So I started naming the names. Whew! That caught his attention. The next day on the bottom of the front page, the story unfolded. Now, several of the neighbors constituted third generations; they were livid. How did I dare hang their dirty linen on the front page! So I made 10 people lifelong enemies, almost; today they're all dead.

I came home from that visit to the *Journal's* offices, called up Jeanette Shoffer, who had a bookstore, and I said, "Jeanette, I want every single book about plants and the wilderness. Just send them all to me." She sent me identification guides and copies of Sigurd Olson's books. I'd read all of John Muir. At the same time, an announcement appeared in the *Journal* that Sigurd Olson was going to be the keynote speaker at the Izaak Walton League meeting. I didn't have any idea about the Izaak Walton League. Fishermen, that's all I could think of. But Olson was coming, and I thought, "Well, maybe they'll let a woman in." So I called and the little man that answered was just so pleased that I'd come. I arrived early because I wanted to speak to him about this situation involving the 20 acres. The table where I sat looked like a squared off "U," and he sat right in the middle, but we were almost close enough that our knees knocked.

Well! I swept Sigurd Olson off his feet. He didn't pay attention to anybody else. So I told him about the situation and said this area shouldn't be destroyed. He said, "Join The Nature Conservancy." At that time we didn't have a Wisconsin chapter; it was the national chapter. And so, by golly, I joined The Nature Conservancy.

One thing led to another, and pretty soon I had joined the Sierra Club and Audubon. One of the biggest and best things that happened to me, however, was that I met UW-Madison botany professor Hugh Iltis. I asked Hugh Iltis to come down. I don't remember how I met him, who got me in contact with him, but I had him walk through the woods with as many neighbors as I could get. And then Hugh gave an inspiring talk afterward to about 100 people in a big old barn at the house on the other side of the ravine.

The following year, I persuaded four women to help me interview all 100 stockholders. Owen had been given a Rolleiflex camera as a professional courtesy gift from a doctor. We hiked through the ravines and took photographs of all the wildflowers that grew around here. I had all of these photographs that I put in an album. Then I walked around and took them to people to show what grew over there. All the people who lived along the lake said they didn't give a damn, that they moved out here to be by the lake. They loved the lake, and they didn't care what happened to the woods. And so half the people on this side would vote to destroy that land. The ones on the other side of the ravine were mixed, but I found about 10 people and got all of their votes.

By this time I met Fred Schmidt who had a little magazine in Milwaukee called *Let's See*. The editorial writer wrote beautifully, and I wanted to meet the person. So I told Fred that I wanted this person to describe Fairy Chasm, an old name given to it. Fred said the writer was Jay Scriba of the *Milwaukee Journal*. So we got together for breakfast here. Jay told me, "You don't have a chance. You're only 12 miles from the middle of Milwaukee. You're not going to save it. You're not going to save the woods."

I said, "Jay, just walk with me. Walk over there."

I couldn't have scripted what happened next. God, it was marvelous! We walked out on the point, started down the ravine, and we looked down on two great horned owls flying side by side like a couple of bombers. We climbed up the bank, and just as we got to the top of the bank, five deer appeared. At that time, you didn't see deer around here. I hadn't seen any deer. I saw tracks once in a while; they just went bounding down ahead of us with their tails sticking straight up. We walked a little farther and a red fox came by. Jay looked at me, he said, "You win. I'll write it up. But I need to get the details, the history." So I gave him the details, and he wrote this wonderful article.

Anyway, the issue came to a final vote, and we won by three votes. Three votes. That was my first big battle.

The chapter didn't end there. A decade later, in 1970, Orrie Loucks and I got together, and we agreed that Orrie would present the idea of adding part of Fairy Chasm to The Nature Conservancy, and I would go to all the neighbors. So Orrie went to Mequon, to their board, and I went to all the neighbors and said, "Let's get this land!" I set up a course in springtime for neighbors only. They had to agree to come one day each week for three consecutive weeks because it changes so much during the spring. So many people signed up for it that I couldn't do it all in one day. Jim Zimmerman used to say, "Not more than eight on a field trip—four on one side of you and four on the other." So, I used to take 10 pounds off every May because I was always out there walking in the woods, translating. Anyway, The Nature Conservancy Board voted to acquire that 20-acre parcel, and I felt marvelous!

> "Our vocabulary stops at the age of six as far as our environment is concerned. If we knew the names of things we're in constant contact with, our language would be much more picturesque. Instead of saying, 'I saw a bird in a tree,' you should say, 'I saw a cardinal in a pine tree with a cumulus cloud behind it.' This is the belief of Mrs. Lorrie Otto. Mrs. Otto didn't know the names of things herself until she and her family moved to Fairy Chasm about eight years ago. Now she can identify all the shrubs and trees and flowering plants, at least 200 of them that grow in the preserve a block from her home.

> "Fairy Chasm Reserve is a wilderness in the center of a residential community on Lake Michigan. Part of the community is in Bayside, part in Mequon. There are a number of botanical finds in the reserve used for study by many students and scientists, and recent finds have been found by Mrs. Otto first. There is the dwarfed prehistoric plant known as horsetail or scouring rush that she found not too long ago. The plant has corrugated green—the silicon on the wall, she explained. This is the first dwarf species to be found. Mrs. Otto will tell you that the plant is sometimes called 'a poor boy's firecracker' because it pops when tossed into a fire. It was also used by the pilgrims for scouring pans and by the Indians as a form of sandpaper, she related....

"'Unusual plant life grows in the Fairy Chasm Reserve,' she pointed out, 'because of climatic conditions. Cool and humid air comes off the lake and up through the deep forested ravines.' A ravine at one side of the reserve has been described by University of Wisconsin-Milwaukee botanist Dr. Alvin Throne as 'the wildest ravine in south Wisconsin.' 'Snow is persistent in the spring in the area,' Mrs. Otto said, 'and in the summer, the rising mists give an oriental quality to the landscape. Trees commonly found farther north reseed themselves in the reserve. There are shrubs and plants common to the Lake Superior region. Nearly all the deciduous trees that are indigenous to Wisconsin and the Great Lakes area are found in the reserve.'"

—From "Beauties of Nature Grow as Chasm Dwellers, Bayside Homemaker Tells Others About Finds in Suburban Reserve" by Laurie Van Dyke, *Milwaukee Journal*, November 27, 1960.

MY BIGGEST AND LONGEST FIGHT involved the effort to ban DDT [*dichlorodiphenyltrichloroethane*] in Wisconsin. When the Wisconsin chapter of The Nature Conservancy formed in 1960, UW botanist Hugh Iltis insisted that I serve on the board, for which UW Professor of Wildlife Ecology Joe Hickey acted as treasurer. Soon, we and many other birders noticed something terribly wrong: American robins were dying in convulsions all over the place after spraying for mosquitoes occurred. And then they sprayed for the Dutch elm beetle from the ground and by helicopters.

The first time I knew anything about DDT came when we lived in Portland. One of the hospitals where Owen worked lay in a valley where all of the shipyard workers lived. Mosquitoes were abundant, and the authorities fogged with DDT. I can remember Owen saying, "This is wrong!" I hadn't given it much thought until I observed robins dying. Then Margaret Reisinger, who also served on The Nature Conservancy board, recommended I call Joe Hickey because he knew more about DDT. So I talked to Joe, and he told me to write to Charlie Wurster, a university biology teacher in Long Island. Charlie was determined to know more about DDT than any person on this earth; he was in contact with graduate students all over the world. So he would send me things. Joe Hickey would send me papers and articles that his graduate students had unearthed, such as one on brown pelicans becoming wiped out in New Orleans. Meanwhile, my village was spraying by helicopter over everything. Well, there weren't any elm trees in the ravines, and there weren't any elm trees on the banks of Lake Michigan, and yet they were spraying over there. I went to the village meeting with all this information, which was a big mistake.

None of these village guys would read through the stack of information I had compiled. They'll read half a page, no more. They would say, "We're following the directions of the Ag Department. What do you want, Mrs. Otto? Birds or trees? It's so cheap, and everybody's using DDT, so why shouldn't we do it too?" It was cheap.

Then Walter Scott called me from the DNR and said, "We can't get a report back from the county. Would you interview the people spraying with DDT in Milwaukee County?" He wanted all the guys responsible for some spraying to fill out a form. He wanted to know what they were spraying and the dosage used. The DNR had sent these forms to them, but nobody would answer them. About four o'clock in the afternoon was the only time when these guys happened to be in their offices. It took me a while to learn that because they wouldn't call you back. You have to catch them! Gosh, it must have taken me at least a month to contact 17 people.

One of the books that influenced me during this period was *Silent Spring* by Rachel Carson. One of my joyful nights occurred when Owen brought home *The New Yorker* from his office with a serialized copy of her book. I was overjoyed because she had got the word out about DDT and other poisons. Before her book, the opposition called us "bird lovers in tennis shoes."

River Hills was one Milwaukee community that stopped using DDT, and Joe Hickey was responsible. Here's a good story. He attended a good friend's funeral in Illinois and was looking out the window at a mulberry tree. There were no robins, and he just kept looking. He took his mind off the funeral, walked out afterwards, then drove around the area, but he saw no robins. And here, mulberries appeared ripe. He had never seen mulberry trees without robins, and in those days everybody knew where a robin's nest occurred. We had robins all over the place. Joe became so upset that he came home and began to investigate the topic seriously, and he began to talk. He talked to the women's garden club of River Hills, a rich area where the minimum lot size is about five acres. Now, I didn't hear the lecture. I don't know what else he talked about, but he convinced those women in River Hills not to spray with DDT. They returned home and told their husbands, "If you vote for DDT, we're going to make a public fuss, get it into the newspapers, and parade around the village hall." Something like that, but they convinced the husbands they shouldn't do it. So River Hills switched to methoxychlor, a much more benign pesticide.

The only other Milwaukee community that didn't use DDT was St. Francis, and I thought that appropriate given that St. Francis was the patron saint of ecology. The communities that used the most DDT were my village of Bayside, and the villages of Fox Point and Elm Grove. Our village manager said, "We have the finest control of anyone in Wisconsin." I convinced them to stop for one year, but they continued the following year, which I read about in our community newspaper. Shortly thereafter, on a Sunday, I read about something called the Environmental Defense Fund. They had come to Michigan to try and stop the DDT spraying. So I called Joe Hickey and told him I wanted to meet with Charles Wurster. Two weeks later Joe and I flew out to Long Island, where Joe went off to The Nature Conservancy meeting, and I met with Charlie Wurster. I had dinner with Charlie, and he said, "We have to get a legal case or we'll dissolve."

I said, "Come to Wisconsin. This is the perfect time. Any later and it will be too late. Our eagle population has declined from 63 pairs down to three, and they're laying thin eggshells." Charlie said he would take it up with the TNC board to visit Wisconsin, where citizens can bring a lawsuit against the state if state waters are becoming polluted.

The next day, Charlie, Joe Hickey, and I walked along the Long Island beach—three Norwegians at play on a hot day. Those two men walked in front of me, and I walked at their heels. They called out the amount of DDT in the breasts of the shorebirds they observed based on the scientific literature they had read. What an afternoon I had! We went to get on the plane, and we were just intoxicated with each other. We could see an opening. We were just about to board the plane when Charlie said, "You know, we're going to need $15,000 to bring scientists in and pay for all the associated costs." Fifteen thousand dollars! We didn't have anything! He could have said $50 million. My face sank. I felt awful. I didn't know anybody who had that kind of money. It was a bucket of water on me.

I returned to Milwaukee with the hopes of raising the $15,000, and so I thought, "Well, I'll go to Audubon. They're concerned about birds, right?" I can't remember where they met, where I had to go, but I remember a great big fireplace and these old guys sitting around smoking cigars after dinner. I told them what was going to happen. Those men looked at me as if I was an angel that had just dropped out of the sky. They gave me $800. It was a start. I came home and thought, "Well, how about bees?" So I called Honey Acres, and the manager said he could give me only $15 because they were poor. Then I thought, "Well, how about fish?" So I called Smith Brothers in Washington. Oh boy, they were just as hard up for money and very concerned because they didn't want the public to know about all that DDT, especially in the fat of the chubs. The head of Smith Brothers—a very nice guy—gave me 10 bucks. A patient of Owen's gave me $600, but that's as far I could go. I simply didn't know anybody else. And I didn't have the credentials. Who the hell is Mrs. Owen Otto? So I brought Charlie in to give a talk at the museum and told Owen Gromme. Fred Ott came. Only about six people came. I was so crushed! We sat around a table and Charlie told them about DDT. It was overwhelming. Gromme took off. Freddy Ott took off. Money started coming in. It was unbelievable.

Fred Ott became the person who got money to pay for just about everything. He'd go over to the phone, call up and say, "Diane, I got $5,000 from Joe yesterday. Now you can make it $6,000 with $1,000 tomorrow morning. I've got to bring this guy in from Sweden." He was referring to a Swedish scientist who had found DDT in mother's milk. That's why we wanted to fly him to Wisconsin. Then I went to Madison and found places to board these people so we didn't have to pay for hotel bills.

Meanwhile, the state Ag Department had formed a committee to decide each year whether they should spray with DDT. Before they voted, Joe Hickey presented them with a report on the DDT in the fish in Lake Michigan and the birds. Then the committee voted. The guy from the DNR declined to vote, but all the rest voted to continue to spray with DDT. This just crushed Hickey. I saw him a half an hour after that because I came into town. I walked up to his office. He was near tears. He could hardly talk. He said, "Lorrie, it's hopeless. Nobody cares."

I said, "Joe, I care! And we'll go through with this! We'll bring in the scientists, and I'll put them in homes in the Madison area. We'll go to people who are members of The Nature Conservancy and ask them to take in a scientist. We'll go to the CNRA (Citizens Natural Resources Association), and we'll ask them." Joe agreed that it would save quite a bit of money.

We went out to the airport to welcome them and make them feel really important. We had a private room in some restaurant and Victor Yannacone, our New York attorney fighting for us, had everything taped. We were not allowed to talk about DDT during the dinner hour. One night, I heard this little hum. "Shh," Charlie said. "Vic is taping this!" He said a microphone hung right underneath the flower bouquet. What a time!

After the dinner meetings, Yannacone would take the materials from whoever was scheduled to be the witness the next day at the hearing and smash him to pieces. I went in with Joe Hickey when he practiced with Joe. It was so painful to watch. I never had nerve enough to go to another one. He just took the material and tore it up, tried to confuse Joe. Here's Joe, an older man, sitting there, and Yannacone just gives it to him. Then he would turn around and build him up so by the time he finished Joe would be mentally prepared.

$$\text{\textit{◢}}$$

BEFORE THE HEARING began on December 2, 1968, I learned that *The New York Times* had a column about the upcoming hearing. This impressed me, and I contacted the author, who wanted us to cover it for him. On the first day, we arrived as did Ag Chemical—all men. They sat on one side, and all of us sat on the other side. Then this blonde with long hair came in, skirt too short, and a little on the heavy side, and she sat with the men. I thought, "Who is that woman? Who wouldn't be on the side of birds and fish?" I wanted to know who the devil she was, so I went over and sat down beside her. She was a reporter for *The Capital Times* named Whitney Gould. She was barely a reporter. She had wanted to be a music and art writer because she had an art history major, but to get a job at *The Capital Times* she became a regular reporter.

Whitney covered the issue thoroughly and wrote so well that the editor turned the front page over to her; it was always the big headline. The next morning she met Charlie as he was coming in the door and asked him if she had made any mistakes. He would straighten things out for her, and that night a correction appeared in the paper. She was just fantastic. I believe without her diligent reporting the state would not have banned DDT so rapidly. She educated the legislators in Madison. Everybody read *The Capital Times*. In 1970, we became the first state in the Union to ban DDT. And then, two years later, the same group of men involved in the state DDT fight all met here in my house. I had men sleeping in the attic, in the basement, all over. They didn't want to separate. They would talk almost all night, and they'd read each other's research. I'd come down in the morning to get breakfast for them and step over bodies all over the living room.

I'd stand there on the balcony, and I'd see sleeping men! That same group of men went to Washington and convinced EPA head Ruckelshaus to ban DDT in our country. The year was 1972.

I can take pride in knowing that I played a role as a catalyst at a critical moment in the campaign.

I remember we were all together and cried with joy when the ban occurred. It was such a long haul. And for me, it just destroyed the best years of my life between ages 40 and 50. These are the years when you're at your peak with everything. You're your most beautiful. You've had enough experience so you're comparatively wise.

After the DDT thing, I was impressed by what one person could do. I really was. And when I tell this story from the stage, I say that. I just say, "You think one person can't make a difference, you remember me!" But then I said to myself, "Can I match it?" I was 50 years old. I thought I'd die when I was 60, or that something awful would happen. My mother died when she was 68 and my father when he was about 71. So I certainly didn't expect to live to be 80! And then Margaret Reisinger, Isabel Lillie, and the Whitefish Bay Garden Club and the Junior League of Milwaukee got together in 1968 and '69, and they started the Riveredge Nature Center, with Andy Larsen as director. The Junior League came forth with $30,000 to pay his salary for two years. He quipped that he thought everyone over 30 was hopeless. And I thought, "Young man. Wait until you meet me!"

He put out the call in 1970. He wanted trained people to serve as teacher-naturalists. So seven of us volunteered, and I was about 15 years older than everybody else. In that first year we studied with him. He sent us off to a prairie conference in Madison. And boy, what a turning point in my life! I was sitting in the audience, and Hugh Iltis was showing these wonderful slides of these flowers that I didn't know about. They were prairie flowers, and afterward I thought, "Oh, I used to walk through those on the way to school." They occurred along the railroad track, and I didn't know those were prairie plants. And then Iltis said that we'd saved only one in five prairie plants, and fared worse with insects. I thought, "Holy smokes! I've got two acres of land. I could save some of those plants. Maybe I can't do anything about the insects, but I could plant prairie flowers on my land."

At the end of the year, Andy sat us down in a little circle in the woods and said, "Now, what would you ladies like to teach?" Two of them took the river, two of them took the forest, and two of them took the soils and the open fields.

But I said, "Andy, I don't want to teach little children. If the adults don't start taking better care of the earth, there isn't going to be anything left when these little children grow up. I want to teach a course for adults."

And he said, "Lorrie, just take the ball and run with it!"

As an aside, Andy Larsen is so courageous and imaginative, a wonderful colleague. Years ago he contracted Parkinson's disease, and at first he was terrible to be around, just stubborn and hostile. He was angry and determined he would do things that he wasn't capable of doing. At the annual Riveredge meeting, he would hold the paper, and then he'd read from it. You wanted to jump up and hold his hand and say, "Alright, Andy, for God's sakes, put your hand in your pocket!" Then something happened. I'm not sure what because he did a real flip-flop. He became gentle, and people started confiding in him. His personality just changed.*

Andy Larsen, sadly for all, passed away on September 22, 2017.

❦

Lorrie's garden has matured over the years with as much grace and vigor as she herself has. It's a showpiece of staying power, an example of all that can be accomplished if you just follow what you believe in. Who would have imagined when it all began that the woman who had to fight for her yard would one day receive accolades from Vice President Al Gore?
   —Lorraine Johnson, *Grow Wild!* Golden, Colorado:
   Fulcrum Publishing, 1998.

❦

AFTER THAT YEAR of training under Andy, I had the summer to think of what I wanted to teach, and I started reading that wealthy suburbia proved ten times worse off than any chemically addicted farmer as far as contributing to runoff pesticides. So I thought, "I've got to try to convince people that they should try to find an alternative to lawns." I didn't care what they used as long as it didn't destroy someplace else and that it didn't waste our precious drinking water. So I decided to teach a course I called "Alternatives to Lawns." I taught at Riveredge for a semester; it proved to be highly popular. And then I did one at the Milwaukee Public Museum for a semester.

At that time, I didn't think anything about native plants. But I began to learn, and eventually I taught a class called "Wild Plants for Tame Places." We started with my property. Then I gave a lecture at Schlitz Audubon Nature Center. A primary grade school teacher was there and turned to her friends, about seven of them, and said, "This is such a good idea. Let's get together and do it! We'll meet every month and help each other." From that lecture, The Wild Ones was born. I've been involved with it now for over 20 years. It has grown from seven people to over 2,500!

When we first formed the Wild Ones Natural Landscaping Club, they were all women. Now, at least half of the members are men.

❧

IN 1972, I landscaped on the grounds at my husband's hospital in Oconomowoc, and I had to drive about 40 miles back and forth. To make it more interesting, I'd take little back roads, every morning and every night. And under the fence lines, I'd see some plants. I would stop and ask the farmer if I could dig that yellow flower out from underneath his fence line. I'd be all dressed up. He would drop everything, grab the shovel out of the shed, dig it up, put it on a newspaper, and place it in the trunk of my car. That's how that collection started on my property corner.

Helen Olney (sister of renowned Milwaukee artist Ruth Grotenrath) with her painting of Bayside wildflowers at Bayside Community Assembly, ca. mid-1970s. Lorrie (at microphone) discusses importance of wild plants. Photo provided to Sumner Matteson by Lorrie.

LORRIE OTTO

One day, Gimbels Department Store put on a cash contest and asked all Wisconsin artists to contribute a painting. A friend, Ruth Grotenrath, wanted to paint wildflowers along a roadside, so she went out to her father's farm. There, however, the roadsides had just been mowed and sprayed. The highway folks had just cut down all of these crabapple trees with grapevines. She couldn't believe it. So she came back, and I said, "Come out to my house."

She said, "You mean you have wildflowers?"

"Yeah, right on the corner. I have quite a few things." So she came out with her sketchbook and painted them. She won first prize!

Ruth said, "You suppose I could plant wildflowers at my house?"

"Well, yes, unless the pollution is too bad on your street, but I have no idea, so why don't we try it?" So we planted her entire front yard. Then Ruth Grotenrath, Hattie Purtell, and I—three women who had volunteered with Andy Larsen—decided that we would plant prairie flowers in our yards. We'd heard that Hal Rock, Director of the Wehr Nature Center, had seeds, so we went out to see him. He was overjoyed. He couldn't believe suburban women wanted to put prairie in our yards.

We also planted prairie and other native wildflowers at the artist Ed Green's place, and then others followed suit. Somehow or another, the *Journal* got wind of this, and they sent a photographer out to do a color shoot at a number of homes. One of those belonged to Ruth Grotenrath and Schomer Lichtner. Ruth had wild roses and wild geraniums, but before it came out in the paper, the garbage man—yes, the guy who comes to pick up the garbage—reported her yard to the weed commissioner. She came home and found this slip saying that they were going to mow everything down. They gave her 48 hours. She called me up and said, "I can't believe this."

I said, "There must be a name on that slip. Who is it?" Sure enough, there was a name, and so I called the guy at night, and I said, "Whatever made you think that those were weeds? If I made a path through them, would that be all right?"

"Well," he said, "you better call the health department."

The next day I called the health department, and they said, "Well, you can't have all that pollen in the city."

"What do you mean, pollen? There aren't any grasses in there, and all the flowers consist of insect-pollinated ones, except the trees. Can't the people in Milwaukee have trees?"

Then-Milwaukee Public Museum botanist David Kopitzke and Lorrie speaking about landscaping with native plants at the Riveredge Nature Center, Ozaukee County, Wisconsin. September 1974. Photo courtesy of Dorothy Boyer.

"Well, yes, they can have trees. You better call the mayor's office." Before I did that, I called the (MPM) Milwaukee Public Museum's botanist, and I got David Kopitzke! I'd never heard of him before. Oh, this wonderful voice! He gave us great support to pursue the matter.

I finally called the mayor's office, but I couldn't get anybody to come and see the yard. So I said, "I want to know when this is going to be cut down, the time—the real time—because on Sunday in the *Milwaukee Journal* on the front page in color, this yard is going to be shown in the women's section of the *Journal*. We want to follow it up with a photograph of a man mowing it down. Mowing it down!"

Well, I got a call about 20 minutes later from the mayor's office saying, "Mrs. Otto, now don't worry about this. We've canceled the whole order."

❦

IN 1974 OR '75, DAVID KOPITZKE AND I started planting the front of the MPM with native plants, and a skinny, white-faced man came over and said, "They won't let me do this in New Berlin." This Donald Hagar told me he had mowed a border, maybe 20 feet wide around his yard, and he said, "I can't do this. There's a little vesper sparrow doing a broken wing act in front of my lawnmower."

I said, "For heaven's sakes, put your lawnmower in the garage, and we'll sue the city of New Berlin!"

But first, we invited city officials—the mayor and alderman among others—for a Sunday afternoon picnic. Mrs. Hagar prepared a wonderful meal, but only the alderman showed. Donald Hagar had about an acre of lawn, and on one end he had an elaborate, wonderful vegetable garden with raspberries all strapped up and his strawberries perfectly mulched. His children had a pumpkin garden. This man was not your ordinary gardener; he worked for the U.S. Forest Service, was a wildlife biologist, and he'd earned his master's degree studying plant succession in New York State. He wanted to know how succession would proceed in Wisconsin. So over seven years, he started with raw dirt on the other side of his lawn, which became New England asters and little oak trees, four feet high. And that's what his neighbor objected to—this plot demonstrating succession. In reality, I'm afraid this proved to be a case of pure jealousy. She objected because everyone wanted to come to the Hagar house instead of her house because children loved the wildness of the land. His daughter had a pony, and they'd pony ride through these paths. It was just an ideal place for kids. But she called the weed commissioner, who came and determined that it was a fire hazard.

My idea of educating them first at this Sunday picnic didn't work. They didn't come. So then I said, "Well, okay, I'll give a lecture on Saturday morning right at the Village Hall." The only people who came included those interested in wildflowers. None of the officials came. But this case acquired a life of its own, and what a great case! It should have been televised. There were stories of how all New Berlin would burn down if the city allowed Hagar to continue with his unkempt yard. We sounded like wicked people by the time the morning was over. Hagar, however, had a friend in the Forest Service who had done fire research for the U.S. government. He knew just how hot it had to be before a house caught on fire.

Anyway, I took the stand as the final witness. There is so much plain serendipity associated with trials like this. Before the trial, I had decided that there had to be weeds associated with this mayor someway or another. He had become so adamant about cutting down Hagar's weeds. So I went to his office. There, junipers grew underneath his office window, and coming through them climbed Canada thistles. That's on the weed list of almost every state in the nation! Then I walked over to his parking lot. Right in front of his car bumper grew ragweeds and thistles. So I took a photograph with his car and his license plate next to this patch.

Then I thought, "Could I be lucky enough to get weeds at his house?" I found out where he lived and drove down this long street where everything looked so neat, cleaner than most kitchens. I came to his lot and observed a big ragweed in full pollen directly below his mailbox. You almost had to reach through it to open his mailbox! And it was the only one for streets and streets. Also, on the front lawn, right against this maple tree, another weed. I took a picture of that, with his house in the background.

Before the trial, someone said, "Oh, Lorrie, this is a tough judge. He's a strict Catholic and a reactionary Republican; you'll never get away with this." But I showed him the photos, and we convinced him! Later, after 25 years on the bench, he retired.

At his retirement party, a reporter asked him what he considered his most outstanding case. "Oh," he replied, "it was this guy who didn't want to mow his lawn." He said he'd received letters from Australia, from all over the world. And the newspapers had such a wonderful time with this; the case made the papers all over, and one of them had as its headline: "Man mows down law, not his lawn."

❧

THE FIRST STEP toward working with native plants is to decide to change your yard and get rid of the lawnmower. We should have ordinances that forbid power lawnmowers. When the ozone is high, lawnmowers stay inside, but why have them at all? And why do we tolerate leaf blowers? The noise alone! I'm terribly aggravated by leaf blowers. Or when I shovel my driveway, listening to snow blowers; they're such an intrusion. When I first moved here, you mowed the lawn with those little push mowers that cut grass and made such a lovely sound.

The other day, a lawn care company came in a good half a block away from me when I was listening to juncos. They flew in all at once, and that sweet twittering was so charming. Then the leaf blowers began—two guys with leaf blowers blowing damp, not dry, leaves. What happened to the good old broom or rake? This kind of noise pollution is intolerable, unacceptable unless we work together to rid our homes of them. Realistically, what chance is there that might happen? Well, conservation efforts always start off with someone raising a little hell.

When people first come to me and say, "Well, where should I start?"

I say, "Are you a sunny person or a shady person?" If you love the sun, and you get a new house out in a naked subdivision, and you have enough nerve to do prairie, go for prairie because we only have a half of one percent left. We can bring back prairie flowers; it's so easy, so distinctive. I also tell them to join a chapter of the Wild Ones. Several chapters of Wild Ones occur around the country. Every other month we have a 16-page newsletter. We also have a handbook that provides a landowner with assistance on how to transform one's yard into a paradise of color through native plant gardening.

The best approach for establishing native plants on your former lawn is to find out what grows in your kind of soil. Barring that, what I tell people is if you're going to go out and get something, go to a native plant nursery and buy a native plant because then you're safe. Once it's established, it will be there for centuries.

I always work with people who specialize in native plants. We've got enough native plant nurseries around in Wisconsin now; this wasn't the case in the beginning. And in the beginning, I wasn't interested in native plants. Gosh, there's a recorded lecture of me at UWM, damn it all, praising purple

Lorrie at the "Indian Hill Native Prairie Garden," River Hills, Wisconsin. September 1998. Photo provided to SM by Lorrie Otto.

loosestrife, saying that everyone should have these purple exclamation marks in their yard! Oh Lord! It took me two or three years before I really understood what to plant and not to plant. When you go into the nursery, you don't want to be buying forsythia either; it's not native, and it doesn't have anything for the birds either.

Once you start, you become so enchanted at the non-lawn part that for some people it becomes a hobby to see what kind of diversity they can get. And some really feel strongly about keeping the genetics in line. Some people say, "Well, I'm only going to find sources of native plants within a 20-mile radius, or a 50-mile radius."

HERE'S WHAT I KNOW. [American] Witch-hazel [*Hamamelis virginiana*] is the last flower to bloom in Wisconsin. And it's not at all particular. It doesn't really like deep shade, but half shade is best. And if there's enough moisture and somewhat of a windbreak around it, it can be in bright sun. Everybody ought to have a witch-hazel.

If you really cornered me, and I could only have one plant, it would be a cup plant [*Silphium perfoliatum*]. It comes up early. When you see that magnificent square stem, you just have to pet it with your thumb and forefinger and rub your hand up and down it. It is so square, and it is so big. I love the shadows of cup plants. Their leaves will come out almost horizontally. Others will come out and make a break. Some of them are more serrated on the edges than others. That's fun to watch.

I have one right next to my kitchen window. I have taken photos of it through the window when bees have made a circle around a tiny cup of water that forms when the leaves come together to make a cup against that square stem. I've watched chickadees come in and drink. Goldfinches come in and drink. Tiger swallowtails emerge at the height of their bloom. All of a sudden there will be four or five tiger swallowtails on one big clump of cup plant. And when it starts coming into seed, the goldfinches can hardly wait to eat those first ones. The ones left become available to juncos, which hit them hard. Seeds fall to the ground where the juncos eat them, unlike the goldfinches that sit up there and pick away.

I wait until November to cut my cup plants down.

As far as favorite shrubs, I like maple-leaved viburnum [*Viburnum acerifolium*] and our native arrow-wood [*Viburnum rafinesquianum*], both of which grow in the shade in the woods. And I also like elderberries [*Sambucus canadensis*]. The elderberries that grow in full sunshine used to occur along the ditches of Wisconsin. The red elderberry [*Sambucus racemosa*], which you see in the woods up north, occurs here once in a great while in the ravine here or at the Schlitz Audubon Nature Center. A good 20 years ago I planted one on the north side of my house and one on the south side to see which would do the best. They are remarkable. When it's so cold and icy out, you'll see these big buds and think, "That's never going to make it." But no siree, they've got to be filled with antifreeze!

Round-leaved dogwood [*Cornus rugosa*], another favorite of mine, is a beauty, but it only grows in the shade. Unfortunately, the deer love it. Don Hagar said they've lost it up north, but we have a few here and there growing through our woods. And then there are the other three dogwoods. If you go with gray dogwood [*Cornus foemina racemosa*], it's going to form a thicket. An ornithologist at the Wehr Nature Center told me one day that he found more birds' nests in dogwood thickets than in any other kind of shrub because those fine, strong little branches are perfect for birds to wind their grass roots or whatever around it to hold the nest secure.

Now if you plant the alternate-leaved dogwood [*Cornus alternifolia*], which has the blue berries, never trim the ends off. The same goes for rough-leaved dogwood [*Cornus drummondii*] with white berries.

If you prune, prune the dogwood stems that no longer have the bright red color. Once the stems have lost that color, cut them off even with the ground. They'll always have these red stems; they'll be so graceful as they fountain out to take their true shape.

High-priced nurserymen plant their shrubs too close together, and then they clip them so they form a continuous wall across. They make a lot of money selling those shrubs, but they put four shrubs where they should only have one. So space them out.

I TALK TO PEOPLE who want to change their lawns when they're going on "digs"—a rescue where either the highway department is going to widen a road that goes through a woods or they're going to put a new road through a woods. Highway folks have been wonderful about letting us come in and dig up plants. I say to people, "Take as much soil as you can. Take along another sled, wicker baskets, whatever you need. Not only are you taking bulbs, seeds, and dormant seeds, but more importantly, you will inoculate your soil with the fungi and the bacteria in this soil so that your home soil will become alive through these microscopic as well as macroscopic elements. They will make your soil healthy and workable again."

I'm very much opposed to saying, "Oh, well, we'll fix up the soil. We'll just bring some peat in." Where's that peat from? What right do we have to destroy wetlands to mine peat? I want people to match the plants to the soil! In the beginning, farmers dug the plants out underneath barbed wire fences for me so I had all the goodies that were in that soil. Also, when I started, no one used herbicides. So when I let my grass grow, I had wonderful asters right away—the first summer.

People ask, "How many different kinds of plants do you have?" Good heavens, I can't even begin to count them. Over the years, people have given me plants, the birds have brought seeds in, and the wind has brought in pollination.

You need to manage and maintain your land without making noise, polluting the air, and using energy. You're not going to use chemicals. You're not going to destroy another place to make your place more interesting. And that means you're not going to go out and steal wildflowers from protected areas and put them in your place. So you have to have that nursery in between you and the wildflowers that does this for you. When I started doing this, we only had two nurseries where you could buy plants. You could buy seeds, so you could grow your own, but in our seminars we always had David Kopitzke, who would teach us how to do cuttings and how to plant. We've had him every single year since we started because he's wonderful at helping people at the beginning.

🍃

I THINK THE GREATEST effect of all from how we have cared for lawns is the loss of food for migrating and resident birds. For centuries, birds have been flying north and south, with immature birds flying south for the first time. Imagine them moving over the countryside, where once abundant wildflowers grew. You would see that they had this big cupboard with all of these shrubs that had fruits, seeds, and berries for them—

a smorgasbord of wonderful things from Solomon's seals and false Solomon's seals, baneberries, blue cohosh, and jack-in-the-pulpits. What a feast! Now they've got a bare cupboard.

People say that these lawn care people have learned that if you cut off the tips of shrubs, it will make them branch or make them fuller. But they also aren't told that those are the growing tips. That's where the flowers are. That's where the berries are. This, of course, impacts the birds. We should have some commitment, obligation, to take care of those birds. I mean almost everybody loves songbirds. And yet many people don't see the whole picture.

The bird doesn't just eat seeds. When they have their young, it's soft, tiny insects that they're feeding those featherless babies in their nests. So, let's preserve and maintain breeding habitats. Such thinking needs to enter more minds of the bird businessmen. The guy who sells birdseed should say, "How many shrubs do you have around? Do you have wildflowers underneath those shrubs? Do you have some nice native trees?" I don't think he usually does that.

Speaking of birds, I used to keep track of bird occurrences on calendars and sometimes in the margins of bird identification books, but mostly on calendars. Then, I'd write down the day that the fox sparrow arrived or the first white-throated sparrow. I did that for years when I belonged to the Phenological Society.

When I moved here, it was the first of September, and warblers hit the windows in a large number. I can remember saying to my husband, "I have to move into a motel. I can't stand this!" I stapled garden fencing around the windows to remedy the situation when mobiles failed, but now there are so damn few warblers, who's going to hit a window? I've lived here almost 50 years and witnessed a dramatic change—a precipitous drop in the number of birds. At first, a big drop occurred during the DDT spraying, followed by a gradual buildup, and now so few numbers.

In the springtime back then, you'd be awakened in the morning by all the fox sparrows rustling and scratching in the leaves. You'd look down the sides of the ravines and see that the color of the leaves and soil and the color of their backs appeared all the same because they occurred in such high number. Now what? I'm up to four! Four fox sparrows.

Another thing. We don't know how many birds are killed by cats. Cats are not a normal thing in our environment. My neighbor next door who

Past the prairie garden and shaded by a conifer ... Lorrie's Bayside home. October 2001. Photo provided to Sumner Matteson by Lorrie.

raised kittens to give to pet shops thought it was wonderful. Her three little children and all the little neighborhood children, and all these little kitties, you know, what a great thing. And the three mother cats roamed around. About every 20 minutes during bird migration, a cat would catch a bird. And one day as I stood out by my mailbox, a cat killed a fledgling catbird on my neighbor's property. This woman is a fundamentalist Christian. And I thought, "You know, God didn't design life to work this way. We didn't have this kind of cat on our continent. The birds don't know how to deal with this, even though eons have passed. Here this cat jumps out from nowhere after that bird was beginning to explore the world. It's not right."

Then there's the woman who lives on the other side of Round Lake Drive, who has a little daughter that became very precious to me because she's a wonderful little artist. I made a videotape with her drawing seedpods from my prairie for a project for a school, so I already knew her and her mother well. One day I looked out the window, and I saw their cat in my yard. She had this teeny-weeny little brown thing I assumed was a meadow vole. So I went out to get it because I wanted to photograph it for another series of slides that I was doing. By golly, it was a little winter wren, dead by the time I retrieved her.

So I went over to her house, rang the doorbell, and the mother and the daughter came to the door. I said, "Some people think this is the most beautiful song that we ever hear around here. This tiny little wren is here for just a short time, and it doesn't come in flocks. Just once in a great while you hear this lovely, lovely call. And it will never call again. I don't know if there are any more winter wrens, and I don't know when the next one will ever appear. But your cat ended its life." Then this woman just stood there wide-eyed. I handed the wren to the girl and said, "You may want to make a sketch of this because it's so nice and fresh. When do you get a chance to have a winter wren in the palm of your hand?"

The mother said, "Oh, well, to please you, we'll try to keep the cat in."

"To please me, nothing. I may have only a few months on this earth. You are the mother of a child. There are two generations here. You have so much longer to live, and your child even longer than you, if everything goes normally. Do you really want to grow up where there are fewer and fewer birds? Or, maybe just one or two kinds of birds? Is that the kind of world you want? That's your responsibility, not mine. You keep that cat in your house because you feel and know that's where it ought to be."

<hr/>

WHATEVER YOU DO, allow the land to come first in your life. I have a hunger for beauty and diversity, and then you think beyond that about how it all begins with the tiniest microorganisms in the soil that are essential to life. The natural world is truly extraordinary! So often, we take away habitat for everything. How do we expect human life to continue? There's no way the earth can sustain the population that is here right now. Why isn't that on the front page? That's so much more serious than the constant news of one tribe killing another that's been going on forever. The whole damn race is going to lose if the world's population continues to grow at present rates. And yet it's not in the headlines; people don't know about it.

Respect for the land is the foundation of our life. When you get these polls about what's the most important thing that Congress should consider, it has to be the environment. Nothing else matters if we don't take care of the environment! But what do we read? Sometimes it's not even mentioned! When you get right down to it, there's too damn many of us. We don't know how to behave. Even if we did know how to behave, we've damn near lost it. But you can't give up. You make life as beautiful as you can wherever you can, and you open your heart and mind to nature's beauty and complexity. While we're here, we have the power and opportunity to make life healthy and diverse.

Where you can manage land, whether it's public lands or private lands, whether it's around your library or your church, there is a role you can play. First, join your local chapter of The Nature Conservancy. I think everybody should be a member. We have to save the examples that are left, or we won't know how to heal. And we have to do it soon on larger scales than what we've done in the past, or we will have lost too much.

❦

IF I HAVE ANY REGRETS about this life, they would involve mistakes I made with my son, George. His body was found a couple of years ago in Loveland, Colorado. He died of grief and guilt under peculiar circumstances. Years ago, there were two mistakes that I made. One, that I didn't run to Canada with him during the Vietnam War. Instead, he came right out of high school and went directly into the army. He was such a gentle boy. I think maybe in the back of Owen's head, going into the army would turn George into a man. He'd see the other side of life. I don't know. Anyway, we let him go. I didn't fight it. He became an army medic, but tragically everyone else in his class was killed in Vietnam. George was the only one who survived because they sent him to Korea instead.

He had received basic training in Texas. Once, close to Christmas, he decorated the entire compound, and no boy had ever done this. I received a letter from his commanding officer. At first I was afraid to open it. I couldn't imagine. I thought maybe he'd been shot by mistake. I opened it and this commander wrote this glowing letter about what this boy had done. When it came time to place these young men, everybody went to Vietnam except George. They sent him to the DMZ (Demilitarized Zone) in Korea as an ambulance driver, so that's where he spent his time.

When he returned, he came home with such a hatred for the government that he didn't vote for years. He wouldn't get married. He wasn't going to sign a contract ever again, and so for 12 years he lived with this wonderful girl until they finally broke up.

George was so bitter that had his father not been a psychiatrist, I'm sure we would have had to commit him somewhere. At the time, Owen served as head of a psychiatric hospital in Oconomowoc, and I was working on the grounds there. Well, after George returned from Korea, the army sent him to Fort Lewis near Tacoma, Washington, to finish off his term. It must have been awful, just awful. At one time, Owen and I had a wonderful relationship with both of my children; we talked about everything. Of his experience at Fort Lewis, George would only say, "I can't tell you what happens when a bunch of men live together."

When George returned, he came to work out at the hospital grounds because I was landscaping out there, and I needed him. I needed his sense of design. He was a very talented artist, and, of course, he was big and strong and a wonderful guy to work with. But George's art changed dramatically when he returned from overseas. It was hideous: dying people and swords going into chests, people standing in an ocean of blood. He decorated his room with his dreadful posters that he brought back from Seattle, so you could see where his mind had gone. In the afternoon, when I would go into his room to take a nap, those drawings looked so terrible that when I closed my eyes, they hurt me. Finally, I said to him, "I cannot stand being in your room; these are so awful." So bit by bit, we would take them out.

For the next 24 years, except during vacations, George would walk with his dad in the afternoon around one of the lakes in Waukesha. They became very close, and then his father developed lung and brain cancer, and George sat with him while he died. A year went by, and I said to him, "Does it get any better?"

"No," he said. "It's worse. I feel as if God has died."

Shortly before Owen died, George finally got married. After Owen's death, they went off to Leadville, Colorado, to open a hardware store. His wife's son—just out of the air force—also helped out. I think they made a million dollars the first year, but the store had been robbed twice, so they had resale guns on hand. One day, the stepson wanted to borrow a gun, and George gave him his handgun. At a party, that man in front of his brother and whoever else was at the party, excused himself to go to his room to get some cigarettes. He came back with the gun, and then to everyone's horror, blew his brains out in front of everybody—with George's gun. So George felt responsible. He stopped eating, and in three weeks, on September 22, 1997, he was dead. They found his body on the bathroom floor.

He was so healthy. He didn't wear glasses. He didn't have any cavities in his mouth. He was this big, strong, gorgeous creature, and only 47.

I've lost some good friends. About every 10 years someone very close to me dies for various reasons. One was a car accident, and another one was suicide because she had Crohn's disease. Another one was through failed bypass surgery. But this! On a Monday afternoon, two days before my daughter's 50th birthday! I was all packed to take off the next morning to fly to Bellingham, Washington, to celebrate her 50th birthday. The telephone rang, and I went over, sat in the chair, and answered the phone. Someone said, "Are you sitting down?"

I've heard it all my life when you get bad news. Well, I was sitting down. But I can understand why they say that because you're involuntary, and your smooth muscles start to quiver like jelly. I just shivered and didn't know what to think. Where was George? All I could think was, well, he's wherever he was before he grew inside of me, so he's now nothingness, and it's forever.

When I started to think about it, I was determined that it was not going to impair my life because I had too few years left. I could not take off a year to grieve. And after all, this occurred in Leadville, Colorado, at such an altitude that I couldn't go to visit him anyway. So I didn't. I took his photographs off the refrigerator. I was all packed to go west anyway. I couldn't get there fast enough. And the other thing was, I had no relationship with his wife. I hardly knew her at all. So neither Patricia nor I went to the funeral.

As I prepared to leave the house to go to the airport, I remembered letters that he had written to me. I had 10 years of letters. I opened up the drawer and threw them all in a shopping bag and got on the airplane. So on the day of his funeral, Trisha and I read aloud his letters. By the time we went to bed, we felt we'd been with him, really been with him. The next day, one of Trisha's friends had a computer we used to create two pages of paragraphs from his different letters. We ran a couple of hundred copies off and sent these to people to let them know that George had died. I wanted to say to everybody, "Well, if you have children, make them write letters to you." That's all I had left of him. I thought about all of those mothers who had lost their sons who were George's contemporaries—kids that had just left high school. They lost their sons before they knew what kind of men they would grow into. But I knew.

I REMEMBER when I thought I was dying a few years ago and had to call 911. I had worked on wildflower-covered berms all day. At that time, the woman who had them had died, and I was taking care of them with a dear friend. We were taking out Queen Anne's lace or something. It was the end of July when all the lawn sprayers were out spraying. I could smell the spray but never thought anything of it. That night I started urinating.

About the third time I got up, I thought, "What in the world did I do to myself? I haven't eaten a watermelon, and gosh I still have to go!"

Finally, maybe it was the fourth or fifth time, I got up and fell against my slide projector. I then righted myself and fell against the door, and I thought, "My gosh, I'm having a stroke." So I got down on my hands and knees, and I crawled to the toilet because I still had to go to the toilet. I came back, crawled on my hands and knees, got up on the bed, and started moving my wrists and my hands. I thought, "Well, I'm not paralyzed." Then I decided to call my daughter, but I couldn't get my head up. Then I thought, "Ooh, this is a 911." So I called 911. They kept me on the phone, but I was losing my ability to talk. They wanted to know if the house was locked. I said, "Nothing is locked. Just walk in."

Four men came. They were standing there, taking my blood pressure, and the head guy said, "We have to take you to the hospital immediately, but we can't put you on a stretcher because we can't get you over the balcony." They had to sit me up. I remember my head falling back as they picked me up. I didn't remember anything until I was stretched out on a stretcher here in the living room. I couldn't get my eyes open, but I could see through my eyelashes.

I had said when we got this house, "You know, I want to die here with my boots on. This is it."

The guy who was taking my blood pressure said, "You're certainly taking this calmly."

I thought to myself, "Why should I not?" You know, I've made my mark. I've done my thing. The bargain isn't for you to live forever, and I'm in the place where I love, so this is it. Then I had that terrible feeling, a sadness that people would miss me, but I still felt ready to go.

So I was lying there, barely conscious, with a policeman bent over me, and he said, "Who's the President of the United States?"

I thought about how funny it was, and I said, "George Bush!" I thought, "By God! I can't die now!"

I think it was a reaction from the pesticides—poisoned by pesticides. They put me on oxygen right away and took me by ambulance to a hospital. The next morning I had a CNRA big day here at my house. In July they always meet here, and I wanted to be with them so badly. In the meantime, I had a student living downstairs, and so she took over playing hostess.

My doctor came in, and they put me through some tests. They wanted to put me through a lot more on Monday morning. Finally, I got some sleep, awakened, walked around, and proved to the doctor that I could walk. So he let me go home.

THERE ARE VERY FEW advantages of being old, but one is all the experience you've had that brings wisdom—an ability to tie things together—that you don't get from reading books. I also like being a catalyst now. Someone will call and ask me about something, and I'll say, "Call so-and-so." Because I've stuck my foot into different spots as the years have gone by, I've come to know many people and how the system works.

Lorrie outside her Bayside home, May 5, 1999. Photo by Sumner Matteson.

Another nice thing too about being older is that the sexual thing doesn't enter in. When you're young, you can't really love men without someone always thinking that there's a sexual thing going on. But when you're older, you're free of all of that. So I can just love them to the marrow of their bones, as I do the women. I have wonderful men friends who are very close. My friendships are very close, as close as marriage because I can talk about anything, but I've always been that way, ever since first grade.

When you're young, you're the spark that lights the fuse, but all the rest of it happens because of your friends. And if you're starting out young, and you don't have a group of devoted friends, you join conservation organizations, and you find them quickly. That's the great advantage of having our kind of people all gathered around some focal point. Today, you have so many different kinds of conservation organizations, with passionate environmentalists, and that helps a lot. And then, when you're old, your greatest treasure, by far, are your friends that feel as strongly as you do and who are there to support you. When we lose a fight, we all lose it together. It's much easier to lose if it's with a group. Each one of those people feeds into the rich current of my life in little streams, and the longer I live and the longer I have those relationships, the richer and more wonderful they become.

I have so many people come up to me now. I'll be at a seminar, or I'll be in the grocery store, and someone comes up and says, "I heard you give a lecture and knew that when I had land of my own, I would never have a lawn. I want to thank you so much!" This sort of thing is because I've lived so long! I have received so many marvelous letters.

When I do die, I'd like to be remembered as a teacher trying to get people to take care of the earth. People have said to me, "Oh, you should write a book." No, the thing I do best is talk. There's something about having this passionate personality; this enthusiastic person has more power than a book. ❇

Lorrie used to jog daily—four miles a night—into her mid-70s, with a Russian wolfhound, until a serious ankle injury befell her. Then she turned to walking a mile, sometimes two, almost every evening when the air was "so much nicer."

In her later years, she moved to Bellingham, Washington, to live with daughter Patricia. After a brief illness, she passed away on Lorrie prior to meeting with visitors at her home, ca. 2000. Photo courtesy of Dorothy Boyer.

May 29, 2010. A green cemetery burial followed, where no embalming occurred and only biodegradable materials were used in her burial.

At her gravesite, at her request, engraved on a river rock, just one word: Lorrie.

CHAPTER NINE 🦅

Francis Hole
(1913-2002)

Dr. Hole plays his violin to UW-Madison Soil Science students
along the banks of the Wisconsin River, April 23, 1983—his last field trip
as a professor. Photo by Sumner Matteson.

WHITE PINE

Chapter Ten~
Francis Hole

My brother and I slept in the attic. That was another way to escape the world of adults. The snow would sift in sometimes when there was a cold winter night. With the wind blowing, snow could get in between the shingles and come down—a little bit of cold powder coming down in our faces. We thought it was great up there....

I wasn't much of a scholar. I spent most of my time studying nature, raising caterpillars and mounting them. Then I became something of an artist. I'd make very careful drawings with India ink and watercolors. Then I did a Leopold kind of thing. I said to myself, "I'm not going to kill these things." I was about twelve. I'd raise moths, and then the promethea [silkmoth, *Callosamia promethea*] would come out, I'd admire it, and let it go....

Climbing trees was terribly important. We had in the back of our house a basswood tree that towered above the house—I suppose it was 65 feet tall—had a big branch, and my father allowed us boys to climb.... From the age of seven on up into my teens, it was a good thing after breakfast to climb up and see what the world looked like. Since I was at the center of the world, I had to look around over the houses.

—FH

CHAPTER TEN

F rancis Doan Hole came into this world on August 25, 1913, as Vivaldi's "The Four Seasons" played in the delivery room and the sun rose clear in the east. This is how I like to imagine his birth, even if it didn't happen that way.

Blessed with a keen sense of wonder and a love for the outdoors, Francis grew up in a Quaker community in rural Richmond, Indiana, where he used what free time he had from a fairly regimented life to explore the hills and woods near Earlham College. Caterpillars were his first primary interest as a small boy followed, naturally, by butterflies. His father, a geologist by training, became curator of the Joseph Moore Museum at Earlham, and here Francis was introduced to a treasure trove of artifacts, including a vast assortment of rocks and minerals, and bird specimens, collected by his father and others from both near and far away places, such as Hawaii.

Influenced also by summer trips with his parents to pristine natural areas and geologic refugia such as the San Juan Mountains, Yellowstone and Glacier national parks, and the Grand Canyon, Francis eventually earned a bachelor of arts in geology and biology at Earlham in 1933. Demonstrating his intellectual breadth, he earned a master of arts the following year in French at Haverford College in Haverford, Pennsylvania (master's thesis: "L'influence de Sir Walter Scott sur Alfred de Vigny"). His real passion, however, was the land—not so much the animal and plant communities, but the bedrock and soil itself. So, after a four-year tour of duty as a teacher at schools in Westtown and Overbrook, Pennsylvania, followed by a year teaching geology at Earlham, he became a graduate fellow in the UW-Madison's Department of Geology during 1941–1942. He obtained his PhD in geology in 1943 and promptly became Earlham's assistant professor of geology, as well as, to his great delight, the acting curator of the Joseph Moore Museum.

During World War II, Dr. Hole went against the grain and chose to be a conscientious objector (CO) due to his Quaker beliefs. As a result, during 1944–1946, he was assigned to the U.S. Department of Agriculture's Soils Laboratory at the Soil and Water Conservation Research Station in Coshocton, Ohio. Beginning in 1946, he began his nearly 40-year association with the University of Wisconsin-Madison when he became an assistant professor of soils.

From 1951 to 1961, Francis directed the Soil Survey Division of the Wisconsin Geological and Natural History Survey while still serving as a UW professor. He achieved a full professorship (professor of soil science) in 1961 and in

1968 became professor of soil science and geography until his retirement from the UW in the spring of 1983. Professor Hole wrote dozens of scientific and popular articles and was best known for *Soils of Wisconsin*, his concise but detailed booklet on our state soils. He also cowrote (with Drs. Ralph McCracken and Stan Buol) a textbook titled *Soil Genesis and Classification*, and in 1968 designed the *Soils of Wisconsin Map* for the Wisconsin Geologic and Natural History Survey.

As a university professor, he merrily applied the playing of his violin (he was classically trained), as well as songwriting, to lectures on the values and pleasures of soil. His unorthodox but brilliant teaching was formally recognized in 1974 when he received the Chancellor's Award for Distinguished Teaching. He even parlayed his musical talents into a grassroots effort that proved to be quite fertile in the establishment of Wisconsin's official state soil: the Antigo Silt Loam. It was officially declared the state soil in 1983, representing the aggregate of more than 550 different soils in the state.

Our soils have never had a better advocate.

I interviewed the gregarious and jovial Dr. Hole at his office on two different occasions in 1982, and I joined his students for his last celebratory field trip as a UW professor to glaciated and unglaciated sites west of Madison in April 1983.

*

I grew up on the edge of the Earlham College campus, a small Quaker institution founded in Richmond, Indiana, in 1847. That's the center of the ragweed belt of the country and also the center of the Quaker population. Many of these people came from the Carolinas to get away from the slavery problem. My father, Allen, was on the faculty of Earlham for 40 years and developed the Geology Department. He didn't publish much because he was so busy teaching. As they say about Jesus: he didn't publish much, but some of his students did.

My dad was a farm boy, a refugee from Ridgeport, Indiana, who had asthma. During harvest-thrashing time it was just about impossible to stay on the farm, so he became a school teacher in the public schools and then in the Quaker schools. He came up here at about age 18 or 19 to LaValle near Reedsburg where there was a Quaker church.

CHAPTER TEN

My mother, Mary Doan, was also from a rural town. Her father was a farmer but also a banker in Westfield, north of Indianapolis. Her mother had been a schoolteacher. Her father had never gone to college because his father had died and someone had to take over the farm, so he was the one who wasn't allowed to go to college. That gave him an extra impetus to read poetry at the table and to urge their seven children to get with it and get a higher education. So she did that and almost got a PhD, but marriage interfered. They were married in 1909 and built a house on the edge of the campus at Earlham.

Earlham College is on a small, level outwash plain and in glacial till—a gently rolling landscape. Within a mile walk of campus I was in Clear Creek Valley, where I was completely free to walk up and down and into the forest beyond. I became a caterpillar collector, butterfly collector, a minnow observer. I had a lot of time in the open.

There was a closeness about the community where I grew up. We weren't allowed to have all that many friends. My mother didn't want her boys mingling with just anybody. To what degree this was snooty, to what degree this was a manifestation of the Quaker concept of leading a sheltered life, to what extent it was fear in the sense of inferiority: a psychotherapist could have a lot of fun! It was chiefly my brother and I amusing ourselves. A friend of my brother's, who later became a psychologist, said, "Allen, I've never seen any two boys so programmed as you and your brother." Because Allen would write in his diary: "Played the piano from 9:00 to 10:00. Went out and high-jumped from 10:00 to 10:45. Mowed the lawn from 10:45 to 11:30. Came back and played the piano until 12:00. Then Mother said come to lunch. Had...." He would write down everything. He didn't have to do this; he just did it. We would walk three or four miles to the Quaker church on Sunday. My brother had a watch, so when it came time to start out for any destination he had a little notebook and paper, and he'd record the departure time. He'd come home and say, "I got to the main street bridge one minute earlier than usual!" Talk about regimented! We were a highly scheduled family.

My brother and I slept in the attic. That was another way to escape the world of adults. The snow would sift in sometimes when there was a cold winter night with the wind blowing. Snow could get in between the shingles and come down—a little bit of cold powder coming down in our faces. We thought it was great up there. Father would come up the steps every morning to announce that it had become "half past six, time to get stirring." Then if we didn't stir, he would simply come to the base of the stairs and, with his two fingers, whistle the sharpest whistle I've ever heard. It was piercing. I never did learn that, and he wouldn't say anything more. We knew that we would die the death of not getting to school if we didn't stir.

🍃

I WAS KIND OF A LONESOME GUY when I was growing up. My brother and I played together. In the attic we had a model railroad. The model railroad consisted of spring-wound trains, well within the budget of my father's low salary. There was a little track that we immediately tossed aside. Father would allow us to buy one-quarter-inch-thick basswood (lindenwood) sheets, four feet long and maybe 12 inches wide. We'd take them down to the workbench, which was grandfather's, and with a coping saw we would saw them into one-quarter-inch strips. These were our rails! We'd nail these rails to the floor. You could bend them on the floor. Very soon the springs in these little locomotives broke, and from then on we'd push them down the rails. We had track 40 feet long and 20 feet wide— it was a big attic—and when they were going, the whole floor became a sounding board. My brother and I played with these trains intensely, even though we were four years apart, well into college. There was a reluctance to grow up.

To get out of the nest was difficult for both of us. I wanted to go barefoot— be the barefoot nature boy. I didn't want to go out into the big, bad world.

🍃

I WASN'T MUCH OF A SCHOLAR. I spent most of my time studying nature, raising caterpillars and mounting them. Then I became something of an artist. I'd make very careful drawings with India ink and watercolors. Then I did a Leopold kind of thing. I said to myself, "I'm not going to kill these things." I was about 12. I'd raise moths, and then the promethea would come out, I'd admire it, and let it go. As George Knudsen knows so well, learning to recognize a cecropia [moth, *Hyalophora cecropia*] or promethea cocoon hanging there among the leaves, becoming aware of these things that most people don't even notice, was certainly important. I did read [William Jacob] Holland's book on butterflies, and everyone was raving about Gene Stratton-Porter, an Indianapolis novelist and naturalist. She was a collector of caterpillars and moths. She lived near a big forest so that all of these gorgeous big moths as well as big butterflies were all over the place, and she was allowed by her publisher to sandwich in now and again stories about this area she called the "Limberlost."

Climbing trees was terribly important. We had in the back of our house a basswood tree that towered above the house—I suppose it was 65 feet tall—had a big branch, and my father allowed us boys to climb. We had no fear. He would talk to us. He would say, "I don't want you climbing that tree unless you are very careful. Remember, when the basswood limbs die they become very brittle. Test every branch you step on." So he didn't instill fear into us, he instilled caution. From the age of seven on up into my teens, it was a good thing after breakfast to climb up and see what the world looked like. Since I was at the center of the world, I had to look around over the houses.

You were communing with the birds up there, and it was an exploration of other parts of the tree: What is a tree like up there in its growing parts? You become something of a philosopher: What is the whole world like? And there's the glorious sunshine and sounds of church bells in the distance. That was an important experience.

EARLHAM was greatly influenced by the natural history movement. One of the pupils of Louis Agassiz was Joseph Moore, who came back and founded the Joseph Moore Museum. My father became an understudy of Moore's and became curator of the Joseph Moore Museum. There used to be great collection trips. For example, they used to go down to Hawaii and come back with kegs of corals, pieces of lava, and stuffed birds. The museum was in the main building on campus, and it occupied a large part of the first floor. He had his office there. I would trot a half-mile from home and go see him. It was like going into a cathedral. There were wooden stairs you'd climb and a platform at the top from where you could view the entire museum. At the end of his day, he would come find me. He would call—and this was very important to me—"All out, all out, the museum is closing!" Well, it was almost like having a daddy who ran a train!

During summers, Dad organized field trips to Yellowstone Park and Glacier National Park in the north, and in the south to the Grand Canyon, the Petrified Forest, and the San Juan Mountains where he had done his PhD work for the University of Chicago. I remember the first trip I went on in 1922 or 1923. I was 10 years old, and it was with a large co-educational group. From then on, I went out with Father for many summers, and then as a student from 1929 to 1933. The blooming of his geology program came later in life. He had a lot of energy and would have lived into his nineties had he had the proper care. He died at age 74, a year after my mother died.

Father loved mathematics and geology, but he was also quite a philosopher who knew German. As a country schoolteacher, he had to know everything. He was also quite a singer. When I do this ham business with my violin and sing the "Antigo Silt Loam Song," I can just hear my dad. He led singing and would have probably loved it. He had a little pitch pipe.

Mother and Father were terribly busy people, always going off to meetings. They didn't have time for more informal things. We were given piano and violin lessons, and they saw to it that these things happened in a scheduled manner.

Mother said to me when I was a kid that geography was the greatest discipline of higher learning because it's so integrated. She liked the way it brought the sciences and humanities together. Mother taught me how to write. She used to say that writing was like playing chess. You try out various things, and you can get down to the winning row by improving the way you set the words in the order in which you place them. It makes a better sentence so that the train of thought is happy. She had been an English professor down at Wilmington College, and she had been teaching this stuff as a professional. Now she was raising two boys. She encouraged me to enter the Lincoln Watch Company contest. The medal they awarded looked like a penny with a picture of Lincoln on it, and so whoever in junior college wrote the best essay would receive the Lincoln medal. I won two years in succession. Most of it was due to the enthusiasm and practical training that Mother had given me. She was a vivacious and highly talented woman in literature and art, particularly drawing. She also carved wood, and she had a lot of social graces. She was tough enough so that she could go at least a few years with my father on college class field trips to national parks. In those days that was pretty unusual. She and Father were in one tent. It was something for Mother, who wasn't a geologist, to be willing to go and not become a cook. There was a student aid instead that became the cook.

Mother's wings were clipped professionally because she was a woman living in a time when a woman's place was thought to be in the home. She really resented that, and that was the cause of a very profound depression she suffered. She died feeling very beat. Psychotherapy was unknown. She had to stew in this, and although Father was helpful, he had no training in how to deal with personal problems. It's too bad because she didn't have the mental and emotional support she should have had that's available nowadays. They both could have flourished and been very happy elderly people together.

BOTH MOTHER AND FATHER were pious people. One could feel a reverence for life in his field trips. At breakfast, he would take out the New Testament. There would be a reading and then a little quiet period. There was a strong, mystical sense of a religious divine presence in his life. It was the cornerstone of his life. During the First World War, Dad received some ridicule for being a pacifist. He was the editor of a very important little magazine called the *Messenger of Peace*, put out under the auspices of the Western Yearly Meeting of Friends, a regional Quaker group. During this time, Mother was talking about the League of Nations. So I knew they were different, that we shook our heads about the First World War. When you're a persecuted minority, it forces you to say one of two things: "Either I'm going to get out of this and be like the rest and go off to war." Or you say, "My people are suffering because of a great moral position, and I believe in it stronger than ever."

The Quaker faith is plain Christianity. It was founded 360 years ago in England as a complete Protestant revolt away from any externals: no stained glass, no ministers. You communicate directly with God. You don't have these people who are paid to talk to God for you. We don't need any translation. So it was completing the reformation, and yet it swung around so far that some people said it swung too far, that it went clear back into the Catholic realm. In a sense, some people say that the quiet moment in the middle of the Mass was expanded upon by the Friends and formed the basis of their meeting together in silence. See, the Quaker faith is written so plain you can't tell it is Christianity. Quakers talk about the *Inner Light*. They also may talk about the *Inner Christ*. The Quaker faith says that there is a spark of God in each person. That means black, white, yellow, red, criminal, saint, child, adult. And that is the reason they were called blasphemous–very dangerous people—by many of the state church people in England where Quakerism developed. The Anglican Church interpreted what Quakers were saying as "We are God!"

So they said, "That's blasphemous! You have to realize that you're probably damned forever!" That's one reason Quakers were persecuted—because they were so optimistic.

The Quaker faith is an extremely interesting hybrid of mysticism and practicality. Some people are activists. They don't understand mysticism, but they do know when somebody is hungry they want to get food for them. As a stranger said, sitting down at a Quaker Meeting for the first time, "Nothing is going on." So the stranger turned to the person next to him and said, "When does the service begin?" The Quaker whispered, "After the Meeting is over." So the practicality side—service, action—is very strong among many Quakers. But the other is very strong also: the extraordinary belief that while you're sitting there, God—if you don't like the word God, then the *Inner Light*—a mystical presence, will communicate to you directly and tell you what spiritual condition you can be in, how you can be flooded with energy and insight and what practical things you should do.

So this combination of people—some quite mystical, some activists, and all manner in between—can be quite powerful in Quaker Meetings. You listen to everybody, anyone who feels a need to speak. Nobody feels submerged. No one feels that they have to have a PhD to say something. What I like about it is the unhurriedness. Everybody moves together.

The concept of the *Inner Light* is not unlike that of the Eastern religions. Actually, you can go to any religious group and they've got some of this. As Gandhi said, all of these religious groups are spokes of a wheel, and the hub is this divine center from which they all have different perspectives. That's why some Eastern people find it comfortable to come to a Friends Meeting because it doesn't offend them. There's no scripture, no externals, no offertory taken up.

You have a group experience, and you have individuals standing up and speaking about what they feel moved to say that day: "What does the spirit tell us today?" They are constantly listening. Of course, it's nice to have read the Bible and know what it told Paul. But we're living now. We're taking in air now. Everybody has to find their own spiritual light. Everybody goes through a revolt of sorts. I revolted away from the pastoral church of Quakerism to what we call the Silent Meeting. Of course, it isn't silent because people can speak. The original Quaker of genius was to have people sit down in quiet and see what happened. A beautiful spirit flowed through. The unimportant stuff fell away. Bitterness fell away. Fear fell away. Hatred and doubt fell away. This is what appealed to me.

One of the people whose philosophy appealed to me was John Woolman. John Woolman was a mystic of sorts. You'd enjoy reading his journal. He was a storekeeper in New Jersey in the 1700s at a time when many Quakers as well as non-Quakers around Philadelphia were becoming wealthy. He said, "No, I can't spend time communicating with the spark within me if I'm going to be spending my time making money." He was a very successful storekeeper. So he closed down his store, spent more time at home with his wife, became a tailor, took care of his orchard, and lived at an absolute minimal level. He's the one who eventually walked up and down the Eastern seaboard from the non-slave owning communities to the slave-owning communities. He walked because he found that if he rode a horse or took a carriage he became separated from the landscape and the people. He felt that he would not be a threat or an interrupter if he walked.

So he would walk in and the plantation owner in Virginia would take him in with great folderol because he was a visiting Quaker. Then John Woolman would sit by the fire and begin to say, "How does ye feel about having slaves?"

"Well, we take very good care of them," the slave owner would say.

Then when John Woolman was leaving, he'd say, "I forgot to leave some money because thy servants have been waiting on me, and I just don't feel that it should be free of charge." He would then give money to the slaves, much to the consternation of the slave owner. It took a lot of guts to do that.

MY DAD WAS A SOIL SCIENTIST OF THE EARLY VINTAGE as well as a geologist. Once, he noticed that the Indiana state geologist was publicly looking for someone to do county soil surveys, so Dad and another person would go to a county and camp in schoolyards, and after a summer or two they would turn out these rather uninteresting looking black and white soil maps—the first soil maps of the county. A group of his students later became important people in the soil survey of the United States. James Thorp, for example, was sent to China in the early 1930s to direct the establishment of soil science there. Earlham College then earned a reputation as a college that turned out soil scientists. So I came along after a master's in French at Haverford College in 1934. My brother, whom I admired so, had done the same thing four years before. He had achieved a master's in French, and so I went and followed in his footsteps.

Then I taught in Philadelphia prep schools for four years: French, physical geography, geology, German, and music. Then I realized that I wanted to get a PhD. One year, when I was teaching at Westtown School, I went to a summer school paid for with a scholarship fund the school had for teachers, so I went to Harvard. I took a courses in French and German. One day, to rest my eyes, probably in 1937, I wandered across to the reference room, and there was a whole row of books on geology. I started looking at them, and this whole rush of emotions came through me. "This is what I love," I thought. "What am I doing taking French and German! I don't want a PhD in that stuff! I don't need to be an authority on all of the poets and all of the novelists of all this junky literature. Why, half-crazy people wrote that! I want to get back where the sage brush is, and the rocks and the fossils!" I told this to my father, and he smiled when he heard me saying that. He had never put pressure on me. He recommended that I go to the University of Wisconsin where there was a strong geology department and a strong soils department. So I resigned my job at Westtown School and came to Wisconsin and got my degree under Professor Thwaites in glacial geology, with a minor in soil science.

THE CHAIRMAN of the geology department, Professor Twenhofel, one day came up to me and said, "Hole, I've heard of a good chance for you in strategic minerals work for the government." The Second World War was on, and the government needed experts to work for them.

I said, "I couldn't do that. Recently, a Japanese ship was sunk, and I felt just as bad as if it had been American."

He stared at me and said, "Get out of my office."

And I thought, "Boy, my goose is cooked. The chairman of the department has told me to get out of his office!"

Then I heard later through his secretary, who talked to my wife, that Twenhofel then walked across the hall to the office and said, "You know, Hole's position is better than mine." Apparently, Twenhofel was wrestling with what to do about war. He was a church man and all that.

I knew I was a conscientious objector. Because of the stance of my folks during the First World War, I knew I wasn't going to take training in shooting people. That wasn't the way this Inner Light wanted people to relate to each other. That wasn't the way you build a better world. It was a real simple position. I knew there was no doubt. The only doubt was what kind of conscientious objector I would be. Would I be one who said I wouldn't even register because that's the machine for getting people into the cannon fodder business, and as a conscientious objector under that system would I simply be getting a special dispensation? Or I could go into the army as my wife's father wanted me to do and be a medic and carry no gun. There were 60,000 of them. Well, I took the middle course. I said I would not put on a uniform. I went to the work camps, which were set up with great effort by the church people working with Selective Service.

It was a strange compromise called Civilian Public Service. It was kind of a glorification of the CCC (Civilian Conservation Corps). These camps were set up under a separate system from the CCC camps. Wherever there was a separate CCC set of barracks sitting conveniently, they were reused. We were in the barracks at the Soil Conservation Service Nursery that were once old CCC barracks. I was in that for two years. Some of my friends were in prison, some were medics, and some were regular soldiers, sailors, and marines. The camps where I worked were about 35 miles southwest of Cornell College in Ithaca, New York. We could walk into the little town of Elmira to church safely, but people, especially drunks, would drive by and call out, "Yellow!" or "Cowards!" I don't think they called us communists, because that was a common thing to say. Once you called a person a communist, you didn't have to think about it. But, as the authorities said, they were going to hide the Conscientious Objectors back in the woods until the war was over and then bring them out. My wife had to live separately from me, and she was certainly given the cold shoulder. People didn't want to talk to her.

I was apart from my wife for the entire two years. During the first two thirds of the war, many ad hoc arrangements were made, especially in the camps out West. Wives would come and live in little huts near their husbands, and their husbands were allowed to go home each evening. In my wife's case, we had a little son, and the camp was no place to bring a son. So we were separated. She was living in Indianapolis with her folks, and I was in Elmira, New York, then Coshocton, Ohio, then Gatlinburg, Tennessee. I had furloughs like any soldier would have. I went home for two weeks at a time.

My wife is a tremendous person. She was a classmate in college. I was not a dater. I looked at her from afar. I was one of these frustrating—as far as she was concerned—hard-to-get-along-with distant young men. Our wedding took place seven years after I graduated from Earlham. Luckily, she was still available to consider a proposal of marriage. She's a sprightly, dynamic, caring person. Her father was head of the sewage treatment plant in Indianapolis and then head of the water treatment plant, so he was the chemist, and she majored in chemistry. She had a lot of charisma at Earlham. She was declared the "EC girl" of Earlham College her senior year, meaning best balanced as a social person, scholar, and outdoor person. She was a great young woman, and I'm glad she was available. She worked as a paramedic, a secretary for two MDs, and I interrupted her career when we got married. We had two children. Ben, born in 1944, is a [at the time of the interview] a budget analyst for the Department of Agriculture, but his real passion is teaching international folk dancing. And Sarah is five years younger and has made a living as a professional potter in Madison.

PUBLIC LIFE tears you away from your family and the religious community and the cause of peace. I've resolved the situation by not doing professional work every evening. I've missed a few scientific meetings and spent time on courses on nonviolence. If I had been spending the time professionally that I spent on these courses on nonviolence these past 10 years, I'd be a much more famous person.

I didn't put professionalism clear at the top, but professionalism still got the lion's share of my time. I wasn't as good a father as I should have been. I was away on the soil survey two weeks at a time. My children didn't see me when they were ages 5 through 12. During summer, I was gone a long time. My father was a much better father than I ever was. His office was only a half-mile away. I could see the building, and he came home for lunch. There was an awful lot of interaction between him and me.

WHEN I FIRST CAME TO UW in 1946 to take charge of a little soil survey operation in cooperation with the Soil Conservation Service, I only had a minor in soil science. I was placed very wisely. They placed me in an office in the Soils building, where I was surrounded by PhD's in soil

CHAPTER TEN

science, career people. Here I was with a PhD in geology and practically no professional experience. So professional fulfillment was something in the future, and I wondered if I would ever attain it. But fulfillment came about through opportunities to survey areas, to publish papers, reports, maps, opportunities to go to scientific conferences, and to interact with others. To get professional fulfillment you have to see the professional tree of your own career grow in a healthy way and bear fruit that is recognized. You have to have respect yourself for what you've done.

I ought to start all over again, however. I ought to know statistics and calculus, which I don't know. I ought to take the latest courses in biochemistry and physics. There's no limit to the amount I ought to know. I'm too much of a Renaissance man and not enough of a modern specialist. To know soils you have to be a Renaissance specialist! You're a committee! The one topic I'm interested in pursuing now is landscape patterns—soil patterns on the landscape. There is much fieldwork that needs to be done on soil landscape analysis. It's the sort of thing that Dr. John Curtis did with plant communities, but soil communities have not been similarly and carefully studied. It would be an endless task, just as with Curtis's work. It will go on and on; it's a career-type thing.

During one of my earliest years here when I was on the Soil Survey, Curtis began to have a very important influence on me because he was a plant ecologist that wanted us to do soil ecology. Professor Sergei "Doc" Wilde, a forest soils ecologist, also had an influence on me. He was a Russian-American, and we were absolute opposites. He was a connoisseur of wines and whiskeys. When I'd go to his house, he'd give me water. He had a wide vocabulary by the way of expletives, and he dealt with women in very unconventional ways. He was a worldly type of man, but he had a heart of gold and was quite a soil scientist. We respected each other's work.

Dr. Norman Fassett had some influence, too. I remember when I was working on the experimental prairie plots that Curtis had allowed us to start in his precious arboretum prairie. I had planted big bluestem seeds the year before, and they were starting to come up. Fassett came walking by—this was a few years before he died—and he said, "What are you doing?"

I said, "I'm trying to get a 12-foot quadrant planted to Indian grass and big bluestem. But I don't know whether these things coming up here are them or not." Fassett was a genius. He could tell from the sprout what it was. He knew what these things looked like when they first appeared. So that made a big impression on me.

WHAT I VALUE LEAST about my profession is knowing the involvement of this university in evil, involvement in a society that wiped out 200,000 people in Hiroshima. That was done with the concurrence of the University

Dr. Hole leads his UW-Madison Soil Science class in singing the "Antigo Silt Loam Song" along the banks of the Wisconsin River, April 23, 1983. Photo by Sumner Matteson.

of Wisconsin and the people of the United States. When I first came here, I was urged to become an advisor to students. I said, "I can't be because they've got ROTC on campus. If I advised students, I would be involved in whether they took ROTC or not." Now ROTC is no longer compulsory. So the conflict there is gone, but there is still some involvement in things of a military nature, for example in what makes a missile operate.

Any college or institution that operates in a way that neglects the personalities and well-being of individuals involved with it, or impacted by it, is acting in a way that does not meet or address people's needs adequately.

You have to *Walk the Light*, as the Quakers say, wherever you are, and open yourself to this tremendous force of Inner Light that can do anything. You just open the window and witness it in the sense that there is an energy, there is a wisdom that could take care of everything. I'm not it, but I am a window unto it. The Gandhian phrase is "Become a zero." That is, there is a Hindu concept that each person aspires to become a zero—the ego isn't there so this Inner Light can shine right through them, and they can become an avenue for letting their window open into a dark world, not because they are anything, but because they are nothing.

In the last 10 years I've become more and more unorthodox, unconventional, in my teaching: by using the violin; by reading poetry, some of which I wrote; and singing songs. The last three years since I became involved with the National Wildlife Federation I've been using songs quite a bit. I'll sing a phrase, everyone repeats it, and we find ourselves singing a rather beautiful sentiment that has to do with the landscape and how we relate to it. For example, the "Antigo Silt Loam Song," is a short lesson on the geologic history of the state, but it also has great emotional power to it. The first verse starts out:

> Great Lakes region, fertile land
> Glaciers spread both clay and sand
> Winds blew silt, then forests grew
> Giving soils their brownish hue.

It's like teaching. The glacier was here and it made the land fertile by spreading ground-up rock material. You know that's a whole year's course! Second verse:

> Great Lakes region, fertile land
> You strengthen us in heart and hand
> Each slope, each flower, each wild bird call
> Proclaims a unity in all.

Third verse:

> Antigo, a soil to know
> Wisconsin's crops and livestock grow
> And forests too, on Antigo.

It's a catchy song. Fourth verse:

> Plant a seed and pull a weed
> The soil will give us all we need
> And plenty more so birds may feed.

The last one addresses the whole problem of world peace:

> Of all the crops, true peace is tops
> It's soil is love that never stops
> It blesses sand and water drops.

When you get to that very emotional portion, you're dealing with the whole thrust of our lives. If our lives are not imbued with love then we're going to have trouble. And the worst trouble comes when we're armed with nuclear weapons.

Humans have to grow up with experiences of how to live in community. We need to ritualize what we do. When I say that people ought to learn to live in community, they need to be aware of not only the human community but the natural world, what goes on between people and the soil. You can't really appreciate the natural world unless your heart pounds and you feel the nature of the surface you're walking on so you relate in every way possible: intellectual, emotional, physical, spiritual. We ought to have a total appreciation for what the land, the soil, provides. I think polarization in terms of competition should not be encouraged. It's unity that's got to be emphasized.

Human beings are in a position to reduce to a minimum, or practically eliminate, competition between themselves and the creatures around them. So I'm thinking rather positively about the relationships between people and the landscapes around them. Peacemaking in a broader sense is what I'm talking about, and peacemaking is the art of training people in maintaining their functioning in a way that conflicts with others, with other creatures, are resolved nonviolently.

IN WISCONSIN, we live on one of the oldest pieces of real estate in the world! Some of the rock here is over three billion years old. How could rock survive the processes of erosion for so long? The ocean bottoms are much younger, and they keep moving just like moving platforms or staircases. Parts slide to the top, and we've got some of those old parts in the north. At Copper Falls, for instance, you see some of the basalt bedrock—old lava flows. Some of these old lava flows, best represented by bedrocks in northern Wisconsin, were on the sea bottom. They pushed out from underneath the water two to three billion years ago. You needn't think of lava as always being formed on the surface of land.

❧

I CAME UP WITH THE IDEA of a Wisconsin state soil after spending years on regional and national committees looking at soil classifications. The north central states produced a bulletin on the soils of the north central region some 20 years ago. We lined up all these soils, thousands of kinds of soils, mapped them, and soil scientists got to the point where you could name them. Then, in opening up the state *Blue Book* you see a state tree and a state everything else, and you say, "Well, these depend on the soil, and it's about time we have a state soil." Soil science is only about 100 years old, but it's old enough to have validity. Many farmers know the names of the soils on their farms and their characteristics. So it isn't just professional scientists that talk about Antigo Silt Loam.

Soils express a connection between rock material, climate, animals, plants, and now human beings. If it weren't for the skin of the earth—the land surface, what we call soil—this would be a dead planet! In mostly the top few centimeters, life is present. So this planet is dead except for that delicate skin on which we live. We see so much greenery that we have

Dr. Hole takes a soil sample with an auger in the Dodgeville area, April 23, 1983. Photo by Sumner Matteson.

the impression that life dominates the planet, but it's just a thin skin! That's why I say our soils are a gift.

We're culturally disadvantaged—the human race is—with respect to an understanding and awareness of the soil. It's not part of our background. The soil is a slow-moving ocean that we live on. We shouldn't take it for granted and just look at the flowers and the trees and the birds and the animals, and the automobiles running over the top of it. If the soil disappeared, we would be on bedrock. We would be on a desolate moonscape—sterile, with no life possible. The soil has got this thin portion in which life is made possible, and to ignore that fact is really a tragedy.

We're losing four tons per acre per year in the agricultural landscape of this state. This is considered by many to be okay. Some places we're losing 40 tons per acre. They say that we're losing a total of 42 million tons of soil off the slopes per year in Wisconsin. I came here 45 years ago as a graduate student, and it's been eroding for 45 years! Most of the soil, actually, is not lost from the state but sits on the river bottoms. Maybe only about 15 percent is getting into the big rivers, and about 3 to 5 percent is actually leaving the state going down toward the delta, and of that, only a small fraction ever reaches the delta or gets anywhere near it. So a lot of it is being lost from the fields, lost from where it was farmed, eroding a short distance, and moving anywhere from 10 feet to 1,000 feet to 10 miles. Soil erosion is like a slow leprosy; it takes apart the landscape bit by bit and doesn't kill the patient right away.

Regarding good ag practices, corn should only be grown on level land, and alfalfa should be grown on sloping land. We're a lot better off than the hog/corn landscape that I grew up in around Richmond, Indiana, because the presence of the cow means that's there's going to be pasture strips and manure present—that makes the soil less subject to erosion. So the presence of the cow has really saved our soil from eroding as badly as it has in corn/hog country. But a step further in the right direction would be not to remove the cow entirely but to make the direct feeding to us more important. We ought to be processing alfalfa just as soybeans are being processed, so that you can't tell, for example, that Dairy Queens are handing out nondairy products that are made from soybeans. They can make soybeans taste like anything. They can make it taste like pork chops. If we can do this with soybeans, then we could do the same with alfalfa to make it palatable. By putting more alfalfa on the land, you practically stop soil erosion dead in its tracks.

But human beings have a very short view. They're not thinking in terms of hundreds of years. What will the child of the year 3000 need? What can I do that will relate to the child of the year 3000? We don't think like that. Four tons of soil erosion a year is okay because we're not thinking about the child 10 years from now. We'll do anything to protect our interests to get what we want right now, and with that shortsightedness we don't really know what we want. Gene Cameron, a retired geology professor—one of the big names in geology, a world authority on the mineral resources of the world—said that the nations don't know what they want. We don't have a public policy as to what we really need. John Woolman would have said, "I'll train you all, if you'll listen to me, on how to get on with the least possible." The economist Kenneth Boulding talks about how the maple forest is an ideal system. It has a maintenance cycle that doesn't demand nutrients like a cornfield. The cornfield is extremely demanding. You're increasing the use of organic matter enormously, and you have to feed in fertilizer elements. It's a stepped-up feverish system!

We need more people—like saints—that are very strong and that take the long view and redo our priorities. Then everything would fall into place. The question would be asked in a society that had the long view, "What is the state, condition, of your soil on the farm?" We should say that we will give the farmer support and respect as long as the soil is as good or better 10 years from now as it is now. But we don't ask that question. We say here are your taxes, and we expect the farmer to turn out as much milk or as much corn as possible per acre.

We haven't gotten to the point where the Chinese have and say that you can only have one child. But there are too many children in a family for the carrying capacity of the ecosystem. Suppose we don't do anything about that, and we just let the population expand. Pretty soon we'll be looking pretty jammed like Europe, and we'll be pouring more fertilizer on the soil to get more crops off the land.

I think that every child that's growing up should go out during weekends and understand how a farm works because the farmers out there that are practicing soil conservation are stewards. The problem is that anybody with money can buy a piece of land and use an insurance company to write-off wall-to-wall corn. For example, in Vernon County some commercial outfit bought farms, and they had wall-to-wall corn. The erosion was rampant. Erosion hadn't been seen like that in Vernon County. So the town enacted an ordinance disallowing such farm practices and stopped those people dead in their tacks. It was local pressure, not pressure from Madison or

Washington. That outfit had intended to mine those farms for 10 years, take the money, and reinvest it in something else, and get rid of the farms.

It is the people's land out there. Just think, if we had included the Menominee or Ojibwe and Winnebago in this picture, we'd have been much better off. We're just lucky that they aren't cutting our throats! Gentleness on the part of a lot of people is the reason the human race has survived. If we involve all people, we'll see an entirely new land ethic.

The soil is a resource that we all can enjoy. I don't think we need to think any longer about the soil as something that only technical people talk about. It's something we can enjoy as we enjoy trees. You don't have to be a forester to enjoy the trees or shrubs or flowers. I emphasize to others that each human being has a response to the soil, a yearning to know more about it, to become closer to it. I would like to encourage people to write poetry about it, enjoy the smell of soil, enjoy thinking about the shapes of all those little channels that run down through the soil. Think about soil even though you can't see under the turf very well, and think about it as the spring comes just as much as we think about the crocus and the wild geese. We are people of the soil—*terra firma*. It's the firm soil beneath us. It's the common ground all around.

❦

I VALUE the privilege of constantly being alive and growing in my interactions with other people. That's why it's important to have young people around. Every year, I learn more, and I'm learning more because I'm with a group of students who are learning more in classes. There's a constant growing going on. I have, and had when I was young, such a diversity of interests. My feeling is that anything you learn—anything you pick up—you can use later in connection to whatever is important to you. One of the famous stories by Rufus Jones, a Quaker leader, is that a man was riding at night on a horse through wild country that he didn't know, and he was going to stay at an inn. He came down into a low place and a voice called out to him, "Come down from your horse and pick up stones, and you'll be both glad and sorry." So he got down from his horse, picked up some stones, put them in a bag, climbed up on his horse, and reached the inn. He could hardly wait to get up to his room, turn up the kerosene lamp, and spill out the stones. To his amazement, they were diamonds and rubies, and he was sorry that he hadn't picked up more, but sure glad that he had picked up what he had. That story has a little moral: you do that in college; pick up whatever you can, and you'll be both glad and sorry.

Teaching soil geography to young people is important to me, and I began to use the violin as a teaching tool very hesitantly. When I began to use the violin in the early 1970s, I brought to class two violins. I said, "I'm going to play a little bit on each of these, and you tell me which violin sounds best." There would be quite an argument in class. I settled it by saying, "Those who thought this one here sounds better are right. And that's the way it's going to be with soils," I told them. Every soil looks alike the first time, and all the names are a jumble. But each one is different for certain purposes. That's what we're here for—to learn how to understand the differences between soils and how they function.

I like to play Bach. Bach is full of gorgeous symbolism. A retired English teacher here at the UW told me once that Bach was getting messages from the heart of the universe like nobody ever got, and he put them into his music. I like to play Bach on the violin because I know I'm getting exposed to these messages. I sometimes see phrases in his compositions that will help me get people to visualize some things about soil. In the midst of my stock violin talk or skit, I talk about how there are interactions between roots in the soil and the plant parts above. Then I take a part of Bach's "Chaconne for Solo Violin" in which he rocks back and forth. You get this really gorgeous down below and up-above feeling, and if it's played just right you practically shiver with delight. So what I am doing is using something that's been part of my joy of life for so many years and putting it to service.

I don't know if a set of exams presented with and without the violin in one group would produce the same or different results. All I know is that people enjoy the presentation more because they are swept into an experience. And that can't be judged by an exam. I think that relating to nature as well as to yourself and a body of knowledge should be a pleasurable experience—a happy thing. The educational system should be shot through with pleasure, which is a very unpopular idea. You're not supposed to be having fun any more than you are supposed to make prisoners too comfortable in prison. We have quite a suffering ethic in this country: If I'm not willing to suffer, at least I want you to suffer.

If you're happy, you learn. I don't know why there seems to be the idea that learning has to be somber and unhappy.

A friend of mine said, "Your work is like meditation." It's true. The closer I get to retirement the more I realize what a privilege it is to be doing my work. When I first arrived here and was drafting lines, I was tense, and then I learned that I didn't have to tense up to draw those lines. So I relaxed and let the pleasure and satisfaction flow through the work. Then the work becomes fun. I must say that I am short on wasting time. The art of wasting time will undoubtedly develop in retirement. I don't spend a lot of time talking to people. The fun for me is walking through the outdoors and observing nature and taking pictures and working my vegetable garden, which is 40 feet by 40 feet.

*

I'M AN OPTIMIST just as a dandelion is an optimist, even though the lawn mower is coming toward it. Until the very moment it is cut off, its mission is to be an optimist. What about the people who were obliterated at Dresden, Hiroshima, and Nagasaki? If they had known they were going to be wiped out, their best choice would have been to go on anyway, naturally, happily, to the last moment, just like the person who is going to drop dead from a heart attack. Better not mope about it ahead of time. Do what comes naturally in the best sense.

I do, however, think about my death quite often. There are several beautiful things as well as the frightening aspects. Two things to think about when approaching death, whether it takes 10 years or so: Is it going to be full of pain and agony and stress? And what is the moment of death like? Gandhi said, "Oh Ram—oh God."

One of Gandhi's great followers, Vinoba Bhave, died saying, "Rama, Hara." Mystical words. Then there's what happens after death. The whole process from the moment of death to after death—as far as I'm concerned— is surrounded by sweetness, perfume, because two years ago my aunt approached me and talked about it. My father had the same feeling, the same attitude. I keep company with these spirits: my dad, my aunt, Gandhi. Therefore, I can't help but have anything but this happy glow about death. And, of course, I have a sense that the spirit does not die. We know that all creatures die and decompose. Of course, the body gets slower and slower, and the thought comes that I'd just as soon lie down and die. This comes naturally more and more often.

When you go to bed at night, you go because you're tired. When you want to die, you feel tired. There's nothing morbid about that; this is very normal. The amazing thing is that when a person gets to be 70, 80, 90, or 100 like my aunt did, to their astonishment the energy keeps flowing. People who don't take care of themselves, then they cripple their lives. It's like breaking an arm. People work themselves into great tensions. They feel so insecure that they've got to have one more honor, one more book. So they're just shattered when they have to retire. They're really scared and they fall apart.

It's a Hindu idea that people are supposed to live to be 120, youthful with energy flowing, but modern civilization tries to break them if possible, make people mistreat themselves so that they drop dead early, unhappy. People should be allowed to bloom!

When it's time to die, what I would like is what happens to a Trappist monk. I had a chance to visit the Trappist monastery near Dubuque, Iowa. One of the brothers, who normally take a vow of silence, was allowed to talk to visitors. We came to a plot of ground between two wings of the building, and he said, "This is where we are buried. A brother dies and we just fold the robe he's wearing around him, pull the hood over, dig a trench in the ground, lay him in, and put the earth back." There's no box. That to me is the way to do it because then you return to the soil the way we're supposed to. Hallelujah!

𝕫

May 10, 1983. State Capitol. There is a packed room for the hearing before the Assembly's State Affairs Committee on Senate Bill 89 and Assembly Bill 60 to designate Antigo Silt Loam as Wisconsin's state soil. Madison Senator Fred Risser, chief sponsor, begins the afternoon session by testifying that a roll call vote in a Senate committee hearing on the same bill was 27 to 3 in favor. He urges executive action and states the following:

"Each of the other so-called living symbols of Wisconsin depend on the soil: the sugar maple, the wood violet, the American robin, the badger, the honey bee, the dairy cow. None of these creatures could exist without the soil. Why the Antigo Silt Loam? There are some 500 different soils in this state. Some are richer than the Antigo Silt loam and some are poorer. However, the Antigo Silt Loam has the distinction of being the only one … that supports the state's three major activities: dairy farming, timber growth, and growing vegetables such as potatoes. It is a soil that is found only in

Wisconsin. It covers some 150,000 acres in 10 counties. It was initially found in Antigo, and that's where it gets its name. It is neither sandy nor clay soil but is rather soft and smooth, the product of glacial advances and retreats some 10,000 years ago.... It is known as one of the better soils in Wisconsin ... the gem of the north."

And then he introduces "one of Wisconsin's most respected soil scientists and the primary proponent of this legislation, Professor Francis Hole."

Wearing a red bow tie and sports jacket, Dr. Hole acknowledges the committee members, the school children of Verona, and other friends present. "This bill is the culmination of 45 years of conducting soil surveys in the state," he says, and "it is not a trivial matter. This bill will save future generations untold millions of dollars because it is symbolic recognition of the importance of the soil resource, and it will lead to better soil conservation. How can we estimate the loss in dollars from erosion of about 42 million tons of soil each year from the hill slopes in Wisconsin? The loss is an affront to our economy now and to posterity. None of us would refuse to take a little time to pay tribute to our own mother, the soil—our mother earth.

"Why is the idea of designating a state soil been so slow in coming? Only Nebraska has taken this action, in 1979, partly from my urgings. We have been slow to take this logical step because many pioneers assumed that the soil would not be worn out and eroded, for there was plenty more to exploit, and because soil science is the youngest of the natural sciences. Soil science is only a century old, whereas botany and zoology, for example, are several centuries old. T.C. Chamberlin, author of the first four-volume report on the geology of Wisconsin, wrote in 1883 that 'There are few subjects on which it is more difficult to make an accurate and at the same time intelligible report than upon soil.' "

Dr. Hole walks over to a map of state soils and picks up a steel auger that he has brought in for the occasion. "We use the auger to drill down into the soil. Since it is not transparent like clear water, we can't see through the soil, so we must drill down and bring up a sample in order to find out what's down there, to tell what the soil is like, and what it can do in terms of supporting crops and trees. This is not my first auger," he says, holding the auger up in the air, "because I have worn out many augers, and the taxpayers of the state have seen fit to supply me with many more! I did bring it along to use as a symbol but also as a pointer." The crowd laughs.

CHAPTER TEN

"My first enthusiasm," he says raising his voice and pointing to the map, "was for the Tamis Silt Loam, a beautiful prairie soil down here in southwestern Wisconsin. 'Shouldn't the state soil be the Tamis Silt Loam?' I said to myself, probably the most productive soil in the state. And yet, it is not located centrally. It's name is from Iowa, and the major extent of it is over there in Iowa. How about the Dodge-McHenry Silt Loam on which this capitol building stands? Why not have the soil around the capitol building itself become the state soil? It is not central, it is southern, and by having the very nerve center of the state here it may not be in good taste!" More laughs. "So I've wrenched myself away from those two soils. How about the Kewaunee? Talk about a beauty for a soil; it's bright red. But it is also only occurring in one side of the state. It also happens to be a problem soil in that it is very clayey.... Wind blows on it in the winter, and the snowdrifts turn red. I just don't feel that it is perhaps the best symbol when it has that particular problem! How about the Antigo Silt Loam? Well, it's located right up here [using the auger to point to central Wisconsin], very central, and for about 200 miles it is present in 10 counties.

"Why are all these soils called silt loam? It is because of the huge dust storms that occurred 10,000 years ago when the glaciers were melting away and exposed a lot of fresh material here. The winds blew across the land, picked up the dust, especially from the Wisconsin River Valley, and so the richness of about two-thirds of our soils is from that dust. It would have been a poor time to be here when that dust was flying, and a poor time to hang out laundry, but we weren't here hanging out laundry or breathing!" More laughter.

"The Antigo Silt Loam, therefore, is a silt loam like the others. It's a soil that doesn't have too much clay or too much sand. It's on the upper level of soils in the state, and geographically it seems to be the better choice. Somebody said to me that the Antigo Silt Loam doesn't occur all over the state like a robin. I would like to point out that almost any grocery store one enters, one can find a sack of potatoes produced on the Antigo Silt Loam, and in that sense it does cover the state.

"It is important to have a state soil not only because of the technical reasons but because it is going to boost public consciousness of the importance of the soil, and therefore lead to a willingness to have more soil control measures. The enthusiasm of school children and adults for the Antigo Silt Loam has been demonstrated by various things such as petitions. I just wonder if the school children have any petitions here supporting the naming of the Antigo Silt Loam as the state soil."

Right on cue, several school children come forward silently and hand Professor Hole a stack of petitions. "Thank you very much!" he says in mock surprise. "May I present these to the chairman? Another evidence of the enjoyment that our people are expressing is in the form of the Antigo Silt Loam T-shirt!" He holds up the T-shirt, which several members of the gathering are wearing and on which are some of the words to his "Antigo Silt Loam Song." He adds, "We're not making money off the T-shirt. It's being sold at cost through the geography department!"

Then he introduces a four-minute puppet play by the Antigo Silt Loam Puppet Theatre, featuring Terra Loam, Erosion, and Bucky Badger performed by Sue Brightson (as the villain Erosion), Cherokee Heights middle schooler Chris Brightson (Bucky Badger), and Madison Memorial High School junior Becky Mead (Terra Loam). After Erosion is convinced to leave Wisconsin and go to the Grand Canyon to "deepen it" because the Wisconsin bill is "bound to pass," Bucky Badger turns to the crowd and asks them to join him in singing the "Antigo Silt Loam Song." Professor Hole starts to play his violin, stops, then says, "I'll sing a verse and you follow."

> Antigo, a soil to know
> Wisconsin's crops and livestock grow
> And forests too, on Antigo!

After most of the people in the room sing the verse, Professor Hole lays down his violin and says, "Thank you very much!" A rousing ovation follows, and the appearances before the committee seem over.

But wait, who is this walking up sheepishly to testify against the bill? As a few boos and laughter precede him, Representative Bradley from the 90th Assembly District walks slowly up to the podium to speak on behalf of the Kewaunee Silt Loam. After a long pause, he asks, "Don't I get a puppet show?" ❊

The bill was approved by committee unanimously that afternoon, and the Assembly later passed the bill. When Governor Tony Earl signed Senate Bill 89 into law on September 9, 1983, it marked Francis Hole's proudest achievement. Years of presentations on the soil's importance continued, with the much-anticipated use of his violin a feature attraction. And he continued to remain active in the Religious Society of Friends, the Quakers, attending meetings across the country.

Dr. Hole passed away quietly on January 15, 2002, at the Oakwood Village West retirement community in Madison, Wisconsin.

Bill Volkert
(1953-)

Bill in the Andes of Argentina, 2008. Photo by Connie Ramthun.
Photo courtesy of William K. Volkert.

SWAMP WHITE OAK

Chapter Eleven~
Bill Volkert

When I moved back to Wisconsin [from Colorado] and to the northern Kettle Moraine area, I realized I had to explore where I grew up, and I was going to learn what the university didn't give me—field experience. I decided the Kettle Moraine was going to be my laboratory. I was going to learn everything.

    —BV

If you could see every bird in the world, you'd see the whole world.

    —Jonathan Franzen, "Why Birds Matter,"
    National Geographic, January 2018

Wisconsin's itinerant naturalist, William Kurt Volkert, perhaps the greatest authority on the ecology of Horicon Marsh in eastern Wisconsin, has always wanted to know as much as he could about the world around him. Born in Milwaukee on March 10, 1953, Bill graduated from Wauwatosa West High School in 1971, attended UW-Superior and UW-Madison, then, disillusioned, dropped out of college during his senior year at age 21 and headed west. After wandering in the Colorado wilderness for the next year and a half, he returned to Wisconsin with new eyes, seeing a land of substantial diversity he had not before appreciated. Immediately, and for the next five years, he set upon a rigorous course of self-education by reading every natural history textbook he could lay his hands on related to the ecology of Wisconsin and the Upper Midwest.

In 1981, Bill began employment as a Limited Term Employee (LTE) for the Wisconsin Department of Natural Resources (WDNR), undertaking a variety of jobs including trail maintenance, wildlife surveys, and presenting a range of natural history talks on the Kettle Moraine State Forest and Horicon Marsh. He remained an LTE for eight and a half years before becoming the WDNR's wildlife educator and naturalist at Horicon in 1988.

Over the ensuing 23 years, before leaving the department in 2011, Bill brought attention to Horicon Marsh like no other, giving more than 3,700 education programs for over 210,000 people that included training scientists from 43 countries. During this time, he also gave over 900 media interviews, including 125 Wisconsin Public Radio shows, and outside his job he presented over 500 lectures on subjects as diverse as birding in Central and South America to travels in the Arctic, Central and South America, Russia, Mongolia, Africa, Australia, and New Zealand. (Parenthetically, the avid birder might be interested to know that Bill has observed more than 3,800 species—over one-third of the world's birds. His personal goal is to see at least half of the world's birds.)

In the 1990s, ornithologist Sam Robbins, author of *Wisconsin Birdlife: Population and Distribution Past and Present* appeared on the Larry Meiller public radio show over the holidays to talk about Wisconsin birds. When he passed away in 2000, Noel Cutright, co-author of *Atlas of the Breeding Birds of Wisconsin*, and Bill were asked to continue this tradition. Over the next 13 years, they did more than 70 programs together. After Noel passed away in 2013, Bill continued the tradition, occasionally with bird artist extraordinaire Tom Schultz. Over the years, he has accrued more than 150 shows with Larry Meiller. For Bill, this has afforded a tremendous opportunity to talk about birds with literally tens of thousands of people.

While at the DNR, Bill assisted experts from the Russian Natural Resources Agency (formerly Goscomecologia, Buryatia) and the Russian Academy of Sciences to further the protection of Lake Baikal in Siberia, Russia. In 1997, he traveled to Washington D.C. to represent Wisconsin as part of the 25th anniversary of cooperative American and Russian conservation efforts—salmon stocking and polar bear and crane conservation, among other initiatives. It was called the U.S.-Russian Conservation Conference, sponsored by the U.S. Fish and Wildlife Service. Bill presented a report on the cooperative Lake Baikal project, and later that year he returned to Russia once more to present a paper on this project at an international symposium on Great Lakes research and management. He offered a proposal for priority watershed protection for the entire Selenga River, which contributes to 56 percent of Lake Baikal's surface water. He argued for establishing a monitoring program above and below the key city of Ulan Ude. The Russian Academy of Sciences has since adopted his recommendations.

In all, Bill made eight trips between 1991 and 2004 to the Republic of Buryatia to work on various projects to protect Lake Baikal and two trips to Mongolia to focus efforts on the Selenga River watershed.

Bill has also worked in the southern hemisphere since 2002 with ornithologists and environmental educators to help develop a National Bird Conservation Education Plan for Nicaragua and to support bird conservation projects in the country. He leads birding trips to Nicaragua almost every winter, and to aid ecotourism efforts he wrote the field book, *Where to Watch Birds in Nicaragua*.

BILL AND HIS WIFE, CONNIE, make their home in the northern Kettle Moraine area of east-central Wisconsin. Here they work together to restore a series of native plant communities on their land, including an oak-hickory forest, a planted prairie community and prairie nursery, and wetlands. From this land, on less than 10 acres, they have now identified over 650 species of plants and animals, including 204 species of birds.

"It's been an experiment, an endeavor," he notes. "It's nice to bring back the integrity of something once degraded, which this land was. You need a piece of land to get your hands dirty and to watch the changes over the years. You spend enough time with it and see it come back. You have an impact, but the land changes you, too, in that you see it in more detail than ever before, which leads to a deeper understanding. I'm starting to listen to common birds in a way that I never did before, listening more intensively, to recognize nuances in their language. For example, with green herons in fall, before they migrate, they do what I refer to as an 'assembly call.' It always occurs in the first three weeks in September. They reserve a very unique call—an abbreviated *keerp*, *keerp*—as they fly around in circles. Right at sunset, others gather to form a flock, and then they all head south. So through this assembly call they are literally calling others, bringing them together, and then departing. The entire phenomenon takes place for only a few minutes in an evening when a cold front is approaching. I don't believe this has ever been documented before."

Bill continues to share his experiences and understanding of the natural world through lectures, presentations, and field trips. He is also working on several writing projects that will give these presentations more permanence and reach an even wider public.

🍂

I SAT DOWN with Bill at his home on November 15, 2000, and again on April 18, 2016, almost a year after he had returned from a once-in-a-lifetime birding trip with Connie around the world. After 233 days—seven and a half months—and over 55,000 miles of travel through 12 countries (South Africa, Madagascar, Zimbabwe, Botswana, Namibia, India, Nepal, Thailand, Cambodia, Vietnam, Malaysia and Borneo), they had racked up 1,328 bird species, of which 1,025 were new to them or "lifers." "One life, one planet, and so many birds!" became his motto. They also observed 124 different kinds of mammals. Bill and Connie ended up taking 35,000 photos to document their observations and experiences.

Did the trip leave Bill optimistic about the state of the world's birds? "I want to be optimistic," he told me, "but I really have some deep concerns because of habitat loss and development, to say nothing about the effects of overpopulation and climate change. Among the many birds I really wanted to see was the giant nuthatch [*Sitta magna*] in northern Thailand but did not. I only saw the silhouette of something shoot over my head. I'm still convinced it was a nuthatch. Only about 200 of these exist in the wild. Will I ever get a chance to see it? Is it still going to be there? I have my concerns. I have a parallel

Bill and wife Connie Ramthun in a dugout canoe in southern Nepal, 2015. Photo courtesy of William K. Volkert.

feeling when I think about the cerulean warbler or golden-winged warbler or the greater prairie-chicken in Wisconsin—all habitat specialists with restricted ranges."

Bill's focus and passion were evident in our interviews, as was an abiding sense of humor.

🖋

My father, Rudolf Volkert, and my mother, Erika Hofmann, were both born in Germany, in what was East Germany. They escaped after World War II. My two older brothers, Egbert (Ed) and Michael, were born in Germany as well. I also have a younger brother, Peter. I was the first person in our family to be born in the United States, only three months after my parents arrived. So, as my dad put it, I was born in the U.S. but made in Germany.

My dad fought in the German army in Yugoslavia during World War II, and my mother went into a work camp and then spent most of the war at home. She tells me about walking down the street in her neighborhood and having an American fighter plane literally shoot at her as target practice. Then, she was put on a train to Berlin, trying to race against the destruction of the railroad by the Russians. For five days she was on that train, and time and again they'd stop, and everybody would run for the woods as they were being fired upon. After the war, my mom illegally crossed the border 21 times to visit family and to gather things so she could get out of Germany. It's hard to imagine. Over the years, we only heard fragments of their experiences. Perhaps some things are just too hard to relive. They always said they wanted to write their story down, but never did.

They spent two years in what was West Germany after the war during a very difficult time. They wanted to start over, to make a new life. Eventually, they went by ship and train and arrived in Milwaukee on Christmas Day in 1952, sponsored by a great aunt and uncle of mine who had come to the U.S. in the late 1920s. For the first three months, they lived with them until they could afford to rent a place of their own.

When my parents arrived, they didn't know the language. They didn't speak English, except Mom, who had once visited a cousin in Texas as a child and so could speak a little bit, but they had no familiarity with the culture. Dad was a glass blower. He made fuses and tubes, but the United States was being automated so they didn't need his skills. As a result, he went into factory work and never got any technical training or a chance to pick up a second career.

✿

BECAUSE MY PARENTS grew up in these small burgs in Germany, they always liked to hike. Germans often speak of the "Thüringer Wald"—the Thuringian Forest—which is the region where they grew up. So we went out to the southern Kettle Moraine, visited Long Lake in Fond du Lac County, and picnicked and camped at Terry Andrae Park on weekends. They never had much money, and the only way to take vacations was to do it cheaply. We couldn't stay in hotels, so we rented a camp trailer. But that got to be too costly, so we bought a tent. Camping became a way of life, mostly, however, for economic reasons. They took us to the Smoky Mountains one year and drove out to Colorado and the Grand Canyon on another trip.

After they left my great aunt and uncle's house, they started moving into what was then an immigrant ethnic neighborhood in Milwaukee. The first thing I really remember is our house on 34th and Cherry, which is now the inner core of Milwaukee. We moved when I was about 6 years old to 54th and Cherry. That's where I went to elementary school. And when I was 11, we finally moved to what I thought was way out on the outskirts, into Wauwatosa, right near the Mayfair Shopping Center at 106th Street. That's where my developmental period began. Mayfair had just been built. There was a four-lane divided avenue coming out to it, and I still remember one of the first comments my mom made. "Well, gee, how stupid are these people? They built this four-lane divided highway, and nobody lives out here. Why did they waste all that money?" Obviously the planners knew something about urban sprawl that my parents didn't see. Over the next few years the area just exploded. Where Mayfair is today is well into Wauwatosa—the Milwaukee metroplex. But we thought we were on the far edge of the city!

Our house was actually a farmhouse before Mayfair was built. Developers started building smaller ranch style houses around it. Where we moved to was kind of a new neighborhood. It was actually two blocks south of Mayfair. Nearby was the George Hanson Park and golf course and Underwood Creek. Underwood Creek was neat because for the first time we had "wild" green space right out our door. Here was this creek and woods, and right across the street, I had a place to explore. I could walk around the woods every day, and we actually had a backyard for the first time. Like any kid, I'd make a fort, roam the countryside, and explore up and down the creek. I'd go out there, carve branches, make a bunch of little spears, and go harass the rabbits, but I never hit anything. I'd also go fishing after little chubs and suckers in the creek.

But houses built there were on the edge of the floodplain. They had problems with sewers backing up and periodic flooding. So, the city decided to re-engineer things, and I witnessed what for me was the first example of environmental destruction. They came and completely rerouted the creek and turned it into a storm sewer. They brought out this big earthmoving equipment and cut down all the trees, except for a real thin belt next to the road, which was mostly box elder scrub. They took this winding little creek, straightened it, channeled it, and gouged it out so you see the heavy blue clay at the bottom. And then they paved the whole thing in concrete. Here I was, 12 years old, and something right there struck me; this just wasn't right. This wasn't good use of the land. I was absolutely outraged, but what could we do? My parents certainly weren't engaged in the community.

⟊

I DIDN'T READ MUCH AS A KID. My folks were not involved with the school. They were busy working and weren't familiar with the American school system, or our studies. In fact, maybe that's why I grew up to be an independent learner because there was never anybody there to guide me. I had to do it myself. Growing up, we spoke a German-English mix at home. My parents spoke mostly German, and us boys grew up speaking German, but hanging around with our friends, it just wasn't cool, wasn't American, to speak another language, and we kind of let it go, although we all remain fluent.

I was a lousy student through most of school. I didn't do homework. I really didn't study. I didn't do much reading. It wasn't until junior high and high school that I started picking up some reading on my own. I started reading a lot of Steinbeck, Hermann Hesse, and those kinds of novels.

⟊

I'VE ALWAYS had one really good close friend, rather than several friends. When I was in middle school, I went to Longfellow Jr. High, which was in Wauwatosa. I had to take a city bus to school. We lived on 106th Street, and the school was on 76th. In school, they seated everybody in alphabetical order, so Volkert was always near the end of the line. Just ahead of me was [now-retired WDNR wolf ecologist, wildlife educator, and author] Dick Thiel. We went to junior high together, and we always sat close together, Thiel and Volkert. Dick and I shared homeroom, which means we also shared detentions—a lot of them. We also were in German class together, and we had the same English teacher. Of course, I took German for an easy grade.

Dick and I were best of friends in seventh and eighth grades. He would visit me because I lived a little more in the countryside, and he lived right in the residential area of Wauwatosa, the older part of town. So, they hardly had much of a backyard. I'd also go over to his house because it was just a short walk from school. What was funny was that neither Dick nor I had a real strong inclination to study nature. We weren't drawn to natural subjects. We didn't go bird watching or anything like that. We just kind of goofed around outside. Then Dick's family moved away, and I didn't see him for 15 years until I was at the first endangered species conference, in Madison.

I didn't realize it was the Dick Thiel I had known until I noticed that he wore a watch on his right hand, and the Richard P. Thiel I had known was left-handed! I kept thinking, "God, that looks like the guy I knew." And then, "No, it can't be." The kid I knew just wasn't into this stuff. I kept looking at him and was so distracted I probably heard only half his talk.

So, after his presentation, I went to introduce myself. "Hi, I'm Bill Volkert."

Before I could say anything more, he said, "Did you go to school at Longfellow?" And right there we broke out laughing.

At the point when Dick's family moved away, there was another fellow that lived two and a half blocks down from me, on Fisher Parkway. His name was Craig Roesler [later a DNR water resources specialist]. He'd been in the neighborhood for some time before me and hung around with a different circle of kids. Craig was always a bit quiet. One day, Craig and another guy came to harass me on my paper route. It was wintertime, and they had a whole wagonful of snowballs they had made, and they just pitched them at me. Finally, I made a few of my own snowballs and charged them. I rolled their wagon over and stomped their entire ammunition into the ground— spoiled their fun. Craig thought that was kind of cool, so all of a sudden we started talking and hitting it off. It turned out he was really into the natural sciences and insect collecting, which was fantastic for a 14-year-old kid.

Craig had this great collection of beetles and butterflies laid out meticulously, and at his house they had this entire collection of *National Geographic* magazines—something my parents probably didn't even know existed. We started hanging around together and going out into the woods. He was very familiar with birds and insects in the area. Then, once we were old enough to get driver's licenses and get around on our own, we went fishing and hunting together. My dad never did hunt or fish, but my oldest brother was quite the fisherman and so was Craig's family. Craig and I did a lot of fishing, and we even did fish taxidermy. We also went out catching things with nets. Craig was collecting insects, and we started catching darters to keep in aquariums to study them. We were junior fish biologists in our own right.

AFTER I GRADUATED from high school, I was basically forced into college. My parents, for some reason, didn't always trust me, so as a result they thought some discipline was necessary. Either I go into the military or to the university; I didn't have a choice. This was the German tradition. I wanted to hang out, take a year or two off to travel and explore, but my parents didn't see any value in that. I was very resentful over it, so I went all the way up to UW-Superior just to get away from home. The problem with Superior was there was a lot of rural land around it, but I didn't have a car so I could never even get out of the city or into the woods. I was stuck on campus, and that was always the paradox about being in school. I wanted to do natural history studies, but I could never get off campus. I had become interested in this largely because of all the hunting and fishing I had done with Craig and my brother. By the time I got into college, I was so interested in fish and fishing that I studied fishery sciences.

In Superior, I was one of the first ichthyology students taught by Bill Swenson, my instructor who had just started teaching there. When I took his course, I already knew the fish species and scientific names for probably a third of the Wisconsin fishes. Swenson was as enthusiastic as me, and we really hit it off. He was at least one person who became a mentor, the first teacher I could have a conversation with and look up to. Because of that it became easy to learn. I pulled the second highest grade in the class, only behind a graduate student who needed the class.

I also had developed an interest in literature, philosophy, and psychology, so I actually took a second major in psychology because I was frustrated and wanted to figure out what I was going to do with my life. I wasn't really looking for a career, I was looking more for a life. I made up my mind that I wasn't going to be stuck in a job as my dad had been. He didn't have the technical skills or a full grasp of the language and ended up with a job that he didn't like but needed to survive. My folks were always struggling, or at least worried about money, both of them working, trying to keep things going. To them the most important thing was to get a good job so I could make some money, but I was looking for something meaningful, something worthwhile to do with my life.

Ornithology seemed to offer some meaning, so I took a class at Superior, and I'll never forget it. I realized three years afterwards that the instructor was one of the worst teachers I'd ever had. He was not a birder, not an ornithologist, not a specialist at all. I think he was reading a week or two ahead of us so he could come up with a lesson plan. He seemed to be making it up as he went, but he kept us busy memorizing all the bird families and orders, memorizing all the bones in the bird body, and so on. Ironically, this was a great experience for me because I developed a good knowledge of bird taxonomy and classification, anatomy, and physiology— all of the textbook bird stuff—but no real field experience. He only offered two field trips. He knew the ducks well enough, but when we came across a flock of sparrows he simply said that they were all "dickey birds." I had never heard the term before and eventually realized that they were just the many songbirds that he couldn't identify. Even so, after this course I figured that I knew birds. I became a little cocky because I had this whole college semester under my belt.

My dad had these German binoculars, and I borrowed them from him for about five years. I thought, "Well, he doesn't use them, and I now have the ornithology background." So when school let out, I took a hike during one of those tremendous warbler migrations. I walked up to George Hanson Park, where I'd grown up, and I went up there confident that I knew birds. Here I found all of these different warblers, but they wouldn't sit still. I was confused because they weren't all stuffed as in the lab. I couldn't identify them. It really humbled me, and I gave up. I'd had all this information pounded into my head, but I couldn't even recognize a bird in the field!

This made me question the value of some of the university learning. So, I went back to studying fish.

One day, I went with my dip net into the Scuppernong Creek in the southern Kettle Moraine. I wanted to net blackside darters [*Percina maculata*]. Along came the Benjamin Goss Bird Club literally led by a little old lady in tennis shoes. I was down in the creek, and I could see them through the bushes. They couldn't see me. All of a sudden, I heard this lady stop and say, "Hold it everyone. I hear a warbling vireo [*Vireo gilvus*]."

I rolled my eyes, thinking, "You heard it? You know what it is?" I wouldn't know one if it landed in front of me. How did she know this? I remember thinking, "Wait a minute. I'm the guy who studied birds at the university, and she didn't look like a college graduate. So how can she know all this and I don't? What does she have that I don't?" Well, it became real obvious: she had experience. She basically had spent time looking at birds. I'd been looking at dead specimens.

⟡

I SPENT the first two years at Superior and then went to UW-Madison. I continued to study zoology and psychology. However, one day, I got into an argument with one of my psych teachers about a paper I had to write. I chose the topic of human values and how it influenced our perception, but he said that psychology as a science couldn't measure human values. I asked if personal values then didn't exist, or if his science was simply inadequate.

I dropped psychology as a second major and tried to focus on zoology. But actually I didn't graduate. I walked out of school because I was so disillusioned by being forced to attend, not knowing why I was there, and some of the unfortunate experiences I had. I was disgusted with that and resentful over the fact that I was stuck on campus. I couldn't even get out of the city of Madison. I didn't have a car and had no way to get out. The fact is I'd already completed all of the course requirements for my majors, but I felt empty, and so I left just before my senior year at age 21.

I was now old enough that my parents could no longer tell me what to do. I finally thought, "I'm going to make up my own mind. I'll go where I want to, when I need to, when I want to." I needed independence, so I moved out of the house. My parents were upset, but I decided I just needed to get away for a while. So I moved out to Colorado for over a year. And that was an interesting experience because the landscape is really dramatic out there, but I didn't find what I was looking for. There were many places to explore, all new to me. I became very much interested in the natural history of the area, but it was all so foreign. I remember, after a long winter, spring arrived and everything was greening up. But about the time it turned green, there was a drought, and everything went brown. It was very arid compared to Wisconsin.

I came back home after a year and a half for my younger brother's wedding. I remember by the time I got into eastern Iowa, everything just looked so lush, so green. The Midwest actually became an attraction to me, and so it was by moving away that Wisconsin became an intrigue to me. By that time, I had taken more than an academic interest in natural history. A degree wasn't important to me. What was important was the knowledge and field experience. So I did a great amount of reading. School had taught me how to study. And so I became an avid reader. I read 50 books a year, mostly natural science textbooks. That's all I read. I read *The Quaternary Geology of Southeastern Wisconsin*, which was an old government study by W.C. Alden, published in 1918—dry as hell but very in depth. He spent years in southeastern Wisconsin looking at glacial deposits, and when he put it all together on a map, he could actually see from these broken moraines, the retreating and shrinking of the ice mass, and he could see a story revealed in the land.

In my library I also have every single thing written by or about Aldo Leopold and by naturalist-author Sigurd Olson, who wrote about the boreal forest and canoeing in the far north. I read classics, such as *Soils of Wisconsin* by Francis Hole, and John Weaver's studies on prairies. I also enjoyed reading *The Physical Geography of Wisconsin* by Lawrence Martin. I read that just before reading John T. Curtis's *The Vegetation of Wisconsin*. I came to realize that most students had used Curtis's book as a reference or read a few chapters, but I had never really met anyone that had read it cover to cover. I decided that's what I was going to do, with that and every other book. The problem for me was that he uses a lot of scientific names for all the plants, and I was not a botanist. So I looked them all up and wrote them down. I kept a pad of paper nearby, and I basically translated the whole book for myself. I'd then re-read a chapter once I had translated it to understand the ecological concepts. When I'd go out for a hike, I'd see Curtis in my mind in these different plant communities. I'd think, "What is it that he saw in this land that he can say this is a particular type of forest with its associated understory?" That's when I started pulling out my field guides and tried to identify every plant I saw. I tried to see and understand the land for myself as these experts had.

These early naturalists spent years studying nature and landscapes and then wrote down their findings and insights. I tried to do the same in reverse, which was to read and understand their findings and then go out to the same areas and learn to see the land as they had. So, as a result of my personal studies, natural history became something very attractive to me, and that's when I decided to become a naturalist. I was really taken by the study of ecology. What fascinated me was seeing not just birds and plants, but the interrelationships in nature. But how could I even begin to comprehend interactions unless I understood the parts? When I moved back to Wisconsin and to the northern Kettle Moraine area, I realized I had to explore where I grew up, and I was going to learn what the university didn't give me—field experience. I decided the Kettle Moraine was going to be my laboratory.

I was going to learn everything.

AFTER READING numerous geology books, I drove around the state with the geologists at my side, so to speak. I would take my geology maps and drive Wisconsin. I'd pull over to a roadside and look around. I'd notice that I was on this particular recessional moraine in this part of Wisconsin. But, how did these people know this when they hiked out here and first described it? I wanted to be able to see this for myself. Besides glacial geology, I also taught myself all the wildflowers, the shrubs, trees, and birds in the Kettle Moraine. I then tried in my mind to find a way to integrate the glacial history with the distribution of plant communities and understand these microclimates and understory plants and see different successional trends. I also wanted to know how this provided a particular habitat for birds and mammals. I wanted to understand the area in its entirety.

During this time, I started making friends with professors at some of the smaller campuses. One guy, Ed Domicee, was a good geologist at the West Bend campus. I never took his classes, but I did help him set up field trips and could ask him a lot of questions. I also took a mycology class there with Sami Saad and spent time in the field with him studying mushrooms.

During this period, in my mid to late 20s, I was bumming. I had job after job just to stay alive. I worked for a while, quit, and hung out reading and buying books or borrowing them from the library, and then I'd spend time in the field. When I ran out of money, I'd get another job. One year I went through nine jobs. I've had 46 jobs in my life because I never stayed very long at any of them. I also had welding skills, so I could get a job somewhere welding. I'd drive by these factories and inquire if they needed a welder. I'd tell them I'd dedicate myself to them for the rest of my life. They'd say, "Bill, you're our man. When can you start? Tomorrow?"

I'd say, "Well, no, I've got another job, and I need to give two-weeks notice." Of course, I didn't have a job, but I'd tell them a two-week notice because that was standard, and that meant I got two more weeks of freedom. After about three months, I'd say, "Look, can I get a day off?"

"No, nobody gets vacation benefits until after a year."

"How about some special arrangement?" I'd ask.

"We don't do that." And finally, they'd say, "Why, we thought you were here to stay."

I'd reply, "I just needed the cash, I'm sorry." I'd then quit and repeat the process all over again.

At home in the northern Kettle Moraine area of east-central Wisconsin, 2000.
Photo by Sumner Matteson.

BILL VOLKERT

The interesting thing from that period of my life was that I was dead set against traveling. I'd already done some of that, having gone to Colorado. I didn't understand Colorado. I was lost there, and my philosophy was, why travel anywhere? Why go to other places when I can't even understand my own backyard? I refused to leave Wisconsin. I was reading 40 to 50 textbooks a year and driving 35,000 miles a year in Wisconsin.

When I came back to Wisconsin, I wanted to create a circle of friends and associates. I became involved with the Fond du Lac County Audubon Society, and that's where I met [bird artist and ornithologist] Tom Schultz. Tom, who was my own age, had his own interest in birds. He and I birded together often and learned a lot from each other. As a result, my birding knowledge and contacts began to grow.

In 1979, an Audubon member named Lew Smith came up to me and said, "Bill, you seem to know an awful lot about birds. Do you think you could teach us?"

I'd never thought about it. I was learning on my own, but I said, "Well, I suppose I could."

He asked, "Would you want to do a short course on birds?" So I did and really enjoyed it. It was fun to talk about what interested me, and people were interested in what I was reading and studying! And, I found another way to make a little money on the side, too, through university short courses and adult outreach classes in Fond du Lac and West Bend. Administrators loved it because they had a fledgling outreach program.

They told me, "Bill, your classes are popular. Are there other subjects you would like to teach?" So I just picked subjects I was studying and organized lectures and field trips. I found that I had to compile several hours of materials for a one-hour presentation, so I could also answer a wide range of questions that might come up. And it helped me to organize my thoughts so that I could express them to others.

At that time, I was also doing beach bird surveys on the Great Lakes, with much time spent on the Lake Michigan shore. This became another subject of interest to me, so I also led some field trips on beach ecology. That proved fascinating to me because this is a very active landscape, and I could actually see changes in just a few years—from a stable dune covered in creeping juniper, to a recent sand blowout. Successional stages were really easy to observe there. I was beginning to feel a sense of confidence because I could start to see patterns and relationships in the land.

In addition to teaching courses, I also began to experiment with radio as a way to promote Audubon events and field trips. I started in Fond du Lac, at KFIZ radio, where if you did say something really stupid, who was going to notice? It was such a small audience. I started with these local radio stations and obtained practical experience. Apparently, I did well since I was often asked back. I can't remember how Wisconsin Public Radio first contacted me, but I'm sure it came about as a listener suggestion, and by the mid-1980s I was appearing on Larry Meiller's show.

✿

IN 1981, my work turned in a different direction. I happened to see something in the local newspaper where they were looking for help in the Northern Kettle Moraine State Forest. Actually, it was just a DNR summer LTE job doing trail maintenance. Up to this point I had never even considered working for the DNR. I didn't know if I wanted to work there as a profession. I just wanted to do something that I enjoyed and understood. They gave me a job where I had to replace the trail marker posts or paint them all the way down the Kettle Moraine. A very mundane job, but the fun thing about it was I did it during the height of the nesting season for birds, so every day I kept a complete bird list. I painted posts while listening to birds sing. I had a little notebook in my pocket at all times, and I wrote down my sightings and then entered them into checklists at home. It provided a great opportunity to census and learn more about the local birds.

During this time, I also kept track of all the prairie remnants I discovered, and I put together my first paper for the *University of Wisconsin-Milwaukee Field Station Bulletin* on prairie plants and remnant communities in the northern Kettle Moraine.[107] This was a complete survey of all the prairie plants and remaining community stands in the area.

At the same time, I convinced a woman with 380 acres in the northern Kettle Moraine to rent me a little cottage after she had asked me to come by and provide land management recommendations. Basically, I had the full run of the land, almost 400 acres. I lived in that cottage for two years and developed a complete list of all the birds and plants I observed there.

Then, DNR wildlife manager Dale Katsma hired me to do some winter deer surveys, looking at food plots and checking wood duck [*Aix sponsa*] boxes. Things took a turn when Dale was asked to complete an endangered species survey. Since he didn't have much information, he asked me to look into it. The Bureau of Endangered Resources (BER) was just getting organized. Since BER lacked staff, they wanted wildlife managers to tell them what species occurred on their properties. I knew, among other things, of five red-shouldered hawk [*Buteo lineatus*] territories in the area and where Acadian flycatchers [*Empidonax virescens*] nested. I quickly realized that I could learn a lot about game management from someone like Dale and contribute my knowledge of the forest with the things I was studying. In addition to my DNR job, I was still teaching short courses at the local campuses, including a six-week class on birds with Tom Schultz and a class on wildflower identification and the physical geography of Fond du Lac County.

Additionally, The Fond du Lac Visitors and Convention Bureau hired me for several years to take busloads of people on tours of Horicon Marsh. They'd invite them from Chicago, put them up overnight, provide a fall harvest dinner, then there'd be a special bus trip down to Horicon Marsh to watch the geese. I had developed a whole story on the area's geology, the history of the marsh, and its wildlife, as well as the life history and migration of the Canada geese. The bus held about 40 people, but there always was another 50 to 100 marsh visitors listening in since there was no interpretive program on the marsh.

At this time, the Ice Age Visitor Center in the northern Kettle Moraine was expanding its programs and needed help. The superintendent asked me to do a few additional naturalist programs because of the many visitors. Roger Reif was the naturalist, and he asked me to lead some of the bird hikes. I started to realize that between Dale and his endangered species survey and Roger and the naturalist programs that I had found a niche. And that's when I really started getting interested in becoming a full-time naturalist.

In the fall of 1984, Walt Adams, the superintendent for the Kettle Moraine, asked me to go to Horicon to assess the potential for interpretative programs. Horicon Marsh was the last property added to the Ice Age National Scientific Reserve of Wisconsin. In the agreement with the National Park Service, it states that we shall "preserve, protect, and interpret the glacial resource." Interpret the glacial history of Horicon Marsh? What did that mean? Do they erect a few signs, develop a brochure, create an education program? Nobody knew.

So I started the education program at Horicon as an experiment to determine its potential. At this point, I realized there was no way I was going to get a permanent job in the Kettle Moraine because Roger Reif was years away from retiring. But I didn't want to move across the state just for a job. I somehow had to prove that there was a demand for another naturalist in the area. The DNR provided money for seven weeks in fall to organize, advertise, and conduct interpretive programs. So as part of my assignment for Walt, I called the federal refuge and said, "Do you mind if I offer interpretive programs on both ends of the marsh?" They didn't, and saw it as a benefit. I knew from my experience with the Fond du Lac Visitors Bureau that I could always attract a crowd there. The program was immediately successful, and I had nearly 2,000 people attend in that first short season. Because I was already with Audubon and doing these outreach classes, I knew how to advertise my programs. I knew the radio stations, the newspapers, and due to the tours I had been conducting for the Visitors Bureau, I already had developed all my lectures before I even came on the job.

The next year, the DNR Parks administrators, in what was then called the DNR's Southern District, became interested in retaining me as an LTE. I worked for 20 weeks and had 4,600 people attend my programs. By the third year, I had crowds for my goose talk of 500–600 people. Bill Moorman and Laurie Osterndorf from the parks program called me up one day and said, "Now wait a minute, Bill, we've got a question on your attendance figures. It says here you had 600 people for an outdoor hike."

I said, "No, no, it's not a hike. You can't take that many on a trail."

They said, "You mean 60 don't you?"

"No, 600," I replied.

They said, "Come on, we've never heard of this before. You say 600 people for a talk?"

I said, "Well, to tell you the truth, I only count those who stick around for the whole hour presentation. There were another 100 or so that came and went, but they really didn't stay.

They didn't believe me, so they came up one day when I did this talk. The first thing I had to do was stand on the railing at the Highway 49 view area. I yelled out, "Can everybody in the back here me? Great!" And I gave an hour presentation on the life history and management of Canada geese as they flew into the marsh for the evening.

Later, Bill Moorman came up and said, "Gosh, Bill, there must have been about 800 people there!"

I said, "Well, I counted 650 of those that stuck around." I said the others only stayed for five or ten minutes.

He replied, "You don't even count those?"

I said, "They came for only a short time but didn't hear my whole presentation, so I don't consider that attendance." He was simply amazed by a crowd of that size for such an event. But at that time there still were large numbers of people coming to the marsh in fall to watch the geese, so I had a readily available audience.

I worked from 1984 through 1987 at Horicon Marsh as the Ice Age naturalist. By that time, I had eight and a half years of LTE work in total. Actually, it worked out pretty nicely. They got a good deal with me because I would start my schedule early in spring, and then to make sure I wouldn't run over six months, I would take off in the middle of summer for six weeks to study and travel. I took a voluntary layoff without pay, and then came back in fall to stretch it long enough when visitors arrived. It was a real sacrifice financially because every time I started up again, I had to go two pay cycles before seeing a check.

During winter, I'd do other outside jobs and whatever else I had to do to survive. I could at least make enough money to drive around and buy books. That's where I was putting my money. I continued to read up to 50 textbooks a year. By that time I'd read, best guesstimate, 625 textbooks.

By 1988, however, I began to wonder if it was worth it anymore. I was thinking that I couldn't keep doing this. Maybe I was nuts to hope for a job that I couldn't even afford to have since it was still only seasonal. Well, Steve Miller, who had been the DNR wildlife manager at Crex Meadows near Grantsburg, and who had designated one-third of the position for biologist Jim Hoefler as wildlife interpreter, now became the wildlife management bureau chief. He said, "Look, education is a big thing. We need this to support our management efforts." So he created an education position in the central office, an outdoor skills program at Sandhill Wildlife Area, which Dick Thiel was appointed to, and also wanted to create an education position at Horicon based on the success I was having. But then all of a sudden the worst news came: the position would be offered first to full-time employees who could transfer laterally. For all my work, it appeared that I had actually created a job for somebody else. My supervisor at the time didn't know what I did and didn't have a clue how to train anybody to do my job. He was a wildlife manager, not an educator. He focused on his job and simply took credit for what I did. So he was worried by this lateral transfer because he would have to train and supervise someone for my work.

To get away from the stress, I took off for the Arctic for five weeks. I traveled to northern Baffin Island, 500 miles above the Arctic Circle. When I came back, the one person who I thought might take the job as a lateral told me he wasn't interested. In the next round of interviews there were five other applicants, and when they heard that I had applied for the job and knew about my reputation, every single one of them pulled out. This entire process lasted nearly 10 months, and in the end, they all but handed me the job. The other funny thing was that the interviewers finally confessed that they were going through my desk and my notes in the evening to try to put together an exam of something that maybe I didn't already know. I was well known for having thoroughly studied subjects of interest to me. Well, I finally got the permanent appointment. Another real funny thing was that the DNR hired Craig Roesler, who's been my best friend ever since I was 14, five weeks before me. So he and I were both in the new employee orientation together. I remember sitting around this table when they said, "Why don't you introduce yourselves to the people you're sitting with."

I looked at Craig and said, "Excuse me, what is your name? How do you spell that? Wrestler?" We laughed and said that we used to have some real confidence in the DNR until they hired both of us. "Do you believe it? What's wrong with these people?" He's now a water resource manager working out of the Spooner office and monitors the lakes and rivers in northwest Wisconsin. He always wanted to get into either fisheries or wildlife, but he didn't think there was a job there, so he went into water chemistry thinking with the Clean Water Act there was more of a chance for work in that field.

Ironically, once I attained permanent status, my supervisor informed me that I could no longer do Wisconsin Public Radio. He told me that our focus was local, not statewide. And he basically forbid me to use state time and money to go on public radio in spite of the fact that I was representing the entire agency and the show was becoming quite popular. This was very disappointing to me, and I recall talking to a friend about it. He said that I was simply out-shining my supervisor and that he stopped me out of jealousy. I didn't want to believe it, saying that this was an agency of professionals and that there must be another reason.

Over the years I have experienced my share of envy and maneuvering from others, and this probably stemmed from the fact that I had so thoroughly thrown myself into my work since this was more than just a job to me. I also know that I can be outspoken, which some people may find intimidating, but I think that is also what has made me an effective presenter. But, I found a way to still do public radio. I stopped working officially at 10:00, drove my own car down to Madison, paid the mileage, and went on the air. I unofficially represented DNR, drove back, and worked a few hours later in the day to make up for my time off. That's what I did, and he couldn't stop me. So I just worked around that obstacle. Eventually, these radio shows became part of my job.

Bill talking to a Chinese delegation of scientists at the state Horicon Marsh overlook—"the old Palmatory Street headquarters," 2003. Photo courtesy of William K. Volkert.

Over the years, I have developed a good rapport with the public radio audience, and audiences in general. I like to refer to myself as an interpretive naturalist due to my knowledge of a wide range of subjects, from geology to plant ecology to ornithology. And as an interpreter, I see my job as an attempt to translate the science and natural history of the landscape and its wildlife and put it into layman's terms. That is to literally take that foreign language of science, ecology, and natural history and make it accessible to the general public.

For the visitors to the marsh, one of the things I always do is tell the history of Horicon Marsh so when people look at it they understand what they are seeing as a result of the past. And, of course, in basic teaching, you've got to take people from what they already know and build on that, so you need to also assess your audience. So I would go through the history of the marsh, sometimes in only a few minutes for younger students, but it needed to be said to set the stage. Other times, I'd take a whole hour to cover the story.

Over the years, I have told the story of Horicon Marsh well over 2,000 times.

Here's the two-minute version:

"The glaciers of the last Ice Age advanced through Wisconsin, gouging out Green Bay, Lake Winnebago, and the Horicon Marsh, and creating the Great Lakes. The advancing glaciers formed the Horicon basin. When the ice retreated, it paused at the south end and deposited material to form a moraine. As the melt waters filled the basin, this moraine acted like an earthen dam to impound the water, and the marsh began as a post-glacial lake. Eventually, the water eroded this outlet to drain the lake and leave behind Horicon Marsh.

"From the end of the Ice Age until modern settlement, every major prehistoric Indian culture known to Wisconsin inhabited or utilized this marsh—an incredibly extensive human history. This was their hunting ground. During all those centuries, people were drawn to the marsh because of its resources, but they never altered it. All the changes to the marsh have come in the last 150 years. European settlers dammed it and flooded it, creating a huge lake, and operated steamboats on it for 23 years.

"Eventually, the dam was removed, and when the marsh returned so did the wildlife, especially the waterfowl. But lacking a sense of conservation, people overhunted the ducks, and when the ducks were gone, they saw no other value to the marsh, so they tried to ditch and drain it for farming purposes. Peat fires raged on for 12 years after this farming effort, and they left behind a wasteland. Eventually, the state and federal government began to acquire the land and restore the marsh for wildlife purposes. What we see today is a restored, or rebuilt, wetland."

Discussing the history of Horicon Marsh. Photo courtesy of William K. Volkert.

That's it. Understand that what you're seeing has been abused and altered time and again. If we don't understand this history, then everything else is without context. And if we forget that history, we might be ignorant enough to try it again—if not here, then somewhere else. Therefore, I use the marsh not only as a unique story about Horicon, but representative of all wetlands and our relationship to them.

After setting the stage with this overview, I also like to get the audience involved to stimulate thought about what I said and what visitors are seeing. One question I like to ask is, "How did the animals ever survive for thousands of years without a professional wildlife manager to take care of them?" It's a simple question, but I am always surprised by how many people are stumped by it.

More than once I've had adults pondering this when a young kid will say, "Well, God (or nature) did that."

So then I ask, "If nature managed everything so well, why are we doing this today?" The answer is because we're also the ones who created all of the problems. We altered the land. Look at the history of the marsh; all the things we did here impacted the wildlife. Management is an effort to rectify this.

And then, the next question I ask is, "So what is the department doing to make things right? What is wildlife management? Look around. Do you see our work? Look at the flooded marsh. We built the dikes to hold back the water and manage favorable water levels. See the extensive grass fields next to the marsh? We planted that as nesting cover for ducks and a variety of songbirds. Our work is often not that visible since we work with the products of nature to re-create wetlands, grasslands, and forests."

What we're really doing is not managing animals but the land on which they live, so we're managing habitats, and that's what people need to see, and I commonly tell visitors we don't feed the wildlife. The marsh will do that. All we do is create conditions to enhance the ability of the marsh to meet the needs of wildlife. That is the art and science of wildlife management.

Another common question I ask is, "If we've been working to restore this marsh for the past 75 years, how do we know if it's working? How do we know if we're doing a good job or not?" The simple answer is because the wildlife has returned. I'll point out, "We know we're doing a great job for geese. Look at how many we have today." But Horicon Marsh is more than a goose marsh. It is a wetland ecosystem, and the birds can tell us a lot about the health of the marsh. Overall, we have now identified 305 species of birds here. And then I'll ask, "How many people here can even name 300 species of Wisconsin birds?" I've rarely ever seen anybody raise a hand.

Once I've set the stage so that visitors can see the marsh for what it is, we then take a hike to see what we can find; we explore. What I want to do is get people to open their eyes and discover our native wildlife. I remember taking a British and Swedish biologist on a bird hike. We were walking through a woodlot, and I couldn't wait to get to the marsh so that I could show them a yellow-headed blackbird. We came across a flock of blue jays, which I pointed out, and was about to lead them to the open water. The Brit stopped and told me he wanted to take a longer, closer look at the jays, which he had never seen before. He commented, "What an extraordinary bird you have in North America." It reminded me just how unique even some of our common birds can be.

I also remember hiking with a group of inner city kids when one of them said, "Oh, what a pretty bird. What is that?"

I replied, "That's a red-winged blackbird." It made me realize that they've probably never seen one before, and it's got to be one of the most abundant birds in the state. Perhaps they've never stopped to look at this bird, or maybe they don't have any habitat nearby where they can see it. So what I'm trying to do is get people to open their eyes and see something of the natural world, and then understand what they're seeing. Whether I am searching for rails and bitterns for experienced birders or showing someone a blackbird or jay for the first time, it is an opportunity to explore, discover, and enjoy nature.

As we walk around I'll also like to ask, "Do we have more wildlife or less wildlife than we did 25 years ago?" I usually hear both answers as some say we've got more, while others say less. The answer is, they're both right. I'll point to deer, geese, raccoons, and gulls as examples of abundant wildlife, as well as the reintroduction of trumpeter swans and wild turkeys as success stories. Then, I'll mention that we have more than 200 species of plants and animals on the threatened and endangered species list. "How come we have so many threatened and endangered species at the same time that others are booming?" People often have a hard time reconciling those two opposing trends. The fact is that when we change the land, we have winners and losers.

I'll mention that Wisconsin is no bigger or smaller than it was 100 years ago. It's the same size, but what's changed is the face, or surface of it. We've cut down trees, plowed under the prairies, ditched and drained wetlands, built factories, houses, and highways, and introduced contaminants, pollutants, and invasive species into the environment.

Every time we do something to the land we're actually creating or encouraging certain wildlife, even if the intent has nothing to do with wildlife. That's what I want people to understand. I want them to see the land as a dynamic landscape. "So what's our place and our responsibility?" I ask. I never try to give them an answer to that question because there isn't a single one. But the bottom line is how can they respect something that they don't fully understand? What I'm trying to do is distill 30 years worth of experience and create a shortcut—to make it easier for others to see the land for its plants and animals and as part of a dynamic process.

Bill holding a female magnolia warbler *(Setophaga magnolia)* he banded at the Horicon Marsh Bird Festival, May 2005. Photo courtesy of William K. Volkert.

FOR A NUMBER OF YEARS, I've conducted spring hikes for an advanced biology class, and one of the things that the teacher always asks me to do is to show the students how I listen to birds and learn their songs. The teacher once asked me what I would miss most, my sight or my hearing. That would be a hard choice. I don't think my hearing is that much more acute than other people, but I've learned to listen to birdsongs in far greater detail than most, and that's improved my level of appreciation.

CHAPTER ELEVEN

Because I am listening, I hear things that others don't, and through years of practice and learning I hear sounds that others miss. It's almost like a conductor of an orchestra who can pick out every instrument in a symphony. He or she has honed that skill to distinguish every individual part of the whole. The rest of us only hear the music. That's one of the problems for conservation. Why should someone care about the loss of a species when they didn't know it existed in the first place? It never affected their life and therefore has no value. What would the problem be if it is gone? So it's important to have experiences to discover what is out there and to let a species or a place grow on you. Then, intimacy begins to develop. Levels of detail become apparent through experience, which translates into awareness and hopefully action.

Talking to the masses about bird-banding. Horicon Marsh Bird Festival, May 2005. Photo courtesy of William K. Volkert.

What I would tell a young person today is, "Spend time outdoors and wander on your own. Find a place that catches you, that talks to you, that attracts you in some way, and see if you can't find a way to spend as much time there as possible. Then learn to look and listen."

I SEE MY JOB as an interpretive naturalist as somewhat different. There are many excellent scientists, including field scientists, but they're not all capable of effectively conveying what they know to a broad audience.

I'm familiar with a wide range of studies in nature; that's why I take the title of naturalist. I'm not a specialist in one particular field, although I have studied birds more than anything else. But I try to be familiar with a variety of topics. In addition to studying nature, for an interpreter, good communication skills are essential. It's one thing to know your subject, it's another to get other people to see it and understand it.

So for me the trick of interpretation is to present complex interrelationships in terms that people can easily relate to, and to leave them hopefully pondering the larger issue of how they can best live with the land. To me, the role of the interpretive naturalist is very much like that of a prism. A prism is nothing more than a fancy piece of cut glass with some unique angles. To take a look at that piece of glass itself is nothing. What's important is what it does. It takes a beam of light and breaks it up into its component parts. It pulls it apart and creates a rainbow. So, the eye is drawn away from the prism to the rainbow, and that's how I see my role.

While I've had some huge audiences and enjoy being before a crowd, I've always felt that I am most effective when I am barely present, when the people ignore the prism and are mesmerized by the rainbow, when I can provide an insight for them to discover the wonder of nature. I am only there to help them see and make it accessible. You don't have to be a scientist to enjoy the natural world, but science brings meaning to what we see.

ONE OF THE THINGS that has compelled me to want to do meaningful, interpretive programs is simply that I'm motivated by selfishness. What I can do is try to teach people to understand so they themselves will protect the land. Why do I think it's important for them to protect it? Because I found something there that's so important to me, and I want to make sure it's still there for all of us in the future. When I was a kid, I had no say when the bulldozers came into our neighborhood and wiped out my favorite haunts. I lost the experience of roaming that land. So I want to inspire people to want to become involved in conservation, in protecting our remaining natural areas, our wild lands and wildlife, so I can always go back to my favorite places wherever they may be. And hopefully they will find something there for themselves as well.

I HAVE CERTAINLY had some exciting experiences as I have explored natural areas. And actually this is one of the things that has encouraged me to want to be a naturalist. I've had some thrilling experiences in remote areas, and I often find that when I'm exploring far away places, such as in northern Canada or Mongolia, I enjoy my solitude but always have this urge to share my experiences with others when I return. My early trips to Canada offered both adventure and a great teaching opportunity.

For many years, after I came back from Colorado, I didn't want to travel because I didn't want to go to more places that I didn't understand. Then, after traveling all around Wisconsin, I began to acquire an understanding of the land. Once I established a foundation, I was ready to see more. Well, in 1980, Tom Schultz and I got the idea of doing some birding farther north to see where our migrants went and search for other birds that we don't see here, such as Ross's gull [*Rhodostethia rosea*], which breeds in the Churchill area on Hudson Bay. He wanted to go right to Churchill and bird there. I said, "Look, why don't we go to Churchill by water? We can take my canoe." So after some planning we finally put a trip together.

We drove to Thompson, Manitoba, and then took the train to Churchill. Halfway there we got off, unloaded our canoe and camping gear and paddled north for nearly two weeks to reach Hudson Bay. Well, in my mind, Hudson Bay seemed like the end of the world. We had made it all the way to Hudson Bay by canoe to watch birds. I had observed the transition from Wisconsin and the southernmost boreal forest through Canada's northern forests into the subarctic and muskeg right to the lower edge of the Arctic tundra and the coastal plain.

When we got back, I thought, "I made it all the way to Churchill. It's almost like being at the North Pole!" But I quickly realized that I had seen only the southernmost sliver of the Arctic. There's a whole ecosystem beyond it, and that's when I became fascinated with what lay further north. Also, I had become intrigued with Ice Age geology in Wisconsin because it was kind of a unifying principle for me. It put everything I saw and studied into a time sequence—like the difference between looking at a picture and watching a movie. It was a way to see how the land evolved over the past 10,000 years.

The Ice Age also gave me an ecological understanding of the Kettle Moraine—why this landscape dictates the composition of our plant communities here as a result of the dynamics of that ice. But we can't go back in time, so how do you get a feel for the Ice Age? Well, go where it's still living; go to the Arctic. The other thing about it is, if I was really trying to understand ecosystem dynamics, the Arctic is the perfect place to visit because it is so simplified and so heavily stressed. It just lays itself out. If you want to look for relationships, there they are, right in front of you. The whole ecosystem is so easily readable. So few things can survive there that you can readily see how they have adapted to it and why. There are not many alternatives or buffers in the ecosystem. That's why there are boom and bust cycles in wildlife populations up there.

In 1983, Connie and I volunteered for the Ontario Breeding Bird Atlas project. We surveyed two areas along Hudson Bay and James Bay. Then in 1986, I traveled to southern Baffin Island and hiked in Auyuittuq National Park. I spent a week walking through a canyon with 5,000-foot walls. I hiked 50 miles—a rugged hike up and down this gorge. For the second part of that trip, I flew to Resolute and then north to Ellesmere Island. Having been right on the Arctic Circle in Auyuittuq, I was now 1,000 miles above it in the most northern land in the world. That was when I began to expand my horizons.

❧

THE ARCTIC is one of the few places that you can go where on the right days there is no sound.

Self-portrait on Bylot Island snowfield in Nunavut, Canada, 500 miles above the Arctic Circle, July 1988. Photo courtesy of William K. Volkert.

In July 1988, I flew up to Pond Inlet on northern Baffin Island. This was when I was waiting to hear about the Horicon job.

My gear doesn't make the transfer in Ottawa, so I have to wait three days for it to arrive. In the meantime, an Inuit family has me stay with them. My guide is Sheatie Tagak. He tells me later me that his wife is a little scared having this bearded white man in their house, but we all get along well. They move their kids out and give me the bedroom.

It's 24-hour daylight up there in summer because we're 500 miles above the Arctic Circle, so the midnight sun is not just along the horizon but quite high in the sky. One day, I walk beyond the village for the longest time and come back to the house at 3:00 a.m. I am tiptoeing in, and as I open the door I find the entire family sitting around watching TV! The village has just received a satellite connection so this is new for them. At the time, all I think is, "Don't you ever sleep?" These people don't have the sense of time as we do since the days are endless.

When my gear finally arrives, Sheatie and I head off by snowmobile and *komatik*—a big sled—on a trip to Bylot Island, just off the northern coast of Baffin Island in Lancaster Sound, where the biggest population of narwhals in the world migrates through. We camp together for four nights. One night, he bags a seal when we're getting out near the floe edge where there is open water. I shoot some pictures, and he looks up at me and says, "You not from Greenpeace?" He laughs. He butchers the seal, lays it down almost next to my tent, and says, "This to keep the polar bears away."

"That close?" I ask.

"We want to make sure they think there's only one food source in the camp." And he laughs again. I think it strange to bait polar bears into our camp, but he is a survivor and has a knowledge of the Arctic that we can barely appreciate.

The next day, we're traveling along the floe edge, which is just amazing because I am sitting in this open sled and there are scads of birds—just flocks like I rarely see—flying up and down the open water, mostly thick-billed murres [*Uria lomvia*]. We then visit a seabird colony with 75,000 nesting pairs of [black-legged] kittiwakes [*Rissa tridactyla*] and murres. Unbelievable. We spend several hours there, and we're sitting beneath the cliffs, which rise 1,000 feet straight up. Sheatie tells me, "You know, I don't climb the cliffs because I'm afraid of heights."

I say, "Well, you know, you're not getting me up there either."

He says, "People go up to collect eggs."

Next thing I know I hear him shouting, and he's 75–100 feet up these cliffs! And he yells, "The birds just starting to lay their eggs. Another week, we collect them."

When he comes down, I say, "I thought you didn't like to climb the cliffs. You were way the hell up!"

He says, "I don't climb like some people. I'm afraid."

I ask, "What do you mean, some people?"

He replies, "They go way up." He then tells me that the previous year someone from his village fell over 400 feet but landed in a deep snow bank and survived.

Next we climb up on a low dome of rock, and everything around us is a sheer cliff face. Sheatie says, "Let me borrow your binoculars." He starts looking around and then says, "I see a polar bear! Look, a big male!" He's almost a mile out, but he says, "We can't get out there. The ice is too rough." I am disappointed, but as we look at the bear, Sheatie then says, "I go to komatik." I tell him I'd be down soon. Birds are nesting right next to me, and I want to shoot more pictures. As I'm clicking away, I hear him yell, "Polar bear! Polar bear!" I am up against a rock wall with nowhere to go. He's down below with the bear on one side and the komatik out on the ice.

What does he do? He keeps yelling, waves his hands, and runs past the bear as I'm sitting there astonished. "What is he doing?" He's going to the sled, where he left his rifle, but fortunately, the bear actually turns and runs away from him.

When I come down from the cliffs, he's laughing. He says, "You wanted me to find you a bear."

I say, "I think he found you!" He then tells me about polar bear behavior and some of his other bear encounters. As I am standing there talking with him, I see the bear over his shoulder coming back towards us. He is climbing up a large block of ice and sniffing the air. I grab my camera and start clicking away. I'm thinking, "Man, this is great. Come a little closer." All of a sudden, three gunshots ring out, and the bear's running away. I am upset since I've never seen a polar bear before. I ask him why he did that because I was just starting to get good pictures.

"Well, I thought the bear was too close."

"Well, you should know," I reply.

"You never see bear?"

"Nope, and now you scared him away."

He then says, "Quick, get in komatik. We go after him."

Bill and Sheatie Tagak on the Arctic's floe edge—where the ice meets permanently open water. They lean against Sheatie's *komatik*—driven by snowmobile over the ice. Sheatie had to use a snowmobile because of a distemper epidemic that had killed most of the dogs in his village. July, 1988. Photo courtesy of William K. Volkert.

So we actually chase him down the ice for about half a mile as I'm sitting in this open sled, with the bear running parallel to us. Sheatie is careful enough to get close to the bear and then back off when he becomes agitated. After this, we turn around and start traveling west along Bylot Island. After a while, we come to an open crack in the ice. From the air, when I was flying in, you could actually see these big cracks, some of them running for miles. Now, they are starting to shift a bit with the tidal movement so they are harder to negotiate. Anyway, he pulls up to the edge, turns the snowmobile, and the sled creaks to a halt. "Stay here," he says as he unties the rope and throws it across a 12-foot-wide open crack. He then jumps on his snowmobile and leaves. Says no more.

I'm thinking, "What's he doing now?" He rides off a good hundred yards and turns around. He revs up his snowmobile and is coming at me at high speed. I think, "You're not going to jump this are you?" All of a sudden he flies by me at over 40 miles per hour. *Phoom!* Right over this opening. "Wow! That's a good trick," I think. "Well, you got over. What about me?"

He then comes back and says, "You sit in komatik and hold on good."

I'm thinking, "We're going to do what?" You see, below us is 800 to 1,000 feet of water. As I look down, the water isn't even blue anymore; it's black. I'm thinking, "I can swim, but I also have 300 pounds worth of gear—all my camping gear and food for five weeks—everything I need and I can't lose that."

He re-ties the sled to the snowmobile and starts off. The sled inches forward and then it pitches a little bit, starting to go down. I am hanging on, and all I see is this black water on both sides. Then, the skis catch the edge of the ice. He pulls the sled up, and we're bridging the gap. As he pulls it a little further, the back end of the sled drops. It's just hanging on the edge. I look back, and he's skidding on the ice, giving it all he's got. Then just like that, the sled tilts forward, slides away, and I see that crack disappear behind me. I think to myself, "We are really pushing the limit now! No one will believe what we just did!" I later realize that for me we are indeed living on the edge. This guy—he does this every day!

We cross five more cracks the same way that day.

After 125 miles of travel, Sheatie drops me off on Bylot Island, where I camp alone for 10 days. He then brings my wife, Connie, to my camp. I want her to see the bird colony, polar bears, and walruses that I had seen along the floe edge, and I tell him, "I'll pay you extra money. Can you take Connie and me out to the floe edge to see the narwhals and the birds?"

He says, "No, I can't. I was out hunting there just two days ago. The ice was bad, really bad. I can't take you."

And then, I think, "What does a guy like you call bad ice?"

Self-portrait taken at 3 a.m. on Ellesmere Island "under a brilliant sun"—the day Bill walked 41 miles in one trek—"the longest hike of my life!" July, 1986. Photo courtesy of William K. Volkert.

CHAPTER ELEVEN

Later, I talked to a fellow back in the village, and he said, "You're lucky that you got out as much as you did with your Inuit guide because most of these guys will never take you out to see much of this, and they'll certainly never take you hunting because when he gets out there on that ice, he needs somebody who can not only pull his own weight but knows what he's doing. He doesn't need you; you're a burden. So consider yourself very lucky!" I did.

I also considered myself very fortunate to be alone for 10 days out there. Essentially, I had a 60-mile long island to myself. It's a large island with a mountain range running down the middle with 6,000-foot peaks.

One day, I hike up to the ice fields 2,000 feet up from my camp and cross over the snow for an hour and a half until the snow becomes too deep. Big boulders appear, thawing out the snow, and as I sit on top of one of those, the wind stops. Looking back over the horizon, I can only see this endless snowfield—nothing but snow and one set of tracks that end right where I am. I remember taking a deep breath, holding it, and straining my ears. There literally is no sound to be heard—nothing. In fact, the only thing I hear is my own heartbeat. I'll never forget that feeling. There are few places on Earth where you can experience total silence.

*

I HAD ANOTHER EXPERIENCE in the far north I'll never forget. When I went to Ellesmere Island in 1986, I went for a hike the first day there.

I really want to see a muskoxen, so I walk about eight miles, and my luck— here are two muskoxen on a hillside. I remember talking to David Gray before my trip. He's a muskoxen social biologist who told me that one of the biggest problems in studying them is that at the sight of humans they'll often start running. It'll take a week to find them.

So I'm thinking, "I better take my time because I don't want them to just get up and run." So I'm sitting there watching these muskoxen, when I look off to my left side. There, far away, I see a white animal approaching. Well, that's kind of cute, here comes an Arctic fox. Cool! All of a sudden, he comes out of a ravine, and I realize this is actually a wolf—pure white! He walks up to the top of the hill and comes down toward the muskoxen because muskoxen like to defend themselves from the top. "He's going to cut them off. This guy's clever," I think. As I sit there, I get a photo across this little valley, muskoxen and wolf, nose to nose. There's barely five feet between them. And then, the wolf turns around, tacks over this hill, and disappears. I think, "Okay, great. If the muskoxen will sit still for a wolf, maybe they'll sit for me. I can move in to get a closer look and maybe get some really good photos." I remember thinking, "What a stupid wolf. I'm sitting here watching this whole drama and he's so fixated on these muskoxen that he doesn't even see me."

So I walk down the hillside. I cut across a little creek and climb up to a plateau before the top of the hill, where the muskoxen are. As I approach, they stand up and I get one bad picture of their backends. I start to walk around to get a better photo, and I look over to my right side. There's the wolf standing there! And I'm now right between the wolf and muskoxen.

This wolf not only saw me, he knew which way I was headed. He knew the lay of the land, went over the hill and cut down to the main river. When I crossed the creek, he came back up the ravine and circled right around behind me! So the first thought that goes through my mind is, "Well, it's never been documented in North America that anybody's ever been killed by a wolf." I look around and think, "Who's going to document it? There's nobody here!" Besides that, they may not attack a person, but I'm standing by *his* muskoxen. I look like the calf of the herd. I start backing off, but the wolf starts following me. I have the camera around my neck with a 400 mm lens on it, and I never take another picture. I am staring right in the face of this wolf, and he just keeps slowly walking, following me.

I back up for 200 yards, and he's still coming, slowly, cautiously. Then, suddenly, he turns around and leaves. Whew! So do I, but I am looking over my shoulder for the next three miles.

Looking into the face of that white wolf was extraordinary, just unbelievable. He just wanted to see who I was. That's all. If he truly intended to kill that day, I wouldn't be here to tell this story.

❧

I'VE HAD SOME WONDERFUL experiences in Wisconsin, too—maybe not as dramatic, but profound nevertheless. One of the most vivid ones occurred when I was with my oldest brother. It's when I knew, or felt, that there was something bigger, more mystical in nature.

CHAPTER ELEVEN

In 1972, we were canoeing the Bois Brule in Douglas County. It was springtime. The ice had just broken. We had paddled for several hours and were coming toward the end of our trip, right near Highway 2. My brother dropped me off and said, "I have to go back and get the car."

It is one of those days where there is still snow on the ground, a real chill in the air, but the sun is warm so you can actually sit outside. I just sit there on the bank of the river knowing I have time to kill. I watch the river flow past and stare at the snow on the side of the river dripping into it, mesmerized. All of a sudden, I begin to see a tremendous volume of water flowing by—the accumulation of all these little drops entering it from the land—and it's not just this day's melt but a continual melt and constant flow.

I look downstream to where this water is flowing and then up to see the open horizon beyond the trees. Lake Superior lies there—this incredible volume of water being fed by all of these streams and rivers comprised of countless droplets. Of course, all of that water is part of a hydrologic cycle, from evaporation to precipitation, but I find myself sitting literally in the middle of this great circle, from the tiniest little drops feeding this river, to all of these rivers flowing to this lake. Here is this vast reservoir where the water is drawn up and falls back onto the land as tiny snowflakes. It is a complete circle, and it flows all around me.

It is one of these experiences when all of a sudden time just stops for me in a beautiful, unexpected moment of awareness. This was a peak experience of sorts.

There is a book by psychologist Abraham Maslow called *Religions, Values, and Peak-Experiences*. In it he suggests that the religious leaders of the world are those who had profound peak experiences and want to share their insights with others. He spells religion with a small and capital *R*. Capital *R* is organized religion attempting to try and share with others these personal experiences of the divine. Small *r* is religion for those who find something mystical or spiritual for themselves in the world around them. Basically, there are a lot of people who are extremely religious and never go to a church, and that's where I put myself. I'm not a Christian. I don't see Christ as any different from Buddha, Muhammad, Lao Tzu, and so on. They're all similar in some way—the same thing in a different culture and time. I still can't figure out why these religions keep fighting each other around the world in the name of God. To me, that has always been one of the oddest paradoxes in human history. I would have to say if there's any temple or church, it lies somewhere in a good walk in the woods, whether it's here or somewhere far away.

I can best relate to the Taoists. I enjoy the ancient writings by Lao Tzu and Chuang Tzu. What I like about them is that there is no name for God. As soon as you start to name it God, it loses its meaning. Take a look at the cycle of the seasons, the intricate interrelationships in nature. They constantly reoccur. Spring ephemerals emerge, the birds migrate, this incredible harmony, these patterns, this interrelationship. Let's just leave it right there. In other words, if you're going in pursuit of God, forget trying to find God because you're not going to see it. Just follow footprints. There's enough evidence. To me, it's just nature, and that's something I think is easier for most people to accept. You can call it God if you want; I don't. And I do that because I've had such a strong difference with institutionalized religion. It has never been a source of answers for me.

If I believe in anything at all, it's probably not what most think. I've long been fascinated with the Buddhists and my friends, the Buryats. These are the northern Mongolian people of the Buryat Republic in southern Russia. They live around Lake Baikal. First of all, there's a genuine quality to their religion with a strong tradition, a cultural root. Take my good friend, Valeriy Golgonov, formerly director of the Natural Resources Agency in Russia, now secretary of state. He works for the president of the republic. Here's a person academically trained, an administrator, a government official, but when we took him to Lake Superior during the ride to Madeline Island in the Apostle Islands, without saying a word, he rolled down the window, reached in his pocket, and threw a coin out. He kept on talking, but I knew what he was doing. That was a sacred site for him, and the coin was his offering. It was more than a superstition to him; this was a necessary ritual.

When we travel across Siberia, we are obligated to stop at sacred sites and leave an offering like a little bit of money or candy or a tobacco offering for the Indians. This has been something that these people have been doing for thousands of years, and it's a unique relationship they have with the land.

I don't know if there's something bigger going on beyond what we see in the seasons' cycles. But the Buryats see the world in an entirely different way, which intrigues me. I'll tell you some interesting stories. Believe this as much as you want, or not. I'm not saying I'm totally convinced either.

In 1992, we are going over a mountain pass in southern Siberia toward Lake Baikal. At the top of the pass is a sacred site. We always stop here. We leave a little offering, and commonly I pull out my pocketknife and shred a handkerchief to make a prayer cloth and tie it to a tree, and that remains there as a symbol of your hopes, wishes, dreams, or prayers.

Here we are, coming up to a site I know very well. We have a driver who is Russian, not Buryat. He says, "We're coming up to the sacred site. Do you people want to stop?"

We say, "If you want to stop, that's fine."

He says, "No, no, you have to understand. I'm not Buryat, I'm Russian. I'm Russian Orthodox. I don't believe in their traditions. But, if you want to stop, we can. Otherwise, I'll drive by."

We say, "Look, you're the driver, do what you wish. If you don't want to stop then go ahead." This is all happening through a translator, and we're in a bit of a rush. So we decide to pass by the sacred site. Literally, 150 yards past the crest of that hill, we blow out the back tire, right off the rim. He jerks his head around and says, "Spirits say we've got to stop." And we all laugh a nervous laugh—very weird.

Okay, once is a coincidence, but twice is suspicious. I went again to Baikal in 1996, invited by my friend Valeriy. He said for everything I'd done, if I could find a way to get to Russia, he'd pay for me to do whatever I wanted for as long as I wanted to stay, which was a heck of an offer. I went for four weeks, and [former WDNR Secretary] George Meyer gave me permission to do that, but without any financial support. I told Valeriy that I wanted to camp for a week on the shores of Lake Baikal, and I wanted to hike to the top of Svyatoy Nos peninsula. So he made all the arrangements for me. He even gave the van driver a week off just so I had somebody to take me up there. My personal guide was the vice director of the national park, and he found a translator for me, too. It was amazing.

So on the ride up, we stop at a river where there's a sacred site. On the way back, it's eleven o'clock at night, as black as can be, cold, and it's raining. I am with a Buryat family and my Buryat driver. The driver says, "We're coming up to a sacred site, but it's really lousy weather, and it's very late. Should we stop?" So we talk it over and decide that maybe we shouldn't because it's so late. I am sitting in the front seat.

As we're driving along, I look up and there's a big coil of wire right in the middle of the road! He tries to swerve, but it literally wraps itself around the drive shaft and jams up the van. We have to crawl out onto the wet road, lie on our backs, and rip this wire out. Of course, these people are absolutely convinced that we had to stop there. The gods are trying to tell us so. I look at my friends with a look that says "You really believe that?" But, when you ask such a question, you already know the answer because there's a deep-rooted belief that this is so, no question about it. I may be somewhat skeptical, but I am also a witness to these events.

A site is made sacred when it's in an area where freshwater springs come to the surface, typically near rivers and where the watershed divides at high promontories. Interestingly, that is exactly where our Native Americans built their effigy mounds. Same sacred sites. This is where the spirits dwell. There's power in the land. People will actually tell you they can feel it. I feel a sense of respect as a visitor, as a guest in that culture. I have also experienced something else though that makes me think that the Buryat people have a connection with something that is foreign to our culture and our way of thinking.

One of my good friends and translators Svetlana Zherebtsova, who's been to Wisconsin several times with groups, is a kindred spirit. I once had to take her and the minister of forestry for Buryatia to northern Wisconsin to meet with our foresters. We were driving along, and I don't remember the conversation, but she very casually remarked that everything in life is 50/50. There's the world we see and the world we don't see. She said that and kind of shrugged it off as a matter of fact, as a matter of reality we all know, but we don't think that way. There's a whole other world equal to what we see. They see the world in an entirely different way than we do.

Let me tell you one more experience from my time in Siberia.

I am traveling with a Russian delegation to the Sayan Mountains along the Mongolian border when I start getting headaches. I'm thinking it might be from exhaust fumes from the Chinese van we're in. It turns out that I'm really sick from drinking contaminated water. We decide to stop along the way and I begin vomiting. This continues throughout the afternoon. Later in the day, they take me to a hotel somewhere. Svetlana, my translator, stays with me. By eleven o'clock at night she looks at me and says, "Bill, you're looking really sick."

I remember thinking to myself, "What do you mean, I look sick now? I've been feeling like hell the whole afternoon. Why now?" Apparently, I started really going downhill because of dehydration, so she calls for a transport to the hospital. In fact, it's only a van with a wooden bench on the side. I still remember that I can't even walk without hanging on to two guys. I can't stand up. They have to all but carry me down the stairs. They put me in this van, and I am so weak and nauseous that my head is spinning and pounding. I look up and see the road with deep ruts and puddles in it after the rain. I remember thinking, "No, no, don't drive down that. You're not going to go down that bumpy road!" Well, the driver pops the clutch, hits these puddles, and I twice roll off the van bench and across the floor and crawl up again. I'm like a piece of cargo back there.

They take me to a hospital and the doctors start giving me water. I think they want to see if I can hold it down. They are holding my head up. I can't even pick up my own head! I guzzle down about eight ounces, turn around, throw it up, and after about the fifth glass I am thinking, "Are you guys seeing a pattern? You pour it in, I throw up." So finally, they take me into this room, give me IVs to stabilize my system, and I stay the night.

The next day our group picks me up, and we go to another sacred site called Arshan. The entire five-acre forest is alive with prayer cloths. Every tree has dozens of ribbons around it, and there's this river they cup water from and offer it me. They say it has healing powers. Then they put me in this room, give me another IV, and the next morning they bring some porridge—the first solid food in almost three days. They take out the IVs, and I try to eat a few spoonfuls. I am so tired of lying around, I think, "I have to get up and move."

I begin to walk the hall of this large sanatorium, a health resort with mineral baths. I watch this old man walk by. He must have been in his 80s, and he passes me up!

I am hanging onto the walls when this nurse and an older Buryat woman begin staring at me. I see that they are talking to each other and pointing at me. I think someone had sent them to my room and I was gone. So this Buryat woman comes up to me, and she says something like, "Stop. Put your hands up." She starts feeling around my head, without even touching me, and then she starts to do these hand motions around my stomach, sweeping something away. Then she taps the floor and grabs my arm motioning me to come along. She takes me up to the fourth floor, and I am crawling up the stairs. She's really pleasant—a big smile—and the only words I understand are "medlina, medlina." Then, in another room, she gives me a full massage, chiropractics, and then performs these hand motions again, making circles around my stomach, sweeping away, and then she taps the floor and says, "I'm done. You can go." I reach in my pocket and try to leave a five-dollar bill on the table, but she wants nothing, as if to say, "This is my job; I'm only here to cure people." So I can't even give her a tip to express my gratitude.

Panoramic view of part of the shoreline around Lake Baikal. Summer 1992.
Photo by, and courtesy of, William K. Volkert.

I leave the room and go down the first flight of stairs, then come around to the second flight. Now, obviously it's easier to go down than up, but I literally stop in mid stride halfway down the second flight of stairs. I am bouncing down those stairs! I stop and look up the stairs and think, "What the heck was that about? What did she just do?" I feel strong, energetic, and I was in there less than 20 minutes!

When I re-join our group, I sit down for a huge breakfast. I have a great appetite, and here I could barely eat even a few spoonfuls of porridge less than an hour before.

So, you know, there's something going on here. These people have a connection to something very unique that is difficult to put into words. Maybe that's why I'm really taken by the Baikal region because it's not just the lake—a wonderful natural resource—but it's also the people who have a unique relationship with it. I believe that they will protect this lake because it's sacred, a living entity to them.

In a toast I once gave the Russians, I said this: "I remember standing on the mountains above Baikal and looking out when it was perfectly calm, just like glass. Looking at that lake, we not only look into its depths, but from the surface it mirrors something of ourselves. In a sense, Baikal talks to us because we're seeing both the lake itself and ourselves in it. It is my belief that if we can't save Baikal, I don't think we can save ourselves."

CHAPTER ELEVEN

I think the entire culture and the Buryat people are tied to Baikal. So their environmental ethic is not just a feel-good type of ethic, it's the root of their cultural origins. Also, I would have to say that my experience with the Buryat people has influenced my thinking toward the land. At times, the things I keep seeing and feeling when I'm out on the land have had an increasingly spiritual quality to them.

In a more humorous vein, when they toast, the Buryats will always take the ring finger of the left hand, use it to sprinkle vodka in the four cardinal directions, or pour a little on the ground or both, because the first offering is always to the spirits. The first time I took the Russians through Wisconsin, we got within sight of Lake Superior and Valeriy tells me to stop emphatically! I'm right in the middle of this two-lane busy highway on a Monday morning as people are heading to work. I ask the translator why he wants me to stop. "Is there something we missed?"

She says, "I don't know, he doesn't say." And then finally she says, "Just stop anywhere."

I pull over to get out of traffic and Valeriy says, "Bill, you have to understand, this is our first sight of Lake Superior. This is your sacred lake, like Baikal. It reminds me of home. We have to toast with the gods." He places a bottle of vodka on the dashboard of the DNR van I'm driving.

I panic and say, "Okay, Valeriy, I understand your traditions, but I'm not going to sit here in a DNR van on a public highway and open a bottle of vodka!"

So I find a dirt road where we can get out. Valeriy borrows my hat, because you do not expose your face to the gods. You humble yourself. He sprinkles vodka around. We have a small ceremonial drink and put away the cups. I then say, "Just do me one favor. Don't ever tell George Meyer that we were driving around in a DNR van drinking vodka on the roadsides!"

❧

MY EXPERIENCE with the Buryat people reminds me that so many people in our society live too distant from the land. I'm lucky that Connie and I have a piece of land to interact with daily. We've been working on our land since 1983, and over the years I have watched the trees grow, and I've cut others down. I feel differently when I have a chainsaw in my hand these days. I used to be quite reluctant to cut anything, but now I know what

I'm going to cut and what I'm not. I've learned how to manage our land. Leopold said something to the effect that the same tools that destroyed the land can be used to restore it. The problem is not that we have efficient tools, but we often don't know how to use them. Management is learning to live with the land. Connie has also become very involved in the work we do. We complement each other.

I got into prairie restoration as an ecologist and as an experiment. Connie's always had an intense interest in gardening and has a green thumb for growing almost anything. I like to watch a prairie grow, but she will actually cultivate plants from seeds and manage the sites intensively. We share experiences working the land here. Mostly she'll work on the prairie and I'll work in the woods. Sometimes I will drop my work to give her a hand with something, but we've got our own corners. So, there's both space for individual projects as well as things we do together.

We share a lot in common, and we travel well together. Quite honestly, I get a lot of people asking me, "Will she allow you to go to the Arctic or Siberia alone?"

"Yes, she does," I reply. And I encourage her to travel alone as well. In fact, six months after we got married, I helped put together a trip that she took on her own for nearly three months to Hawaii, New Zealand, and Australia.

I had people ask me, "So how's married life?"

"I don't know," I said, "I haven't seen her in two months!"

AFTER TRAVELING IN THE ARCTIC, learning about the far north and having some tremendous adventures, I wanted to learn more about birds around the world. While the Arctic is a wonderful wilderness, not too many animals live there. So in 1995 we took our first trip to Belize and Costa Rica in Central America. I was astounded by the variety of birds.

Over the years we continued to explore the tropics, making our way to Venezuela and eventually taking nearly 25 trips to visit most of Central and South America. I also wanted to learn about this complex ecosystem and see the many birds, but I wanted to explore South America in a methodical way. So we made plans for our trips to visit neighboring countries to see some familiar landscapes and build on those experiences. We worked our

Examining an elephant bird (Aepyornithidae) egg at a small local museum in southeast Madagascar. Elephant birds became extinct around 1000-1200 CE. Photo by Connie Ramthun, 2014. Photo courtesy of William K. Volkert.

way down the Andes, through Ecuador, Peru, and then Chile, Argentina, and Bolivia on subsequent trips. Once Colombia settled down and became safe to visit, we made two trips there as well.

I have come to realize that foreign travel can be intimidating, and many people are hesitant to go out of their comfort zone, but it also can be tremendously rewarding, and once you get over that reluctance, good travel can become habit forming. The more you see of the world, the more you want to see. The same holds true of birds for me. And I've often said that if you follow the birds, they will take you to some of the wildest, most beautiful places in the world.

Okay. That would have been a good place to end the chapter, but I can't end without including one story from Bill and Connie's 2015 round-the-world trip. The place: South African bush in Kruger National Park. The date: early October.

THE FIRST DAY OUT, Connie and I see this huge elephant coming down the road towards us. We back up five different times to give him room. He's towering over our little car. When we return to the camp that night, one of the staff says, "You want to respect the elephants, even in a car. You've got to give them room. Six months ago, we had Japanese tourists here, and they did not give any room to an elephant. He flipped their car over and destroyed it."

So I realize right then and there you have to respect these massive animals. Some of these bulls have actually developed a bit of an attitude toward people because of the high poaching rate. The survivors seem to be the ones that are more aggressive.

About four days later, we are driving down one of the dirt roads in the park. In Africa, there's what they call the big five: elephant, rhino, lion, leopard, and Cape buffalo. These are the five mammals that the tourists wants to see. The lion is especially big on the list. If you meet anybody who's sighted a lion, it's shared with everyone else.

Soon a car pulls up and the driver asks us if we are interested in seeing a lion. Two are resting just down the way.

Connie and I already had a good morning of birding, and it's getting hot. We drive over, and there's a small area to pull off. Sure enough we see two lions lying on their backs under some tall bushes. Not the best view, but good enough. After a quick look we decide to do a little more bird watching—something more rewarding. We drive from there and find a nice vulture roost with three species of vultures.

As we are driving back, we come across a large herd of elephants along the roadside—almost 20 of them, including three small young. We cautiously drive past them. We drive a short distance when we realize that we are at the turn-off where the lions occur. It is the middle of the day and close to 100 degrees, and we decide to go down and see them. Sure enough, they are still there lying on their backs. We take a few pictures and then decide to go down the road and take a break—to a dead end with a 30-foot drop to a dry riverbed.

We pull under a big shade tree, roll down the windows, decide to have a little snack in the car, and put the seats back to relax a little bit.

As we are sitting there, I hear this trumpeting of an elephant really close behind us. When I sit up, I'm getting ready to turn around to see what's going on. I look in the rearview mirror, and here I see this male lion bounding down the road right toward the car! I can see its mane moving up and down, like something out of a Tarzan movie. "Oh my gosh!" I exclaim (not my exact words). "We've got a lion coming up on the car! He's charging us!" Then I suddenly realize we have the windows rolled all the way down! So we quickly put them up, and he walks right to the car. He stands there— barely 10 feet from the side of the car. People will drive days hoping to see a lion halfway across the savannah, and here is one right next to us!

He passes slowly by the side of the car and then walks down the ravine, toward this dry riverbed, and disappears. Connie and I are both astounded by the experience. "There's no way we can top that!" I say. Just as I say that, I sit back in the seat and look up in the rearview mirror again. I see a large herd of elephants coming up the road. There are six to eight elephants across, 18 in all, and they are coming right at us! I quickly think back to giving elephants respect, giving them room. We are on a dead-end road with a 30-foot drop off ahead of us. The only way out is the way we came in, and the elephants have us blocked in. I then realize what had happened: The elephants were roaming around, grazing for the morning, with these young

Herd of elephants coming Bill and Connie's way. Photo courtesy of William K. Volkert.

ones mixed in the herd, and stumbled across these lions. They trumpeted to chase them away. After the lions left, the elephants started to come our way.

So we sit in the car as they approach, and I remember Connie asking me, "Should we put our seatbelts on?"

"Well, you can, but I don't know what good it's going to do!" I replied, laughing.

"Well, then what are we going to do?"

"We're going to sit in the car quietly, cross our fingers, and hope nothing happens! It's up to them. I can't do anything!"

At this point the matriarch is right behind our car. They are looking for a place to continue their walk and their grazing. I realize that elephants are rather top-heavy. They can't go down a real steep incline. The only decent path to the riverbed is right behind the car. So we sit there as they shuffle around right by our car. The whole incident takes about 25 minutes. Finally, she starts making her way down a path, a very short distance behind the car. We look out the back window, and one after another they all slowly start to follow.

When the entire herd has just about passed, I look to the side and here are three young bulls. They just don't like something about this situation. I remember one of them actually walking toward us, shaking his head and trunk and flapping his ears—a sign of aggression. I am thinking, "Oh boy, this guy does not like this! Something has got him nervous. He's young but still four times the size of our car. I've got to try and do something." I remember saying to Connie and the elephants, "Okay, let's be calm."

I turn the key and start the engine, and fortunately the elephants don't react. I don't want them to panic and charge. So I put the car in gear and start slowly moving along this turn-around clockwise. As I do so, I give them the clearance they need, and the last three pass without any further incident. Pretty amazing!

During our travels we saw and experienced so much, but this was one of the top experiences for this grand trip. That's the fun of birding; you never know what else you might find! ※

LeRoy Lintereur
(1920-1995)

Examining a catkin on a beaked hazelnut *(Corylus cornuta)*.
"No one should step outdoors without a hand lens," says daughter Judith.
Photo courtesy of Judith Lintereur Johnson.

TAMARACK TWIG WITH NEEDLES AND CONES

Chapter Twelve~
LeRoy Lintereur

I cannot imagine the misery that would be mine were I to give up my dream of knowing as much as possible about the natural world.
—LJL, July 8, 1994

If there was ever a person destined to be a naturalist, it was LeRoy Joseph Lintereur, who embraced the moniker with relish. Born November 22, 1920, in Two Rivers, Wisconsin, to a German mother and a French-Canadian father, he was remarkably skilled at observing and describing the natural world. What he had in common with the best of Wisconsin naturalists past was a fastidious attention to detail and nothing less than an obsessive desire to understand and describe the biodiversity in locales he frequented, in his case in northeastern Wisconsin and Michigan's Upper Peninsula.

LeRoy recorded what he observed in personal journals that he used as a basis for over 700 written essays and articles published locally. Extraordinary were the breadth and depth of these typewritten journals—26 volumes in total, over 3,000 pages—entries written almost daily, certainly weekly year-round from 1963 until October 8, 1995, the day before he passed away. (He first began tinkering with journal writing when in his early 20s.) These journals not only convey the careful, detailed observations of natural history observations at marshes, bogs, fens, old growth woods, rivers, estuaries, sandscapes, pine barrens, grasslands, and along roadsides, but they contain far more—poignant descriptions of his relatives and townspeople, farm life, commentaries on habitat changes to sites he frequented over the years, and philosophical musings influenced by Darwin, Thoreau (Henry in his journals), the French scholar Jean Jaurès, the monastic Thomas Merton (TM), philosopher and geologist/ botanist and Jesuit priest Pierre Teilhard de Chardin (PT), and his political heroes, Abraham Lincoln and Franklin Delano Roosevelt.

LeRoy was the oldest of five children. Ruth followed in 1922, then Maryon in 1926 (with whom he grew especially close due to their mutual love of literature and writing), Donald in 1927, and Bernice in 1929. Among his older relatives, LeRoy became very fond of his grandmother (father's side) Hereaux, who arrived in America speaking only French, and who stubbornly cared to learn just a few English words in her lifetime. She lived in Green Bay, where she took him on forays to the public library to peruse the nature, history, and music sections. Libraries at Green Bay and Two Rivers became favorite haunts that he visited throughout his lifetime.

As a young lad growing up in Two Rivers. Photo courtesy of Judith Lintereur Johnson.

Growing up in Two Rivers (TR throughout his journals) first on 16th Street, then on 20th Street, only a stone's throw from the West Twin River, afforded ample time to explore the marshes and nearby shores in a wooden skiff he dubbed "The Seaweed." So began his love affair with wetlands and his abiding search to understand its flora and fauna. He took great delight in his discoveries, no matter what age. On October 8, 1993, after an outing somewhere in Marinette County, he wrote:

> I traversed creek no. 2, it still has a trickle of water. A hope of tracks, other than deer and raccoon, mink, perhaps or even otter—none. But two wild duck, near the river now, went shrieking down the stream. They are dark, but noted a flush of red, almost the first ducks to come out of eclipse. Then the prize. I seldom lift logs or disturb ground

shelter, but there's this inviting piece of bark. I lifted it carefully hoping for ants—lo, in a slot between two chips, was a blue-spotted salamander [*Ambystoma laterale*]. The cold was getting to it; there was no effort at escape, and when I lifted it, the sensation was chill, like a hand thrust in snow. It seemed quite thin, nothing plump about it whatsoever; one can hope it finds a well-insulated site, not too cold, and that next season on a glorious day in late winter, when the pools thaw just a little, in what it sees as life all over again, it may crawl to the edge of a pool, and either set out a little cone of sperm, or grasp one, whatever the case may be. And that hundreds of years from now, its progeny will cozy up under bark in this very woods, proclaiming that *life* still lives, that it is one, and that the world will always need salamanders [and] the cover they demand if it is to survive. The opposite is too awful to contemplate.

LeRoy, early on, did not much care for institutional schooling, neither in grade school nor high school, but one cannot fault his thinking. When at the St. Luke's Grade School, he was relentlessly bullied and abused by Catholic nuns because of his heritage. LeRoy wrote painfully of his time at St. Lukes, experiences that haunted him throughout his life and which affected his self-esteem. Remembering this period 61 years later, as if it happened yesterday, he wrote these entries on back-to-back days:

November 22, 1992

So, anyway, made it to 72; the same kid who looked out the window in the 5th grade at St. Lukes. That would be 1931, under SR [Sister] Eustachia's lash. I look longingly out the windows and wonder if ever I would get out from under this terrible tyranny and join those fellows in the factory. How I hated that grade, and all the rest of them also. Wonder how many psychic [psychological] marks I, [and] all of the poor students, carry from those dreadful, fear-filled years.

When, in the 8th grade, SR Florian would stomp the floor in nunnish fury, and in one black streak head for my desk, shouting to the class, "That darn Lin-ter-er!" I would all but collapse in dread. When it came time to have the class picture taken, she had told me I would not graduate....

They had told us how tough the teachers would be in high school, and when Lile Watkins our English teacher treated me kindly and remarked on my fondness for literature, I did not know how to respond. All I knew of teachers is that when they came near—duck!

November 23, 1992

The sisters who taught me were mainly from German rural areas in central Wisconsin. Their Mother House was in Fond du Lac. I think they had a dislike of all French people, and despite my German ancestry, some of that descended upon me. They could never pronounce my name, and from the 4th grade on I ended up in a far corner where those cast into exterior darkness were stuck and forgotten. Coincidentally, all had French names, and not coincidentally, most vanished before the 8th grade, transferred to other schools, and then to vocational school. Anyway, we were an interesting lot, and some I recall fondly—Tety La Fleur, who ended up with a little rug-weaving business on the east side.

That some were woefully ignorant cannot be questioned. I recall a girl, she was sort of awkward, the poorest of the poor in this depressed blue-collar town. Some there could not live in conventional flats, but rather existed in rented basements, or made-over chicken coops that entrepreneurs created in backyards. Anyway, this girl could not understand, and when she would go to the board and stand there frightened witless, the sister would mock her: "Well, Mademoiselle, (actually, she said it with venom, this bride of Christ) don't you understand that one either?" She had a brother named Lawrence, who was a good sort, but finally the family just disappeared and no one knew where. There was no father.

But back to the 5th grade. We were given an assignment, an essay on a subject we had read, but with it went strict instructions. We were not to copy from any book we might have in our desks. Right up my alley. I had just finished a book on camels, and my head was full of them. I dashed off a paper on the difference between Arabian and Bactrian camels. First finished and with a flourish, and carried it in triumph to Sister's desk. The pets were still struggling to get something on paper. Sister read it, and her face darkened. She said in a threatening voice, "You were told not to copy!" I protested my innocence and was sent to the principal's office for this putative crime—so heinous.

Sister hustled me back to the class, where in consternation I noted that my desk was stripped down, and the exasperated Sister was complaining she could find nothing that I might have copied from. Well, wouldn't you know, I was kept after school, filling the blackboard with "I must not copy." But most miserable was to listen to the winner grope through a miserable reading, while my shredded effort was in the wastebasket....

From those days on, [I] cherished my Canadian ancestry like a fragile flower. Anything those characters despised had to, in my book, be good.... Gradually, I built up my own world. My father was from up north, a military hero in my eyes, and an all around nice guy. How could I be so fortunate? And he oriented me toward a fondness for the north, for forests and streams, marshes and lakes. That was the motif for my life and remains so to this day.

LeRoy took Latin in high school and learned to appreciate it, which led to a lifetime study of Linnaeus's binomial nomenclature and his subsequent common usage of Latin names for plants. His daughter Judith commented to me, "His attachment to it was already in place from the Catholic liturgy. Latin was a beautiful sounding language. He had to find out what 'they' were saying. When he did find out later, he said it sounded a lot better in Latin. Latin and Greek were both languages that showed up in taxonomic keys. He did later learn Greek, started with practice writing the alphabet. Those Latin and Greek names really did mean something descriptive to him."

Plowing fields in Tisch Mills, Wisconsin, ca. 1937. Photo courtesy of Judith Lintereur Johnson.

LeRoy dropped out of high school in his sophomore year—a decision he later regretted—and worked on a farm in Mishicot, and later at a farm in Tisch Mills where he plowed fields with horses and used them to remove logs and maintain roads. Throughout his life, when various circumstances led to a certain despondency, he would reflect back on those farm experiences with nostalgia and reverence. In his late teens and early 20s, he joined hundreds of other local laborers at the largest factory employer in Two Rivers: Aluminum Goods Manufacturing Company (later changed to Mirro Aluminum Company), known locally as "The Goods." Here, in a noisy and dusty work environment, he helped create pots and pans and other aluminum products.

LeRoy left the factory to enlist in the army in May 1942 and soon rose to the rank of sergeant, in charge of an ordinance unit at Gainesville, Texas. During this period, which lasted to war's end in 1945, LeRoy continued his readings and entertained his interest in observing wildlife, especially birds.

On October 17, 1992, LeRoy reflected on a seminal moment during his army service:

> What was the most defining of [my] life? I can't point to anything ... definite. Have an early memory of someone lifting me up in the entrance of an old school house, and holding a lantern aloft, show[ing] me some tiny birds, mouth agape. I would have been about six at the time. But more immediate, when I was about 24, and in the army, I struck up a friendship with Miller, the curator of the museum in Dallas. One morning we were sitting in his office, and he said to me, "Don't consider anything else but being a naturalist. You have the interest, and that's all it takes. If you can't get into college, get yourself a camera, practice writing and observing. That's all it takes. You'll do ok."

Newly enlisted, 1942.
Photo courtesy of
Judith Lintereur Johnson.

Returning home to Two Rivers after the war, LeRoy focused his energy on resuming his scholastic career and found a college that would accept someone without a high school diploma—St. Norbert's College in DePere, Wisconsin. His sights, however, were set on the University of Wisconsin-Madison, and he transferred there a year later in 1949, rooming for a brief time with George Becker, who later taught ichthyology at the University of Wisconsin-Stevens Point and wrote *Fishes of Wisconsin.*

In fall 1949, still a UW student, he married Joyce Copeskey, whom he had met at The Goods, and they moved into a housing unit near Baraboo called Badger Village. He was really not sure any woman would ever have him.

Though a man of modest height and rugged good looks, he did not take kindly to his outward appearance, a regular theme throughout his writings, perhaps influenced by his childhood years, remarking once that he cringed when observing his reflection in a department store window. In 1981, he wrote: "A description of myself—totally nondescript from head to foot. A face dominated by a bald head and red nose. The chin, as if nature said, 'We won't give him any,' and then at [the] last moment changed her mind. The relationship between neck and head, rather like a turtle, unless it be, say, a grotesque tulip. No chest, just enough room for a pocket. An ass best described as huge. Legs knock kneed and crooked. Feet the flattest imaginable. I walk on the side of my feet. Our doctor at home burst out laughing when he saw them."

The following June 1950, the couple announced the birth of twins Judith and Julie.

While at the UW, LeRoy enjoyed the teachings and field trips of botany professor, Dr. Norman Fassett. (Fassett's successor, Hugh Iltis, later encouraged LeRoy's study of wetland plants.) LeRoy graduated with a degree in zoology in 1952. Son Daniel was born that year, followed by Gregory in 1954, and Philip in 1959. Each of his children would spend many a day in the field with him learning the names of plants, handling fox (pine) snakes, watching birds, turning over logs to snare salamanders, conquering a fear of spiders. And later, son Greg participated in deer and coyote surveys and woodcock, mourning dove, and ruffed grouse counts.

After graduation, LeRoy spent the summer working at the Badger Ordinance Plant in Madison, but his dream was to work for the Wisconsin Conservation Department, which later became the Wisconsin DNR. Late in life, on June 7, 1995, he looked back on this aspiration:

> I, an anachronism, still have a profound sense of belonging. It has been the lodestone for my life, indeed, the one and only reason why I'm here as a wildlifer. For surely my interest in wildlife via a fondness for the woods tradition that my father regarded as his own—he loved this northland, Canada, everything about it—this his true homeland that in a very real sense he never left. I never seriously considered living in any other place, somewhere in NE Wis, and when I conferred with Bill Grimmer, Chief of Game in the forties—this when I was a JR in college—and he a kind and gentle man asked, "Where would you want to be stationed?" There was no other possibility than my rejoinder: Marinette County. He looked at his map, pointed to a flag pinned into

Wausaukee, and said, "Well, there'll be someone there someday. Do well in school, take the tests, and keep in touch with us." This I did, and here I am in my mid-seventies still tied by a bond that was forged 70 years ago. This upper lakes has and always will be my life, and St. Léon and Quebec, too.

His determination paid off. He entered the Wisconsin Conservation Department in September 1952 as a conservation aide, moving his young family to the Burlington area. He continued reading and studying natural history and worked hard on menial tasks, such as posting public hunting grounds, mowing the grounds, fencing, and generally performing whatever was assigned to him. It wasn't long before his skills as a well-organized and skillful naturalist garnered praise, and he was promoted to assistant area game manager after two years.

In 1956, Bill Grimmer's words proved prophetic when LeRoy was given the game manager job at Wausaukee. Two years later, he was assigned to Marinette as area game manager, supervising all wildlife programs and staff for Marinette, Oconto, Shawano, Florence, and Menominee counties in northeastern Wisconsin until his retirement in 1983.

The new game manager in Marinette examining a black bear (Ursus americanus) skull, 1958. Photo courtesy of Judith Lintereur Johnson.

Notably, LeRoy's love of marshes, estuaries, rivers, and streams fueled his desire to protect Green Bay's west shore wetlands and sandscapes in Marinette and Oconto counties, leading to the creation of the 90-acre Seagull Bar Wildlife Area in 1959, the 1,300-acre Lake Noquebay Wildlife Area in 1960, the Seagull Bar State Natural Area in 1962, the Lake Noquebay Sedge Meadow State Natural Area in 2008, and ultimately to the DNR's Green Bay West Shores Project, with an acquisition goal of nearly 1,400 acres.

His drive to know as much as he could about the area's flora and fauna served him well when he was called upon to represent the DNR in a landmark case involving wetland protection. In 1967, he had been a Marinette County committee member that had drafted a county ordinance (Marinette County Shoreland Zoning Ordinance Number 24) defining a wetland as an "area where groundwater is at or near the surface much of the year and where any segment of plant cover is deemed an aquatic according to N.C. Fassett's *A Manual of Aquatic Plants*." Six months after the ordinance became effective, Mr. Ronald Just ignored the ordinance and filled in part of a wetland he owned along the shores of Lake Noquebay. Marinette County sued, and the case went all the way to the Wisconsin Supreme Court (*Just v. Marinette County*), where LeRoy's expert testimony proved pivotal in the 1972 decision upholding the county ordinance and preserving thousands of wetland acres in the state. The court opinioned "... swamps and wetlands serve a vital role in nature, are part of the balance of nature and are essential to the purity of the water in our lakes and streams. Swamps and wetlands are a necessary part of the ecological creation and now, even to the uninitiated, possess their own beauty in nature."

One could imagine LeRoy smiling when he read that part of the decision, but curiously, he makes no mention of this case in his journals. Instead, it was the DNR's 1977 legal battle with Scott Paper Company over the pollution of the Oconto River and Green Bay that he chose to note.

December 22, 1977

We point out that Scott [Paper Company] ... had a $10 million advantage when they polluted the river, but that's not enough—no money in it—so the river flows back, a stinking mess to the bay, where the shit is slowly strangling a lovely body of water.

I met all the lawyers coming out of the courthouse, all elegant in their business suits, headed for the three-martini lunch, which of course goes a long way toward making life bearable. I hope that on the way they would glance to the left at the river, where the corruption from their mill is now frozen into an ugly mess. Perhaps it might be just if this crap was painted onto their boardrooms and set in bowls in their dining room, wherever it may be....

Writing on December 12, 1992, he also said:

Recall one meeting with great relish. It was at Oconto, and along with Chamber of Commerce types, who were looking for a way out for Scott [Paper Company], I was state witness. Scott's lawyer was in full dress uniform, grey with white shirt and cuffs. He had the finest, longest fingers—pale and adroit in taking papers, one after another, out of a beautiful and expensive briefcase. [Then it was] my turn: "The entire Oconto below Stiles is an open sewer."

He: "Do you mean to tell me that you've inspected every inch of that river?"

Me: "No, but if Point X is swirling, then Point Y downstream is certain to be the same, and so on down to the bay.

He: "How do you identify pollution? You are no chemist."

Me: "No, but I do have a nose and can smell the stuff. Come on outside, everyone, and we'll take a sniff of the river."

He: "I wasn't expecting that type of testimony."

Me: "Well, no, I suppose, but can you argue it?"

[His] long white fingers creep all over the table gathering up papers. Meeting called off, and the next week Scott notified the DNR that they would, being a civic-minded group, acquiesce to the new [water quality standards] code.

But the legal quagmire Scott Paper Company found itself in was not resolved until 1979, when the DNR, joined by the EPA, settled with Scott out of court for one million dollars. The DNR was awarded over half of the settlement to implement a management plan to restore aquatic habitats along portions of the Oconto River and Green Bay polluted by Scott's paper mill, which Scott had shut down the year before.

From a less contentious perspective, LeRoy also took note of an obscure decision by Governor Tommy Thompson:

June 26, 1995

Praise the Lord, oh my soul, the Guv [Tommy Thompson] signed the Bloch option this noon, and all the land is now in public ownership. The guvs office called me at [about] 2:30 this afternoon, after I called them, fearful that the option would run out without being exercised. So we have a nice new tract of land in public ownership; now I hope we can protect it from our own developers.

June 27, 1995

Well, in a sense, the Bloch acquisition is the peak of my professional career at the [Peshtigo] Harbor [State Wildlife Area]. When I first got to know the project area, there were certain areas that it seemed were imperative [to protect]. The Bloch lands were high on the list, fine woods, and river frontage, but they were outside the project boundary, and my relationship with the family was not that great. They allowed their cattle to pasture our land—no fences—and there was once I drove them off the Singer tract; they were right down to the bay.

There are still two tracts I think we should get: the 40 [acres] south of the barn, which will certainly be a home site some day, and the Surk tract, an integral aspect of our wetlands complex. But all these are nothing compared to the Bloch lands. For some reason, they [the family] never exploited their woods, and the farm is such a pleasant sweep of fields, woods, and river frontage. The day will surely come when a society, hemmed in and needing a fine horizon, will find it here; the trend on all such similar in the county is to develop, and this trend will surely accelerate.

The interior of the Bloch lands stirred something almost primeval in LeRoy. On June 5, 1991, he wrote:

> The a.m. in Blochs, so windy and cold I went back for my jacket. Man, has the woods ever greened up. Stepping in, you've no idea what kind of woods it is, such is the wall of green. And we, or at least I, like to think of wild lilies as sort of prima donnas, but when you consider they, through *Maianthemum* [*canadense*, Canada mayflower], dominate the forest floor, with a little help from the various true and untrue Solomon's-Seal [*Polygonatum* and *Maianthemum*].... Imagine the O$_2$ floating up into the air from this woods. When young, I used to imagine the prayers ascending into heaven from our church, like steam from a street in the rain.

No less important to LeRoy were areas just across the state line in Michigan's Upper Peninsula, particularly a place (about five miles west of Carney) he called Carney Bog, one of his favorite all-time haunts, and a place to which he often retreated (with family or alone), prominently mentioned throughout his journals. In time, his name became practically synonymous with the place as he sought to publicize it through newspaper accounts, public lectures, and field trips—to protect it. Michigan wildlife managers and conservationists took note. On one Carney visit, a Michigan wildlife manager made an unexpected, urgent plea:

June 18, 1985

Yesterday to Carney Bog, on an ideal day, cool, high wind, spattering rain, a wonderful summer day. And some shocking news. Roger [Amundson] introduced me to a Mich wildlife mgr, a fine fellow, who wanted to discuss a most crucial matter with me. The Carney Bog is to be cut for timber, unless something is done about it, and he said it must come from me.... To the foresters wood is wood, and whether it be a bog unique with its plants and bugs, or a pine plantation makes no difference. "We need it." So there we sat, out in the meadow, while whitethroats sang in the tamaracks, and a wind sent the tufted cotton grass swaying, discussing our strategy to save the swamp from depredation by the resource person as **Vandal**, unthinking, destructive, only because before him there is only a cash balance sheet, bucks in his eyes.... Engineers versus the butterfly collectors. Who will win? I think we'd all better stay tuned.

Although LeRoy would not live to see it, he would have been delighted to know that the Michigan DNR legally dedicated and set aside the Carney Fen State Natural Area in 2009—an area 2,325 acres in size in Menominee County.

LeRoy, as with most renowned naturalists, was a creature of habit, who especially preferred alone time in the early morning hours while his family slept. As his early journals show, he would rise while the constellations were still bright, note what he saw, then he would go upstairs to his small study and start his journal entries, beginning sometimes with the previous night's dreams or with thoughts and reflections carried forward from the previous day. He would also transcribe tape-recorded observations from the day before, recall memorable moments, or type up the previous day's field notes.

Whether observing spiders with a hand lens, studying bees, birds, plants, snakes, shrews, and everything from ants to stars, LeRoy had an indefatigable love for it all, including both living and nonliving elements that comprised a landscape.

❧

I FIRST HEARD about LeRoy when working for the Wisconsin Department of Natural Resources (WDNR) as a nongame biologist in 1981. I knew that he was highly revered for his broad knowledge of the state's flora and fauna and was a much sought-after speaker. His colleagues within the WDNR's Bureau of Wildlife Management (BWM) often called upon him at statewide wildlife management meetings or on other occasions to present his views extemporaneously on a wide range of subjects. The late Steve Miller, former BWM director, described LeRoy as having the greatest impact on him of anyone in his profession.

In the early 1980s, LeRoy and I had talked occasionally over the phone about Forster's and common terns in the Green Bay area while I was planning statewide endangered tern surveys. In 1985, we finally canoed Oconto Marsh in search of breeding Forster's terns. It was a rewarding day with far-ranging discussions (some of which were captured by a tape recorder that I had lying on the bottom of the canoe). His typical field attire (worn that day), as noted by son Gregory, resembled that of a dairy farmer: striped bib overalls with a train engineer's cap to match. One time, when he and Greg

"Son Of The Soil" canoeing Oconto Marsh, Oconto County, 1985. Photo by Sumner Matteson.

were returning from a field trip, they stopped to have lunch. Greg smiled broadly in remembering the moment. Standing outside his car, LeRoy was approached by another man similarly dressed. "Oh my God," exclaimed the man, "another Son Of The Soil!"

A lifelong conservationist before the word was popular, this Son Of The Soil touched everyone who knew him. He led countless numbers of field trips for Audubon chapters, UW-Marinette, women's clubs, nature organizations, and after he retired, for Elderhostel groups. In many ways, he was and is Wisconsin's best kept secret—an extraordinary repository of natural history knowledge that endures through his writings and those he influenced. And he won't be forgotten by posterity. LeRoy is a member of the Wisconsin Conservation Hall of Fame, inducted April 30, 2016.

The writings that follow represent journal selections from each of the decades spanning the 1960s through the mid-1990s. These selections are organized by season and decade, beginning with winter. They reveal a man rooted in his faith but searching for an interpretation of God he could

Explaining deer browse to UW-Green Bay (Marinette campus) students at Eagle Creek Deer Yard, NE Wisconsin, 1971. Photo courtesy of Judith Lintereur Johnson.

embrace in all that he experienced in the outdoors. He was never quite satisfied. Throughout his journals, however, his passion and reverence for the natural world stand out as a beacon of hope and inspiration, transcendent and singularly lucent among the writings of Wisconsin naturalists.

Except for corrections to spellings and some punctuation (to make entries easier to read), and editing that shortened some passages, the entries selected here are as he wrote them. Some of these passages are also especially poignant, such as when he observes in spring the last remaining greater prairie-chickens in northeastern Wisconsin, and comments on the assassination of JFK—both in 1963. Or this especially emotional and evocative entry, presented here, and written November 4, 1992:

> A winter walk, with tatter of what was summer, fluttering, or swaying helplessly in the strong November wind. There's so much grim about this month: weather, poignancy for all that has vanished, sadness for a season lost. I think of all the emotions flesh is heir to; this is one issued to me in spades. Early on, I can recall the last night spent in the house on 16th Street, rocking in our big chair, singing sadly some hymn as I recall.

Then there's one I'll never forget:

> The big esker along 163, ripped up and hauled away when they improved the highway. I was unbelieving when it vanished and could not believe it when others marveled that I cared so much for a gravel

pit. From then on it's been one after another. Woods vanished, houses and barns torn down, even old stone fences disappearing. My world has always been slipping away, for as long as I can remember. I think my dad had it. Recall his exclamation when, after a long absence, he saw his favorite swamp timbered off. Uncle Nap[oleon] chided him: "Why, that was just an old swamp!" Not to my dad, though; he talked of it for the rest of his life.

I'm thinking of this because another came to mind this a.m. It was the old cemetery where I took frequent walks at this time of year. On a hillock, grown up and disregarded, there was a small stone, topped with a lamb and the simple inscription, "Georgia," and the year, "1912." Well, every year, right before Xmas, there was a bundle of balsam branches bound with red ribbon, placed, one can guess, with touching tenderness upon it. Then, inevitably the year came when some brother or sister who remembered a long lost sister, vanished.

Finally, the time came and the stone, too, disappeared. I searched and searched, but it was gone. Then, a couple of years ago, [I was] walking the ridge, [where there] was a dump where old stones were carelessly tossed, and there right on top was the little stone with the lamb upon it. The cemetery staff simply wanted to cut down the acreage they were responsible for. It really got to me, and for some time I thought to return it to the proper place, which I still recalled. But I did not, and am afraid to go back for fear it may be gone for good, and that's it. Anyway, it gets to me, and there's no sense attempting to explain it to anyone. This sense of irretrievable loss really hits me at this time of year; am always happy when the holidays are over and the new year begins.

❧

Winter 1960s

December 25, 1963

Christmas day, and like any happy one-half Frenchman and one-half German, I have been to Mass and am drinking wine with my family. A rather dull morning really, and I cannot help but contrast it with those so long gone by. We have, you see, no relatives in this city, and my children will never know the doting circle of aunts and uncles that I had in the city of my youth. Everyone on Christmas morning went to my Aunt Diana's (née

Lintereur) house. I can hear her voice now, rather loud over the din that only my relation could make. I would enter the house, no one would notice me until she spotted me in the crowd, and she would call out for me to come to her. I was, you see, her godchild; she was my sponsor, and it was she who chose my name, LeRoy Joseph, an odd combination surely, but she liked it. I had, over all the cousins, first pick from the candy dish, no small favor in these years immediately after Hoover's abolition of poverty. And there we would be, eating, us younger ones, the older drinking and kissing the younger cousins and the older ones, too, if I remember rightly. They all got home somehow. I suppose the religious overtones of the day were subordinate to its more secular aspects, if the term must be used, but for this day at least above all days, all worries and cares were forgotten.

December 26 and 27, 1964

To Two Rivers for weekend. Visit with [sister] Maryon and have fine discussion on Russian authors. Maryon certainly one of the most perceptive persons I know. She told me that her idea of a perfect novel is Jane Austen's *Emma*, which I will try to get a hold of.

January 4, 1969

This is the day of Lewis's woodpecker [*Melauerpes lewis*]. Lindberg saw it first and asked if I'd care to look the bird over. Indeed so, and this morning in the freezing cold we drove up to Porterfield. The place where the bird has chosen to spend the winter is a farm, with some apple trees, some oaks, and a row of pines. It hardly seemed worth the effort of coming this far east for. After all, I'm sure this could easily be duplicated in South Dakota.... But any[way], there the creature was, first quiet on an oak, and then in straight flight to another, and finally from one fence post to another, a delicate colored bird with a stout bullet-shaped body and a sense that he did not want to leave this farmstead, for whatever reason. The world's probably all the same for him, and if his inimitable Lewisness did not tell him different, he would probably do as well in Wisconsin as in the far West. Anyway, there he was, flying from fence post to orchard and then to white pine....

January 10, 1965

This morning out to Seagull Bar in a world utterly dead, or it seemed so until a flock of blessed snow buntings, certainly the most welcome and lovely of all our winter creatures, swirled out of a sedge meadow and circled about glittering in the pale sunlight and the freezing air. I don't know how much Greenland and the Arctic receives from us, but we certainly daily are presented with a priceless gift from them—all those who love our landscape, that is.

January 16, 1966

Florence County for the last two days looking over deer range.... We were in the Goodman timber, the country of the big hemlocks and maple, although at the rate they are going, there won't be much hemlock left. Too bad it doesn't have more value, and I might say too bad we don't have something to say about the harvesting of timber on private lands. A hemlock is more valuable than a deer, and when they are gone it will be for good. Imagine the north without its hemlocks.

Surprisingly, no birds. We saw two pileated woodpeckers and that was it. Not one single hawk nor grouse. The timber was a joy in itself, the towering maples and yellow birches—the favored ones are worth money—and the doomed hemlocks. Everything in these woods bears the imprint of deer. Not a young maple that does not have a scar or twist or torn off bud, and the shrub understory is almost gone. The swamps are loaded, but this is alder, a species they do not like. Deer, as much as the foresters, are going to determine the future of these woods.

January 25, 1969

Yesterday, Lloyd [Sebero, LL's field assistant] and I up to Long Swamp and the eastern part of the county. The county is cutting out the swamp where I found the orchids on the Mullaney Creek Road, and it is with sorrow that I note this. It would be absurd for me to go to John and say, "Look, you're ruining some good orchid habitat," because the orchids are not worth money, and the pulp now decked along side the road [is] waiting for its trip up to Green Bay to be ground up into toilet paper. I just wonder when the day will come, if ever, that orchids would be put on an equal par with toilet paper. I recognize the utility of both. It would be a happy day when the same can be said for society. Think of it. What values would have then come to the fore—a love of living things, all living things, a regard that goes beyond money, an antidote for all the woes that are going to bury man, something beyond the material, something that does only one thing—it exists and beautifies this world hidden, and therefor akin to God, or perhaps God himself, and behold He became all things....

January 28, 1963

Out with Tex this morning early for our usual walk. Stars beautiful but already getting light at 6:15. Antares bright but spray of stars in front blanked out by light. Mars far to the west and almost setting. My favorites, Arcturus and Spica—nice and bright in the early morning sky.

January 29, 1965

This morning outside at 6 with temp 15 below. Antares glowing really red in the south, and in the southwest Mars, well named, certainly high, bright, and glowing in the sky. To the east, the cross and Vega clear and white and high on the meridian with the handle of the dipper pointing to it, as it should. Arcturus still my favorite. They seem so far away and remote from us. Like the age of the earth and the glacier, I cannot imagine their distance and their magnitude. Such is this world and such is life on it.

February 11, 1965

Up in air today looking for deer and admiring our geologic formations. I think that I finally can grasp the difference between a lateral and ground moraine now and just how the glacier did work. These formations are really striking. The Cataline rocks have a true mountain appearance, weathered and aged beyond all imagination. There may be no such thing as the everlasting hills, but should there be such the Cataline rocks would qualify.

We were cruising over the Brazeau Swamp, when in the distance, like a huge dark mountain—Thunder Mountain—truly a giant from the air. Deer threaded throughout the countryside, and in one creek, remote from any road, a perfect network of otter tracks. Only one flock of birds—these in Long Swamp, and I could not tell what species they were. We were in the air for about two and one half hours, and I was glad to finally get down, but there can be no denying this is the way to see the country. The spines and twisting eskers, the soft ground moraines, almost like a flock of bedded-down sheep in the distance, the massive sharp and really huge lateral and terminal moraines, and finally the plain along the shore.

February 16, 1966

Royal and I brushing out lines on Oconto Marsh, and right now my tractor is slowly becoming part of that marsh, by now into a solid block of ice right where we left it after a futile effort to extract it after it broke through the ice. The job was finished, we were on our way back. I was walking ahead when I heard the tractor roar and Royal curse. That was it. A day of brush and marsh, with a little off-site aspen—now black spars.... Coming back along the Hale road, two pine grosbeaks feeding in the road. Sky grey and dark all day, with snow that you could feel toward evening. A few flakes fell, but otherwise there was only a foggy mist chill in the air.

Tomorrow, we have to dig out the tractor. I've seen enough of Oconto Marsh for this winter.

February 17, 1966

I well recall a book *One Day on Teton Marsh*. Well, I wonder how many pages the author would have written about the marsh I spent the day on. Our tractor is still very much part of Oconto Marsh, and now it has been joined by Buck Durand's 22-ton bulldozer, which managed to bury itself a scant forty off the road while on the way to fish my tractor. One minute it was purring along as only a cat can; the next it was floundering as helpless [as] a turned-over tortoise. And there we were for the day helplessly trying to coax this now totally inept monster out of the mud, in a temperature that did not hit five above, and with a wind right out of Ungava sweeping the marsh.

Oddly enough, there were other live creatures on the marsh besides ourselves. Five snow [buntings] shimmering so in the February sun that I took them at first for flotsam, sweeping against the chill wind as oblivious to the day as if along the Gulf. And then late in the afternoon, a falcon—a real rarity, sickle wings and all—cutting very business-like across the desolation. It wasn't much of a day. I ate out of Royal's bucket, fell into the open water twice, and have nothing to show for it except that now there are two tractors, mine and Buck's frozen solidly into the marsh.

February 19, 1966

Our tractor is now free, having been wrenched from its frozen prison by Lloyd's bulldozer at about 11 a.m. this morning. I hope it is none the worse for the experience. It was a bitter cold day, with temperature that registered ten below when we left Marinette. Going onto the marsh, we flushed two hen pheasants, poor devils, scrounging for food on that desert. No other life except for one set of mouse tracks. The politician went whipping by in his car as we were horsing the tractor up on the trailer. Suppose that is one thing he didn't care to see—game managers in the cold, and on Saturday at that.

Marsh 8, 1966

Admire the fine stands of timber in the northern part of Marinette County and wonder why I don't spend more time up there. The beeches in the western part of the town of Silver Cliff, the fine spruces in Long Swamp, the hemlock forests on Del Santo's land—all of them. When is the last time I really looked them over. There's something about hemlocks, the soft wind singing through them, I think, that sets them apart. Solemn, quiet, dignified. All these could be applied to any grove. And the potbellied beeches, always gnarled in this country, looking like they had a tough time of it, which is always the case.

🍃

Spring 1960s

March 23, 1968

If green is the color of June, and red is that of October, then certainly grey is March's own color. That is about all I saw today on Seagull Bar. Grey sky, grey ice, and grey water in little ponds and leads, which have only recently opened small patches, rifled by the wind, a freezing full breeze right out of the north. A flock of goldeneyes in the pocket, and I thought it empty until I swept it with my glasses, and then I noted the prize—a pair of whistling [tundra] swans, calm and sedate, graceful on the grey water, feeding with their long necks twisting, and then as the wind rose, in self defense, contrasting them almost to the height of the bow in their backs. One was last year's young, the other a full grown, cream-white bird, brilliant even in the dull light of this March day.

There was no other life but this was enough.

March 26, 1968

Where there was only a dead silence there is now a chorus of blackbirds, and where there was a solid sheet of life ice there is water, and where there is water there is life. It was along the bay in quantity today that rafts of ducks, mainly hooded mergansers and goldeneyes, the latter pumping their necks up and down with a vigor that could only be bought on by the noble passion, which has evidently put the hooks on them.

Back in the brush, the still song of song sparrows, muted by the distance and positively delicate when compared to the liquid gurgling of the blackbirds. Through it all, there was the haunting feeling that only life can bring the certainty that great things are going on, that ancestral rites are being performed, that a great act is going on in front of us, which we can only dimly understand, like a poem, let us say, whose meaning eludes us, that leads us on and on through the clamor of birdsong, the waving of green grass and the leaves, the color of flowers, and then the slow disappearance and silence once more....

April 4, 1965

With Lindberg to Green Bay today. Attend meeting of bird club and gave talk on waterfowl migration, which was well-received, if I may say so. The stated purpose of the tour was to observe [tundra] swans, and such is our spring this year that I was ready to bet Lindberg that we would see none. For once I was prudent on these matters because there they were, about 400 of them, feeding and roosting happily on the ice and open water as they must have done on these spots for thousands of years indeed since the glacier left. The region is now pierced by belching stacks, the marshes have all been filled in, and the river polluted beyond all recognition, but there they were as they must have been in ages past, with only the Indians to welcome their coming, and indeed before the days when their presence here was some thousands of years away. This pattern was well established by the time these Asiatic men came trickling across the straits. And there they were once more impatiently awaiting the disappearance of this ice. Is this the ten thousandth floe of ice they have waited out? What a chronology if only there would be some swan historian to write it out.

CHAPTER TWELVE

April 10, 1969

Lloyd and I looking over the emergency spillway at Lake Noquebay, where water is running freely. There is a glint in the washed soil at our feet that I note just as Lloyd reaches down to pick it up. A perfect quartz arrowhead, sharp, to the point that it hurt when I ran my finger along the edge. It was only appropriate that someone like Lloyd, who hunted this marsh so intensely, should find the sign left by a hunter long ago, who probably hunted it with the same skill and pleasure he did.

The past suddenly seemed very close just there in that little piece of well-worked quartz. The mind reels to the original piece of quartz, to the hand that fashioned it, to the day a shot was probably missed on these marshes.

April 13, 1963

This may well have been the last time prairie-chickens were observed in this part of Wisconsin [Pensaukee, Oconto County], so will go into some detail on the event. Walter Krause, Harold Lindberg, and I arrived on the grounds about 5:30 a.m. We heard birds but could not see them until two flushed in a westerly direction. After a bit, we could hear them, and after stalking through some brush fields had no trouble spotting one of them on a flattened ridge in full display. The other bird, also a male, displayed only sporadically, and both finally flushed when I walked up to the [booming] ground. No female was evident. These probably are the same two birds we have observed twice previously this season.

Only a miracle can prevent this population from becoming [extirpated] this year, and we can be quite certain they will not be on the grounds next spring. As a rough rule of thumb, it could be stated this population has been halving inversely each season for the past three years. Year before, ten; last year, five; and this year, two. One will have to look for factors other than edaphic to account for their disappearance. The openings are still there, brushed in perhaps, but still chicken habitats. It almost seems that once they hit 15, there was no holding them back—they were doomed.

No one will miss them except I. Most of the old timers express surprise that there are any left at all. They thought them lost a long time ago.

[LeRoy returned a year later, almost to the day, and reported:] Lindberg and I back to Pensaukee this morning early to look at the chickens. We arrived just as dawn was breaking, one of those grey misty bayshore mornings, and heard the birds almost immediately. Spotted them in a weed patch, two males again, displaying madly and I believe futilely to each other. It was a magnificent and I think fruitless display—don't think there is a hen chicken within 200 miles of here. Had they been born 10 years ago, there may have been a dozen admiring and willing females in attendance, but there was no one except Linberg and I to admire their efforts, and there's not much we could do to help them out.

May 5, 1963

This morning out to Seagull Bar. Noted an old man digging out what he called a boomstick—actually a pine log, rough, with a deep notch in the middle. He was to take it home for firewood and said that he had his father's wedges yet to cut it up. In a way this was only justice. He and his father were both old lumberjacks, and how much more proper that he should get the use of it rather than it ending up as part of a ranch house decoration.

May 8, 1963

Stepped out of my car in a woods north of Oconto, and a sound hit my ears. Like an easily recognized face it came back to me instantly—this was the sound of our summer's woods—the flycatchers, kingbirds in a distant field, wrens, towhees, but above all, the [great] crested flycatchers crying in the treetops. Walking along a creek, flushed a vesper sparrow off its nest and without even searching for it, spotted it tucked in a crevice along the river bank. Heard a doglike and faintly swanlike noise on the lake through the brush to the bayshore, and there they were: five swans in so close that one of them had to walk in the shallows. They flew off after awhile—probably the last we will see this year.

Stopped at Langills. Warblers in profusion, mainly mourning and palms. By the way, I heard Maryland [common] yellowthroats and yellows whenever I passed a brush patch, and saw a yellow at Langills. Also, in a willow, a half dozen white-crowned sparrows feeding quietly and intently on the willow catkin. Coming back through our woods road, flushed a Cooper's hawk off tree along edge of road. He flew down the road a bit and took a perch in another tree, where he sat intently scrutinizing the ground in under the tree. After a bit it flew further up the road, giving its wings a singularly sinister beat. No matter how glorious the day, this creature was intent on only one thing—doing away with some of the birds that were singing in the trees.

May 10, 1968

This was the week of the shorebirds return to Seagull Bar and warblers to our wood and brushlands. Now that the marshes are quieting down, the main waterfowl migration having passed through, the rest of the area is coming to life. A palm warbler, all subtle colors and one line of red, working over the new leaflets on a willow. The brushlands are buzzing and ringing with yellow warblers. Orioles crying in the woods. Reports of sandhills coming in from all directions.

The second wave of spring flowers, roadside ditches and flooded swamps yellow with *Caltha* [marsh-marigold]. The whole business looks just fine, and compared to the months that have passed, simply incredible. What is more unbelievable than a fine day in May. The woods were frozen and dead, and now they are a blaze of fine color, ringing with music instead of frozen silence, and everywhere hope springing out of the dead wood and ground.

I wonder if it is a coincidence that those cultures most advanced are those where spring is at its finest—where each year they have a living example of hope, of a promise fulfilled, that there is an end to everything, finally, and things eventually turn out for the better. Even our northern springs and winters finally disappear in a avalanche of color and sound.

May 12, 1963

Pack a lunch and take family out collecting fossils along Escanaba River downstream from Boney Falls Dam. No sooner hit the spot when we found a slab of crinoids—solid with them—the first real fossil beyond a thumbprint of brachiopod I've ever found. We found several brachiopods and one anterior portion of a trilobite. It just doesn't seem possible that millions of years ago a warm reef flourished here, that these crinoids lived and died there, and in this year of our Lord, 1963, my children and I come along on a chill day in spring and batter them from their resting places. Wonder what they would say if by some time machine you could ask them. A tale they could tell—not of pines and jacks but one that would put Monsieur Bunyan to shame—as indeed all nature's tales could. As much as our pine stumps, they tell of a different day, one when man was eons removed, when warm waters lapped these bays, of starfish and sharks in a drowned Escanaba! Imagine the dinosaurs, man was long in the offing when these creatures flourished. Why, these were good crinoid lands for a longer period than they were good pine lands.

May 21, 1967

We had our first real flight of warblers, the first sign of leaves, also the first mosquitoes and wood ticks. The warblers came in Wednesday morning after the first warm day in weeks. I stood in Long Swamp, where a road has killed all the conifers, and watched a stream of them—blackburnians, black-and-white, black-throated greens, and chestnut-sided visit each spar, search it eagerly, and then depart for another section of the swamp. The blackburnians colored in tones almost neon in brightness, their orange showing an almost smoldering intensity, glowing like no other color in nature. All of them with lines so trim and that incessant activity, all against the stark spars and the columned green of the spruces.

Out on the Coleman Lake openings, spring was just the call of the [upland] plovers, plaintive with all that is pensive and fleeting in a bird call, and one bearberry flower. Otherwise, the plains were a pattern of dark and light browns, unrelieved by any color save the backdrop of jack pines. It was so bitter cold, spattering rain and low grey skies, [and] two sharptails clattering off a food patch.

May 24, 1966

There is something special about a day in May. It was always a haunting month, so much so that one longs for a lesser day, March let's say, when there wasn't so much going on and it is impossible to waste a minute because March is just a month to be passed through while May and June, too, are months to be lived to the full with every wasted moment begrudged with a real sense of loss and with the shock that every minute passed is one never to be lived again, that what is gone is gone for good.

Somehow standing there in the woods this morning I felt that the whole business was too good to be true, that I was missing something, that here was the answer if I could only catch on, or think of the proper question. And there they all were, unheeding, the flycatchers, the flowers, the trees spreading out their leaves—everything welcoming the sun, just as they have for the past thousands of years, ever since the glacier receded and exposed this esker to the sun....

Tonight with boys out to Seagull Bar. Actually warm, even along the bay. Hoped to find some shorebirds and took a station on a log opposite the sandspit. A small flock of turnstones and a semipalmated plover along with a sanderling. Something special about these birds, not the least being that they have so far to go before they can nest. Think of it, their nesting areas are still under ice and snow.

Bay a fine blue with just a touch of the waves, sky cloudless. As I left, a pound boat was pulling into shore lifting nets. An archaic trade, a page out of the past. Take away the motor and put on a sail, and this is the way their ancestors would have handled things in Sweden. Different fish perhaps, but same men.

June 5, 1966

This morning with the boys out to Carney Bog. One yellow lady's-slipper open, a lovely thing that we all exclaimed at as if it were the first we ever saw. It rained during the night, and the yellow shoe was gleaming in the green sedge as if it had been formed from wax. The ram's-head [*Cypripedium arietinum*] at the full now, both on the ridge and in the bog. These are plants for connoisseurs only, with shape and form both delicate and subtle. So fine are they that they tremble in the slightest breeze. The sepal covering the lip really conceals the plant from view.

Admired some fine *Carex* [sedge] in the woods, [C.] *castanea* [chestnut sedge], I believe, with slender filament and seeds strung like miniature beads. Afternoon to Kleinke Park. Joyce and I walk along the beach where I took picture of *Potentilla anserina* [silverweed cinquefoil or common silverweed], now in full flower, yellow with basal leaves giving them an almost artificial appearance. Here is a true dune flower, growing where there is not one trace of humus, nor a square inch of shade or protection of any sort. Here it finds its home in this alternately burning and freezing sand, now exposed to the heat of noon, than to the chill of night. *Carex cryptolepis* [northeastern sedge] in full seed now. How is it that I never noted how pretty these sedges were until now?

June 6, 1965

This morning with Boyle out to Carney Bog, where the ram's-heads are now in full bloom on the hemlock ridge and in the muskeg also. This is the event of the year. Their value is that of all things rare, like a coin let us say, except that their rarity is compounded by an exquisite beauty—theirs alone that the rest of the *Cypripedia* do not have. There they are trembling in the breeze, an associate of nothing except for a sedge or two that finds its niche on these barren sands, purple and white, shining to attract the bugs that are necessary to their survival, small for an orchid really....

Surprising absence of warblers, and I am beginning to wonder whether in fact these creatures are disappearing. Heard several whitethroats [white-throated sparrows], and finally, when we were walking out, the sizzling notes of a black-and-white [warbler]. Trilliums now out of phase, their glory now long gone. *Linnaea* [twin flower] just ready to come into flower—my favorite of all of them. Not many bugs yet. The bog is too cold.

June 7, 1964

This afternoon Danny brought home a *Heterodon* [eastern hognose snake] from the cemetery, but alas it took no time at all for one of our more timid neighbors, of which we are really blessed, to call the police. Said officer said the snake would have to be released because it was disturbing the peace.

June 17, 1963

Coleman Lake openings. Thick with *Amelanchier laevis* [Allegheny serviceberry or smooth serviceberry] and blueberry. Trilliums in full, white bloom! Right out in the openings without a bit of shade. Back through the Goodman timber, where the slaughter of the hemlocks continues. The owners and the jobbers are making a bit, and society loses a stand of hemlock that were old before any one ever heard of an investment. There is something wrong with a society that allows this to happen.

June 20, 1964

While in Walsh swamp, heard my children screaming, and indeed they had something to shout about—a 3-foot fox snake in my butterfly net, which I made them release. Judith was turning over logs looking for bugs when out came this creature, which Danny promptly grabbed and popped in the net....

Summer 1960s

June 21, 1964

Along beach at Cedar River, a killdeer nest in the sand, and about a half dozen adults crying out along the water's edge, seemingly more concerned about each other. *Junci* [rushes] in bloom, the flowers really quite beautiful. The stamens being bright yellow, and the pistils red. Kids caught a *Storeria* [red-bellied snake], which looked pregnant. This beach has a fine variety of bugs and spiders. We caught three fine lycosids, and Julie picked up at least three instars of monarch. Greg caught a *Cambarus diogenes*, [crayfish] put it down, and was in tears when the creature made off. He didn't think a crab could move that fast. They normally can't, but *diogenes* can!

July 2, 1964

Last two days with James Z[immerman] working on the genus *Carex* in Oconto and Marinette counties. We found a goodly number, mainly in the bogs, which would be expected. These sedges have a beauty and grace all their very own, a bit subtle perhaps, but it's there nevertheless.

July 4, 1966

This afternoon with boys to the Lake Noquebay outlet, they wanting to catch some metallic wing damselflies which we did without any trouble. The path through the woods was loaded with all sorts of odonatids, all except the big *Anax* [*junius*–common green darner], which for some reason was absent. Anyway, almost each leaf had a fragile appearing damsel, hovering like a little helicopter without any effort whatsoever. Something there is about *Anax* that seems to come right out of the Carboniferous, with the metallic crackle of his wings and snapping jaws. There is nothing of this in the damsels with their soft, gentle flight, yet they are every bit as efficient and deadly as the larger forms, being able to capture and hold a mosquito with all the dispatch of the big fellows.

Late this afternoon, Joyce and I up to take a picture of the *Orchis rotundifolia* [*Amerorchis rotundifolia*, round-leaved orchid]. The grass pinks (*Calopogon pulchellus*) are in full bloom now, with their petals spread out like the wings of a butterfly, as if to catch every bit of sunlight, or more likely to attract every bug.... The *Arethusas* [*Arethusa bulbosa*, dragon's mouth orchid] are fading now, but the showys [*Galearis*] are putting out new flowers daily and will for some time to come. Oddly enough the sundews [*Drosera spp.*] still aren't in flower—each one still coiled like [a] watch spring and ready to pop, although they are in no hurry. Something should be said of the *Arethusas*; they are so beautiful, and it just doesn't seem proper that in a world thirsting for beauty such as ours, that these plants should grow and die there unseen, falling over, pink petals, and face into the moss to become more unincorporated humus.

July 15, 1965

Tonight with boys walking, or rather canoeing, down our ditch at Peshtigo Harbor. Several bitterns flushed—one with a mouse in its bill. Poor mouse! Imagine being speared by a shipoke's bill. Talk about the A bomb. And then there were the black terns—hundreds of them, flying over the marsh— for what I wonder.... Two black-crowned night-herons, flying along and complaining as they always do about our showing up in their domain.... One sora rail very quiet and rather sneaky, I thought, moving through the sedge on the bank. Deer flies, hundreds of them, and mosquitoes, too. One deer fly nailed me through the hat, and it hurt.

July 29, 1967

It's Saturday morning, and we are making our final preparations for the trip to Canada, or more properly, Quebec province, and it seems incredible that I am writing the word. We have no idea what it will be like, how we will get along with the people, where we will camp, or for that matter just where we are going.

Perhaps the Quebec of my fathers is gone forever, and all we will find is a bit of watered down USA, although I hope not. I trust we will find little farms and villages, surely some horses in harness, and if fate smiles on us, even a yoke of oxen. We are looking forward to the seabirds along the St. Lawrence, the new rock formations, a new landscape, new everything. I know we will like Canada....

August 1, 1967

We are on our way to Louiseville, to the north of this town, where sits the village of St. Leon, my ancestral home, from whence the Laterreurs sprang. We reach Louiseville, and there plainly marked is a directional sign—

St. Leon. With increased excitement we head north, and finally there is the church spire and the town. The cemetery has one Laterreur stone, which we photograph. A group of chattering children come out of the school, and regard us with only a mild curiosity. I go up to an elderly gentleman sitting on a porch and ask him, in English, if he knows the name Laterreurs. He speaks only French and does so at a rate that frightens me into a totally monolingual state. I write the name Laterreur down, and he spews out a discourse on the Laterreurs in the area. I make out the words "white house," so now all we have to find is a white house.

Since all the houses are either white or unpainted this will be a problem; but anyway we start down the road and there full on a mailbox is the name Georges Laterreur and, moreover, Georges is on the porch. He promptly disappears when it looks like we will drive into his yard, leaving me with a barking dog.

He reappears with his wife, and I make a halting attempt first in French, and then in English to explain that I am his relative, although my name is spelled differently, and that we are from Wisconsin. Both give me a blank stare, although the wife gives some indication that she thinks Wisconsin is in Canada. By this time, I am getting panicky, and so quite obviously are they. A desperate final effort is made to communicate, I in English and they in rapid French, the wife repeating over and over a French sentence, which I gather was pigeon, and of whose meaning I had not the vaguest idea. The failure was utter and total, and finally with a desperate gesture I fled the scene leaving Georges to wonder what stranger, from what planet, had pulled into his yard. So ended my effort to contact the Quebec Laterreurs, and I'm happy that my grandfather saw fit to leave....

August 8, 1964

Tonight, Dan came in the house with a tiny garter snake, a suspicious bulge in its midriff. From time to time it would gape, and gradually the gaping became almost continuous. It was apparently attempting to vomit up its supper, and I confidently said it could not do this, the lump being past the midriff. Gradually, its effort became almost frantic, and the lump visibly moved forward. Finally, with an almost audible gasp of triumph, the creature cast out the lump, a frog, quite large for such a small animal, the hind legs already digested, the front part just recognizable.

August 12, 1969

This beaver had dammed up water that flooded a sand road leading through a woods, where its ancestors had lived for some thousands of years. Berry pickers use the road, but could not do so when it was flooded. So there was an outraged complaint, and we trapped out 5 young and the male, but the mother eluded us, and it was she who night after night repaired the dam that kept the road flooded. Finally last night we trapped her, but such was her strength that she did not drown, but rather, weight, trap and all, struggled back onto the dam—her dam, let it be said.

Lloyd advanced on her with a club, and now in terror she floundered into the water. Too late, and a blow descends on her head, the water boils now in her agony, and then another and another. The water is quiet and stained with blood. Lloyd pulls her onto the dam, and she is motionless, a full forty pounds of animal.

She had in her life wrung off one foot and pulled a part out of her hind foot. Lloyd was telling the aide, "Don't be afraid of them, they'll never attack you."

Now, there are no more beaver in the dam; it is blasted out, and the berry pickers can move along the road without getting their cars wet.

August 16, 1964

With Boyle up to North Lake this morning, and while waiting for Mr. Myers, his contractor, had a chance to look the woods over. Praise the Lord my soul for things that creep and crawl on the ground and under bark, for ground beetle larvae and rove beetles tucked away in the folds of rotten mushrooms, for slimy little salamanders spending their summer under the bark of a prostrate popple, for slender, sinuous centipedes speeding away from the light, for ambush bugs and flower beetles prowling through the jungle on the cyme of a goldenrod.

August 21, 1963

To Pensaukee and Charles Pond today. The pond isn't holding much water, but it did have a goodly number of ducks. At Pensaukee, *Chelone* [Turtlehead] and *Pedicularis* [Lousewort] in full bloom. Along the dike, clouds of tiger beetles. Watched them through my glasses and they certainly are striking creatures—like bulldogs rather, rearing at the front, ready to spring on any bug or little piece of material that moves. They have no tolerance for each other—just so close and then a rush. Clearly saw two of them catch small insects. Their movements and reflexes are incredibly swift—almost too quick for the eye to catch. Some Bembi on the dike, rather small; they land, there is a spurt of sand, and a flurry of legs and lo, they are gone. Are these burrows that they are uncovering? Everything is full to repletion. Flowers are ranked high along the roadsides and fields; grasses, *Spartina* [cord-grass] and *Andropogon* [bluestem], in long graceful lines, and along the bay solid white of wild buckwheat....

August 21, 1966

Throughout winter we carry the image of the late summer and fall woods in our minds, and it struck me yesterday how long it takes to load up.... It's the fall composites and ferns that do the trick. Nothing innocent and fleeting about them. They just take over and hold the stage—a bit battered and jaded, but they will be there until spring rolls around, some of them still standing, others prostrate on the forest floor. Right now, they are beautiful in the mass, in the solid front they present. Joe Pye weed takes over whole marshes, a tossing restless assemblage of red. Boneset bright and then dirty white; the asters an unwieldy aggregate of species that few bother to identify—not I certainly. Then the fungi, out of this world, the real mystery plants of the forest, varnished, some of them dead white, changing swiftly to a sodden mass that I hesitate to touch.

Right now our open hillsides are full ranked with bracken, a real aggressor, taking over as no plant does, shading out all others. Their particular brand of green dominates the openings now, not only the openings but much of the forest also. Some ferns are as delicate and retiring as any spring ephemeral, but not bracken—it believes in a true pan-brackenism: the world is clearly to be dominated by bracken. Its duty to somehow maintain the dominance that all ferns held in the Mesozoic. Let anyone who thinks that they have lost this position contemplate the bracken each year at this time....

Mosquitoes and heat that made the summer woods miserable gone. *Linnaea* blooming a thousand fold.... Now a welcome coolness, every insect too busy with its own affairs to even notice a human; the hustle of creatures, who must be about their affairs and finish them before the night and dark descend. To seek and find the right caterpillar ... [on a] bit of bark [an] egg can be laid in time to hatch while the earth is still warm, or perhaps it can, in torpor, tough out the Arctic winter.

Most impressive of all I think is the stillness, the quiet of these late summer woods. Much of nature has clearly finished its work; the cycle is just about complete, no time now or no need for the rituals that dominate spring and early summer. Storing and gathering of food is infinitely less exciting than finding a mate ... the joy and ecstasy are long gone....

Just returned from Seagull Bar. Strong wind, spattering rain, black clouds, waves pounding against the shore. Semipalmated and least sandpipers, turnstones, feeding along the edge of water asking only to be left alone and understandably reluctant to take to the air. Out on the point, a coterie of every species of gull and tern known to the area, riding out the storm, taking to wing at the last moment with a wild cacophony of sound, a racket really all tacking and veering in the strong wind, the lighter terns just about holding on. Walking away I could not help but admire the wild scene—the heavy low clouds, white crest of waves pounding against the shore, roar of wind, and the gulls and terns all against the wildly swaying green of the cottonwoods and willows.... Don't imagine the scene would have been different 100 years ago.

August 21, 1968

Today and yesterday through our pleasant Kewaunee countryside, and revel in, as always, the log barns, the fine old houses, the much-used hills and fields and the surprising woods.

I love most of all, I think, the rock-strewn fields and the stone fences, the old rails and stumps, the cemeteries with the Czech and German inscriptions, the pioneers who moved into this land who wrested a living from it, who lived in a world so different from mine. I always like to think that they loved this land like I do, and am sure they did, but probably in a different way.

There are those who will think of this county as backward, who will be repelled by the barren, stony hills, the dark little farmsteads, the unpronounceable Czech names. I hope the county never becomes popular, and that in the minds of all except the favored few such as myself, it remains so.

Tonight the news that the Russians have moved into Czechoslovakia. Those damn unspeakable fools. How could they? Damn everyone in this world, whether it be the pope, an American general, or a Russian, who tries to impose his will and his ways on other people....

CHAPTER TWELVE

August 23, 1969

Saturday morning, and I have just finished my quart of beer, after having several downtown. Anyway, the German record that Joyce picked up last week has just finished, and since they were mainly folk songs, not many were new to me. My mother used to sing them, and we, in our fixation on the French, would tease her. I think somewhat bitterly now that none of us ever asked her to repeat the words, or even wondered what they meant. I wonder what to this day she thinks, and more than anything right now I think of my grandmother, my mother's mother. She was born a Duve in West Preussen [province of West Prussia - today within Poland].... I never remember her as anyone but an incredibly withdrawn and remote person. Her loneliness in this land must have been beyond belief, and I cannot think of her as a person. Ma said that from the time she was 40 she was fading, and so it was the terminal effect of her condition that was part of my youth. I see her now, a face pale, hair grey, drawn tightly about her head, always a grey dress that tailed to the ground, a look that was always abstract, an expression changeless, but this was, after all, part of her condition. I think now how she tried to respond to us and could not, or at least we could not respond to her; she was, even in Two Rivers, a person so foreign and remote, utterly beyond our culture.

Her life that counted was in her church, and when she no longer took that walk down 22nd Street to Jefferson ... in Two Rivers, her daughters knew that she had indeed lost her mind.

When she died, I was at the university, and Ma didn't notify me, figuring that we couldn't make it home anyway. Anyway, the day after the funeral, my mother and her sisters were going through her personal effects, which were indeed the family's lot on this earth. My Aunt Martha tossed my mother a pin cushion and said, laughing, and I am sure not without a bitter humor, "Mary (this is my mother, named after her mother), here's your inheritance!" She used the German word, and my mother told the story with a laugh. That just shows you how little my mother expected out of life and how much she gave to all of us.

In my mother's house ... there was a picture, a lithograph in gold mainly, of the Blessed Virgin dying, surrounded by angels swinging censers. Everyone assured me that this was indeed the way she [grandmother] had died, and had been carried up into heaven. Ave, ave, Maria, and to my grandmother, ave.

September 2, 1965

This morning out to pocket in Benson tract early, and wade out into the wild rice. I was forewarned, could hear some gabbling, but hardly prepared for the mallards. Wave upon wave, roaring up until there must have been 2,000 cutting through the air, a startling if not downright overwhelming sight. As I walked through, they continued to flush in 2 and 3's and am certain there were birds left.

Several cranes, out of place it seemed, giving their harsh call, and one bittern, [which] acted like I was really after him. A yellowlegs, all white and grey, landed delicately in a pool and chose not to notice me at first, but after a while I got the best of him, and he flew crying into the air. There were perhaps a dozen wood ducks and about 30 blue wings. The mallards really go for the wild rice; it must be at its peak now as provender. Some of them flew suspiciously, heavy-loaded with rice I suppose. Swamp candles still in bloom beside the composites.

For life you can't beat a marsh, and I guess I saw as much this morning, or more, than I will all winter in the woods. It was a fine day, cool enough for a coat at first, with a fine September sun.

September 16, 1963

Just returned from walk with Tex near armory. Vast bank of fall flowers, and strung between two goldenrods noted a web and suspended from the web, arms spread as on a cross was a bumblebee, dead at first I thought, but upon close examination noted a faint movement. I turned him loose, and after a minute or so he vibrated his wings and was gone. I had save[d] a life, my good deed for the day.

Now to find the murderer. I lift up one leaf, then another—no one at home. Suddenly, a folded leaf, low down. I lift it up, and there is the culprit, a huge *Araneus trifolium* [shamrock orbweaver], so replete that it never bothered to come out and look at the victim in its web. With the rings on her legs, she was gaudily bespangled as any madam, and for the present as indifferent as a replete madam should be. Here this worker, this hero, came buzzing along, intent only on provender; it blunders into this net, fights his heart out, finally hanging there, resigned to this fate, while she, loaded with the juice of this morning's bug, sat groggily in her leaf parlor, letting our hero snared on his gibbet.

Yesterday to visit Maryon at Sandy Bay through Namur and Brussels. Is there any part of rural Wisconsin more beautiful, more authentic, than this Belgian country? When I was a kid, that's the only term I ever heard used for them, the Belgian settlements, despite the fact that they came here before the Bohemians. I always like to think that the neat high gabled brick farmhouses reflect a Flemish influence. The weathered log barns are of purest Wisconsin vintage, and with the green and scattered trees, and the lovely slender church spires, make a singularly harmonious picture. These crosses and names on the mailboxes really belong. This is a culture that has remained relatively pure for a hundred years.

Fall 1960s

September 30, 1962

Notes on Seagull Bar at 6 a.m. on a fine autumn morning. The sun, a red ball just barely visible through the murk and fog. The willows, still bright green, shiny bright with first bright light of the early sun. Song sparrows and robins faintly singing, almost as on a day in spring. Seagulls, brown young of the year, tearing at rotten fish. The bay, calm and quiet, looking like it must have when there were only Indians to behold it. Gulls, as large as geese through the fog, resting on the water. On the pocket, ducks heard but not seen. Four golden plovers, subdued in their fall plumage, beachcombing through the flotsam on the shore. They fly off crying. A domain of dead fish, natural debris, gulls, shorebirds, and ducks.

September 30, 1964

Fall really is upon us and summer is gone. It was in retrospect a wonderful year—this spring glorious as few have ever been. I can feel the first warm sun out on Seagull Bar, hear the gulls cry, the gentle waves and the sudden spattering rain, the golden summer and now the bitterness and bleakness. The leaves that came out so green are now gone, the gulls have long flown, and now all there is—tomorrow and tomorrow and tomorrow.

October 1 and 2, 1966

Opening of grouse season and spent the weekend checking hunters, of which there were many, and their grouse, of which there were few. Weather and woods also beautiful. Frost both nights and woods was wet and chill in the morning. Saw two asters growing in a bog, but otherwise all flowers are gone. Ferns and marsh sedges have all lost their color. Chipmunks scurrying all over the place—the warm sun of mid-day really perked them up. Flocks of migrating warblers and whitethroats, the latter with their little white bibs that look like they've just dipped into a saucer of milk.

Scattered fox and song sparrows reluctant to move out of the sedge, and at the brook, Prince put out no less then 4 towhees. Must say something about Prince. It's Sunday night now and he's sprawled out on a rug. He was given to us last Thursday, having come to Marinette by a rather devious route including Okauchee and the Alphonse Monette farm. He's a boxer, as bright and nosey as a dog can be, loves the woods and generally seems to be fascinated by just about everything. In color he is fawn, with a dark streak down his back and black muzzle right up to his eyes. He minds beautifully, has been well trained, and will be a wonderful field companion for me.

October 3, 1964

I note where the gravel men are really chewing up the esker at the [Highway] 64-141 intersection. Don't imagine that many people hereabouts really care if we have eskers or not. The world, it can really be said, can get along well without them. All they are, after all, is a ridge of stone and sand laid down by some under glacier torrent some 15,000 years ago, and why bother with that when there are things so much more interesting— the Braves and the Beatles, for instance.

October 13, 1964

Shorebirds—mainly sanderlings and a few Bairds—feed vigorously along a sandbar, even a few killdeers with them. Come to think of it, the killdeers disappear early and really disappear. Have you ever seen many killdeers in fall?

Some shorebirds didn't do too well today. A hunter stops and says, "Any luck?"

"No," I said, "How about you?"

"A couple yellowlegs." I was incredulous, but he did indeed have two of them in the back of his car and seemed to have no idea that they were protected by law. I have them now but did not arrest him. He had no idea as to the illegality of his action. Said that hunters in Green Bay shoot them regularly. We'll have to look into that.

October 16, 1964

To Waubee this afternoon hunting woodcock, of which I shot three, having flushed six and fired at four. Struck by the gold, really golden, of the tamaracks. Just as their flush of green is so welcome in the spring, so now their startling yellow, vivid against the muted browns and greens of our swamps, almost an unearthly color when contrasted to those others that make up our swamps now. This is a color really out of step. There you have it—tamarack is a non-conformist.

Standing, watching Tex cast for a woodcock, noted a tiny slip of a brown shadow against a rotting log, a little *Sorex cinereus* [masked shrew or common shrew] fleeing from one dark world to another, for this instant in the dangerous light of day. Just as man seeks the light, so *Sorex* the dark.

November 3, 1967

It finally happened—a hunter shot a bird right out of the crate, some four feet to the right of me. I had pulled the slide, and the first birds were flying out. Suddenly, a shot—I whirl around and am staring into the muzzle of a smoking shotgun held by the trembling hands of a duck-clad old-timer, and I do mean old. I remonstrate with him, and when I turn about, see a dead pheasant laying in front of the crate. The old son of a bitch couldn't wait and shot the bird when my back was turned as it walked out of the crate. He was going to get his bird at all costs, even if it meant my life. Such is the hunter that we are faced with today, the monster that we have given birth to; this is conservation!

November 8, 1969

Some comments on deer.

There are few animals that elicit the antipodal reactions evoked by the sight of a deer. Approximately one-half of our public would have the animal crash to earth with a well-placed bullet in its heart or head; the other half could not even imagine themselves or anyone else, for that matter, perpetrating an act so cruel. Both factions agree on only one point of discussion—there can never be too many of the creatures, and woe to him who doubts this premise.

I am a game manager, a fact which automatically puts me in the minority of those (there are less than 40 of us in the state) who are convinced that there can be too many deer....

We have no animal more beautiful, more graceful, nor for its size more fecund and more capable of eating itself out of house and home. I think that this sentence, if I may say so, sums up the trouble deer are causing today.

We have no hoofed animal that can reproduce with the speed of the wily white tail and none with its almost total lack of natural enemies, unless we include man in that category....

I have shot only one deer in my life and was never moved to shoot another. If there is anything I am not, it is a deer hunter. Nevertheless, this does not blind me to the fact that in the absence of any other predator, man is the only one who can control this species. If the day would come that hunting as a sport would, for whatever reason, disappear, we would find it necessary to hire men to control them. Let anyone who regards as anathema he who would kill Bambi ponder this fact.

The only time I ever saw deer actually starve was in the year 1948 in the Black River Falls country. The forest looked like a well-kept English park. There was no brush whatsoever, and trees had been trimmed as high as a deer could reach. Fawns were laying dead on piles of hay that had been hauled to them in a futile effort to forestall the inevitable. These animals had in a very literal sense destroyed their range. The next year, after almost a decade of furious struggle, a season that could control these animals and bring their numbers to reasonable levels was passed. That was almost twenty years ago. The battle still rages. Terrence, the ancient Roman put it this way: "You may throw nature out with a pitchfork, but still she returns."

While the politicians fulminate, the deer just go on breeding and chomping away just like they have for ages. Both are moving might and main to dominate the world they know. Sooner or later, one will be caught up short. The deer cannot be blamed, the politician can.

CHAPTER TWELVE

November 22, 1963

Tonight, Orion and Gemini ride high in the sky, just as they have for these millions of years, and tonight the president lies dead, a brother to the stone and soil to which he will alas soon become. So may a great intellect be snuffed out.... A crank scares up twelve bucks to buy a rifle. He finds a place to shoot it, and the leader of the free world lies dead as if he were a deer in our Wisconsin woods. That's the way things go in this world—of mice and men indeed. All this turmoil, all this waste, just because a screwball couldn't get what he wanted, or maybe he just wanted a little attention. It doesn't make much difference if you are bright or dumb, a Harvard man or a high school failure, a president or a roustabout; as long as you have a gun, you can get the other guy, which is the way it has always been. All you need are the guts to do it, and it's really no different than if you were a leopard in the jungle, even if you are a child of God and heir of Heaven, as the saying goes. Guns can always clean up on brains.

November 28, 1963

This morning again to Pensaukee.... Swans still on water near shore so chased them all away lest some deer hunter decide to see how far he could shoot! Wish our English language had more descriptive words—the only ones I can think of to describe our swans are "stately" and "noble." "Serene" is another, although this is mainly an illusion, an image they project to the world. In reality, they are quite excitable birds. Some were so far out in the bay that they looked more like fish stakes, with bodies below the line of vision.... The next time we see the swans it will be spring. Now, they will fly to the Chesapeake and then once again back to our Green Bay, the bay of the French fathers and the Indians, alas so long ago. Imagine this lovely land with its forests and untamed rivers. The Menominee [River], before the dams, was the equal of any western stream, and they had no forests to equal ours. But this land was livable, people wanted it, and they killed the wilderness—it's gone, never to return again. It had everything, which was, I suppose, its undoing. The wilderness is long gone, but the swans do not know this, and so they return year after year. This land, which now is really for making money, is to them what it has been for so many thousands of years—a stopover to Ungava of course.

December 1, 1966

Tonight late, just as the sun was setting, out to Seagull Bar. Bitter cold now, the frozen sand like a pavement. The light was poor, and I could not determine the extent of the ice, but the shore zone at least is frozen. It was an Arctic landscape, grey white and buff on the beach, the only color the pale, wan red light of the setting sun, not glistening but just showing on the stark branches silhouetted on the dunes. No birds—no life of any kind, certainly not in the plants now being whipped and shredded by the freezing wind. All things come to an end, and this summer's glory is long gone....

December 7, 1966

Take the afternoon off and walk with Prince out to the end of Seagull Bar. I hoping to spot a snowy owl, and Prince just asking for a clear place to run. He was successful. I was not, but it was a fine walk anyway. Heavy clouds, sharp wind, and pounding black water rimmed with ice. A pair of mergansers and one lone golden eye spattered off the water laboring into the strong wind, gulls tilting, and that was about it. Not quite. One flock of [snow] buntings feeding out on the ice, on what I've often wondered—wind-blown material, but that would seem to be pretty bleak pickings.

Skeletons of gulls frozen into the sand now, all of them young who will never reach the one-half score that the books say they have coming. There seemed to be something particularly appropriate about dead buried in the sand by the last winds. The whole thing fit in with the general pattern—the barren beach, the freezing water, and ice rimmed along the shore, and the biting wind right out of the Arctic.

If the world must eventually come to an end as indeed it must, this can be regarded as reality, a foretaste of a future condition that will someday engulf this earth and all living things; unless, of course, the world shall end in fire and not in ice....

December 14, 1968

Yesterday, if one cares to record such things, was a real landmark in my life. Thanks to Barbara Neverman's efforts, I sold one of my columns—the one on snow fleas, for $12, the first income I get from my writings. So the snow fleas [springtails—*Hypogastrura nivicola*] and I have one thing in common—we are both worth $12, or it can be looked at another way—I as their publicity agent am worth that amount. Anyway, no matter how one cares to look at it in this eminently practical age, we are both worth something.

❦

Winter 1970s

December 28, 1971

To the harbor on this ... cold morning, notable enough because the sun is shining in a bright blue sky, and for this once there isn't a cloud in sight. A light snow fell during the night, making a perfect clean page on crust that remains from the first snow.

Deer moving in and out of the food patches and through the woods. A fox looked the county over thoroughly but must still be hungry, or at least he did not feast. Prettiest pattern of all was the short-tailed shrews [*Blarina brevicauda*]—a staggered series of little prints wandering aimlessly over the snow, now over, then under, finally ending in a plunge hole, or rather a little cluster of three, into which he disappeared and stayed down.

There is a phenomenon of shrews, as well as man. It is a series of erratic and nervous wanderings through the woods; tunnels on top of the snow, little tracks almost fading away, an animal in ceaseless movement, an animal that really leaves its mark. The landscape had the crisp, clear, uncomplicated simplicity that is ours at winter's best; a matter of green pines, the symmetry of dark branches, the snow, and left over from last year, the skeletons of weeds and grasses. No birds; there was nothing on the bay, now a very quiet sheet of ice, locked up for the next months.

December 28, 1977

How to make the world a sacred thing in a society that sees nothing wrong in exploiting the good Lord for profit. What's a mountain or stream to a world that sees dollars sticking out of everything. It goes without saying that just as we need a restructuring of our society and its institutions, so do we need a restructuring of our attitude toward the world around us.

It is recorded that the ancients felt sorry and asked forgiveness from the animals and plants they killed, for they were so close to them. By this, I take [it] is meant physically close. There's a key here someplace. Neuman speaks of a total fusion between man and nature, both the plant and animal world, identification between a man and his totem. Just to mention this is to grasp at the depth of the modern problem....

Megalopoly will continue to sprawl over the countryside, and nature as we know it [will] disappear. The hills are being ripped apart out West. It is only a matter of time before the tropical rainforests disappear. When will it all end, and how can we convince man that with the ruination of the planet our days as a species are numbered—a new weather god speaking not from a burning bush, or whirl of dust, but rather from a stripped and plundered hillside, or from the depths of a polluted lake.

January 2, 1973

Today for the first time in memory we saw the sun, a beautiful bright vision that reflected from every facet of our landscape. To the Eagle, and snowshoe in on a crust so slippery I had to crash it at each step or take the chance of sliding as on skates. The deer are already in the yard; they look so well fed and innocent. Fortunately, they have no way of knowing what is in store for them because things are going to be rough. I could see it in the trails already well-packed and [in] the trimmed browse. A heavy snow and sleet has weighted down the trees, and this is what they are hitting, hemlock in particular. The crust has a fine skiff of tracking snow, and the mice and canid sign showed beautifully.

No birds, except for the constant call of ravens, and along the highway one pine grosbeak.

So here we are in the quiet and the white, the brutality of it all, bitter cold, and deer breaking through the crust—each step a noise like a shot. The grouse cannot snow-roost, and there is an influx of goshawks.

January 2, 1979

My first field trip of 1979, to the harbor in something like 15 below at noon, complete with wind. That driving indifference of nature, each plant on the marsh now with an individual ridge of snow, sculptured lightly there— a little shadow in the pale Jan[uary] sun....

January 7, 1978

Saturday—we have had no sky or stars for over a week. Driving, biting snow, grey amorphous clouds, and today, freezing rain. Some time in the woods. On Wednesday, coming along the Lake Noquebay dike, there was suddenly this mink, leaping along, swimming under the snow, dark startling brown in all the white. I squeaked—whereupon he stopped as if struck, and then there was only a flash of mahogany streaking under and up, out of the snow, and then down until he vanished for good. I saw his track all over the woods; he had really looked it over, and one can only guess at his desperate search for food. Other than that, there were ravens wherever I went, marking dead deer and rabbits—always that sudden, angry, frantic swirl out of the snow.

I continue with my study of astronomy, and say with some pride that I have a certain grasp of it....

January 9, 1973

Today I walk into the northern end of Long Swamp on an old snowmobile trail. Bitter cold and clear, no wind with a fine sky. The whole thing was beautiful, with the snow and the sun shimmering on bits of ice on the trees, fragmenting the atmosphere into every possible color combination in the spectrum. I hated to leave—it was so still; only once a crying of ravens in the distance, and in my winter clothes there wasn't even a chance of chill.

So in a perfect mood I drove back, looking over the hills, and the dark forests, pines particularly, and it occurred to me I've never given the world its due, loved it in the sense that Teilhard was fond of mentioning....

I felt warm toward the hills, felt I would get out of the car and pat them. I think tonight I can say as never before—Earth, I love you, and have loved you all my life.

January 11, 1971

Tonight with Prince after the sun had gone down in the beautiful simple quiet, a universe of slight pink and white, a glow over everything; no sun, no stars, no clouds, just the sky and world that I could see before me.

January 14, 1972

This afternoon I watched the sun lowering itself out of sight, silhouetted behind pines, a vivid blackness and pale brightness over everything, and the most inhuman cold imaginable. I spent the day in something very close to minus 10, and I'll bet that in the wind, which was simply unbearable, it must have been close to minus 50.

It struck me how terribly inhospitable the world can be, how brute nature is, and when I stepped into our warm house, how fine, how unique, how necessary it is to be human. A partridge [ruffed grouse–*Bonasa umbellus*] in a scrub oak a perfect balance of colors, a certain brilliance even in that cold sun. Three birds must have spent all of yesterday and part of this morning feeding on the hillside—it was woven with their floundering tracks in the deep, soft snow, and I found at least 4 roosts, little tunnels in the snow, each with its telltale pile of droppings—the grouse calling cards that we will search for in spring, which I don't think will ever come. Someone has set an otter trap, where all the sign is at Lake Noquebay. I wish him ill luck. Those tracks are worth infinitely more than his money.

On one spot near the second flowage, the mice had a frolic last night, and the snow was just laced with their trails, all looking very exuberant. What else could send them careening around and over the snow in such reckless and apparently patternless pattern.

Tonight, Prince's feet were freezing, and he tried to shake the cold off as he ran along.

I should record that this morning, for the first time in my life, I definitely saw Mercury, and through the glass at that. I'm one up on Copernicus now.

January 18, 1975

A beautiful week, our northern winter at its best. Most of the time out of the office, which is of course enough to make any week beautiful....

Our days have been spectacular, fine sun against the trees, that soft glow—the winter condition in all the stillness and quiet of our woods; my world and I love it.

January 22, 1975

This morning in severe cold to Abrams, where someone is trying to put a bridge over the Pensaukee. They've taken a nice old farm, stripped it clear, and degraded it into a golf course. The original forest must have been a beauty—the old farm a reasonable compromise. But now it's nothing, complete with the realtor's sign up front. It will never again be an old sand farm—sprinklers and fertilizers will maintain an illusion....

Walked out the pond at Charles Pond and also the flowage at Oconto. Not much alive in either. Was surprised to note that there was a nesting colony of black-crown[ed night-herons] in the willows on the flowage. They are there yet—little platforms of twigs, very primitive, but I'd guess workable. How else would these birds have spread all over the world?

January 24, 1971

This Sunday had just a touch of warmth—a grey sky and slight snow in the morning. It was a morning of excellent Mass, perfect meditation, peace in the family, and then in afternoon, out on the pocket at the harbor.

A solitary runner [musk]rat wanders aimlessly across the glare of ice. Then with a roar, three snowmobiles came out of nowhere. They spot the creature now humping for the distant line of brush, and for the moment the boredom of tearing about on the ice vanished. They bear down on him, cutting close, and one boldly boots him. Before he recovers from his roll, one of the machines roars over the rat, now struggling, stunned on the ice. I am running, shouting, waving my hands, but so intent are they on their fun that I go unnoticed. Now they sweep again and then one, somehow, spots me. They roar off in [a] cloud of vapor, and are gone, leaving the animal to limp painfully for the shore, which he makes, and finally comes to rest under some willow.

So there is man, whom I am to love, but I find it easier to respond to the rat, in this case, than to man. No more compassion towards the animal than had they been cats with a mouse. We have a long, long way to go.

I am reaching a stage where I can easily define ... those people with a passion for compassion, justice, mercy, empathy with the world, not only toward man but everything in it—be they muskrats, man, or elms, not as a matter of sentiment, although there is nothing wrong in that, but rather as a realization that this is man at his most human, and one might say least animal, becoming really as another Christ. We have no alternative if life is to survive on this planet. Let all those of good will gather, all of us who love this world.

February 3, 1970

This was the antithesis of a day in June, and the only word that might apply is merciless. Parked north of the Eagle yard, and with snowshoes under arm and scarf tight around neck, headed south down the road. An occasional puff of wind that would have froze a person in midstep had it been just a little prolonged, but I finally reached the swamp.

Now for the snowshoes, no luck; the harness had to be relaxed because the leather was frozen.... Deer starting to tear balsam along the trails. Things obviously were not going well for them, or me either because my snowshoe fell off, and the leather was frozen so, and my hands also, that I just couldn't get them back on and had no recourse but to flounder out. Glad for the road, but now a wind that would have sent all Novosibirsk [Siberian city] indoors hit me square in the face. Over the hills were agony—face, fingers, everything frozen, cold soaking through the clothing, only my feet reasonably warm. Over all, the brilliant sky, sun glaring on the snow, and the sound of the wind, which was really something to listen to. Ravens sailing about and calling; now there's a bird.

Long Swamp just a little warmer. Tracks in the snow: shrews, grouse, a snowshoe hare, white and innocent ... and that was it....

I think I see why most of the world's great religions developed in warm countries. How could anyone even visualize a deity who was beneficent, kind, and gentle in a universe that threatened your life at every step, everything steel and ice?

February 13, 1974

To Pensaukee on this cold thoroughly wintry day. Strong wind whipping over the bay; a sky that could only threaten more of the same; a dark landscape.

I admire jack pine, twisted there on these snowy openings, as green now as they are in summer, not minding heat nor cold. That is the being of jack pine. I buy T[homas] M[erton]: all being is from God. There is a spirit that weaves a net through the universe, that makes hawks search, jack pine so nice and green, and Antares shine there so red in the early morning sky.

Nothing can stand by itself, so it's obvious there is one being that exists in the universe; we all partake of it; there it is, glowing, whistling, calling,

CHAPTER TWELVE

now a bird, then a tree, an old battered stem from last year, those bones on the ground, or that constellation marching ... across the sky.

February 16, 1974

To the harbor. Sun bright on the snow, almost blinding. Sitting in my car just looking over the horizon, and there was this instant flash of white on the white. It was a weasel—a little fellow, flying over the snow in an extended gallop, into the bank and out, through the canary grass, consumed with a total curiosity over his world. There's something sacred, I think, about every animal's environment, and his case particularly so. And they are entitled to it, even as we are to life, liberty, and pursuit of happiness by the same law. His was the dead canary grass, the snow, and whatever mice there were underneath. Don't look on him as an abstract, but rather as this totally adapted animal. The snow, the mice, and the dead grass—they mean as much to him as his teeth, and flying feet.

February 28, 1978

Nice letter from my mother. She wrote a sad little note of her mother's birthday on the 22 Feb, said how tough her life was, and then added, "I remember her in my prayer's every night." The sheer beauty of it all—whatever could possibly replace that in extending the human spirit.

My mother has a link with her mother, the same I am sure that my grandmother, removed from Germany and all her people, had with hers. Mama said she never said anything of the old country. She sailed without relatives and landed in a town where there was no one she knew. And the situation hardly changed in the 60 or so years she lived in TR. Until her [LL's grandmother's] mind failed, she never missed Mass, almost daily. I see her yet walking down Jefferson Street, coat and hat always black, even in midsummer, blue dress trailing. There was something shy and yet strong-willed about her face. Impossible to think of her as a young girl, and yet she surely was. I guess Grandpa broke her spirit. My mother said she was always old to her. May she, may we, may all the souls of the faithful departed, rest in peace....

March 2, 1973

I lament the passing of our fine stands of hardwood along the bay. Dumke is slashing the elms and ash in Pavlin's tract—a once beautiful stand, now being reduced to a shambles. I counted out ash that were over 150 years old. Of course, Pavlin got 7,000 bucks for this. There must be some way out before all the big trees are gone. For those who say we need the wood, what will they do within the decade when the trees are gone? In the meantime, we could have the wood; at least ration it out somehow. How can we all be so blind?

March 15, 1977

I spent part of the afternoon on the Noquebay Marsh. The water is running freely through the tube, and from what I can see, the ice has vanished from the inlet. No ducks though, surprisingly, and while I heard cranes in the far distance, there were none in sight on the marsh.

Mosses and lichens are at a peak of perfection—the influence of the fog, and every stump and log was some shade of emerald.

The economy of an old shredded pine stump. There was one spot where, with the toss of a stone, I could encompass the territory held down by nine of them for these past 300 years or so—I could easily imagine the tall trees waving in the sky. Think of it—there were no whites here; this was Indian country. They may well have had a path under these very trees, or since this was the end of the lake, maybe even an encampment. Then along we come, wreck everything—we needed land and money; neither pines nor Indians had any rights; we did the whole works in, even as we are now in the process of wrecking land all over the globe.

Spring 1970s

April 11, 1977

Everything hit, with a blast of heat and roar of wind, and there was our north, suddenly frying under temperatures that went over 80 deg. The snow, except for little vestiges, is gone. There is a flush of green in the water, and in the woods at Pensaukee. Flowers of hazel are common.

There is that Mesozoic chuckle of frogs—music from days gone by, so to speak, before there were birds to take up the chorus, and they, the frogs that is, do very well.

Big flocks of ducks on Oconto Marsh. A bakers dozen of shovelers going through their Hell's Angels routine—perfection in form and flight.

First dragonflies—one aeschnids and several libellulids, looking over the old fief with a most practiced eye, next to the road in the rotting woods, easily the most practiced. We even had summer clouds—those ephemeral cumuli, vague and indistinct on the horizon, complete with a hot wind. There's the Tao of a summer day, less than a week after we shivered....

April 19, 1971

Pleasant and warm; no coat or cap and into the woods for dead deer check. Eleven, no less, on a 40 [acre spread] near Campbell Lake, nested in there own torn and shredded hair, victims of our winter and stupidity. They, the deer, have in a literal sense shredded the countryside, chewed cherries and juneberries to the point where they are girdled and beyond return. Balsam stripped of branches to the point of total reduction, and there is not a sprout of any kind left in the country—even the blackberries have been trimmed. It will take a long time before this all recovers, and some of it never will. The deer leave their mark on the countryside, as surely as do we, another animal able to breed without restraint.

Call of winter wren bursting onto the world, singing frogs and *Hylas* [tree frogs] spring song at its most welcome.

April 24, 1972

Clear and very cold early this morning so that I froze through the Eddie Bauer [clothing]. Huge flock of scaup diving and posing, and far out a half dozen redheads, not quite colored as they should be; there was not that much light, but their heads had that carved decoy look, very distinctive, with that light grey.

Then to the dike, right now a thing of beauty, and I hope a joy forever. The bay broke up during the night—the terminus of [a] slow and agonizing process. Ice piled up in huge bergs along the shore, and rafts of it float[ed] out toward the peninsula. There was a solid line of Canadas [geese] forming a border on a floe that had lodged against the shore—a pattern of black on the ice, heads lifting up and then down. Suddenly I was sighted and the whole works went into the air in panic, a mass of flapping, honking animals, put out by the intrusion, and for this moment at least not yet ready to fly. The entire group planed off and landed on another raft; their muttering away and assuring each other that this will not last.

The impoundment is loaded with ducks, flying, sitting there, courting, or just doing nothing. Shovelers! Could see their green sheen and the huge bills when they flew, and there's something positively beady about those eyes. Ringbills—beautifully line[d], shaped heads, bobbing flight, and in the right light a purple sheen. Eared grebes and a long-billed Holboell's grebe [red-necked grebe], calling....

The birds are bringing the dead woods to life. Kinglets flashing their colors, myrtles flicking onto the road, and always the call of flickers and [their] loping, gliding flight.

It was a day of joy, one to relate [to], one that made me think what it means to be a naturalist: Challenge the world; this has a value to you; this can give meaning to your life; the world's existence and your own depends on how these creatures are treated. Or more properly, your attitude towards them.

April 24, 1979

Lake Noquebay Flowage, where out of the ice and snow—gone only for a matter of days, a new world is flowing forth, through the air [and] the water, and under the cold waves. They made me fight for life in my canoe this afternoon.

First, this osprey sweeping along in a most grand fashion, teetering in the air just a bit, carrying a snake I thought. But no, in my glass it turned out to be a long trailing wad of nesting material that he was hurrying along in a fashion almost painful. He flew the full length of the flowage, then along the woods, and finally over and out of sight. He had that harried, unkempt look osprey always have—an image of great power and determination.

Then, back near the dike, a suffocating blanket of leopard frog snores, yelp of wood frogs, and slicky trill of chorus frogs—all together in an excited chorus that shouted: things are really happening here in these murky waters.

There were flocks of ducks—mainly ringbills [ring-billed ducks] and paired buffleheads, and scattered pairs of teal and mallard, the last residents who will stay the summer. In the woods, first *Hepaticas* [round-lobed hepatica, *Anemone americana*] and *Luzula* [wood-rush]—bright white and new green in the dead leaves. Two mourning cloaks [butterflies] at their insouciant ease—loafing on oak leaves, when suddenly, they blunder into each other. Face to face, wings frantic, they mount into the air. They fly at each other, locked by an instinct cable-strong. Now they still soar, high over the trees. The wind is catching them, and it takes every beat they can give it not to lose each other. One minute pumping their wings slowly, and I'd guess contentedly, in the bright sun and quiet of a forest floor; then suddenly high over their woods in a maelstrom of wind and thrashing branches.

May 3, 1974

To Florence, running the woodcock counts and grouse also....

All the early flowers are out—*Hepaticas, Anemones,* and, above all, the moosewood [*Acer pensylvanicum*] now, the glory of the woods, and no one, alas, there to see it. But there it is in the light green and darkness, little tears of yellow suspended there in the distance, seemingly in midair, high yellow in every sense of the word.

May 4, 1979

Sharp cold—a strong wind right out of the Arctic, bringing I'm sure the spring breath of the tundra and Lake Superior right here into the center of the lake states. If a chickadee, a tachinid fly, a far-off hawk, and tentative call of chorus frog, is a woods coming to life. Well then, in sun and wind I saw a woods come to life this morning. It had rained for two days, and were it not for the cold, this woods should have been a fury. And well it may be—the mosses are very green, and lichens newly sorediate.

Also, there is just a touch of gossamer on the red osiers before me. But it's hardly the spring of which poets sing—this is the northern lake states in May. But in the dead fallen grass and the new spears of green, I saw a sinister, hair-raising sign. There, sneaking haltingly and carefully along, was a huge fox snake—he was over 4 feet long, and in my glass he looked like a python. Head, amazingly clear eyes, his tongue darting into every little fold and crevice in the ground. His search quietly frantic; he would disappear and then suddenly out of the dead grass there would be that darting tongue, and those eyes. I tried to think as a naturalist, but my humanity and the archetypal man kept me in check. I felt a twinge of horror for any little family of mice that could have come under the flick of that tongue. He never noticed me, and in my glass, was so close I could see the slot in his lower jaw for the tongue and feel his stare when he glanced in my direction. Face compared to body—surprisingly bright and new....

May 5, 1974

This morning, walking home from Mass in chill and bright sun, was struck by dew recently melted from frost, gleaming with every shade in the landscape.... In one flash it came over me—how many angles I as a human can consider it? [As] An artist of course, I was first held by its beauty; [as] a scientist, at very least I could classify the grass and reflect on what this dew means to the ecosystem ... we—the grass, dew, and I are components in this world. And then, last and surely not least, the Being we share—the water, the plant, and I; the oneness we have ... in everything.

May 8, 1973

This was a day that in rain, and a swamp awash, I found *Primula mistassinica* [bird's-eye primrose], for me until now a denizen of the far north and Isle Royale. On this old root, moss-covered, and with the flood forming a bank for the stream, there were these little flecks of pink, and at first I gave them the bewildered stare that we reserve for plants that somehow have escaped from a garden and, amazingly, are doing well in a swamp. But there was this something, a memory of Isle Royale, I'd guess, and now for the second, totally incredulous look. There was that yellow circlet, and the basal, incised leaves, and the overall innocence we associate with mountain and arctic flowers.

It was *Primula*, until now known in only a few choice spots in the state. [Also] There in the mud and washed mosses, a *Thuidium* [fern moss] is hanging on ... enclosed by new sedges, this little masterpiece, far from the sandstone cliffs and limestone outcrops. A root is good enough, an old one at that.

Tao indeed; Tao in an old root and a fleck of red, looking up from the mud, within a whisper of Smith Creek, alive with new rain, and plummeting on its course, via the Peshtigo, to the bay, and then somewhere, in eternity. If they could only know [that] I bring them in existence, proclaim them to the world, or do I? They affect me more than I do them, although somewhere in the long vanished past, which is right now, we are related and one in the world.

May 13, 1973

Cold these last days, with only a slight glimpse of the sun, so remote that one hardly noticed. This afternoon stop on the esker across from [County Highway] W and was counting the rings on a felled hemlock. There were 100, but this all came later because when I reached 90 there came this horrible, fractured scream, and over my head there was a red-shoulder[ed hawk] shouting bloody murder to the world: Don't you harm this nest! And there was the nest: a rickety platform of branches in the crook of a white birch, high silhouetted against the sky—the perfect place for the manufacture of hawks.

The woods are fine now, even in the chill, leafing out nicely with that delicate array of new colors that marks our northern spring, fresh flowers— this woods had *Hepatica*, blue really of heaven, and the net regularity of *Mitella diphylla* [two-leaf miterwort or bishop's cap], with its array of white flowers, and always those subtending leaves.

Sacred earth, sacred *Mitella*, and holy red shoulder. Divinity hides in you, or maybe not even hidden—there it is, for all of us to see, if only we open that third eye. Or better, close the ones we use.

May 14, 1971

Gary Jolin knows of a [northern] goshawk nest, so today in the course of regular work, of course we inspected the setup. It was in a maple woods, now coming to life with a tender show of color, and a faint, elegant breath of new life. The lower part was wet and given to ferns getting ready to unfurl.

First, there was this darting shadow, right down out of a tall balsam. Then, high in a tall ash was the nest, a stratified pile of sticks; wild architecture at its finest, set right there against the sky. The shadow was now nowhere to be seen. Then out of the swamp came this aggravated clamor, a call out of the depths. Just get out of here. Don't harm this future for my race, and it was coming closer—a royal procession. Then there it was—this grey eminence, the destroying angel, the death of partridges, a formidable creature, even in her desperate pleading. The mother herself. After a while, she let on the nest. I could see her bright red eye, the spread of her tail, the delicate grey color, all the power, and then she was gone, and only an agitated voice, deep in the swamp.

May 16, 1977

A day on the marshes, where the very life itself is bursting ... the air is loaded with pollen. Brilliant green is bursting through the dead stems of last year, now in the way, refusing to face facts, for they too had their day, and where they are now so will this green.

Our tropical birds are here now—the flycatchers, the orioles, the cuckoos, besides those birds equally tropical—the shorebirds, innocent little flocks bent only on living.

I saw a pair of black mallards, the first of this year. I was bitten by a bee and stung by mosquitoes, and upon removing my overalls, Joyce picked a tick off my leg. Life, as they say, goes on. I am not only an observer, I am a vector and giver of life also.

The new willows are decorated with the fairest of them all—little yellow warblers. Where are the tropics through all this? We, the town of Peshtigo— the tropics, complete with 80 plus temp, and humidity you could cut through....

I was stripped to the waist for the day, and the wind and sun felt beautiful. After all, I, too, am their child, every bit as much as these deer and sedges. Incidentally, the marsh was loaded with deer, getting away from the mosquitoes. And the sedges are coming along nicely. *Carex stricta* [common tussock sedge; hummock sedge; tussock sedge; uptight sedge] is [in] full flower, and the rushes are just beginning. Few butterflies—one *V[anessa] cardui* [painted lady] and numerous Camberwell beauties [name given to species in British Isles; here it is known as the mourning cloak, *Nymphalis antiopa*].

Now its grey and threatening out, and I hear thunder. All fine; we can use rain....

May 18, 1972

May, I just must say this: Your very name is beautiful; you speak of so much of the beginning of everything, the bursting flowers, the leaves twisting out of the once dead branches.

CHAPTER TWELVE

This is the month of soft color, a newness on the horizon, and [a] matter of 5 days or so out of 365—a softness and promise we will not see for another year. Orioles, bright orange in the trees, beautiful in the touch of green and blazing sky. Each branch has a touch of it now. There is nothing commonplace; perhaps there never really was, but now the whole world shouts with it.

The ditches are yellow with *Caltha*; those same ditches that a matter of days ago were just there and dead, nothing. Now they call out to the world, to anyone who will listen.

May 19, 1976

I walked late in the afternoon through the birch forest near Holt Farm. It was a world alive in white and green, fresh wind, bright sun under an intense blue sky....

On the way out, I noted that one of the giant pines near the old fields has been recently toppled by wind. The needles were still green, but it is done—ripped from the stump in one towering slash.

I gazed into the galleries like into an old ruined building; huge old rooms bored and dug by animals long gone, the interior an atrophied column of compressed wood and old grass, some of it undoubtedly hundreds of years old. I am glad it was not cut; this is the way it should have gone—that one giant wind in those hundreds of years; the wind that had swayed it so often, sang through its branches when there was probably no one in the area to hear. But then the right combination—power and age—and there she is, all her secrets bare; this animal, this bug, this bird had once lived here.

June 5, 1971

We have ripped this world to hell, burdened it terribly, and after these millennia of depredation still think it our absolute right to do so. I looked over the torn up elm stand north of Steve Parrish last year at this time. It was a most beautiful forest; now it is just shambles on the ground. The pine stumps from the first mutilation are still there, side by side, with the remnants of the latest crime. Crime it is and a terrible one, and there isn't a way in the world to check this thing. Our large forests are just disappearing, and it's terrible, but no one stays their destructive hands. This is private property, so the right is absolute, even when it applies to these delicate communities that have been abuilding for these hundreds of years. Such is life....

June 6, 1973

Today, ran the dove count in Oconto County through the German country north of Hinz. I aroused the curiosity of two farmers, who finally shouted their exasperation to me: What would a man be doing, silent, looking over their farm at 5:30 in the morning? Well, what's a man to do? What in the world would they have said had I shouted back to them, "Listening for mourning doves!" So all I said was, "I'm from the DNR," letting them puzzle what that somewhat ambiguous acronym might mean....

June 7, 1974

To our Dunbar unit yesterday ... walked the length of the openings and ended up on a hill with a magnificent overview. Thinking to spot maybe a badger (there being sand piles below me), I knelt down and fumbled for my glasses under the jacket. Suddenly there was a move, felt, not heard, and out into the open in full view strides this bobcat, feet and head high like a hackney, smooth gait, all ears and eyes, and a coat of brightest red. We stared at each other for a matter of seconds, and then in wild panic he flushed across in front of me, and disappeared into a stand of poppies. I was stunned by the whole business.

Soon, I realized there was something else going on; two deer ambling toward me from a distance, joyous, graceful creatures, playing, browsing, happy with the morning. On they came ending up close to the spot where the cat had stood. In helping himself to blackberry, one of them got a whiff of Bob, and you never saw a turned-on deer like that; he whistled, barked, stomped his front feet [so] that I could plainly hear the thuds, swung about, and then actually took [to] the track, to lose it at the point where the cat took off.

His companion didn't know what to make of this turn of events. In any event, he was not about to fight bobcats, and said so by, alternately racing away and then returning. Finally, unable to stand the tension, he fled for the far hills. His companion still stomped, but watched him intently, first refusing to follow and acting as if he'd stay on the original course. But the pull was too strong, and soon he, too, hightailed it across the draw and disappeared.

I had spoken to him quietly in French so as not to frighten him, but he never gave any sign of my presence.

It was an animal encounter of the first order.... I walked along the road back, in rain and mist. There were sharp-tail tracks in the thick mud, and just when I arrived at the car, a sharp whistle out of the sedge. No problem here, and an upland sandpiper flew up and out over the sedge. Three species on the endangered list in one area in a half-hour. There are indeed more there than the juneberries, sand cherries, and groves of oak.

June 10, 1973

Last night, just before Mass, I glanced at [a book by Isaac] Asimov, and read his speculations on the eventual demise of the solar system, one 40th gone now. The thought of Antares and Earth drifting into nothingness. I suddenly felt the terrible importance of being human, and the sheer necessity of our Latin phrase *in aeternum* [forever] fell on me like a ton of bricks.... In me a world lives, me—a center—and also the little *Capsella* [*bursa-pastoris*] [shepherd's purse] I'd just admired coming up through a crack in the sidewalk.

Tomorrow, we leave for the land of my father's, Canada, always a magic name for me: sacred land, the little farms, the old cities, the churches, the language, those old hills—right to the dawn of everything. History, life, this very world all tied up in the mountains [and] the hills and shores of the Gaspé....

June 13, 1972

I think the world [has] gone mad in a fashion never anticipated. No one believes in anything anymore. But there is just one little ray. The ... EP[A] man in the Nixon administration has banned the use of DDT in the U.S. So Rachel Carson, wherever you may be, let all mankind honor you. Respice you saint of the world, you lover of all things that crawl on the ground, man included....

June 19, 1974

It would seem that this month should always be written with a caress gently ... the gentle green, the bright flowers, the soft wind, birds singing, bees everywhere. Where there was only death and quiet, there is now life, bursting at the seams, taking over the world....

Monday, after 4 days of rain, there was a break in the clouds, and suddenly everything was flooded with the purest light, as if it were a new creation seen for the first time sweeping over these fields and forests; this is what you have all been waiting for.... Everything else was just an interlude. It is the sun and water that counts.

✐

Summer 1970s

June 22, 1974

Green Bay, thanks to us, is a sloppy mess. I suppose that it was predictable by our very makeup that we should demolish this ecosystem and bring to total ruin what was once the bay. Our brain gave us not only the sense of need, but a feeling of dominance also. We never will realize just what the bay is, but that it will in no way stop us from making a big dumping ground out of it. There should be a day of mourning for this all—someone to show pictures of bright, clean water, uncluttered shorelines, fine quality fish. Then, everybody, gather and listen to the water [lap] against the shore.

June 22, 1976

In the afternoon to Charles Pond, where I was assaulted, mobbed, and practically left for dead by the most vicious horde of mosquitoes.

Oconto Marsh, where the birds are. Three ruddys [ruddy ducks] with one female; one male following her so lewd I could see the gleam in his eye. The dainty, fairy-like step of snow[y] egret feeding on the little island, a tread so light, absolutely like no other bird. I saw him fly out of the alders trailing golden shoes. Then an ibis—right out of Egypt, sacred bird, huge somewhat ungainly curved bill, royal, exotic color, right out of the East. I can see why the ancients deified the creature.

Constant flight of blackcrowns [black-crowned night-herons]—they with the cry, and greens [green herons], with their orange feet. Then there [were] the [common] gallinules—the individualists. I watched two of them feed on the island, formally polite to each other, just so close and just so much togetherness. Bright red, light on their feet, brainly birds, more advanced than the others.

There are Caspians [Caspian terns] on the lower bay.

No way to enter a bird's world, and I believe it counterproductive just to try if all we can do is use our own points of departure. Here is where the prajna [wisdom] comes in—approach them without even thinking the word "bird," with all its connotations....

July 7, 1975

On Stephenson Lake today with my canoe—a surprisingly nice little body of water and happy are they who have it, for there lives background. It is really one series of little patterns with crowded, perfectly designed leaves of water shield—each leaf perfect and glowing in emerald green. *Potamogeton amplifolius* [big-leaved pondweed; broad-leaved pondweed; large-leaved pondweed], forests of it, color faded to a sort of neutral buff, seeds up to the surface now. Then the perfection of *P. natans* [common pondweed; floating pondweed; floating-leaf pondweed]—ovate, olive leaves, so quiet in the clear water. And then the backdrop—a true northern forest, tamarack and spruce, a quaking bog of cattails, *Eleocharis* [spike-rush], and sedges that were beyond me. No one has built on it yet, but the time will surely come. Praise the Lord for quaking shorelines and bugs that keep people away....

I am reading Hermann Hesse with a sort of shock. He is a powerful man. The parallels between his early writing and Zen are almost too good to be true....

July 14, 1975

The book on Emily D[ickinson is] exciting, and I'd give anything to have someone who I might discuss it with. She really lives for me, like [Thomas] Merton and Henry [Thoreau], the people who I know best on this earth. The mystery indeed; Emily, we share it together. Flowers are the thing, and so are birds....

So then, love the earth, for it is our mother, Terra Mater, sacred too, sacred as anything; it bore us just a surely as did our mothers at home. All these living and nonliving things, none to be subtracted, none to be said why this is really it, all dependent on each other, all bringing each other into being— the jeweled web, indeed.

July 15, 1970

Up north for the day, which broke dark and sultry, and finally sent me flying in a most welcome but still pouring rain. This is the day I made the acquaintance, after all these years, of *Riccia frostii* [Frost's crystalwort], at first just a tiny spot of green in the mud, and then under the mike a glistening, almost sugary rosette of leaf, a decoration almost as intricate as a snowflake. And there it was—just a fleck in the mud, living away until I came along....

July 17, 1970

Today to the Black Sam [to] work over the beech forest. Trunks straight into the sky, crusted over with lichen and moss, rather like an old stone in a churchyard, and they made this part of the woods seem incredibly ancient. I hope the foresters let them alone. Just think, they could go on for centuries, see the collapse of our technocracy, perhaps even see man in despair turn to these trees ... live with them, live with the whole earth. There can possibly be no alternative if man is to survive. The only thing is will the trees and hills still remain?

August 15, 1979

Tomorrow at 6 my father will have been dead 30 years ... and was 50 when he died. He took an awful lot with beside our hearts. We all live in his memory, but I wonder how many of us, my mother included, really knew him. I was never quite sure what he wanted out of life, or what his expectations were.

He came of a group that with two or three exceptions had their sights set very low, at least in a financial sense. They lived almost without hope. My mother said he never brought home 2 hundred a month. That would mean his salary never topped 2,500 a year. He was, nevertheless, a happy man, and I think reasonably contented with his lot—enough for a walk downtown and a couple beers. Once a year, perhaps, or twice if lucky, a ride up north to visit Coleman, a town he dearly loved but never saw much of. His fondness and attachment to this county was real and deep.

September 17, 1979

A dream of my father last night. Some sort of gathering, and Ray Kyro and I began singing WWI songs. We break out loudly into "Hinky Dinky

Parlez Vous," oddly enough a full chorus of sorts. But we need help, and then I realize my father is in the next room. He helps us along, playing an accordion of all things. Then he and I walk slowly along a country road. We try to communicate, but no words come out, and nothing makes any sense. So it ends....

September 20, 1972

I think that PT and I have this in common. That as young men, he and I were overcome by the beauty and wonder of the world around us, and that this deepened to a point where we felt the world simply could not be this wonderful, else how could mankind be so casual about something with such depth, so divine, a holy thing ... as we saw it. Then in late life, it dawned on us that the world was of greater beauty and depth than we ever dreamed; we saw what others could not see. And we arrived at it through an attachment to this nature, realized in solitude, and remote from those around us.

🍃

Fall 1970s

October 3, 1970

One of those beautiful, delicate evenings. The landscape lit as if by searchlight. The clouds light pearl and dark on the edges reflected properly on the quiet water where a muskrat was cruising along.

Then on the horizon three specks, closer now and the sun is glinting on the white of their wings.

The wings set, and there is a roar—a dumbfounding series of blasts. One bird falters and pitches into the marsh; the other two separate in an uncertain zig-zag flight. A cry, "You fucking asshole!" careens across the water, and then all is still, and once again there is only the marsh and the water.

This was the duck season opener, and how it will be a benefit to society escapes me now more than ever, and all I can say is that I cringe for the birds.

October 5, 1972

Fine day, and I spent part of it at Miscauno. For one vivid existential moment, the landscape flickered with juncos, nuthatches, and creepers, mixed with the falling leaves. Then suddenly all was quiet, the wind faded, the birds were gone, and there was only the slight rustling of leaves as they fluttered to meet their final destiny on the earth.

October 6, 1972

There is something fine about song sparrows flighting happily to a high branch in an old orchard, bright with color in an autumn sun. There is sheer objective beauty in a roadside wild with blackberry colors, and a field of asters abuzz with bees, and whipped into a purple haze....

October 6, 1975

Carry my canoe through the woods and onto the water at Charles Pond in just a very slight sweat. Canoe had a bit of bounce in the brisk wind and waves; it was just glorious. I paddled out to the sandspit. They were covered with shorebirds—mainly black-bellied plovers. They of the melodious piping and gentle whistle, something that seems to hold all that is melancholy in our northern fall. Then, as I stood there in admiration, there was just the slightest little sound in the air, and a flock of dunlins, newly arrived I'm sure, settled down breathlessly and immediately began to forage over the sand. The whole business [was] very serious—befitting birds who cannot waste a moment, and who have much to do, far to go indeed.

Took a short walk through the woods, everything drifting down now, all those leaves floating through the bright sun, their time past, and a new one coming up. Under the old elm bark, placid colonies of *Asellus* lumbering about there in the dark chewing their wood; a little frantic in the light, but not too much—it not being their nature to get excited over anything....

October 8, 1972

Mrs. Reineman told me the other night that the little Nicklaus girl, who is slowly becoming immobilized by dystrophy is alone now. Her mother died last week, and Dag was here for the funeral. We all hate and dread the word alone, and all fear loneliness, but where is the word that can even hint to the condition of this bright little girl ... faced now with certain death, which she knows to be coming, and deprived of her loving mother. Put yourself in her place, a crucifixion that may drag on for years. And how basically insensitive we are to each other that she must feel alone.

November 1, 1970

We have just returned from Madison and a lichen trip to the western part of the state. For the better part of the day, Joyce and I, along with a group of perhaps the finest people in the state clustered around Dr. Thomson and listened to him discourse and pass around the lichens he felled off trees, chiseled off rocks, lifted from the ground. Doc must be one of the most unique men in the business. Not only is he expert, but where else would you find a man who, without talking down to his group for an instant, explain to this group, not one of whom was a botanist in the excepted sense of the word, all the intricacies of this difficult group of plants, with absolute enthusiasm on the part of both, undiminished throughout a chill, grey day.

We followed him up sheer cliffs, crawled over rocks, burst though pine, and finally, the piece de resistance as he saw it, at the end of a special 20-mile drive, the Icelandic moss, *Cetraria islandica*, which looked rather like a dried and dead leaf from some other plant, and I'm sure I'd not even recognized it as a lichen.

Then there was the uniqueness of the Driftless Area, the ranges of hills, the plains in between, the vistas; this part of the state has without end the towns, Avoca, Blue Earth, Lone Rock, almost forgotten by everything, tucked away in these hills and flats, almost, one might say, beyond the reach of modem civilization.

November 2, 1973

Tonight, I am a little less proud to be human and mildly revolted by the very thought of my profession. It was the day of our mid-season pheasant plant, the moment when we throw up in the air, let's see now, for the what, pleasure, assertion of manhood, something akin to the brute, or what? Anyway, we force these pheasants out of the crates, they take to the air, and then some human—a child of God, no less, blasts the creature into oblivion, and reduces this streaming beauty to the stew pot. Well, rest at ease, bird; ultimately it will happen to all of us, and while society may well relegate you to nothing, I'm not at all sure that ultimately this is not the fate awaiting all of us.

I watched one young lad in the presence of his father blast three of them off the truck, just like that; they were done for and tumbling into the forest that was meant for them in all eternity. But not now, not in this world anyway; there was no place to hide.

November 3, 1978

I have been out each morning to welcome Arcturus, reappearing in the eastern sky, admire Algol and the double nebulae, and the Praesepe in Cancer, now marked by Jupiter. [Praesepe is the name of a star cluster in Cancer, also known as The Beehive as LL has noted under his entry for December 11, 1977.] Orion sliding down. Soon it will be in the evening sky. Endless stars just beyond the grasp of my glass, even as the whole system is beyond that of my mind....

November 5, 1977

A beautiful November day, clear, not even cool, nice sun. Above all, I just talked to my mother on the phone. I believe of all voices this one is most dear to me. It is one in my core, closer to me than my own, and the most beautiful [thing about] my mother's voice is this: She will be 80 next September. I would challenge anyone to cite her age. Just listening to her on the phone, you could say 40, 30 whatever, but it is just and clear and lucid, with a flow of words that any young person would envy.

Her writing, incidentally, is exactly the same—her penmanship that of a schoolgirl. Pa always said proudly she was a stock clerk, hence her ability; words just like that. I bet she does not hesitate one second over any of them. I must admit that in this past year I have a foreboding, that sooner or later something will happen, that somehow her age will begin to show. I, we, all of us, should count our blessings. There is not the slightest sign; she is the equal of stability in all of us. Perhaps I might be more concerned about the rest of us, rather than her....

November 26, 1975

We have a fine clear day out. Last night, everything in the world froze, and I can put my canoe up for storage. Only five months, and I will have it on the water once more.

CHAPTER TWELVE

I note with joy that the little *Misum[ena*, flower crab spider] that had appeared on my desk pad has established residence on my lamp and has a web spun across it. Welcome for the winter, sir; we will share this together.

Dear Fritz—Daddy ... it sometimes escapes me, though never for long, that you are the only person who ever lived that I can call that name. Tomorrow, you will be 77, and I want you to know that so long as I live, so will you, and then I would ask nothing more of my children that you live in them, in their love for this same beautiful Wisconsin, these lovely streams, these lakes, these forests, the marshes, that you so impressed on me were really something. We, you, they, them, were, are, always one; none of us will ever be separated.

November 28, 1973

Yesterday spent in the rain, wading the Lake Noquebay littoral, picking up mud. Then in the afternoon to the center, peering at the stuff through a mike, seeing just what, if anything, was at home. Segment after segment showed only bits of leaves, resting cells of something, and a fineness all set to enter some recycling machine. And then in the murk there was this bright red eye, tiger burning bright indeed; it glowed, literally with life, and it turned out to be a copepod, aggravated by the light, churning way in his little world, fit to be tied by it all; then another—twisting jaws on a delicate head and a transparent body—a chironomid. And that's the denizen of the Lake Noquebay mud. Either of them enlarged and on land would give anyone a fit, and perhaps it's best that their lives are lived outside our vision....

December 11, 1977

This morning up early and onto the porch, looking at the sky. It was clear and cold; there was no sound, and above all no clouds. There, overhead, was Leo, bright, in clear outline, crouched there looking at Cancer, except that if he could see the crab, I could not. So then I swept with my glasses, looking for the Beehive, and there it was suddenly—a huge open cluster, bright I almost said, with life....

We stare at the fringes, unable yet to fathom what it means to us. We know what happened but I don't think we'll ever quite grasp it's meaning, unless it be nothing. How we have constricted the whole thing—5 billion years or so to produce the planet, 2 billion to produce a cell, another billion to produce a nucleus. There nature has fashioned the key to the lock forged in the sun. Then the swift rush, finally backboned animals flounder up on shore, then the scales, skin, hair, then us. It took a little over 4 billion years. Then, in considerably less than a hundred, only a hundred, here we are talking glibly about wrecking the whole thing, pounding it into a lifeless mass, as if this indeed were not only our destiny, but the destiny of the earth herself....

December 15, 1978

This was the week I finally received my Leitz Trinovids [binoculars]. They are beautiful and graceful as a good glass should be, but I have still to see a bird through them because it is also the week something went wrong with my left eye on precisely the day I received the glass. It all began up here. I thought it lint in the air, but no, it refused to go away. Then when I turned out the light, it seemed there was a little bright light flashing on the lid of my eye. It increased in frequency and intensity. The dust became a swarm of lint floating and darting before my eye, so here I sit, home, somewhat scared, a patch over my eye, with my good right eye doing herculean duty. It may well be that not my Ammerman feet but rather my Ammerman eye will be my undoing. I have been to the doctor; he held out no hopes of being able to do anything.

Funny how cold, icy, and chill it seems outside now, a world gone awry. This could be a test of the interior life I've always hoped to build up ... with the outward search now somewhat curtailed. In [the] long run, it's not the books and walks that are it. What do you do with them? What impact, what synthesis [occurs] in your own mind. Lo, the kingdom is within you. It is the one word of Christ's that should be emblazoned [in] our minds and hearts. So, we shall see. I long to look at a bird, some bird, any bird, with my new glass, not yet....

🍃

Winter 1980s

December 26, 1988

How I look forward to the woods. I thirst for them, like Israel for the Lord, and have but one request, that I end my days in them, and that finished, my ashes sink slowly into the humus of a stand of hemlocks....

December 29, 1980

Return after two days in TR on ice-glazed highways, driving really scary. It was our Christmas visit. My mother presented me with an afghan she had knitted, something to keep me warm, she said. How fitting that she, who kept me warm in body and spirit, should think like that. It must have taken her hours—a really neat weave—and joins my field glasses and journal in that special group I would take with me.... Yesterday, when I wanted something, a spontaneous "Mama" came to my lips. "Mama, Mama," just like that. Bless the Lord for this, oh my soul.

January 13, 1986

This is the time to relate to a landscape. Now you see the forest, not the trees; there is nothing but you and the universe, consisting now of sky, some clouds, snow, trees, and dead sedge. That's it—nothing comes between you and your world; there is just you two. And getting around! Slow, steady, crunch, crunch of snowshoes; there's no obstacle here. Places in summer jammed with brush, mud, water are now all the same.

January 15, 1982

The paper states Sigurd Olson dead at 82. And most importantly he died while trying out some snowshoes. Last week, as I floundered along, the thought came to me, as I gasped along, wouldn't this be the way to go. Clear white and cold, in under cedars, with no one but deer and the chickadees to witness your passing. Compare that to a hospital, with all its people and paraphernalia.

January 17, 1983

On this very cold, windy morning [I go] to the woods across from Terreins. There's a heavy blanket of snow there now, one that both the other animals and I could negotiate with ease. There was a surprising level of movement, tracks all over the place. Life, for those of us who love the woods, is a series of indentations in the snow. Weasels, out of the woods, into the fields, curve, circle about ... squirrels, digging up ... in a style that impressed me as frantic calling cards all over the place, proclaiming not that Kilroy was here, but coyote, shrew, and Mr. Mouse. The coyote track was most vivid. They tracked through the woods across from Terreins, two of them, practically in each other's track, except that they would diverge every 25 yards or so. At one point, on a birch they scratched and pissed mightily, a yellow flecking high on the tree, and a forceful scratching, right down to bare leaves in the snow, which they sent flying in all directions. I took the track through the woods, figuring I could find out what they were up too, but all they did was walk. One might say all they did was live, in the snow and birches, and mouse tracks.

A shrew track so light it might have been made with the head of a pin, an incredibly delicate tracing, just barely making its mark. I heard nor saw nothing alive until, when leaving the woods, out of a patch of weeds flew two birds I took to be tree sparrows. They were just up in the air and then vanished quickly in the snow-swept field.

January 31, 1983

This weekend a party for J and I, my retirement from the DNR, in style. All my people from TR here—my brother, the Martinis, Kenny and Ann, and all the rest. I am delighted and grateful to see everyone. Greg came from Madison. We all—the twins, Greg, J and I at the front table—the only time ever that this will happen. Everyone amazed at my mother's vitality.

My mother ... [in] good spirits. This morning she was talking of her life in TR, and for the first time ever, really told us of FX. She said her childhood was misery, that it was an ordinary event for him to come into the house drunk and beat up the family. This all continued until Uncle Joe was about 16, when on a Sunday afternoon, they called Joe from his Uncle John's stable, where he always hung around, and he rushed home and pinned FX to the wall, threatening him that if he ever touched anyone in the family, he, Joe, would kill him. That, she said, took the fight out of FX, and from then on he, at least, would not beat up on the family.

I was questioning here—"Weren't there any fathers who were nice to their kids? Were they all the same, German, French, Polish, and so on?" She said the French were definitely different; she said most of them ... were easy to get along with. She went on—When she was a little girl, women had to take whatever their husbands handed them; there was nothing for them to do. She said now, men, even if not nicer, don't get away with it—they simply leave them and get a divorce. There's no question what system she thinks is best!

February 18, 1988

This morning I bid a sad and fond farewell to the County Line Woods. A road has been punched into it, the trucks are squatting to be loaded, and the very spot where I so often checked for first sedges is a splintered, battered ruin. Seemed so grotesque—my spot, my trees, my area, sullied, with the equipment required to wreck a woods, the world, and ourselves in the process.

February 26, 1988

I crossed to Block's Island, stepping carefully, alert for any fracture in the ice, and then walked up the flooded timber to the south. Thought to cross back at an angle, and lo, my path blocked by a freshet, from springs up above. It was hardly frozen, and there were areas where very dark water was boiling up, tearing away at the thin ice. I followed along on the slough side, the freshet becoming progressively quiet and solid enough to hold snow. And there was my otter family, all four, bellies traced on the snow. They had clearly hunted on the far end, and this was the path taken home. I noted one hole in the ice. They must have broken through after a long dive under the ice. They really have utmost confidence in their own river ability. They headed back to Block's Island; their den must be off in there somewhere. Hope with all my heart that no trapper finds it. So far the only tracks there are my own. Hope whoever sees it will think, "Oh hell, someone is already trapping there."

And to end the morning, a happening. Stuck my snowshoes to dry in the bank along road, and sat in car eating apple. There comes a snowplow, [and] I cleverly swung car to other side of road. Then thought of sacred snowshoes, ran in front of snowplow, stopped it, and rescued them. Judy thought I was crazy to do that. Well, perhaps, but the family has orders that they are to be cremated with me. I've had them for over 33 years now. They took me through all those swamps and deer yards, and it was the least I could do....

*

Spring 1980s

April 27, 1987

In the afternoon, there was general agreement, even enthusiasm that we should look for the pine snake we saw yesterday. So we picked up Judy and Ira, and all down to the harbor. The first sighting was a big snake smashed on the road. My heart sank; there was my animal. But, I walked to the badger burrow, and 6 feet from it stretched out in full, ominous length and

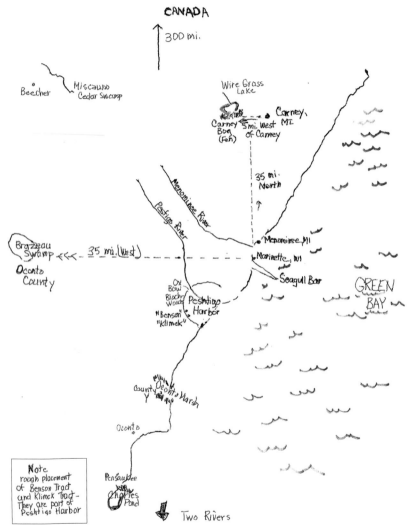

Judith Lintereur Johnson's hand-drawn map of LeRoy's favorite haunts in northeastern Wisconsin.

CHAPTER TWELVE

quiet, was a pine snake. In a trice there was an eager, but wary line in back of me, and [then came] the quavered query, "Is he alive, Grandpa?" As if to answer, the snake reared its head slightly, and began buzzing its tail. The reaction from the children was instantaneous. David Joseph began to cry in mounting crescendo, soon becoming a hysterical scream. I had not touched the creature. Suggested that the kids be ushered away from the scene—a trauma seemed indicated—then I picked up the animal. By now, Marie Ann, and then Paul David, came timidly forward—Marie in particular being very good about it. I returned the snake to its burrow ... [and it] incidentally showed signs of coiling and uncoiling in the loose sand. Julie occupied the kids in a search for garter snakes, which seemed to be numerous.

Then we returned to the car, but Danny Johnson wanted to look at the dead snake I had removed from the road and stretched out in the woods. He shouted, "Snake!" and lo, another had come up to this dead one, attracted by the scent I'd guess. This was a big fellow, coppery snub head, angrier than hell at being interrupted in what he must have thought was a sure thing. We checked him out, and he coiled off into the new grass and disappeared.

April 30, 1985

Yesterday to Long Swamp with Roger [Amundson]. A grim and somber day. What was a beautiful sweep of swamp is now a shambles of slash, muddy logging trails, a litter of logs and carnage, strewn over what was the finest swamp in the Northeast. It is an ecologic crime shouting to heaven, but there's no one to listen, surely not in heaven, and not likely on earth either. It's gone—Long Swamp is no more.

But we were not the only ones on U Lane. Down from Clay Curve there was a puff adder [hognose snake] crossing the road, with aplomb and great dignity. I picked him up, and he flattened his head in best cobra fashion, making no effort to even swing his head in my direction. His color was fascinating, muted olives and buffs, with an ideal pattern of stripes. His eyes and flicking tongue fitted this ensemble with perfection. How could nature arrive at such a blend, ideal as my hand and foot, just right....

This is so sad to say, but even the stretch of woods where I always parked and walked to the stream is gone. The big tamarack spars have either fallen or been knocked down, and I don't recognize the spot. The big rock must be covered with slash. Damn, when we humans decide to obliterate we have it in our power to do a bang-up job in a hurry. Now, just like that, presto, it's gone, no one to even give a backward glance.

May 7, 1982

Around the dike yesterday, in beautiful spring weather. It was just slightly cold off the bay, but once the shelter of the woods was reached, I took off my coat, and basked alone in the sun. One cerulean blue [eastern tailed-blue butterfly]—a love form, hutching through the grass and bright blue against all the green, a beautiful little scenario. First green heron of the year, flight of thrashers over the road, and trembling in the wind, the first *Arabis* [rockcress]—bright white in the new green, crosses, crucifer well named.

May 7, 1985

Every aspect of our culture blocks us from seeing nature, the one and only source of everything, our being, our structure, our life—in short, the attributes that we grant to God. Just think of it, were we to grasp that simple, existential fact, we would see nature as God. Is that what Spinoza saw?

May 7, 1987

This magic, most mystic of all our months.... With flush of green, shades of red, and the first flowers, we are at that surge of mystery, nature softly declaring her might. Some swamps bear the burden of winter—ferns, remnant green, flattened from bearing a weight of snow. Everything woody and in reach, hit hard by deer. At Wells Park, first flowers already gone, the next stage waiting, I think due to drought and sharp cold, which still strikes us each night. The canopy is shifting beautifully, but the ground story isn't going any place....

But everything is charged with excitement. Monday, May 4, we saw a blackburnian warbler, blaze orange, larger than life, technicolor, would you believe in a leafless maple. And then one [American] redstart, all dart, flash, and fight, flew into the tree, and in a scrap with a base in the Cretaceous or before, sent the blackburnian in full flight out of the tree and sight.

Roger and I yesterday, the 6th, on waterfowl count on Peshtigo Flowage. The woods along the flowage white with Trillium. What can you say about a pure-white woods and an eagle. He flushed from the forest at the launch sight, then settled in a leafed tree, and all there was to be seen were two patches of white, one head and one tail—not even recognizable as an eagle....

May 15, 1987

Found a spot where I could sit with back wedged against a giant pine in Stanley's Woods, nice sweep of new green before me. Just sat there admiring the woods, looking up at the pine. Hope with all my heart no one comes in to saw it down. How nice if it and the others in this woods could live out a normal span. Stanley hasn't cut anything. When I asked him about going in his woods, he said it was one to enjoy. Which it is. Now there's a rare man. Stanley's in his 80s. Wish he were, for the sake of the woods, in his forties.

May 17, 1989

Today to the beech woods in Ingallston. Warm enough for warblers to sing and move through branches; the *Claytonia* [spring-beauties] are in full flower, and the first maple leaves just beginning to show. Beech very copper colored; they are just beginning to unwind. The trunks appear so solid and firm. One can wish them their hundreds of years. Earth to triple in population by 2100. I will have long been an island in dishonored grass who none but beetles know (Emily D.), but I express a fervent hope that our forests will not be overcome by the flood, that they will still flourish, raise those leaves to the sky, flowers in incredible pink and blue facing the bright May sun. I hope that man in his folly doesn't think of them as building sites, and that finally, it will dawn on him, that these woods are the source of his life, and all good upon earth.

May 19, 1982

There are dunlins along the bay now, little blizzards of them, hurtling in perfectly coordinated flight, low over the water, a perfect combination of bay and bird. They live in perpetual motion—a sleeping or even resting dunlin seems to be a contradiction.

May 23, 1989

Can you imagine anything more meaningful to the spirit than a stand of towering hemlocks and a forest floor newly springing into its primitive green, sedges all in seed, and grasses, with newly crowned stalks? And tiny violets, a fleck of shocking white buried in the green, with wide-eyed *Coptis* [goldthread], looking surprised to be thrust once more into this ancient world, new now, as the eons that brought it into being.

May 24, 1986

To the harbor on an absolutely ideal day. Bugs were rough, but we had just the right degree of coolness. There was a nice bright sun, and in the open enough wind to sweep the biters away. Forest a flood of green—the leaves so painfully new. I had a feeling of witnessing their first full day in the sun—the antithesis of that day when they spiral down to earth.

Had a happening. There was this odd form moving over the forest floor, and my glasses fogged when I bent down to look close. It was a wasp moving rapidly over the leaves, a fresh spider clamped in its jaws. It dropped the creature and fled, leaving me with a fine fresh specimen I can check at leisure. No worry of resurrection or decomposition. What a boon for an arachnologist—to have a trained wasp that might function as a collector....

May 25, 1985

Every once in awhile, I have an encounter in nature that makes me rub my eyes and wonder, how can this all be? Where could it have come from? Thursday I turned over a hazel leaf, or rather a witch hazel leaf. There was this speck of life, that even in its minuteness I knew to be a weevil. My glass determined this to be true. Further it, by a most delicate and efficient beak, was attached to a vein, sucking up a ration of witch hazel extract. At home under the mike it came across as an incredible animal. Beak so fine and efficient, eyes needle point size and capable of taking in their world nicely. Feet with claws hooked ever so proper. Everything just perfect, proper for this creature's world. And I think most of all a structure so refined and intricate, bespoke of a sensory structure capable of responding to this system, a world beyond anything we might grasp, even, or more so particularly one beyond our comprehension. I just looked at it once more. There it is, a compact little miniature, odd in its own way as any dinosaur, quite simply out of this world. The antennae are elbowed and laid very neatly in grooves along the beak. Everything fits here like a very delicate lock and key. Or one might say, everything here was designed and patented for this little beetle.

And a spider. This was a salticid beauty that I plucked out of a leaf. I've watched spiders fumble about in their webs; shrink in terror from assaulting wasps; make furtive passes, and then blunder away from prey. All of which seems inept and even comic. But a spider under 20x mag[nification] is a creature of wonder and terror. Those piercing, gleaming eyes, mechanical and yet so alive; the deadly fangs; the hooks and complex brushes on all eight feet. And the hairs, magnified suddenly into spikes, stuck at a formidable and wicked angle, each a base we are told for no less than three sensory nerves. This is the original ogre, the monster—everyone's dream in pure and adulterated fright. One marvels; it's a good thing the bugs don't know....

May 27, 1989

Up to the Carney Bog with Judy and Wendel, Greg and Julie, and Joyce. Absolutely perfect, cool breeze, not even a touch of discomfort. Judith found them first: ram's-head on King Ridge. Then to top it all, she found another stand on the ridge (leading out to the main road), which shall hereafter be called Judy's Ridge. It's the west-facing slope of the ridge, back of the borrow pit. She found at least a half-dozen plants there. These were open in all their orchid finery; come on bugs! King Ridge plants still had their caps on so to speak.

Everyone had a good look at a crab spider's eyes, but listen to this, the real prize. Wendel is approaching the culvert crossing the Nathan Road when he hears a buzzing noise, at first taken to be bugs. Closer now, here are two pine snakes, with one, the larger of the two, locking his jaws around the head of the other. They buzzed in anger, at each other I'd guess. The attacker refused to release his grip, even when Wendel closed in with a close-up camera. Finally, they separated. Both were huge, the dominant one being close to four feet, the other, who had one blur of blood where the grip was locked, about half a foot less. Both prime specimens, newly shed, sleek, gleaming ominous in the grass. Judy pulled one out of the willow, Wendel the other. We, or rather Greg, took pictures of the two, freed from each other, both heads lined up.

June 3, 1981

Long Swamp is a shambles. Those magnificent firs and spruce that made this the finest swamp in our area, are decked now, awaiting their final trip to the mill. Those that were huge ... those that were just growing, the whole works. Those tops that stood there so fine in cold winter dawns are now just brown rubble on the ground—nothing. And so there they are, converted, as we do with everything, to cash, and let it be said they might as well be rags stacked there, or scrap iron; we do, indeed, make all things one—cash is the great leveler.

I fled the place after an hour. All that remains are little groves of cedar. The little feeder still runs toward the main creek, but it's a grotesque rivulet through the shambles of what was once a swamp.

June 7, 1987

Perfect morning on Oconto Marsh. Sun breaking through some ragged clouds in the east, with fresh wind rolling in from the west.... The marsh was alive—yellow-headed blackbirds, black-crowned night-herons, continual call of coot and grebe. And out of a hawkweed there came the flurry of tiny wings: my first least skipper of the year. Wings in deep beat threaded through the grass with great care, and then another hawkweed. I saw another down the path—this one favoring mouse ear chickweed. [Common] yellowthroat warbler, mounting up into willow not 10 feet from me. He throws back his head, delicate throat pulses, and out pours his song, again and again. I walked to the beaver dam, which has been refurbished in the past week; it's now more solid than ever. A willow has fallen into the flooded area, and on its recumbent trunk a kingbird was building a nest, really an untidy mess of feathers and bits of bark. From what I could see he just stuck a bit into the pile, and then shaped it by swiveling about in it.

June 17, 1988

Our days are so sunlit, so bright and brilliant, cloudless, breezy, akin to perfection, except that under all this something terrible is happening. We are on the edge of a terrible drought, and if it does not rain within the next week, a good share of the Midwest crop will fail. The woods are not showing distress yet; they are quite green. But many of the plants growing in the open show signs of stress. The streams are way down. I note in particular that the milkweed, all ready to flower, will in many cases be a little over a foot high.

Glen has the pump going on Oconto Marsh, so at least there we have a good head of water. Huge, open raft of mallards, males mainly, in open formation on the far end. The females are fighting for the life of their broods, but nature has released the males from that stress, and now all they need do is last out the summer, winter, and then be all set to go next spring.

CHAPTER TWELVE

June 18, 1985

Keyed out the ants plucked from the mound on the edge of Carney Bog. *Acanthomyops interjectus* [*Lasius interjectus,* larger yellow ant] comes very close, right to the fringe of hairs on the clypeus. The ant itself is an impressive creature; triangular jaws with strong serrate edge, eyes, antennae, claws, sensory hairs, the latter important in setting them apart from other ants. Color clear bronze, an efficient, perfect ensemble. The mound they lived in is a striking flat pile of well-sifted black humus; its surface pleated with a sulci of runaways, padded down by a billion little footprints—raw humus, smooth as a child's cheek, by miniscule feet. Surely one of the major art and engineering projects that have taken place in our area.

I believe the colony has been present for years. It may well be old as the swamp itself, with a tree ring of humic sand added on each season. One probe with my hammer and there was a system of runaways, choked with ants, swarming in subdued disarray over the disturbed area. There [were] the ends of a labyrinth of tunnels. Who knows what that humus hides. Who knows what goes on down there, in this subterranean darkness. What signals sent, what received, filtered through those antennae and sensory hairs; why they may well be sensitive as my fingertips. And what do they mean? What do ants have to say to me? Well, for one, they "be," they are existing in a powerfully integrated community with mechanics and interactions we can only glimmer by a correlate with ours. Secondly, they hold the world together, part of the complex we all depend upon, for surely they are an integral aspect of this bog, with an impact going back to its beginning. We all impact the world—some build, others tear down. I won't say where we are, but they definitely are builders, and have been so since the age of dinosaurs. In other words, if this world is something of wonder, beauty, utility, they were a factor in making it so, and still holding up their end.

June 19, 1986

Yesterday, Roger, Adrian, and I went to the scientific area in Shawano. This is an awesome stand of old timber, beech, and hemlock mainly, with some pine and sugar maple. You lower the voice in a woods such as this and clamber over the fallen trees with foreboding, fearing that this may be in store for the entire stand. When they hit ... they hit not only the ground but anything in the way: hemlock, maple or whatever. There is no ground story here, the shade is too heavy ... the floor was empty. Lots of leaves, though the duff struck me as shallow and rather sterile. We found two frogs—one *Hyla cru* [*Pseudacris crucifer,* spring peeper], and another, *Rana sylvatica* [*Lithobates sylvatica,* wood frog]. The logs, or rather those decayed enough, seemed rich enough. I found a goodly number of centipedes and carabid larvae, the latter mean looking devils that magnified could scare the hell out of anyone. Lots of ogres are to be found here. Slab city, sawdust, and decayed bark of beech and hemlock converted ultimately to the final bug, from what I see mainly carabid beetles....

One swift, shadowy movement on the floor, then it flew low into a tree; we had disturbed an ovenbird. Soon there were two, deeply disturbed birds; we mercifully fled.

At the car all turned to admire the stand. It was silent; the gigantic trees holding their own secrets. Sapling beech take over the sites where giants have crashed to earth. This community bears its future, its own continuity within its own structure. It is in fact a process. Indians surely moved through here, cougar crouched on these branches. It would be a senseless cliché to say only the trees remain, because they do, just barely and entirely by our sufferance. For this is the only stand of old growth in the area, indeed in NE Wisc, and a change of feeling in Madison could finish it off tomorrow. Such is life....

June 20, 1989

The pure joy of botany. I stumble through the mud on the edge of the bog at Stanley's, and there, at my foot, *Carex pauciflora* [few-flowered bog sedge; few-flowered sedge; star sedge], sort of trembling on its delicate threads, the neatly colored floral parts, subtle, as nature can be. This bog's offering to whom—the world, surely, and we too, if we only care to notice. It's worth waiting the year for, particularly when there is so much in between. Like *Cornus c*[*anadensis,* bunchberry] white, and those shades of green, a perfect pattern. They all are, I'd guess, but bunchberry seems a little more so. Walk past *Viburnum acerifolium* [dockmackie; maple-leaved arrow-wood; maple-leaved viburnum], just a little pink with the flowers ready to break out. *Danthonia* [wild oatgrass], little sods of thread grass; there's the seed itself, now, this very minute.... Richness of our northern woods. *Rubus* [blackberry; dewberry; raspberry] just now flowering. Tiger swallowtails, very businesslike, looking that situation over, a yellow and black wonder, the tropics surely, on a little sand hill, probably an old dune left by the bay, right in the middle of the forest. I actually heard warblers sing, and grosbeak songs were ringing throughout my walk....

Summer 1980s

June 24, 1989

Yesterday, Steve Miller, now wildlife director, and once my assistant, drove me up to the Carney Bog. Steve is a dear friend, and let me say, the epitome of concern, appreciation, compassion, just about any positive human quality you can think of. We had a fine morning together. *Arethusa* [*bulbosa,* dragon's-mouth] are at peak; imagine that pink in all the green. The sedges, exquisite in their complexity, subtlety and beauty. And the profound mass of green, shouting in a very quiet way its message of life.... Here's the mystery we will never grasp. The showys are twisting out of the ground, late this year, and the swamp saxifrage has just about peaked, with the gold flowers tipping the tall stem. Steve, committed to the principle long ago, wanted to talk about biodiversity, the bottom line we both agree to

Happy after a morning amid the sedges. Photo courtesy of Judith Lintereur Johnson.

all resource management.... When we walked out, he told me of the strong influence I'd had on him and other game managers also, and I admit it's nice to think this might be possible....

June 25, 1987

A shocking sight. Up ahead was the little hemlock woods across from Tony Kopish, and there parked before it was an array of heavy equipment trailers. I caught my breath. Maybe this was the town working on the road. No such luck. The hemlock woods is gone, shattered for a building site—what a dreadful happening. Coolness of hemlock woods in summer, defiance of their dark green to winter, white flowers of *Mitchella* [partridge-berry] on the floor, certain sedges, and warblers flitting through the branches: all of the past—it's patios now, and power mowers.

I wonder how can I be concerned about my own mortality when woods that have so much to offer life, now and in the future, are crashing down, literally ground to bits in shredding machines.

I walked through Stanley's Woods, and all the while there was that mechanical, scary whine of machinery—man the destroyer. I suppose it's but a question of time before Stanley's Woods becomes a building site. Both he and his father protected and treasured this woods, but Stanley's in his 80s, and it's only a question of time before he passes on. We should treat our forest tenderly, with love and compassion; they have so much to offer. And forbid use of the word resource. Never let it pass our lips, unless to curse those who see in these forests nothing but resource and investment.

June 25, 1989

Judith drove me to Oconto Marsh. Bit of a brisk wind, not overly warm, nice sun—perfect summer day. A field trip with Judith is different. I look at the leaf; she peers under them. I admire a blue flag, she's down into the core of the plant. I step on the rocks along shore; she turns them over. And from these sites come a host of larvae, flat worms, blobs unknown to me, beetles I've never observed, and a sense of wonderment; what a sharp observer she is. She carefully picked a dragonfly, or rather a damselfly larva and insisted I admire its caudal gills through my glass. Talk of a delicate, neat, very workable, and surely very ancient structure. Here was one of nature's earliest and most persistent, therefore, successful patents. Those light blue *Enallagma* (damselflies), in such carefully controlled flight, hovering, now here, now a plant ahead, going through their intricate rituals, male and male, male and female, lived by those little leaves. As Judy pointed out, you can see the water pulse through them. And they, the larvae, have that mask, the extending and grappling jaw—another one of nature's very successful, and most ancient patterns, evolved long before any land vertebrate we recognize appeared on earth.

July 8, 1988

Years ago, when this summer sun would rise up, we would call out, "There she comes, the Old Haymaker." Now, there is no hay; sun, is rather the hay burner, destroyer of hay and corn, oats, everything. We are in the grip of a most dreadful drought, our nighttime temps have been close to 80, daytime on the edge of a hundred. We've had a week of this, and there is no relief

CHAPTER TWELVE

in sight. The long-range forecast is for more of the same. I've been out on Seagull Bar these past two days. It is, if not quite a riot of birds, a real haven for them. The receding waters of the bay are setting up a series of marshes and sloughs, and even one extensive wet sand community.... One of the shallow ponds had a wealth of shorebirds. Phaleropes, dowitchers, and above all, greater yellowlegs, tilting and balancing along, all so dreadfully earnest, absorbed in a eager search for whatever is in the mud they need.

July 9, 1985

Spiders might well be a metaphor for our attitude toward the natural world. They shock, some they horrify. No one gives much thought to them. And once you know and understand them, they become creatures of surpassing beauty. They surprise and jolt you close up. Two collected yesterday were of such supreme beauty under the [magnifying] glass that you want to proclaim them. How can you tell the world about spiders?

One was rolled tightly in a leaf—a sort of cigar spider.... The legs, head, and abdomen in their several divisions looked like a nautilus. Under the mike, it leaped up at me as a creature of pure fantasy. The color stippled like a very fine, rare marble in a pattern of white and grey. The head was dominated by eight bright eyes, a lurid gleam that death had no effect on. Its fangs were something to wonder at—this was *Pachygnatha* [thickjawed orb weaver spider]—thick jaw, with a powerful brace holding the wicked, sinister fangs, a work of art no kris or dagger could equal, no matter how finely worked and polished.

July 12, 1981

To TR this weekend, mainly to see my sister [Maryon], who is still very ill, although it seemed to me she was much more alert than the last time we were there. She talked evenly of the future and calmly of her condition. While we were there, Father Becker came in and gave her communion. We all received together, a lovely little ceremony. Most moving, my mother. Right before the priest gave Maryon the host, my mother—with unspeakable tenderness—moved quickly and placed her hand behind Maryon's head and held it until she received, then with German practicality, gave Maryon a little sip of water.

Mama is fine. She talked of TR most of yesterday morning. She talked of her dad and the French—his dislike of them, of course. She said one of the bravest things she ever did was to invite Grandma Heroux to her house for a meal. It must have been something.... She couldn't understand why her dad disliked a nice young man like my father.

July 21, 1985

Nice spiders in Tony's marsh, one a *Misumena* [flower crab spider] in splendid white and pink that on [a] woman would be ravishing. I collected her and felt guilty for it. *Misumena* affects me that way and want to go into some detail about her here, assuring myself at least, and anyone who may read this later that she died not in vain.

Afield to collect butterflies in northeastern Wisconsin ... and to search for spiders. Photo courtesy of Judith Lintereur Johnson.

I won't begin with her colulus, but it's the first thing I searched for—in her case a little flap adnate to the spinnerets. Her eyes are most remarkable glittering points of black, except the two median anterior row, which flash and re-flash a deep red, a signal to whom? Then the jaw, neat, fine, each burnished scimitar, sporting its own tooth, as it were, high polish, dark, almost black at the tips, but right to the end a deepening of the bronze. Her form had its own perfection, legs terminated by the most delicate and perfect claws, protected by a series of fine brushes. When I first saw her, she was swaying, suspended from a thread she had spun, swaying slightly in the wind, one pair of legs stretched out in cruciform pattern as she twisted rigid in the form nature buried in her neurons—how long ago—thousands certainly, millions? When did the *Misumena* first scramble onto a flower?

August 2, 1987

Mother Nature gave us all a demonstration of her might last night. For three hours, we cowered in heat and semidarkness, broken by a continuing flash of lightening and boom and blast of thunder. And rain, a good share of it ending up in my basement. We've not had any rain for a month, and this is most welcome. Even the lawns are struggling to a semblance of green,

CHAPTER TWELVE

breaking through the dead brown. It was hot and humid early today, but now, in midafternoon, there's a touch of cool, with rattling maple leaves. Stiffness of late summer is overcoming them.

Reading of the destruction of forests the world over, and the efforts at replanting. Why can't we let nature take over, in her own way. Why do we fear the word *wild*. The "wild" produced every aspect we hold dear, not only our bodies, but our minds. It produced everything we see about us and depend upon to sustain existence. Why are we like nouveau riche, disdaining and disowning a parent, for we have but one in a long run: Mother Nature, the process we see around us....

August 6, 1986

I am lost in admiration for the dragonfly collected last week at Carney. He (Judy determined it a male) is a huge graceful bug, wingspread of 4-1/2 inches, and what wings they have, the texture of strong gossamer that ... glints in the light. The most striking aspect of these wings—they are a marvel of nature—is the two nodal veins. They are much more than thickened areas; rather, they are built buttressed into vanes, vaned and angled, as if designed by a engineer who really knew his stuff, a perfect mechanical structure. And the darts at the end of the abdomen are really flatted leaves. The eyes, the assortment of hooks, jaws tucked under their flaps, and above all the grass green sheen, just the thing for a creature spending much of its time, clinging, wings adroop from grass. This is an incredible animal. When we humans think we are unique, it might be well to contemplate the big dragonfly, *Anax junius* [common green darner].... It is said that of all dragonflies, *Anax* is most modern, most advanced. And that's what we think of ourselves, mainly because we dominate this earth so totally. And *Anax*, skimming high over the marsh and forests, can witness the same....

August 25, 1986

Morning cool and so quiet [on Oconto Marsh]. There was a reflection of the far bank on the water, exactly like a Corot painting. Discordant bird activity—cormorants flying, full length. One massive mixed flock of blue-winged teal mixed with green-winged, the young now same as the elders. The minority of downys that got to fly cut the air, a far cry from peeping over the water, ecstatic over a fleck of green duck weed. So things change. And most surprising of all, a racket at my feet, and two least bittern young, callow as spring itself, flapping over the slough almost into the water, struggling then for a grip on a cattail. In my glass, there was the natal down, sticking up from the head like an Indian headdress. They appeared terrified by the world, abristle with fear, still at the mercy of the universe. Life is a tremendous struggle, just to grapple with a cattail. Later, an adult with sureness and skill, flapped over the far marsh, and vanished.

September 2, 1985

Already the second day of this most blessed of months. This morning walked through the oak woods at the harbor in a sort of wonder—the woods just perfect, cool, green, absolutely perfect balance, nice bright sun, the leaves waving so firm and secure. This month in the air, next month the duff; that's the way it goes for all of us.

Good look at the strong white oaks in Klimek Woods. They must be well into their second hundred, and still they wave there so strong. All the fires, powerful winds, the bugs that could have got to them, men that surely looked them over, and thought, no, we'll take that tree and let this one here. I hope they can be secure for the next hundred or so.

A morning with the spiders. That lovely little white specimen that I uncover in hazel leaves is close to *Cheiracanthium* [yellow sac spider], a clubinoid. It has two very neat hooks on each foot—eyes, bright and black all alike. Fangs that seem to be in sheaths—something odd about them. But the color is what is most beautiful and subtle: very delicate, yellow and white with sort of herringbone striping on the back. Then, poking around in a goldenrod patch, there were three big leaves plastered together, and an awful lot of web—a big fellow. Sure as hell, a huge *Epeira* [*Araneus*–common orb-weaving spider], the one with a swollen, lozenge-shaped abdomen, tumbled out with something akin to hasty terror that sort of embarrasses me. After all, such a formidable creature. Well, I found her, poking around on the ground and got her head in my glass. Now there is an animal: four pairs of eyes sharp as tacks, and shrewd, and a set of fangs almost scary in visage. Oddly enough the fangs move independent of the boss; they were working around in a sort of probing manner. She finally nailed me with the claws on her feet, which sort of startled, and I dropped her. She is an absolutely wondrous creature.

And just one more: a *Pisaurina mira* [nursery web spider], warm brown and black, good size, one cm, with the black stripe bordered by the most delicate line of white, a refinement almost without equal. Why would

Gaia even think of something like that? What need, why, how, why that nice warm color, why that delicate white border, the sort of thing a careful and imaginative seamstress might build into a product. And there it was tucked away under a leaf, no one to admire all that except other spiders. It's a design for catching flies in the long run, that's it, and for replicating same. Energy transfer indeed....

September 12, 1980

Last night to a wake at Coleman, my second cousin Reuben Ammerman.... He spent his entire life on the town of Brazeau farm, where he died of a heart attack. He was one of the important personages in my life. I liked him for his quiet ways and because, when I was a kid, he treated me as an adult and suffered my love of horses. It was he who took the team to a tub on Saturday and bathed them with a cloth, because they liked it, he said. I recall working with him long ago when he was plowing some strong turf with a walking plow, and how he patiently trod down the furrow because the team could not pull fast enough to turn it over. He didn't have much to say these past years, and would fall asleep as I talked to him, probably part of his condition.... Well, Reuben, old friend, rest in peace.

🍃

Fall 1980s

September 23, 1981

A terrible trip to TR. My sister, Maryon, with a mind as crystal clear as a grad student is laying there watching, feeling her life ebb away from her. No complaint, no wistful talk, nothing. She lays there and talks about anything you wish to broach—history, my mother's potato pancakes—anything but her illness.

My mother was with her when she received the sacraments last week. Tears came to Maryon's eyes. She has been so honest with everyone including the Lord. She wants to live; that is all she asks of the world.

She called to me in such a firm voice as I left: "Come see me again, Lee!" How I hold her in my affections. Her face is thin now, and she looks so much like my father, the effect is startling. Daddy, I could kneel right now, if I were only able.

October 4, 1981

The living praise God and beg his mercy. Then they drive home to dinner. The dead stare silent, sightless into eternity.

This morning, on a rainy Sunday, at 8:30, my sister Maryon joined her father. She's gone, and the bell indeed tolls for me. Daddy is gone so long; he seems like a dim mystery, a rumor that was a part of my life. One by one, we fade, first in sorrow; then the memory slowly fades. All of us step into line. Weep for yourself too, LJ, and all your folly.

October 14, 1982

This afternoon picking stone on the road at the harbor. The world was so beautiful I turned away from it, unable to stand all this no longer. There was a strong flight of dragonflies, the big fellow *Anax,* and they were hawking up a storm on the road before me. In the slanting sun their wings were not clear, but actually bronze, so intense that at first I thought this a new species. But no, when they were directly overhead, their wings were clear, without trace of color. So they glinted along, hawking with quick movements best described as deft, snap and chew, quick little aside movements, hitting the little flies, who were also taking advantage of this last, almost certainly, sun.

November 3, 1987

Two new bugs this a.m. I was plodding down the woods road, when it struck me there was some little speck flying about. Or it did not seem to fly but rather was progressing, so learnedly I took it for a goldenrod seed with remarkable control.... But then I chased one with my cap, and lo, first I took it for a moth. Delicate, dusty, wings folded along back. Then the truth dawned on me—this was a *psychodid* fly, a moth fly. Such a little speck, flying through this chill woods in fury. Then, while inspecting some mosses, there was this creature—not an ant, possibly a mimicking salticid spider. I wet a finger and placed it under my glass. It's a scorpion fly—*Boreus brumalis*, black and shiny, with vestigial wings sprouted from its pronotum.

December 2, 1983

It would seem that a person who asked no more out of life than a more or less steady stream of visits from her children, grandchildren, and great grandchildren, especially the latter, while she held them, served them something, or knit something for them, would go on forever, but this was not the case. I record here in deep sorrow that my mother, Marie, passed away at noon, on Nov 29. And I finally realized in shock ... that this time it was her they were wheeling down the length of her parish church, and ... did she ever remain faithful all her long life in you oh Lord through all the tragedies and trials of her life. Her middle years were laden with crisis—the commitment of her sister, Annie, to a mental institution, where she lived out her life. My mother, after visits to her, would come into the house literally bowed over with grief. And [then there was] the senility of her mother, who in time became dangerous and brutal, while my mother tried to calm her, in her arms.

Her father's death—she came home and sobbed, "Now our home will be broken up." I learned the news from her as she was walking swiftly down the street, arms tucked under her apron, as she ran to be with her sisters. And that night, when the angelus rang, she sat at our table in stricken horror, and said, "Now they are going to ring for my dad." Suddenly, over the city, came the ominous toll of the bell, while we all sat in deathly silence, counting each toll of the bell. All this was against the grim background of the Depression, when she never knew from one month to another whether we would keep our house. She said, "LeRoy, if you don't go to work, we are done." And you can bet I went to work.

Then on August 16, 1949, she was dealt one massive blow—my father died at age 50, and she was left with nothing. Faced a world as a widow, stripped of everything—my father's love and companionship, the limited income she lived on so very well, no income whatsoever, and her house in debt. But now something new entered her life: a steady stream of grandchildren that became her joy, her pleasure and concern, especially the latter. And it was to them, in the most literal sense of the word, that she dedicated the rest of her life. She never ceased to grieve for my father, never even considered the companionship of another male, and not a month before her death, she told me happily and with relish how the girls she worked with would say, "How did you land such a handsome boyfriend?" The thought of this situation over all those years, no less than 65 of them, still brought a pleased smile to her face.

But one more shock came into her life. On October 4, 1981, her daughter Maryon died, and while outwardly she was unchanged, something deep within her said that she would join her and my father, someplace.

One year ago she, on her own, quietly left the home she and my father set up over 50 years ago and ... moved to an apartment. She asked me in August if I didn't think she was getting thin and told me then she had no appetite. It was the beginning of a condition that took her away.

The last time I talked to her was on my birthday; she had sent me a card, signed Mom, two bucks, and a note. She sounded ok, hopeful certainly, talked about her plans for Thanksgiving with Ruth. She took sick on Saturday, but told her daughters not to tell us—Donnie and I—about it because we would come down and the weather was poor. I'd planned to go to TR Wednesday, but by then she was gone.

I have a thousand images of her, and there's no sense in sorting them out here. But there is one I shall certainly carry to *my* grave. That was when Maryon received communion about a week before she died. My mother, as the priest held the Host to her, swiftly put her hand behind Maryon's head, raised it up with unspeakable tenderness, then gave her a sip of water, and said, "Now lay back, Maryon." Then she and I and Joyce received. So let's give Maryon the last word on this—She told me the nicest thing about being sick is having mother take care of you.

*

Winter 1990s

December 21, 1992

Here's the first of the new season, and already we are deep into it. This morning, along the Ox-bo, had a most graphic demonstration in grey and gloom of how the Northerners could have worried of the sun's return. It was at first nothing, then a blur of light just making it through the clouds, a tiny globe, as if someone, Woton or whomever, may have been strangling it. Then, by the time, now in deeper woods, I got to the river, it had vanished without trace, and there was only the dark forest, a sky

A morning coffee in first light. Photo courtesy of Judith Lintereur Johnson.

of almost desperate, helpless grey, and me trudging along, wondering why in hell my feet were so cold....

January 1, 1993

Well, I came up here [private study] a little before 7, and there was light filtering into the room—an omen for the coming year? Anyway, was up early, going through Jimmies [Jim Zimmerman's] book on sedges, they being always my bête noire, and then to the early composites in the back of the book. Of course, that's all some time away. We have three months of weather before us ... just came over radio—it's -4 out and will stay in the singles for the day....

January 3, 1995

Yesterday unaware of the cold. Down to the tracks. Nothing there, but it was horribly cold. Came back with frozen fingers, and right now my fingertips are a mass of cracks, some of them bloody. Now, today, we are only going to have 8–9 above, and tonight the temps will plummet, with wind chills of -50 in some areas north of here. Well, there will be no field for me in the days to come....

January 4, 1993

It's dark and chill out this a.m. There is a promise of snow, and we are still coated with ice, a very mean world outside.... I remember very well when after a three-day weekend, we wended our reluctant way to the factory, and there suddenly in the violent glare of factory and roar of machinery was our reality, day in and day out.

February 6, 1995

I often wonder—will anyone read what I have written long after I'm gone? If anyone should, I welcome you. And I hope you love humanity, and Mother Earth, for if this be your inclination, I have something to say to you. For I, too, have a deep regard and fondness for both. This has been the leitmotif of my life. I am now 75 and will one of these years be finished. And right now, people like myself are in retreat and eclipse in this country. We are in the grip of reactionaries, some of them in positions of great power; their cosmology and view of the universe and man is based on a Stone Age pattern of myths, addressing the dark and irrational side of human nature—those fears, dreads, and hates that still bubble up and out of our unconscious. They do not hesitate to attack the very basis of our civilization, and the rational structure that has so painfully and slowly evolved over the past 500 years.... These men are leading us to ruin—powerful forces who see dominance and money in this misalliance are fostering it. I wonder now, from your vantage point, how, or to what extent they will have succeeded, whether they have finally vanished, or if fear and hate, ignorance and the dark, have established them in high places.

February 19, 1994

Just for the hell of it last night, took down my D[onald]C[ulross]P(eattie's] *Green Laurels*, [*The Lives and Achievements of the Great Naturalists*] and began to read it. I've not looked at it for years, and page after page it came back to me—my joy at receiving this book (I sent for it through Wards in TR), my shock that anyone would write on such a topic, and my struggle with the fact that after all, I was but a factory worker trapped in a hopeless situation. I was just getting to know a little. Gary and I were doing some fieldwork; I marveled that such a world existed.

In a perverse way, I assured myself that it all begins with woods and marshes; this was basic, and I had them in spades, all around me, for the taking so to speak. In those days, I fantasized myself in the tradition of the Fr[ench] naturalists, esp. [plant biologist Jean-Baptiste] Lamarck and [Constantine Samuel] Rafinesque, above all Raf. I've forgot that now, but that sentence "he too knew the flashing finny..." always resonated with my longings. Because clearly, I was already at 18 a failure, rightly disliked by most, a freak of which no good could come—exactly what the frontier society thought of Rafinesque. [And botanist André] Michaux, dead on a tropical island [Madagascar], far from our forests. Somehow or another I always regarded them as the baseline. Of course, I still do.

I first read the book over 50 years ago; my situation has changed immeasurably. I am, in fact, a naturalist, a professional I might say, far away indeed from the days when I thought a sedge a joke, an abstraction beyond everyone's grasp.... I know most of them now, but still there is something that eludes me. My response is all on the surface; the depth—what that sedge or frog, or bug, *really* is eludes me. Sometimes I get just a glimmer, feel I might hit it, and then it fades away. I sometimes think that, for myself, I'd do more good just to sit like a monk and meditate, rather than reading and "observing." But, I'm obsessed with time and nailing my knowledge down, fearful there is something not known well enough, material that is at least in my purview. I don't know why this should be—guess it's my search for something to write about. After all, once you strive for the depths, unless a poet or expert essayist, like Annie [Dillard], or Diane Ackerman, you flounder.

Sometimes in the turmoil of my family relations, with all its cares and problems, I sit and review all the sites where I'll relate this summer—Block Woods, Carney, the harbor generally, Penn, the bay—and a wave of joy comes over me. My salvation: Mother Nature, *Salvator* [savior]. Then, I could easily recite the Litany of Loreto [Litany of the Blessed Virgin Mary—first documented in 1558], inserting Gaia for the Blessed Mother, blessed Gaia; *spes nostra* [our hope], *vita* [our life], *dulcedo* [our sweetness] indeed. *Ad te clamamus* [To thee we cry]....

February 21, 1993

Yesterday, Joe and I into the Ox-bo forest; it was an ideal winter day, temp in the low 20s, no wind, and bright sun. The going was perfect on snowshoes, and conditions absolutely ideal. The crust strong but covered with a layer of light snow that was of such texture that even the creases on the smaller animal tracks showed. I had a feeling of being in a tableau, if not vivant, then mostly so, every step framed as a picture; the sun gleaming in through the hemlocks, reflecting on the dark trunks, glinting on snow that was all but covered with animal tracks. Most common are coon ... close to the river runaways show, padded down so that the tracks individually are obliterated.... A close study reveals tracks of every side, some totally perfect with even the ridges on the claws etched into the packed snow. Their claws are formidable, not quite up to badger speed, but close. Only one series led to what could have been a den tree; the others wandering about the woods in what seemed to me erratic patterns, going nowhere. Then, again, close to the river, there are colonies of microtines, and in some places, webs of *Peromyscus* [deer mice], racing from one hole in the snow to another; some, but not many [*Sorex*] *cinereus* [masked shrew], and at least two *Blarina* [*brevicauda,* northern short-tailed shrew]. These latter not classic enough—the trough in the snow, to say for certain. There along the river, are still identifiable wild rye and reed canary, with the twisted leafless stems of *Smilax* [greenbrier]. Pleurocarpous mosses on trunks that I turn away from; they have confounded me for so long. I don't care to consider them. But mainly it was the perfection of the day that was overcoming. Sun, snow, forest, then the vast, inert expanse of the river, with mile long vistas in either direction.

February 23, 1994

Continue with my review of the [Cyperaceae]. Taking Jim [Zimmerman] and going through all species listed in our range, my state of knowledge is thus: sight recognize reasonably 26 species; with Jim and glass, another 27; know, but never with certainty, 6; finally, 16 with little or no acquaintance. Not much for the time spent with them. I had too little method, too desultory, too many gaps. But my interest never flagged. A challenge at first. As I felt my way along and began to know the group, they became close friends of mine, and I regard them so to this day. *Carex pedunculata* [long-stalk sedge] seems to be first, and I watch for it eagerly, as once I watched for orchids.

February 24, 1994

Judith called last night and told me that Lloyd is dead. That is Lloyd Sebero, for over 15 years my assistant and good right hand man. He was 83, almost to the end a hard tough woodsman, who had literally spent his life there, and knew no other occupation save those centered in that milieu: logger, trapper, fisherman, and hunter. He was a consummate expert in all these, but was not beyond admiring and asking of flowers we passed in the woods.

He was born in Oneida, had some fracas with his father, and came to this part of the state. He lived with the Wickmens. Then on an election day in the thirties, a raw April day, there came this family moving to the north part of the county. The family was driving the cattle, and all the family's goods were loaded on a hayrack, and the team driven by a pretty girl. It was Clarice Berg, of a family of Norsk out of Iowa, and in time they were married. They raised a big family of big boys, all of whom are still to this day centered around Lloyd's home in the town of Wagner.

He worked as a farmer and logger, and when he was in his thirties, began for FP, first at Pembine, and then at Pound. He worked off and on for [DNR's] Fish and L[aw] E[nforcement], and in 1962 I put him on, eventually making him a tech. Then he took off, loving the responsibility that he finally had, beaver-trapping equipment operating, and above all a woods boss. He worked on all my dikes, woods' roads, ran the timber sales, built my roads, often literally, he being the one who handled the equipment. He had a strong attachment to his work, and was very proud of his accomplishments. He retired at age 65 plus (He was retired for 20 yrs.), and after that my glory days were over—my district never the same. There was no replacement for him. He always logged on the side, and now it became a full-time occupation. For over 15 years this was his occupation, and he worked so long as he could.

He was a moose hunter, who hunted up in Canada and Alaska, loved to travel in wilderness country. I saw little of him after he retired. We never visited, and in time drifted apart. I heard he had a heart condition, and this eventually got to him. Well, rest in peace, Lloyd, although the word seems strange when applied to you. If there's anything that he was never up to, [it] was resting.

In all our years we had exactly one argument, and I gave him one direct order. There were some hemlock in the Eagle, and against my orders he marked them for cutting. He told me some years later he had no idea I could get that burnt up over trees. Well, we all had our proclivities.

March 3, 1995

I was thinking: No matter what I or others may think, there can be no argument that since I was twenty, I knew that somehow I'd be a naturalist. All thought there was no idea how this might be carried out. But anyway, in the summer of 1941 my factory closed down. The government had requisitioned all the aluminum for the military, and there was no work in Two Rivers. So I went on the farm until fall, when the factory called me back until the end of October.... That winter was the most significant in my life. When it began, I was floundering. When it ended, I had a goal, or at least a target to shoot for, and for the next 50 plus years have not deviated from it.

I was always odd in that my tastes were not those of others. When I was a sixth grader on the farm, and all excited, shouted to the hired man, "That was a kingbird in the orchard!" (I recognized it from the figure in [Ernest Thompson] Seton's *Two Little Savages*, where Yan was shown peering at a kingbird.) He [the hired man] said, "There's something wrong with that guy—he should be locked in a cage of birds!" I recall the remark very well, but then had no idea what generated the animosity toward bird watching in my society. Anyway, that was it. From then on, I was tagged: there was something wrong with me. This all reached a peak when my dad apologetically asked me not to collect butterflies ... my mother, less circumspect on such matters, simply said that was "nuts stuff" in the certain belief that interests such as mine were a sure road to the asylum. And so it went.

But by [age] twenty, criticism such as this meant nothing to me. My friend Gary [Daetz] and I mapped out our future together. He was then down at Madison in the university, taking some bio courses, among them a course with Leopold. He became interested through these in bees and owls and urged me to work with him on both. Thus we set up beehives, and then throughout that winter, with a padded number one pole trap, we captured owls....

And above all, I began reading [Henry David] Thoreau seriously, particularly Henry Seidel Canby's bio of Henry—still one of the cornerstone books in my library. He defined Henry's problem, which I quickly grasped as my own: What to do when society has no use for your talents. Henry's response was to simplify his life, and this became in effect my agenda.

I also, with my Kodak Monitor, tried my hand at wildlife photography, but never had the proper equipment to make anything out of it. Gary, much more rigorous than I, saw nature photography as our future. The first books—Edwin Way Teale's *Grassroots Jungle* and *The Golden Throng*—both on insects, were new on the market and were a revelation to both of us. So that was it. We would be nature photogs, except that I had it in the back of my mind to become a writer, and from winter '41–'42 on, began keeping a journal, a composition book that cost a quarter, now unfortunately lost.

But anyway, the die was cast. Gary became a nature photog [wrote a book titled Rookery Island], but I did not follow him to Alaska or Oregon, despite his lifelong urgings. He died in 1972 under the most tragic circumstances [suicide], which grieves me to this day. I eventually entered the university, and became finally a programmatic naturalist, now hiding nothing from anyone, even the people in TR, who, as our neighbor told me later, thought that I would "never come to anything." But, he said, "You surprised them." Well, I am not so sure of that. I never did become a recognized author, but with some 26 volumes of my journal on the shelf, can think of myself as a writer; then there are my 500 plus newspaper columns. So, win some, lose some.

But this is for certain—I still remain faithful to my naturalist's instincts; this remains my one true and abiding interest, and hope to remain so until I die. There are certain difficulties looming on the horizon. My reading and mike ability are fading with my eyes, and I foresee that my driving will, one of

CHAPTER TWELVE

these years, be over. And my feet pain me no end, so old age is catching up on me. But to balance that I have developed a philosophy I can live with, am learning more each season; so what the hell, as we say in TR.

March 17, 1993

Yesterday, a pleasant surprise. A big, bearded man approaches me as I'm heading for the store—it was Emmet (Polish name)[Judziewicz]. We had a pleasant hour going over my sedges, and he is taking some to Madison. I was going to give him all of them, but am keeping some of the more attractive ones, for "further study." Anyway, it was pleasant to talk with someone who loves *Carex* as I do. I look forward to another year with them. The very first will be *pedunculata*, somewhere in the southern part of the area....

🖋

Spring 1990s

March 28, 1993

Up in the UP with Judith yesterday p.m.... to the muskeg. Hummocks in the open, channel's frozen with soggy snow over the ice. As Judith pointed out, the hummocks' southern slopes are really warm, I think 25 C, compared to the ambient of 20. And we saw our first moth—swarms of them bursting out of the cotton grass tussocks, settling onto the depressed shrubs, then another swarm into the air. It was a grand, exhilarating experience. There is something so classic about floundering through a northern MI bog, negotiating shoals of soggy snow, slipping still on ice. There are the old familiar plants with some months to go, and here [are] these fragile moths, rushing the season, unable to withstand this spring sun....

I have the moth home, and spent the evening without any success trying to figure it out. It's small, not two cm in wingspan, golden bronze, legs spinulose, wings—particularly the lower, m2 area, fimbriated. You'd think that being so early, and in such restricted habitat, it would come easy, but nothing came close and haven't a clue.

Put a sprig of *Andromeda* under my mike; shocked at the beauty of the bundle scars and the structure of the stem. It's a struggle working through the muskeg at any time, more so now than any time of the year. But, you can make it, and there's surely a reward. Man as witness, transcending our primitiveness, by finally recognizing our origins, deconstructing ourselves, transcending our origins by relating to them. We step into the melting snow and the glazed ice, right into the glacier's tracks, and should we have any, our future....

March 29, 1993

In something close to spring splendor up to the muskeg west of Wells. The moths were out, collected three, and throughout the a.m. there was continued call of cranes, rattling on every horizon. It was over an hour before I saw them, exactly two, making all that racket, straight across the meridian, and then cutting across the southern horizon. As luck would have it, in a sort of exuberance, I almost fell off a hummock, braced myself, and tore a ligament or something in the gastrocnemius area. Geez, did it ever hurt, still does. It was a shirtsleeve day, the muscle bit ended my bogging, so to the Hayward lake outlet. A muskrat swimming the open channel, and was searching the river, when there came this long, slender shadow on the dark water. Looked up and there was a long silent file of geese, very determined, no nonsense, onto the northland. No city suburb for these birds. The snow will really go now—even the bank before our house is vanishing, and the wood negotiable. So it's here, here it is, *exultavit* [be joyful].

The little brown moth keyed out to a tortricid [tortrix moths or leafroller moths]—checked with several foresters, and entos, and none know of a moth flying this early. It struck me that it was more numerous near the road, where the bay is more waterlogged.

April 20, 1994

I avert my gaze from the monstrous crimes that have been committed in the past year along the bay. For one, a fellow has filled in a large section of marsh, right on the shore, blacktopped it, and erected two horrible houses, multistoried, painted a dark varnish, utterly destroying the sweep of horizon that the other cottages built there didn't even touch. I wonder how permits were handled here. I hope with all my heart that they are flooded out in the next rise—in the '70s this land was under water.

Then the destruction of the woods on our north border; a huge pile of sand, and atop this angled to break horizon max, a trailer, raised up as a sort of monument to the brainless destruction we bring to all values related to the wild. Save for public land, it's gone. It's going to be dead as a doornail. All the bay shore will be totally urbanized within the next decade. There seems to be no brake on all this. And that oak woods is a shambles, slash and spoil, all the large trees gone, the smaller doomed to windthrow.

We are all, in matters such as this, Attila the Hun redux, monsters of stupidity. Nature does so very well in establishing habitat for everyone and thing, man included. Why must we be so damn destructive, so valueless, so blind to what we are up to. It said in Sunday's paper that all the hills in Sauk County will eventually be crowned by a house; people from Madison fleeing their wrecked city, now doing the same to one of the most pleasant and ecologically sound landscapes in the Midwest. It's just all so sad! We are vandals.

April 28, 1994

When I read of the unconscious, and above all childhood associations, seeming so simple and facile in some, I wonder of my own. For, no matter what, I do have a powerful, abiding link to the natural world, one that took hold of me when very young, and that I have developed ever since. To say that it dominates my life is an understatement. I have lived it and often wonder why. First of all, my habitat. Until fourth grade we lived a block away from the mouth of the rivers and the lake, waves booming against the pier, fog horns blasting; even when not beside it this was a presence to me.

Gulls, always gulls, obviously different types, which no one knew. "What's a seagle?" Fear of dragonflies and fascination of bees. The former fascinated me, even when filling me with dread. We all knew they sewed up ears—some said mouths also. Fish tugs with Fr[ench] names. (Bon Jour, Bon Ami, Manville LaFond, The Allie Brothers: All Fr[ench] Canadian families who came to TR in 1830–1840s.)

Then when we moved to lower 20th St. We lived but a block away from the river; huge, we thought, as the Miss[issippi], with broad marshes and a horizon that still to this day has to be one of the most striking in the state—farms, forest, and of course, a marsh. Surveys saying it's one of the most extensive on the western shore of Lake Mi. Within a year we had a rowboat, *The Seaweed*, and we spent the rest of my TR days on the river, with its ducks, coots, herons, bitterns, gulls, terns—an endless and enduring succession. Then there was my father, a F[rench] chauvinist; father a lumber jack. He brought up on a pioneer farm, 16 years old when he left his ancestral Canadian village in the forests of Marinette Cty—a place that in some ways he never left because the people he knew, all his relatives and friends, talked it endlessly—it was my spiritual milieu, and remains so to this day.

Then my reading, solid Ernest Thompson Seton, and of the Indians, James Willard Schultz, and always westerns—such was my life. The one given I had was a certain curiosity that just led me on and on. I was a rarity in my town, a kid equally at home in a library, always loved books, and on "the crick." It was a good combination, leading me on and on. To this day I cannot pass anything in the woods without wondering of it, except now I know how and where to find out. And this, I think, it was [that] separated me from others. No one ever said I was smart. I am in fact, unless interested, appallingly dumb. But I do have a capacity for liking things and wondering, plus a curiosity that holds me in good stead to this day. And that's why I still shuffle about in the woods and sit here puzzling out bugs and plants; I cannot help myself.... I do love to write and always thought of myself as a writer, and am interested in ideas, although grasping very few. See, it really all falls into place. Nothing clashes. Were I smart this w[oul]d have led me into some specialty, but am not, and it did not. So it goes—my dad, the lake, the river, the forest in Canada, plus the TR library. And the people in TR— they thought I was nuts and said so.

May 6, 1993

It was forecast to be perfect and it was—an absolutely stunning spring day. It began just slightly cool and ended hot enough that I doffed my bug shirt. First to Pensaukee, my old station for *Draba* [whitlow-grass] and *Arabis* [rockcress] in that sandy opening between the two woodlots. Well, the foresters arrived first and neither is present, having joined that infinite long line of communities degraded by man. The foresters were really active this winter, and the loggers. What remains of the forest is piled or scattered on the opening, functioning now not as a home for *Arabis*, but rather a park for equipment, which of course does gouge. So that's it for Pen[saukee] and I, our relationship goes back to '56, when I set up the area. The forester who set up the sale wouldn't even know me—a strange old man, lamenting the lost.

May 9, 1995

A nice accolade [for] Hugh Iltis (Emmet sent to me). He was born in Bohemia, Brno no less. His father was an early Socialist teacher/botanist, who tried to make plants a reality to ordinary people (There must have been many such in Brno), and as a refugee Jew, [Hugh] came to the U.S. in the late thirties.

He was educated in southern schools, never hit the big time academically, taught at Tenn(essee) and Ark(ansas) before coming to Madison. It's odd that the Botany Department passed over eastern educated WASPs for him, and I think it shows the strong power of his personality, which he really has. He was, from the first [time] he met me, a good friend. For years he insisted I try [to develop] a flora of Marinette County, and it was he who emptied out the Marinette County maps that are still in my desk drawer. He was, in the end, the only one on the Madison faculty who greeted me. I hope he's around for a long time to come. Our state needs men like him. What am I talking of, the country needs men like him.

May 15, 1994

Imagine my pleasure, when this a.m., re-reading some old notes on my desk, I found out this—that trout lily is a sink for all minerals, particularly K, gathered from spring runoff, then released to other plants, trees included throughout the summer. Can you think of a more noble position, a place on this earth more valuable, a life more positive? Compare her contributions, first the sprightly beauty, then her pollen and nectar to all bees, ants, beetles, then finally to the trees. They freshen the atmosphere, making for us, an environment, all life possible....

May 17, 1994

Met Judith for lunch; back to the harbor. Klimek Woods, heaven help us; the path was an avalanche, a cascade of birds, surely arrived only the night before. Along the path, swooping low and for half the length, a [great] crested flycatcher, all blaze, yellow, red, sweeping expertly in hawking flight, grabbing his bugs out of the air, pursuing them right onto the ground. Same for Baltimore orioles; thrushes, more sedate, and then finally an ovenbird, pacing nervously along, first a trunk, then the ground, figuring things out, I'd guess, in this temporary home, where they really must have chilled out last night. Well, they're welcome to this northern latitude. Keep the process going. May there be no coons in your life up here.

I've never seen such a cascade of birds. Unfortunately, Judith had to return by two. Some chores for J this a.m., then I'm returning.

This is finally the spring of the poets, with color, leaves, birdsong that even I with wretched ears could hear. It must have been glorious for the good ears. I left the woods haunted by the beauty, the natural glory of it all.

May 22[?], 1994

Y-day a wasted day in May. No field, and none of the work set out to do in the garden. In the afternoon, when finally I made it out there it was simply too hot—that's right—hot. For the first time ever, I think, Marinette was warmer than Philip's home in Fla. We had over 90; they had 79 as tops, and last night our temps were to be the same. It felt awful; a hot, dry wind as out of the desert. There must have been a top fire danger all over the state; we are virtually on the edge of drought. It has one spinoff—we are low on mosquitoes. And one does not sink up to the neck in a swamp.

May 27, 1995

Marinette the Cosmopolite! It happens every year at this time; the shorebird migration is here, and the Seagull Bar is awash with a host of dunlin, turnstones, and one huge whimbrel. They are the most trusting of creatures; humans mean little to them. My first sighting was thus. The sun was glaring on the water, and I walked along head low, the brim on my hat pulled down. Suddenly, at my side, between me and the waves, was this

In bliss at "Carney"—Michigan's Carney Fen State Natural Area, only about a 40-minute drive for LeRoy, into the southern Upper Peninsula. Photo courtesy of Judith Lintereur Johnson.

CHAPTER TWELVE

dense mass of life. A flock had settled down beside me, and now raced part, one by one, pursuing the elusive bug tossed ashore by the waves. That wave zone is their habitat. They recede and advance like the wave itself, up and down the beach, flying mainly to gain on each other, since #1 gets there first. Never in repose, their leg and wing muscles must be marvels of endurance.

June 2, 1993

I thought of my true occupation last night. I am a sedge welcomer. There is much talk of welcoming our spring flowers; it's commonplace amongst nature people. But I've never heard of anyone out there welcoming our various sedge species. I have done so now for several years, so by default, why not me? In other words, c'est moi. Well, there was not much to welcome yesterday. Several clumps of *Carex gracillima* [graceful sedge] and of course, lots of *pedunculata* [long-stalked sedge]. Of these, the fertile culms are starting to fall, which is exactly what they should do. And in the swamp, all flooded now, there is no sign of *leptalea* [bristle-stalked sedge], or *disperma* [soft-leaf sedge]. Just slender leaves, with the fruit some distance off. Goldthread still in the cedars and *sphag*[*num*], and as of June 2, that's about it.

June 13, 1993

So in love with the *Cornus c*[*anadensis*, bunchberry]. I saw yesterday [at Stanley's Bog], thought of a fine motto for all us northern conservationists: *All we ask is a world where Cornus c. is safe; all else will follow.* I can't imagine a finer flower, and the ones on Stanley's land, right on the bog edge are the finest. And then before me, the lead, and on this edge is *Carex paupercula* [bog sedge]; it never fails. This would be everyone's favorite sedge, if they only knew, with its delicate little pedicels and bright scales; a little green miracle in its watery home, popped right out of the *sphag*[*num*]. The cotton grass is gone, and the *Kalmia* [*polifolia,* bog laurel] down to a few spots of pink. But across the opening are large banks of *Ledum* [*palustre*], [*Rhododendron groenlandicum* Labrador tea] and if one looks closely, still *Viola lanceolata* [lance-leaved violet], a white wonder, in its freezing, watery world.

The main sedge here is *oligosperma* [few-seeded sedge] and *lacustris* [lake sedge], the latter still not in flower. Along the edges are tufts of *interior* [inland sedge], and in at least two spots, *trisperma* [three-seeded sedge]. I hoped for *angustior* [*Carex echinata*, star sedge], but have never found it there. Across on higher land grades is *C. stricta* [tussock sedge] and *V. myrtilloides* [velvet-leaf blueberry] in some sites, with a bright floral wonder, *Aronia* [chokeberry]; here just a small plant, almost an herb, but on the south border it forms a hedge, say 6 feet high. Most interesting is a huge clump of *Ilex verticillata* [common winterberry], a good twelve feet high, a solid clump extending over 20 feet, with the interior stems forming a 10-foot thicket. I have never seen anything like it up here; most of the stands up north have been long dominated by deer and snowshoes. One can guess that this clump came into its majority when there were no deer in the area, say 40–50 years ago. Wonder how far back a clump like that would go. Besides the moskeets [sic], who were awful, there were not many bugs; no dragonflies, a surprise, because the day really warm, nor butterflies. Some *bombi* [bumblebees] working over the *Ledum* [*groendlandicum*, Labrador-tea] and the remnant *Kalmia*. Then there's cranberry, now showing, but it's really a sedge meadow. With all that [it] implies. Stanley's Bog is really a wonderful place.

June 13, 1994

A strong rain during the night; we are soaked this a.m. And further, the same pattern—thunderstorms and rain [are] to dominate the week, through Friday. I was going up to Carney, but it's soaked up there, so I think it'll be Oconto Marsh where we were yesterday, meeting Julie and Greg.

Greg is a perfect field companion, knows his plants and birds well, and of course, his training is in ent[omology]. While the rest talked, we bird-watched; this marsh superlative for that. One black crown, and later an A[merican] bittern flew high over the marsh. Without my glass, I called it b[lack]c[rown]. Greg said quietly, "I thought it a bittern," which it was. Then walking back, J noted this spot of white—an egret deep in the marsh. While we watched, it picked itself up and flapped over into the shallow water, where it began to stalk. Did it ever, the neck in a tense S, that flew out like a spring, straight out, and one good gulp. We disturbed a blackbird, enough that it flew up to us, or rather about 20 ft away. I put a glass on it—such a blaze of black, satiny sheen, and a flaming of epaulets. Greg put up his glass and exclaimed in amazement. When the bird flew up, the blend of feathers, black and red, was startling.... One thing for sure—it goes best if we remain in the background, out of it, save just a touch.

June 16, 1995

Well, it looks like Ox-bo and I separate for the season. I threw myself in heavy cover there yesterday, falling with a violent blow to the face. Thought sure I'd broken my nose; the bridge was bleeding and glasses covered with blood. I found out when I arrived at home that there was a dried stream of blood down my cheek.

The cover there is so heavy—ferns just up to the top of my head—these huge *Osmundas* [royal ferns] that make the "imaginating" of Triassic landscapes unnecessary. There they are, the gigantic fern forests. And just about bereft of resident bugs, there being almost none upon them, but not quite. When I glanced down my pants legs while sitting in the car, there was this race of twenty plus wood ticks up my pants legs; was shooing them out of the car with both hands. When I arrived home was still loaded. I am welted and scarred, scratched and bitten like never before, and last night was really uncomfortable. To top it all, I ruined my eyes on the trip to Green Bay. Now this Sunday must drive J down to TR for J's Father's Day celebration. This will blind me for the week.

Ox-bo is now full green, except under the beech; its ferns all the way, mainly *Osmundas*, with a scattering of *Dryopteris* [wood-fern]. The sedges and grasses except for the creek bank and the mud spots are not that great. There is a scattering of *Carex brunnescens* [brownish sedge or green bog sedge] and small tufts of *C. pensylvanica* [common oak sedge or Pennsylvania sedge]. But along the stream banks there are strong stands of *intumescens* [greater bladder sedge; shining bur sedge; swollen sedge], *gracillima*, *lupulina* [common hop sedge], even some *interior*.

I checked the hemlocks over carefully, but the spiders have not located there yet. The bug buildup, mosquitoes excepted, does not hit there until later in summer. One skipper, almost orange save for black border, and a black marking ... no satyrs yet, but my eyes are getting so poor that I'd not stake my reputation on any sightings now.

I think my days in the field are coming to an end. My balance becomes poorer every year. Yesterday was a warning to me. My eyes are definitely awful ... haven't used my beloved stereo mi(croscope) for two days now, a grievous situation for me. Well, hell, I'm hitting 75 now. Lots of people my age are unable to hit the brush like I do, so not to complain, but damn, it bothers me.

June 19, 1995

We are in a heat wave. Already at six [a.m.] it's 80 plus in GB, and J said our house temp is 80. Superior, our coolest city normally, had a record 102 temp yesterday; such a dreadfully unreal world. Unlike winter, there's no escape from this. Snuggling down into warm blankets on a cold winter night is one thing. Awakening to a sweat as last night is clearly something else. It was so humid there was a light haze over the landscape. It was rather like driving through Georgia for Florida at this time of year. Every bit as dreadful....

It's odd, how we longed for summer. Well, it's here now, and I just turned off the radio, unable to listen in on the dreadful forecast they continue to repeat: hot, humid, and muggy for the "period," with record highs. GB at seven [a.m.] already into the 80s; can't stand the thought of Titusville weather up here. Wisconsin as the deep south—how horrible.

Summer 1990s

June 23, 1993

To Carney on an absolutely perfect day—light wind, cool, or not hot anyway—enough haze to hold the sun down. The fen and its swamps are now one glory of green ... sedges, in all their intricate patterns are at peak, a dazzling sight—[Carex] leptalea, interior, trisperma in neat, crisp mats—one must look close. Carney fen is a sedge seed producer of the first rank, doing everything possible to keep fens agoing.

Around 10:30, I noted a nice dry tussock formed by a pine. Wedged my back against it and luxuriated there, wind in pines; even the mini-threads of C. limosa [muck sedge] trembled in it. It was a chance for total relatedness, in this style once a year. Right next to me a clone of S. hudsonianus [Trichophorum alpinum, alpine cotton-grass], wisps of cotton. All of these are plants extending their range into the Arctic. Here, pressing around me, was the Process, going once more through these ancient forms....

There's always in this country a vision of horizons—true north speaking so quietly and determinedly, here's the classic at its peak. I've tried to put down what a day in the north means to me, and as usual, failed. A poet could, or painter, photo also. Words fail; they apply to everything, and there's nothing like this, at once so simple and so intricate, so subdued, indeed commonplace as green, yet so alive and with such power.

CHAPTER TWELVE

June 25, 1993

To please J, I remained inside yesterday, vacuumed the rugs, tidied up the front room. Then, came upstairs here and worked over my collections, on my day up in Mich. I could have shouted for joy; a new *Carex*; this in the *sphag*[*num*] north of the fen, and another lost for some 10 years. *Tenuiflora* [*Carex tenuiflora*, small-headed bog sedge or sparse-flowered sedge] was the new and *chordorrhiza* [creeping sedge] the old. Both are so unique in their own way, and so secretive, just as unobtrusive a plant as can be imagined. Both were found while looking closely for another. What the hell is this little wisp. Now, I think save for *angustior*, my sedge search of Carney fen is complete....

And then, there is always in my mind how to justify, this "collecting." After all, it's a euphemism for killing, and it bothers me. I guess that, like this writing, it's a compulsion with me. I've been this way since 6th grade, only more so then—i.e. the killing did not bother me; in fact, was avid as any hunter, more so. It's my nature, but now an old man, I need more than that....

July 2, 1993

Oh, can't forget the [spring] peeper experience in the big hemlocks at Wells. J noted it first, a tiny fumbling of brown in the twigs ... materialized into a peeper, cross and all, leaping up with magnificent precision onto a hemlock chip, whence he swiveled his neck about calculating the next move. It was down and out, into the twigs and shadows once more. On the chip it was less than an inch, imagine, with legs to match. Why the bones couldn't have been thicker than a paper clip, and the brain measured in grains, but all perfectly adequate for a look around, and then one, long, graceful leap, just right to propel the tiny structure into cover and safety, complete with snack of bugs. It's month(s) until winter, then 5 of freeze and frost to be endured, when the peeper's song will burst onto the world once more, singing one message—more peepers. All else is surplus.

July 8, 1994

Doggone, but these months are merciless in their progression. My eyes hurt terribly this a.m.; meet with an OD Monday to have the glasses checked— hope he can find something. If not, I'll need [to] curtail my time with the mike. There and in driving seem to cause the most problems. I often wonder, am I close[r] to just sitting around than I think? Nothing would please J more. She cannot figure out what the point is in "just looking at flowers."

Well, I do much more than that, but sticking to that point, what is one to say? What does one do, what does one accomplish *just looking at flowers*? This question is never asked of a golf player, say, or a baseball fan, for this is obviously recreation, and *this* is an old man's prerogative. But I myself would hate to think of what I do as "recreation," and cannot think in that manner. Were I to concentrate in one field, I could make a real contribution to say, some herbarium, or museum, but that, too, is foreign to me.

I cannot walk through a community without wondering of everything, or at least that within my grasp. I wanted to become, in Walton's phrase, "a compleat naturalist," and think within limits I am very close. With more to come, if I choose to do so. Now, the kicker—what good is it, and that is not so easy. It gives me a great sense of belonging to say, casually, [I] know the willows, or the sedges, or spiders and beetles, too. Everyone knows birds and mammals, and most of the herps, so they do not enter here. I can't imagine a plantsman blind to tanagers, but I do know some who are very good at plants, while not knowing or showing the least interest in butterflies. But, they know what they are up to—whatever the motive may be, they are furthering the knowledge of plants.

I once thought there was surely [a] need for a man like myself, but now know better. And always there is the worrisome intrusive—I'm not at all what I perceive myself to be. I can say a lot here, as an unprincipled dilettante what can I expect.... I cannot say I delude myself, and in self-defense, point out this is a compulsion with me. I cannot imagine the misery that would be mine were I to give up my dream, of knowing as much as possible about the natural world.... And perhaps that can be my goal, to achieve this, somehow, myself, and then pass it on via my strings to those, who in the future, might want to know what a person such as myself thought of the world. To which some will say, "Well, what the hell's so different about you?" This could apply to anyone. All true, but I take the trouble to write it down and at least formulate my thoughts. And between that, the compulsion, and the pure joy of recognizing a new or an old friend in the woods, is the best I can say. There are surely more like me in the state, but would be surprised if there are such here in the Upper Lakes. And that is my province, my life and excuse for being. And let anyone who could criticize me for dodging my normal responsibilities, whatever they may be, or isolating myself, reflect on this—how many springs does the old fellow have left?

CHAPTER TWELVE

July 10, 1995

I learned over the weekend of Increase Lapham's statement in defense of forests, and an effort to limit exploitation, that they affected climate, and the air, water, and built soils. What a modern statement, [but] they hooted at him, and in twenty years slashed our forest to ribbons. By 1900, there were those who regretted that someone had not slowed them down; indeed, and the battle goes on to this day. Our situation both national and state is hopeless given the domination of the political system and the indifferent public. The leg[islative bodies] on both levels are busily dismantling all the environmental legislation of the past 30 years—getting the government off our backs, as the exploiters and pols put it.

July 13, 1994

A grievous happening today. I drove up to Carney in bright sun to meet Kenny and Ann. They arrived at ca. 10:30, as prearranged. It was to be a great day. They are my favorite companions anyplace, and here esp[ecially]. We made our way slowly through the fen. Ken and I talk a lot—DNR stuff mainly—and finally we arrived at the little cedar Island. I was standing there talking to Kenny, when suddenly the world turned. First, a light yellow then white, as in an over-exposed film. At the same time, I became nauseated and in pain. It ran down my midline and to the center of the abdomen. I lay down before falling down, stretched out, and covered my eyes. I just barely held on to consciousness, thinking, "Perfect, I'm going to die in Carney fen."

I asked Ken to go back to the car and get my sunglasses, not having them in the fen. After several moments, I struggled to a sitting position. My view had now turned to normal, but Ann, who was with me, insisted I lay down, and take it easy. Ken returned with the glasses and a thermos of cold water. I took a sip and he bathed my bandana in it, and I placed this under my hat. By now I was OK after a fashion, a little shaky at first, more chagrined than anything. It put a damper on the day, and we headed back to the cars. We sat and talked until close to two. They wanted to drive me home, but I made it ok. Ann called up at 4. Was I resting? "OK, Annie," I said. "I'm OK."

Now, at ca. 10 p.m. My eyes are still burning from the day. I feel odd and strange. Is this it, or what the hell? I know this for sure, long drives of any kind are out for me, and that for now my days of my driving up to Carney, or any place in the UP are over. I'd feel better of this if I knew how long to live, but I don't want to hang around here, just doing nothing, and fretting about not being up north. Think I'll stick with my agenda, not driving any heavily travelled roads, the possibility being, of course, that had this happened while driving, I might have hurt someone. I always knew that the day would come when I had to give up, it may be here now. I'd like to consult with a specialist for eyes, and for heart in GB. I suspect both are involved here.

July 19, 1991

Well, my aluminum canoe, the one given to me by my people as a retirement gift is gone, sold to Betty Cherry's brother in Wagner, so in a sense it is still in the family. I could not lift it after my illness. In its place I have a Old Towne, 12 foot, at 33 pounds, and I can handle it without difficulty. Yesterday, for the first time, we, the canoe and I, had our maiden voyage on the pocket at Seagull Bar. It was a hot, humid day inland, but comfortable out on the water. The canoe handles perfectly. I think we will get along very well together.

Paddled to the end of the bar. It's grown mainly to *Sonchus* [sow-thistle], not quite my sort of plant. But they were loaded with *Syrphids* [hoverflies], that dark type, my favorite. Then in the sand, a flurry of blue *Sphecids* [thread-waisted wasps]. The first was dragging a *Geolycosid* [burrowing wolf spider], and as I moved to collect, both spider and wasp disappeared down a burrow. I waited 10 minutes, but she did not re-appear. Soon there were several on the same patch of sand, all hustling busily about, searching I'd guess for spiders. One, however, after a brisk orientation, vanished into a burrow, already constructed....

July 21, 1992

Oconto Marsh—cloudless, brisk cool wind, nice bright sun. There were no ducks in sight, so I walked down to the control, thinking to sit there a bit. Not much doing. Then there was a movement to my right, and a doe appeared, strolling slowly down the dike. On she came, looking up toward the road, sensing the wind, totally alert but always on the road. She never not[iced] me. When twelve feet away—now I have her head in my glass like a portrait—she turned slowly, walked back some yards, and then with great deliberation, and I might say, quiet skill, swam the creek, pulled up on the shore, and began to nip at the green. But no, there was more than that to life. She began to nuzzle, lower jaw upturned, stroking her head and neck against the dangling heads of the tall *Scirpus validus* [*Schoenoplectus tabernaemontani*, soft-stem bulrush], giving every impression that she was enjoying herself, more playful by the minute. She neatly nipped off the flower head from a purple loosestrife, and then gradually lost herself in the tall sedge.

When I turned back to the water, there was an otter swimming along, diving in progress like a dolphin, total grace. And a helldiver [pied-billed grebe], young by its zebra stripes, its back loaded with milfoil from its last dive. There were [great] blue herons in every direction and distantly one huge great egret. I had to get on to Pensaukee, vowing to come back for lunch.

Pen[saukee] fine—that striking *Libellula pulchellus* [twelve-spotted skimmer], designer dragonfly, angling to display wings perfectly, and some *Sympetrum* [meadowhawks], the first of the year. Sedges in profusion, some nice and green, mainly *Carex rostrata* [beaked sedge] and *lupulina* in the wet spots, with *normalis* [intermediate sedge] and *bebbii* [Bebb's sedge].

Back to the marsh, eat my lunch, but nothing doing on the dike. Driving back now. There is something in the road, some yards ahead. A truck blinks its lights to caution me; what the hell, it's a deer, still, struggling. It's the doe, grasping feebly at the road, no blood but a thin, serous fluid running from her nostrils. Public service truck drives up—I felt in a dream, walked to the car. "Do you fellows have something to kill her? She's still living." So one took a maul to her, and that was it. A violent struggle, then she gave up her spirit. Quiet now, the eye so sharp and bright, distorted.

We dragged her off the road, and that was it, just like that. There must be somewhere a theology of killing, where man justifies himself, to kill a lovely creature like this. God, was she alive and vibrant.... She must have been some kind of pinnacle nature set out to produce, a peak of the selective process. I never observed a wild deer that close, fawns maybe, but not adult. One must avoid being mawkish with something like this, but for me her spirit will always float over the marsh, in the swaying, trembling *Scirpi*.

July 26, 1993

I cannot recall when there was not a marsh, a river, a forest in my life. I felt at home on the river. For some reason being closed in by the woods scared me as a child. It may reflect back to the terror Ruth and I felt when it seemed we were abandoned in Lake Shore Park, of a Sunday morning. Or the tales central Europeans spun of creatures; no, demons abiding there. Spirits, spooks, were real to me, and deep forests were their home. Huge snakes, too. But, they were my world to the exclusion of all others.

My first Tisch Mills summer, when I first encountered woods with giant trees, vast fields, the swamp, stone fences, even with the nameless fears, or perhaps because of them, was for me a defining experience. It has been, for my life, no matter where, my milieu—different forest, streams, fields, marshes—all have been one in my life. I've always thought of them as threatened, and 60 years later my terror dream is to find that some favored haunt has been settled, some skyline irrevocably altered. I should never doubt myself on this and have never asked anything of it, save awe and wonder.... My bitter disappointment is living in a world rejecting these values.

July 29, 1994

I have finished my notes on *Salix* [willows]; counted out 12 species normally run into here, with a probability of two others on dunes.... Hooked on the willows still, and very proud that I can walk down the line and toll them off. They have the damnedest growing patterns—two species, practically out of the same square of ground, good valid species, too, say *bebbiana* [beaked willow] and *discolor* [pussy willow]. It would seem that about 10 percent are beyond me. They have a complex of character[istics] that do not add up, but at least half can be told at a glance, and the rest either cannot be identified, at least by me, or require close study with my glass. But they are all fascinating. I wince to think I walked past them all my life without knowing them. It's not that I could not name them—I never even would note the difference, except for the most obvious, sand willow say, and then *lucida* [shining willow], this latter still my favorite.... I'm so damned hooked on the willows that I hardly note anything else. Well, I know them now anyway. The goldenrods will be out soon. Have set up my notes on them, and hope to pursue the same course as with the willows....

July 31, 1992

Well, this a.m. out to Seagull Bar.... Walking through a sea of green, mainly *S. Americana* [LeRoy's sense of humor on display]. A medium dragonfly sets down on a stem—wings a lovely shade of orange and yellow, two transverse stripes, one lateral. He angled around the stem. Now there's his side: delicate yellow, with patterned black stripes. When he lifted off, it was a gauzy, dreamy design, all power packed into all that delicacy. Going through the book, *Celithemis eponina* [Halloween pennant dragonfly] seems close enough. Had no desire to collect him, a design of such perfection....

CHAPTER TWELVE

July 31, 1995

A dreadful day, followed by a miserable night. It was 90 in our garage at 6 p.m., and it stayed close to that. It's 6 a.m. now, and our house is hottest I've ever seen. This is the way it must feel in Manilla, although I'd guess they are more used to it than us northerners.... A bit of serendipity. I am in the garden, in desperate heat, picking berries. There is a continuing and agitated clamor from a robin—it's going on for half an hour. J comes out with her clothes basket, and I learnedly explain to her that a cat is stalking a robin, probably in Brickert's yard, and she is raising the alarm. J suddenly calls to me, something about a garbage can. In alarm, I go to her. "No," she said, "there's a little robin in there." Sure enough, it must have fluttered, or fell from the fence. There it sits, mouth agape, pin feathers bristling. I scoop it out, and lo, instantly, they are agonizing around me; first two, then three robins. The young bird scuttles into the raspberry patch, and the calls subside. Then I move in to pick [it up] once more, and the calls, in great concern, sound off once more. So at J's prudent suggestion, I quit, walk out, and quiet resumes once more. I'm up in my room, and the sweat is pouring off me, as it has not up here for years. We are in an unusually miserable weather pattern. No escape....

August 10, 1994

I wish there was someone who would listen to me sing of the willows. Now that I can toll them off, they seem so individualistic, their response to site so delicate; they are simply so painfully ecological, with individual sensitivity to site.

I was yesterday up in MI, the first time since toppling over in the fen. Stopped at Baileys, the hemlocks, and the Cedar Road bog. I looked mainly at willows. Almost all exist on the sands and ridge along the bay, but their habit is variant from what I see at the lower bay. For one, they have less tendency to form those big clones, and many are dendritic in habit. This applies esp. to *bebb* [*Salix bebbiana*], both in the bog and shore. It has a dendritic habit, with smaller leaves that intensify the characteristics that serve to separate them. The two exceptions are *exigua* [sandbar willow] and *petiolaris* [meadow willow or slender willow]. They seem to grow in about the same style no matter where found. *Petiolaris* seemed subdued in the bog, but it was there, I think about as tolerant a species as we have. *Mira coides* [*Salix myricoides*, bayberry willow or blue-leaf willow]—I first found it at Baileys years ago—is common there. It is truly a sand species. All these sites are so painfully northern. They all have black spruce, with its silhouette. This forms the bog at Cedar Road. I wish I could get over my reluctance to drive, or that I lived closer to these sites. Perhaps it's best that I reduce my fondness for all three because the day is close at hand when I will be unable to drive the distance. Then I will sit at home and lament that I never took advantage of them like I should.

August 24, 1994

To Oconto and then the harbor. Going through the woods, there's a different *Solidago*, finally. I thought it to be *nemoralis* [gray goldenrod], for some reason, but at home with the mike it's *juncea* [early goldenrod], and further I think my characterization of the goldenrods along Woods Road as *juncea* is wrong—was going strictly by the axial leaves in the inflorescence mentioned by McKinney. Incidentally, none of the manuals mention this. Also, I'm certain I can call the smooth-stemmed, three-nerved plant *gigantea* [giant goldenrod; late goldenrod; smooth goldenrod]. Keyed one out using Grey. Can you imagine? I've reached that point, and it only took me—let's see, 45 years!

September 5, 1993

J and I along the tracks for the first time since spring, and into a naturalist's bonanza. The railroad has not used the tracks all summer … right now it is a strong growth (I use the word deliberately) of bull thistle, Canadian thistle, goldenrod, and some aster. The tracks are encroached by *Acer negundo* [box elder] and *Rhamnus* [buckthorn], and the stream has its own growth, although the water still is very crumby. It was cool enough to suppress bugs, and the only ones in quantity were *bombi*, frantically working over the bull thistle, some long gone to seed, others with bright red flowers. But most responsive were the goldfinch, and we saw a half mile of them, ripping and tearing at the thistle heads. The fur was flying, seeds ballooning in all directions, mayhem, a win-win situation. Goldfinch filched the seeds. Bull thistle was dislocated and sent flying into the Sept air, ballooning up into the sky, victory over the city and country side—exactly as bull thistle evolved—asking only that seeds and more seeds hit the silk, so to speak, up and away from the mother plant.

September 6, 1994

I think that ants more than any other creature, demonstrate our ignorance of what the natural world means to us. Nature could not exist without them; they are indispensable as soil manipulators, as insect predators, as vectors for plants, for most of us it's a win-win situation. But we regard the whole works with something akin to horror. People stooped over applying poison to the cracks in the sidewalk are an ordinary Sunday sight. Housewives confronted with ants any place in the house go nuts, and carpenter ants, much maligned, are public enemy number one....

September 8, 1994

Up early, glanced out the door, and there for the first time in months were the stars—mankind's markers.... Orion, really glorious; almost overhead, Auriga, the Pleiades, Taurus. Man, there is really an array of constellations. There is our past, and I'd guess our future also—that's us.

September 15, 1993

Well, by Gar, let's hear it for beach grass (*Ammophila*) sand-lover, a grass without equal or peer, the one and only that can struggle all over a sand dune, as formidable a challenge as any plant in our area. And this is its function—an inhabitant of the coastal mid-Atlantic dunes, to Newfy, and the Great Lakes. Everything of it is stout and sturdy. The manuals all testify to that, and I can also. It is one flowered, blessed with close relationship to *Calamagrostis* [reed-grass], glumes lemmas, even the paleas strong, daggerlike, of good size—a rigorous study of spike of flowers. They are all straw-colored now, but the culms are full-green, anchored, and nourished by a root system with a nose for water like no other plant in this upper lakes area. I love that term, and here is our quintessential shore plant.

And let's hear it for fringed gentian [*Gentianopsis crinita*]. We, Joy and I, found a stand of it today in wet sands, a sort of flooded old field type, in a rise that's part of the musket on the Cedar River road. We had been exclaiming on the *Spiranthes* [ladies'-tresses] and *Gerardia* [*Agalinis sp.*]. All is soaked from the rain; it poured all day yesterday, and these are perched water tables that will not dry this year. There, heaven help me, was the most solid of royal blues, deep, profoundly so, and soon we had a stand, hundreds of them, a floral display [leaving] one helpless, what to do, what the hell should one do to immortalize this scene? A picture, better yet a poem, something to immortalize this tableau vivant.... Is this necessary to pull in the bugs at this time of year? ... Well, bug, if it's blue you want of the heavenly variety, one that might be the blessed Mother's own color, here it is, blue so deep that one more hit and it would be purple, but no, it's blue.

It was a cold a.m. J and I in full fall gear and on the water, still chill. But inland it was warmer. Trees are fading. All rushes are a deep brown, and if more were needed, at high noon a racket high up, and a huge clamoring flock of Canadas, hell bent for Horicon, shouted the season.

September 17, 1990

Today, at mid morning, I touched the primordium. It happened thus: I was walking down a cold lane at the harbor, when up ahead there was this patch of goldenrod gleaming in the sun—the rest of the road chill and shaded by trees bordering the road. I walked up to it, and instantly there was that sense of gentle warmth, a sense suddenly of liveliness in the proper meaning of the word. Up to now there were no bugs, but here they were gearing up, which for most would quite literally be the end time, there being no tomorrow. But now bees landed on goldenrod. There were long horned beetles, even one phymatid, a striking yellow type. As I watched a dragonfly, one of the green darners flew in, sicked himself at a *Bombus*, who flew off and stretched full winged on a leaf, all but sighing to himself in the warm sun. There were some syrphid flies there, basking, wings stretched to the full, their abdomen not raised but touching the leaf, as if to absorb every bit of heat....

Finished off the morning across from the barn, scraping through duff with my trowel, admiring the fine soil we have and the process bringing it into being....

September 19, 1994

Joyce and I, in these final days of our fading northern summer, to the marsh. Everything faded now; the sedges and cattails are brown, and the goldenrods all but colorless. There was one aster on the dike—a rich, purple plant, nothing but vigor and color, and well, richness.... These are the days when everything comes to the fore, either actually, or the nostalgia relating to the season. Lumberjacks would be leaving now. This was the time of year when my father and I longed for the north. Oh to be there. My dad would be consumed with longing for his homeland, here in the north, which for him was always a region of small farms and forest populated with French-speaking people, men in red shirts and boots.

The sky is glorious today. The woods just beginning to turn with the ashes and some oaks brown and crinkly. How suddenly it all goes. Why, only yesterday there was all the green; now it's lost, crackling, where it once sighed when tread upon.

*

Fall 1990s

September 21, 1990

One should not be morbid about these things and say that summer has flown. It's there, some of it anyway. The leaves are for the most part green, the sedges in the sloughs flourish, and while the flowers are gone, there are plenty of plants on the forest floor to make you marvel—just look at that. But this afternoon at Stanley's, there was a sky, low, gloom, threatening, and a chill wind out of the east. There were almost no bugs, and only a few spiders. And working through the trees, a vast horde of warblers, but all at the top, overhead in the pines, just a dark blur in my glass. Then I slushed to the head of the muskeg, found a dry spot and sat down, back wedged to a pine tree. Soon, on my right a flurry, and there in the pine, bright red rust, almost flaming with it, and decked with spots, a wood thrush. I sought my glass, and he vanished. Then a motion on my left; there it was gorging on *Viburnum lentago* [nannyberry]. Up came my glass, that feeling of breathlessness—astounded by its clear lines, bright colors, sharp eye. Now there is one neat design.

Met a fellow, married into Stanley's family. I voiced my fears that Stanleys might give up the woods. The fellow told me, never, his son will get it and vowed that he will keep it always. Now exultavit, exult, all of you. It's a woods any logger dreams of: perfect oak, pines, some maple, all easy to get at. They could wreck it in one winter. I hope with all my heart that it will be saved....

September 24, 1994

Thought to stick to the house yesterday, so spent it with the mike and two spiders collected the day previous. They always startle, the *Theridion* [tangle-web spiders] particularly. Those jaws and spines, and refined spinnerets, and the eyes. Man if [one] could meditate on them.... For they are denizens of hazel leaves almost exclusively. Imagine to have as your true home, your niche in this world, a hazel leaf.

Brush we crash through, check early for flowers, later for fruit; "buckbrush" the hunters call it. And there each fall out of the blue, suddenly these hordes of smallish spiders, living out short lives ... snare a ration of tiny flies. Search and lure of a mate, hardwired little head, world of shadows and sudden forms ... an ability to detect shifts in wind currents. Then the cold and down into the duff for another season, a life lived between duff and hazel leaf.

Does *Theridion* go back to the origin of our modern forest? Did it too follow the glacier, out of some refuge, say, in the Appalachians? What holds *Theridion* back? There are so many unoccupied hazel leaves. It has delicate colors and unbelievably exquisite claws; they [are] the epitome of mechanical grace. A grim visage with those powerful, strongly toothed fangs; the latter as stiletto, folded against an array of strong teeth. And there they are, thousands in each woods; we all live a life unaware they exist and collectively dismiss them as spiders. A man could spend a life pondering them ... what power in all that seeming delicacy.

September 25, 1995

Return from the Hermas; the p.m. temp now up to 65, and the bug world has responded very well. A horde of small *bombi*, knocking pollen off the goldenrod. The *Solidago* [goldenrod] is indeed the northern fall plant, and one would guess that hereabouts *Bombus* and any number of [hymenopterans] evolved together; it seems one cannot do without the other.... Muscids, too, all on the blessed goldenrod, up here a true bread and butter plant for most of our wasps and bees. Then there was a scurrying in the underbrush on the edge of the park. First, a yellow and dark gray fall warbler, pretty good size; then a song sparrow, and the prize a white-throat, with its bib, always as if it were a child with milk on the bib; a fall flurry, and then suddenly all [is] quiet. They are at this time of the year, communitarians—all seeking comfort from each other, happy to be near something recognizable as a friend.

All the flowers, save *Sol[idago]* and some of the *Polygonum* [knotweed; smartweed; tearthumb] are gone for the season. Joyce put up my bug shirt and red bandana. I wear it for 4 months out of the year; now come the 8 when nothing bothers save cold and colder, ice and more of it, snow and more snow, until finally the world is locked away from me, and I look forward to the first spongy struggle through a lifeless forest, wondering when will this woods come to life. It will be 7+ months before the bandana and bug shirt come out of storage. Wonder how, or if, I'll be by that time.

September 26, 1995

It promises to be a fine day, and I'm to Seagull Bar this a.m. Last night continued with the bio[graphy] of Lincoln. If there ever was a national hero, it must be him. Unlike Wash[ington], he had nothing. One can only speculate on what he thought of the cartoons and remarks portraying him as an ape. He had less than a year of education, yet his is some of the most graceful prose ever written in the country. He had a strong sense of the Union and never entertained the idea of splitting it asunder, innately realizing that it would be the end of America were this to happen.

October 2, 1995

Clear out this a.m. At 5, Orion is behind the maple, and its place now centered by Gemini....

A dream last night. I was standing in the midst of our forty at Tisch Mills, the "other farm" as we called it. It was evening, there was a slanted sun, and the landscape spread before me unbelievably beautiful. I was grieving—to think I'll never see this again. It's gone, forever. Left me really shaken. This is where in an old orchard surrounded by a stone fence, an acre perhaps, that I ... having already read Fabre in a youth's book on insects ... recall sitting ... say at age 11 [watching] ... as wasps assaulted the bruised fruit. I always longed for it; how nice that it showed up perfectly in a dream.

October 3, 1995

I had a fine afternoon at High Banks, which, if I live into next season, will surely appear more and more in these notes. These are dry, xeric plains overlooking a triangular bend of the Peshtigo, at the apex of the broad triangle. The Peshtigo splits at the island. This is the tip where the river rejoins into a broad stream.

First bugs. Was startled to see a *Lycaenid* certainly *phleas* [*Lycaena phlaeas*, small copper or American copper or common copper], and so far as I can see a late record. The bug fluttered uncertainly over the road, sat there pumping its wings in the warm sun, then took over, refreshed, in very *Lycaenid*-like flight down the road.... Again on the road, there's this big, rather gross, beetle on the road; a long neck, big round soft body, loading my hand with an orange fluid when I picked it up. It had no wings, save swallow-tailed structures that covered perhaps a third of its abdomen. First, I thought, an aberrant carabid, but then down the road there was a cluster of 6 more, one pair in coitus, really absorbed. Then it dawned on me— these are meloids; checked it out at home: *Meloe angusticollis* [short-winged blister beetle or oil beetle]—the narrow collar, well named indeed.

Walked in the hard mud on the river shore. It was well padded with coon, but oddly no mink or muskrat. There are not many beaver here; found only one very old tree downed and not harvested. Hiked up the road and noted a medium snake. Beautifully striped, rigid, with its head raised several inches. Nice to contemplate them. So much history in those lost limbs and most radical departure from what we consider the vertebrate type ... like Emily D[ickinson], I have never seen one without a "tightening of the bone." And if it's, say, a pine snake, then the chest really tightens up. There is something about them that gets to all of us.

But most of the time I spent just looking around at this beautiful fluvial and forest horizon and the lichens in the sands. It's, for here, a truly remarkable community.

October 4, 1992

Shocked to read in paper that Jim Z[immerman] is dead. His book on sedges is unfinished, sadly.... There was no one who knew plants like he. Quite simply he knew them all and whatever was known about them. He is close to the last link with [Prof. Norman] Fassett. We were of different worlds—he was of the community centered in Madison. Not even the DNR Madison staff could touch him. I was remote from all of them, and of course never close to him in knowledge, not of plants and birds anyway. He was an activist without equal; people listened when he talked, but then he moved in circles who would grasp what he said....

October 7, 1994

The gall we picked up on Seagull Bar—a tiny round apple off a willow—is a sawfly, so restricted to willow that it bears the name *Salicaceae* in its name. I wish now I had spent more time with them. They surely are interesting, the heads in particular, showing up beautifully under the mike. It has an intricate pattern of scoring and spouting labia and antennae. But I must admit to a certain uneasiness in all this. When I cut the creature out of its home and dropped it in alcohol, a twinge of remorse came over me. By what right do I subject an animal to this horrible torture. I know that a scientist has no problems with this and can justify it with his work. But, I cannot do that; this is purely for my own knowledge, and in this context it would seem unthinkable, my own enjoyment. I suppose I can salve myself by thinking, "Well, this is part of my thrust vis à vis the public." I can transfer the knowledge gained to others, who, one might hope, would benefit from it, and in an infinitesimal way, Mother Earth herself. Perhaps with my writings, ultimately.

Anyway, these two forces, my Buddhist respect for life and my strong needs as a biologist, really clash in my mind. Well, hell, often I wonder whether my head is nothing but clashes. None will win and the eventual loser will be me, and what's that worth fretting over.

Just now returned from Seagull Bar. It's awful windy and quite warm, with a glare of sun. I was uncomfortable, eyes watering, flinching from the sun. Scanned the water; nothing doing, save some gulls on shore. My intent was to find the possum skull that Wendel had set down, but nothing doing. It will keep until next year. Looked over some willows and collected galls of the sawfly, these the tiny, miniature apples. Some willows are loaded with them, all on a solitary leaf on a branchlet.

In the strong wind, and over the mowed grass, there was this monarch struggling to stay with it. The wind was giving it a hard time, wings faded and battered a bit. It will never make it to the sunny south.

The willows all coming into fall nicely. *Salix lucida* [shining willow] just a little yellow, but still that fine, burnished green. *S. amygdaloides* [peach-leaved willow] perhaps hit the hardest. It's really drooping now, and branchlets losing their bright summer red. In the wind, everything beat, whipped and blown; most of the grasses have long given up their seeds; all *Carex* vanished, and rushes a mess.

So endeth the year; they will all return—will I?

LeRoy's Final Journal Entry:

October 8, 1995

Strong wind, and bit of chill yesterday, not much doing. Read excellent article in *Discovery* on new concept, Hypersea, stressing the importance of fungi in evolution and extension of land communities. Almost Gaia, and my guess it will receive the same treatment. But anyway, it's one of these concepts that places an emphasis on elements in community that we, or at least I, seldom give thought to—fungi ... I still think of as bread mould.

Weather today promises to be fair and will remain so for most of the week. Leaves are coming down. How a season does fade away.

🖋

LEROY'S FINAL DAY, as recalled by daughter Judith:

"On Sunday, October 8, I stopped to visit Mom and Dad. I was on my way to my classroom to prepare for Monday. We had rolls and coffee and a great time discussing the warm days ahead, political scene. Dad was very interested in my classroom. After I left, he went for a walk to a little creek about six blocks down Mary Street. On the way back, his leg hurt and he went to the emergency room at our local hospital. I didn't find this out until evening. He thought he had a blood clot in his leg. The attending physician had him raise his leg, proclaimed him fine, and he came home.

"The next morning I got a call from my mom around 6 a.m., and she said Dad was in the ER. I went over and Dad was in a semi sitting position on a bed with oxygen and IV. He had had a heart attack. We talked to his physician and decided to move him to the cardiac unit in Green Bay. Dad was taken by ambulance, and Mom and I followed in my car. Once there, he was calm and just happy to have Julie and Mom and I with him. Around two in the afternoon Dad was stable. Mom said we could go back to Marinette, and we told Dad we would see him tomorrow. I wanted one more goodbye. I hugged him. He was concerned more about our drive. I told him I loved him, and he said, 'I love you, too.'

"We drove to [sister] Julie's, and about an hour later, they said Dad coded. We drove back, frantic. At one point I got out of the car and directed traffic to clear our route; it was pretty congested. When we got back to the Cardiac Care Unit, they were still working on Dad, and we couldn't see him.

CHAPTER TWELVE 🦅

"An hour later, a physician came in and said Dad was gone. He had a blood clot that dislodged from his leg and moved to his heart.

"There is still this slump of sadness that hits hard.

"When I got back to Marinette with Mom, I went up to his work area. There, his canvas pack was set to go out into the field for the morning of October 9. Some spiders were set aside next to his dissecting microscope, as was his personalized key for *Solidago*. He left so much of his interests with us, but not ever enough because he took that LeRoy star with him." ✳

BALSAM FIR

Lois Nestel
(1921-1995)

Lois at Cable Natural History Museum entrance, Cable, Wisconsin, 1981.
Photo courtesy of Deb Nelson and Cable Natural History Museum.

SUGAR MAPLE

GJK

Chapter Thirteen~
Lois Nestel

I grew up on a farm near Cable and spent all of my childhood rambling through the woods. Nature was simply a part of my life that I took for granted as much as I took for granted eating or sleeping or anything else. It was my teacher, my friend, my guide.

—LN

Except for one and a half years spent in Chicago, after she had turned 19 and married Charles Alfred Nestel, Lois Nestel's life revolved around the observation and study of Bayfield County's flora and fauna near Cable in northwestern Wisconsin.

One of the most quiet, humble individuals I've ever met, there was no mistaking her passion for natural history, particularly her enthusiasm for varieties of edible wild mushrooms and woodland wildflowers, and for the life associated with streams and bogs. Beginning when I was 16, I remember well the evening summer lecture series held in the Cable Town Hall, where even fully open windows did little to dissipate the summer heat trapped inside. Cable's community leader at the time, Reverend Jenkins, a bespectacled little man, with a high raspy voice and bright smile, often introduced Lois, and she proceeded to enthrall the audiences (and beat the heat) with slideshows on wildflowers, birds, mammals, or some other feature of the local flora and fauna.

Born February 21, 1921, in the Ashland General Hospital to Nellie Anderson Rasmussen, of Norwegian and English descent, and Walter Rasmussen, of Danish descent, Lois Rasmussen grew up on a small family farm carved out of the land near Cable at the end of Wisconsin's logging boom in the early 1900s. "Smoke was a part of my life as a child," she once told an Associated Press reporter in 1981. "People [were] trying to burn off pasture and space for fields. I recall especially the pitch pines. The fire would burn down through the root system, burning for years, and afterward, the potholes were filled with water. "It was heartbreaking," she said, "to see all the work put in on land not fit for farming by people too broke to leave."[108]

Lois attended the Cable Union Free High School, graduating in 1939. She did not go to college. Except for a correspondence course or two, she was self-taught and trained in taxidermy, mycology, botany, ornithology, mammalogy, and entomology. Her expertise caught the eye of conservationist Mary Griggs Burke, who asked her to serve as coordinator of an environmental education initiative known as the Forest Lodge Nature Program, and as curator at the Cable Natural History Museum from its inception in 1968 until 1988, when she retired to her farm. Severe arthritis had made working at the museum and leading field trips very difficult.

During the course of her work, Lois made hundreds of detailed plant and animal sketches, including pen-and-ink drawings of over 300 different mushroom species. Lois's watercolors of mushrooms hung from a corridor connecting the museum to the adjoining Forest Lodge Library, and accompanying the watercolors was a description of how to identify mushrooms in the field by making spore prints.

In 1975, a collection of Lois's nature writings for the newspaper *Cable Commentator* was privately published in a booklet titled *Wayside Wanderings*. Author-naturalist Sigurd Olson wrote the Introduction. Among other things, he said, "No one can truly evaluate the impact of the Forest Lodge Nature Program on the cultural life and enjoyment of those who live in the Cable-Namakagon area. Nor can one fully understand the many facets of the full program—the summer lectures by visiting scientists and workers in various environmental fields, the Natural History Museum, the Forest Lodge Library, and the famous nature trail itself—until one has been there and taken part in the activities coordinated by Lois Nestel. Her *Wayside Wanderings* ... give an insight into her feelings about the wonders of nature as they unfold during the four seasons of the year.... With the eyes of a naturalist, artist, and poet ... she has recorded ... the beauty of flowers, trees, and animals. Her essays build awareness and open the eyes of children to a world of wonder and delight they may not have known before. Teachers and many summer visitors, who also come to see and learn, share her insight and understanding of a place they have begun to think of as their own."

I've included seasonal selections from *Wayside Wanderings* at the end of this chapter.

🌿

ON A RAINY DAY in mid-August 1980, and again on a cool bright day in early May 1981, I interviewed Lois at the museum where much of her artwork, including plant dyes and watercolors, accented displays of the flora and fauna of northwestern Wisconsin. Her ability to make plant dyes was legendary among local residents, for she used a wide variety of plants, including cranberry, elderberry, blueberry, baneberry, blackberry, dandelion, sumac, mullein, garden beet, black cherry, hazelnut, white birch, alder, dogwood, hemlock, and lichens such as beard, deer, and rock tripe.

Lois makes a detailed sketch of great St. John's wort *(Hypericum pyramidatum)*. Photo courtesy of Deb Nelson and Cable Natural History Museum.

Her taxidermy specimens included a hognose snake, common nighthawk, rough-legged hawk, osprey, otter, bald eagle (killed when it became caught in a trap and brought to her by a warden), a great horned owl and barred owl (both road kills), a long-eared owl, and a snowy owl, which had died from a disease affecting its lungs. Also present were a common raven, American crow, pied-billed grebes, black ducks, bufflehead, three window-killed cedar waxwings, and a variety of other passerines. One forest exhibit

Surrounded by her own taxidermy specimens. Top: bald eagle. Bottom left to right: great horned owl, snowy owl, barred owl, and (bottom) long-eared owl, 1981. Photo courtesy of Deb Nelson and Cable Natural History Museum.

featured a standing snowshoe hare, an adult and young coyote, and a red fox. Another exhibit included deer fawns; black bears; a bobcat; fisher; porcupine; great gray owl; gray, red, and flying squirrels; woodchucks; weasel; jumping mice; shrews and voles; bog lemmings; and red-backed mice.

Yet another exhibit contained a statuesque golden eagle (shot years ago) and two immature northern goshawks—one found dead after flying into a building and the other recovered dead from a lake, apparently shot through the eyes. A wetland scene featured mink, muskrat, great blue heron, tundra swan, and American bittern.

Other displays and exhibits at the museum included bottled specimens of frogs; snakes and salamanders; animal tracks set in plaster casts; a rock collection containing Lake Superior agates and other stones; Ojibwe Chief Namakagon's ceremonial shawl, hand-embroidered in intricate bead patterns; Ojibwe arrowheads and flints; a small but meticulous insect collection; and a large bald-faced hornet's nest hanging above an exit.

Amazed by the variety of specimens exhibited, I asked her how long it took to do her taxidermy. "It takes a bit longer with the larger ones," she replied quietly. "Take the coyote. First you have to skin it, and then you have to tan and cure it, and that takes several months. Then you put the animal back together again and sew it up. The smaller a thing is the harder it is to do, as with the voles, moles, and shrews. The actual mounting, apart from curing time, may take three to four hours for small specimens, and up to many days for large birds, animals, or fish."

🖋

WHEN I INTERVIEWED LOIS—a gracious, sunny woman of medium height and short, curly auburn hair—she spoke in a disciplined, soft-spoken voice, her words chosen carefully. Wearing jeans and a brown smock, she complained about a pile of paperwork that she had to wade through, but that the interview came at a time "as good as any." She ushered me into her herbarium office adjoining the museum displays and talked first about her early years.

⟋

I grew up on a farm near Cable and spent my childhood rambling through the woods. Nature was simply a part of my life that I took for granted as much as I took for granted eating or sleeping or anything else. It was my teacher, my friend, my guide. One of the first things I remember as a child was hearing my father whistling back at the birds and talking to the animals as he would go to the barn in the early dawn. He had a song for every bird that gave him a song back.

I was always so interested in everything. When the first flowers bloomed in the spring and the first mushrooms showed up, I was there.

My father was a small-time family farmer. Our farm, like others, came into existence in the early 1900s when it was cleared of trees, and the stumps were pulled or blasted from the earth. We ran the type of farm that everyone around here had at that time: cattle and pigs, horses and chickens, and a few field crops. We raised oats, potatoes, and hay—just enough to help keep us going. It was not self-supporting, and nearly everyone needed an outside job. We had a small herd of about 15 cows, and we sold milk. There used to be a cheese factory in town where we sold the milk, but after it went out of business, my father hauled the milk someplace else. Everything was done the hard way in those days. Nothing was automatic. By the time you had milked the cows in the morning, fed them their hay and grain, and cleaned the barn by hand, you had a pretty good start on the day.

There were no blacktop roads back then, and in the spring there was mud. Lots of mud. I can remember how often people got stuck in the mud going past our place, and how they would come in for Dad and ask him to hitch up the horses and pull them out of the muck.

Once the weather became warm enough for the cattle to go out, I drove them to pasture and brought them home in the evening. On the way back

I'd pick flowers. I was always looking for the first spring flowers. I had less to do in the fields in spring than in summer, except when we had great big fields of rutabaga potatoes and I had to thin them out. I hated that job. But during the spring, I had more free time to ramble than at any other time of the year. There were paths through the woods in all directions that the animals had made, and I used to go down to Big Brook, a few miles west of Cable, paddle around in the water, and catch some fish. I taught myself how to swim down there. Mostly, I was alone when I did these things. I think I've always been pretty much of a loner, except when I was very small, and then I followed my brother and his friends. Later, once in a while I brought someone along, but most often I did things by myself.

I had favorite stretches of woods that I roamed around in. I liked to follow the old railroad grades west of town along streams and bog lands. I'd go for miles, but I don't think I ever went out with any particular purpose in mind; it was just goings [sic]. The land has changed incredibly since then. There were lots of forest fires and cutting of pine when I was a child, so I witnessed the coming of the second growth of timber. This growth has matured to the extent where it's being cut off again. I've seen the full cycle.

In summer, we were almost always up by 4:30 or 5:00 in the morning. We all had chores to do: clean the barn, milk and feed the cows, and, as always, it was my job to drive the cows to pasture. That was something I loved. I took the dogs and made a few side excursions to look for berries or flowers. There was garden work to do, too; we always had large gardens. As I got older, I helped in the fields. The work was all done with horses then. I cocked and pitched hay, drove horses and shocked grain, and worked in the silo during silo-filling time. I did as little as possible in the house, although I did learn to cook and love to cook now, but I was never really very domestically oriented. I'd rather have been out with the cattle, or just rambling around.

I USED TO KEEP A JOURNAL about what I saw, but I'm a moody person, and every once in a while I'd go into a blue funk and destroy everything, and then start over again. Now, I keep a journal to record observations. You always think that you're sure to remember things, but you don't, and it helps to have something to refresh the memory. Impressions and ideas change over time, so it's good to be able to go back to the original source.

Fall was a busy time because there was always the harvesting to do. We had to harvest the hay and the grain, and I had to pull and top the rutabagas. I remember standing there with my hands freezing, wagonloads full of huge rutabagas to top and tail and to be hauled into the barn for winter storage because they were going to be used for winter stock feed.

Winters were a lot harder when I was a child than they are now. We had longer spells of very cold weather, and we had far more severe storm weather. Three-day blizzards used to be a natural part of life. Storms would be shrieking for days, and afterwards the snow would be packed so hard that my friends and I could run across the drifts pretending we were running across big ocean waves. We'd run from wave to wave without ever going through. I remember that Dr. Neer, our closest neighbor, had a driveway that I suppose was a half-mile long, and my father would help him shovel that because there weren't any snow plows around at that time to do the job. You depended on your friends much more for things like that back then.

The snow would be so deep and so hard packed that they would cut blocks of snow just as the Eskimos did for building igloos.

I love winter and always have. There wasn't all the fancy heating that you have now. We lived in an old, cold, wooden farmhouse and carried tons of wood into the house to try to heat it up. And we pumped our water outside and carried it in by bucket. I loved it. I'd get up in the dark of the morning, do whatever chores were necessary, and then walk to school, which was about a mile and a half away. After school, I walked back and knew that I had to fill the wood boxes before supper. I can still see myself coming home from school and see in the distance smoke coming out of the chimney and the lamplight in the kitchen window. Of course, we didn't have electric lights then; it was all kerosene. By the time I'd get home it would be nearly dark, and I would have just enough time to carry in the wood.

After supper, we all read until bedtime. There was a lot of reading, but we weren't the kind who read in bed. I slept upstairs where it was cold and was glad just to get up there and get into bed, pull the blankets up, and go to sleep. But I read constantly whenever I had the time.

When I was still in my crib, I remember lying awake at night as my parents read aloud. We had no radio then, and they took turns reading different books. The first book that I ever remember them reading was Gene Stratton-Porter's *The Keeper of the Bees*. Another book that I remember someone reading to me when I was very small was Thornton Burgess's *Peter Rabbit*. Reading was the principal activity in our spare time, but I also drew. I got interested in drawing partly because of my mother's influence—she was a fine painter—and partly because there weren't many other things to do.

Skiing was another fun activity. We had homemade skis that my father had made out of pine or popple. He steamed them to fashion a curve, and then put single toe straps on them. We explored the woods with these and fished and trapped. I had learned to be quite observant of everything around me. I'd hear the coyotes, birds, owls, see the shadings of the shadows on the snow. Everything was as natural as breathing.

❧

I NEVER RECALL AT ANY TIME thinking that I would become a so-called naturalist. It was something that never even entered my mind. To me, a naturalist was someone who went off to college and learned all kinds of great things and got a diploma. I was just me. I wasn't anything in particular.

The year after I graduated from high school I got married, and I didn't get any further formal education after that. My husband worked for the telephone company for many years and is now retired. My life was extremely quiet. I still rambled in the woods when I had time, and I had a big garden. I always have had, in various combinations, chickens, pigs, cows, rabbits, bees, and, of course, cats and dogs. My life would be incomplete unless surrounded by plants and animals, whether wild or domestic. I don't know an animal with which I don't have some feeling of kinship.

❧

I'M NOT, in the standard way of viewing things, a religious person. I belong to no organized church and never have. My parents belonged to churches. My father was raised a Lutheran and became part of the Christian Missionary Alliance, and my mother was a Congregationalist all her life. I went to Sunday school occasionally and to church off and on, but it was never a compulsive thing. I do have very strong religious feelings, however, and feel closer to God in nature than probably many people do in church. I find many things in the old Indian religions that are far closer to my own feelings. I know that there is some kind of Being—I don't know what you want to call it, but call it God—and it's everywhere. I can't see a plant or a bird or anything that I don't have some kind of religious feeling for. I feel like saying, "Thank you, God," for the beauty and all of the good things and sometimes even for the bad things, because sometimes beauty comes out of the bad things.

I think that our lives should express a constant thank you for all that we have. I have my own foolish way of doing these things. I think that if you kill an animal for food, asking its forgiveness is not a ridiculous notion at all. Even if you aren't asking the bear or deer, or whatever it is you've killed, for forgiveness, you're saying, "Thank you, God," for providing this food. I always express a mental thank you when I go out and find some berries. It's a thanks for creation coming from a fullness of the heart.

I'VE LEARNED MORE ABOUT THE NATURAL WORLD outside the classroom than in it, and no one has given me any personal guidance along the way. There have been people, however, through my lifetime that have inspired me, like Ernest Swift, former game warden with the Conservation Department [Wisconsin DNR]. He was the local hero around here. People laughed about his exploits because he was sort of a Robin Hood figure, and in his capacity as game warden he had quite an ability to catch poachers [once facing down a gangster shooting game with a machine gun[109]]. And he was quite a woodsman. He could walk deer down and had the endurance to continually keep on the move. He, more than anyone, personified my feelings for the outdoors.

Principally, writings have influenced me the most. Writings like *The Girl of the Limberlost* by Gene Stratton-Porter. Virginia Eifert is another woman writer whose work has been inspirational to me. She used to be the head of a natural history museum in Illinois, and she wrote books like *Land of the Snowshoe Hare*, which was written over in the Rhinelander area. I fell in love with her writings because I felt as if I was walking right along with her—walking through the bog lands. Her philosophy and feeling for the outdoors were so similar to my own that I identified closely with what she experienced.

Whatever I know, I attribute to my drive to know, and I simply have to know for my own personal satisfaction. It's a hunger that I can't completely satisfy. I get as excited now as I ever did whenever I find something new or unusual.

CHAPTER THIRTEEN

I first started learning about wildflowers. I'd find something new, then I'd locate all the books I could to find out what it was, and then learn about its relationship to other plants and how it fit into a plant community as a whole. Once I found out what it was, I kept a mental record of it. It's only been in recent years that I've written down names, dates, and classifications. Quite often I would do a pen and ink drawing of a flower, and this would help me remember it, especially those that I didn't want to disturb. If I could remember to, I would do a watercolor of it afterwards.

Lois painted and catalogued over 300 mushroom species, including this one—formerly named *Boletus aurantiacus*, now known as *Leccinum aurantiacum*—the (edible) red-capped scaber stalk. Illustration courtesy of Deb Nelson and Cable Natural History Museum.

I'm probably more knowledgeable about mushrooms than the average person is around here, but I'm far from being an expert because there are still many things that I don't know. What is it about mushrooms? I don't know. They give me an endless fascination. There's such a variety of birds and flowers, too, but the mushrooms just seem to catch my fancy. I get a lot of fun out of discovering what they are, making drawings, and writing down all the details about them.

☙

BACK IN THE LATE 1960s, the town of Cable started having these nature lectures in the summer, and I was asked to give a lecture on mushrooms. And it was at that first lecture that the idea for the Cable Natural History Museum came about. At the time, I had just started taking slides. So for the presentation, I had to make great big charts and drawings of mushrooms. As it turned out, Mr. and Mrs. Jackson Burke, who had a home on Lake Namakagon, attended that first lecture. Mrs. Burke came up afterwards and asked me if I'd be interested in helping to start a nature trail. I said, "Well, I guess so," and after we worked on getting the trail started, she asked me if I was interested in starting a small nature museum. I said, "Sure." She rented a little storefront on Main Street, and we started the museum there, where we remained for nearly two years before the present building was built in 1971. It's all grown from that.

Sometimes I will hear people talk about an exhibit and will join their discussion. They may need a further explanation or just a story to help them understand something. But the groups vary and must be handled differently. As a general rule, I do not give prepared talks to school groups unless teachers request them because, chances are, the kids could care less about something that's presented to them.

I prefer to circulate among the kids and let them ask me what they want. If they're really interested in something, they'll ask me about it. For example, how plant dyes are made: I tell them the roots, berries, bark, or whatever it is you use are boiled, then you soak white wool yarn in a solution of cream of tartar and alum, or in the dye product itself to preserve it. Then you simmer the wool in the dye until it reaches the color shade you want, and then rinse it with clear water until no more color comes out of it. Some of the lichen dyes I soak in an ammonia and water solution for several weeks to develop different colors, such as the purple from rock tripe, for instance.

The hognose snake, among other things, is a curiosity to students. It commands attention because it looks like a cobra ready to strike. But it isn't poisonous. It makes itself look very deadly because it throws out its mantle, raises itself, hisses horribly. If you pester it some more, it will roll over on its back and play dead. If you continue to bother it, it will vomit up everything it has eaten. It primarily eats toads with teeth about the size of a minnow. They're just big enough to prevent the toad from escaping.

During the weekends—and they're pretty typical—there's washing, baking, cooking, and gardening. I really wouldn't know how to live in the summertime without a garden. I spend a lot of time there—probably six to eight hours—far more than is required, but I have to visit the plants even if there's nothing to do for them. I'm a devout organic gardener. I pile on the mulches and don't use any commercial fertilizers or poisons. I garden intensively. It looks like a jungle, but it really produces. I start all my own plants from seed, so actually my gardening season begins the first week of March. Some of the early garden things like beets, onions, peas, and carrots go into the garden in April. I won't put tomatoes in before the first week of June, and even then I have to worry about frost.

I do a tremendous amount of canning, freezing, and drying of just about everything that is possible to grow in this area. I figure that I'm raising enough potatoes, onions, carrots, beets, and corn so we don't have to buy anything except occasional fresh lettuce or fresh fruit during the winter.

Harvesting annual wild rice *(Zizania aquatica)* in northwestern Wisconsin, fall 1982. Photo courtesy of Deb Nelson and Cable Natural History Museum.

I can't think of anything that gives me more pleasure than working in the garden or walking all day in the woods collecting things and taking pictures. I do needlework, too, and I make all my own designs—crewelwork from designs of grasses, flowers, mushrooms, and that sort of thing. I bring home samples of grasses, then draw them onto fabric and embroider them.

THERE ARE SOME PEOPLE who never think about nature because they've never explored or studied it. I know people around town, who with the best intentions in the world toward the land, don't know one plant from another in the woods. They've simply been preoccupied with other parts of their lives, and a study of what's around them has never seemed important. And it's a completely new experience being exposed to what's in the natural world.

I think that anyone who owns some land or has some control over it, should leave it in as good or better a condition as when they found it. Stewardship— to me that's the answer. Using it—yes. I approve of making use of the land and what it has to offer, but never to the extent that you are abusing it, or that you are taking away from the land itself, or from future generations. You have to be aware of the consequences of any action you take when you use the land.

Land is the greatest thing the world possesses, and it's up to everyone to do his or her part to maintain and nurture it. Some of the careless logging operations send me into a tizzy. Logging itself I don't object to because there are trees that need to be harvested. Trees are a crop. But it has been the crude, careless, indiscriminate logging operations that have angered me to no end. Terrible destruction by skid equipment is a real problem up here. Ski trails made by equipment that haul logs out have resulted in total destruction of anything that existed along the equipment's path.

There are better ways ecologically for the loggers to do what they are doing, but there's probably no better way financially. Naturally, loggers are trying to make the most profit at the least expense. I'm talking about private logging operations on private lands, where there's nothing anyone can do. Such logging has destroyed many of the places I used to love to wander.

Sometimes I see where livestock have been pastured in a fragile bog and have trampled all over everything. This sickens me! I talked to a neighbor about it once, and as a result, he hasn't spoken to me in 15 years. He pastured livestock in a bog, where there was really nothing for them to eat, and they destroyed it by turning it into a mud flat. The bog used to have orchids, liverworts, and ferns, which I treasured. If it had been good pasture, I wouldn't have said a word about it because I would have thought that he would have had the right to utilize it, but when it was nothing of any value to his stock, I thought it was a shame.

You know, I've had to compromise all my life, but I don't do it gracefully. I might in the long run have to say all right, we'll sacrifice this piece of land for that piece, but I wouldn't do it happily. To me, the thought of destroying one square foot doesn't make sense. Land is a precious commodity, and I begrudge the destruction of any of it, especially since we're rapidly losing so much of it these days. Once something is destroyed, it's awfully hard to replace it. It may eventually be replaced by something, but it will probably never be the same as it was unless it's land that will then remain undisturbed for centuries or millennia.

People who know little of the natural world can't develop an ethical regard for the land unless they have a real desire to because it's the desire that's going to make it happen. Other than that, you can't force it on anyone.

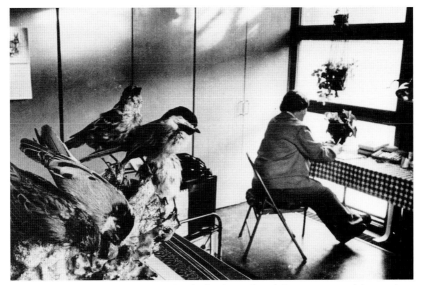

Lois working at the "old" museum (that had to be replaced due to structural damage); some of her taxidermy specimens are in the foreground, 1981. Photo courtesy of Deb Nelson and Cable Natural History Museum.

People need to get out and experience nature in person—I think that's the only way. You can go to the books afterwards, but I think that you need to have the personal experience first.

The easiest way to begin to change people's thinking about how they see the natural world is to show them beautiful pictures of what's around them. Very few are going to go on that first walk with you, but if you can show them pictures of orchids or rare, unusual plants, beautiful things that they were never aware of, and explain their importance to a plant community, then their understanding begins to grow, and their minds begin to change.

I feel that I'm not nearly helping as much the people of Cable to understand what's around them as I am the visitor from out of town. It's always nice to find kindred spirits and see a response to what I've done. I need that. I need to see people getting something worthwhile so that I feel as though my work has been done for a reason, other than for my own satisfaction. I want people to leave the museum thinking they now want to know more. I want to see people look at the collections of things in here and say, "What a great world we have! I want to learn how to be a better part of it!"

Selected Seasonal Excerpts From Lois Nestel's *Wayside Wanderings* (privately published in 1975; limited edition)

WINTER
Blinding Wild Snow
Blows, Whirls And
Drifts About Me ...
In This World Alone
　　—Chora

Most people are aware of the beauty of summer flowers and often bemoan their passing as winter approaches. This need not be a cause for regret because, while much color may be lost, there continue—as seeds, pods, and capsules—many forms that rival the flowers in beauty and grace. Many of these seed containers last throughout the winter, serving as food for wildlife and pleasure for humans.

There is a sculptured beauty in the pods of various milkweeds and wild iris, evening primrose, cockle and Indian pipes. Delicate grace is exemplified in airy sprays of sweet cicely, papery clusters of wild hops and feathery virgin's bower (wild clematis) twining over bushes, and in the dried grasses and sedges, each with individual form and style. Many fall-blooming flowers (weeds if one must call them that) retain their form if not their color through the winter months. Goldenrod, tansy and yarrow are sepia-toned replicas of summer's gay colors. Flowers such as asters lift clusters of tan star-like sepals above the snow.

Touches of color do remain in scattered places; the dark velvety red of sumac heads, the red-orange of rose hips, and the brighter red of highbush cranberries and hawthorn frozen on their shrubs.

To enjoy these and many other beauties of winter there are few requirements; namely these: get outside, have open eyes to see and an open mind, receptive enough to appreciate what is seen....

On winter walks when much plant life is hidden beneath snow, one of my favorite plant families stands out in plain view: the little known and less appreciated tree-dwelling lichens. These patches of soft color on the tree trunks, everyone has seen them, yet have they really? Have you ever looked closely at the rosette forms of *Parmelia* lichen, like embroidered doilies in pearly shades of green or blue or muted yellows, pinks and tans? Their textures and designs are not less beautiful than the most elaborately designed lace.

Rough-barked trees like pines may have from a few to hundreds of lichens, from dot size to those larger than dinner plates. Smooth-barked trees such as aspen often have golden patches of yellow shield lichen, its fruiting bodies minute saucer shapes on a foliose background.

Numerous species of shield lichen and twig lichen abound, some with leaf forms, some coral-like, others granular, curded or leather-like. Beard and hair lichen hang in tufts from many trees and are especially noticeable in bog evergreens.

Thousands of species exist, creating a miniature world too seldom noticed, a world of surprise and pleasure. For full appreciation, try viewing them through a magnifying glass and add a new dimension to your world.

Had I been one of the druids of old I believe my worship would have been, not for the mighty oak, but surely for one of the evergreens. While other trees have dropped their ruffled gowns and stand in shivering nakedness, the evergreen reaches out with well-clothed arms to offer shelter from the cold. We would be bereft without this royal family of the northern climes.

Here stand the spruces, maids in waiting, dark, slender dancers of the skyline; and here the balsams, reserved aristocrats, rich in their own perfume and decked with icicle and frost jewels. Here are the tough, gnarled jack pines, outcasts and black sheep of the family, fighters for their share of the earth. What they lack in grace they make up in sheer tenacity....

Here are the hemlocks, full of queenly grace and serenity from seedling to massive and dignified old age, replenishing the earth beneath them and pouring forth their largess in multitudes of cones to benefit the wildlife. Here, too, the sinewy cedars, crown princes of the swamplands and benevolent overseers of the delicate orchids.

And here, head and shoulders above the rest, stand my beloved white pines. Like lanky, callow youths in their early years, they develop the symmetry of handsome adulthood, and in the fullness of their years are craggy, unconventional and full of character. There is strength in the clean lines of great limbs and tenderness in the soft-whispering blue-green plumes of needles. As I see them now, mantled with snow, it is as the cloak of ermine tossed carelessly across the shoulders of the king. Towering in stately dignity, no other tree adds such distinctive beauty to the sylvan scene.

If I were a druid, to this world would I bow down. But as I am not, I can only gaze in awe and admiration and think, "What wonders God has wrought!"

There are times when the winter woods are so still, so empty, that walking in them, one feels like the last living creature. Not a track mars the snow; not a sound stirs the air. Where has everything gone? It is strange because a few days earlier there may have been an abundance of life in many forms.

On one of these livelier days I set out with a definite purpose in mind. I was stalking a pileated woodpecker whose calls and rapid-fire hammerings seemed to come consistently from one area of trees not far from the house. These big, wary birds are not easy to pursue so reasonable caution was necessary. In line with the hammering of the woodpecker was a pine grove and, approaching this I was greeted with one of the woodland's loveliest sounds. Like the chiming of myriad crystals, a flock of juncos was gossiping among the branches. Their notes were so fragile and unbelievably pure they seemed to float on the air. They fell silent as I passed beneath them but resumed immediately as the intrusion passed.

Silence ahead seemed to indicate that the big bird had flown, but the apprehension was dispelled as, from a pine stub ahead, there came a staccato burst and bits of flying wood. A stealthy approach, timed with the pecking, ended abruptly when a large black beak topped by bright eyes and a flame red cockade was suddenly thrust around the side of the stub. With much scuffling of feet the crow-sized black body came into view. Unaware of being watched, the bird seemed to talk to himself with soft *kooking* notes as if trying to decide where to drill the next hole.

Some unwary movement or sound on my part suddenly alerted him. There was a brief eye-to-eye confrontation; then the broad wings spread, and with a few swooping beats ... the great woodpecker [flew] into the safety and seclusion of the forest.

The pine stub bore evidence of much work. Large openings had been chopped through the shell and into the honeycombed interior. Breaking open a piece of this riddled wood revealed the dormant bodies of large black ants. This was what had attracted the woodpecker and would undoubtedly bring him back again. I might not be around to see, but the sound of the drumming would bring to mind a clear picture of a great black bird with a flaming topknot—a memory to treasure.

When a winter wind is sculpturing the snowy waysides, I am inclined to stay indoors and do my wandering in memories of younger days. Of all the elements, strong winter winds are what I like the least, and yet, in retrospect, even these have brought their measure of satisfaction.

Perhaps it is because houses are more tightly constructed that these days I do not hear the wind in the same way as in my childhood. Then the winter wind seemed a living thing that shrieked and moaned around the corners and clawed at the windows. But that soulless wail was great to hear when curled, warm and comfortable, beneath the patchwork quilts. It was exciting then to see the sheets of snow driven relentlessly across the fields to form drifts that curved and swelled like ocean surf frozen at its crest. That wind-packed snow could hold the weight of a man and beast, and meant untold hours of shovel work as an aftermath, but while it lasted it was thrilling and challenging.

Now there seems a desolation and bitterness in the wind as though it mourns the sadness and injustice in the world. But the wind is not governed by political upheavals, poverty, or crime. It is as it always has been; only the listener, the endurer, has changed.

These days I shiver with the birds huddled in more sheltered spots. I start nervously at sudden, violent gusts, as do the animals. The wind was once my playmate; I could run with it and contend against it, but now it no longer is my friend. The loss is mine.

🍂

On the night of the last full moon the winds were quiet and the sky clear following heavy ... snow. Awakening in the night I sat by the window gazing out at a familiar world made strange and new by moonlight and shadow. The trees were stark silhouettes against the sky, and their shadows were blue-inked traceries upon the sparkling snow. As I watched, one dark form and then another emerged from the shadows as two cottontails came out to eat the food scattered on the ground for them each evening. They fed quietly for a while before moon madness struck them and they began to leap high, twisting and kicking heels into the crystal air. They would chase madly around the trees, in and out of the shadows, stop, facing each other, and then be off again, often with one leaping over the other to begin the race.

LOIS NESTEL

How long this would have continued is hard to say, but suddenly, quite close by, a coyote wailed, and immediately the voices of several others rose in chorus.... Several times the yipping wails of the coyotes rose and fell; then all was silent.

Nothing lasts forever and winter is waning. There is a new warmth in the sun, and each day brings changes so that even the seeming setbacks of late winter storms cannot alter the fact that spring is in the air.

An occasional fly now basks on a sun-warmed wall, a spider creeps lethargically from a crevice, and a warm afternoon may find a mourning cloak butterfly emerging temporarily from hibernation to flit over receding banks of snow.

The sight of a snowshoe hare crossing the yard made me realize that its great spring transition has begun. This is the time when the hare turns, over a period of several weeks, from winter white to brown. Long white guard hairs are dropping out, to be brushed off during its passage through the bushes. The white tips on the soft underhairs have become worn and frayed, and as they break off the snowshoe is no longer solidly white. The entire coat becomes tinged with tan, and brown patches appear, first on the face and forelegs, then spreading back over the body. If the hare is lucky, these changes will keep pace with the melting of the snow so that the white animal of the white winter becomes the mottled animal of the thawed spots and, finally, the brown of leaves, grass and earth. A sudden warm spell, taking too much snow too soon, can leave a white hare in sharp contrast to a dark background and so in constant peril from predation. A very late snow can leave the darkened animal in the same precarious position.

SPRING
> *Now Wild Geese Return*
> *What Draws Them*
> *Crying Crying*
> *All The Long Dark Night*
> —Roka

Poor weary, battered spring, after many reversals, seems to have finally arrived. The time of emergence is upon us. The hibernators are out.

Chipmunks, tails straight up, scurry enthusiastically about as if checking up on last year's unfinished business. Gophers and woodchucks search for succulent green spears or drowse dull-eyed in the sun. The deer have left their wintering yards, and the tracks of bears once again mark the forest trails. Skunks dig for grubs in the softening soil and leave muddy imprints of slender paws on receding snow.

The sap is rising in the trees. The pines have taken on a brighter, livelier hue, and the buds of aspen and maple are swelling. On a recent day I watched purple finches drinking sparkling sap droplets from winter-damaged twigs of the box elders. This member of the maple family has sap only slightly less sweet than the sugar maple.

Every day brings new flocks of migrating birds, some to pause briefly before continuing north, others to remain and build their nests. Meadowlarks and bobolinks, birds common to this area in the days when farming was more extensive, have made brief appearances and moved on to the hayfields beyond.

The lakes are not yet open, but ducks, herons, and shorebirds wing their way from open stream to stream and search the still brown marshes for likely nesting sites....

The water world is slowly awakening as warmer days and spring rains clear the ice from lake and marshland. May brings the bird-like calling of the spring peepers (hylids), which, to me, is the truest sign of spring. Swelling the chorus for "frog song" will come the leopard and wood frogs followed by the toads, the pickerel and green frogs. It takes a little time but one who cares can learn to recognize the individual calls of the different species.

In lakes and streams the spawning runs of some fish have begun. Walleyes begin their migration soon after the ice goes out, and spawning generally occurs in flowing streams or along lakes shores where waves over gravel keep the water in motion. Most of the migration occurs during the hours of darkness with the fish resting quietly in deeper waters during the day. This, in general, applies to the annual sucker run as well. There is a special thrill in standing on a quiet, dark lake shore and suddenly hearing a mighty rushing of waters, knowing the waterfall-like sound is caused by the powerful thrashing of hundreds of spawning fish. The spawning of most other local fish is less spectacular, some making nests in sand or gravel; others like the northern pike, preferring grassy or marshy vegetation in the high, shallow water of spring.

Activity of all types will speed up rapidly as the water warms. Humans translate much of this into [the rites] of fishing: the fish that will bite the minnow, frog, or worm bait, and the hordes of aquatic insects that will bite the fisherman. The cycle of life goes on, the food chain remains in tact. As in all the worlds within our world, life, procreation, and death continue in the water world....

All the tender shades of spring are now unfolding. All the hues of autumn are here, only in tones more delicate and subtle. Soft shades of pink and wine and the daintiest of yellow blend with the sheerest of green as buds unfurl and fragile leaves and blooms unfold.

At a distance, forest and brushland wear watercolor shades and soft-washed pastels. Tree blossoms, seldom noted, are small perfections deserving closer examination and appreciation. Well known are juneberry, cherry and plum blossoms, hawthorn and red elderberry; less commonly recognized, though equally beautiful in a miniature way, are the flowers of the maple and oak—delicate clustered flowers of russet, rose, and yellow dangling on slender pale green stems—or the willows, their catkins now masses of gold and chartreuse.

Beneath the trees the ferns lift the scrolled perfection of their still furled fronds, some tan or silvery with down, some stemmed in soft maroon in contrast with the shaded greens of others. Wood flowers bloom now before leaf shade from trees cuts down their light. Bloodroot leaves embrace the stems of snowy, golden-eyed flowers and *Hepaticas*, spring beauties and wood *Anemones* nod heads of lavender, pink and white, while trailing arbutus perfumes the air from clustered blossoms of pink and white. Soon trilliums will dance beneath the trees, and the marshlands will glow yellow with marsh marigolds, rosy with bog laurel, and white with Labrador tea.

Shade on shade, tone on tone, the palette of nature is spread with her most gentle colors. The harsh, the gaudy, may come, but now is the time for tenderness.

The high tide of bird life is upon us. Some early migrants have already passed through on their way to nesting grounds in the north, but the cold spring has slowed the movement so that those who seldom cross paths are temporally brought into close company.

Some of the loveliest warblers have appeared in our yard, though they seldom use the feeders. Perhaps the most beautiful has been the magnolia warbler, but there have been others: yellowthroat, chestnut-sided, blackburnian, and myrtle [yellow-rumped]. Orioles are dining on crumbs and orange halves—that is, if the squirrels don't carry them away and hang them high in the pine branches....

The pattern of bird life changes from day to day as some depart and others make their seasonal appearance. The dawn chorus swells to its maximum in late May and the vespers touch a responsive chord in human hearts. Treasure the birds. The place they fill in our lives can never be duplicated.

SUMMER

Little Silver Fish
Pointing Upstream
Moving Downstream
In Clean Quiet Water
      —Soseki

Wetlands are places of fascinating variety; yet except for some hunters and a few avid bog-hoppers, they are less well known than most other types of terrain. Marshes, swamps, and bogs all come under the heading of wetlands, and of these, the bogs are my favorite. These may also be divided into groups: one, the older bogs, shaded and sheltered by cedar or tamarack, black spruce and alder; the other, the more open, sunny bog which may or may not have a pond in the center.

It was one of this latter type that I recently visited, as I try to do two or three times a year. The surrounding hill drops sharply and it is a slipping, sliding, tree-grabbing jaunt to bog level. The outer edges are ringed with leather leaf, Labrador tea, and clumps of blue flag, with occasional stunted spruce and dead snags. Dry weather has bleached the upper surfaces of the sphagnum moss, but it is nevertheless a floating bog; stepping upon it means sinking into darkness, and standing still finds cold brown water seeping into shoes and around ankles as the bog settles under pressure.

The bog is filled with pitcher plants, which were, at this time, lifting dozens of intricate wine and green blossoms above the pitcher-shaped leaves. These are insectivorous plants and near them in the sphagnum grew other plants with the same unusual habit. These are the sundews, whose sticky-tipped hairs on reddish leaves catch and hold gnat-sized insects, which the plant digests.

Bog rosemary, sedges, bog beans and scores of other ... plants grow in and around the moss. Wild callas were just past their prime, with the fruiting center growing large within the still fresh spathe of creamy white, and the delicate tracery of wild cranberry laced the entire bog with trailing stems and dainty recurved pink flowers.

I had hoped to find, as I did last year, calypso and calopogan orchids but the timing was wrong. This could cause no more than momentary regret when so many other elements were present. Delightful plant life surrounded me, veeries and thrushes sang from the hillsides, while kingbirds on dead stubs awaited insects, and blackbirds cried from the cattails. Life at such a time can seem very full and satisfying. One becomes, not a superior creation, but a part of the fabric of life, attuned to rather in competition with nature.

⁂

The night watch has been in frequent session lately. I am not an insomniac, merely a light and fitful sleeper, and the wakeful periods are pleasantly spent in absorbing the night—its scents, its sounds, its movements all so different from those of daytime. Musky, earthy, fecund odors seem to rise and drift on the night air—basic life aromas no longer masked by day's activities....

Against the night sky I have watched the erratic black flutterings of bats and heard the taffeta rustlings of their wings sweeping close to my window in the quest of insects. Nothing sinister here, just small, busy mammals helping hold the insect population in check.

The other enchanting creature of the night is the firefly, and watching the winking greenish lights against the darkened trees and lawns my mind drifts back to childhood evenings when the things of nature were an unquestioned part of life. In retrospect, I smell again the fragrance of the fields of clover and alfalfa and my mother's roses. I feel again the dew-cooled grass beneath bare feet while racing up and down the lawn to capture fireflies and lock them in a jar. There was endless fascination in those cool winking lights. Sometimes they seemed to flash in unison, sometimes helter-skelter. But the insects that could light the pages of a book at night were disappointingly dull, grubby insects by morning's light when they would be released. Come evening, though, the chase would be resumed.

⁂

Soft breezes may provide a background for a serenade of crickets, or on a moonlit night, the half-phrased notes of a drowsy bird. The hum of insects, the soft rustle of a bat's wings, a whip-poor-will, a distant barking dog, the measured hooting of an owl blend to produce the heartbeat of the night.

Even without the wind the night is seldom silent, and the sounds are music to my ears. A rabbit thumps his feet in alarm, and a deer blows sharply at some unseen intruder. Raccoons chur in conversation or raise their voices in tremolo wails as they contest over a choice tidbit, and perhaps most delightful to me is the vocalizing of the coyotes in a wild and haunting madrigal of freedom and solitude.

Who listens, I wonder? Who hears, or senses the pulsing cadence of the elements? Our ears are tuned to different sounds, and behind closed doors we listen to man-made, machine-made din: radio, television, records and endless, pointless small talk. For some this will suffice, and for these I am truly sorry, though I know they would consider my pity an affront to their tastes and logic. To each his own. As for me, nature's song brings me a special peace and serenity. I ask for no more than that.

❧

I wonder—does anyone watch clouds anymore, just for the sake of cloud watching? To me, these are some of nature's most beautiful formations, never twice the same, always amazing, whether puffy fleeces, shredded mare's tails, or threatening banks jeweled with lightning.

In the habit formed in childhood I still see in the cumulus clouds a fantasy world; human faces and forms, animals, landscapes, ever changing and reforming, sometimes in such majesty that it seems that I must glimpse the face of God.

Sunrise and sunset add a new dimension to cloud formations, adding tints and strengthening contrasts. The towering castles and turrets of thunderheads in an evening sky overwhelm one with awe as the high-piled vapors glow with snowy whiteness tipped with crimson, rose and gold and shades too evanescent and fragile to describe. Small wonder that artists have depicted angels sailing along on heavenly cloud ships in a blue, blue sky.

It is satisfying, I suppose, to name the clouds scientifically—stratus, cumulus, cirrus, cumulonimbus—but to really see the clouds, to know their beauty and their meaning has far greater satisfactions. A mackerel sky at evening means more to me than to identify altocumulus clouds, and the fat dumpling wind clouds, the slatey snow clouds, the boiling masses of summer storm clouds are familiar friends who need no names.

Lift up your eyes, not to look for storm and trouble but to see the magnificence that fills the sky. Rejoice that such beauty, such grace is free to all.

Although summer is far from over, there are many signs of the advancing season. Days are noticeably shorter, and the dawns are now greeted by few spasmodic and seemingly unenthusiastic birdcalls. Many of our local birds have already molted into fall plumage, and migration from the north is in progress. The confusion of yellowish-green warblers drifts through....

Blackberries are ripening and a few mushrooms, encouraged by recent showers, are fruiting in favorable areas. In searching for some of these I have beheld an amazing array of flowers that only this season can bring. In deeply sheltered woods I occasionally see blackberry blossoms while adjacent sunny glades hold dead-ripe fruit. Late

Wayside Bounty

A collage of nature's bounty—a sketch from Lois's wanderings in northern Wisconsin. Illustration courtesy of Deb Nelson and Cable Natural History Museum.

wild roses and bluebells dance in the moss beneath trees, and wintergreen provides a double delight as last season's fat red berries mingle with the pearly bells of the current year.

Roadsides and fallow fields defy description. The blues, purples and magenta of asters, ironweed, and fireweed swirl through the sheeted gold of tansy and goldenrod, and all are white-embroidered with fleabane, late daisies, and pearly everlasting. Kaleidoscopic colors shift and glow through changing light and changing days. The heyday of the flowers is now, before their radiance is dimmed by the fullness of seedtime. In some instances

CHAPTER THIRTEEN

that time is here, as indicated by the ripening grasses and the heavy crop of hazelnuts, which chipmunks are busily harvesting, although the shells are only faintly brown within green husks.

There will still be days of smoldering heat and days with the balmy caress of spring when autumn will seem far away, but the die is cast. The flower-decked green mantle of summer is becoming a bit tattered at the edges, and her brown undergarments are showing. Before her finery becomes tarnished and drab, take time to experience her abundant attractions.

AUTUMN

White Autumn Moon
Black-Branch
Shadow Patterns
Printed On the Mats
　—Kikoku

While I may not go to the wood to fetch back words of wisdom, I do by choice traverse it alone on most occasions. There may be many reasons for my going. I may be searching for specific plants for photographic subjects or equally practical purposes, but most often (and most rewarding) I go for the soothing, healing peace the solitude of a quiet woodland brings to me.

At this time of year the tranquility of nature seems most apparent. It is the deep-breathing pause between the hectic days of growth and fruition and the chilled dormancy of winter. Fallen leaves carpet the earth in hues that rival and outshine the crafts of the Orient. Mosses, at their greenest now, seem to glow with an inner radiance on rock and stump and fallen tree. The beauty of these lowly plants is equal to the fairest flower or mightiest tree. Mingling one with another, they clothe the raw earth and decaying wood in protective emerald garb.

Beneath tall evergreens one can move in cat-footed silence over moss and needle-cushioned ground, seeing, hearing, feeling the serenity of a natural world. Being alone in this way is not being lonely. Freed from the need for conversation and the distractions of everyday affairs, one can open the doors of the mind, airing out the pettiness, discord, and annoyance.

Truly there is great wisdom here if willing hearts and open minds can accept it: the endless patience of forest and earth to renew themselves despite the many violations wrought upon them by man; the lack of malice among wild creatures who prey upon one another only to sustain life but never in spite or rancor. And there is hope and faith, for even as the dying leaves color the earth, the trees and shrubs are putting forth new buds for the year to come. The seed, fallen to the ground, bears the germ of the plant yet to come, and the bulb beneath the earth bears within its heart next summer's flower.

These things speak to me in my solitary walks. They speak in the still, small voice of the spirit, and I am strengthened and renewed.

***

The little, isolated lake lay serene and unruffled in the autumn sunlight, its surface reflecting with a silvery sheen the blue October sky. It was wrapped about by [a] quaking bog studded with leatherleaf, sedges and pitcher plants, and encircling the water like a ruby necklace were the wild cranberries growing in careless profusion. Woven throughout the bog, especially on the narrow open strip approaching the water, were animal trails, well used; scattered droppings along them indicated habitation by a variety of animals. Back among the leatherleaf clumps lay the well-cleaned skin of a porcupine, quills down—mute evidence of an encounter with a fisher. Chewed lengths of plant stems on the bog edge and in the water seemed to indicate the presence of muskrats.

All through the bog there appeared no movement. Although bright eyes may have been watching from any number of hidden nooks, it seemed likely that most of the inhabitants were nocturnal.

The lake presented a different picture, for soon after our arrival the glassy surface on the far side was broken into silvery rings in three places, and in the center of each ring appeared a dark post-like object. Soon the forms converged and in long, undulating glides approached our side of the lake. Otters, of course. As they came near they again separated to view the intruders from different vantage points. From here, from there, curious and alert, they scrutinized us. Showing no fear but boundless interest they kept pace with the progress on shore while performing an intricate water ballet. Looking almost boneless in their fluid movement, they would dive and roll, rise high in the water, then dive again.

At last, bored or satisfied, they swam off in the direction from which they had come, and we lost track of them. Again the water lay smooth and quiet with only a small dead bluegill floating near the bog, awaiting perhaps a scavenging raccoon in the approaching darkness.

The first snow of the season blanketed the ground and reflected back the moonlight with unaccustomed brightness. Looking out, I thought the world seemed empty of life, silent and pristine. The illusion was soon shattered as from somewhere in the shadows of the trees came the piercing, quavering cry of a rabbit, rising to a shriek and then ending abruptly. My first thought was, "Oh, the poor thing—what a pity." I believed it to be the work of the locally resident great horned owl, and I pictured the silent swoop, the clutch of talons, and the great, tearing beak. Then, lying back, I mulled over the subject. The death was but a link in the chain and sad only for the rabbit. For the owl, as prime predator, it was cause for fierce pleasure and satisfaction, a sustaining of life. Lesser creatures would glean crumbs from his table, bits of flesh and bone to be gnawed by mice and shrews, to be picked by birds; nests would be lined in spring with scattered hair. Remnants of body wastes and liquids would sink into the earth to nourish next year's blade or twig, which in turn would nourish, perhaps, another rabbit in the passage of time.

Left to its normal management there is no waste in nature. Everything uses and is used, is changed and converted but never lost. Part of the owl flying in the night sky and the beetle beneath dead leaves is the rabbit who ate the twig whose nutriment came from other death and decay.

I regret that human standards have removed us from the natural chain. Human civilization has come to mean constant taking, seldom returning. How long will nature tolerate us? ✻

Lois passed away quietly on March 7, 1995, but true to her wishes there was no funeral service and no obituary, so that many people weren't aware that she had died for months. Her legacy, however, is evident today in the continuing educational work conducted by the capable Cable Natural History Museum staff. Stop by the museum, if you can, when in the Cable area.

BIGTOOTH ASPEN

GJK

Marion Moran
(1927-2016)

Marion's favorite photo that she selected for this chapter.
Photo courtesy of Gene and Marion Moran.

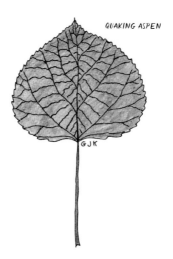

QUAKING ASPEN

GJK

Chapter Fourteen~
Marion Moran

When I was a child and my father went hunting, I would ask him to bring me back a fawn—alive. I wanted one badly. He didn't ever bring one back, but he did bring back gifts of the forest—wintergreen and pine cones—things that began to tell me of another place.

—MM

When a tree is cut down and reveals its naked death—wound to the sun, one can read its whole history in the luminous, inscribed disk of its trunk.... Trees are sanctuaries. Whoever knows how to speak to them, whoever knows how to listen to them, can learn the truth.

—Hermann Hesse, *Wandering: Notes and Sketches.*

The tree which moves some to tears of joy is in the eyes of others only a green thing which stands in the way.

—William Blake, letter to Reverend
John Trusler, August 23, 1799

M arion P. Moran, born February 4, 1927, in Fond du Lac, grew up in a large Swiss family at the foot of Lake Winnebago near the Eldorado Marsh. She graduated in 1945 from West High School in Madison and attended the University of Wisconsin-Madison for two and a half years before dropping out. Disillusioned and not sure in what direction to go, she returned home to help her recently divorced mother care for her younger siblings and help run the household.

Marion married for the first time in 1948 and spent the 1950s and most of the 1960s raising three children—Sue, Beth, and Rob—in Chesterfield, Missouri. Throughout this period, she also took neighborhood kids on nature walks into the Missouri River bottoms, where she began to develop a skill teaching others about the diversity and beauty of the natural world. She returned with her family to Madison in 1968, but the marriage did not survive; she was divorced in 1971.

From 1968 to 1976, Marion worked as a naturalist for the Madison School District, leading a program for children she called "Come Walk With Me." She also led tours at the UW-Madison Arboretum under the direction of naturalist Rosemary Fleming. In 1974, Marion became certified to teach natural history courses through the UW-Madison Extension system. She had found her calling.

Marion's UW-Extension natural history courses (later taught through the Madison Area Technical College and Edgewood College in Madison), with their emphasis on ecology and Native American spirituality, became highly popular. These included "Walks on the Wild Side," "Learning Together," and "Tracks in the Snow." She also began a long association with The Clearing in Door County and the Durward's Glen Retreat and Conference Center in the Baraboo Hills, where she conducted weekday and week-long retreats titled "Touch the Earth," and "Discovering a Sense of Place." Another popular session she led called "Spirit of the Land" occurred over a weekend at Upham Woods on Blackhawk Island, north of the Wisconsin Dells. And in the Baraboo area she occasionally taught about Native American history and culture at nearby schools.

I first interviewed Marion at her then-arboretum home in November 1981. She later moved with second husband, Gene, in 1986 to a secluded old farmstead—a place she called High Meadows—in the southern Baraboo Hills in 1985. I visited her there in April 2001 to catch up on her life. This chapter is a composite of both interviews.

My family was very much into the natural world. We spent a lot of time recreating in the outdoors, and my mother loved to garden. Quite early on, I used to wander the shoreline of Lake Winnebago for miles. I collected things, observed organisms in the wild, and had the freedom to roam. There were fields all around us where I watched honeybees and bumblebees and spiders making orb webs. There are times when I'm out in a field or prairie now where the smells are similar. I can see myself running through a similar meadow when I was younger with my younger brothers and sisters.

I learned a great deal about nature from my parents and grandparents. My grandmother, Eliza Bernett, came from the French part of Switzerland and was a self-trained botanist. My grandfather, Robert Bernett, came from the German sector of Switzerland and worked as an engineer. My mother was Pearl Evelyn Burnett, and my father, John Trummer—also German-Swiss—was a hunter who painted murals of marshes on our walls. He would have pursued a career as a biologist if that career had been a possibility at the time, but instead he started his own plumbing and heating business.

When I was a child and my father went hunting, I would ask him to bring me back a fawn—alive. I wanted one badly. He didn't ever bring one back, but he did bring back gifts of the forest—wintergreen and pine cones—things that began to tell me of another place.

❧

I WAS THE FOURTH of nine kids; an older brother died at age two. Special moments occurred whenever a younger brother or sister was born. At those times, my big brother or sister would take us into the outdoors while Mother gave birth. She didn't ever go to the hospital. She wanted to have her babies at home. Each of those birthdays I now associate with a particular activity, place, or thing, and I gave each day a special name. For example, my last sister, Heidi, was born on *The Day of the Blue Flag Iris*. Do you know where I was that day? In the marsh. My brother, Dick, was born on *The Day of Snow Ice Cream*. We made snow ice cream that day in the middle of winter.

Mother used to tell me that I always wanted to be in the garden. There's a photograph of me when I was two where I'm looking at flowers or into seedpods. When she brought me out to the garden, we would often sit quietly and watch insects. She allowed me to put my hands into the soil and help her plant flowers. And she bred canaries. She had as many as 30 at one time. We had one room called the bird room, and I went down and helped her feed the birds and take care of the fledglings. My interest in bird-watching grew out of that experience.

My mother taught me reverence for life, for the life forms around me.

She always told me that there was something special about me. I was unplanned, and she thought she would never have another child before I arrived.

My mother wasn't the only woman to influence me early on. When I was in the fifth grade, I had a teacher named Nellie Mitchell. She was my teacher for two years, and she loved nature. She had us recite poetry and tell her about things in nature that excited us.

🌿

MY CHILDHOOD from the age of 12 on was a very difficult one. It was a stressful time because my father was not spending much time at home; he was an alcoholic. I remember him as someone who would take me to church and sing songs to me, and was always kind to me. Mother used to say he cherished me because I was born after a long period when she wasn't able to have a child. But I can't forget what happened.

One night he came home, and Mother confronted him. I remember sitting in a chair nearby and listening to their conversation, which became very heated. The next thing I saw was my father attacking and choking her. She became so distraught that she broke away, ran to the neighbors, and called the police. Having witnessed that, I shook like a leaf. A policeman came—a friend of my father's—and stood beside me. Glaring down at me, he said, "Your father didn't do that, did he?"

I had to say, "Yes, he did." From that point on, everything fell apart, and Mother decided to pack us all up and move to Madison, where my sister was going to college. I was the oldest of six kids at home. My older brother stayed behind because he was working as an apprentice to my dad. From then on, I became the responsible child, the one who helped my mother through this time. I was expected to come home and not linger at school because I had to help with the other children.

I remember going outside often after that incident and finding my only comfort there, with the wind and the trees. I turned to nature for solace. This was during the Second World War, and times were tough. Mother rented out our garage to a neighbor for five dollars a month, and I was sent to the store to buy groceries with that rent money. Once, with my two brothers, we brought along a cardboard box sled with two barrel-slats for runners. As we were coming home, however, we spilled a ten-pound bag of sugar. I was afraid to go home because there was no money to buy more sugar. So with the innocence of a child, I returned to the store and told the grocer I had broken the bag. He showed compassion and gave me a new, ten-pound bag of sugar. I have never forgotten his act of kindness.

FROM THE TIME of ninth grade on, Mother kept moving us to make ends meet, so it was very hard to make and keep friends. It was Fond du Lac to Madison for seventh, eighth, and ninth grades; tenth grade to Fort Atkinson; eleventh grade back to Fond du Lac; and finally back to West High School in Madison for twelfth grade.

Tenth grade was probably my best high school year. It was a smaller school, and the teachers were able to provide students with more personal attention. They even allowed me to bring my younger sister, Heidi, to school during times when Mother became ill. I had the good fortune of having a wonderful teacher that inspired me. I was struggling with math, but my math teacher, Dorothy Wagner, taught with such excitement and wonder that her spirit lifted mine. I got A's in that class. I haven't forgotten her.

Another teacher that helped me immensely was Beth Sutherland. High school girls are easily embarrassed, and I did not fit in with the crowd. One day, Miss Sutherland called me up to her desk between classes and said, "Marion. I've been watching you. Don't ever change. Don't feel like you have to be like the other girls." They were all typical teenagers. I had responsibilities, and there wasn't time for joining them. I'll never forget Beth Sutherland either. I named one of my daughters after her.

BOOKS have always been an important part of my life. They have been a great source of inspiration and knowledge. My mother used to read *Hiawatha* to me at night and in the afternoon. We took it paragraph by paragraph. That was the one thing I always wanted her to read.

As a child, books carried me away to special places and adventures. I recall mystery books such as the Nancy Drew series and several about outdoor adventure. One of the first nature books I read was Virginia Eifert's *Essays on Nature*. I love all her books. All of Sigurd Olson's books are included in my library as well. They have been very meaningful to me over the years. And John Muir—all of his writings, such as *The Story of My Boyhood and Youth*, have inspired me. Did you know that he was one of the few naturalists that dared to use the word "divine" when writing about nature? I love the way he talks about things. You can see that he has a deep love and appreciation for the earth.

Leopold's *A Sand County Almanac* is a book I always include in my teachings to help people ponder a land ethic. Then there are all of my many Native American books. More recently, a book that's inspired me is *Spiritual Healing in a Scientific Age* by Robert Peel. Another is *The Compassionate Universe: The Power of the Individual to Heal the Environment* by Eknath Easwaran—a tremendously empowering book.

⌒

I HAD NEVER THOUGHT of becoming a naturalist, though my childhood interests certainly pointed in that direction. I remember that Mother tried to discourage me from taking science courses. I wanted to take meteorology once, and she said, "Women just don't go into this field. I don't want to see you do this." Nowadays, there are a great number of women who do a terrific job reporting the weather.

So I went into Letters and Science. But I was an out-of-doors person. I liked sports. I became a figure skater, played basketball, and loved to hike. So I thought, "Gee, I'll become a gym teacher." And yet when I got into school at the University of Wisconsin, I became lost. After two and a half years, I quit. I was 21. Instead, I stayed at home to help my mother—alone with five younger children because of the divorce. I became the "man" of the house. I did all the yardwork. I stoked the furnace. I was the one responsible for the care of younger children when Mother became ill. But that intense interest in nature never left me. I continued my education at my own pace through studies at the UW-Extension. I also took classes in public speaking and writing at Madison Area Technical College. My best teacher, however, was the earth herself and all that I learned by observing her closely.

As an example, when you think of pollination and the survival of a flowering plant, it's quite remarkable. Once, when I was in a Piper Cub airplane over Lake Okeechobee in Florida, flying above the wood storks at 1,200 feet, the air was permeated with the scent of orange blossoms. I then realized how the pollinators find the trees: the fragrance is up there!

I took a fern course with [botanist] Olive Thomson once, and I can remember how excited I was to look through the microscope for the first time and observe all the minute parts of the sporangia. The diversity and growth amazed me.

🪶

I FIRST BECAME a paid naturalist in 1968. We came back to Madison after living in Missouri for a while. My first husband had just lost his job with a pharmaceutical company, and we needed a source of income to tide us over for a while. I approached Curt Bliss, head of the Madison Public School Recreation Department. Having worked for the department before my children were born, I hoped he might have an opening for me. I told him I had an idea about taking children on nature excursions. With his encouragement, I started a summer program I called "Come Walk With Me," which ran for eight years.

I worked all summer long with several groups of children, taking them into marshes, prairies, and woodlands, giving them the same kind of experience I'd had as a child, including dumping polliwogs out of our wet boots! About this time, [naturalist] Rosemary Fleming was beginning to lead the arboretum's tour program, and I became one of the few people asked by her to lead tours in the arboretum. So I worked for the Madison School District during the summer and gave tours in the arboretum other times. I also began teaching for the UW Environmental Resources Unit and for the Madison Area Technical College.

Once, I took a Memorial High School botany taxonomy class out into the woods during spring, and the teacher wanted the kids to know all the monocots and dicots. I said, "Fine." So the kids got on the trail, and we saw all the spring wild ephemerals, but I felt so empty because I was just pointing out all these plants. So I decided to try something. I said, "Let's talk about what we saw today. Can anyone tell me one of the monocots?" The response was quick: trillium. But when I asked what it looked like, nobody could tell me. They hadn't really looked at the plants; they had only put a name on a piece of paper. So afterwards I told the teacher that I would like to try a different approach. I told her I wasn't satisfied; the kids weren't getting anything out of the experience.

The next time I asked the kids to get down on the ground and really look at the plant—look at the stem, leaves, and petals. So they did, and I said, "Now we can give the plant a name. This is a trillium. What is it characterized by?" They could tell me, and I told them that now they were beginning to see. After a while, they began to enjoy looking for all the clues that would help them know a flower by its name.

You can have all the book-study you need, but it isn't until you get out there and experience the natural world that you really learn.

Sigurd Olson once talked about business guys coming from their big corporate worlds, coming to him for a break from their busy lives. After three days, they'd come up to him and say they were seeing ants crawling around, birds moving among branches, and other forms of wildlife—listing them. He'd pause, smile, and say, "Now you have arrived!" It takes time and a letting go of our everyday attachments—and a willingness to begin to see—if we are to develop some awareness and understanding of our natural world.

❧

IN 1976, I began to teach classes at a place called The Clearing in Ellison Bay, Door County. Jens Jensen, a Danish-born landscape architect, founded The Clearing in 1935 as a place where city people could renew their contact with the soil, renew their spirit. He was 79 years old at the time. Here, a succession of art and natural history classes occur from May through October. In my "Touch the Earth" class, I ask participants, during the course of the five days I am with them, to go out and find a tree—or let the tree find them—while they're out walking. I take them on various field trips to natural areas first and say that perhaps they will find a tree that appeals to them for one reason or another. Then on the last day of class, I ask them to look at that tree in terms of their own personal growth. What does that tree tell you about yourself, what your expectations are, what your vision or goals might be? People, who at first were hard as shells, began to open up and talk about their tree. The most beautiful words and feelings came from these people.

One 80-year-old woman stood out over the Niagara dolomite escarpment in Door County on a tree that was growing out of a rock, and she said, "This tree is like my life. It's been a hard life, but I hang on and keep on going." Another woman, struggling with alcoholism, chose a paper birch tree growing in a meadow. The branches were twisted, but one young branch grew straight up. She said that the branches represented her struggle, but she had found new growth.

At Durward's Glen near Baraboo, when I am teaching there, I take my group over to a 400- year-old white oak, and that's when I talk about my life. I tell them that I have persevered like this tree. The tree has lost some of its branches—they are part of the old ways, and they need to be let go. I say, "If you look up at the crown of this tree, it is reaching for the sun. It's still reaching for the sun, and it's still growing, as we all are."

The most important thing for my participants to come away with is appreciation and awareness. I can hand out all the factual material they want, but what I need to know is, am I touching them in the right place? People tell me that I'm just as effective in raising awareness as I am in teaching them about nature. The raising of people's consciousness—awareness—is essential right now to create greater harmony. I realize more and more that we need to heal ourselves. I ask people in my classes to close their eyes and allow the wind to speak to them. I ask them to realize that the wind that touches them today has touched many, many other people. I want them to realize that they're not alone; they are a part of this wondrous circle of life.

ONE OF MY MENTORS was an Ojibwe elder named Keewaydinoquay, who taught botany at UW-Milwaukee. She would visit here [High Meadows home] once in a while, and she would bring with her an old drum that was 500 years old. She didn't want to sleep in the bedroom, but rather on the davenport where she could put the drum in the nearby captain's chair and watch over it. She told me she was charged with the safekeeping of it, so she kept it with her at all times.

When she first came into our house, she said, "You know, I feel there's a special being around here." There was—a ruffed grouse would follow Gene around whenever he was outside, and it followed her around as well whenever she appeared. This bird would dance and strut around her. She called him "Siyo."

Kee taught me much about Ojibwe ways—a way of life that included how to live honorably and to the fullest, a concept known as *bimaadiziwin*. When one of my brothers passed on, Kee comforted me by saying, "We Indians do not believe in death, but when we pass over we go to dance among the Northern Lights."

Marion at peace in the Hills. Photo courtesy of Gene and Marion Moran.

EVEN THOUGH THE ARBORETUM was a nice place to live, it is here in the Baraboo Hills that I have found my sense of place. I think when I came here, it was not hard to let go of my family homestead in the arboretum because I realized our being here is part of the healing of the land. The first thing I did here—and it was run-down—was plant prairie flowers that I brought from home. We have cleaned up and taken all the junk out of the streams, filled in the erosion ditches, and generally tried to give the land a sense of itself again because it was so abused. There was nothing but debris and junk laying everywhere, even in the woods above. According to the original land surveys, the land was oak openings. Every once in a while I'd find a remnant of prairie flowers. And so I would just hang seeds in trees around the perimeter of the meadows and let them blow in. And now, we have some nice prairie meadow. Rosemary Fleming came up here from Florida and was really impressed by what Gene and I had done, mostly alone, with one burn by an International Crane Foundation crew.

Everything I've done here has been an effort to achieve restoration, and it's blessed us. Where else can you wake up to silence in this busy world of ours? There's something about being in the Baraboo Hills that's actually magical. Whenever I drive into Madison and then return, when I see the Baraboo Hills I say, "There are my beloved hills." It's a wonderful sense of renewal. I have become so intimate with this land. I know every plant, every bird. If I hear a noise in the corner of the outside kitchen wall, I know it's the downy woodpecker taking the seed from the birdfeeder, taking it up to where the boards are mired together, and cracking it open. To see the stars here at night when the sky is razor clear is beautiful beyond description.

THOSE WHO TEACH about the environment have to serve as role models. But we don't have much time. We're really in a mess right now. Quoting from Thoreau: "If a man goes to the woods half of each day for the sake of enjoying them, he is considered a loafer. If he goes to the woods and makes the earth bald before its time, he is considered an enterprising citizen." That's the kind of mentality that has prevailed for too long in this country despite environmental gains. Native American prophecy says that our sore and tired earth and its people will suffer great destruction. But the saving grace, according to Black Elk, is that prayer is more powerful than prophecy, and that's the thread I hang on to; that keeps me going.

Interestingly, the Judeo-Christian ethic dictates that man has dominion over the earth. You know what dominion means? It means to care for; it means to respect life, to honor it. Everything in nature is representative of something more beautiful beyond what we can intellectually comprehend. I want my grandchildren to experience the special beauty that nature offers, but it just tears me apart to think that this world might be lost because of man's greed or nuclear wars.

If I had it my way, I would not be one to compromise. I think if we are to continue with any quality of life, we have to make every effort to preserve what land resources we have now without further exploitation. What we have around us right now has to be maintained. We need a spiritual revolution—people coming together in large numbers, coming together as one voice to make the important changes in how we get along and care for the earth.

🌒

WHEN GENE AND I first moved here [High Meadows] in August 1986, we had not yet walked the boundaries of the 83 acres of land. We feel we are only caretakers here. We don't own this land, and I've never felt that we do. In January 1987, a friend of ours came up and started walking the land with us. I had been hearing chainsaws up in the northeast corner. When I got up there, I heard the trees cry. To my great despair and shock, the entire northeast corner had been logged off, except for one oak tree standing in the middle. There were stacks and stacks of logs, and there are no words to describe the crying. It was a great, distressful, mournful sound, with a heaviness in the air, and the stench was like the smell of death itself.

We found the post where the lots came together and found that this private logging operation had logged property to the north of us but had come in way beyond the property line. So we came down after using ribbons extensively to mark the property lines to make them obvious. We knew they'd be coming back; the skidder was still up there, as was other heavy equipment. The next morning we walked up there, and these guys were surprised to see another person. They asked me what I wanted. I looked around and saw they had taken red spray paint and had sprayed within where they had cut to make it look like they were within their jurisdiction. So I said, "We're here because you obviously have logged out trees that were not on the right property." They tried to point to the spray paint, but I quickly pointed to the post separating the property lines. So we talked, but I broke down and cried. One of the guys looked at me and said, "Lady, why are you crying? They're only trees." There was no understanding. He told me that I would have to speak to his boss about it.

I went up there almost every day to keep my eye on them. The good thing about that was that I began to know the land. I had not ever had the chance to walk up there before. I had not taken time to do so, and what had happened lay heavy on my conscience. I felt that I needed to do something about this. In the meantime, they had let the landowner know. One week later, on a Sunday, the log boss showed up at our door and said he was sorry for cutting some of our trees. He said, "I'm on my way down to Mass at the

[Durward's] Glen. I would never do anything dishonest. You probably need to talk to Mr. Singer, the landowner, and see what you can do to get money from the trees." I told him that money wouldn't bring the trees back, and when we had bought the land, I had hoped that future generations might know the big oak trees on the property.

Coincidentally, through the mail came an article titled, "Death of a Forest" in a Catholic newsletter, about another situation. I sent it to the log boss, along with photos of all the cleanup debris—beer bottles, booze bottles, oil cans—that Gene and I found up there after they'd left. I still have all the pictures. Nina Bradley told me later that I could have gotten eight times what the logs were worth through a lawsuit, and in retrospect we probably should have sued, but we didn't have any money at the time for a lawyer.

When the log boss got the letter, he came right to the house, said he would make it up to us some day, and bring us a load of firewood. Well, one day, his men brought us a truckload and sat here on the front lawn. They said, "You know lady, we thought you were crazy, but you know we have to make a living."

I replied, "I understand, but if you're going to cut—wipe out a big part of somebody's woods—you need their permission." We talked, and by the end of our discussion I think they had a better understanding of how I could feel such a loss.

One day in late March, Bonnie, a friend of mine, came up, and I told her I wanted to take her up to the place where I heard the trees cry. There was a little bit of snow on the ground, and the sun was coming from the west. It was shining through the trees into the forest. Now, our property is long and narrow. You go through a meadow, some woods, and you come out into another small meadow, where actually we have found an Indian crescent mound that a Madison archeologist told us goes back to ancient times. So, from that meadow, I looked up into the trees and I see these gray-green round, gossamer circles—concentric rings—different sizes like the growth rings of trees, and they're flowing and weaving through the tops of the canopy of what I now call the graveyard. They had cut down 800 trees on the property beyond us, plus ours. I looked down at the ground for a moment because I thought I was hallucinating. I looked up again, and they're still coming, but I didn't want to say anything to Bonnie because she knew I was emotional over the cutting. But pretty soon her hand was on my shoulder, and she said, "Do you see what I see?" She was seeing it, too.

I told this story that summer, still not quite sure about what I saw. I participated in a workshop at the Sigurd Olson Institute. One night we were at Ojibwe leader and Northland College professor Joe Rose's lodge on the shore of Lake Superior. He began to talk about animals and all the beings out there who have a right to life, and who have this quality of life that we fail to see. He asked if there was anybody in the group who had ever had any experience of realizing the life forces of other beings. I swallowed a little bit and told my story. Afterwards, he looked straight at me and said, "Marion, I sense in you a great spiritual awareness. You were privileged to see the life forces leaving the trees. And you did hear the trees cry."

Even with this affirmation, I still was not sure. The next month we were guests of former Sigurd Olson Environmental Institute Director Mark Peterson. That night at dinner I told this story again, and there was another woman there who said, "I have a feeling that you still feel doubtful about this. I have to tell you that my husband quit the logging business because he couldn't stand the crying anymore."

❧

[WRITER AND NATURALIST] HENRY BESTON said: "We need a wiser and more mystical concept of living things." Sigurd Olson had it. I admired him most of all the naturalists I respected. All were men because, until recently, it was a male-dominated profession. I am more in his corner than the rest of them. I do, however, have a great respect for Aldo Leopold. I think, had he lived, that he would have reached a higher level of consciousness in dealing with the natural world. But Sigurd Olson's first and last books were my favorites, but especially *The Singing Wilderness*. What can you say when the wilderness—when wild land—is a part of your life, and someone else puts it into words as he did? And how did he pass away? In touch with the earth, literally and metaphorically, while snowshoeing.

❧

I'M NOT AFRAID of death. I don't think that dying brings us into perfection. It's not unlike a flower blooming in a prairie. You come and do what you are here to do, and then you let go to make way for others. But I feel that I'm not ready for that yet because I've got a lot of things I need to do. When it's my time, I won't have any regrets. Hopefully, I will have made the world a better place. Like a ring of bright water, you hope that the circle you've started will keep reaching out toward others. And if it's true that we go to dance among the Northern Lights, I'm looking forward to that! ✳

Surrounded by her family in Reedsburg, Wisconsin, Marion passed away peacefully on August 31, 2016. She was 89.

CHAPTER FOURTEEN 🦅

Joseph Martin Rose
(1935-   )

Joseph Martin Rose with ceremonial drum—an important element of the Anishinaabe culture. Photo courtesy of Joseph M. Rose.

NORTHERN WHITE CEDAR

Chapter Fifteen~
Joseph Martin Rose

I think we have to teach our young people about the sacredness of the land. We have to get them out there and let them experience the natural world.... If they begin to experience the natural world, they'll begin to understand it. From an understanding comes respect. From that respect comes love. And when they begin to love that natural world, when they begin to feel that in their own spirit, then they'll stand and defend the natural world.

—JMR

In the year 2000, I asked biologist Joe D. Rose of the Bad River Band of the Lake Superior Chippewa Indians who he might recommend from the tribe for inclusion in the *Wisconsin Naturalists Project*. I had met Joe through the Wisconsin Trumpeter Swan Recovery Program in the mid-1990s. He didn't hesitate. "Why don't you interview my father?" he said.

When I called Joseph Martin Rose (Joe Rose, Sr.), an Ojibwe elder and associate professor of Native American studies at Northland College, he didn't hesitate either. "Sure," he said. "Come on up."

A review of not-too-distant Native American history reminds us that the Ojibwe people of the Upper Midwest witnessed the loss of their lands to the U.S. federal government in the nineteenth century. Treaties in 1836, 1837, 1842, and 1854 led to the establishment of ceded territories and a reservation system that continues today.

At Odanah, near Ashland, the Bad River Band occupies a reservation that includes one of the Upper Midwest's largest and arguably least disturbed coastal wetland complexes—part of the Kakagon River and Bad River watershed. Sixteen thousand acres, or 25 square miles, (65 km^2) are recognized as a Ramsar Wetland of International Importance.

Joseph Rose, born April 1935 to Carl and Mary C. ("Dolly") Rose, grew up on the Bad River Reservation during the early 1940s. Here, he learned mainly through his grandfather how to trap, fish, and hunt, and to become acquainted with the animals and plants that inhabited the area.

Joe attended local schools in the Ashland area, graduating from DePadua High School in 1953 and from Northland College in 1958 with a bachelor of science degree in biology and secondary education. For ten years after graduating from Northland College, he worked as a high school science and math teacher and athletic coach. During 1970-1974, he was employed as a counselor for Bad River students at Ashland High School. In 1971, he received a master of science degree in education from Black Hills State University in Spearfish, South Dakota. He began teaching Native American Studies at Northland College in Ashland in 1974. He retired in 2012.

Our interview took place at his office at Northland College during a bright morning on October 6, 2001. Later that afternoon, I joined his students for a field trip to the shore of Lake Superior, where Professor Rose has a cabin and sweat lodge, and where he taught his students about the sacred aspects of a sweat lodge ceremony.

*

My culture is Anishinaabe. I can go back at least five generations. In 1852, President Millard Fillmore rescinded the order of President Zachary Taylor to remove Native Americans from their lands. And that led to the Treaty of 1854, which established reservations for all of the Lake Superior Ojibwe in Minnesota, Wisconsin, and Michigan. My grandfather—Dan Jackson, Sr.—had two grandfathers that signed the Treaty of 1854. One was Chief Condecon from Ontanogan and the other was Chief Blackbird from Bad River. In fact, the administration building at Bad River is named after him: The Chief Blackbird Center.

Blackbird was quite an orator; he often stood up and spoke at the councils. There were certain issues—such as distribution of moneys and goods— that they discussed. These fur traders that had extended credit to Indian people were always there with their hands out whenever the Indians received their annuities or any payments for the land that they had given up. They wanted the government administrators to pay them before paying the Indians. Blackbird, on one occasion, arose and insisted that money goes to the people first and then to the fur traders.

The Treaties of 1837, 1842, and 1854 were all land cession treaties where millions of acres of land were given up, but the right to hunt, fish, and gather was retained in the negotiations between the Indian leaders and the commissioners of the United States government. The ceded territory is pretty large, pretty big—about the northern one-third of the state of Wisconsin, about the northeastern one-quarter of the state of Minnesota, and most of the Upper Peninsula of Michigan. These treaty rights, however, were violated by the government for several generations, but finally reaffirmed by a decision of a federal court in 1983. This was known as the Voigt Decision.

Indian people did not have the financial resources to fight for their rights for many years. Also, native people were not educated formally in the white man's way.

I remember over 30 years ago when the Great Lakes Intertribal Council had a subcommittee called the Great Lakes Intertribal Council Education Committee, which represented all the Indians in the state of Wisconsin in matters of education. I remember in 1971 or 1972 we did a survey to find out how many Indians had earned a college degree. At that time you could count them on the fingers of both hands. I was fortunate enough to be one of them.

HISTORY OFFERS THE WISDOM OF PERSPECTIVE. A little known fact is that the United States Constitution is based on many of the principles of the Iroquois and Algonquin confederacies that operated on the Eastern seaboard prior to European presence. By the time George Washington and Thomas Jefferson came along, there had been 150 years of relations with the tribes. Washington and Jefferson came from a monarchy, and when their forefathers came over, they had never encountered the idea that leaders were servants of the people.

Leaders were representatives of the people. These leaders could be recalled if they didn't support the wishes of the people. So some of these ideas were incorporated into the Constitution of the United States. Benjamin Franklin, for one, was quite knowledgeable about the way these Indian confederacies operated. Indians aren't given credit for that because they were considered pagans, savages, and heathens in 1789 when the Constitution was ratified.

The irony is that Native American people are some of the most patriotic in this country. In the two world wars we've fought, to the best of my knowledge, there have been a higher percentage of Native Americans per capita who have fought in the armed forces of the United States than any other ethnic group. This is their homeland. They didn't immigrate here from somewhere else. That bond with the land is very strong.

My mother left the reservation to attend Haskell Indian School in Kansas. Upon graduation, she was sent to work as a medical stenographer at a veterans hospital in Muskogee, Oklahoma. Muskogee is where she met my father, who in high school had played on the Oklahoma State Championship football team and made the Oklahoma All State Team at the Left End position. He was offered a full scholarship to play football for Louisiana State University—LSU. He passed up a chance to play Division One Football and instead married my mother.

Joe's parents: Mary Dolly (Jackson) Rose and Carl M. Rose, Sr. Photo courtesy of Joseph Martin Rose.

*

I WAS BORN IN MUSKOGEE, OKLAHOMA, and shortly afterward, my mother and dad moved to Odanah, Wisconsin, because of the strong cultural and family ties that Mother had.

I'm a mixed-blood Ojibwe. My mother's Ojibwe and and my dad is white. I experienced discrimination when I was growing up, mostly from white society. In fact, I think it's even worse for mixed bloods because the dominant society knows that if you have a choice you can go either way, and you're not choosing their way. There were a few Indians when I was going to grade school that saw me as white rather than Indian. I knew there was a pecking order, so I fought my way to the top of it and was then accepted as Indian. I was a good street fighter.

We had relatives all over the reservation. The clan system was still pretty strong. I remember the sense of community was so much stronger when I was a boy. Families used to visit each other. In fact, I grew up in my grandfather's old house. We had visitors almost on a daily basis there. And there weren't any locked doors. Sometimes people would rap on the door before they'd come in; other times, they'd just walk in and sit down.

We didn't have indoor plumbing. We used to haul our water from the town pumps. We didn't have central heating; we heated with wood. We'd sit around the old wood stove in my grandfather's living room. The old people would come in. Their first language was Ojibwe, but they spoke broken English. We'd listen to many stories about Native American traditions. My grandmother also had the old wood kitchen range. She'd put out a bowl of soup or something or maybe go into the bedroom and dig out a jar of canned blackberries and serve them with homemade bread. They'd sit there and visit. You knew every person in the community, from the little kids on up. That's not true anymore. I don't know why it has changed. People just don't get together like that anymore perhaps because of all the new technology, from automobiles to television to computers.

Grandfather's mother was from Bad River, and his father was from Ontonagon, Michigan, along the Upper Peninsula Lake Superior shore. Those families moved back and forth between the two reservations pretty often. He said they used to travel back and forth between Ontonagon and Bad River in birch bark canoes. When a storm would come up, he said they would just beach the canoes and camp out there.

We didn't have electricity in our homes when I grew up on the reservation. My mother used to read by kerosene lamp to my brother and me every night before we went to bed. I remember studying by kerosene lamp.

Growing up, there were probably about a dozen cars on the Bad River Reservation; people walked everywhere they went. Kids spent most of their waking hours out-of-doors, and you had your chores every night when you got home from school. After chores, we might go out and look at our rabbit snares after dark. I always had a little pack with a flashlight in it. We'd go out, back in the woods, and check the rabbit snares with the flashlight.

There wasn't any television. A few people had battery-operated radios. Kids would get together at somebody's house with a radio and listen to the Green Bay Packers football game on Sunday. The rest of the time we were outside. We were in excellent physical shape. Nowadays, the kids sit indoors. You get some of these kids out in the woods, and they can't tell the difference between a popple tree and a birch tree. It's an altogether different lifestyle than what we had.

We have to teach our young people about the sacredness of the land. We have to get them out there and let them experience the natural world and pull them away from these boomboxes, Nintendo, TV, soda pop, potato chips, and even in some cases alcohol and hard drugs. Give them a chance to experience the natural world. If they begin to experience the natural world, they'll begin to understand it. From an understanding comes respect. From that respect comes love. And when they begin to love that natural world, when they begin to feel that in their own spirit, then they'll stand and defend the natural world. They'll challenge those who would upset the balance, pollute, degrade the earth, the water, and the air. Challenge those that are responsible for all of those species that are becoming endangered or extinct.

SOME OF MY EARLY OUTDOOR EXPERIENCES and understanding of the natural world happened with my grandfather; he's full-blooded Ojibwe. He used to take me out rabbit hunting even before I started school. I remember the snow felt very deep; my legs were pretty short. We'd be walking in the woods and I'd fall behind. I'd be way back there. He'd turn around and look and wait for me to catch up to him. He'd then put me on his back and walk until I was rested. He'd set me down again and let me walk a while 'til I got tired. Then he'd pick me up and put me on his back again. That was a part of my early education.

Through my grandfather I learned how to track and set snares. I learned about all the plants and animals in the woods at an early age. While I was growing up, especially in my grade school years, I spent more time with my grandfather than I did with my dad because my dad was a construction

Joe Rose, Sr., and his grandfather, Dan Jackson, Sr., on Pine Plat Road, Bad River Indian Reservation, early 1950s. Photo courtesy of Joseph Martin Rose.

worker, and northern Wisconsin was an economically depressed area. Dad worked in Milwaukee or wherever he could find work. But he was one of my teachers, too. He grew up in northeastern Oklahoma and hunted and fished with the Cherokee and Creek Indians. He had many of the same skills that my grandfather did, so I grew up in a family of hunters.

I understand from the stories my grandfather told that his family lived completely off the land, engaged in hunting and all the seasonal gathering activities. Every fall, they'd get ready for winter. They'd dig these circular shaped pits in the ground, somewhat like a cylinder. Then they'd line them with birch bark. They'd put a layer of potatoes in there, then a layer of straw, and then another layer of potatoes. They placed saplings over the top, covered that with boughs, and then when it snowed, they could dig into that cache. They'd get potatoes, or whatever they had buried there, all winter long. They made food caches in trees also.

Grandfather said when they got ready for winter they always took deer and bear. It was late enough in the season that it was starting to freeze, so they could preserve the meat. They used to set snares for deer and deadfalls for bear. Of course, they'd skin those animals out, save the hides, and then they'd butcher them and hang them up in a shed where they'd have meat all winter long since that meat would freeze. And then whenever they wanted fresh meat, they'd just go and saw a piece off, bring it in, and thaw it out. That was supper.

I remember we had a shed out behind my grandfather's house when I was a kid. I'd go out to that shed, bring in a hindquarter of venison, and my grandmother would take a hacksaw to saw a piece off. Then I'd take it back out and hang it up again. Very seldom did we ever have meat from the grocery store or the supermarket. We usually ate wild game: venison, bear meat, muskrat, quite a bit of rabbit, ruffed grouse, and a lot of ducks and fish. Usually the main course consisted of meat and potatoes from Gurney, Wisconsin, where they had big potato farms. Several 100-pound bags of potatoes were your potatoes for the winter.

I remember Grandfather drank some of the wild teas gathered from the woods. The old-timers didn't drink coffee. They called it *makade mishkiki wabo*, or black medicine water. They drank tea for breakfast. Some of the teas they made came from sumac, wintergreen, rosehips, and cedar they collected. There are all kinds of wild plants out there. Even in the dead of winter you can go out and collect sumac, cedar, or rosehips. I like the tea made from wild raspberry leaves.

🍃

I REMEMBER WHEN I GOT MY FIRST DEER. I was probably a freshman or sophomore in high school. Going after my first deer seemed to be pretty important to my grandfather because he started taking me out almost every weekend after it got cold. I remember it was in late November, right around Thanksgiving time. He took me out and I hunted with a single-barreled, 12-gauge shotgun. I got that for a Christmas present when I was in the sixth grade. That's what I hunted with until I was an adult. My grandfather had a model 94 Winchester, the lever-action carbine, .30-30 caliber.

I remember we'd go and spend all day in the woods. At that time you could spend all day in the woods on the reservation without running into a logging road or a clear-cut area. But this particular evening, we happened to run into a logging road. He knew the reservation so well he knew where it led to. He said, "This goes out to the road. We have to head back. It'll be dark in about an hour. Let's trade guns. You take my rifle and you go ahead." So he stayed back and let me go ahead by myself on that logging road.

As I walked, I looked down the road. There, I saw a couple of deer standing up on their hind legs, eating buds from this tree. It must have been a couple of hundred yards down the trail. I took a shot at one. My grandfather heard me shoot, so he was there in a few minutes. He looked down at the tracks, and he told me, "Well, you shot this one, and you hit it right in the joint in the front leg." It was getting pretty late, starting to get dark. So he said, "We'll come back soon as we get good daylight tomorrow. And then we'll start tracking."

It must have been around eight o'clock the following morning when we started. There were several good trackers on the reservation at that time, but I never saw one as good as him. He was the best that I've ever been around. We started tracking that deer. The deer quit bleeding, and then it ran on some well-trodden trails where other deer were running. To this day I don't know how Grandfather was able to pick out that one track from the others, but he was doing it. He could track on a dead trot. I've never been able to do that. I've never seen anybody else that could. We caught a glimpse of the deer that morning.

Anyway, it was getting toward noon, and I was getting anxious. He said, "Well, let's have some lunch." He always did that; he always stopped about noon, built a little fire, took off his pack, heated up our sandwiches, and made some hot tea. Of course, I was anxious to keep on tracking. He told me that the deer would lie down. After we got through eating, he said, "I'm going to put you off to the side here, further behind me, and I'm going to go ahead. What's going to happen is that the deer is going to circle around, and you'll get a shot at it." Sure enough, that's what happened. The deer did circle around. I got a shot at it. That was my first deer. Months later, I asked him how he knew that the deer was going to circle around. He said, "When you are tracking a deer, they will usually circle downwind from you to catch your scent. I put you behind me and downwind from me. I knew the deer would circle toward you." He was so knowledgeable about the habits of the animals, he could predict what they were going to do.

❧

I'VE LIVED MOST OF MY LIFE by the Big Lake. And, in fact, where I live at Waverly Beach I'm three and a half miles from the nearest powerline or telephone line. I live right on Lake Superior, and the seasons and weather conditions change from day to day. Sometimes the lake is as smooth as glass, not even a slight breeze, and other times it can get pretty wild. So I guess living like that kind of stirs the blood. Keeps you alive, I guess.

I think the Gaia Hypothesis is real: the earth and everything else—the water, the air, the land, the animals—are part of a living organism. Everything is interconnected. And I guess I can feel that when I'm out there. I can go elsewhere into an area that's been clear-cut, and it's a pretty emotional experience, one that almost brings tears when you see that old growth timber that has been taken. And it seems like the spirit, or essence or mood of that place, has been forever changed. I'll never see such a place—that

Joe walking at Sugar Bush Lake, Bad River Indian Reservation, 1990s.
Photo courtesy of Joseph Martin Rose.

particular site—again in my lifetime, and my grandchildren will probably never see it. So it makes me feel pretty sad.

With all of this new technology—these skidders, harvesters, and all of this equipment—the logger has to probably invest half a million dollars, so it's necessary to go in and clear-cut in order to pay for that investment. Fifty or sixty years ago they were still cutting with crosscut saws, axes, skidding with horses, and taking over-mature popple and leaving the evergreens and the hardwoods to stand.

Prior to clear-cutting, we had more wilderness and biodiversity.

*

I'VE BEEN LUCKY to have had a number of really good teachers: my grandfather, my dad, my mother, my uncle, as well as my grandfather's relatives on the Bad River Reservation. I learned a great deal from those Indian elders.

In more recent years, I have had friends from quite a few different tribes that share their knowledge and experiences. I guess it's a situation where you never stop learning. I also like to meet new people and sit down and listen to them. Some of them have a lot of knowledge and wisdom that they are willing to share.

The wisdom that has come my way has come through the elders. Now I am an elder. We acknowledge that everything out there has a spirit: Mother Earth, the wind, the water, the trees and all plants, the birds and animals, as well as all humans.

As human beings, we are interrelated to all things in the Web of Life. ✳

Michael Van Stappen
(1956-2000)

Trapping raptors occurred as part of a fall 1993 bird migration study on Outer Island in the Apostle Islands, Lake Superior. Here, Mike releases an immature female peregrine falcon (*Falco peregrinus*). Photo by William Smith. Photo courtesy of Julie Van Stappen.

BIGTOOTH ASPEN

GJK

Chapter Sixteen~
Michael Van Stappen

I have a strong feeling of involvement with the landscape, and I have
tried to convey this through my writings. It's a conscious involvement:
really trying to get to know a place, trying to know the birds and plants,
and being inside the landscape.

—MVS

Bayfield County's Michael Francis Van Stappen, born May 19, 1956,
in Kaukauna, Wisconsin, grew up in Little Chute, a small Dutch
town south of Kaukauna in eastern Wisconsin. Here, he explored
pond edges and the nearby Fox River, a meandering and tranquil stretch of
river that was not yet developed as it was to the north in Green Bay. Mike
graduated from the University of Wisconsin-Oshkosh with a bachelor of
science degree in geology in 1979, married Julie Urbain in 1981, and took
graduate courses in biology and writing at UW-Stevens Point from 1982
to 1983. At various times during the 1980s, they lived in Seattle, Colorado,
and Nebraska, before settling permanently in 1988 in northern Wisconsin,
where Julie became the resource management specialist for the Apostle
Islands National Lakeshore on Lake Superior.

While Julie worked, Mike stayed at home in Washburn and cared for their children, daughter Jessie and son Casey. At the same time, he continued to pursue a keen interest in the natural world, becoming intimately acquainted with Lake Superior's wild lands. His love for the north found an outlet in natural history writing, poetry, and photography, and he conducted biological contract work, including Breeding Bird Surveys for The Nature Conservancy, the Natural Resources Research Institute, the DNR's Natural Heritage Inventory, and the Wisconsin Society for Ornithology's first Breeding Bird Atlas project. As a volunteer, he assisted Julie's programs by performing migratory, breeding, and colonial bird surveys.

In 1998, Prairie Oak Press published a collection of Mike's essays titled *Northern Passages, Reflections from Lake Superior Country*, lyrical accounts of his natural history observations in the Lake Superior watershed. This work earned wide regional acclaim and resulted in the 1999 Sigurd F. Olson Nature Writing Award from the Sigurd Olson Environmental Institute in Ashland, and a 1999 Outstanding Literary Achievement Award from the Wisconsin Library Association. Mike also wrote a chapbook of poetry titled *A Handful of Stardust*, self-published in 1997.

I occasionally spent time with Mike in the field during the 1990s surveying cormorants and gulls in the Apostle Islands. His keen eye for detail was evident when he observed from afar a ruddy turnstone rolling/robbing a herring gull egg from an Eagle Island nest. I last visited him in August 2000 at his hillside home northwest of Washburn. He was surrounded—occasionally interrupted—by his children, who engaged in various activities upstairs and down, with Julie nearby. This was Mike's final summer, having returned home from yet another surgery in a lengthy battle with brain cancer. Mike sat in a long chair that allowed him as much comfort as possible. He talked quietly about his life and his love for family and the Northwoods.

My mother, Theresa, is Dutch, and many of my relatives came from the Netherlands. My father, Frank, came to Wisconsin from Chicago, so he's a real outlander. After he and Mom met, they went ballroom dancing once, and that was it!

Nature was important early on. It became a tradition every spring to go out to Seymour in Outagamie County and look for wild asparagus along the way. It was hard work, but Mom and Dad really looked forward to it. I remember reading a book later by Euell Gibbons titled *Stalking the Wild Asparagus*, which motivated me to find it on my own. I remember feeling so proud about finding some and bringing it back to my parents.

Little Chute, where I grew up, was originally called Port du Chutes, a river of chutes—small rapids. Here, there was a large park in town where a bunch of muskrats, mallards, leopard frogs, green frogs, and garter snakes thrived. I'd follow the edge of the park and try to catch many of these and bring them home. I also brought perch back to the house and put them in some steel drums that Dad had.

Embarking on a trek into the northwoods, 1994. Photo by, and courtesy of, Julie Van Stappen.

Dad took me fishing on the Fox River in a rowboat, so I spent a good deal of time in and around water. On the terra firma side, my mother liked to garden, and that got me into looking at things in the soil. She also liked all birds. She did not discriminate.

But the Fox River was special to me. There was a canal built in the 1800s so that barges pulled by mules could get up and down the river. When they drained the canal in the fall, you could go in it and catch little bullheads by hand, rusty crayfish, and aquatic insects as well. I once read the writings of a U.S. Army lieutenant who rode by horse along the Fox. During the course of his ride, he noted that broad stretches of savannah occurred along the upper edge of the riverbank. There were some beautiful stretches of oak and hickory. I always found the area fascinating—so many beautiful flowers. All aspects of life caught my eye. I took out field guides from the local library trying to figure out what I was seeing. I even used to bike to Kaukauna where an excellent library awaited me. I learned that the original name of the Fox River is *rivière aux Renards*, which means River of the Foxes.

I WAS somewhat of a loner growing up. Even now, I'm more comfortable being by myself, but it's not that I'm shy. I just need a great deal of personal time. I'm sure I escaped to the river for solace, or if I got into trouble. It was a refuge.

Back home, though, I was busy. Up in my room I had a laboratory of sorts. Once, I dissected a frog that I'd caught. I learned how to pith it, which made me feel kind of bad, so Mom and Dad bought me some preserved frogs for Christmas; these I could dissect and examine without feeling guilty about killing something.

I'll never forget the time they gave me a chemistry set. I did something with a burner and a tube, and the whole thing blew up, painting the ceiling. They were surprisingly tolerant about the whole thing. One

On the North Country Trail near Grandview, Wisconsin. September 1992. Photo by, and courtesy of, Julie Van Stappen.

year, I entered a contest for kids building things, and I won. I brought home a motor scooter, and Dad let me sell it, so I bought a nice telescope. I spent a great deal of time on the flat roof over our kitchen looking at stars. I had an intense interest in astronomy. I wanted to see how everything in the universe went together. What really made an impression on my young mind was a fellow who built his own telescope. By the time I had reached fourth grade, I really believed I was going to be an astronomer. But as it turned out, I had too many other interests.

Electronics was also an area that intrigued me. My dad used to bring home spare parts from his job as a millwright, repairing everything from refrigerators to forklifts; he's very mechanically gifted. So in sixth grade I built quite an electrical contraption, complete with a fan. But electronics was merely an intellectual pursuit. I was eventually drawn back to the earth, you might say literally. After graduating from high school, I went to the

University of Wisconsin campus at Appleton and then transferred to UW-Madison. But I was a small town kid, and I didn't make it. I felt really out of place. So I came home to my folks and went to school at UW-Oshkosh.

I had a good friend who said I could make a decent living as a geologist. The first course I took at Oshkosh was in environmental geology. I found it tremendously fascinating. Here was something dealing with the landscape. What appealed to me was examining the impacts people had on landscapes, even my river. I took another course where I looked at the effects of natural processes on landscapes, learning about glaciers, for example. Gene LaBerge was an incredible professor there. His specialty was mineralogy, and he conveyed his enthusiasm for minerals to the class. He also provided a great deal of support, encouraging me. Another guy, Chuck Fedder, was a hydrologist. He especially caught my ear because he proposed blowing the dams out of the Fox River. Let it run free. There were many wonderful courses at UW-Oshkosh, including a great invertebrate zoology course in which I learned about the evolutionary history of invertebrates. As far as books that influenced me during this period, *A Sand County Almanac* was huge. This wasn't required reading, but somehow it came into my hands. Also, some of Sigurd Olson's books, such as *The Singing Wilderness*, were important. My best friend, Larry Schiebel, was reading Sig O before I was, and he suggested some of Sig's books to me.

In high school, I read August Derleth's works and learned about southern Wisconsin landscapes. Later, through college geology field trips, I drove down there looking for fossils in the Black Earth area and visiting Devil's Lake.

As part of my geology studies, and before graduating, I had to go to a geology field camp in La Rue, Sauk County. You learn how to map sections of rock. The following year, in 1979, I was rock climbing and camping out at La Rue. It was there that I ran into Julie. We had actually met first at a geology student farewell party in Oshkosh. Love at first sight.

After I graduated from Oshkosh, I worked as an engineering technician for an Oshkosh soil-testing lab, a private company. Julie was finishing up her undergraduate work in geology. When she got her degree, she wanted to see what it would be like to work as a geologist in Alaska. So she managed to get a summer job near Fairbanks with a gold mine. I didn't want her to go alone, and so I applied and was hired as well. A week before we departed, we got married.

CHAPTER SIXTEEN

The gold mine company flew us up there, and we stayed in a camp with miners, who, we found out later, really hated environmentalists. It was kind of strange because I belonged to the Sierra Club. I felt very uncomfortable there. We'd get dropped off by helicopter way out on the tundra, and all you could see were huge gashes across the tundra by bulldozers looking for gold. It was also dangerous because you never knew what the weather would do, and we had no radio. Well, we could see what was really going on, and we didn't want to be a part of it. One morning after being dropped off, Julie was in tears. So we let them know that we wanted to leave, but they weren't going to fly us back to Wisconsin. They said that they would drive us back to Fairbanks, but no further. So we hitchhiked from there to southeast Alaska, where we boarded a ferry for Seattle, and we then shipped most of our gear back to Wisconsin.

On the way back, we camped near St. Petersburg [Florida], where we got eaten alive by no-see-ums. I was just amazed by the number of eagles—as many eagles as crows—and also the life in the waters with sea *Anemones* and the sea stars. We learned what a wonderful and rich place the ocean is.

🌿

DURING 1982 AND 1983, I attended graduate school at UW-Stevens Point and had wanted to go into landscape restoration, but my adviser was trying to turn me into a wildlife manager, which I didn't want to be. I've never been much of a game hunter, although I do shoot deer in the fall when my health allows me. We like venison, and I do believe that they're having a big impact on the landscape up here. But Stevens Point didn't quite work for me because of this game manager thing. I was interested in much more. On my own I learned about grasses. I always wanted to look at the bigger picture, and I was hoping that someday I could work for the Nature Conservancy, which actually occurred. I did Breeding Bird Surveys on contract after we moved to Washburn in 1988. We've been in Bayfield County ever since.

🌿

I BEGAN WRITING when I was a kid but didn't begin nature writing until much later. Robert Finch's books were an important influence; he wrote about the Cape Cod area. Henry Beston's *The Outermost House* and John

Hay's *The River* were two other important books. I wanted to capture some of the things I felt and saw on the landscape as these authors had, and I liked to write because it gave me an opportunity to express myself clearly. At first, I would write things down but then realize that they didn't really express how I felt, so I would heavily edit what I wrote, but writing allowed me to examine things closely.

I remember once in high school when my English teacher embarrassed the daylights out of me. I had written a few essays or poetry, and in front of the whole class he said, "Mike, you're an uncut diamond." I shrunk to the size of a peanut. Fortunately, most of the kids didn't know what he was talking about, but I think more than anything he could tell that my heart was in writing. He always gave me a great deal of encouragement to keep writing. He told me I didn't have to do it just for classes.

As a kid, I kept little notebooks and stories of what I felt and thought about. I have a field notebook today, but I don't write every day. I find that the best time of day for writing is when I have quiet time. I used to get up at 4:00 a.m. before we had kids and they needed attention. Then the best time became right after I got them off to school.

Gathering blueberries in the Moquah Barrens, Bayfield County, northwestern Wisconsin, 1993. Photo by, and courtesy of, Julie Van Stappen.

CHAPTER SIXTEEN

I have a strong feeling of involvement with the landscape, and I have tried to convey this through my writings. It's a conscious involvement: trying to get to know a place, the birds and plants, and being inside the landscape. Having moved quite a bit in my life, I've seen degraded landscapes and can only imagine what they must have looked like back in time. As you learn more about the land, you have to bear some of the pain involved with what you see. I see the continued harvesting of pulpwood as a problem. On one level it has a tremendous impact on the soil; it's akin to mining the soil by taking minerals out of it. I'm talking about clearcutting specifically. There is a place for logging if you do it right using selective cutting, for example. But what's needed is to look at logging from the perspective of its effect on the natural community. Many people, unfortunately, don't have any regard for that view. The Forest Service is doing some things for rare species, but they could do better, in my opinion, by taking a landscape-scale perspective in their management.

And deer have had a major impact. In some places you can see browsing on yew, and in our own forest you can see where browsing has occurred on hemlock. At other places, spring ephemerals have been hit hard and obviously eaten. We have to look at the whole system and the impacts that are occurring.

🍂

THROUGH MY STORIES I write about what I see, and hopefully I will teach others to have a greater respect for the land. In my stories, I talk about the outdoors in a way that will get readers to think. Many of the stories in *Northern Passages* were written for the people who live here, to get them out of their houses and go look at things. The best way people can get to know the land is—as the poet and essayist Gary Snyder would say—to get on your knees and crawl; crawl through the land that you inhabit.

People have to get out, pick berries, look for mushrooms, hike, bushwhack, and so forth. Leave all the burdens of your life at home. Around here, the times I have been out to Outer Island in the Apostle Islands have been overpowering. When I conducted fall bird surveys on the island, I had a peak experience, and I wrote about this in my book in the chapter titled, "Grasping a Bird Lens." The wildness of the lake around you, the waters crashing around you, listening to the waves at night. Just to be there and aware of the history—how many people have come and gone—then to be up early in the morning and see the migration and the birds that come and go. I didn't feel like someone present merely to conduct a brief survey, but someone who was there as an observer for a very important reason, a reason that connected me to the spirit of the place.

I have argued for some time that the Apostle Islands be designated a wilderness area. I wrote a letter to Gaylord Nelson, and he responded by calling the Apostle Islands National Lakeshore office, and the need for a wilderness study was eventually included in the park's General Management Plan.

I've had some wonderful times outdoors in Wisconsin. Just out of high school, on spring break my freshman year, my best friend, Larry, and I were dropped off in northern Wisconsin, and we bushwhacked across the Pine River country. We had our pants up, shoes off, crossed the river, and went into the wild. We took basic food items, a cheap tent, and took off. We went through all of these old pines, and one day we came across an old saw blade just stuck in the ground. We realized that we weren't the first people to walk through the area. But being on our own like rolling stones for a few weeks was a peak experience. We got eaten alive by mosquitoes, but it was fun.

A plant ID lesson with daughter Jessie and son Casey in woods near Washburn, Wisconsin. April 1992. Photo by, and courtesy of, Julie Van Stappen.

CHAPTER SIXTEEN

Pause during a Breeding Bird Survey, Sand Island, Apostle Islands National Lakeshore, June 1998. Photo by, and courtesy of, Julie Van Stappen.

I CAN TALK about peak experiences in the outdoors, but the most significant peak experience in my life is having children. It's a major biological thing, you know. Your whole life you want children, and you go through this process, this wonderful process. Then, one day there's your baby boy or your baby girl. Right there. Suddenly you're a family. And my kids love being outdoors. When we took a trip to the West Coast recently, the kids loved exploring and finding things. Once, Casey was swimming and got real close to a baby seal. He pet it and removed a piece of kelp from its head. Then it followed him to shore, and when he got out, it followed him. Not to anthropomorphize, but it was a nice experience for Casey to be that close to a wild mammal of the ocean. It's like sitting up in a tree in the woods and, all of a sudden, having a chickadee land on you, looking at you closely. Something he'll remember for the rest of his life. I wonder if the seal will.

My family has a temporary relationship with animals, particularly reptiles. We save turtles when we drive down roads. When we see them crossing, we hit the brakes and try to get them across. If they look like they're imperiled, we'll take them down by the Sioux River or someplace like that. This reminds me, one of my best essays, which was rejected, had to do with finding a sick great blue heron along a roadside on the Skagit Flats in Washington. The story was rejected because I didn't provide enough new information about

Mike with Casey, Julie with Jessie in the North Cascades, Washington, 1994, during a family vacation. Photo courtesy of Julie Van Stappen.

great blue herons. It was goose season out there, and we stopped when I saw it. I examined the wings for gunshot wounds and decided to pick it up and take it out to the end of the Flats and set it down where people couldn't see it. I was trying to respect its dignity. I suppose in one way it was comical: a great blue heron sitting in the back seat of a Volkswagen. But on the other hand, the bird was very ill.

🍂

REMEMBER THAT OLD BOOK, *Man Not Apart,* published by the Sierra Club, written in the 1960s? I've always felt close to what *is* in nature. I see it all as one great thing, not individual little spirits; we're a part of something together. It's interesting how quarks—among the smallest known physical matter—make up all these little particles that are you and how fleeting all of it is. The major structure of everything is space. Gravity is actually just a curvature of space around the planet. It's not anything else. You realize then that what you are, what your children are, what the sandstone and clay bluffs are along the bay, are all something that comes from the same source, however changed it may be over time. When you look at the physics of who we are, there is not much there because all the particles are changing all the time. According to relativity theory, everything is in motion. I remember once that there was this famous physicist, though his name escapes me, who was afraid to leave his house because he felt there was no firm place to stand. He was afraid he'd fall through the particles!

WHEN I BREATHE, everything is breathing all together—one breath. I'm not outside of the story. Then you think about the physics—the gas exchanges—argon floating around the atmosphere for thousands of years that has gone through Wisconsin plants or plants in the tropics. We're not separate from this whole place we call earth. We are not apart.

I often sit *zazen*—a Zen practice of sitting peacefully, breathing and just being—a Buddhist way, which is one way Gary Snyder influenced me. At other times, when I am in the woods looking for rare plants, looking for warblers, I am doing my animal thing among the other animals. But my Buddhist practices have made me more aware of my relationship to the land. As I said, we're not apart. You don't have to go to Mount Rainier to experience a wondrous place. If you're outside, you can experience it right now where you are.

I don't know if my illness has added or not to this experience of the outdoors, but it has made me aware of how ephemeral I am. How so? Because it is so. It's going to happen, and in that sense I fit into the landscape like a dragonfly or mayfly. It's not so unnatural. Most people see a really serious disease as something not natural, but I don't see it that way, so I can be a little more accepting about how things will go, but also take comfort in being part of the land.

There have been times when I've been too sick to get out, which is part of the reason we're living in this house up here. I can always, at least, open the window and hear indigo buntings or scarlet tanagers. And I can see the weeds! I know the weeds better now, and once in while I hear the coyotes at night, or the foxes barking.

I'm happy being here right now, breathing, and trying to live a good life. I can't say I'm at one-hundred percent acceptance of my condition, but I've done a lot of work to keep my head above ground. I know that whatever we are together depends on individual effort. It's hard to describe. I've been going over this myself lately trying to understand Buddhist ideas about returning. I was raised a devout Christian, and I went through a period where I was a devout atheist. But I shifted back to Buddhism because it seems more real.

When I think of my kids, what I want for them is happiness and a close relationship with the world, that they'll be able to do good things. No one has a perfect life, but I wouldn't want them consuming too much and wasting too much. Of course, Julie knows this. She has been a great inspiration in my life. When I started out as a writer, she gave me a great deal of support. She saw that if I could write, everything would be good in the sense that my enrichment from the writing would become richness for the family. There's a kind of music and harmony between us. We both love the land, and we share everything together.

We've been together almost 20 years. Makes me think of the sandhill cranes. I'm ready to dance, yet! ✳

In the early morning of September 26, 2000, with Julie by his side at home, Mike quietly passed away.

On December 8, 2004, 80 percent of the Apostle Islands National Lakeshore became federally protected wilderness, set aside officially from any future development as the Gaylord Nelson Wilderness.

Eric Epstein
(1946-   )

Devouring a can of *Bush's® Baked Beans* by a campfire on south
Outer Island, September 1991. Note the sneaker (lower left) perched
and drying out. Photo courtesy of Eric Epstein.

BLACK SPRUCE

Chapter Seventeen~
Eric Epstein

The longer I was at the DNR, the more I became aware of the task of not only cataloging inventory data but in applying this information in a variety of ways that might improve management, point us toward sustainability, and hopefully avoid the common pitfall where we were simply documenting the decline of the natural world around us.

—EE

Eric Epstein, born August 13, 1946, in Laconia, New Hampshire, moved around often with his family early on, but grew up in Milwaukee. He played music professionally from the age of 18 until he was in his mid-thirties, "mostly American roots stuff." Professional gigs were sporadic at first. Then between the ages of 22 and 30, he was engaged full-time as a musician. As he entered his thirties, however, he turned his attention to bird study and ecology.

Armed with a degree in biological aspects of conservation from the University of Wisconsin-Milwaukee, he entered the Wisconsin DNR (WDNR) workforce as a WDNR research scientist in 1980. Then, in 1985, he became the ecologist for the WDNR's Bureau of Endangered Resources and spent the next three decades surveying, evaluating, and recommending areas of the state for long-term conservation and management. He retired in 2011.

Eric became well known among Wisconsin conservationists and biologists for his unparalleled and detailed understanding of Wisconsin's natural history. This understanding is evident and on full display in a masterful compendium describing Wisconsin's 16 ecological landscapes, written as an online publication (when it became two thousand pages long) for the Wisconsin Department of Natural Resources, with co-authors from the department's interdisciplinary Ecosystem Management Planning Team, particularly founding team member and leader, Gerald Bartelt. Their prodigious work is titled *The Ecological Landscapes of Wisconsin, An Assessment of Ecological Resources and a Guide to Planning Sustainable Management.*

Not as well known, except to those who have worked with him, is his wicked, imaginative, sense of humor. For example, I once wrote to him and asked, "What should I wear biking to work when I learn of a particularly brutal winter forecast?"

He replied, "A minimal loincloth and plenty of sunblock? Or, jam yourself into a pre-paid mailer addressed to the Hawaiian god of fire, and try to make it to the nearest post office. Imagine how bad things must have been in the 'old country' to have made the Gathering of Waters seem like an appealing destination! In my case, that would have been the area around Gdańsk. Or perhaps, my ancestors were simply misinformed? 'Alternative facts' are nothing new! Now, about cashing in on those 72 virgins my grandparents must have eschewed. Which reminds me, I got a notice that my 50th high school reunion will be held this year. I will go as a Mormon. But I want to out-conservative the inhabitants of blood red Wauwatosa. So first I'll get a flat top—maybe 'Chicago boxcars' and a cheap brown suit. But to ensure that I'll push a button or three, I'll wear a brightly colored sash and bring at least six of my wives, perhaps more—I'll need a couple of 'rent-a-wives'!"

My chance meetings with Eric in the field occurred on Lake Superior, where I was studying the state endangered piping plover and common tern. Longhaired, mustachioed, broad-shouldered, with thick eyebrows that protected a penetrating gaze, and dressed in faded, ripped jeans, I was somewhat surprised when this biologist bandito accompanied me to a common tern colony near Ashland with an umbrella. Only Eric would have thought of bringing an umbrella out to a tern colony and considered its utility the previous night ("spent in a bar—no connection, I'm sure"). And very functional the umbrella turned out to be as it prevented the marauding adults from striking his scalp and defecating on him ("Sumner and wildlife manager Fred Strand were irreparably soiled and sent to the nearest car wash."), and it afforded protection from the bright summer sun.

Always prepared (holding empty egg carton for nonviable tern eggs) ... at the oldest active Wisconsin common tern colony site (near Ashland). July, 1986. Photo by Sumner Matteson.

Notable are the accolades (and there have been several) Eric Epstein has received from The Nature Conservancy and other organizations for his dedication to identifying and cataloging the state's biological diversity. But just as important, there are few as insightful, visionary, and fierce in speaking eloquently for the conservation and protection of Wisconsin's natural heritage.

I WAS THE FIRSTBORN, and my father, Herbert Hofmeister, died when I was two, three. I have no memories of him. I was a timid little kid. You don't ask people about the dead at that point. Or I didn't know how to do that. My father had rheumatic fever in his teens, so he had a weak heart, which is ironic because he was one of two outstanding athletes in the family. He was long, lean, and red-haired. I looked like the other half of the family—burly Prussians. I never saw a picture of him until I was in my early teens, when I finally talked my grandmother back east into showing me a picture. I always had this feeling that her life pretty much ended when her only child died. I remember looking at her sometimes, and she just had this odd expression that looked vaguely like a person who had been shocked and traumatized in some way, carried it with her always, and had nowhere to go with her grief.

Our family moved around a lot because my father was a writer of fiction. He wrote all kinds of background material for the government during

World War II. He couldn't serve in combat because of his bad heart, so he turned to writing as his contribution to the war effort. Shortly after I was born, we moved from the New Hampshire farm to a blueberry farm in Kenilworth, Connecticut, then to Manhattan in New York City, and from New York City to Tucson. He was young and still trying to get established and probably bouncing from position to position. He also had his underlying health condition, which, he had been advised, would best be handled by living in a healthier climate; that's how Tucson came into the picture.

After my father's death, my mother went back to Milwaukee, her city of birth. She remarried a guy who had served as the family doctor. He was my mother's third husband, and he adopted me when I was eight. He was our pediatrician—the doctor my mother found for me because as a little kid, I was small and sickly. I was physically weak and terrified of everything until those wicked hormones kicked in a few years later. I wasn't really on the same playing field with the other kids. Except that I was a good softball player. That was my one saving grace. I was pretty introverted. I read a lot. Everything. I'd read encyclopedias and novels. I would go through phases where I'd read western histories or war stories, or I'd read biographies. At the time, it never seemed as if that was a displacement activity. It was just something that transported me to a safe and engaging world as a latchkey kid. And it was a pretty good stand-in as a way to satisfy my curiosity.

My mom, Marianne, was a single working mother in the early 1950s, from the age of three until I was eight. So I was alone most of that time. My maternal grandmother would come over and take care of me sometimes, but she also worked. She was remarkable in that she had been a single mother with three kids during the Depression, worked the whole time, and put all her kids through college, which wasn't that common then. She encouraged me to read. One of the books I read was *Birds of America* by T. Gilbert Pearson. A copy of that came down from my grandfather. I remember going through it, reading the text, and while there was some anthropomorphizing, the descriptions of plumages and behavior really brought the birds to life. And the illustrations, by Louis Agassiz Fuertes, knocked me out. They still do. And when I was ten, in 1956, for a birthday present someone gave me a subscription to *Natural History Magazine*. I used to devour that thing cover to cover. Here was a rag that not only covered the natural world but bridged it culturally: How people lived in their worlds and what effects they had. I found that fascinating.

From the age of six or seven through high school, I looked forward to visiting the Milwaukee Public Museum. You could go down into the sub-basement and pull out these huge trays of exotic butterflies and beetles, things like that. It was dark and warm and no one ever hassled you. It was a secret and very personal place of discovery.

*

IN HIGH SCHOOL, there was no social network that I could connect with or plug myself into. I hated the whole experience. I ended up in a different high school every year, and I was still introverted and really shy but also not willing to take crap from people whether they were other students or teachers. My parents were concerned that I was becoming a problem as those same hormones that made me large also had effects on my behavior. I did get into a fight once in a while.

For a period of years you either stagnated, or were transformed into something else, or you emerged from this cocoon as something new. You likely became an organism that neither you nor anyone else around you recognized or related to, and that must approximate the natural order of things because a lot of people I know went through the very same thing.

I needed a girlfriend, which I didn't have. I needed a car that made a lot of noise, which I also didn't have. I still liked going outside but wasn't sure why, and I wasn't really paying attention because I had been side tracked by music and cars and sex—mostly with imaginary partners.

*

ONCE I STARTED, my first big personal breakthrough occurred when I decided that adults might not have my best interests in mind. Whatever I was going to pick, engage in, or be swallowed up by, it had better be something I chose, not them. So the demolition derby began.

During a prolonged bout of insomnia in the early '60s, when I was in my mid-teens, I'd often spin the radio dial late at night. One evening, after midnight, I heard this great voice—a big booming baritone—say, "This is John R., way down south in Dixie." And then he played a string of tunes from artists I'd never heard of, like Sonny Boy Williamson, Little Junior Parker, Slim Harpo, Lightnin' Hopkins, Lowell Fulson, and Howlin' Wolf, and I was like, "WTF is this?" I couldn't get that station—WLAC, out of Nashville—every night, but I always tried. About that same time, one of the neighborhood delinquents was given a guitar, an old Gibson acoustic, by his mother. Once he figured out that his mom wanted him to play as a means of redirecting his more vicious and antisocial instincts, he wanted nothing to do with music, and he gave me the guitar.

So, it was right back to the radio, where I'd try to play along with what seemed at the time to be the simplest tunes—simplicity is so often deceptive! Following months of ghastly fumblings, my breakthrough came when John R. put on a Jimmy Reed tune in the key of E—right where my lower string was tuned—and I was able to copy the bass line, and then one of the rhythm guitar parts—one of three, I figured out later! And from then on that's what made the bed springs creak....

Eventually I escaped my institutional shackles, got a job parking and washing cars in downtown Milwaukee, bumped into a low-end electric Gretsch, which I paid 40 bucks for, and started going to offbeat record stores. I began running into other musicians in a similar gravitational field. I was able to trade the Gretsch and a few cases of beer for a Fender Jazzmaster and Showman amp; I wish I still had that amp. I didn't like the Jazzmaster and traded it for a Gibson electric—an ES-335 for those who get such things—or care. And that was it. It's been Gibsons ever since.

When I was in my late teens, the music thing took over. I had pretty much taken a vow that I was not going to allow myself to be institutionalized ever

Eric (age 20, left) and singer, songwriter, guitarist Dave Ray, who "possessed the sharpest and most wicked sense of humor I've ever encountered in another human being" (EE). Performing at the Avant Garde Coffeehouse, East Side of Milwaukee, 1967. Photo courtesy of Eric Epstein.

ERIC EPSTEIN

again because high school was such a waste of time—yeah, yeah, in part that was my doing—and such a negative experience. I got good enough as a picker that I could start playing with other people who had similar interests and tastes and capabilities. At age 18, I began playing occasional gigs with my betters. Most of them are still my betters, even those who have passed on.

So I started working semi-professionally, initially. Then, when I was 23, someone asked me to play in a band, and I had never really considered that, but I liked the kind of music they played, and it became overwhelmingly a full-time plus endeavor. We played together for seven or eight years. Milwaukee had a pretty good live music scene, in that you could actually make a living playing music. For most of the guys I played with at that time, music was their sole source of income, so you had to work gigs. It wasn't like you did something else. I played lead guitar in our band—a band I called Stuffed Shorts. But its real name was Short Stuff. It was literally picked out of a hat. I hated that name, but it was a really good bar band.

(Ed. Note: Good enough to be inducted into the Wisconsin Area Music Industry's Hall of Fame in 2017. Eric received a WAMI! Of this honor, he told me, "Yeah, I got a WAMI statue of sorts. More of a paperweight, actually. Hefty, and rather lethal, I'd say. By way of contrast, DNR gave me a '10-year' length of service pin—after I'd been there for 22 years. Always a hoot and a half.")

We worked probably 200 to 250 nights a year, mostly bars. Every once in a while you'd have this very awkward situation where you would open for a name act and blow the headliner off the stage. But usually that can't happen, because the audience isn't there to see you. They're there waiting for you to get out of the way. But the money for those sorts of jobs was usually good, and the hours were really short for college gigs and special events like Summer Fest.

Every place we went, I always drove because the other guys were hopeless. There was always a six-pack of Miller longnecks and a bag of dope on the front seat, and usually, when I could find them, a bag of oranges for balance. That's how you maintained and kept things level. There was no room for anything else. It was great in a lot of ways, almost nothing like it. We had a circuit of places in Illinois, Iowa, Minnesota, Michigan, and occasionally we would go east as far as Toronto or west to Boulder, Colorado.

Being hooked on music, you are naturally influenced by many. Too many to name. In my case almost all of them were rootsy Americans. In addition to blues, jazz, and hardcore country, there's the Tex-Mex stuff, Afro-Cuban music, Irish murder ballads, and some Hawaiian music. Pickers I liked a lot included Scrapper Blackwell—a Cherokee, who was singer-pianist Leroy Carr's guitarist; Freddy King—the blues riff-master; Wayne Bennet—Bobby 'Blue' Bland's guitarist, who used beautiful chord voicings; Kenny Burrell, a jazz guitarist with a big fat soulful sound; Albert Collins—incredible power and drive and an inimitable, quirky style; Lonnie Mack—a plump hillbilly from Indiana and the master of the Gibson Flying V; Roy Nichols and then Redd Volkaert—great guitarists who played with Merle Haggard; and about a thousand and one others.

But I had to get out of the music scene. One of the reasons I stopped, believe it or not, was the realization that I hadn't read a book in seven years. I was about 30. And, you know, I had loved to read. I wanted to read. I also realized I didn't want to drive 400 miles to go to work to end up in a bar and have the same conversation I'd had the last 350 nights. I didn't want to be around people who were usually drunk, stoned, or some combination of both, which sometimes included me, at least not all the time.

❧

IN THE MID-1970s, shortly after I quit playing music professionally, I drove back to the Northeast to see relatives in Boston, then went up to New Hampshire to see the house where I lived as a child. It was right in the center of the state outside of a town called Center Harbor, which was on Squam Lake—the lake that was used as a backdrop for the movie *On Golden Pond*. Someday I'll watch it just to see if I can spot my house. "How could anyone ever have left this?" I'd ask myself. It was this old, sprawling New England farmhouse where every building was connected to every other building through this system of sheds and tunnels because they got so much snow in the winter. Right behind the house was a 2,000-foot granite mountain called Red Hill, which had a raven's nest that I remember well.

❧

LOOKING BACK, there are little things that are still there 60 years later. I can still pull them out. They left an imprint that I think probably did shape or, in some way, guided my subsequent interests. Odd things. Like staring out our four-story walkup apartment building in Milwaukee on a snowy day in winter and realizing that something was looking back at me from the treetop I was staring into. It was a screech owl. Here's this little kid on the couch, staring out the window at nothing in particular. It's gray and gloomy and depressing. There, across the way, are these yellow eyes looking at me—looking into me, watching every movement I made. That stuck with me.

My mother had a twin, Carl Holtz, my uncle. One of UW-Madison's 50 greatest athletes in crew. (You think you've seen muscles and stamina!) He worked for Patrick Cudahy on the southside of Milwaukee. He had taken a course or two from Aldo Leopold when he was at Madison in the 1940s. He had been a bombardier in World War II, and following the war, the greatest sin in the world to him was killing for pleasure, which included all hunting, except for subsistence hunting. So he had strong views. His ambition was to have his own farm. So he would sometimes come pick me up, and we would drive all over the state looking at farms. We'd be driving around the state, and if there was a hawk on the side of the road he'd stop and look at it. He usually knew what it was, but by the time I was eight or nine I was better at that than he was.

Birds, at first, were a challenge.

Once, going through the huge ancient tome by T. Gilbert Pearson with the great watercolors and line drawings by Louis Agassiz Fuertes, I hit the wood warblers, but that was all a blur. It was just too much detail for me to absorb at age 12. There was a Peterson Guide out at that time, but I didn't have it, or even know that it existed. Then, early one foggy and cold May day, I went down to the Lake Michigan shore, where I often spent a lot of time. The big lake was near where we lived on the lower east side of Milwaukee— right there, like having a huge void, with no one to mess with you. So I was walking down these stone steps to the lake, and I suddenly realized that the shrubbery around me was in motion. Birds everywhere. I didn't know what any of them were because I couldn't carry the huge Pearson book around with me—I could barely lift it. Then I started remembering some of these things I'd only seen in the book, and I decided that I would try and put names to some of those tiny but vividly colored and patterned birds I was seeing. So I'm stumbling down the steps toward the lake, and I remembered that the male chestnut-sided warbler had a yellow cap, and there it was! The males had these bright chestnut streaks on the side. I saw a redstart for the first time and it was like, holy shit, this is amazing! When I got home that day, I got out that ancient, and by now dilapidated, copy of the Pearson book, and I started looking at the wood warblers. A few things clicked, and they began to make sense—no longer a mystery—the kind of revelation that made me want to know more. A door had opened, and behind it? Many more mysteries!

Similarly, one morning, years later, I remember coming home at about 4:30 in the morning after playing at a local bar, and it was just starting to get light out when I heard all these little chipping noises in the air. So I went down to the Lake Michigan shore as usual and realized that there were hoards of birds flying in over me toward land from the lake. If you see the radar images taken during periods of heavy migration, these birds aren't just following the shoreline at night, they're all over the place, and at first light they head for the nearest land, if they're lucky enough to find land. It also made me wonder about what was going on and how this all worked. Where were they going? Where did they come from? What are they?

I had become pretty good at identifying birds by the time I decided to quit playing music professionally. I thought that if I really wanted to know more about them, how they live, where they live, and what was happening to them—good, bad, same, whatever—I needed to go back to school. It wasn't as if everything began to coalesce. I simply decided it was time to get a degree, or at least do some serious reading to go along with the mad cross-country dashes I'd made in my teens and early twenties. So I talked myself into going back part-time, which I did at UW-Milwaukee. I was going to go to Madison, then arguably the best public school in the state, but when I found out that people stood in line for a week trying to get the classes they wanted, I thought, "You've got to be kidding!" *And I was 30.* Milwaukee was set up better to handle adults, which I was—marginally. And there was work in Milwaukee, so I could play a night or two a week and make the rent. I pursued the interdisciplinary degree, biological aspects of conservation, which pulled in all kinds of stuff, and I had a double major, the other being botany. It wasn't that I was so interested in plants per se. I simply thought you couldn't understand what was going on with the birds without understanding more about the vegetation of the state, so I started peeling the onion or opened Pandora's box! The only reason I wanted to get a degree at all, which I received in the early 1980s, was that it became clear at some point I wasn't going to be employed unless I had some kind of credential, or at least that's what I talked myself into. I think there are ways around that, but if you're going to be a player at the table, you need someone to want to offer you a chair.

MY LAST COUPLE OF YEARS PLAYING MUSIC, I'd started reading more across a broad array of subjects. I read Curtis's *The Vegetation of Wisconsin* in the late '70s. I thought it was a really good read, but I am apparently in a minority. But I read it and thought, "How did this guy do all of this? How did he come to these conclusions, and where are these places?" He mentioned the State Scientific Areas Program, and Curtis was on the very first State Scientific Areas Board along with Aldo Leopold. So reading that book made me think that I really needed to get out and see some of these places. Trips to the scientific areas—and many other places—discovered in a variety of ways, and what I experienced there became my Rosetta Stone.

I also read Leopold's *A Sand County Almanac* and some of his other essays and was struck by how you could read something this guy had written in 1933 about a trip to Germany, about forests then and what had happened there, and how they were being managed, and especially how they had been altered by their different land use histories. It was illuminating. Some of the imagery he used to paint word pictures really spoke to me because I had observed and puzzled over similar or parallel situations in Wisconsin. I found it easy to relate what he had seen and how he had described that to what I had also seen. He made the science and natural history live and, as a bonus, provided insight.

Another book *Those of the Forest* by Wallace Grange was a very creative way to approach forest interrelationships through the eyes, mind, and life of an ancient rabbit, with all the changes that are part of the great cycle of life. There was something comforting as well as revealing in that. It was the kind of book that, if I'd had kids, I would have read passages to them frequently—my dogs love stories about rabbits.

I often liked reading correspondence between authors because it was less self-conscious than many of their more formal published efforts. Also, I was reading a lot of published scientific papers. There's no end to that stuff! Most of it, no matter how good the idea is, I don't enjoy, but it gives the background needed to say certain things or to make points effectively, and it's absolutely crucial in terms of enrichment, understanding, and personal evolution. Technical writing is certainly not my forte, neither by inclination nor ability. But I've been lucky enough to work with several individuals who excel at such endeavors and owe each of them a great debt. (Most of you know who you are.)

CHAPTER SEVENTEEN

Finally, for anyone more interested in beetles, birds-of-paradise, orangutans, and biogeography than finches and tortoises, check out Alfred Russel Wallace, whose birthdate was January 1823. Wallace suffered because he was poor his entire life, though he did a lot of hard traveling! He collected insects and birds in the Amazon for four years. The ship on which he sent ALL of his specimens back to England burned and sank during that voyage. All was lost, and those specimens were his livelihood! But he went out again! At least one biographer described Wallace as Darwin's satellite—Darwin's moon or competitor. That struck me as horribly off target. Darwin was "establishment" and a classic gentleman naturalist, albeit one with brilliance, and who knew that he was in fact a revolutionary, which must have given him many a sleepless night. Wallace was quite the opposite, and became something of a spiritualist late in life. No one was more fiercely independent or persistent than Wallace. His book *The Malay Archipelago* influenced me, which in addition to being a great story, includes nifty maps and some lovely reproductions of woodcuts. As a most worthwhile bonus, his positive take on the lives and cultures of the indigenous people he encountered in the mid-nineteenth century was way out of the mainstream.

And for those interested in seances ... well, never mind. There's something to be said for swaying in a hammock while marooned in the Spice Islands while running a high fever! An incredibly keen observer who was working in exactly the right place, Wallace was semi-delirious in that hammock when the concept of evolution by natural selection suddenly made sense from the patterns of distribution he had been observing throughout the archipelago involving beetles, birds-of-paradise, orangutans, and other organisms as he traveled between the islands.

Both Wallace and Darwin arrived at their insights into the theory of natural selection independently! It was Wallace who contacted Darwin by letter, letting the genie out of the bottle. To the credit of both, they shared in the announcement of their discovery. But Darwin agonized, literally for decades, over whether or not he had enough data, what the presentation of his findings and the theory he had derived from it would mean for society, and how his formidable and intimidating relatives, particularly his grandfather, Erasmus, would regard him. And he probably worried about anything else he could think of, as well, including the possibility of getting scooped by Wallace. Would *On the Origin of Species* ever have been published had Wallace not written that letter?

IN MY EARLY THIRTIES, I started submitting bird observations to *The Passenger Pigeon*. Occasionally, someone would contact me to tell me how full of crap I was: "There's no way you saw a burrowing owl," and, you know, I did. One of the people who contacted me was my future boss, Bill Smith, and a case history unto himself, about Cooper's hawks. It had been listed as a threatened species in Wisconsin post-persecution and DDT effects, and Bill had started working at DNR's Bureau of Research in 1976. He was looking for information on Cooper's hawk nests, and I knew where several active nests were. So Bill came up to my wreck of a house in the Driftless Area to band Cooper's Hawk nestlings.

If you want to watch a man in labor, watch Bill Smith climb a tree.

But the nest was occupied, Bill was ultimately successful, and afterwards we had a big dinner at my house. I kept in touch with him. He was going through his major bout of raptor psychosis at that time. He was a falconer, he was banding, and he was successfully getting studies funded. Bill then told me that there was this project coordinated by his office in DNR Research called the County Natural Area Inventories. The way he explained it was that a DNR advisory body—the *Scientific Areas Preservation Council*—had decided that they needed a more systematic means of identifying and prioritizing candidate state scientific areas beyond selecting some professor's favorite teaching site, which was, you know, how a lot of these sites were picked early on. To be fair, many of these sites were favorites for good reasons. So it was decided by the council that they would begin these systematic statewide inventories using blocks of counties as the geographic units. That started in 1969 as a modest, chronically underfunded effort but with some good people participating, all of whom I learned a lot from.

IN 1976 OR 1977, the DNR published a technical bulletin that listed most, if not all, of the State Scientific Areas that had been designated up to that time—a modest number. So I decided that I would try and look at some of these sites and see what I could see, which created a template that I would try to apply later as I was trying to envision, for example, what the stand of old hemlock hardwoods on the Flambeau River State Forest would look like from the air. (It was leveled in a violent downburst in 1977—one object lesson among many.) Then, I would wonder if other places in that landscape or in the counties in that landscape had parallel or similar signatures. And if not, why? Did the ecosystems change, or were their use histories different? How would you separate such differences? And what did they mean for the future? So you start broadening your perspective, then try to focus back on what it is that you think you want and need to know. In many respects it became clear that much of what had represented the landscapes in Wisconsin for millennia only a century or so ago, was gone. Either it had been destroyed, like most of our prairies and oak savannas, or it had been logged and severely burned, often multiple times. These things we unfortunately accepted as routine.

Right now, the general landscape conditions are not representative of the way things were when European settlement began. So that whole question of comparative signatures became interesting to me.

∅

IN 1979, I got a call from Bill Smith. He told me that Monroe County, where I lived, was one of the counties that would soon be getting survey attention for the County Natural Area Inventory project. He asked if I was interested. I think they were interested in me because Bill knew I was engaged by the subject matter and had some familiarity with that part of the state. But mostly, I lived here so there were minimal support expenses.

Cliff Germain, who was head of the State Scientific Areas Program in DNR and working within the state bureaucracy, tried to keep things as focused as he could to look for potential State Natural Areas and never overlooked the opportunity to save a nickel. I say that with great fondness, of course!

The first year I started with the County Natural Area Inventory, I worked only in Monroe, Jackson, and Trempealeau counties. That was easily several seasons worth of fieldwork—I had about three months! I was surveying geology, landforms, soils, hydrology, and vegetation. Plus I was on the lookout for a target group of plants and animals that were thought to be rare in the state and likely to occur in that group of counties—now that's called multi-tasking. I would always start, however, by looking at stereo pairs of air photos for an entire county. A few days of that was enough to make your eyes pop right out of your head. I learned how to do this partly through coursework, but, like anything else that interests you, you learn mostly by doing and learning from others who know more than you do and have practical experience. Finding those who could help you understand or explain what it was that you were seeing became an invaluable skill.

The only people I encountered who had expertise in air photo interpretation were some of the foresters, especially some of the older foresters. That seems to be a skill that's declined considerably, too, or has been deemed irrelevant and replaced with other methodologies and technologies. A couple of those guys were really good, and a subset of them would even talk to people in our program. So I learned how to do that, and I looked for areas that hadn't been developed or subjected to a recent cutover or been degraded in some discernible way. Learn to recognize the differences from the present norm and interpret the signatures on the photos. I regret that the methodology we used wasn't better documented because several of my co-workers and I got pretty good at identifying sites that had a high potential for supporting sites with intact vegetation or other attributes of interest to our program. Looking at so many air photos, which almost always depicted much larger areas than we were used to examining on the ground, also forced us to think more about scale and context, and what it was that likely made sites viable over the long-term—or not.

Now, sometimes in concert with surveys to identify potential State Scientific Areas, our shop would also survey a county, region, property, or landscape feature such as a Great Lakes shoreline, a national forest, or Driftless Area cliffs for selected groups of rare organisms. Early on, most of this work was focused on plants. In the 1980s, there were some surveys for rare plants that were restricted to habitats along the Great Lakes coastal areas of both Lake Michigan and Lake Superior. We also collaborated on surveys for areas proposed for major development. One of these occurred in the Driftless Area's Kickapoo River Valley because of the large dam proposed for construction near LaFarge, which would have inundated many miles of cliffs, some of which were known to harbor rare organisms. I was very glad that some of the farsighted local folks came up with a much better idea for this unique area than constructing that dam and flooding the river valley! Incidentally, it was projections of poor water quality in the reservoir and an extremely unfavorable cost-benefit analysis that did the project in— not rare species.

CHAPTER SEVENTEEN

DURING THE EARLY TO MID-1980s, when I was doing basic inventory work, I had almost no contact with anyone else in the Bureau of Endangered Resources or the department. My boss, Bill Smith, was my primary contact. But finally I ended up in Madison in GEF 2 at a time when there was a bureau meeting scheduled. I didn't know what a bureau was, really, or what transpired during their meetings. I was one of those peripheral people who sat in a chair on the side of the room. You know, the real employees got to sit at the table.

The first ten minutes bored everyone to paralysis, and then the great debate started. This began as an argument over whether we should serve hamburgers or wieners at a planned party to recognize our bureau's supporters. It became this war of words and wills between two of my now new bureau-mates, whose names shall remain nameless. Here's a section chief and here's his opponent who, at that time, was planning and leading the management of State Scientific Areas in Wisconsin. It was a hopeless debate on the relative merits of serving those citizens who had propped up and breathed life into our program. Had any of them been in attendance they would have jumped ship immediately. As intense and unrelenting a displaying male as one of the protagonists could be, there was no moving the other from his position—classic irresistible force and immovable object. But it just went on endlessly, and there was no movement. It was like being in an Off-Off Broadway play with these two entities representing "Dark" and "Darker."

I don't know if the lights dimmed or something happened, but I just slipped out and left. I reaffirmed my vow, the one vow I took when I got out of high school: I'm never going to be institutionalized again! So what did I spend the next 32-plus years doing? Working for the State of Wisconsin—the DNR. Irony of ironies.

My only other memories of work in Madison involve smashing my head against concrete in the GEF 2 stairwell. I did this each morning upon entering the building hoping to injure myself severely enough to prevent me from reaching the rat maze of cubicleland. But it was like being caught in a Star Trek tractor beam and trying with futility to avoid being drawn into the Borg cube. My head still hurts when I think about the DNR. Especially those who think they run it [referring to the pre-Preston Cole days].

*

WHEN THE WISCONSIN NATURAL HERITAGE PROGRAM started in Madison, there were no positions. There were no offices. We didn't have chairs. The bucks were abysmal, and they were LTE jobs. So we tried getting this Natural Heritage Inventory program going with Bill Smith, who was coordinator and also lead (and only) zoologist, and we also had a botanist, ecologist, and data manager. And that was it. We went through this very intensive training because The Nature Conservancy had developed a standardized and extraordinarily detailed methodology, which all heritage programs had to use. They bestowed upon each of us this enormous operations manual that you pretty much had to commit to memory and then get periodically tested on—and embarrassed semi-publicly, repeatedly. Those manuals still show up occasionally on eBay, or in my nightmares.

I know and worked with some biologists who definitely have a passion for the work they're engaged in, but it's almost as if that passion is transferrable to the next problem or the next taxon. Bill Smith is a classic example of this. When I met him, he was engulfed by pondweeds and was, at the time, one of the state's experts in that field of endeavor—a small and select group to be sure. Then it was on to tiger beetles, then raptors, then mussels, and now he's emerged as Mr. Odonate. When I began working at the DNR his knowledge of Wisconsin's flora was incredible. He was very influential in his way. He's an extremely talented biologist, but he's also like "The Dude" in the movie *The Big Lebowski*; he could at times be the laziest individual I'd ever met in my life! Until he'd engage in his passion of the day.

BOTANIST AND GEOGRAPHER Emmet Judziewicz is another person who defies description. I liked working with him a lot, in part because he knew so much more than I about things I felt that I needed to know more about. Both his academic and field credentials were impeccable. Even though he's not one of God's most patient critters—an understatement—we got along well. He has an active lively mind. He's very creative and an extraordinarily productive botanist if you look at the number and quality of publications (and students) he's cranked out at UW-Stevens Point—pretty much off the charts, and things that other people wouldn't touch because they're undoable by someone who doesn't have his knowledge, drive, or energy.

No botanists I've worked with move the way he moves. Most tend to plod ahead with great care, their eyes fixed on a couple of square meters just ahead of their toes. Emmet sort of explodes across a landscape like a prairie fire on a windy day. You would learn a lot and cover a lot of ground. For projects that had a major scale aspect to them, where you had an impossible amount of ground to cover, there wasn't a more ideal person. In addition, he was, or had been, a Milwaukee Braves fan, like me! I'd skip school for two reasons: to screw around down along the Milwaukee River, and to see Warren Spahn pitch. Emmet was from the south side of Milwaukee, one of our state's special cultural landscapes. While with the DNR he did things that I know were extremely difficult for him, such as take groups of troubled teens out into the field with him—successfully! They all got along great. These are things he got no credit whatsoever for at the time.

THERE WERE ALWAYS THINGS I saw as core tasks of my ecologist's position that I thought were important and basic and required constant attention at some level, such as development and continual refinement of a vegetation classification system or identifying which natural communities have become rare, which were trending that way, why these things were

Eric amid swamp white oak *(Quercus bicolor)* and wood-nettle *(Laportea canadensis)* at what is now Wauzeka Bottoms State Natural Area, featuring an extensive stand of older floodplain forest. June 1985. Photo by, and courtesy of, Michael J. Mossman.

happening, and which species would be affected—all of which led to the need for better information to make appropriate long-term conservation decisions. The larger questions were what could we and should we do within our landscapes? What's really been lost? What's really restorable? And what are the benefits of restoration? Over the long-term, the social benefits of grappling with, rather than ignoring, such questions were potentially enormous. And the likely price of not dealing with such questions was likely to be of equal magnitude. Fortunately, the information and inspiration to be obtained from others I knew and worked with, like you, Mike Mossman, Emmet, Bill Smith, and so many others who individually and collectively have this fantastic wealth of knowledge that's taken them at least one lifetime to amass, was often accessible to me. This wasn't just book learning; it had some juice!

Some people I worked with in the Natural Heritage Program, however, saw projects as these very finite sorts of things: You do the work, there's a report written, and that's the end of it. But much of what we did never had such sharp boundaries because the ongoing collection and interpretation of data at local, state, and global scales are primary functions of a heritage program. Inventories, if they are to be of any value, are dynamic processes, not static end points. But who is going to interpret these data if we didn't? We've had past administrators who thought that you just throw raw information out there, and the managers, planners, politicians, citizens, and others who use the data would somehow do what we want. Well, what do we want? The longer I was at the DNR, the more I became aware of the task of not only cataloging inventory data but in applying this information in a variety of ways that might improve management, point us toward sustainability, and hopefully avoid the common pitfall where we were simply documenting the decline of the natural world around us. And always remember, our work was science-based, not dogma or ideology.

I've come to realize that whatever path you take in our field, you also have to feel that the work is worth doing for its own sake. You've got to like it, or really love it and have a passion for it, or it's a sham and you end up in a government office with a figurative rubber stamp of some sort, or you become someone's political appointee—the latter was never the life for me.

IN 1999, I was asked to join the department's Ecosystem Management Planning Team, which [now retired DNR Research Scientist] Jerry Bartelt had joined in 1996, and which had been a standing interdisciplinary WDNR team with reps from the Bureaus of Forestry, Facilities and Lands, ER, Wildlife Management, and one of the water bureaus. The idea was to have representation from each of the programs in what is now the WDNR Fish, Wildlife, and Parks Division. You start off with, or come to, this idea that to be effective you need to be more comprehensive in outlook, more broadly encompassing, and emphasize actions that make the most sense in a given location rather than trying to do everything on the same property or acre of land. Well, too often the reality with teams was that you ended up in endless meetings where you didn't get anything done and then came out the other end with some version of the prevailing status quo. We've all spent a good part of our careers figuring out ways to circumvent that stuff because we can't get anything accomplished otherwise. It's the classic clash between what seems good in theory and what works in practice. Anyway, this particular team—they were in vogue for a while—was one of the few I was involved in that pretty much got it right (that and the Old-growth and Old Forests team, which desperately needs to be revitalized).

Jerry and I were the only members that outlasted our teammates, and the focus at the end of our careers became the completion of a book titled *The Ecological Landscapes of Wisconsin*—a mammoth undertaking if ever there was one. If we had only known!

The first chapter, "Principles and Landscape Scale Management," gives thumbnail descriptions of each of Wisconsin's 16 ecological landscapes, basic definitions, and suggests who the users might be. There's a chapter that provides a summary and assessment of current conditions and another on comparisons of ecological landscapes across the state. You get basic information on what kinds and how much of various natural features occur in each ecological landscape, such as how much and what kinds of forest occur there, how much native grassland and savanna, how many miles of stream, how many lakes and acres of lakes, and there's background information and basic references on soils, geology, geography, aquatic habitats, vegetation, animals, and plants. We also look at what the major opportunities are for conservation and management within each of these ecological landscapes, especially those opportunities that don't occur elsewhere. There's also a chapter on current and emerging resource issues. And then the big one: We grouped some of the communities, species guilds, species geological features, and tried to compare the opportunities within different parts of the state. As an example, do we really want to emphasize prairie and other grassland management up in Forest County? Maybe not. Do you want to try to do something with the endemic Great Lakes coastal communities in Madison? Probably not.

We also try to broaden what Wisconsin has to offer within a regional and continental context, so certain choices and actions will hopefully make more sense, not just locally but at broader scales. For example, where are the best opportunities for pine barrens management? And why? Wisconsin probably has the best opportunities in the world to do effective pine and oak barrens management, which includes maintaining viable populations of sharp-tailed grouse, usually the focal species as a surrogate in areas managed to restore and maintain barrens. If we protect and sustainably manage viable populations of sharp-tails, what else is protected? What falls through the cracks? Can management be adjusted to conserve what's missing?

The inherent challenge we faced with *The Ecological Landscapes of Wisconsin*[110] had to do with the sheer size and scope of the project, the time it would take to get it done, and the fact that the team never had adequate representation from several key programs, especially those that deal with water. At times we lacked a representative from Wildlife Management, though Jerry's 35-year career had been spent in wildlife research efforts. There were times when the team had eight people on it; four of them from forestry—all good reps by the way. This chronically skewed representation, trying to figure out how you were going to include really important information when you don't even have a liaison, let alone an expert, on your team. Well, it often came down to expanding your own work. That being said, several individuals from programs where we sought additional representation, who were never formal team members, were extremely generous in providing us with missing information and their perspectives. And administering the occasional correction!

When it comes down to presenting this thing, now and in the future, we need to start out by recognizing what Wisconsin has to offer, not only in and of itself, but compared with other places on the planet. So we need to identify and acknowledge those opportunities that exist here and understand how they stack up against opportunities elsewhere in the state, the Upper Midwest, and across the continent, and then make the best decisions we can when faced with the omnipresent economic and political challenges.

Each time I'd start focusing on an ecological landscape, my approach would be to take a map of Wisconsin, cut out the landscape we were working on, and consider and figure out what's really lost, what's no longer there, and what can't we get in other places. If we write about the Southern Lake Michigan Coastal Ecological Landscape and cut that out of a state map, what are we really missing? Is there anything there that you can't do or get any place else? That's what you focus on and emphasize so that those features aren't irreparably damaged and lost, and then you look at how that

Ecological landscapes are based on the National Hierarchical Framework of Ecological Units (Cleland et al. 1997) to aid efforts to manage ecosystems. Map creator: Nina Janicki. Map courtesy of Wisconsin Department of Natural Resources.

The Ecological Landscapes of Wisconsin Area Descriptions*

Central Lake Michigan Coastal: Lake Michigan climate influence; Great Lakes shoreline features; level to rolling topography with clay soils; large insular wetlands; Niagara Escarpment; dominant agricultural and urban land uses.

Central Sand Hills: hilly topography, sandy soils; land cover is a mix of dry oak forests, mixed pine-oak forests, agricultural fields, and wetlands; small barrens and savanna remnants; glacial end moraine with springs and coldwater streams.

Central Sand Plains: huge glacial lakebed, level topography, sandy soils, sandstone buttes; extensive dry oak, pine, aspen forests; barrens remnants; extensive acid peatlands; commercial cranberry production, agriculture based on center pivot irrigation; surrogate grasslands. Recreation and forestry are important land uses.

Forest Transition: rolling to flat topography with productive silt loam soils; historically forested, now dominated by agricultural uses (including ginseng production); extensive hemlock-hardwood forests limited to the east, pine-oak forests to the west; urban areas concentrated near the Wisconsin River.

North Central Forest: rolling topography with loamy soils; most extensive forests in Wisconsin; forested watersheds, numerous wetlands, lakes, and headwaters streams; striking bedrock features in northwest (the Penokee Range); huge public land base. Forestry and recreation are major land uses.

Northeast Sands: rolling topography with sandy soils; extensive forests are primarily oak, aspen, and pine, some hemlock-beech; large northern white-cedar swamps; coldwater streams; igneous and metamorphic bedrock outcroppings.

Northern Highland: rolling to flat glacial outwash plain, sandy or loamy soils; depressions contain many lakes and wetlands; uplands dominated by mixed hardwood-conifer forests, mostly of pine, oak, and aspen; large boggy peatlands; wild rice marshes.

Northern Lake Michigan Coastal: Lake Michigan climate influence; Great Lakes shoreline features; gently rolling to flat topography with loamy soils; mix of agriculture and hardwood/conifer forest; extensive marshes along the west shore of Green Bay; exceptional concentration of rare species and natural communities associated with the Door Peninsula, Grand Traverse Islands, and Niagara Escarpment.

Northwest Lowlands: gently rolling topography with loamy and organic soils; land cover is primarily mixed hardwood-conifer forests; large open peatlands; many headwaters streams and the corridor of the St. Croix River and associated habitats.

CHAPTER SEVENTEEN

Northwest Sands: rolling to flat topography, sandy soils; primarily dry oak and pine forests; pine barrens, vast sedge meadow/marsh complexes; several concentrations of lakes.

Southeast Glacial Plains: rolling topography with productive silt loam soils; outstanding array of glacial landforms; agriculture is the dominant land use; numerous wetlands including large fertile marshes; the Kettle (Interlobate) Moraine is a major repository of globally rare communities such as tallgrass prairie, oak savanna, Calcareous Fen; diverse warmwater rivers and streams, and marl lakes.

Southern Lake Michigan Coastal: Lake Michigan climate influence; Great Lakes shoreline features; gently rolling topography with clay and loam soils; most populated and heavily urbanized landscape in Wisconsin; intensive agriculture.

Southwest Savanna: unglaciated ridge and valley topography; agriculture is the dominant land use; extensive grasslands include prairie and savanna remnants; patches of hardwood forest on valley side-slopes; spring-fed streams.

Superior Coastal Plain: Lake Superior climate influence; Great Lakes coastal features include freshwater estuaries, sandspits, lagoons, wave-carved sandstone cliffs, Apostle Islands archipelago; rolling to flat topography with heavy clay soils; rugged tip of the Bayfield Peninsula; mixed hardwood and spruce-fir forests; spring-fed trout streams; some agriculture, including orchards.

Western Coulees and Ridges: unglaciated ridge and valley topography; frequent outcroppings of sandstone and dolomite bedrock and associated rare communities; silts and silt loams on ridges derived from windblown loess; agriculture is the major land use on ridges and in valleys; extensive mesic and drymesic hardwood forests; conifer bluffs; high gradient headwaters streams. Major rivers with broad well-developed floodplains such as the Mississippi, Wisconsin, Chippewa, and Black are major repositories of diversity and the source of many social benefits.

Western Prairie: gently rolling to flat topography with many depressions forming lakes, ponds, and wetlands; silt loam soils; extensive grasslands; uplands are used primarily for agriculture; rapid urbanization; ecologically important lower St. Croix River.

A more detailed comparison of ecological landscapes can be found in the book's Chapter 3, "Comparison of Ecological Landscapes," and even more detail is described in each of the book's chapters.

landscape is used and how likely is it that these natural features will be maintained or perpetuated over time. What will it take? Are there things that can be done differently to better ensure that conservation measures will be effective? Then, of course, over time, is climate change likely to affect these features? If so, how? There are certain species or groups of species, or natural communities or aquatic features that are more likely than others to be affected by climate change. You hope that you can make some pretty good projections and then at the very least identify some things that should be priorities for monitoring.

Let's glance at Superior Coastal Plain, one of these 16 state ecological landscapes, to give you a better feel for what I'm talking about. Many unique natural features occur here, including several major forest communities and numerous shoreline features—the later visibly evident and often best represented in the Apostle Islands archipelago and along the mainland coast.

This landscape probably has the greatest concentration of intact freshwater estuaries in the western Great Lakes, which may mean anywhere in North America. So here's a climate change conundrum: It's the landscape where management for a conifer-dominated boreal forest is probably most appropriate and practically implemented, but there may be some difficulties in actually achieving that if the climate continues to warm. On the other hand, areas near the Great Lakes may have some of these climate-induced changes moderated or mitigated by proximity to the lake, or the lake itself may warm up, which Superior has been doing rather rapidly in recent years at its western end.

The sandspit and lagoon complexes that are part of the coastal estuaries are really important and not replicated anywhere else in Wisconsin, and at very few places farther east because of the way the Lake Superior basin is rebounding from the departure—and weight—of the last glaciers. You've got all these estuarine wetlands with the coastal marshes and fens and other peatlands, but farther east on Lake Superior many of those coastal peatlands are now disconnected from the lake, and they've become more acidic and bog-like.

The Apostle Islands, coastal estuaries, and the river corridors of the Bad, the Brule, the Nemadji, and the St. Louis are very important. They offer a number of aquatic resources, wetlands, and associated terrestrial communities that are generally not found in other places in northern Wisconsin. The constellation of sandscapes that occur in the Apostles and to the west along the mainland shore are not limited to Wisconsin's Lake Superior coast, but they receive little pressure there, unlike some areas east of the Keweenaw Peninsula in Michigan, where, for example, the tombolo—a rare type of sandscape—hosts a heavily visited state park.

A major opportunity in the Superior Coastal Plain would be to maintain these functional complexes of natural communities that are better represented here than anywhere else. The opportunity for boreal forest management here, however, would entail considerable restoration, which we don't know how to do yet. A lot of this landscape is now managed to perpetuate aspen. This is an area that was almost entirely forested historically, but now it's got a checkerboard pattern of forests and fields, that is, it's highly fragmented, mostly by pastures and other openings related to past and present agricultural use. Things that you might expect to be in an interior forest, particularly an interior boreal forest situation, just aren't there. In addition, there's serious overbrowse on the forest understory from deer.

Regarding old-growth boreal forest, I'm not sure there is any in this landscape, though in a few locations conditions are headed that way. Mostly, however, they're going the other direction. The best opportunities to conserve and manage toward the historically common but now all but absent old-growth forest conditions in the Superior Coastal Plain are at a few sites within the Apostle Islands National Lakeshore, the northern half of the Bois Brule River State Forest, perhaps in parts of the Bad River and Red Cliff Ojibwe reservations, and in the city of Superior's Municipal Forest.

Boreal Forest management opportunities in the short- and mid-term on the Bois Brule River State Forest are limited by the small number and limited acreage of remnants that resemble the pre-European settlement condition, all of which are second-growth, but which have significant coniferous cover of white spruce, balsam fir, eastern white pine, and very rarely, northern white-cedar. This forest, however, has virtually all of the conifer-dominated boreal stands on state land in the Superior Coastal Plain, and would be a logical place for us to make appropriate designations and encourage experimental management to increase and encourage more boreal conditions. This could create opportunities to promote some of the now rare vegetation that was formerly widespread here.

Lots of alder on the uplands, meaning wet soils or a high water table, making forest management tricky. There are local swamping issues when some stands are heavily cut, inhibiting the regeneration of trees. Golden-winged warblers love these conditions and might love it even more if the overall abundance of forest and alder thicket increases.

Forest cover on the Bois Brule River State Forest is now mostly aspen-birch maintained by clearcutting, and plantation-grown pine. Much of this is in areas that supported diverse pine barrens vegetation into at least the early 1940s–1950s. If you want a glimpse of what parts of the Brule used to look like, check out the Cedar Island Estate, the Winneboujou Club tract south of County Highway B, and the deep ravines near McNeil's Landing in the northern part of the state forest. Keep in mind that much of this land is privately owned and posted and not accessible to the casual user. You can see a lot of this from the river, though.

It's not young forest that needs exclusive attention here. The department's "Young Forest Initiative" has its place, here and in other parts of northern Wisconsin, but the department is not being responsible if it presents that as addressing a "need." It may be addressing something people want because there may be more deer or grouse available locally for recreation. But it does not address an ecological need or a forest trend, which is going very much in the other direction for old forest. As presently conceived, such a program is of limited scope and focused almost entirely on aspen, or in a few areas, on the tall shrub, speckled alder.

Today we have almost no old growth compared to a historical situation where it was abundant throughout most of the north. And not only do we have almost none, but what we do have upon closer scrutiny is something that's increasingly dysfunctional and no longer currently supports regeneration of the dominant trees or some of the more sensitive species associated with the oldest stages of forest development. So this is where the landscape picture becomes very important. The department's Young Forest Initiative, however, is mainly a game-related initiative. It's really a "young aspen initiative," and should be so named. Where is the concern for other early successional forest types that clearly merit attention due to their widespread decline? Examples include forests of jack pine, naturally occurring red pine (as opposed to monotypic plantations), scrub oak, tamarack, black willow-cottonwood, and several other types.

To just proceed with promoting young forest wherever we can is short-sighted. You have to look at the entire landscape to determine the best fit for any given program: where, how much, and at what cost? It's a very gnarly issue, but not all of the perspectives among the many stakeholders are given equal weight.

We could *easily* implement well-conceived programs to maintain early successional forest in many locations and landscapes of Wisconsin. These programs, of course, already exist, but are they well-conceived? A citizen scientist from Baraboo once lamented the "remarkable incuriosity" of the DNR regarding what used to inhabit the lands and waters they are charged with managing. She had a point. At times we seem only to lament the passing of the conditions that were prevalent following the worst excesses of the Cutover.

As far as the DNR's Forestry Division, some agency foresters don't embrace old growth because they see it as conflicting with their personal values. They see that, or have been trained to see that, as improper or wasteful management—allowing trees to die in the forest. Despite all of the information that has been amassed in recent decades on the special values of old growth—old growth species composition, unique structural features, and functional processes dependent on old-growth conditions, the need for research areas so we can identify, measure, and monitor, and better understand some of these characteristics—we continue to ignore or minimize the importance of old forests. Wisconsin is alone among the other Great Lakes states and provinces in totally lacking large functional areas of intact, unharvested forest.

The best opportunities for old growth restoration management are places where 1) you have a lot of forest to start with; 2) some old growth remnants persist; 3) you have enough control of land to potentially keep deer densities at levels where they're not going to make management for characteristic important and sensitive plants such as hemlock, white cedar, yellow birch, Canadian yew, and numerous native herbs impossible; and 4) there is support, especially locally, for managing these older successional stages or older forest developmental stages. The only two places I can think of that meet these criteria are our national forests and a few of our state forest lands.

What the tribes want to do is another question. Is this something they would want to do, and if so, at what scale? Some NGOs have projects that focus on old growth. The Nature Conservancy has a border lakes project on the Wisconsin-Upper Michigan border, which is pretty good. That's an example of a good start. Along some of the major river corridors, especially in southern Wisconsin, there is strong sentiment for protecting and maintaining connected areas of continuous forest, but these tend to be somewhat linear corridors rather than the big blocks of unfragmented forest habitat, sometimes covering entire watersheds, that still occur in the north.

Both are important—critical really. Both are needed, as they represent very different ecosystems, which in turn support different vegetation and associated plants and animals. One of the many benefits to be realized by such projects would be in connecting areas of mature forest for additional watershed protection.

In Wisconsin, we remain in the early stages of integrating various kinds of active management and land use in more compatible and sustainable ways, and at multiple scales.

I'VE ALWAYS FELT that if you kept your eyes and ears open you would learn something potentially astonishing every day. I had a job that was not like any other. I think it was the best job in the department, and maybe the only one for which I was suited, but it did require spending almost all of my time alone in nature—almost always.

Each part of the state offers something quite different, at varying scales, with some experiences that cover and are embedded within broad themes and others that are up close and personal. Some of those unique experiences were fleeting and ephemeral, never to be repeated.

Decades ago I was on Long Island in the Apostles, and I had been staying in the old Sivertsen cabin.

One morning before dawn, I walk to the Sand Cut, which, as you know, Sumner, is a fair piece of walking in deep sand. (During years when water levels are high, you'd often be walking in the lake.) At the time, the Sand Cut is still very open and sparsely vegetated. I think it's a low-water year, and in addition, the seiche is out.

On the Chequamegon Bay side of the island there's a small lagoon, partially enclosed by two curving sandy horns. I sit there waiting for the sun to come up. Just before sunrise, a flock of marbled godwits flies in and drops into the lagoon not far from where I am sitting.

Then, for just a moment after they land, the birds lift their wings simultaneously just as the sun appears, as the first rays of sun come across Chequamegon Bay.

As the rays shine through their wings, the most incredible cinnamon gold color I've ever seen appears, but lasts for only an instant. The sandspit and bay are in the foreground, and Oak Point is in the background. Never have I seen anything like it, and the scene, with its perfect timing and lighting, is just stunning. A stunning and indelible vision.

ON A MORE RECENT JOURNEY, I visited Lake Superior in late May 2014. The remnants of winter were refusing to let go along the coast. The western end of the lake—as far as I could see with 10.5x binocs—was still full of ice. Broken in places by short leads of open water, the ice still covered well over 99 percent of what I could see beyond the outer beach of Wisconsin Point at the Twin Ports. I watched a flock of about 30 dunlins and a few pectoral sandpipers several hundred meters offshore picking at debris on the ice floes. A lone ruddy turnstone was closer in, working its way along the shore.

Upended blocks of ice on the west end of the lake were eight to twelve feet thick, lending the whole scene an eerie, but strangely beautiful, aspect. By contrast, inside of Wisconsin Point, Allouez and St. Louis bays were entirely open, and it felt almost balmy! Many common terns were fishing, an olive-sided flycatcher was hawking insects from a bare treetop near the Coast Guard Station, and I could hear leopard frogs calling from the warm shallow bays!

Most interesting were the many flocks of wood warblers and others moving through and feeding in the pine forests on Wisconsin Point. Eighty to ninety percent of the birds were in red maples, which were in full bloom— the only blooming plants on the point of any use to a warbler. Many of the warblers had their heads buried in the maple flowers. Whether they were after nectar, small insects, or both, I don't know. It made me think about the scorn so many in the conservation community have for red maple. It's treated by some—especially the pyromaniacal—as a pernicious invasive in many cases and some places for good reason. But I suspect that the migrating warblers, vireos, and flycatchers on Wisconsin Point that day would have offered a very different take on red maple. At least under that year's conditions!

HERE'S AN APOSTLE ISLANDS TALE. In the past, I'd had myself marooned on the islands to kick my smoking habit. If I was feeling sociable, I'd find a way to get myself to Long Island, not too far off the mainland shore. If I didn't want to see anybody, I'd go to Outer Island. So one fall when I was grouchy and out of sorts after a long field season, [AINL ecologist] Julie Van Stappen dropped me off on Outer Island. I had some task I was performing for her shop, so the Park Service was getting free work out of me, but more importantly, I was further cementing my interagency relationships while striving to improve my health, which were good things!

It's late September. This is just before the time when the lake typically begins to turn ugly, but I haven't checked the weather, and I decide to take a long walk from the spit on the south end of Outer, where I am camped, up along the west side of the island. So I am maybe three to four miles from the spit, and I come around the bend on the island's west flank, and the crisp vista and clear horizon of water, waves, and sky I had been seeing have vanished. They have been replaced by a boiling black mass, and I'm thinking to myself, "What the hell is that? Whatever it is, it's heading straight for me!" It's like this huge black snout working its way down the west coast of the island. So I turn around and I run!

I run wildly, which is not easy for various reasons, including all of the deadfalls, so half of my route is in cold water, and then jumping over things that I can't even dream about jumping over these days. Every once in a while I turn around, and this thing is getting closer to me. It is like footage I've seen of dust storms from the 1930s, where you have this wall of impenetrable black, and it looks as if life on earth—yours especially—is about to end. So I run and run, passing the big boggy lagoon, and manage to reach the spit. This "wall of obliteration" is now right on top of me. I get to the campsite. I have a couple of extra tent pegs that I tether my tent to and jump inside just as the storm hits. It is incredible. It kept up all night. An evil night. The world IS ending. Gale force winds! I can hear trees crashing. There are thunderclaps exploding right above me, and the lightning flashes are nonstop.

Following a lightning flash there would be an instantaneous explosion, and then sometimes a thud as a tree hit the ground. I am lucky that night not to have gotten crushed by a falling tree.

Finally, the storm abates, and I am exhausted. Somehow my tent pegs have held. I'm still there, and I fall sleep. When I awake again, it's getting light, and my surroundings are almost calm. I get up and venture out. The sandspit on the south end of the island is just loaded with migrating birds. It is actually very pleasant. So I build a fire, make coffee, and I'm sitting writing up my field notes and reading. Then 8:25 a.m. comes around, and I pick up my Park Service radio to call in lake conditions as all the rangers and various riff-raff who are stationed out on the islands are required to do.

Though my campsite is serene, the lake is wild after this gale. From the north and west it looks nasty, but I am pretty sure that no more trees are going to fall. I have food for probably a week, and I'm not worried. In fact, I like it because I know I am not going to get any company. But my radio is dead. They gave me no spare batteries, so I have no way to contact the offices on the mainland. So I know at that moment that the Park Service, aware of what a hellacious storm just passed through, is likely worried when they can't contact me. And I worry about them because I know there is no reason for them to even think about me, or do anything on my behalf. "Wait until the lake calms down and then come out!" ... but I had no way to let them know.

So the lake stays wild, and there is nothing I can do. The radio is dead. Birds are flying, singing, feeding, running up and down the beach. It's really great. I can see waves hitting Stockton Island several miles to the south of my location—parts of the coast that are rocky. There are these geysers, these jets of spray and foam, created when waves hit the rocks, that must be reaching 50–60 foot heights. There didn't seem to be any real pattern to the lake's wildness. How would anyone navigate through or negotiate waves like this? In a small boat? But the [Outer Island] sandspit curves, and there's always one side or the other that is relatively calm. In fact, it is much easier to land a boat on one side or the other of the spit than up on the north end where the lighthouse is, where you could be dashed on the rocks and crushed.

So I take a walk and then go back to reading. It's about 10:30. Then I hear a noise that isn't part of the background noise of crashing waves. I know what it is right away. I look out, and here's some poor, miserable, rookie ranger in a little bathtub boat, and it's going up and down like a child's toy in roiled bath water. He's by himself (because no one would go with him!), the boat half disappearing from sight, and finally he gets around the tip of the spit and into calmer protected waters. He lands on the east side of the spit. Poor guy. He looks shell-shocked. But he has come out just to see if I am okay. In a lot of ways that really impressed me even though I thought it was kind of foolish. I gave him a cup of coffee. I think he wanted to stay!

One other time, Tom Doolittle, when he worked for the Park Service, came out *during* a storm to pick me up at the same sandspit. When he arrived, I asked him if he really wanted to head back to shore. This was a storm that convinced me that God—or whoever—did indeed protect drunks, babies, and Doolittles. Or at least one Doolittle.

It was wicked. Before Tom got us into the sheltering windbreak that Stockton Island can form, sometimes a trough between waves would develop, and you'd be up on top of a big wave with nothing but a void in front of you. And that little bathtub toy of a boat would just come smashing down into that trough! It would hurt your spine it would hit so hard! At that point, I thought we would never make it to Stockton, let alone back to the mainland docks. There was a point at which I looked behind me, and it was one of those times when waves from different directions seem to synchronize and come together. There was this huge wave that had formed directly behind us, and it must have been 15 feet high. It started breaking, and I thought, "This thing is going to fall on us and sink this boat!" Somehow, we just went up the face of another wave, the 15-footer broke apart, and all was fine.

Doolittle was like Doolittle throughout—very engaged but not quite as nonchalant or talkative as usual. He was really paying attention. Thanks, Tommy!

***

ANOTHER SUPERIOR TALE. Years ago, as part of a Lake Superior basin wetland inventory, I was surveying a remote part of the huge Bibon Swamp. I had come in from the far southwest side, which is very difficult. It was difficult to the point of stupidity. I think I'm headed for a conifer swamp that is composed of old white cedar, fairly extensive, and thought to be in good condition based on an examination of air photos and forest recon data. To get there, I had to slosh through an extensive swamp of black ash.

It's between 4 and 4:30 in the morning and very dark. Well, it's a wet year, and there are pools of standing water between every ash tree. The ashes are all on hummocks. On the sides of each hummock there is poison ivy everywhere. I know that under these conditions the oils and compounds from poison ivy are likely to be in the water. I am already soaked to the gills. I react badly to poison ivy, even worse to poison sumac, though that's a tale for another time. I have given up on wearing a rubber suit to work, so it's old sneakers and jeans and stuff that I didn't care much about. I know

I'm going to be trashed for probably the rest of the summer because of the dermatitis that results from the ivy exposure. But, there are some cool birds here. Many northern waterthrushes are singing in the ash swamp, along with many other songbirds of the deep woods.

The fog is dense. I'm not really trusting my compass, trying to head for what I think is a bend in the White River, which should take me right to my objective—the center of this cedar swamp. But I can't see more than 40 feet in front of me. My pores are open, and I feel as if they're the size of quarters. I know that all of this toxic ivy sap is getting into my head as well as all over my body and probably going to make my brain swell and maybe explode.

I slog on and stop every five minutes or hundred meters to do a BBS [Breeding Bird Survey] point count, then soldier on. All of a sudden I'm in the cedars—a beautiful old cedar swamp. The fog is swirling through the trees, and it's starting to get light out, but I still can't really see. It's so very foggy and dim. I am trying to time my arrival to get the most birdsong and am rewarded with a nice assemblage of wood warblers—northern parulas, Nashvilles, yellow-rumps, Canadas, and also yellow-bellied flycatchers, blue-headed vireos, winter wrens, white-throated sparrows, and hermit thrushes.

I start looking around through the swirling mist. Then through the cedars, I see a clump of showy lady's-slippers. I start looking around some more, and there are hundreds of showy lady's-slippers everywhere, but I can't see very far. Then I notice that what I have initially taken as hummocks of *Sphagnum* moss are instead the carcasses of deer that died during the past winter. A deer graveyard. This had probably been their last chance to find food and escape brutal weather. There must have been 30, 40, 50 deer carcasses within my limited viewshed.

So there I am within this gorgeous but eerie forest of old twisted cedars with the swirling mist, soaked to the gills, amid hundreds of clumps of one of our most beautiful native plants, and then ... there is all this death. Very moving—a dramatic but sobering slice of reality. I've never come across anything like that before.

🍃

SOMETIMES WHAT YOU THINK YOU MIGHT SEE or hope you might see but don't, happens when there's a disruption caused by our presence on the landscape. It's almost as if there's a palpable interference that keeps you from connecting in some meaningful way. I've had a couple of things happen, one of which I attribute to hypothermia. One June morning, when the air temperature was less than 40 degrees, ornithologist and friend Joan Elias and I threw a canoe into the Bad River. We were going to do Breeding Bird Surveys in two separate areas north of Highway 2, and the way we decided to cover the most ground was for her to drop me off, and then I would follow a compass line through the vast wetlands and hopefully meet her hours later at a pre-arranged spot on a topographic map. She would go survey another portion of this huge sedge meadow and marsh, and we would attempt to convene at the pre-arranged place and time.

So we reach the point where we agreed to split up. Joan drops me off, goes paddling off into the mist, and disappears from view. It's 40 degrees. It's uncomfortable, and my shoes—Chuck Taylor high-tops—and socks are already soaked. I take three steps and immediately fall face first into a pool. I'm soaked from head to toe. Did I mention that it's 40 degrees? So that is suboptimal. I think, "Well, at least I am tired. Maybe the discomfort will keep me awake and thinking about other things real hard so I don't have to dwell on the miserable conditions I've chosen to work under in this chapter of my life." So I'm taking BBS points all along a compass line that's semi-randomized—a pretty good, soundly designed survey. I am amazed at how many second-year male redstarts there are out there in the alder and even in stands of small tamarack. It's second-year male redstarts galore—scores of them!

I go on for a while, and I come to a channel shrouded in swirling mists. I see a figure that looks vaguely human. At first, I am kind of startled because who the hell is going to be out here in the middle of the night? It's probably five in the morning by then, maybe five thirty. But it's dark, misty, cold, and windy. So I see this human figure. He is bent over, and he can't be harvesting rice because you don't harvest rice in June. But he's in a rice bed looking down at the rice doing something and never looking up at me.

I decide to try and get closer to see who I am seeing out here, and the point comes where I am probably within 30 feet of this individual, who is separated from me by this deep channel of moving water. I can clearly see him—an Ojibwe—still bent over and intent on doing something. I can see facial features, high cheekbones, straight black hair, and clothes a lumberjack might have worn a hundred years ago—heavy plaid shirt and baggy slacks. Then, what I don't expect actually happens. All of a sudden he starts receding; he just vaporized. Really eerie. I'm not frightened but think,

CHAPTER SEVENTEEN

"What am I seeing here?"

I am beyond the point of being highly functional. I'd fallen into really cold water and am probably not terribly astute or otherwise functional. I go on automatic pilot and somehow end up about where I said I was going to be, and after a bit Joan comes paddling up, probably between seven and eight. A short time later [botanists] Jim Meeker and Emmet Judziewicz pull up in a johnboat with a small outboard so we can do some vegetation sampling a mile or two farther on, around Honest John Lake near Lake Superior.

We spend the day out there, but I don't tell anyone about the incident with the phantom Ojibwe in the rice beds because I thought I must have been hallucinating. Maybe I was. Or maybe that's literally what happened. But why *that* vision, in that place? Although it seemed appropriate, it did seem like a time warpage of some sort—like this individual belonged there and had always been there but wasn't quite corporeal. Was it just hypothermia? I looked semi-normal in retrospect.

⟋

THIS IS A SHORT ANECDOTE. Occasionally you bump into someone who you feel is a kindred spirit, even in the middle of nowhere. I ran into [ornithologist] Mike Mossman in Florence County. We'd both been in the field—the barrens—for several days straight. We had both been doing various kinds of biological survey work in the three big barrens and bracken grassland areas out there on either side of the Pine River. So we conspired to explore the possibilities of collaborating, enabling us to cover more ground. But we also decided to have a real dinner, and there are not a lot of options in Florence County. But one or both of us remembered an Italian restaurant in Florence that was pretty good.

So we're in this dimly lit Italian supper club, and the waitress is bringing us more and more drinks, and we're waiting for a couple of pizzas. Then I notice that our tablecloth appears to be "animated," which, in fact, turns out to be the case. Now, the northeastern Wisconsin barrens and bracken grasslands are one of the state's tick hotspots. Mike and I are shedding ticks like crazy! There are scores of the fearsome beasts—wood ticks fortunately—and they are crawling all over us and everything around us.

I start to see people at nearby tables looking sideways at us. I feel this movement on my head, and I'm looking at these eight-legged vermin crawling all over our table. I see that the arrival of our pizzas is imminent. I'm looking around, and here's a nice jar of red pepper flakes. In a dimly lit room those flakes look a lot like ticks, but I want to deal with this dangerous animal-at-large problem before dinner, not afterwards, when I would have to wonder what it was that I was ingesting!

So I stab one with my buck knife, and it becomes like a parlor game. Did you ever see the Polish flick *Knife in the Water*? There's an amazing scene with a knife that was reprised in the spooky film *Aliens*, by the android. It's kind of remarkable, and here in the Italian supper club it almost goes like that—one of those days when my hand-eye coordination is good, and I am locked in on the task at hand. I am just slicing the things up left and right. I see the waitress staring at us as she walks by, and she starts laughing. She knew what was happening, and she says, "Good, good. Keep it up. Don't stop."

So, short story long, eventually the problem seems to be at a manageable level and our pizzas arrive, and we lived happily ever after to talk about it. I'm not sure I've been back to Florence County since then. I guess I have. And, of course, as always, it was worth it! ☀

After a long day afield ... notebook snug in shirt pocket. No bugs. Wauzeka Bottoms, Crawford County, June 1985. Photo by, and courtesy of, Michael J. Mossman.

CHAPTER SEVENTEEN

Sigurd Olson
(1899-1982)

Sig Olson at his cabin on Listening Point near Ely, Minnesota, 1970s

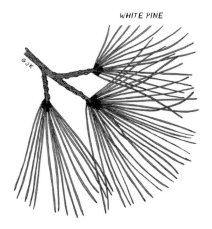

WHITE PINE

GJK

Chapter Eighteen~ Remembering Sigurd Olson

If we lose our wilderness, we have nothing left, in my opinion, worth fighting for.

—Aldo Leopold, Letter to Wallace Grange, January 3, 1948

Something will have gone out of us as a people if we ever let the remaining wilderness be destroyed.

—Wallace Stegner, "Wilderness Letter"
to Congress, December 3, 1960

A mere fifty centuries of "civilized" life can barely be expected to have changed the wild blood that still rushes through our veins.

—Michael Van Stappen, *Northern Passages,*
Reflections from Lake Superior Country

One goes to wilderness in an attempt to transcend [the] ordinary world, self, and manner of perception.... Thus, to enter wilderness is to leave behind the profane, changing, man-dominated world for a perfect world, which is a manifestation of sacred power.

—Linda H. Graber, *Wilderness as Sacred Space*

I have not stopped loving that which is sacred in this world.

—Albert Camus, *Notebooks 1951–1959*

The sun reigns, I am drowned in light. At this hour, sitting alone at the focal point of the universe, surrounded by a thousand square miles of largely uninhabited no-man's land, I cannot be seriously disturbed by any premonitions of danger to my vulnerable wilderness.

—Edward Abbey, *Desert Solitaire*

Give us one clear morning after another and the one whose work remains unfinished.

—Rumi

Sigurd Ferdinand Olson, born in Chicago on April 4, 1899, the second son of a Swedish Baptist minister, lived along the rocky coast of Sister Bay near Death's Door in Door County, Wisconsin. At age ten, his father's calling brought the family to Prentice in northern Wisconsin. Three years later they journeyed farther north to Ashland on Lake Superior, where Sigurd attended Ashland High School. After high school, Sig enrolled for two years at Ashland's Northland College. He, however, completed his undergraduate education in Madison at the University of Wisconsin, receiving a bachelor of science degree in animal husbandry in 1920.

One summer, while working on the farm of Soren Jensen Uhrenholdt in Seeley, Wisconsin, Sig became acquainted with his future wife and lifelong partner, Elizabeth Uhrenholdt. They married in 1921 and eventually had two children: Sigurd, Jr., and Robert.

In 1923, the Olsons moved to Ely, Minnesota, where he taught high school biology and became a wilderness guide during summers. In 1926, Olson began dual teaching stints at Ely High School where he taught biology, and at Ely Junior College, where he taught animal biology and human physiology.

A determination to achieve an advanced degree resulted in a move to the University of Illinois in 1931, and in 1932 he obtained a master of science degree in plant and animal ecology. For his master's thesis he completed a pioneer study on the predatory relationships and life history of the timber (gray) wolf based on fieldwork he had initiated in the Superior National Forest in 1930. Aldo Leopold took note and attempted unsuccessfully to lure him to Madison in the fall of 1933 as his first doctoral student in game management.[III]

Had it not been for a technicality—namely that Olson was still employed as a teacher and ineligible to apply for a public works program—Sig might have indeed become Aldo's first doctoral student, and this could have altered Sig's career path. (He harbored reservations about pursuing a master's program.[112]) He resumed his high school teaching at Ely and at the junior college, and then by fall 1934 taught solely at the junior college, where be became dean in 1936.[113]

While serving as a teacher and dean at Ely Junior College until 1947, and thereafter as a professional conservationist and writer, Sig spent nearly 60 years campaigning to preserve the Quetico-Superior wilderness of northeastern Minnesota and western Ontario. With conservationist Ernest Oberholtzer and others, he labored to keep massive road building projects, hydroelectric power schemes, intensive logging, and aircraft out of the Quetico-Superior. His vision became synonymous with the cause to preserve the Quetico-Superior, so much so that *Time* magazine and other national media singled out his opposition to mechanized vehicle use in the Boundary Waters Canoe Area (BWCA).[114]

During the 1950s and 1960s, Olson was instrumental in the efforts to establish the BWCA and to include it in the Wilderness Act of 1964. His most satisfying political moment came in 1978 when President Jimmy Carter significantly limited the use of motorboats and snowmobiles, authorized a permit system for recreational access, and restricted logging and mining activities across the entire 1,075,000 acres of the BWCA.[115] The year had been a lively one for the town of Ely. Residents had slashed tires, smashed car windows, and blocked canoe access routes with pickup trucks in angry protest over the legislation to protect the BWCA.

Many of northeastern Minnesota's residents had protested vehemently against preserving more wilderness because of the worry that a struggling local economy, partially depressed by tax exempt lands, would eventually be strangled by government land use restrictions. Olson, instead, believed wilderness preservation to be the best economic insurance policy for Ely's future. Time is proving him right: wilderness is becoming more scarce and an increasingly valuable resource. Ely, as gateway to the Quetico-Superior canoe country, conducts a profitable summer business serving canoeists and fishermen from all over the world.

Despite his noted activism (which also included serving as president of the National Parks Association, president of the Wilderness Society, the Izaak Walton League of America's wilderness ecologist, and adviser to the

President's Committee for the Quetico-Superior and the Department of the Interior), Olson is perhaps best known for nine distinguished books on travels in and observations of the Quetico-Superior and Canadian far north. His first and perhaps most widely read book, *The Singing Wilderness*, published in 1956 by Alfred A. Knopf, was highly acclaimed (making *The New York Times* Best Seller List). It established his national reputation as a premier nature writer and spokesperson for wilderness values. Other works that followed—each published by Knopf, except one—were *Listening Point* (1958); *The Lonely Land* (1961); *Runes of the North* (1963); *Open Horizons* (1969); *The Hidden Forest* (Viking Press 1969/Voyageur Press 1990); *Wilderness Days* (1972), mostly a compilation of essays from each of the previous works, but with four new essays; *Reflections from the North Country* (1976); and *Of Time and Place* (1982, posthumous).

Songs of the North (1987), a collection of writings from previously published works was published posthumously by Penguin Books and republished in 1995. Additional books, published posthumously by the University of Minnesota Press, include *The Meaning of Wilderness* (2001), and *Spirit of the North* (2004).

In 1974, he was awarded the John Burroughs Medal—the nation's most prestigious award for outstanding nature writing.

Sigurd Olson became a friend, mentor, and father figure to my dad, Robert, whose parents died tragically in a Florida automobile accident when he was 21 years old and a junior at Carleton College in Northfield, Minnesota. What brought them together initially, in the 1950s, was a passion they shared for canoeing and wilderness preservation. (And both were very fond of the poems of adventurer Robert Service, who described scenes and events from the Yukon and the Canadian wilderness.) Together, in 1972, they founded the Sigurd Olson Environmental Institute in Ashland, Wisconsin, to institutionalize their concern for environmental conservation and education in the north. And, since one of Elizabeth Olson's two sisters, Johanne Johnson, lived at the old Uhrenholdt farmstead in Seeley, Wisconsin, ample opportunities presented themselves for Sigurd and Robert to get together, since my parents lived at the time on nearby Lake Namakagon.

Sigurd was a complex, persistent, and tenacious individual, not unlike my father, who became wonderfully relaxed and at ease around Sig in a reverential way. I remember fondly the summer visits Sig made to our Lake Namakagon home during the early 1970s. Especially memorable was one sauna we took together on a clear, still night. My dad had moved an old Finnish sauna hut—much like the one at Olson's retreat at Listening Point—to a secluded hillside spot beneath sugar maples, hemlock, and balsam fir, quite a distance away from our house. On this particular August night, we steamily emerged from the hut, slowly and carefully walked down to the lake edge, then plunged into the cool mercurial waters. Somewhat light-headed (perhaps only me) after the lake baptism, we climbed back up the hill to the hut, where Dad and Sig, towels over their shoulders, beers in hand, sat back against the sauna's outer wall and reminisced about canoe trips in the far north. I was old enough to remember, and imagine.

Walking back to the house, Sig occasionally paused and pointed out different constellations through gaps in the forest canopy.

🍃

I visited Sig once in 1979 at his home in Ely, Minnesota. This was two and a half years before he snowshoed off alone into the woods, and then suddenly, naturally, fell over into a fresh snow, never to rise again.

The steamy July day I spent with him, recalled below, included an unexpected invitation for me to spend the night alone at his Listening Point cabin. And what a night. It was wonderful beyond words—a meditation within a pine-enshrouded temple, where the only sound was the wind coming and going through long, white pine boughs and the wide-open cabin windows.

July 12, 1979

A gravel road leads to a two-story wood house half-hidden by pines. Voices and the scraping of metal come from around back. Following these sounds, I find Sigurd Olson wearing baggy khakis, shirtless, with his shoulders pink from the sun. He is shoveling dirt. A baseball cap turned upward covers chalk-white hair, but does little to shade sunlight. His weathered face is ancient and kind. Furrowed lines run across his forehead, and ocher tinged with raspberry colors his nose and cheeks.

He has just finished planting a white pine sapling between his home and his neighbor's, where the town of Ely had cleared vegetation to get at broken sewer lines. He levels a mound of soil and smooths the ground with a rake.

A gray-haired friend of his in overalls stands a few feet away, hands on the end of a shovel, and watches. Standing nearly six feet tall, Sig slowly raises his back from its arched position, and stares down at the sapling.

It seems fitting that he would be repairing this small space of disturbed land. He has dedicated his life to caring for land.

"Let's go to the cabin," he says on greeting me. "We can take a swim and talk there. Might be cooler, too."

This is the famed cabin located on land known throughout his writings as Listening Point. It is land that borders the BWCA and a place many have come to know well through his books.

The dirt road into his land is hilly and slow, as it should be, he says. When we arrive at a cut-out parking area, and I open the car door, the forest air is humid, tropical. Cedar, pine, birch, fir, and maple surround us, and songs of black-throated green and Wilson's warblers are near, with wood thrushes, song sparrows, nuthatches, and chickadees farther away. A brief shower has passed through, and beyond, through a stand of cedar and aspen, I can see lake water.

"The cabin?" I ask.

Sig says it lies about 200 yards to the west over a slight rise in the terrain. "Closer by is the sauna." He starts down a narrow footpath rutted with veins of white cedar. *Sphagnum* grows between and over stones. The trail passes by clusters of violets, goldthread, and wood sorrel. Soon, a Finnish sauna, built in the 1920s, comes into view. Sig moved it here over snow and ice decades ago.

The sauna is dark and cool inside. We pass through a room where bathers undress and walk into the steam room. Here, a pile of stones lay encased in a steel crib next to a barrel stove. Cedar boughs (switches) tied by twine hang from an iron nail. Sig laughs recalling those souls unaccustomed to the whip of the boughs on their backs. "The use of cedar switches opens up one's pores and hastens the cleansing process," he says, "and leaves you rejuvenated." He points to the walls and roof, and asks me to get close and examine how dark the logs are.

Taking hundreds of saunas, especially when no stovepipe was present, just a hole in the roof, are the cause of the logs' deep mahogany color, he explains. "This place smells so good when it gets going. And nothing is more exhilarating than a dip in lake water after sitting in temperatures of 175 degrees," he says, smiling. For seconds, after the plunge, one feels neither heat nor cold, nor any temperature sensation, he says. "It's as if one's body has become part of the liquid—bones and flesh suspended in ether. Afterwards, one emerges tranquil." Lingering pungent odors of cedar tempt him to start up the sauna fires, but the day is already too hot, and he decides against it.

"Let me take you to a favorite spot of mine." The narrow footpath winds toward the lake. A few yards off it he locates a depression in the ground guarded by dwarf dogwood, violets, and mosses. Here is a spring well, with a round flat stone covering the opening. Overhead, a red-breasted nuthatch calls—a soft nasal drone high up a cedar branch. Sig kneels and uncovers the well—a small black pool.

"The purest water around. No chemicals. No nothing. Here, have a sip." The thin, clear water from a tin cup is achingly cold.

Rising slowly, he glances at his hands for a moment, then examines the trunk of a white cedar an arm's length away. "These trees are old friends."

Sig turns and walks on. The path leads to the foot of a bay and a pine deck with two weathered-gray wood chairs facing southwest. He steps up to look over the bay for a moment, then turns back to the path again, but something catches his eye. He stops in his tracks.

"Wild strawberries! The first of the year. Here, have one."

Walking on, he talks of the downed trees now coming into view. "Now you're beginning to see the results of the tornado that blew down an enormous number of trees last year. Nothing hit the cabin or woodshed. We were very lucky." The footpath narrows and traverses a slight depression a few meters from the water's edge. He stops to listen. An ovenbird, numerous blue jays, and a black-throated green warbler are present, but these aren't the sounds

Gathering wood for the fireplace. July, 1979. Photo by Sumner Matteson.

that have captured his attention. Instead, it is a deep, resonant voice from the water's edge. He turns to walk again, but the green frog bellows.

"Oh, come on! We'll be back," he says, smiling.

Soon, coming into view is an open-faced woodshed, where split wood stands neatly stacked. Sig wipes perspiration from his forehead and stares at the rows before him. The tail of an old stump sits nearby. It serves as a block for splitting logs. His log cabin is about 30 meters west of us. "There's more wood here than I could possibly ever use. This chopping block has seen a lot of good use over the years. It's rock solid and will last for years to come." He points to a huge balsam fir that just missed striking the shed roof and shakes his head, then laughs. "It's enormous, isn't it? Would have been quite a mess if it had hit."

He removes a handful of keys from his pocket and surveys the cabin. Ivy runs along and up the stone chimney. The rest of the cabin is slate-gray with hand-hewn logs and windows almost two meters wide on each of three walls. Keys jangle, and the door opens.

"There's lots of tradition in this old place," he says, stepping into the coolness. "I've had it for almost a quarter century. Let's open the windows and get what breeze there is." A latch opens in the middle of each window. We swing them open and tie each to a nail with a leather cord. The rolling whistle of a veery breezes in, and at first I cannot tell from which direction. It's as if an open tent encloses us, not a cabin.

Kerosene lamps hang from three walls, and one sits on a cedar table by the west window. There is no electricity here; the only amenity to remind one of modern life lies against the east wall. It is an oven-sized refrigerator powered by natural gas. Birch pegs on the north wall serve as a hat rack, and here I recognize a hat, gray and soft as felt, worn by Sig in book photos from his days as a guide. Pine bookshelves line the tops of four walls, and they are full with accounts of regional folklore and history. Two beds, on the north and south sides, lie under the windows. Hudson Bay blankets and patched quilts cover both.

"It was built [likely in 1899], and I bought it from a family about 10 miles south of our home in Ely. It was standing unused at an old homestead site, and the young people there were building a new house. They didn't want anything to do with this one. I went out there one day and said, 'What'll you take for the old one?'

'Well,' they said, 'would 200 bucks be too much?'

'Sold!' I replied. We tore it down, hauled it away in the wintertime, stacked and marked the logs one by one, and brought it out here."

Winds from the southwest drive cumulus clouds toward us. Will there be another rain today? Sig wishes to take a swim. We change into swim trunks in the sauna and walk to the foot of the bay. The pine boards of the deck are hot to bare feet. Anticipating this, he wears an old pair of sneakers, laces left untied. Sig slips out of them, sits down, and dangles his feet in the water.

For a few minutes I turn my back to the sun to catch sight of a singing blackburnian warbler. When I turn around again, Sig is standing in the water and has moved one-third of the way out parallel to the point. Can the water be so shallow? It is sandy along the bottom, and this helps explain the ribbon of beach lining the shore. I watch him now moving slowly, still walking out. Then he descends into the sun-brightened water and begins to swim out toward the center of the bay, only the back of his white head visible in the sparkling, broken surface. When he returns, he rises out of the shallows, steps up onto the dock, drapes a towel the color of red clay over his shoulders and sits in a chair.

After a few minutes of silence, I ask him about his earliest recollections of the Quetico-Superior. "An easy question to answer," he says. "During the First World War, which I was in briefly, I lived in Ashland. I'd always heard of that beautiful country across Lake Superior from the Apostle Islands, along the famous north shore. And I'd always had a yen inside of me to get over there. In 1916, '17, and '18, I'd canoed all around Ashland and used to keep a canoe down at the waterfront near Fish Creek Slough. Sometimes, I would canoe out to Long Island at the head of Chequamegon Bay. I also used to canoe the White River, the Bois Brule, and the Namakagon. At that time, the Namekagon was boiling with brook trout. Nowadays you hardly catch a brook; they're all browns.

Sig, after a late afternoon swim at Listening Point, reflects on his early Wisconsin days. July 1979. Photo by Sumner Matteson.

"Eventually I went to the Quetico-Superior in 1920 after graduating from the University of Wisconsin-Madison. I taught high school in

CHAPTER EIGHTEEN

Nashwauk, Minnesota, a small mining town in the northeast corner of the state, and spent my free time exploring rivers and lakes around the area. I immediately fell in love with this country and decided that this was where I was going to live!

"I began to cruise around the area on my own and finally learned the country well enough to become a guide in 1923. I guided parties without knowing most of the country. There were big sections of the area that weren't mapped. I often had to climb a tree, spot some blue, cut out a portage and keep on going. That was the way most of this country was mapped before aerial surveys.

"In my early days of guiding, I dreamt of emulating the feats of older guides who had been to Hudson Bay. Hudson Bay was an impossible dream to me. But eventually, I went a lot further than any of them had ever dreamed of going. I came to know the whole north, including the Yukon in Alaska. But I no sooner got up here than I got involved in the preservation of this wilderness from the 1920s to the present.

"I remember the 1920s well. In the early years of that decade, the Forest Service had a plan to build a series of roads into all the border lakes, and that's when I first got involved. The Ely Chamber of Commerce and all the Chambers of Commerce across northern Minnesota trumpeted the slogan: 'Let's make this country the playground of the nation.' Well, I was guiding at the time, and I didn't spend much time thinking about the concept of wilderness. But I did have a strong feeling about wild country, and it disturbed me to think that if they built a road up to Basswood Lake, up to Crooked Lake, Lac la Croix, and Saganagons lakes, the wilderness would be ruined; it would be gone. And I had enough perception to realize that if the wilderness disappeared, I would lose something very precious to me. Those old men at the Chamber of Commerce in Ely—they were probably in their 30s or 40s—thought I was crazy, absolutely insane. Why on earth could I object to bringing prosperity to the country and really making it the playground of the nation? I tried to explain in my faltering way—I hadn't yet formulated my concept of wilderness—why wilderness, in time, might help the local economy. They couldn't understand.

"In 1922, with the battle beginning to rage over the roads issue, I met a young forester by the name of Arthur Carhart. He was the first landscape architect employed by the Forest Service. I met him up on Saganagons one night, and we had a long talk. He had not seen the country before and was enthralled by it. He came back from that trip and met with the Ely Chamber of Commerce and told them that the best thing they could do was to keep the land in its wild state and not build any roads. And he recommended to the Forest Service that they abandon their project. They had $50,000 put aside to build all these roads, and they finally cancelled the project. The reaction: the old diehards here in Ely thought I had ruined the country. That was the beginning of my demise as a citizen.

"The Secretary of the Forest Service in 1926, William Jardine, signed a proclamation designating the areas in question as the Roadless Areas into which there were to be no roads. You could hunt, fish, cut timber, use motorboats, etc., but it was a primitive area and a primitive area it was supposed to remain. It went through a whole series of names. Once, it was called the Superior Primitive Area, then the Roadless Areas, then the Boundary Waters Canoe Area in 1968, and finally the Boundary Waters Canoe Area Wilderness in 1978. The important designation here is the word 'wilderness.'

"Wilderness was a growing concept for me. I gradually became aware of its importance to posterity. And I gradually became aware of developing a spiritual relationship to land as Native Americans did and have done for centuries. Everything they have comes from the land, and they feel they must use its resources and never waste them. That is the way I feel about the land, and the land belongs to God. Therefore, we cannot hurt the land without hurting our relationship to God. So when it comes to the matter of wilderness, wilderness being what the land originally was before we desecrated it, we are trying to preserve the purity of the land as God intended it for our spiritual welfare as well as for our psychological well-being. We belong to the land, and we cannot divorce ourselves from it. When you divorce yourself from the land, you cut your roots. Those who cut their roots are lost souls, and the world is full of them grasping, looking desperately for something to hold on to. If they would only realize that all they have to do is feel one with the land, and feel one with God. They're one and the same thing.

"So wilderness, too, is a state of mind. You can find it even in small areas, such in a city park screened from traffic. Once there, if you're in the proper state of mind, you'll discover your wilderness."

Gusts of wind sweep across the bay, and Sig intently watches the clouds drift overhead. Talk turns to his final days as a guide and the decision to sell his Border Lakes Outfitting Company in Winton, Minnesota.

CHAPTER EIGHTEEN

"I sold out my interest for peanuts because I wanted to counter the criticism that I had made money off the wilderness so why shouldn't everybody else. I can still see the fingers pointing at me: 'You're making your money off this. Of course you want to preserve it!' So, to counter that, I sold my business for $5,000, which was ridiculous. I could have gotten $100,000 or $200,000 if I had waited a few years. But I wanted to be clean. I wanted to be out of it, and I got out of it, and I shut the mouths of those who had been criticizing me. The most rabid critics said, 'You damn fool, what'd you do that for?' Well, I said I had to get out of it.

"They replied, 'You're crazy.' " He laughs quietly and shakes his head at this no-win situation. Then he looks up at the sky.

"Is that thunder?" He suggests we move to the cabin. Once inside, he lies down on the bed against the north wall, his hands behind his head. Lake breezes greet us with fresh pine scents.

"Let me tell you a little about the battle to ban aircraft from the Roadless Areas after World War II," he begins. "Pilots came in from the war to discover that every lake here was like a landing field. There were planes in here all the time, and the work that we had done up to that time to preserve the Quetico-Superior was threatened by the airplanes and fly-in resorts in both Canada and the U.S. Well, what were we to do about it? The Quetico-Superior Committee sent me down to Washington to look up the Air Commerce Act of 1926 to see if there was anything that could be used as a key to the situation. Nobody had ever controlled private aircraft over the country. Well, I found that under Section 4 of the Act, the president of the United States had the power to establish an airspace reservation for national defense, government installations, etc., *and for other governmental purposes*. I read that last part of that line with delight. I discovered that 'other governmental purposes' was a determination for which the United States had spent money. Fine. We could show that from Teddy Roosevelt's proclamation of the Superior National Forest in 1909 up to the recently passed Thye-Blatnik Act of 1948, which gave the Forest Service the power to purchase recreational lands for wilderness protection, there had been a consistent government record to protect the Roadless Areas.

"I went to President Truman's staff and asked them if it was possible to get an executive order on the matter. They said, 'Sure,' and drafted the order. The order gave the president the power to establish an airspace reservation over this area for the protection of wilderness. Then the big question was whether we could have the executive order signed. It had to be signed by at least six cabinet members. So it was sent out to the cabinet members, but nothing happened. I didn't hear any more about it.

"Russell Andrews, a friend of mine and an assistant to Truman, was getting worried.

"He said, 'Let's sit down, call all the departments, and see where this thing is. It's been lost somewhere.' We spent a whole day looking for the damn thing. No soap. Then it was discovered that the Secretary of Commerce was still to be heard from. Well, Russ had a hunch that it was probably on some underling's desk in the Department of Commerce and told me he was going to go over there personally. There it was on an undersecretary's desk under a pile of stuff about a foot high. Russ brought it back to the White House, and I looked at it with awe and delight. We started the calls all over again, and this time Russ had it hand-carried around all the departments until finally it came back to the president.

"Truman was just about to leave office. He was busier than hell. He had all kinds of things to take care of before he got out of office, so he went to his favorite summer place in Key West, Florida. That was before the days of San Clemente. It was just a simple little place. Russ went down there with him and the precious signed document. And on the last day before Truman was to come back to Washington, Russ waited for him as he came off the beach wrapped in his towel. The president was dripping wet. Russ handed him the document, and Truman said, 'Well, what's this?' Russ told him it was about the Superior National Forest, and the president said, 'Oh, yeah, I know all about this. This is the battle between the beaver and the airplane pilots. Well,' he said, 'let's give it to the beaver.' And he signed it right there. That's the famous airspace reservation of 1949.

"There have been so many battles over the years that I'm glad we finally got the law in 1978 establishing the Boundary Waters Canoe Area Wilderness. It is a much better wilderness than any of the Quetico-Superior Committee had envisioned that would have included motorboats, cutting of timber, mining, snowmobiles, and more. Our bill wasn't perfect, but darn near. It has phase-out periods on various snowmobile and motorboat routes, so in five years about 1,250,000 acres will be all wilderness. No mechanized uses.

"As far as the Canadians are concerned, they have stopped all motorboats and snowmobile traffic in Quetico Provincial Park [located adjacent to Superior National Forest in Ontario, established in 1913] as of May 5, 1979. There's no mining, no logging, nothing. It's a wilderness park. I met with the Canadian Quetico-Superior Committee in the spring of 1979, and they and the prime minister reaffirmed that Quetico Park would remain a wilderness park. The Canadians have enlarged the park by 250,000 acres on the east side and have added great wilderness chunks near Lake of the Woods. You know a lot of us wanted a treaty between the United States and Canada protecting the Quetico-Superior region. I spent almost 15 years trying to secure such a treaty. But the original treaty precepts were not as all-inclusive as the provisions of the law we have today. I once was bitter about not getting a treaty, but events have worked out pretty well.

"Unfortunately, there will never be completion of the work to preserve the Quetico-Superior. The old opponents of the new law are going to sue the government saying that the law is unconstitutional. They threaten to go through all the court procedures, not realizing that to reach the Supreme Court today will cost them millions of dollars. Furthermore, Congress will not retrace its steps. The legislative process has acted, and all the agony of getting this measure through is over with. I'm happy with it, but nothing is perfect. It seems that the battle will always rage.[116]

"The future looks pretty good except that there are too many people, but I don't know what you can do about that. The only hope lies in the fact that there is more canoe country to the north, far more than there is here. It's most difficult to get to and harder to travel. The Boundary Waters Canoe Area Wilderness is cursed with easy accessibility and ease of travel: short portages and long chains of lakes. And like many vulnerable areas, it's beautiful. You won't find this kind of beauty in the far north. You won't find towering red and white pines and beautiful campsites on rocky ledges like you have here. But the north has its advantages in its tremendous space and solitude."

Sig sits up as he speaks, then says we should sit on the cedar bench outside the west window to watch the sunset. Black-gray clouds hide all but slashes of golden light along the horizon to the west. Islands appear as moles to the far west. Sig's attention turns briefly to the subject of wilderness management.

"The concept of multiple-use management is not compatible with the concept of wilderness management. The use of wilderness means no multiple use. Wilderness can only have one use: enjoyment for itself. As we look ahead 10 to 20 years, this land will be more beautiful than ever. The results of fire and logging are still evident, but everything is coming back. This little place here was logged and burned about 1890 and look how big

Stealing a moment alone. July, 1979. Photo by Sumner Matteson.

the trees are now. Give them another 100 years, and it will look like a virgin forest. I'll never live to see it, of course, but somebody will."

Across the lake, a cloud has broken from the rest and carries sheets of rainwater toward us. I can't feel or hear any wind, and the noise of rain on the still lake is strangely loud, almost like the muted sound of gravel poured from a distant barrel. I ask Sigurd if he hears it. At first he doesn't respond, but tilting his head in the direction I'm pointing, he rises, excited.

"Ah! Let's go and watch it!"

About 200 meters to the southwest, a rain curtain moves in our direction—closer and closer it comes. "Sounds like an express train in a subway," he says, chuckling. Seventy-five meters, fifty meters. Still we are dry. Right up to our feet roll beads of rainwater. Instantly we feel cool droplets. In seconds, the shower passes by and continues inland as it taps across the woodland canopy. To the west, long strands of sunlight stretch across the water.

"Listen!" whispers Sig.

Near the center of the lake a common loon calls—a mournful, slow, hypnotic wailing.

Then Elizabeth, his devoted and tireless wife, too calls. She has arrived with dinner. ☀

CHAPTER EIGHTEEN

Think back

through the silence,

of the life that was and is not here now,

of the strong pastness of things—

shadows

of the end and the beginning.

—John Haines

Acknowledgments

I must begin by thanking each of the fine naturalists who allowed me into their homes to endure my many questions about their lives and work (and some agreed to allow me to accompany them in the field). It was my privilege and honor to spend time together.

Over the course of 40 years working intermittently on this project, there are scores of additional individuals and several organizations to thank whose support has been instrumental and invaluable to both the development of the Wisconsin Naturalists Project and the writing and production of *AFIELD*, Volume One. Listed in alphabetical order, they are as follows:

Karen Agee, Aldo Leopold Foundation, Mary Allen, Tom Allen, Bil Alverson, Jane Anklam, George Archibald, Jeb and Barb Barzen, Sarah Bass, John Bates, Dale Becker, David and Patti Becker, Kenneth Becker, Sylvia Becker, Katie Beilfuss, Judson Bemis, Bird City Green Bay, John Bielefeldt, Jeffrey Bodony, Sarah Boles, Dorothy Boyer, Charles and Nina Bradley, Maria Brandl, Alan Brew, Bill Brooks, Mary and Phil Brown, Darren Bush, M. Terese Campbell, William Carlson, William Castro, Charlotte and Walter Kohler Charitable Trust, Daryl and Sherry Christensen, Noel Cutright, Jane Dennis, Virginia Dodge, Adelaide Donnelley, Elliott Donnelley, Catherine Drexler, Velga Dunis, Emily Earley, Tom Erdman, Les Ferge, Mary L. Griggs and Mary Griggs Burke Foundation, Caroline Foster, David Foster, Edward (Ned) Foster, Elizabeth (Betty) Foster, Henry Dutton Foster, Michael Foy, Scott Fulton, Clifford Germain, David Gjestson, Ron Grasshoff, Owen Gromme, Betsy Guenzel, Rebecca Haefner, Inga and Woody Hagge, James T. Harris, Lisa Hartman, Bob Hay, Hazel Hiemstra, R. Tod Highsmith, Gerald Hoague, Randy Hoffman, Emma Hoffmann, Ben Hole, Sarah Hole, B.J. Hollars, Wellington "Buddy" Huffaker, Hugh Iltis, Harriet Irwin, Michael Jaeger, Johnson Family Foundation, Sam and Imogene "Gene" Johnson, Wendell and Judith Johnson, Winnifred Marquart-Johnson, Emmet Judziewicz, Randle and Barb Jurewicz, Darcy Kind, Orlando Kjosa, Virginia Kline, Ellen Klusmeier, Brad Knudsen, Terry and Mary Stewart Kohler, Mary Korkor, Harold Kruse, Holy Kuusinen, R. Michael LaBelle, Gretchen LaBudde, David Laden, Ken Lange, Andy Larsen, James Lenfestey, Albert Lindeke, Chip Lindeke, David Linderud, Divya Ma Lovingly, Roy and Charlotte

Lukes, Charlie Luthin, Caitlin Matteson, Mark and Sue Martin, Fredric Matteson, Jane Matteson, Liam Matteson, Liz Matteson, Robert Matteson, Robert Matteson, Jr., Sean Matteson, Peter Matthiessen (for critical advice and helpful suggestions), Jim McEvoy, Robert C. Mead, Curt Meine, George Meyer, Mike Mossman, Wade Mueller, William Mueller, Nancy Nabak, Susan Nehls, Deb Nelson, Nelson Institute for Environmental Studies, Mary Ann Neuses, David Noble, Robert Olson, Connie Otis, Mark Peterson, Gretchen Petraske, Charles Pils, Kate Redmond, Renaissance Charitable Foundation, Katherine Rill, Richard Ringelstetter, Eugene Roark, Betsy Robbins, Rick Robbins, Shirley Robbins, Robert Rolley, John Ross (who made me a better writer; he critiqued in the early 1980s a primordial thesis iteration titled "Voices For Wisconsin"), Kenny and Mary Kay Salwey, Phil Sander, Irene Schmidt, Susan Schumacher, Schwab Charitable Fund, Carl and Barbara Schwartz, Penelope Shackelford, Shackelford Family Fund, James Shurts, William Smith, Stephen Solheim, Julie Van Stappen, Emily Stone, Chuck Stonecipher, Jack and Marjorie Swelstad, John and Olive Thomson, Laura Tiffany, Marjie Tomter, Mary Tracy, Pam Troxell, Lori Uihlein, Lynde Uihlein, Robert Wallen, Donald Waller, the Walter Kuhlmann Award from the Diversity Inventory Group, Inc., WE-Energies Foundation, Karen Weiss, Wisconsin Wetlands Association, Adrian Wydeven, Barbara Zellmer (who, as my WDNR supervisor at the time, approved a six-month sabbatical leave to focus on the project after the turn of the century), and Elizabeth Zimmerman.

For their munificent support, I am especially indebted to Karen Agee and Scott Fulton, Inga and A. Woodson Hagge, Tod Highsmith, Gerald Hoague, Terry and Mary Kohler, Mary Ann Neuses, Jack and Marjorie Swelstad, Lynde Uihlein, and to the Diversity Inventory Group, Inc. For their years of dedicated support and encouragement: Charlie Luthin, James T. Harris, Nancy Nabak, Mark Peterson, Carl Schwartz, and the Twin Cities Foster Family—especially Ned and Dutton Foster. And a special thank you to David Laden for his timely and impactful contribution.

The following foundations and charitable entities were critically important to the sound financial footing and progress of the *Wisconsin Naturalists Project,* culminating in this first volume: Mary L. Griggs and Mary Griggs Burke Foundation, Johnson Family Foundation, Charlotte and Walter Kohler Charitable Trust, Aldo Leopold Foundation, Renaissance Charitable Foundation, Schwab Charitable Fund, and the WE-Energies Foundation.

There were two seminal moments in the life of the project. The first occurred in 2000, when The Wisconsin Wetlands Association, under the direction of Charlie Luthin, agreed to serve as the nonprofit organization sponsoring the Wisconsin Naturalists Project, then titled "Wisconsin Naturalists: Readers of the Landscape." Curt Meine, then research associate with the International Crane Foundation, wrote a letter of support to assist fundraising efforts. I am especially grateful to Curt for his long-standing support and for the fine Foreword that begins the book.

The late Samuel C. Johnson was the first person in 2000 to back this book project financially with a modest check, writing just a few words: "A small token for your good efforts." His signature took up much of the rest of the page.

A six-month sabbatical from WDNR bird conservation work followed in January 2001 that allowed me to focus on this project at an office provided by Eileen Hanneman of the UW-Madison's Nelson Institute for Environmental Studies. Did I expect to complete the project during this period? At first, yes, but when I delved back into tapes and filed material that I had started archiving beginning in 1979, I soon realized that the sheer volume of material made completion of the work impossible in six months. Not only did I realize that I needed to reconnect with several naturalists after I had first sat down with them, but several individuals strongly suggested I include others: Lorrie Otto—the champion of converting our Kentucky bluegrass-dominated front yards to landscapes and gardens of native plants and the pioneering founder of the innovative Wild Ones Natural Landscapers; George Becker—author of *Fishes of Wisconsin*, whom I visited in spring 2001 at his home in Eureka Springs, Arkansas; and LeRoy Lintereur, a former Wisconsin DNR wildlife manager and naturalist whose personal journals amounted to more than 3,000 pages. I shall be forever grateful to daughter Judith Johnson and LeRoy's widow, Joyce, for turning over to me all of his original journals. Judith and her husband, Wendell Johnson—both fine naturalists in their own right—have provided invaluable support and encouragement over the years, and to them I am especially thankful.

The second critical moment in the project's life occurred in 2015 when I entered into a relationship with Northland College and the Sigurd Olson Environmental Institute—directed by the unflappable Mark Peterson and his successor, the inspired Alan Brew. Mark wrote an important letter asking for donor support of the project. Northland played the pivotal role of nonprofit sponsor, allowing me—working early mornings, evenings, and weekends—to complete Volume One.

With the first draft completed, what followed were several months of chapter reviews. So ... to borrow a phrase from my friend, Duluth interpretive bird artist extraordinaire, Clare Cooley, *a thousand thank yous* to the following family members for chapter reviews (and photographs): David and Patti Becker (son- and daughter-in-law), Elva Hamerstrom Paulson (daughter), Patricia Otto (daughter), Sarah Hole (daughter) and Ben Hole (son), Judith Lintereur Johnson (daughter), Brad Knudsen (son), Robert Olson (son), Shirley Robbins (widow), Betsy Robbins (daughter), Rick Robbins (son), Julie Van Stappen (widow), and Elizabeth Zimmerman (widow).

Additional and much appreciated thanks for the photos contributed by: The Becker Family and Patti Becker, Dorothy Boyer, Ryan Brady, Eric Epstein, Lisa Gaumnitz, Thomas A. Meyer, Gene and Marion Moran, Michael J. Mossman, Deb Nelson and Cable Natural History Museum, Milwaukee Public Museum, Lorrie Otto, Joseph M. Rose, Connie Ramthun, William Volkert, and the Wisconsin Historical Society.

I am also very grateful to the following individuals for reviews: Carol Chew (Otto chapter), Michael Dombeck (Becker chapter), James T. Harris (Preface and Prologue), Paul G. Hayes (Lapham chapter), B.J. Hollars (Zirrer chapter), Emmet Judziewicz (Lintereur chapter, and a speical thanks to Emmet on plant taxonomy questions), Curt Meine (Preface and Prologue), George Meyer (Volkert chapter), Matthew Perry (Hamerstroms chapter), Mark Peterson (Moran and Olson chapters), Charles Pils (Hine and Knudsen chapters), and Bill Volkert, Eric Epstein, and Joseph Rose for making corrections, additions, and improvements to their own chapters, respectively.

I am especially grateful to Dave Gjestson, who spent an untold number of hours reviewing, editing, and making suggestions for improvements to several chapters. His comments and reviews were exceptional.

And a special thanks to retired WDNR wildlife manager Mike Foy and the Knudsen family for providing a collection of original George Knudsen plant and animal sketches. George's botanical sketches start each of the naturalist chapters. A special thank you as well to Lise Goddard for helpful comments and insights about Midland School, mentioned in the Preface, and for the book on founder Paul Squibb, and for her own booklet on Midland. A special thanks to: 1) the University of Wisconsin-Madison's Dr. David Mladenoff and Monika Shea for providing the historic land cover map featured at the end of the Lapham chapter; and 2) to the

Wisconsin DNR's Michelle Jesko for arranging the use of the Ecological Landscapes of Wisconsin map in the Eric Epstein chapter.

Thank you, Clare Cooley for allowing me to quote from your fine, unpublished writings. A special hats off to Elva Hamerstrom Paulson and Dr. Stanley Temple for determining who (Robert McCabe) took the back cover photo of *AFIELD* provided by Elva, and a grateful thank you to Nancy Nabak for the photo of SM taken at the Crex Meadows Wildlife Area in Burnett County.

The staff at the Wisconsin Historical Society were extremely helpful and supportive. Many thanks to Reference Archivist Simone O. Munson and Lee C. Grady for the special attention they gave to the project.

Thank you to Terrell Hyde, Eric Epstein, Richard Staffen, WIlliam Smith, and Andrew Stoltman for assistance in compiling resources listed in the Appendix.

Thank you to Ronda Jolma, Kristin Liphart, and Jennifer Watson of Northland College for their much-appreciated help with administrative support of the project.

A hearty and special thank you to Kristin Mitchell of Wisconsin's, Little Creek Press for embracing this project, for the book's design and for putting up with my many changes and last-minute additions.

Finally, a most grateful thanks to the typists over the years who helped me transcribe scores of cassette tapes: Pat Adair, Genny Mittnacht, Shannon Booth, Jeanne Zwaska, and especially Jill Olson, who spent hundreds of hours laboring over exact word-for-word transcriptions of the tapes. I can't thank you enough for your extraordinarily fine work, captured on CDs, which made writing the chapters a less challenging endeavor.

Last, but certainly not least, a special hats off to Carla Thomas, who painstakingly compiled the Index, and to my fine editor, Shannon Booth (no relation to John Wilkes Booth), who superbly edited the entire manuscript—as daunting a task as one might imagine. Any errors that remain are mine alone. ✳

About the Author

Sumner Matteson has worked as a nongame biologist, conservation biologist, and avian ecologist for the Wisconsin Department of Natural Resources since 1981. He has authored and co-authored many papers and reports on nongame birds, and for 25 years led the successful effort to restore trumpeter swans to Wisconsin, working with a diverse team of partners in the public and private sectors. A graduate of the University of Wisconsin-Madison (BA, MS), he has lived in the Madison area for nearly 50 years. Also, he is a past president of the Wisconsin Society for Ornithology. His longtime interest in the history of Wisconsin conservation and in those interested in natural history study led to his development of the *Wisconsin Naturalists Project*, which resulted in this first volume. ✳

Scoping waterbirds, Crex Meadows Wildlfe Area, Burnett County, Wisconsin.
Photo by Nancy Nabak.

Endnotes

Preface ~ To Catch a Naturalist
NOTES

1 J. Muir, *The Story of My Boyhood and Youth*. (Madison and London: The University of Wisconsin Press, 1965).

2 S. Flader, "Leopold's 'Some Fundamentals of Conservation': A Commentary," *Environmental Ethics* (1979), (1): 143.

3 A. Leopold, "Some Fundamentals of Conservation in the Southwest," *Environmental Ethics* (1979), (1): 131–141.

4 "The Land Ethic" is the final essay in *A Sand County Almanac and Sketches Here and There*. (New York: Oxford University Press, fifth printing, 1960. The book was originally published in 1949).

Prologue ~ Revelations
NOTES

5 Discussions between Curt Meine and SM in fall 2017 underscored the importance of greater awareness of indigenous/traditional ecological knowledge systems.

6 A.C. Jenkins, *The Naturalists, Pioneers of Natural History*. (New York: Mayflower Books, 1978).

7 Jenkins

8 K. Heard, *Maria Merian's Butterflies*. (London: Royal Collection Trust, 2016).

9 J. Kastner, *A Species of Eternity*. (New York: Alfred A. Knopf, 1977).

10 A.C. Jenkins, *The Naturalists, Pioneers of Natural History*

11 Jenkins

12 C. Darwin, *Journal of Researches into the Geology and Natural History of the Various Countries Visited by H.M.S. Beagle, Facsimile Reprint of the First Edition*. (New York: Hufner, 1952).

13 L. Barber, *The Heyday of Natural History*. (New York: Doubleday, 1980).

14 The most penetrating and insightful portrayal of Alexander von Humboldt's life and work is presented in *The Passage to Cosmos, Alexander von Humboldt and the Shaping of America* (Chicago and London: The University of Chicago Press, 2009) by Laura Dassow Walls.

15 A. Leopold, "Some Fundamentals of Conservation in the Southwest," *Environmental Ethics* (1), 131–141.

16 M. Edmonds, 2018. *Taking Flight: A History of Birds and People in the Heart of America.* (Madison: Wisconsin Historical Society Press, 1979).

17 Edmonds

18 W. Hanley, *Natural History in America.* (New York: Doubleday, 1977).

19 Hanley

20 P.G. Hayes, Personal communication with S.W. Matteson (2017).

21 M.J. Mossman, "H.R. Schoolcraft and Natural History on the Western Frontier, Part 2: The 1820 Expedition." *The Passenger Pigeon* (1992), 54(1): 59–84.

22 A.W. Schorger, *Some Wisconsin Naturalists.* (Madison: Wisconsin Society for Ornithology, 1946).

23 A.W. Schorger

24 A.W. Schorger

25 A.W. Schorger

26 A.W. Schorger

27 A.W. Schorger

28 A.W. Schorger

29 A.W. Schorger

30 A.W. Schorger

31 A.W. Schorger

32 A.W. Schorger

33 A.W. Schorger

34 L. Kumlien and N. Hollister, *The birds of Wisconsin.* Bull. Wis. Nat. Hist. Soc. 3(1–3): 1–143; published in same year in one volume with the cooperation of the board of trustees of the Milwaukee Public Mus. (1903). Reprinted with A.W. Schorger's revisions, Wis. Soc. Ornithol. (1951).

35 Curt Meine, *Aldo Leopold: His Life and Work.* (Madison and London: University of Wisconsin Press, 1988).

36 A. Leopold, *A Sand County Almanac and Sketches Here and There.* (New York: Oxford University Press, 1960, fifth printing).

37 Curt Meine, *Aldo Leopold: His Life and Work.* (Madison and London: University of Wisconsin Press, 1988), 519–520.

38 I.A. Lapham, *The Antiquities Of Wisconsin, As Surveyed And Described.* (On behalf of the American Antiquarian Society.) The Smithsonian Institution, Washington D.C., 1855.

39 "NOTE.—The startling intelligence was brought to the City yesterday, that Prof. I.A. Lapham, late State Geologist, had been found dead in a boat, on Lake Oconomowoc...." *Wisconsin Free Press,* Oconomowoc, Sept. 15, 1875.

40 I.A. Lapham, *Report on the Disastrous Effects of the Destruction of Forest Trees, Now Going on So Rapidly in the State of Wisconsin.* With J.G. Knapp and H. Crocker. (Madison: Atwood & Rublee, 1867).

41 I.A. Lapham, "A Catalogue of Plants and Shells Found in the Vicinity of Milwaukee, on the West Side of Lake Michigan." *Milwaukee Advertiser, 1836.* Milwaukee's first newspaper.

42 I.A. Lapham, *Wisconsin: Its Geography and Topography, History, Geology, and Mineralogy: Together with Brief Sketches of Its Antiquities, Natural History, Soil, Productions, Population, and Government.* (Milwaukee: I.A. Hopkins, 1846).

43 I.A. Lapham, Unpublished autobiography. (Madison: Increase Lapham Archives, Wisconsin Historical Society, 1875).

44 P.R. Hoy, "Increase A. Lapham, L.L.D." *Transactions of the Wisconsin Academy of Sciences, Arts, and Letters* (1875–1876), 264–267.

45 M. Haines, "Fertility and Mortality in the United States." EH.Net Encyclopedia, edited by R. Whaples. (2008). March 19, 2008.

46 Barbara and David Barquist, *Oconomowoc, Barons to Bootleggers* (Oconomowoc: Leitzke Printing, 2006). Also: Paul Hayes, personal communication, January 22, 2018.

47 Editorial—*Death of Prof. I.A. Lapham*; The Oconomowoc Local, Friday morning, September 17, 1875.

Chapter Two ~ Francis Zirrer
NOTES

48 This chapter draws from three articles I penned for *The Passenger Pigeon* in 1990 (Volume 52, Nos.1,2,3). *The Passenger Pigeon* is published quarterly by the Wisconsin Society for Ornithology. For more information on the life and work of Zirrer see *Flock Together, A Love Affair with Extinct Birds* by B.J. Hollars, University of Nebraska Press, 2016.

49 F. Zirrer, "The Great Horned Owl." *The Passenger Pigeon* (1956) 18(3):99–109.

50 Owen Gromme letter to S. Matteson, January 30, 1989.

51 F. Zirrer, "The Great Horned Owl." (1956).

52 F. Zirrer, "Wisconsin's Smallest Owl." *The Passenger Pigeon* (1944) 6(3):62–65.

53 F. G. Wilson, *E. M. Griffith and the Early Story of Wisconsin Forestry.* (Madison: Wisconsin Department of Natural Resources, 1982), 67.

54 F. Zirrer, "The Goshawk." *The Passenger Pigeon* (1947) 9(3):79–94.

55 A. J. Schoenebeck, "The Birds of Oconto County." *The Passenger Pigeon* (1939) 1(6):79–88.

56 O. Gromme, Field notes. Feb. 1934–Dec. 1935. Vol. 13:1667. Unpublished manuscript. (Milwaukee Public Museum, 1934b).

57 F. Zirrer, "The Goshawk." (1947).

58 O. Gromme, Field notes. Feb. 1934–Dec. 1935. Vol. 13:1670. Unpublished manuscript. (Milwaukee Public Museum, 1934c).

59 O. Gromme, Field notes. Feb. 1934–Dec. 1935. Vol. 13:1713. Unpublished manuscript. (Milwaukee Public Museum, 1934d).

60 F. Zirrer, "The Goshawk." (1947).

61 O. Gromme, Field notes. Feb. 1934–Dec. 1935. Vol. 13:1719. Unpublished manuscript. (Milwaukee Public Museum, 1934e).

62 "The Goshawk *(Astur atricapillus)* Nesting in Wisconsin." (1935) *Auk* 52(1):15-20.

63 O. Gromme, Field notes. Feb. 1934–Dec. 1935. Vol. 13:1593–1850. Unpublished manuscript. (Milwaukee Public Museum).

64 F. Zirrer, "The Goshawk." (1947).

65 F. Zirrer, "The Goshawk." (1947).

66 F. Zirrer letter to A.W. Schorger, August 24, 1941.

67 S. Solheim, Notes regarding Kissick Alkaline Lake Bog (Sawyer Co.). WDNR files. (1981) 2 pp.

68 WDNR. Kissick swamp wildlife area draft management plan. WDNR. (1983) 9 pp.

69 F. Zirrer letter to A.W. Schorger, July 7, 1944.

70 F. Zirrer, "The Ring-Necked Duck." *The Passenger Pigeon* (1945) 7(2):41–46.

71 E. Epstein, personal communication, October 10, 1989.

72 F. Zirrer, "The Ring-Necked Duck." (1945).

73 F. Zirrer letter to A.W. Schorger, July 12, 1944.

74 H.H.T. Jackson, *Mammals of Wisconsin*. (Madison: The University of Wisconsin Press, 1961) 249.

75 S.W. Matteson, "Francis Zirrer: Unheralded Naturalist of the North Woods" (Part 3). *The Passenger Pigeon* (1990) 52(3): 233–250.

76 F. Zirrer letter to A.W. Schorger, March 12, 1942.

77 A.W. Schorger letter to R. Works, July 11, 1968.

78 F. Zirrer, "Bittern." *The Passenger Pigeon* (1944) 6(2): 44–46.

79 F. Zirrer letter to A.W. Schorger, October 27, 1946.

80 A.W. Schorger letter to F. Zirrer, October 30, 1946.

81 F. Zirrer, "The Great Blue Heron." *The Passenger Pigeon* (1951) 13(3): 92–98.

82 F. Zirrer, "The 'Great' Pileated Woodpecker." *The Passenger Pigeon* (1952) 14(1): 9–15.

83 F. Zirrer, "The Great Horned Owl." *The Passenger Pigeon* (1956) 18(3): 99–109.

84 F. Zirrer, "Life and Death in Northwoods; Animals That Hibernate Solve Food Shortage Problem, but Others Are Having Hard Time This Winter. *Milwaukee Journal*, (1958a) 1 p.

85 W. E. Scott letter to A.W. Schorger, July 7, 1968.

86 C. Kemper, In memoriam. *The Passenger Pigeon* (1968) 30(2):67.

87 R. Works letter to A.W. Schorger, July 27, 1968.

Chapter Three ~ George Knudsen
NOTES

88 Known also as "Brazee Lake," "Brazee Swamp," "Patrick Lake," and "Old Lake." Drained in the mid-1960s, Brazee Lake was lost for three decades but was restored in the 1990s due to Department of Transportation expansion of Hwy 151 from Sun Prairie to Columbus, with ownership transferred to the Wisconsin Department of Natural Resources. Today, it is known as the "Patrick Marsh Wildlife Area."

Chapter Four ~ Jim Zimmerman
NOTES

89 Libby Zimmerman commented (personal communication to SM, January 6, 2018) that Jim's mother had lost twins, so she wanted to make sure his birth was successful. She added, "Jim's family already lived in the Storybook House in Madison, which his mother had built before her marriage, so he was really a Wisconsin native. She kept the building records, including those showing that the excavation was done using, yes, horses."

90 Libby commented (personal communication to SM, January 6, 2018): "The sedge book is slowly being brought to a finish. It represents to me a third of Jim's professional life output— teaching, sedges, conservation—and I want to see it published, before it's all online! I was the illustrator originally and saw most of the species in the field with Jim."

91 Libby commented (personal communication to SM, January 6, 2018): "The Wisconsin Wetlands Association was co-founded by Jim, me, Attorney Bill Lunney, and Dan Caulfield at an evening meeting on our lawn that Bill called a 'mosquito festival.' Originally it was an ad hoc group dedicated to stopping the new beltline from going through the Upper Mud Lake Marsh (a partial victory), as the Dane County Wetlands Association, later becoming the Southern Wisconsin Wetlands Association."

92 Libby commented (personal communication to SM, January 6, 2018): "The garden was on Madison's west side, on land Jim's mother owned in what was then the country. He often mentioned how he biked out there. This ended when urban expansion caused the city to assess the large lot for sewer and water, forcing Jim's mother to sell."

93 From a poem Libby wrote after Jim died. Personal communication to SM, January 6, 2018.

Chapter Five ~ Ruth Hine
NOTES
94 "Ruth Hine, 1923–2010, Inducted 2010," The Wisconsin Conservation Hall of Fame, wchf.org.

Chapter Six ~ Frances and Frederick Hamerstrom
NOTES

95 H.M. Corneli, Mice in the Freezer, Owls on the Porch: the Lives of Naturalists Frederick and Frances Hamerstrom. (Madison: University of Wisconsin Press, 2002).

96 E. Paulson, personal communication, September 1, 2017.

97 P.L. Errington, F. Hamerstrom, and F. N. Hamerstrom, "The Great Horned Owl and its prey in north-central United States." Research Bulletin 277. (Agricultural Experiment Station, Iowa State College of Agriculture and Mechanic Arts, 1940).

98 F.N. Hamerstrom, and F. Hamerstrom. "A guide to prairie-chicken management." Technical Bulletin Number 15. (Madison: Wisconsin Cons. Dep., 1957).

99 Frances Hamerstrom's books include An Eagle to the Sky (1970); Walk When the Moon Is Full (1975); Adventure of the Stone Man (1977); Strictly for the Chickens (1980); Birding with a Purpose: Of Raptors, Gabboons, and Other Creatures (1984); Eagles, Hawks, Falcons, and Owls of America: A Coloring Album (1984); Harrier, Hawk of the Marshes: The Hawk That is Ruled by a Mouse (1986); Is She Coming Too?: Memoirs of a Lady Hunter (1989), Wild Food Cookbook (1989), and My Double Life, Memoirs of a Naturalist (1994). She also wrote a booklet titled Birds of Prey of Wisconsin (1984), published jointly by the Wisconsin Department of Natural Resources and the Madison Audubon Society.

100 E. Paulson, personal communication, September 1, 2017. D. Gjestson, personal communication, October 13, 2017.

101 Frederick Hamerstrom, 1909-1990, Inducted 1996. Frances Hamerstrom, 1907-1998, Inducted 1996. The Wisconsin Conservation Hall of Fame. www.wchf.org.

102 Thomas L. Friedman, Thank You for Being Late, An Optimist's Guide To Thriving In The Age of Accelerations. (New York: Farrar, Straus and Giroux, 2016.)

103 F.N. Hamerstrom, F. Hamerstrom, and O.E. Mattson, Sharptails Into the Shadows. (Madison: Wis. Cons. Dep., 1952).

Chapter Seven ~ Sam Robbins
NOTES

104 Material adapted and edited from an article I wrote for *The Passenger Pigeon* (Vol. 60, No. 1, Spring 1998: "Samuel D. Robbins, Jr. at 75: An Interview with the Author of *Wisconsin Birdlife: Population and Distribution Past and Present*")—forms the basis for the chapter presented here.

Chapter Eight ~ George Becker
NOTES

105 *Fishes of Wisconsin* is available online at: www.seagrant.wisc.edu/greatlakesfish/becker.html. An update of Becker's book is titled *Wisconsin Fishes 2000: Status and Distribution*, by John Lyons, Philip A. Cochrane, and Don Fago. It is available through the University of Wisconsin Sea Grant Institute in Madison, Wisconsin.

106 C.A. Long, "In Memoriam, George Charles Becker 1917–2002." *The Passenger Pigeon* (2002) 64(4): 325–327

Chapter Eleven ~ Bill Volkert
NOTES

107 W.K. Volkert, "The occurrence and distribution of prairie-associated plants and remnant prairie communities in the Northern Kettle Moraine State Forest." *Field Station Bulletin* (1984) 17(1): 23–31.

Chapter Thirteen ~ Lois Nestel
NOTES

108 Dion Henderson, "Preserver of nature" Wisconsin State Journal, Section 3, Monday, March 9, 1981.

109 Dion Henderson, "Preserver of nature," March 9, 1981.

Chapter Seventeen ~ Eric Epstein-
NOTES

110 Cleland, D. T.; Avers, P. E.; McNab, W. H.; Jensen, M. E.; Bailey, R. G.; King, T.; Russell, W. E. 1997. National Hierarchical Framework of Ecological Units. Published in: Boyce M. S.; Haney, A., ed. 1997. Ecosystem Management Applications for Sustainable Forestland Wildlife Resources. Yale University Press, New Haven, CT. Pg. 181-200.

Chapter Eighteen ~ Remembering Sigurd Olson
NOTES

111 Letter from Aldo Leopold to Wallace Grange, January 3, 1948, cited in Curt Meine's biography, *Aldo Leopold, His Life and Work*. (The University of Wisconsin Press: Madison and London, 1988).

112 Mark Peterson, personal communication to SM, November 1, 2017.

113 David Backes, "A Need for Recognition," *The Life of Sigurd F. Olson*. (Minneapolis: University of Minnesota Press, 1997) 97.

114 Madeleine Nash, "Storm over Voyageurs' Country," *Time* magazine. September 11, 1978, Vol. 112, No. 11.

115 Mark Peterson, November 1, 2017.

116 A new threat (at the time of this book's publication) to the sanctity of the BWCA is sulfide-ore copper mining—which can leach sulfuric acid, heavy metals, and sulfates into the air and water. Mines are also proposed along the borders of the BWCA. The local economy will likely suffer as a result of the proposed mines due to the expected decline in tourists and canoeists, to say nothing of the possible pending catastrophe awaiting aquatic ecosystems. Forest fragmentation will be another effect, and mercury contamination of fish is probable.

Appendix: Taxonomic Online Resources for Scientific and Common Names of Species Mentioned in *AFIELD*.

The most comprehensive taxonomic resource recommended by some within the Wisconsin Department of Natural Resources is the governmental *Integrated Taxonomic Information System* (ITIS): **https://www.itis.gov/**.

There are, however, other online sites specializing in a particular taxon; these are listed below. For taxa not covered below, please refer to the ITIS website. **NOTE:** If an organization's website should happen to change, simply type in the organization's name on your computer to find the new website and search for a taxonomic list or checklist.

1. Wisconsin botanists prefer to use the University of Wisconsin Herbarium website: **http://wisflora.herbarium.wisc.edu/**.

2. For Wisconsin bird species, I recommend the Wisconsin Society for Ornithology's *Checklist of Wisconsin Birds*, which is updated regularly: **https://wsobirds.org/checklist-of-wisconsin-birds**. Or alternatively: the American Ornithologists' Union (AOU) Checklist of North and Middle American Birds: **http://checklist.aou.org/taxa/**. Updates to the online AOU checklist are made annually as new supplements are published in AOU's *The Auk*.

3. For Wisconsin reptiles and amphibians, check out this North American source of herptile taxonomy from the Society for the Study of Amphibians and Reptiles: **https://ssarherps.org/publications/north-american-checklist/** – a frequently updated site.

4. For Wisconsin mammals, there are apparently no online taxonomic resources, but both the *Journal of Wildlife Management* and *Journal of Mammalogy* use this resource for current nomenclature: **http://www.nsrl.ttu.edu/publications/opapers/ops/OP327.pdf**.

5. For odonates (dragonflies and damselflies), the best regularly updated source comes from the Dragonfly Society of the Americas: **https://www.odonatacentral.org/index.php/PageAction.get/name/NADragonflies**.

Sumner Matteson

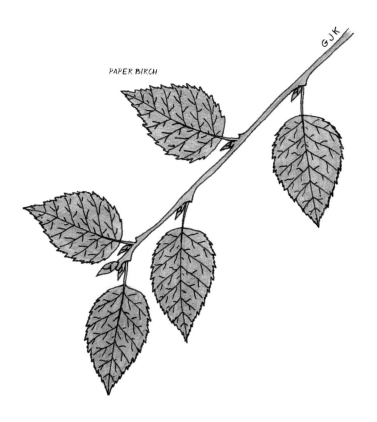

PAPER BIRCH

GJK

Index

A

H

L

S

V